Money and Capital Markets
The Financial System in the Economy

PETER S. ROSE
Texas A & M University

Money and Capital Markets

The Financial System in the Economy

 1983

BUSINESS PUBLICATIONS, INC.
Plano, Texas   75075

ISBN 0-256-02708-0
Library of Congress Catalog Card No. 81–71919

Printed in the United States of America

2 3 4 5 6 7 8 9 0 MP 9 8 7 6 5 4 3

To my family

Preface

This book is focused on a study of the financial system—the money and capital markets—of the United States. The financial system, where bonds, stocks, and other financial instruments are traded, is one of the most important of all institutions that serve the public. It is also one of the most misunderstood. The financial system performs several absolutely vital functions in the economy. It channels savings into capital investment to spur economic growth. It supplies credit to expand the current purchasing power of businesses, consumers, and governments and provides a mechanism for the making of payments. The financial system offers a means to store purchasing power (wealth) for future contingencies and to protect against many different forms of personal and property risk.

The great importance of the financial system and the money and capital markets to business, consumers, and governments clearly makes them a worthwhile and compelling area for study. Each of us interacts in the financial markets in a wide variety of ways during our lifetime. Some of us will be called upon to carry out financial transactions as the manager of our own business firm or as a hired manager for another firm. Many, if not most, of us will be placed in the role of home buyers, requiring mortgage credit from the cheapest source available. Nearly everyone at one time or another will be compelled to borrow money from a bank or credit union to purchase a new car, furniture, or home appliance, or to finance a dream vacation. Others will accumulate substantial investments in stocks, bonds, and other financial instruments as a reserve of liquid funds or to prepare for retirement. All of these activities require a knowledge of how the financial system operates and what causes interest rates and the availability of credit to change. Helping the reader achieve this kind of understanding is one of the most important objectives of this book.

Equally important for each of us as citizens is the key role played by today's financial system in the economic policies of government. In recent years the United States, Great Britain, Canada, and many other nations have conducted their economic policy principally through the financial system, manipulating interest rates and the availability of credit to all sectors of the economy. For example many of the world's central banks, including the Federal Reserve System, have pursued "tight money" policies in recent years in an effort to control inflation and slow the growth of borrowing and spending. If we are to understand these government policies and their probable effects on our everyday lives, we must grasp more fully how the financial system affects the health of the nation's economy.

The 28 chapters of this book present a survey of all the major money and capital markets and institutions which form the American financial system. While these chapters are grouped into eight different parts, in reality the text divides quite naturally into two main sections. The first section, covering Chapters 1 through 10, is designed to set the stage for a thorough study of individual financial markets later in the book. These first 10 chapters provide a *conceptual framework* for understanding how and why money and capital markets operate the way they do.

For example, Chapters 1 and 2 introduce the concept of a financial system and explain the essential role of markets within that system. They illuminate the factors which lead to the creation of financial instruments and the channels through which loanable funds are routed from savers and lenders to borrowers and investors. Chapters 3, 4, and 5 highlight the key role played by financial institutions in the daily workings of the financial system. Included in these chapters are analyses of the functions performed by commercial banks, credit unions, savings banks, savings and loan associations, insurance companies, mutual funds, pension plans, and other financial institutions.

An explicit framework for understanding the fundamental forces influencing security prices and interest rates appears in Chapters 6 through 9. The key functions of interest rates are presented, and the principal theories of interest-rate determination reviewed. The most popular methods used in today's financial market place for calculating and measuring interest rates and security prices are presented. There is a review of the theory and uses of the yield curve, the measurement of risk, the effects of inflation on interest rates, the impact of taxation on financial instruments, and the roles that call privileges and convertibility features play in influencing relative interest rates. This analytical portion of the book concludes with an extended discussion of the sources of information available to students of the financial system on interest rates, security prices, the financial condition of borrowers, and the health of the economy and financial markets. The Flow of Funds Accounts and their companion set of social accounts, the National Income

Accounts, are discussed and analyzed at the conclusion of this first major part of the text.

The remainder of the book, beginning with Chapter 11, is devoted to a study of the essential features of all major markets in today's financial system. There are whole chapters or major portions of chapters devoted to the markets for U.S. Treasury bills, repurchase agreements, federal funds, certificates of deposit, commercial paper, federal agency obligations, bankers' acceptances, financial futures, consumer credit and savings, residential and commercial mortgages, corporate notes and bonds, bank business loans, common and preferred stock, stock options, Treasury notes and bonds, state and local debt securities, foreign currencies, Eurodollars, Eurobonds, and international commercial loans. Thus, the reader is presented with a wide menu of modern financial instruments to study and compare. And each financial instrument and market is analyzed in terms of its key features, methods of calculating yields, principal investor groups, and recent innovations in trading and lending.

While the principal focus of this second section of the text is upon individual financial instruments and markets, the key role played by government policy in today's financial marketplace is also examined in detail. For example, Chapters 21, 22, and 23 present a detailed study of central banking and the Federal Reserve System. The principal functions of central banks in controlling the money stock, stabilizing the financial markets, ensuring a smooth flow of payments, and supervising the banking system are explored along with an explanation of how the Federal Reserve System performs each of these important functions. Considerable attention is paid to the Fed's daily activity in the money market, controlling reserves and monetary growth through open-market operations.

The key indicators of Federal Reserve monetary policy are discussed at length in this text, principally from the vantage point of market investors. The discussion attempts to provide a deeper understanding of what the Federal Reserve is trying to accomplish and the problems that beset monetary policy today. The nation's principal economic problems, particularly inflation and unemployment, are examined, and potential monetary and fiscal remedies (including supply-side economics) evaluated. In a subsequent chapter, the policy options presented by government fiscal and debt-management policy are also discussed. Among the most important topics introduced here are the effects of government borrowing and debt retirement on the financial system and the economy, and a discussion of the latest techniques for marketing U.S. Treasury securities.

This book has a number of features designed to aid the reader in achieving a deeper understanding of the material presented. These features include an expanded use of diagrams, figures, and exhibits to reinforce major points, along with references for further reading listed at the conclusion of each chapter. Questions appear at the end of each chapter to facilitate class discussion and problem solving. A number of topics often overlooked in the field are explored in depth—for example, consumer credit, financial futures, creative financing in the home-mortgage market, Eurobonds, Eurodollars, and trading and hedging in foreign currencies.

The text combines both a conceptual and an applied perspective, reflecting the author's philosophy that the student of the financial system needs *both* viewpoints. A good grasp of analytical concepts relating to the financial marketplace is essential if we are to understand the problems that may confront us in the future. But we must also be able to apply analytical concepts to understand our current financial problems. Therefore the text provides ample descriptive material on financial institutions and markets operating today as well as a framework for analyzing tomorrow's important financial trends.

This book is designed primarily for courses dealing with money and capital markets, and with the financial system, and for financially oriented money-and-banking classes. It is also suitable for those working in such disciplines as commercial banking, investments, business finance, marketing, economics, and accounting. Each of these fields touches the financial system in a variety of ways, and each would benefit from the combined analytical and applied approach traced out in these pages. Readers who have had introductory courses in business finance, economics, and perhaps money and banking will find these preparatory courses helpful in understanding the material in this book. But these courses are not mandatory prerequisites for reading and understanding the major points presented. The use of quantitative analysis is limited, being confined almost exclusively to Part 3, which deals with interest rates and security prices.

A book of this size reflects the contributions of many individuals and institutions in providing essential data, helpful comments, and criticisms. Organizations which provided assistance with data and other pertinent information include Moody's Investor Service, Standard & Poor's Corporation, Dun & Bradstreet, Inc., the American Council of Life Insurance, the Insurance Information Institute, the Credit Union National Association, the United States League of Savings Associations, the National Association of Mutual Savings Banks, the Chicago Board of Trade, The First Boston Corporation, and Dow Jones Reprints. The author is also indebted to Professor Ivan T. Call of Brigham Young University; Professor Eugene F. Drzycimski of the University of Wisconsin; and Professor Timothy Koch of Texas Tech University, who reviewed the entire manuscript and made many useful comments and suggestions. Mrs. Mary Anne Frederick and Mrs. Susan Beene typed and retyped the manuscript and responded cheerfully to all deadlines. The author also owes a debt of gratitude to his colleagues at Texas A&M University and to his family, especially his wife Kandy, for their patience and essential support in making this book possible. While the encouragement and support provided by all of these individuals and institutions was absolutely essential to completion of the project, the errors that remain and the opinions expressed belong, of course, to the author.

Peter S. Rose

Contents

part three
Interest Rates and Security Prices

Functions of the Rate of Interest in the Economy. The Classical Theory of Interest Rates: *Saving by Households. Saving by Business Firms. Saving by Government. The Demand for Investment Funds. The Equilibrium Rate of Interest in the Classical Theory of Interest.* The Liquidity Preference Theory: *The Demand for Liquidity. The Supply of Money. The Equilibrium Rate of Interest in Liquidity Preference Theory. Limitations of the Liquidity Preference Theory.* The Loanable Funds Theory: *Consumer Demand for Loanable Funds. Business Demand for Loanable Funds. Government Demand for Loanable Funds. Total Demand for Loanable Funds. The Supply of Loanable Funds. The Equilibrium Rate of Interest in the Loanable Funds Theory.*

Units of Measurement for Interest Rates and Security Prices: *Definition of Interest Rates. Basis Points. Security Prices.* Measures of the Rate of Return, or Yield, on a Security: *Coupon Rate. Current Yield. Yield to Maturity. Holding-Period Yield. Calculating Yields to Maturity and Holding-Period Yields.* Yield-Price Relationships. Interest Rates and the Business Cycle: *Relative Movements in Short-Term and Long-Term Interest Rates and Security Prices.* Interest Rates Charged by Institutional Lenders: *The Simple-Interest Method. Add-On Rate of Interest. Discount Method. Annual Percentage Rate (APR).*

The Maturity of a Loan: *The Yield Curve and the Term Structure of Interest Rates. Types of Yield Curves. The Expectations Hypothesis. The Role of Expectations in Shaping the Yield Curve. Relative Changes in Long-Term and Short-Term Interest Rates. Policy Implications of the Expectations Hypothesis. The Liquidity Premium View of the Yield Curve. The Segmented Markets Argument. Policy Implications of the Segmented-Markets Theory. Research Evidence. Uses of the Yield Curve.* Default Risk and Interest Rates: *The Premium for Default Risk. The Expected Rate of Return or Yield. Expected Default Loss and Market Risk Premiums. Factors Influencing Risk Premiums.* Inflation and Interest Rates: *The Correlation between Inflation and Interest Rates. The Nominal and Real Interest Rate. The Fisher Effect. An Alternative View. The Research Evidence.*

Marketability. The Call Privilege: *Calculating Yields on Called Securities. Advantages and Disadvantages of the Call Privilege. The Call Premium and*

part four
The Money Market

ing Yields on Paper Issues. Advantages of Issuing Commercial Paper. Possible Disadvantages of Issuing Commercial Paper. Principal Investors. Commercial Paper Ratings. Dealers in Paper. Federal Agency Securities: *Types of Federal Credit Agencies. Growth of the Agency Market. Terms on Agency Securities. The Marketing of Agency Issues.*

Bankers' Acceptances: *Why Acceptances Are Used in International Trade. How Acceptances Arise. Recent Growth of Acceptance Financing. Acceptance Rates. Investors in Acceptances.* Eurodollars: *What Is a Eurodollar? The Creation of Eurodollars. Eurodollar Maturities. The Supply of Eurodollars. Eurodollars in Domestic Bank Operations. Benefits and Costs of the Eurodollar Market.*

The Nature of Futures Trading. General Principles of Hedging: *Opening and Closing a Hedge. Why Hedging Can Be Effective. Risk Selection through Hedging.* Financial Futures: *The Purposes of Trading in Financial Futures.* Securities Used in Financial Futures Contracts: *U.S. Treasury Bonds and Notes. U.S. Treasury Bills. GMNA Mortgage Pass-Through or Mortgage-Backed Securities. 90-Day Commercial Paper. Bank Certificates of Deposit.* Types of Hedging in the Financial Futures Market: *The Long (or Buying) Hedge. The Short (or Selling) Hedge. Cross Hedging.* Traders Active in the Futures Market. Potential Benefits to Financial Institutions from the Futures Market. Social Consequences of the Futures Market.

**part five
The Consumer in the Financial Markets**

Consumers as Lenders of Funds: *Financial Assets Purchased by Consumers. Government Regulation and Returns to the Small Saver.* Consumers as Borrowers of Funds: *Is Consumer Borrowing Excessive? Categories of Consumer Borrowing.* Credit and Debit Cards: *Growth of Credit Cards. Credit-Card Users. Operational Problems in Offering Credit Cards. Debit Cards.* The Determinants of Consumer Borrowing. Consumer Lending Institutions: *Commercial Banks. Finance Companies. Other Consumer Lending Institutions.* Factors Considered in Making Consumer Loans. Financial Disclosure and Consumer Credit: *Truth in Lending. Fair Credit Reporting Act. Fair Credit Billing Act. Consumer Leasing Act.* Credit Discrimination Laws: *Community Reinvestment Act. Equal Credit Opportunity Act. Fair Housing and Home Mortgage Disclosure Acts.*

Recent Trends in New Home Prices and the Terms of Mortgage Loans. The Structure of the Mortgage Market: *Volume of Mortgage Loans. Residential versus Nonresidential Mortgage Loans.* Mortgage-Lending Institutions. The Roles Played by Financial Institutions in the Mortgage Market: *Savings and Loan*

part six
Businesses in the Financial Markets

part seven
Government in the Financial Markets

Creation of the Federal Reserve System. The Early Structure of the Federal Reserve System. Goals and Policy Tools in the Early History of the Federal Reserve System. How the Fed Is Organized: *Board of Governors of the Federal Reserve System. The Federal Open Market Committee and Manager of the System Open Market Account. The Federal Reserve Banks. The Member Banks of the Fed's System.* Many Roles of the Federal Reserve System Today: *The Clearing and Collection of Checks and Other Means of Payment. Issuing Currency and Coin and Providing Other Services. Maintaining a Sound Banking and Financial System. Serving as the Federal Government's Fiscal Agent. Carrying Out Monetary Policy. Providing Information to the Public.*

Motivations for State and Local Government Borrowing. Uses of Borrowed Funds. Types of Securities Issued by State and Local Governments: *Short-Term Securities. Long-Term Securities. Types of Revenue Bonds. Types of Securities Issued by Different Governmental Units.* Key Features of Municipal Debt: *Tax Exemption. Credit Ratings. Serialization.* How Municipal Bonds Are Marketed. Problems in the Municipal Market: *Problems and Proposals Regarding Tax Exemption. California's Proposition 13. The Growing Burden of Local Taxes and Debt. The Need for Alternatives to Fixed-Rate Municipal Bonds.*

part eight
The International Financial System

Enter the International Field. Foreign Banks in the United States: *Recent Growth of Foreign Banks in the United States. Types of Organizations Operated by Foreign Banks in the United States. Federal Regulation of Foreign Bank Activity. Foreign Banks and the International Banking Act of 1978.* Regulation of the International Banking Activities of U.S. Banks. Problems and the Future of International Banking: *The Risks of International Lending. Public Confidence and Bank Failures. The Energy Crisis and Petrodollars. Prospects and Issues in the 1980s.*

part one

The Financial System
in Perspective

1

The Role of the Financial System in the Economy

This book is devoted to a study of the *financial system*—the collection of markets, individuals and institutions, laws, regulations, and techniques through which bonds, stocks, and other securities are traded and interest rates determined. The financial system is one of the most important inventions of modern industrial societies. Its vital task is to move scarce loanable funds in the form of credit from those who save to those who borrow for consumption and investment. By making funds available for lending and borrowing, the financial system provides the means whereby modern economies grow and increase the standard of living enjoyed by their citizens. Much of the credit thus obtained goes to purchase machinery and equipment, to construct new bridges, highways, factories, and schools, and to stock the shelves of businesses with inventories of goods. Without the financial system and the credit it supplies, each of us would lead a very different and probably less enjoyable existence.

The financial system determines both the *cost* of credit and *how much* credit will be available to pay for the thousands of different goods and services we purchase daily. Equally important, what happens in this system has a powerful impact upon the health of the nation's economy. When credit becomes more costly and less available, total spending for goods and services generally falls. As a result, unemployment rises, and the economy's growth slows down as businesses cut back production and reduce inventories. In contrast, when the cost of credit declines and loanable funds become more readily available, total spending in the economy usually increases, more jobs are created, and the economy's rate of growth accelerates. In truth, the financial system is an integral part of the economic system and cannot be viewed in isolation from it.

THE ECONOMY AND THE FINANCIAL SYSTEM

Flows within the Economic System

In order to better understand the role played by the financial system in our daily lives we begin by examining its position within the nation's economic system.

The basic function of any economy is to allocate scarce material resources in order to produce the goods and services needed by society. The high standard of living most of us enjoy today depends fundamentally upon the ability of the nation's economy to turn out each day the enormous volume of clothing, food, fuel, shelter, transportation services, and other essentials of modern living. This is an exceedingly complex task because scarce resources must first be procured in just the right amounts to provide the raw materials of production and combined at just the right time with labor and capital to generate the products and services demanded by consumers. In short, any economic system must combine *inputs*—land and other natural resources, labor and managerial skills, and capital equipment—in order to produce *outputs* in the form of goods and services. The economy generates a flow of production (goods and services) in return for a flow of payments, usually in the form of money (see Figure 1–1).

FIGURE 1–1
The Economic System

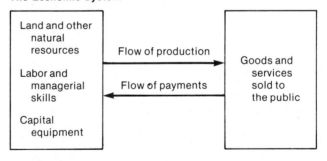

We may also depict the flows of payments and production within the economic system as a *circular flow* between producing units (mainly businesses and governments) and consuming units (principally households) (see Figure 1–2). In modern economies households provide labor, managerial skills, and natural resources to business firms and governments in return for income in the form of salaries, wages, rents, royalties, dividends, etc. Most of the income received by households is spent to purchase goods and ser-

FIGURE 1–2
Circular Flows of Income, Payments, and Production in the Economic System

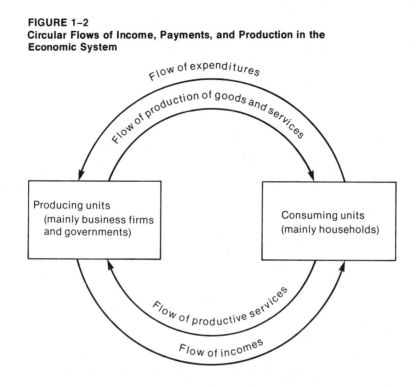

vices. In 1980, for example, about 95 percent of the $2.2 trillion in total personal income received by individuals and families in the United States was spent for consumption of goods and services or paid out in taxes.[1] The result of this spending is a flow of funds back to producing units, which stimulates further production and creates income in future periods. The circular flow of production and income is, thus, interdependent and never ending.

The Role of Markets in the Economic System

In most economies of the Western world, including the United States, *markets* are used to carry out this complex task of allocating resources, distributing income, and producing needed goods and services. What is a market? It is an institution set up by society to allocate resources which are scarce relative to the demand for them. Modern societies use markets to allocate labor time, raw materials, energy, managerial skills, and capital in order to produce the thousands of goods and services necessary for survi-

---

[1] In percentage terms, U.S. households in 1980 allocated about 80 percent of their total personal income for consumption expenditures; nearly 16 percent went for federal, state, and local taxes and fees; and the remainder—almost 5 percent—was set aside as personal savings.

val and growth.[2] Markets are the channel through which buyers and sellers meet to exchange goods, services, and resources.

The marketplace determines what goods and services will be produced and in what quantity. This is accomplished essentially through changes in the *prices* of commodities and services offered in the market. If the price of a commodity rises, for example, this stimulates business firms to produce and supply more of it to consumers. In the long run new firms may enter the market (in the absence of government restrictions) to produce those goods or services experiencing increased demand and rising prices. A decline in price, on the other hand, usually leads to reduced production of a good or service, and in the long run some firms will leave the marketplace. Markets also distribute income. In a pure market system the income of an individual or business firm is determined solely by the contributions each makes to production. Markets reward superior productivity, innovation, and sensitivity to customer needs with increased profits, higher wages and salaries, and other economic benefits.

Types of Markets

There are essentially three types of markets at work within the economic system: (1) factor markets, (2) product markets, and (3) financial markets (see Figure 1–3). In *factor markets* consuming units sell their labor, managerial skills, and other resources to those producing units offering the highest prices. The factor markets allocate the so-called factors of production (land, labor, and capital) and distribute incomes in the form of salaries, wages, rental income, etc. to the owners of productive resources. As Figure 1–3 shows, consuming units use most of their income from the factor markets to purchase goods and services in *product markets*. Food, shelter, clothing, medical care, automobiles, books, theater tickets, gasoline, and swimming pools are among the many goods and services sold in product markets.

The Financial Markets and the Financial System

Of course, not all factor income is consumed. A substantial proportion of after-tax income received by households each year—$101 billion in 1980—is earmarked for personal saving. In addition, business firms save billions of dollars each year to build up equity reserves for future contingencies and to support long-term capital investment. For example, in 1980, U.S. corporations earned $163 billion in after-tax profits, of which $107 billion was set

---

[2] Of course, scarce resources may be allocated by government order and central planning as well as by the marketplace. In the Soviet Union, for example, resources flow to those uses predetermined by a central government plan. While most industrialized economies in the Western world use markets to allocate the majority of their scarce resources today, these economies are really *mixed economies,* with market mechanisms and government-directed planning operating side by side.

FIGURE 1–3
Types of Markets in the Economic System

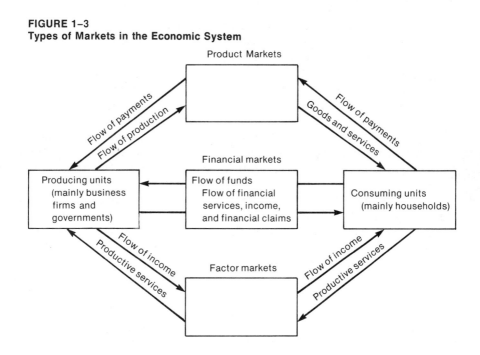

Product Markets

Flow of payments
Flow of production

Flow of payments
Goods and services

Financial markets

Producing units
(mainly business
firms and
governments)

Flow of funds
Flow of financial
services, income,
and financial claims

Consuming units
(mainly households)

Flow of income
Productive services

Flow of income
Productive services

Factor markets

aside (undistributed) for possible future needs. It is here that the third kind of market—financial markets—performs a vital function within the economic system. The financial markets channel *savings*—which come mainly from households—to those individuals and institutions who need more funds for spending than are provided by current income.[3] The financial markets are the heart of the financial system, determining the volume of credit available, attracting savings, and setting interest rates and security prices.

Most of the funds set aside as savings flow through the financial markets to support *investment* by business firms and governments. Investment generally refers to the acquisition of capital goods—buildings, machinery, and equipment—and the purchase of inventories of raw materials, semifinished goods, and finished products.[4] Modern economies require enormous

---

[3] As we will see in Chapter 6, the definition of *saving* differs depending upon what type of unit in the economy is doing the saving. For households, savings are what is left over out of current income after all current consumption expenditures are made. In the business sector, saving includes current net earnings retained in the business after payment of taxes, stockholder dividends, and all other cash expenses. Government saving—a rare event—arises when the current budget runs a surplus of revenues over expenditures.

[4] The makeup of *investment* varies with the particular unit doing the investing. For a business firm, expenditures on fixed assets—buildings, machinery, and equipment—and inventories are investment expenditures. Households invest when they acquire residential housing. However, household purchases of furniture, appliances, automobiles, and other durable consumer goods are generally classified as consumption spending (i.e., expenditures on current account) and not as investment (i.e., expenditures on capital account). Government spending for buildings and other public facilities is another form of investment.

amounts of capital equipment—ships, drill presses, warehouses, residential housing, trucks, schools, bridges, airports, and thousands of similar items and facilities—in order to produce goods and services. Investment in new equipment increases the productivity of labor and ultimately leads to a higher standard of living. However, investment generally requires large amounts of funds, often far beyond the resources available to a single firm or governmental unit. By selling financial claims—stocks, bonds, etc.—in the financial markets, though, large amounts of funds can be raised quickly, and the loan repaid out of future income. Indeed, the financial markets operating within the nation's financial system make possible the exchange of current income for future income.

Those who supply funds in the financial markets receive only *promises* in return for the loan of their money. These promises are packaged in the form of attractive financial claims and financial services—stocks, bonds, checking accounts, savings deposits, insurance policies, etc. (See Figure 1–4). Finan-

FIGURE 1–4
The Financial System

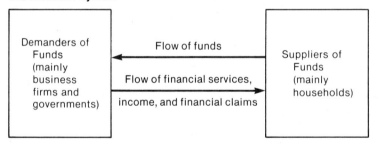

cial claims promise the supplier of funds a future flow of money income, which may consist of dividends, interest payments, capital gains, or other returns. Of course there is no guarantee that the expected flow of future income will ever materialize. However suppliers of funds to the financial system expect not only to recover their original commitment of funds but also to earn additional income as a reward for waiting and for the assumption of risk.

The role of the financial markets in channeling savings into investment is absolutely essential to the health and vitality of the economic system. For example, if households were to set aside savings and those funds were not returned to the spending stream through investment by businesses and governments, the economy would begin to *contract*. The amount of income paid out by business firms and governments would not be matched by funds paid back to those same sectors. As a result, future payments of wages, salaries, rents, and other forms of income would begin to decline, leading to reduced consumption spending. The nation's standard of living would fall. Moreover, with less total spending going on, the need for labor and management skills would be curtailed, resulting in higher unemployment.

SERVICES PROVIDED BY THE FINANCIAL SYSTEM AND THE FINANCIAL MARKETS

Credit Services

In addition to facilitating the flow of savings into investment, the financial markets provide other important services as well. These markets furnish *credit* in thousands of different forms for thousands of different purposes, not all of which are related to investment.

Credit consists of a loan of funds in return for a promise of future payment. Consumers frequently need credit to pay their taxes, purchase groceries and fuel, repair home appliances and the family automobile, enjoy vacations, and retire outstanding debt. Businesses draw upon their lines of credit to meet payrolls, pay taxes, repair equipment, pay interest to bond-holders and other creditors, and grant dividends to their stockholders. State, local, and federal governments frequently borrow to meet payrolls and cover daily cash expenses until tax revenues flow in. Clearly, while the financial markets provide an outlet for savings, they are also the source of credit without which modern, industrialized economies simply could not operate.

The total volume of credit extended through the financial markets of major industrialized economies today is huge and growing rapidly. Businesses, households, and governments have become far more skillful at using credit and taking advantage of favorable opportunities to borrow money than was true even a generation ago. Continuing inflation has encouraged the development of a "buy now on credit" philosophy. The fact that interest payments on debt are a tax-deductible expense in the United States has further stimulated the use of credit as a means of enjoying a higher standard of living. As shown in Exhibit 1–1, households in the U.S. economy borrowed almost $101 billion in 1980, while businesses borrowed another $133 billion, and governments, $147 billion. All told, the various sectors of the U.S. economy raised more than $400 billion in credit during 1980, or about 15 percent of the nation's gross national product (GNP), or total output of goods and services.

Payment Services

The financial system also provides a mechanism for making payments for goods and services. Certain financial assets, principally checking accounts and NOW (negotiable order of withdrawal) accounts, serve as a medium of exchange in the making of payments. Commercial banks—the principal institutions within the financial system—create checkbook money for public

EXHIBIT 1–1
Total Funds Raised in U.S. Financial Markets by Major Sectors of the Economy, 1980

Sector		Amount of Funds Raised ($ billions)
Households		$100.8
Business firms:		
Farms	19.0	
Nonfinancial corporations	101.1	
Other businesses	12.5	
Total—all firms		132.6
Private financial institutions		23.3
Governments:		
U.S. government	79.2	
Federally sponsored agencies	47.5	
State and local governments	20.7	
Total—all governments in United States................		147.4
Total funds raised by major sectors in U.S. financial markets		$404.1

SOURCE: Board of Governors of the Federal Reserve System, *Flow of Funds Accounts,* 1980.

use by making loans. In recent years, mutual savings banks and savings and loan associations along with commercial banks have offered NOW accounts which bear interest, as a savings account does, and permit the customer to draft the account to pay for goods and services, just like a checking account. Since 1977, credit unions have offered "share drafts" which, like the NOW, earn interest and can be used to make payments. Plastic credit cards issued by many commercial and savings banks, credit unions, oil companies, and retail stores give the customer instant access to short-term credit but also are widely accepted as a convenient means of payment.

Another type of plastic card—the debit card—is also used to make purchases of goods and services today. Debit cards, currently issued free by about 10 percent of all banks in the United States, are used to charge a buyer's deposit account for purchases of goods and services and transfer the proceeds instantly by wire to the seller's account. Debit cards and other electronic means of payment, including telephone transfers, cable hookups through in-home TV sets, and computer terminals in retail stores, are likely to displace checks, currency, and other pieces of paper as the principal means of payment in the years ahead.

The Service of Providing Liquidity

The system of financial markets provides liquidity—the ability to raise cash quickly with little risk of loss—to those who save and acquire financial claims. The investor can place funds in stocks, bonds, and other financial assets which earn income and, through the financial system, quickly convert those assets into money. In modern societies money consists mainly of deposits held at commercial banks, savings and loan associations, savings banks, and credit unions. Money has the advantage of *perfect liquidity;* it can be spent as it is without the necessity of converting it into some other form. However, money generally earns the lowest rate of return of all assets traded in the financial system, and its purchasing power is seriously eroded by inflation. That is why savers generally minimize their holdings of money and hold stocks, bonds, and other financial assets instead until spendable funds are really needed.

TYPES OF FINANCIAL MARKETS WITHIN THE FINANCIAL SYSTEM

As we noted above, the financial markets where financial claims and financial services are traded are the heart of the financial system. These markets may be viewed as a vast pool of funds, continually being drawn upon by demanders of funds and continually being replenished by suppliers of funds. The level in the pool rises when the volume of funds contributed by households, businesses, and governments exceeds the amount of funds demanded. At such times, an ample supply of credit is available, and the cost of credit—the rate of interest—tends to decline. On the other hand, when the inflow of funds is small relative to the demand for funds, the level in the pool falls, and the relatively scarce supply of credit available usually leads to higher interest rates. The price mechanism at work in the financial system serves to adjust the demand for and supply of available funds until all those seeking credit and willing to pay its cost are satisfied.

The Money Market versus the Capital Market

The pool of funds represented by the financial markets may be divided into different segments, depending upon the characteristics of financial claims being traded and the needs of different groups. One of the most important divisions in the financial system is between the money market and the capital market.

The *money market* is designed for the making of short-term loans where individuals and institutions with temporary surpluses of funds meet borrowers who have temporary cash shortages. By convention, a security evidencing a loan which matures within one year or less is considered to be a money market instrument. One of the principal functions of the money market is to finance the working-capital needs of corporations and to provide governments with short-term funds in lieu of tax collections. The money market also supplies funds for speculative buying of securities and commodities.

In contrast, the *capital market* is designed to finance long-term investments. Trading of funds in the capital market makes possible the construction of factories, office buildings, highways, bridges, schools, homes, and apartments. Financial instruments traded in the capital market have original maturities of more than one year.

Who are the principal suppliers and demanders of funds in the money market and the capital market? In the money market commercial banks are the most important institutional lender to both business firms and governments. Nonfinancial business corporations with temporary cash surpluses also provide substantial short-term funds to commercial banks, securities dealers, and other corporations in the money market. Finance companies supply large amounts of working capital to major corporate borrowers, as do money market mutual funds which specialize in short-term, high-grade government and corporate securities (see Exhibit 1–2).

EXHIBIT 1–2
The Money Market and the Capital Market

Money Market*		Capital Market†	
Principal Suppliers of Funds	Principal Demanders of Funds	Principal Suppliers of Funds	Principal Demanders of Funds
Commercial banks	U.S. Treasury	Pension funds	Businesses
Nonfinancial corporations	Commercial banks	Insurance companies	Households
Finance companies	Nonfinancial corporations	Households	Governments
Money market mutual funds	Finance companies	Savings and loan associations	
State and local governments	Security dealers	Commercial banks	
Federal Reserve System	Federal Reserve System		

* Securities one year and under to maturity.
† Securities more than one year to maturity.

On the demand-for-funds side the largest borrower in the American money market is the U.S. Treasury, which borrows several billion dollars weekly. The largest and best-known U.S. corporations are also active borrowers in the money market through their offerings of short-term notes. Major securities dealers require huge amounts of borrowed funds daily to carry billions of dollars in securities held in their trading portfolios to meet customer demand. Finally, the Federal Reserve System, which is charged by Congress with responsibility for regulating the flow of money and credit in the U.S. financial system, operates on both sides of the money market. Through its open market operations the Fed both buys and sells securities to maintain credit conditions at levels deemed satisfactory to meet the nation's economic goals.[5] Due to the large size and strong financial standing of these

---

[5] Chapters 21, 22, and 23 examine in detail the role of the Federal Reserve System in U.S. money and capital markets.

well-known money market borrowers and lenders, money market credit instruments are considered to be high-quality, "near money" IOUs.

The principal suppliers and demanders of funds in the capital market are more varied than in the money market. An institution must be large and well known with an excellent credit rating to gain access to the money market. The capital market for long-term funds, in contrast, encompasses both well-established and lesser-known individuals and institutions. Families and individuals, for example, tap the capital market when they borrow to finance a new home or new automobile. State and local governments rely upon the capital market for funds to build schools, highways, and public buildings and to provide essential services to the public. The U.S. Treasury draws upon the capital market in issuing new notes and bonds to pay for federal government programs. The most important borrowers in the nation's capital market are businesses of all sizes, which issue bonds, notes, and other long-term IOUs to cover the purchase of equipment and the construction of new plants and other facilities.

Ranged against these many borrowers in the capital market are financial institutions which supply the bulk of long-term funds. Prominent here are life and property-casualty insurance companies, pension funds, savings and loan associations, mutual savings banks, finance companies, and commercial banks. Each of these institutions tends to specialize in a few different kinds of loans consistent with its own cash-flow needs and regulatory restrictions. For example, life insurance companies are major buyers of corporate bonds and commercial mortgages. Property-casualty insurers stay heavily invested in state and local government (municipal) bonds, corporate stock, and corporate bonds. Pension funds are major buyers of both corporate equities and bonds, while savings and loan associations are principally home mortgage lenders. Mutual savings banks emphasize investments in mortgages and corporate bonds. Finance companies and commercial banks provide large amounts of capital funds to both individuals and businesses through direct loans and lease financing. Commercial banks are probably the most diversified of all lenders in the capital market since they provide long-term funds to all major groups in the economy.

Divisions of the Money and Capital Markets

The money market and the capital market may be further subdivided into smaller markets, each important to selected groups of demanders and suppliers of funds. Within the money market, for example, is the huge U.S. Treasury bill market—the largest market for a single security in the world. Treasury bills—an IOU of the United States government—are a safe, stable, and popular investment medium for financial institutions and nonfinancial corporations of all sizes.

Even larger in total dollar volume is the market for $100,000+ negotiable certificates of deposit (CDs) issued by the largest, best-known commercial banks. These interest-bearing deposit receipts are bought avidly by corporations, wealthy individuals, and state and local governments. Banks use the funds raised from CDs and other sources to extend loans to corporations and other borrowers. Two other important money market instruments evidencing loans to corporations are bankers acceptances and commercial paper. Acceptances are promises issued by a bank to pay a fixed sum of money on a specified date in the future and usually arise from the creation of loans to finance exports and imports of goods. Commercial paper is a short-term IOU issued by a large, well-established corporation, usually to finance purchases of inventory or meet other near-term obligations.

Still another portion of the money market is devoted to trading in federal funds, which are essentially reserve balances of commercial banks held at the Federal Reserve and with other commercial banks. Federal funds are unique in being immediately available money, easily and instantly transferable from one bank to another by wire. Transactions in the money market generally are carried out in federal funds due to their speed and safety.

Another segment of the money market reaches around the globe to encompass suppliers and demanders of short-term funds in Europe, Asia, and the Middle East. This is the vast and largely unregulated Eurocurrency market, where the world's major trading currencies—the dollar, the franc, the pound, the yen, and the mark—are loaned to multinational corporations and governments.

The capital market, too, is divided into several major sectors, each having special characteristics and its own collection of suppliers and demanders of funds. For example, the largest segment of the capital market is devoted to mortgage loans on both commercial and residential properties. A mortgage is a certificate evidencing that a loan has been made, with real property—land, buildings, or equipment—serving as security for the amount of the loan. Mortgage loans outstanding in the United States total well over $1 trillion—more than half the size of the nation's annual GNP. It is a market which encompasses individuals and families as well as some of the largest financial institutions, nonfinancial corporations, and units of government. State and local governments sell their tax-exempt (municipal) bonds in the capital market, principally to high-income individuals, commercial banks, and insurance companies. Consumers borrow well over $100 billion each year in the capital market for purchases ranging from automobiles to home appliances. There is also an international capital market closely linked to trading in Eurodollars and other major Eurocurrencies, represented by the Eurobond market.

Probably the best-known segment of the capital market is the market for corporate stock represented by the major exchanges, such as the New York Stock Exchange (NYSE) and the American Stock Exchange (AMEX), and a vast over-the-counter (OTC) market for individual stocks. No matter where it is sold, however, each share of stock (equity security) represents a certificate of ownership in a corporation, entitling the holder to receive any dividends which may be paid out of current company earnings. Corporations also sell a huge quantity of notes and bonds in the capital market each year to raise long-term funds. These securities, unlike shares of stocks, are pure IOUs, evidencing a debt owed plus an obligation to pay interest to the holder. A list of the principal financial instruments traded in the U.S. money and capital markets today is shown in Exhibit 1–3.

EXHIBIT 1–3
Principal Financial Instruments Traded in the U.S. Money and Capital Markets, 1980 ($ billions, end of period)

	Amount
Principal money market instruments:	
U.S. Treasury bills	$ 216.1
Certificates of deposit ($100,000+)	265.8
Securities issued by federal agencies	193.2
Federal funds sold and repurchase agreements*	109.5
Eurodollar deposits†	205.3
Commercial paper	125.1
Bankers acceptances	54.7
Principal capital market instruments:	
Mortgages	$1,451.8
Common stocks	1,244.5‡
Corporate and foreign bonds	455.7‡
U.S. Treasury notes and bonds	407.0
State and local government bonds	281.0‡
Consumer installment loans	313.4

* Bank borrowings from nonbank institutions.
† Liabilities owed to foreigners payable in U.S. dollars reported by banks in the United States.
‡ Figures are as of year-end 1979.
SOURCES: Board of Governors of the Federal Reserve System, *Flow of Funds Accounts* and *Federal Reserve Bulletin;* U.S. Department of Commerce; *Survey of Current Business;* and U.S. Treasury Department, *Treasury Bulletin.*

Risk in the Money and Capital Markets

As in the money market, each of these segments of the capital market is differentiated from the other segments by regulations, customs, and the unique characteristics of financial instruments traded there. For example, some financial claims carry more risk of borrower default—*credit risk*—than others. At one extreme are U.S. Treasury bills, bonds, and notes, regarded as virtually riskless because the federal government can always tax its citizens or print money to pay its debts. In contrast, debt securities issued by private corporations carry varying degrees of credit risk, and each year thousands of firms fail to meet all of the promised payments of principal or interest on their loans. Some of these firms are forced into bankruptcy. The failures of such major corporations as Penn Central Railroad in 1970, Electrospace in 1973, and W. T. Grant in 1975 suggest that even the securities issued by some of the largest, best-known corporations may quickly lose their value. The collapse of major banks like United States National Bank of San Diego in 1973 or Franklin National Bank of New York in 1974 suggest that even bank deposits and bank stock can be risky.

Financial claims issued by demanders of funds also differ greatly in their degree of risk due to fluctuations in market price—*money risk*. For example, most short-term money market securities are quite stable in price, holding their value well even in periods of considerable economic turmoil and uncertainty. In contrast, long-term capital market securities frequently experience large price fluctuations due to changing economic conditions, political developments, and so on. Some securities are more easily marketed than others, and there are vast differences in maturity. For example, all U.S. Treasury bills mature within a year. In contrast, most home mortgages and many corporate bonds carry original maturities of 20 to 30 years. While, in theory at least, the financial markets are one vast pool of funds, quite clearly the financial system is divided into many segments, each with special features. Many of these unique features and financial characteristics will be considered in subsequent chapters of this book.

Open versus Negotiated Markets

Another distinction within the financial system which is sometimes useful is that between *open markets* and *negotiated markets*. For example, some corporate bonds are sold in the open market to the highest bidder and bought and sold any number of times before they mature. In contrast, in the negotiated market for corporate bonds, securities generally are sold to one or a few buyers under private contract and held to maturity.

An individual who goes to his or her local banker to secure a loan for a new car enters the negotiated market for auto loans. However, a broker instructed to buy a few shares of GM stock will attempt to fill the order by contacting a seller in the open market. Most state and local government securities are sold in the open market, but a growing number are sold under a privately negotiated "treaty" with one or a few buyers. In the market for corporate stocks there are over-the-counter (OTC) sales and the major stock exchanges, which represent the open market. Operating at the same time, however, is the negotiated market for stock, in which a corporation may sell its entire equity issue to a large insurance company or pension fund.

Primary versus Secondary Markets

The financial markets may also be divided into *primary markets* and *secondary markets*. The primary market is for the trading of new securities never before issued. Its principal function is the raising of financial capital to support new investment in buildings, equipment, and inventories. You engage in a primary-market transaction when you purchase shares of stock just issued by a company, borrow money through a new mortgage to purchase a home, negotiate a loan at the bank to restock the shelves of your business, or purchase bonds just issued by the local school district to construct new classrooms.

In contrast, the secondary market deals in securities previously issued. Its chief function is to provide liquidity to security investors—an avenue for converting stocks, bonds, and other securities into ready cash. If you sell shares of stock or bonds you have been holding for some time to a relative or friend or call a broker and place an order for shares currently being traded on the American Stock Exchange, you are participating in a secondary-market transaction.

The volume of trading in the secondary market is far larger than trading in the primary market. However the secondary market does not support new investment. Nevertheless, the primary and secondary markets are closely intertwined. For example, a rise in interest rates or security prices in the secondary market usually leads to a similar rise in the prices or rates on primary-market securities and vice versa. This happens because investors frequently switch from one market to another in response to differences in price and yield. Many financial institutions are active in both markets.

Factors Tying All Financial Markets Together

Each corner of the financial system represents, to some extent, a distinct market with its own special characteristics. Each segment is insulated from the others to some degree by investor preferences and by rules and regulations. Yet when interest rates and security prices change in one corner of the financial system, *all* of the financial markets will be affected eventually. For example, a rise in money market interest rates, sometimes after a lag of several weeks, leads to a rise in capital market rates and usually affects the stock market as well. This implies that, even though law, regulation, tradition, and investor preferences tend to split up the financial system into many different markets, there must be forces at work to tie all of these markets together.

One unifying factor is the fact that the basic commodity being traded in all financial markets is *credit*. The money market, as we have seen, provides short-term credit, while the capital market provides long-term credit. Borrowers can switch from one market to another, seeking the most favorable credit terms. It is not uncommon, for example, for an oil company to finance the construction of an oil rig and drilling platform through short-term money market loans because interest rates in the capital market are unusually high, only to seek long-term funding of the project later on when capital market conditions are more favorable. The shifting of borrowers between markets helps to weld the parts of the financial system closer together. It brings the cost of credit in any one market into proper balance with its cost in other markets.

Another unifying element is the profit seeking of suppliers of funds. Speculators in securities are continually on the lookout for small differences in interest rates attached to different securities. A temporary rise in interest yields in one corner of the market quickly sends funds flowing toward that point. This is the force of *arbitrage,* in which professional investors watch for profitable opportunities and respond instantly by adjusting their portfolios whenever prices and rates on certain financial instruments are unusually attractive. Eventually, after all security buyers and sellers have made their desired portfolio adjustments, a condition of equilibrium is restored. All security prices and interest rates are then consistent with one another, and there is no further reason for change until something happens to disturb the financial system again. As noted at a later point in this book, the money and capital markets are highly efficient markets where security prices and interest rates react quickly to new information and changing economic circumstances.

THE PLAN OF THIS BOOK

This text is divided into eight major sections, each devoted to a particular segment of the financial system.

Part 1 of the book provides an overview of the financial system—its role in the economy, major sectors, and basic characteristics. The emphasis here is on providing the reader with a broad-brush picture of the fundamental nature and purpose of transactions in the financial marketplace. The vital processes of saving and investment, lending and borrowing, and the creation and destruction of financial assets are described, and their critical importance to economic growth, employment, and the nation's standard of living is stressed.

Part 2 is devoted to the study of financial institutions. Commercial banks, credit unions, savings and loan associations, savings banks, insurance companies, pension funds, mutual funds, finance companies—these and other financial firms dominate our financial system today. Moreover, each plays a leading role in different markets within the financial system. For example, commercial banks are the key financial institutions active in the short-term money market on both the borrowing and lending side of that market. Savings and loan associations and savings banks are the principal sources of funds in the market for home mortgages. Insurance companies, pension funds, and mutual funds dominate activity in the corporate bond and stock markets, while finance companies vie with commercial banks for direct commercial and consumer loans. We will encounter each of these institutions, not only in Part 2 of the book, but also later on as we discuss the particular money and capital markets where they are most active.

Part 3 examines in detail the forces that shape and influence interest rates and the prices of financial instruments. These fundamental driving forces within the financial system include savings and investment, the demand for and supply of money, and the demand for credit. The rate of interest is the key price in the financial system, channeling savings toward their most profitable uses and continually bringing the demand and supply for credit into balance. For this reason Part 3 of the text devotes considerable space to developing analytical tools that aid our understanding of what sets the levels of interest rates and security prices at any point in time. The section begins in Chapter 6 with a review of major theories of interest-rate determination. The "real world" measurement and behavior of interest rates and security prices is then addressed in Chapter 7. The next two chapters in Part 3 are devoted to the factors that cause the interest rate and price of one security to differ from those of another. The section concludes with a discussion of the major sources of data available today to students and researchers interested in following movements in interest rates, security prices, and the volume of borrowing and lending going on in the financial system.

Part 4 is aimed at the money market, beginning with an overview of the principal institutions and instruments which dominate money market activity in the United States. Subsequent chapters in this section examine the characteristics of major money market instruments—U.S. Treasury bills, federal funds, repurchase agreements, bank certificates of deposit, commercial paper, federal agency securities, bankers acceptances, and Eurodollars. Principal buyers and sellers of each financial instrument, its maturity ranges, methods of calculating yields, volume of trading, and recent innovations in the market are discussed. The section concludes with a chapter on one of the newest of all short-term financial instruments—financial futures.

The borrowing habits and financial characteristics of consumers—families and individuals—are considered in Part 5. There are two chapters in this section of the book. The first presents an overview of consumer financial affairs, examining the major categories of consumer debt outstanding today and recent changes in laws and regulations affecting the consumer. The second, Chapter 18, is devoted to the largest of all consumer debt markets—residential mortgages—where innovative new financial instruments are being developed today to make home ownership more affordable for individuals and families.

Part 6 focuses upon the activities of nonfinancial business firms in the money and capital markets. Chapter 19 covers business borrowing, principally the marketing, pricing, and trading activity surrounding the issuance of new corporate bonds and notes. Special attention is paid to the critical role played by investment bankers in the modern-day marketing of corporate securities. The final chapter in this section, Chapter 20, is concerned with the market for common and preferred stock. This chapter opens with a discussion of the basic characteristics of corporate stocks—the rights, responsibilities, and risks attached to stock ownership—and then proceeds to examine the structure of today's equities market.

The often dominating role of governments—federal, state, and local—within the financial system is taken up in Part 7 of the text. The first three chapters in the section are devoted to monetary policy and the Federal Reserve System. In terms of day-to-day financial market activity the Fed—the central bank of the United States—probably has more impact on the American financial system than any other agency of government. A brief history of the Federal Reserve System is presented, including a discussion of the weaknesses of our financial system which resulted in the Fed's creation early in this century. The operating structure of the Fed, its major policy tools, and its policy indicators are then addressed in subsequent sections and chapters. Recent problems in the pursuit of the nation's major economic goals are examined, and their implications for the future considered.

The fiscal operations of federal, state, and local governments are examined in Chapters 24 and 25 of the text. Fiscal policy—the taxing and spending activities of the federal government—and the management of the huge public debt of the United States government are reviewed in Chapter 24. State and local government financial affairs are the subject of Chapter 25. The market for state and local government debt (municipals) has been one of the most rapidly growing segments of the U.S. money and capital markets since World War II.

Finally, Part 8 of the text is devoted to the international financial system. Topics covered here include the economic benefits of international trade and finance, the history of changing monetary standards, and the balance-of-payments accounts. The markets for foreign currencies are examined in considerable detail, including the mechanics of modern foreign exchange trading. Part 8 concludes with a discussion of international banking institutions.

Throughout this book there is a strong emphasis upon the innovative character of modern financial systems and institutions. There has been a virtual explosion of new instruments and trading techniques within the financial system in recent years. Examples include financial futures, new types of home mortgages and tax-exempt revenue bonds, instant electronic transfer of funds and other financial information, and major changes in laws and regulations affecting financial services offered, prices charged, and returns paid to savers. Moreover, the pace of innovation in financial services and methods appears to be accelerating under the combined pressure of increased competition, rising costs, and burgeoning demand. As we will see in the pages and chapters that follow, these forces of innovation, competition, rising costs, and growing demand are profoundly reshaping the structure and operations of our whole financial system today.

STUDY QUESTIONS

1. Why is it important to understand how the financial system operates? In what ways is the financial system linked to the economy as a whole?
2. What are the principal functions of markets within the economic system? How do the financial markets fulfill those functions?

3. What is the *rate of interest,* and what is its role in the financial system?
4. Explain what is meant by *saving* and by *investment.* Why are they important to economic growth and the nation's standard of living?
5. Describe the payments function performed by the financial system. In recent years a number of new payments devices have been developed. Describe some of these.
6. Distinguish between the money market and the capital market; between open and negotiated markets and primary and secondary markets. What are the principal divisions of each?
7. Why do interest rates and security prices in the various segments of the financial system tend to move in the same direction? What forces seem to bind the various parts of the financial system together?

SELECTED REFERENCES

1. Carson, Deane, ed. *Banking and Monetary Studies.* Homewood, Ill.: Richard D. Irwin, 1963.
2. Dougall, Herbert E., and Jack E. Gaumnitz. *Capital Markets and Institutions.* 4th ed. Englewood Cliffs, N.J.: Prentice-Hall, 1980.
3. Moore, Basil J. *An Introduction to the Theory of Finance.* New York: Free Press, 1968.
4. Polakoff, Murray E., Thomas A. Durkin et al. *Financial Institutions and Markets.* 2d ed. Boston: Houghton Mifflin, 1981.
5. Smith, Paul F. *Economics of Financial Institutions and Markets.* Homewood, Ill.: Richard D. Irwin, 1971.
6. Van Horne, James C. *Financial Market Rates and Flows.* Englewood Cliffs, N.J.: Prentice-Hall, 1978.
7. Woodworth, Walter G. *The Money Market and Monetary Management.* 2d ed. New York: Harper & Row, 1972.

2

Financial Assets, Money, and Financial Transactions

The financial system is the mechanism through which loanable funds reach borrowers. Through the operation of the financial markets, money is exchanged for financial claims in the form of stocks, bonds, and other securities. And, through the exchange of money for financial claims, the economy's capacity to produce goods and services is increased. This happens because the money and capital markets provide the financial resources needed for investment. While it is true that the financial markets deal mainly in the exchange of paper claims and bookkeeping entries, these markets provide an indispensable conduit for the conversion of savings into investment, accelerating the economy's growth and development.

The present chapter looks closely at the essential role played by the financial markets in converting savings into investment and how that role has changed over time. We begin by observing that nearly all financial transactions between buyers and sellers involve the creation or destruction of a special kind of asset—a *financial asset*. Financial assets perform a vital role in the behavior and decision making of businesses, consumers, and governments. Moreover, financial assets possess a number of characteristics which make them unique among all the assets held by individuals and institutions. In the next section we consider the nature of financial assets and how they are created and destroyed through the workings of the financial system.

THE CREATION OF FINANCIAL ASSETS

What is a *financial asset?* It is a *claim* against the income or wealth of a business firm, household, or unit of government, represented usually by a certificate, receipt, or other legal document. Familiar examples include stocks, bonds, insurance policies, and deposits held in a commercial bank, credit union, or savings bank. Financial assets do not provide a continuing stream of services to their owner as does a home or an apartment, an automobile, or a washing machine. These assets are sought after because they promise *future* returns to the holder and serve as a *store of value* (purchasing power). As noted later in this chapter, money too is a financial asset.

How are financial assets created? We may illustrate this process using a very rudimentary financial system in which there are only two economic units—a household and a business firm.

Assume that this financial system is *closed* so that no external transactions with other units are possible. Each unit holds certain assets accumulated over the years as a result of its saving out of current income. The household, for example, may have accumulated furniture, an automobile, books, clothes, and other items needed to provide entertainment, food, shelter, and transportation. The business firm holds inventories of goods to be sold, raw materials, machinery and equipment, a building, and other assets required to produce its product and sell it to the public.

The financial position of these two economic units is presented in the form of balance sheets, shown in Exhibit 2–1. A balance sheet, of course, is a financial statement prepared as of a certain date, showing a particular unit's

EXHIBIT 2–1
Balance Sheets of Units in a Simple Financial System

Household
Balance Sheet

Assets*		*Liabilities and Net Worth†*	
Cash	$13,000	Net worth	
Furniture	1,000	(accumulated	
Clothes	1,500	savings)	$20,000
Automobile	4,000		
Other assets	500		
		Total liabilities	
Total assets	$20,000	and net worth	$20,000

Business Firm
Balance Sheet

Assets*		*Liabilities and Net Worth†*	
Inventories		Net worth	
of goods	$ 10,000	(accumulated	
Machinery and		savings)	$100,000
equipment	25,000		
Building	60,000		
Other assets	5,000		
		Total liabilities	
Total assets	$100,000	and net worth	$100,000

* Accumulated uses of funds.
† Accumulated sources of funds.

assets, liabilities, and net worth. Assets represent the accumulated *uses of funds* made by economic units, while liabilities and net worth represent the various *sources of funds* which economic units have drawn upon to acquire the assets they now hold. The net worth account represents total savings accumulated over time by each economic unit. A balance sheet must always *balance*, meaning the total assets (accumulated uses of funds) must equal total liabilities plus net worth (accumulated sources of funds).

The household in our example holds total assets valued at $20,000, including an automobile, clothes, furniture, and cash. Because the household's financial statement must balance, total liabilities and net worth also add up to $20,000, all of which in this instance happens to come from net worth (accumulated savings). The business firm holds assets amounting to $100,000, including a building housing the firm's offices, equipment, and machinery, and an inventory of unsold goods. The firm's only source of funds currently is net worth (accumulated savings), also valued at $100,000.

By today's standards the two balance sheets shown in Exhibit 2–1 are most unusual. Neither the household nor the business firm has any outstanding liabilities. Each unit is entirely self-financed, because each has acquired its assets by saving and spending within its current income and not by borrowing. In the terminology of finance, both the household and the business firm have engaged in *internal financing*—the use of current income and accumulated savings to acquire assets.[1] For most businesses and households, internally generated funds are the most important resources for acquiring assets. For example, in the U.S. economy approximately two thirds of all investment in plant, equipment, and inventories carried out by business firms each year is financed internally rather than by borrowing. Households as a group save substantially more than they borrow each year, with the savings flowing into purchases of real assets—homes, automobiles, appliances, clothing, etc.—and into sizable purchases of stocks, bonds, and other financial assets.

Suppose the business firm in our rudimentary financial system wishes to purchase new equipment in the form of a drill press. Due to inflation and shortages of key raw materials, however, the cost of the new drill press has been increasing rapidly. Internal sources of funds are not sufficient to cover the equipment's full cost. What can be done? There are four likely alternatives: (1) postpone the purchase of the new equipment until sufficient savings can be accumulated to cover its cost; (2) sell off some existing assets to raise the necessary funds; (3) borrow all or a portion of the needed funds; or (4) issue new stock (equity securities).

---

[1] In the case of the household, it has accumulated savings by taking some portion of each period's income and setting money aside rather than spending all of its income on current consumption. The business firm has abstained from paying out all of its revenues in expenses (including stockholder dividends). Instead, some portion of the firm's cash inflow each period has been set aside in the form of retained earnings (accumulated savings).

Time is frequently a determining factor here. Postponement of the equipment purchase probably will result in lost sales and lost profits. In the real world where there is not one business firm, as in our example, but many serving the same market, a competitor may rush ahead to expand operations and capture some share of this firm's market. Then, too, in an environment of inflation, the new drill press surely will cost even more in the future than it does now. While selling some existing assets to raise the necessary funds is a distinct possibility, this may take some time, and there is the risk of substantial loss, especially if fixed assets must be sold. The third alternative—borrowing—has the advantage of raising funds quickly, and the interest cost on the loan is tax deductible.[2] The firm could sell additional stock if it hesitated to take on a debt obligation, but equity financing is usually much more expensive than borrowing and requires more time to arrange.

If the business firm decides to borrow, who will lend the funds that it needs? Obviously, in this two-unit financial system the household must provide the needed funds. The firm must engage in *external financing* by issuing to the household securities evidencing a loan of money. In general, if any economic unit wishes to add to its holdings of assets but lacks the necessary resources to do so, it can raise additional funds by issuing financial liabilities (borrowing)—provided a buyer of those IOUs can be found. The buyer will regard the IOUs as an asset—a financial asset—which may earn income, unless the borrower goes out of business and defaults on the loan.

Suppose the business firm decides to borrow by issuing a liability in the amount of $10,000 in order to pay for its new drill press. Because the firm is promising an attractive interest rate on this new IOU, the household willingly acquires it as a financial asset. This asset is intangible—a mere *promise* to pay $10,000 at maturity plus a stream of interest payments over time. The borrowing and creation of this financial asset may be shown on the balance sheets of these two economic units. As shown in Exhibit 2–2, the household has purchased the firm's IOU by using some of its accumulated cash. Its *total* assets are unchanged. Instead of holding $13,000 in noninterest-bearing cash, the household now holds an interest-bearing asset in the form of a $10,000 security and $3,000 in cash. The business firm has increased its stock of machinery and equipment from $25,000 to $35,000 after purchasing the new equipment but also has incurred new debt amounting to $10,000. The firm's total assets and total liabilities plus net worth increase due to the combined effects of borrowing and the acquisition of a productive real asset.

---

[2] An added advantage associated with issuing debt is the "leverage effect." If the firm can earn more from purchasing and using the new equipment than the cost of borrowing funds, the surplus return will flow to the stockholders in the form of increased earnings. Earnings per share of stock will rise, increasing the value of the company's stock and the value of the stockholders' investment. The result is *favorable* financial leverage. Unfortunately, leverage is a two-edged sword. If the firm earns less than the cost of borrowed funds, the stockholders' losses will be magnified as a result of unfavorable (negative) financial leverage.

EXHIBIT 2–2
Unit Balance Sheets Following the Purchase of Equipment and Issuance of a
Financial Asset

Household
Balance Sheet

Assets*		Liabilities and Net Worth†	
Cash............................	$ 3,000	Net worth	$20,000
Financial asset	10,000		
Furniture.....................	1,000		
Clothes	1,500		
Automobile	4,000		
Other assets	500		
		Total liabilities	
Total assets	$20,000	and net worth	$20,000

Business Firm
Balance Sheet

Assets*		Liabilities and Net Worth†	
Inventories of goods	$ 10,000	Liabilities	$ 10,000
Machinery and		Net worth	100,000
equipment:			
Existing equipment	$ 25,000		
New equipment..............	10,000		
Total machinery			
and equipment	35,000		
Building	60,000		
Other assets....................	5,000		
		Total liabilities	
Total assets	$110,000	and net worth	$110,000

* Accumulated uses of funds.
† Accumulated sources of funds.

FINANCIAL ASSETS AND THE FINANCIAL SYSTEM

This simple example illustrates several important points concerning the operation and role of the financial system in the economy. First, the act of borrowing simultaneously gives rise to the creation of an *equal* volume of financial assets. In the foregoing example, the $10,000 financial asset held by the household lending money is exactly matched by the $10,000 liability of the business firm borrowing money. This suggests one way of defining a financial asset: *Any asset held by a business firm, government, or household which is also recorded as a liability or claim on some other economic unit's balance sheet is a financial asset.* Assets which meet this definition of a financial asset include common stock and preferred stock (which are financial claims but not debt), corporate and government bonds, deposits and loans held with a financial institution, insurance policies, and shares in a retirement plan.

For the entire financial system the sum of all financial assets must equal the total of all financial liabilities and claims outstanding. In contrast, *real assets* such as automobiles, furniture, machinery, and buildings are not necessarily matched by claims or liabilities somewhere in the financial system.

This distinction between financial assets and liabilities, on the one hand, and real assets, on the other, is worth pursuing with an example. Suppose you borrow $4,000 from the bank to purchase an automobile. Your balance sheet will now contain a liability in the amount of $4,000. The bank from which you borrowed the funds will record the transaction as a loan—an interest-bearing financial asset—appearing on the asset side of its balance sheet in the like amount of $4,000. On the asset side of your balance sheet appears the market value of the automobile—a real asset. The value of the real asset probably exceeds $4,000 since most banks expect a borrower to supply some of his or her own funds rather than lending the full purchase price. Let's say the automobile was sold to you for $5,000 with $1,000 of the cost coming out of your savings account and $4,000 from the bank loan. Then, your balance sheet would contain a new real asset (automobile) valued at $5,000, a liability (bank loan) of $4,000, and your savings account (a financial asset) would decline by $1,000.

Clearly, there are two equalities which hold for this transaction and also hold whenever money is loaned and borrowed in the financial system. First,

$$
\begin{array}{c}
\text{Volume of financial} \\
\text{assets created}
\end{array}
=
\begin{array}{c}
\text{Volume of liabilities} \\
\text{issued by borrowers}
\end{array}
\tag{2-1}
$$

$$
\begin{array}{c}
\text{In this case, a bank} \\
\text{loan of \$4,000}
\end{array}
=
\begin{array}{c}
\text{A borrower's IOU} \\
\text{of \$4,000}
\end{array}
$$

Second,

$$
\text{Total uses of funds} = \text{Total sources of funds}
$$

$$
\begin{array}{l}
\text{Purchase of a \$5,000} = \text{Issue of a \$4,000} \\
\text{automobile} \qquad\quad\; \text{borrower IOU} + \\
\qquad\qquad\qquad\quad \text{\$1,000 drawn from a} \\
\qquad\qquad\qquad\quad \text{savings account}
\end{array}
\tag{2-2}
$$

Every financial asset in existence represents the lending or investing of money transferred from one economic unit to another.

Because the sum of all financial assets created must always equal the amount of all liabilities and claims outstanding, the amount of lending in the financial system must always equal the amount of borrowing going on. In effect, financial assets and liabilities (claims) cancel each other out across the whole financial system. We can illustrate this fact by reference to the balance sheet of any unit in the economy—business firm, household, or government. The following must be true for all balance sheets:

$$
\text{Total assets} = \text{Total liabilities} + \text{Net worth} \tag{2-3}
$$

Because all assets may be classified as either real assets or financial assets, it follows that

$$\text{Real assets} + \text{Financial assets} = \text{Total liabilities} + \text{Net worth} \quad (2-4)$$

Because the volume of financial assets outstanding must always equal the volume of liabilities and claims in existence, it follows that the aggregate volume of real assets held in the economy must equal the total amount of net worth. Therefore, for the economy and financial system *as a whole:*

$$\text{Total financial assets} = \text{Total liabilities} \quad (2-5)$$

$$\text{Total real assets} = \text{Net worth (i.e., accumulated savings)} \quad (2-6)$$

This means that the value of all buildings, bridges, highways, machinery, schools, and other *real assets* in existence matches the total amount of *saving* carried out by all businesses, households, and units of government. We are not better off in real terms by the mere creation of financial assets and liabilities. These are only pieces of paper evidencing a loan or investment of money. Rather, society increases its wealth only by saving and thus increasing the quantity of real assets, for these assets enable the economy to produce more goods and services.

Does this suggest that the creation of financial assets and liabilities—the basic function of the financial system—is a useless exercise? Not at all. The mere act of saving by one economic unit does not guarantee that those savings will be used to build or purchase real assets which add to society's stock of wealth. In modern economies saving and investment usually are carried out by different groups. In the U.S. economy, for example, the bulk of saving is carried out by households, while business firms account for the majority of investments in productive real assets. Some mechanism is needed to ensure that savings flow from those who save to those who invest in real assets.

The financial system provides the essential channel necessary for the creation and exchange of financial assets between savers and borrowers so that real assets can be acquired. Without that channel for savings, the total volume of investment in the economy surely would be reduced, and the growth of investment and production would be diminished. All investment by individual economic units would have to depend on the ability of those same units to save (i.e., engage in internal financing). Many promising investment opportunities would have to be foregone or postponed due to insufficient savings. Society's scarce resources would be allocated less efficiently than is possible with a system of financial markets. Growth in the nation's income and employment would be seriously impaired.

LENDING AND BORROWING IN THE FINANCIAL SYSTEM

Business firms, households, and governments play a wide variety of roles in modern financial systems. It is quite common for an individual or institution to be a lender of funds in one period and a borrower in the next or to do *both* simultaneously. Indeed, financial intermediaries, such as banks and insurance companies, are in the business of operating on both sides of the financial markets, receiving funds from their customers by issuing attractive financial claims and simultaneously making loans available to other customers. Virtually all of us at one point or another in our lifetime will be involved in the financial system as a borrower or lender of funds and probably both.

A number of years ago two economists, Gurley and Shaw,[3] pointed out that each business firm, household, or unit of government active in the financial system must conform to the following identity:

Expenditures out of current income − current income receipts
= Change in holdings of debt and equity during the
current period − change in holdings of financial assets
during the current period

In symbols,

$$E - R = \Delta D - \Delta FA \qquad (2-7)$$

If our current expenditures (E) exceed our current receipts (R), we usually make up the difference by (1) reducing our holdings of financial assets ($-\Delta FA$)—for example, by drawing money out of a savings account; (2) issuing debt or stock ($+\Delta D$); or (3) using some combination of both. On the other hand, if our receipts (R) in the current period are larger than current expenditures (E), we can (1) build up our holdings of financial assets ($+\Delta FA$)—for example, by placing money in a savings account or buying a few shares of stock; (2) pay off some outstanding debt or retire stock previously issued by our business firm ($-\Delta D$); or (3) do some combination of both.

It follows that for any given period of time—week, month, or year—the individual economic unit must fall into one of three groups:

Deficit-budget unit $E > R$; and so, $\Delta D > \Delta FA$
(net borrower of funds)
Surplus-budget unit $R > E$; and thus, $\Delta FA > \Delta D$
(net lender and investor of funds)
Balanced-budget unit $R = E$; and, therefore, $\Delta D = \Delta FA$

A net lender and investor of funds is really a net *supplier* of funds to the financial marketplace. It accomplishes this function by purchasing financial assets, paying off debt, or retiring equity claims (stock). In contrast, a net borrower of funds is a net *demander* of funds from the money and capital markets, selling financial assets, issuing new debt, or selling new stock. The business and government sectors of the economy tend to be net borrowers (demanders) of funds, while the household sector, composed of all families and individuals, tends to be a net lender and investor (supplier) of funds. This

---

[3] See references 5 and 6 at the end of this chapter.

is shown clearly in data on purchases of financial assets and increases in liabilities compiled each year by the Federal Reserve System for the U.S. Flow-of-Funds accounting system.[4] For example, as Exhibit 2–3 reveals, in 1980 households acquired almost $282 billion in financial assets and issued

EXHIBIT 2–3
Net Acquisitions of Financial Assets and Liabilities by Major Sectors of the U.S. Economy, 1980
($ billions)

Sector of the Economy	Net Acquisition of Financial Assets during Year	Net Increase in Liabilities during Year	Net Lender (+) or Net Borrower (−) of Funds
Households	$281.8	$110.1	$+171.7
Nonfinancial businesses	72.6	139.3	−66.7
State and local governments	19.9	27.1	−7.2
Federal government	26.0	88.8	−62.8

SOURCE: Board of Governors of the Federal Reserve System, *Flow of Funds Accounts,* 2nd Quarter 1981, Statistical Release of the Division of Research and Statistics.

$110 billion in liabilities, making this sector of the U.S. economy a net lender of funds to the financial markets in the amount of almost $172 billion. In contrast, nonfinancial businesses were net *borrowers* of more than $66 billion, while the federal government borrowed net almost $63 billion during the year.

Of course, over any given period of time any one household, business firm, or unit of government may be a deficit, surplus, or balanced-budget unit. In fact, from day to day and week to week, our major institutions in the business and government sectors fluctuate from being deficit-budget units to surplus-budget units and back again. Consider a large corporation such as General Motors or Exxon. One week such a firm may be a net lender, supplying monies for short periods of time through purchases of U.S. Treasury bills, bank CDs, and other financial assets. The following week a dividend payment may be due company stockholders, bonds must be refunded, or purchases made to increase inventories and expand plant and equipment. At this point the firm may become a net borrower of funds, drawing down its holdings of financial assets, securing loans by issuing financial liabilities, or selling equity securities. Most of the large institutions that interact in the nation's financial markets continually fluctuate from one side of the market to the other. This is also true of most households today. One of the most important contributions of the financial system to our daily lives is in permitting businesses, households, and governments to adjust their financial posi-

---

[4] See Chapter 10 for a description of the method of construction and uses of the Federal Reserve System's Flow of Funds Accounts.

tion from that of net borrower to net lender and back again, smoothly and efficiently.

MONEY AS A FINANCIAL ASSET

What Is Money?

The most important financial asset in the economy is *money*. All financial assets are valued in terms of money, and flows of funds between lenders and borrowers occur through the medium of money. Money itself is a true financial asset because all forms of money in use today in the United States and in most other countries are a claim against some institution, public or private, and are issued as debt. For example, one of the largest components of the U.S. money supply today is the checking account, which is the debt of commercial or savings bank. Another important component of the money supply is currency and coin, or pocket money held by the public. The bulk of currency in use today in the United States consists of Federal Reserve notes, representing debt obligations of the 12 Federal Reserve banks. In fact, if the Federal Reserve ever closed its doors (a highly unlikely event!), Fed notes held by the public would be a first claim against the assets of the Federal Reserve banks. As we will see in Chapter 23, some definitions of the nation's money supply today include savings accounts at banks and credit unions, shares in money market mutual funds, and even overnight loans between financial institutions and their customers—all forms of debt, giving rise to financial assets.[5]

The Functions of Money

Money performs a wide variety of important services. It serves as a *standard of value* for all goods and services. Without money the price of every good or service we might wish to trade would have to be expressed in terms of exchange ratios with all other goods and services—an enormous information burden for both buyers and sellers. We would need to know, for example, how many loaves of bread would be required to purchase a quart of milk

---

[5] The principal definitions of the money supply in use today in the United States include: (1) M–1A, the sum of currency and coin in circulation and demand deposits held by the nonbank public; (2) M–1B, the sum of M–1A plus NOW accounts, automatic transfer service accounts at banks and thrift institutions, credit union share drafts, and demand deposits at mutual savings banks; (3) M–2, which includes M–1B plus savings and small-denomination time deposits at all depository institutions, overnight repurchase agreements at commercial banks, overnight Eurodollars held by U.S. nonbank residents, and shares in money market mutual funds; (4) M–3, including M–2 plus large-denomination time deposits at all depository institutions and term repurchase agreements at commercial banks and savings and loan associations; and (5) L, which is M–3 plus various liquid assets such as term Eurodollar deposits held by U.S. nonbank residents, bankers acceptances, commercial paper, U.S. Treasury bills, other liquid Treasury securities, and U.S. savings bonds. See especially references 1, 3, 7, 12, and 14 at the conclusion of this chapter.

or what quantity of firewood might exchange for a suit of clothes. To trade just 12 different goods and services, we would have to remember 66 different exchange ratios. In contrast, the existence of money as a common standard of value permits us to express the prices of all goods and services in terms of only one good—the monetary unit. In the United States that unit is, of course, the dollar. In France the official monetary unit is the franc; in Mexico, the peso; in Britain, the pound sterling; and in West Germany, the deutsche mark. Whatever the monetary unit is called, however, it always has a constant price in terms of itself (i.e., a dollar always exchanges for a dollar). The prices of all other goods and services are expressed in multiples or in fractions of the monetary unit.

Money also serves as a *medium of exchange*. It is usually the only financial asset which virtually every business, household, and unit of government will accept in payment for goods and services. By itself, money typically has little or no use as a commodity (except when gold or silver, for example, is used as the medium of exchange). People accept money only because they know they can exchange the monetary medium at a later date for goods and services. The monetary unit itself need have little or no intrinsic value as a commodity once it is widely accepted. This is why modern governments have been able to separate the monetary unit from precious metals like gold and silver bullion and successfully issue *fiat money* (i.e., pieces of paper) not tied to any particular commodity.

Money's service as a medium of exchange frees us from the terrible constraints of a barter economy. Money allows us to separate the act of selling goods and services from the act of buying goods and services. For example, we can sell our own labor skills for money and then later convert the money earned into food, clothing, and shelter. A medium of exchange readily acceptable to all saves enormous amounts of time. We do not have to search around to find a seller who is offering exactly the same goods and services we need and is willing to buy precisely the goods and services we are offering. With a medium of exchange, buyers and sellers no longer need to have an exact coincidence of wants in terms of quality, quantity, time, and location.

Money serves also as a *store of value*—a reserve of future purchasing power. We need not spend dollars right away but can hold them until circumstances are right and our need for goods or services is imminent. For example, we may wish to buy bonds and stocks, but their prices are falling, and it seems logical to wait for a lower price. Purchasing power can be stored in currency or in a checking account until the time is right to buy. Of course, money is not always a good store of value. The value of money, measured by its purchasing power, can experience marked fluctuations. For example, the prices of consumer goods represented in the U.S. cost-of-living index increased more than 2½ times between 1967 and 1981. If individuals or families had purchased in each of these years the identical market basket of goods and services represented in the U.S. cost-of-living index, they would have found that the purchasing power of their money had decreased by more than half during this period.

Money functions as the only *perfectly liquid asset* in the financial system. An asset is liquid if it can be converted into cash quickly with little or no loss in value.[6] All assets—real and financial—differ in their degrees of liquidity. Generally, financial assets, especially U.S. Treasury bills, bank deposits, and stocks and bonds issued by major corporations, tend to be highly liquid, while real assets, such as a home, an automobile, clothing, furniture, and diamonds, may be extremely difficult to sell in a hurry without taking a substantial loss. Money is, of course, the most liquid of all assets since it need not be converted into any other form in order to be spent. Unfortunately, the most liquid assets, including money, tend to carry the lowest rates of return. One measure of the "cost" of holding money is the income foregone by the owner who fails to convert his or her money balances into more-profitable investments in real or financial assets. The rate of interest, which is the price of obtaining credit in the financial system, is a measure of the penalty suffered by an investor for not converting money into earning assets.

TYPES OF FINANCIAL TRANSACTIONS

Financial markets are never static but change constantly in response to shifting demands from the public, the development of new technology, and changes in laws and regulations. Competition in the financial marketplace forces financial institutions to respond to public need by developing new, better quality, and more convenient financial services. Over time, the system of financial markets has evolved from simple to more complex ways of carrying out financial transactions. The growth of industrial centers with enormous capital investment needs and the emergence of a huge middle class of savers have played major roles in the gradual evolution of the financial system.

Whether simple or complex, all financial systems perform one basic function. They move scarce funds from those who save and lend (surplus-budget units) to those who wish to borrow and invest (deficit-budget units). In the process, money is exchanged for financial assets. However, the transfer of funds from savers to borrowers can be accomplished in at least three different ways. We label these methods of funds transfer: (1) *direct finance,* (2) *semidirect finance,* and (3) *indirect finance.* Most financial systems have evolved gradually over time so as to place less and less reliance upon the

---

[6] A liquid asset possesses three essential characteristics: (1) price stability, (2) ready marketability, and (3) reversibility. An asset must be considered liquid if its price tends to be reasonably stable over time, if it has an active resale market, and if it is reversible so that the investor can quickly recover his original investment.

direct and semidirect financing techniques and greater emphasis upon the indirect financing approach.

Direct Finance

With the *direct* financing technique, borrower and lender meet each other and exchange funds in return for financial assets. You engage in direct finance when you borrow money from a friend and give him your IOU or when you purchase stocks or bonds directly from the company issuing them. We usually call the claims arising from direct finance *primary securities* since they flow directly from the borrower to the ultimate lender of funds. (Figure 2–1 illustrates the process of direct financing between borrowing units and lending units.)

FIGURE 2–1
Direct Finance

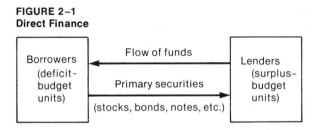

Direct finance is the simplest method of carrying out financial transactions. However, it has a number of serious limitations. For one thing, both borrower and lender must desire to exchange the same amount of funds at the same time. More important, the lender must be willing to accept the borrower's IOU, which may be quite risky, illiquid, or slow to mature. Clearly, there must be a *coincidence of wants* between surplus- and deficit-budget units in terms of the amount and form of a loan. Without that fundamental coincidence, direct finance breaks down.

Another problem is that both lender and borrower must frequently incur substantial *information costs* simply to find each other. The borrower may have to contact many lenders before he finds the one surplus-budget unit with just the right amount of funds and a willingness to take on the borrower's IOU. It should be no surprise to discover that direct finance soon gives way to other methods of carrying out financial transactions as money and capital markets develop.

Semidirect Finance

Early in the history of most financial systems, a new form of financial transaction appears, which we call *semidirect finance*. Some individuals and business firms become securities brokers and dealers whose essential function is to bring surplus- and deficit-budget units together, thereby reducing information costs (see Figure 2–2).

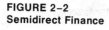

FIGURE 2–2
Semidirect Finance

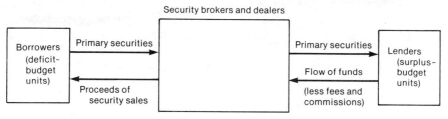

We must distinguish here between a broker and a dealer in securities. A *broker* is merely an individual or financial institution who provides information concerning possible purchases and sales of securities. Either a buyer or a seller of securities may contact a broker, whose job is simply to bring buyers and sellers together. A *dealer* also serves as a middleman between buyers and sellers, but the dealer actually acquires the seller's securities in the hope of marketing them at a later time at a more favorable price. Dealers take a "position of risk" because, by purchasing securities outright for their own portfolios, they are subject to risk of loss if the securities decline in value.[7]

Semidirect finance is an improvement over direct finance in a number of ways. It lowers the search (or information) costs for participants in the financial markets. Frequently a dealer will split up a large issue of primary securities into smaller units affordable by even buyers of modest means and thereby expand the flow of savings into investment. In addition, brokers and dealers facilitate the development and growth of *secondary markets* where securities are offered for resale. When the current holder of securities is short of cash and needs to sell off a portion of a portfolio, the secondary market gives those securities a measure of liquidity and marketability.

Despite the important contribution of brokers and dealers to the functioning of the financial system, the semidirect finance approach is not without its limitations. The ultimate lender still winds up holding the borrower's securities, and therefore the lender must be willing to accept the risk, liquidity, and maturity characteristics of the borrower's IOU. There still must be a fundamental coincidence of wants and needs between surplus- and deficit-budget units for semidirect financial transactions to take place.

---

[7] The meaning of the term *position of risk* is discussed in greater detail in Chapter 12, where the activities of U.S. government securities dealers are examined.

Indirect Finance

The limitations of both direct and semidirect finance stimulated the development of *indirect* financial transactions, carried out with the help of financial intermediaries. Financial intermediaries active in today's financial markets include commercial banks, insurance companies, credit unions, finance companies, savings and loan associations, mutual savings banks, pension funds, mutual funds, and similar organizations. Their fundamental role in the financial system is to serve as intermediaries between ultimate lenders and borrowers, but in a much more complete way than brokers and dealers do. Financial intermediaries issue securities of their own—secondary securities—to ultimate lenders and at the same time accept IOUs from borrowers—primary securities (see Figure 2–3).

FIGURE 2–3
Indirect Finance

Financial intermediaries

Ultimate borrowers (deficit-budget units) → Primary securities / Loanable funds → [Financial intermediaries] → Secondary securities / Loanable funds → Ultimate lenders (surplus-budget units)

The *secondary securities* issued by financial intermediaries include such familiar financial instruments as checking and saving accounts; health, life, and accident insurance policies; pension plans; and shares in a mutual fund. For the most part these securities share a number of common characteristics. They generally carry *low risk* of default. For example, most deposits held in U.S. banks and credit unions are insured by an agency of the federal government up to $100,000. Moreover, the majority of secondary securities can be acquired in *small denominations,* affordable by savers of limited means. For the most part secondary securities are *liquid* and therefore can be converted quickly into cash with little risk of significant loss for the purchaser. Financial intermediaries in recent years have tried to make savings as *convenient* as possible through mail transactions services and transfer of funds by plastic card, computer terminal, and telephone in order to reduce transactions costs to the saver.

Financial intermediaries accept *primary securities* from those who need credit and, in doing so, take on financial assets which many savers, especially those with limited funds and limited knowledge of the market, would find unacceptable. For example, many large corporations require billions of dollars in credit financing each year—sums which would make it impractical to deal directly with thousands of small savers. By pooling the resources of scores of small savings accounts, however, a large commercial bank or other intermediary frequently can service the credit needs of several large firms simultaneously. In addition, many primary securities, even those issued by some of the largest borrowers, are not readily marketable and carry sizable risk of borrower default—a situation usually not acceptable to the small saver. By issuing its own securities, which are attractive to ultimate lenders (savers), and accepting primary securities from borrowers, the financial intermediary acts to satisfy the financial needs of both surplus- and deficit-budget units in the economy.

Portfolio Decisions by Financial Intermediaries

In acting as a middleman between savers and borrowers, the management of a financial intermediary is called upon daily to make *portfolio decisions*— what uses to make of incoming funds and what sources of funds to draw upon. A number of factors affect these critical decisions. For example, the relative rates of return and risk attached to different sources and uses of funds will affect the composition of the intermediary's portfolio. Obviously, if management is interested in maximizing profits and has minimal aversion to risk, it will tend to pursue the highest-yielding assets available, especially corporate bonds and stocks. A more risk-averse institution, on the other hand, is likely to surrender some yield in return for the greater safety available in acquiring government bonds and high-quality money market instruments.

The cost, volatility, and maturity of incoming funds provided by surplus-budget units also has a significant impact upon the loans and investments made by a financial intermediary. Commercial banks, for example, must derive much of their funds from checking accounts, which are relatively inexpensive but highly volatile. Such an institution will tend to concentrate its lending activities in short-term and medium-term loans in order to avoid an embarassing and expensive liquidity crisis. On the other hand, a financial institution, such as a pension fund, which receives a stable and predictable inflow of savings is largely freed from concern over short-run liquidity needs. It is able to invest heavily in stocks, bonds, mortgages, and other long-term assets. Thus, the *hedging principle*—the approximate matching of the maturity of assets held with liabilities taken on—is an important guide for choosing those financial assets that a financial intermediary will hold in its portfolio.[8]

Decisions by intermediaries on what loans and investments to make and what sources of funds to draw upon are also influenced by the *size* of the individual financial institution. Larger financial intermediaries frequently can take advantage of greater *diversification* in sources and uses of funds than smaller institutions. This means that the overall risk of a portfolio of securities can be reduced by acquiring securities from many different borrowers.

---

[8] See Chapter 13 for further discussion of the hedging principal.

Similarly, a larger intermediary can contact a broader range of savers and achieve greater stability in its incoming flows of funds. At the same time, through *economies of scale* (size), larger intermediaries can often sell financial services to both borrowers and ultimate lenders at lower costs per unit and pass those savings along to their customers.

Finally, regulations and competition—two external forces—play major roles in shaping both the sources and uses of funds for a financial intermediary. Because they have the bulk of the public's savings and are so crucial to economic growth and investment activity, financial intermediaries form one of the most heavily regulated of all industries. Examples abound. Commercial banks are prohibited from investing in corporate stock or in speculative debt securities. Insurance companies must restrict any security purchases to those a "prudent man" would most likely choose. Investment companies must make full disclosure of their management goals, fees, and financial position to prospective customers. The maximum interest rates paid on savings deposits by banks and credit unions are regulated by state and federal law. Most regulations in this sector pertain to prices charged, assets which can be acquired, adequacy of net worth, and services which can be offered to the public. In theory, at least, such regulations are designed to promote competition and ensure the safety of the public's funds.

Disintermediation

One factor which has had a profound influence on intermediary portfolios in recent years is the phenomenon of *disintermediation*. Exactly opposite from the intermediation of funds, disintermediation means the withdrawal of funds from an intermediary by ultimate lenders (savers) and the lending of those funds directly to ultimate borrowers. In other words, disintermediation involves the shifting of funds from indirect finance to direct and semidirect finance[9] (see Figure 2–4).

You engage in disintermediation when you remove funds from a savings account at the local bank and purchase common stock or U.S. Treasury bills through a broker. The phenomenon is more likely to occur during periods of high and rapidly rising interest rates when the higher returns demanded by savers outpace the interest rates paid by financial intermediaries. Clearly, disintermediation forces a financial institution to surrender funds and, if severe, may lead to losses on assets and failure. While intermediaries are forced to be more liquid and reduce their credit-granting activities during

---

[9] Some authorities in the field broaden the definition of disintermediation to include the shifting of funds from one financial intermediary to another. For example, if commercial banks are offering more-attractive terms on money market certificates of deposit than savings and loan associations, the public might shift a significant portion of its savings deposits from savings associations to commercial banks. In this instance savings and loans would experience disintermediation while commercial banks would be the beneficiaries of intermediation. See Dougall and Gaumnitz (2), Polakoff et al. (9), and Smith (13) for a further discussion of disintermediation.

FIGURE 2–4
Financial Disintermediation

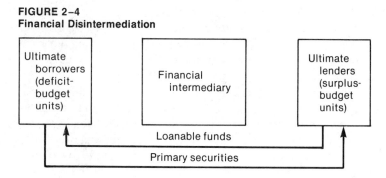

periods of disintermediation, there is no evidence that the *total* flow of credit through the financial system is reduced during such periods.

Types of Financial Intermediaries

Financial intermediaries differ greatly in their relative importance within the U.S. financial system. Measured by total assets, commercial banks dominate the system, as shown in Exhibit 2–4. The $1.7 trillion in assets held

EXHIBIT 2–4
Total Assets of U.S. Financial Intermediaries, Selected Years ($ billions at year-end)

Financial Intermediary	1950	1960	1970	1975	1980*
Commercial banks	$168.9	$257.6	$ 576.2	$ 964.9	$1,702.7
Savings and loan associations	16.9	71.5	176.2	338.2	629.8
Life insurance companies	64.0	119.6	207.3	289.3	476.2
Property-casualty insurance companies	n.a.	30.1	58.6	94.1	156.7†
Mutual savings banks	22.4	40.6	79.0	121.1	171.6
Finance companies	9.3	27.6	64.0	97.7	180.1
Investment companies	3.3	17.0	47.6	42.2	58.4
Credit unions	1.0	5.7	18.0	38.0	71.7
Private pension funds	7.1	38.1	110.6	148.9	264.8
State and local government pension funds	4.9	19.7	60.3	104.7	200.4
Real estate investment trusts	—	—	4.7	21.3	13.6
Money market funds	—	—	—	3.7	74.4
Totals	$297.8	$597.4	$1,402.5	$2,264.1	$4,000.4

n.a. = not available.
* Preliminary data.
† Figures are for year-end 1979.
SOURCES: United States League of Savings Associations, *'81 Savings and Loan Sourcebook* (Chicago: 1981), table 55; and Board of Governors of the Federal Reserve System, *Flow of Funds Accounts: Assets and Liabilities Outstanding, 1969–79.*

by U.S. banks at year-end 1980 represented 43 percent of the total resources of all American financial intermediaries. The huge size of the banking industry relative to other financial industries reflects the tremendous variety of essential financial services offered by commercial banks—a diversity of function unmatched by any other financial institution.

A distant second in relative size is the savings and loan industry—another deposit-type financial intermediary active in the nation's mortgage market. Savings and loan associations held nearly $630 billion in total assets at year-end 1980, or about 16 percent of the aggregate resources of all U.S. intermediaries. Very similar in sources and uses of funds to savings and loans are mutual savings banks, headquartered mainly along the Atlantic seaboard and in the New England area. Mutuals held $172 billion in total assets at year-end 1980, about 4 percent of total intermediary assets. Both savings and loan associations and mutual savings banks were started in the early 19th century to provide an outlet for funds accumulated by small and medium-sized savers. The fourth major kind of deposit-type financial intermediary, the credit union, was also created to attract small savings deposits from individuals and families. Credit unions have been among the fastest-growing U.S. financial institutions in recent years, due principally to their low interest rates on consumer loans and the offering of many new services.

When the assets of all four deposit-type intermediaries—commercial banks, savings and loans, mutual savings banks, and credit unions—are combined, they represent about two thirds of the total assets of all U.S. financial intermediaries. The remaining third of the sector's total assets are held by a highly diverse group of financial institutions. Life insurance companies, which protect their policyholders against the risks of premature death and disability, lead the list of nondeposit financial institutions. U.S. life companies held $476 billion in total assets at year-end 1980, representing about 12 percent of total intermediary resources. The other type of insurance firm—property-casualty insurers—held a much smaller asset total, just $157 billion. Property-casualty insurance companies offer their policyholders protection against a wide variety of risks related to loss of property or injury and death to others.

One of the fastest-growing intermediaries is the pension fund which, like an insurance company, protects its customers against risk. Pension funds provide protection for workers against the risk of living too long following retirement and outlasting the individual's accumulated savings. If we combine pension funds in the private sector with those operated by state and local governments, we find that these institutions held more than $465 billion in assets in 1980, or 12 percent of total intermediary resources.

Other important financial intermediaries include finance companies, investment companies, and real estate investment trusts. Finance companies lend money to both businesses and consumers to meet short-term working-capital needs and for long-term investment. Investment companies pool the funds contributed by thousands of investors by selling shares and then invest mainly in common stocks, corporate and municipal bonds, and, recently, money market securities. Related to investment companies are real estate investment trusts, the smallest member of the financial intermediary sector. REITs invest mainly in commercial and residential real estate projects and distribute all but a small portion of net earnings to their shareholders.

Classification of Financial Intermediaries

Financial intermediaries may be grouped in a variety of different ways. For example, we can identify *depository intermediaries* (commercial banks, savings and loan associations, mutual savings banks, and credit unions) and *contractual intermediaries* (insurance companies and pension funds). Depository institutions derive the bulk of their loanable funds from deposit accounts sold to the public, while contractual intermediaries attract funds by offering legal contracts to protect the saver against risk.

Other methods of classification focus upon the form of organization used by an intermediary. For example, *mutual* organizations (prominent in the insurance industry and among savings and loans, mutual savings banks, and credit unions) legally are owned by their policyholders, depositors, or borrowers. In contrast, *stockholder-owned* intermediaries are owned, as is any private corporation, by their stockholders, and the depositors or policyholders are simply creditors of the organization. Commercial banks, finance companies, investment companies, real estate investment trusts, and some insurance companies and savings and loans are stockholder-owned corporations.

We may also classify an intermediary as a *unit,* if it operates out of only one office, or a *branch,* if it conducts its business from several office locations. This distinction is especially important in the commercial banking industry and in savings banking, where both state and federal laws prohibit or restrict some forms of branching activity.

Some authorities find it useful to distinguish between *local* intermediaries and *regional* or *national* intermediaries. A financial institution is local in character if it receives the bulk of its funds and makes a majority of its loans and investments in the surrounding community (usually a city or county area). Most credit unions, savings and loans, and smaller commercial banks are locally oriented intermediaries. Other financial institutions—especially insurance companies, finance companies, larger commercial banks, pension funds, and investment companies—tend to be regional or national in scope. Their sources of funds, loans, and investments in securities tend to cover wide geographic areas and may even reach into foreign markets. This distinction between local, regional, national, or international intermediaries is especially important in trying to assess the degree of competition prevailing in the financial institutions' sector and in evaluating how well each institution is serving the public in its chosen market area.

CONCLUSION

In the next section of the book we will explore in more depth the role of financial intermediaries in the money and capital markets. We will discover that their role has been expanding rapidly in recent years in response to the rise of the small saver and the massive needs for credit coming from businesses, consumers, and governments today. In most years the process of financial intermediation accounts for about four fifths of all savings flows in the American economy. Thus, while direct financing and semidirect financing techniques are still important ways of carrying out financial transactions, indirect financing through financial intermediaries is clearly the most important route for financial transactions in the modern world.

STUDY QUESTIONS

1. What is a financial asset? How does it arise within the workings of the financial system? Why must the volume of financial assets outstanding always equal the volume of liabilities?
2. Explain the difference between internal and external finance. When an economic unit—business, household, or government—needs funds, what are its principal alternatives? What factors enter into the choice among different sources of funds?
3. How is the creation of financial assets and liabilities linked to saving and investment activity in the economy?
4. Define lending and borrowing for an economic unit. Are these two necessarily equal to each other?
5. Define the terms *deficit-budget unit, surplus-budget unit,* and *balanced-budget unit.* Which were you last month? Why?
6. What is *money?* What are its principal functions within the financial system?
7. Distinguish between direct finance, semidirect finance, and indirect finance. Which is most important today in the financial system? Explain why.
8. What are primary securities? Secondary securities? Give examples of each. Why is the distinction between these two kinds of securities important? What are the principal characteristics of each?
9. List the major kinds of financial intermediaries in the American economy. Which ones on your list can be classified as depository intermediaries? Contractual intermediaries? Mutuals? Stock companies? Local? National or regional?

SELECTED REFERENCES

1. Board of Governors of the Federal Reserve System. "A Proposal for Redefining the Monetary Aggregates." *Federal Reserve Bulletin,* January 1979, pp. 13–42.
2. Dougall, Herbert E., and Jack E. Gaumnitz. *Capital Markets and Institutions.* 4th ed. Englewood Cliffs, N.J.: Prentice-Hall, 1980.

3. Garcia, Gilliam, and Simon Pak. "Some Clues in the Case of the Missing Money." *American Economic Review, Papers and Proceedings,* May 1979, pp. 330–34.

4. Goldsmith, Raymond W. *Financial Institutions.* New York: Random House, 1968.

5. Gurley, John G., and Edward S. Shaw. *Money in a Theory of Finance.* Washington, D.C.: Brookings Institution, 1960.

6. _____. "Financial Intermediaries and the Saving-Investment Process." *Journal of Finance,* May 1956, pp. 257–66.

7. Hafer, R. W. "The New Monetary Aggregates." *Review,* Federal Reserve Bank of St. Louis, February 1980, pp. 25–32.

8. Jacobs, Donald P., Loring C. Farwell, and Edwin Neave. *Financial Institutions.* 5th ed. Homewood, Ill.: Richard D. Irwin, 1972.

9. Polakoff, Murray E., Thomas A. Durkin, et al. *Financial Institutions and Markets.* 2d ed. Boston: Houghton Mifflin, 1981.

10. Pyle, David H. "On the Theory of Financial Intermediation." *Journal of Finance,* June 1971, pp. 737–47.

11. Rose, Peter S. and Donald R. Fraser, *Financial Institutions.* Dallas, Texas: Business Publications, Inc., 1980.

12. Simpson, Thomas D. "The Redefined Monetary Aggregates." *Federal Reserve Bulletin,* February 1980, pp. 97–114.

13. Smith, Paul F. *Economics of Financial Institutions and Markets.* Homewood, Ill.: Richard D. Irwin, 1971.

14. Wenniger, John, and Charles Siversind. "Defining Money for a Changing Financial System." *Quarterly Review,* Federal Reserve Bank of New York, Spring 1979, pp. 1–8.

part two

Financial Institutions in the Financial System

3

Commercial Banks and Money Creation

The dominant financial institution in the United States and in the economies of most major industrialized countries is the commercial bank. This institution offers the public both deposit and credit services and is the major financial intermediary involved in making payments on behalf of the public for purchases of goods and services. The name *commercial* implies that banks devote a substantial portion of their resources to meeting the financial needs of business firms. In recent years, however, commercial banks have significantly expanded their offerings of financial services to consumers and units of government. The result is the emergence of a financial institution which has rightly been called a "financial department store" since it satisfies a broad spectrum of credit and deposit needs in the economy.

The dominant importance of commercial banks may be measured in a number of ways. Banks have about two fifths of the total assets of all financial institutions headquartered in the United States. While this is significantly less than the 70 to 80 percent share of total assets held by commercial banks during the 19th century, it actually reflects a gradual rise in recent years as banks have become more innovative and more aggressive in pursuit of the customer's business. Commercial banks hold the principal means of making payments in the U.S. economy—the check or demand deposit. About four fifths of all transactions balances held by households, businesses, and governments in the United States today consist of demand deposits in commercial banks. And banks are uniquely important because of their ability to create money from excess reserves made available from the public's deposits. The commercial banking system can take a given volume of excess cash reserves and, through the making of loans and investments, generate a multiple amount of credit—a process explained later in this chapter.

Banks today are the principal channel for government monetary policy. In the United States, the Federal Reserve System carries out its policies to affect interest rates and the availability of credit mainly through altering the level and rate of growth of bank reserves. Today, U.S. commercial banks are the most important source of consumer credit and one of the major sources of loans to small and medium-sized businesses. In most years, banks are the principal purchasers of state and local government debt obligations and are one of the major buyers of new security issues by the U.S. Treasury. For all of these reasons commercial banks play a dominant role in the money and capital markets and are worthy of detailed study if we are to understand more fully how the financial system operates.

THE STRUCTURE OF U.S. COMMERCIAL BANKING

The structure of U.S. banking is unique in comparison with other banking systems around the globe. The term *structure* concerns the number and array of sizes of banks operating in the thousands of different banking markets across the United States. While the banking systems of most other nations comprise a few large banking organizations operating hundreds or thousands of branch offices, the U.S. banking system is dominated by thousands of relatively small commercial banks. For example, at year-end 1980 there were nearly 15,000 commercial banking institutions headquartered in the United States compared to only 11 domestic chartered banks in Canada and less than three dozen in the United Kingdom.

Not surprisingly, most U.S. banks are modest in size compared to banks in other countries. Roughly half of all American commercial banks have total assets of under $25 million each, while only about 1 percent hold assets of a billion dollars or more and actively compete in global markets for loans and deposits (see Exhibit 3–1). While smaller banks predominate in numbers, the

EXHIBIT 3–1
Number and Size of Insured U.S. Commercial Banks, December 31, 1980

Asset Size Group*	Number of Banks	Percent of Total	Total Amount of Assets* ($ millions)	Percent of Total
Less than $25 million	7,220	50.0	$ 94,844	6.2%
$25 to $50 million	3,546	24.6	125,799	8.2
$50 to $100 million.................	1,969	13.6	135,521	8.8
$100 to $500 million	1,354	9.4	259,622	16.9
$500 million to $1 billion	159	1.1	107,845	7.0
Over $1 billion	187	1.3	809,344	52.8
Totals	14,435	100.0%	$1,532,975	100.0%

* Domestic assets only. Columns may not add to totals due to rounding.
SOURCE: Federal Deposit Insurance Corporation, *Annual Report*, 1980.

larger banks have a disproportionate share of the industry's assets. For example, the roughly 1 percent of all U.S. banks with a billion or more dollars in total assets have about 50 percent of all assets in the industry. In contrast, the numerically dominant small banks with less than $25 million in assets have only 6 percent of banking's total assets.

Most commercial banks in the United States are chartered by the states rather than by the federal government. As shown in Exhibit 3–2, of the

EXHIBIT 3–2
Number of Operating Commercial Banks and Branches in the United States, December 31, 1980

Category	Number of Banks	Number of Branch Offices
Insured banks:		
National banks	4,425	19,620
State-chartered member banks	997	4,759
Members of the Federal Reserve System—total	5,422	24,379
Nonmember state-chartered banks	9,000	13,923
Total—insured banks.............................	14,422	38,302
Noninsured banks	414	51
Total—all U.S. commercial banks	14,836	38,353

SOURCE: Board of Governors of the Federal Reserve System, *Annual Report,* 1980.

almost 15,000 commercial banks in operation at year-end 1980, close to 10,000 were state chartered. The remaining one third, classified as national banks, were chartered by the federal government. National banks, on average, are much larger and include nearly all of the nation's billion-dollar banking institutions. All national banks must be insured by the Federal Deposit Insurance Corporation (FDIC) and be members of the Federal Reserve System. State-chartered banks may elect to become members of the Fed and also elect to have their deposits insured by the FDIC if they are willing to conform to the regulations of these two federal agencies. The vast majority of U.S. banks (about 97 percent) are FDIC insured, but only a minority have elected to join the Federal Reserve System. Nevertheless, Fed member banks hold more than two thirds of all bank deposits and assets in the United States. We will have more to say about the roles of the Fed, the FDIC, and other bank regulatory agencies at a later point in this chapter.

A Trend toward Consolidation

A number of interesting structural changes have affected the banking industry in recent years. One of the most important is the drive toward *consolidation* of industry assets and deposits into larger and larger organizations.

As we noted above, the United States is still essentially a nation of small banks. But great pressures are operating to form larger banking organizations in order to make more efficient use of resources. Recent studies by Bell and Murphy (3), Benston (4), Daniel, Longbrake, and Murphy (13), and others suggest that as banks grow their costs increase more slowly than output, resulting in cost savings. In general, a 10 percent rise in deposit and loan accounts results in only a 9 percent increase in the cost of bank operations. When automated bookkeeping and computer processing of accounts are used, substantial economies of size characterize bank installment and real estate lending and the offering of checking accounts. Under pressure from a cost squeeze, declining profit margins, and increased competition from bank and nonbank financial institutions, many U.S. banks have viewed the strategy of growing into larger-sized banking organizations as an "escape" from some of these pressures.

Branch Banking

The drive toward consolidation of banking organizations is most evident in the shift toward branch banking. Until the 1940s and 1950s, the United States was basically a nation of *unit banks,* each housed in only a single office. For example, in 1900 there were 12,427 banks, but only 87 of these had any branches. By 1975, however, there were 14,632 commercial banks of which 5,521, or 38 percent, were branch-banking organizations. And the number of branch offices has increased dramatically in recent years. In 1950 there were approximately 4,700 branch-banking offices in operation; by 1980 the total reached more than 38,000.

The growth of branching has been aided by the liberalization of many state laws to permit greater use of the branch office as a means of growth. Prominent examples of states liberalizing their branch-banking laws in recent years include Florida, New Jersey, New York, and Virginia. Another factor is the massive shift of the U.S. population over the last three decades to suburban and rural areas. Many of the nation's largest banks have followed their customers to outlying markets through branching and mergers in order to protect their sources of funds. The trend toward more and more branch banking is likely to continue in future years provided restrictive state and federal laws can be changed.

Bank Holding Companies

Paralleling the rapid growth of branch banking has been the growth of bank holding companies. The bank holding company is a relatively old organizational form in the industry, having its origins in the late 19th century. A bank holding company is simply a corporation organized to acquire the stock of one or more banks. The company may also hold stock in certain nonbank business ventures.

Fearing danger to the safety of banks, Congress first attempted to regulate the bank holding company movement during the 1930s but was largely unsuccessful. Then in 1956 the Bank Holding Company Act was passed. The new law required all holding companies controlling at least 25 percent of the stock of two or more banks to register with the Federal Reserve Board. In addition, a holding company seeking to acquire additional shares of a bank was required to obtain Fed approval.

The Bank Holding Company Act left an unregulated opening for holding companies which held stock in only one bank. As a result, many of the nation's largest commercial banks formed one-bank holding companies during the late 1960s and began to reach out and acquire nonbank businesses far removed from the business of banking, including steel mills and meat-packing plants. Congress closed this loophole with passage of the 1970 amendments to the Bank Holding Company Act. From this point on, all holding companies seeking to acquire even a single bank had to register with the Federal Reserve Board and gain Fed approval for any new bank or nonbank business. Nonbank business ventures acquired must now be so "closely related" to banking as to be "a proper incident thereto." What business activities are "closely related" to banking? To date, the Federal Reserve Board has approved for acquisition businesses engaged in the making of loans (such as finance companies), the writing of leases (for example, equipment-leasing companies), insuring the repayment of credit (such as firms selling credit life insurance), and the recording and transfer of financial information (such as data-processing firms).

Bank holding companies have grown rapidly in the United States. In 1960 registered holding company organizations controlled only about 6 percent of all domestic banking offices. By 1980, holding companies controlled about half of U.S. banking offices and about three quarters of the nation's bank deposits. Most of this dramatic growth was due to the requirement after 1970 that one-bank holding companies register with the Federal Reserve Board. The growth of nonbanking business activities of holding companies also has been extremely rapid. Insurance agencies, finance companies, mortgage companies, leasing firms, factoring companies, data-processing facilities, consulting firms, and other financially related businesses have been started or acquired in substantial numbers by bank holding companies in recent years. These ventures represent an attempt to diversify banking operations geographically and by product line in order to reduce risk and gain access to a broader market. They are also an attempt to gain the advantages of increased size and market power and to skirt around those state laws which forbid or restrict branch banking.

International Banking

The growth of larger U.S. banking organizations at home has been paralleled by accelerated growth of American banks abroad. This expansion overseas has not been confined to the largest institutions in such established money centers as New York, Chicago, Los Angeles, and San Francisco, but today includes leading banks in regional financial centers such as Atlanta, Dallas, Houston, and Miami. Several of the nation's largest banks receive half or more of their net income from foreign sources.

These big U.S. banks have penetrated overseas markets for a wide variety of reasons. In many cases their corporate customers expanding abroad have needed multinational banking facilities. The huge Eurodollar market which spans the globe offers an attractive source of bank funds when domestic sources of funds are less available or more costly. In most instances, foreign markets have also offered fewer regulatory barriers and less banking competition than are found in the United States. On the other side of the coin, foreign banks have grown rapidly in the United States, with many of the largest European, Middle Eastern, and Asian banks viewing the 50 states as a huge, economically and politically stable common market. Congress responded to this "invasion" by foreign banks by passing the International Banking Act of 1978, bringing foreign banks under federal regulation for the first time.[1]

Bank Failures

One undesirable side effect of all these recent changes in the banking community is an apparent rise in the bank failure rate. For most of its history, the banking industry has experienced an extremely low failure rate due to extensive government regulations and conservative management practices. Studies show that the failure rate in U.S. banking is less than 1 percent of the total banking population, compared to about 10 times that figure for private industry as a whole. However, the number of commercial bank failures and the average size of failing banks has advanced sharply in recent years.

For example, a postwar record for the number of bank failures in a single year was set in 1976, when 16 insured U.S. banks closed their doors. However, during 1982 a new record was in the making with close to 30 failures recorded. The largest U.S. bank ever to fail was Franklin National Bank of New York, which ranked 14th in the nation in total assets at the time of its closing in October 1974.

The reasons behind this apparent acceleration in bank failures are numerous. Many bankers today are willing to accept greater risk in their operations, in part because of intensified competition from bank and nonbank financial institutions. More leniency in the interpretation and enforcement of banking regulations, such as standards for the maintenance of equity capital, has also been a factor in the overall trend of increased bank failures. Some analysts argue that the dominant cause is the increased volatility of eco-

---

[1] The provisions of the International Banking Act and the recent growth of international banking are discussed in Chapter 28.

nomic and financial conditions, especially interest rates and the prices of foreign currencies.

Changing Technology

Banking today is passing through a technological revolution. Computer terminals and high-speed information processing are transforming the industry, stressing convenience and speed in handling such routine banking transactions as making deposits, withdrawing cash, repaying loans, and cashing checks. Most of the new technology is designed to reduce labor and paper costs, making the industry less labor intensive and more capital intensive.

Among the most important pieces of technology in the industry are automated teller machines (ATMs). ATMs accept deposits, dispense cash and information, and accept payments. For many banking transactions they perform just as human tellers do, with the added advantage of 24–hour availability. Most ATMs during the 1970s were placed on bank premises, but their future growth probably will be centered in retail stores, shopping centers, airports, and train terminals. In these locations they are known as remote service units (RSUs) and serve to lower transactions costs for the customer and to reduce the need for conventional branch offices.

Related to ATMs are point-of-sale terminals (POS) located in retail stores and other commercial establishments. Connected on-line to the bank's computer, POS terminals accept plastic credit and debit cards, permitting the customer to pay instantly for a purchase without the necessity of cashing a check. For those customers who do want to cash checks, a store can use the POS terminal to verify that a check is good. Customers have not accepted POS terminals as enthusiastically as they have ATMs. Part of the problem is the customer's loss of checkbook float when payments are made instantly. In the United States, POS terminals have run into serious legal challenges in the courts on grounds that they violate antibranching laws in several states.

Another important new piece of machinery in the industry is the automated clearinghouse (ACH). An ACH transfers information from one financial institution to another and from account to account via computer tape. In the United States, more than 10,000 financial institutions—commercial banks, credit unions, savings and loan associations, and mutual savings banks—are members of about 30 regional ACHs. They are used principally for handling payrolls, dispensing welfare payments, and processing federal government transactions. In the near future, check truncation systems will be used extensively alongside the ACH. Such a system transmits images of checks electronically from one financial institution to another, eliminating the need to transfer paper.

On the near horizon is in-home banking via TV screen and telephone. In 1980, Bank One of Columbus, Ohio, began experimenting with cable TV outlets in approximately two hundred homes. A special adapter unit permits information on bank accounts and installment payments and even data from an encyclopedia and the card catalog of the local public library to appear on an ordinary home TV screen. Using a special keyboard, the customer punches in a request for information or conducts financial transactions over the telephone. Such systems, in effect, make every customer a branch, provide greater convenience, and cut down on paper flow. Telephone bill-paying services are expected to proliferate in great numbers over the next two decades.

These recent technological changes have profound implications for bank costs, employment, and profitability. In the future, customers will find less and less need to enter a bank building, and the need for brick-and-mortar branches will decline. Routine financial transactions can be handled by terminals and telephones in homes, stores, shopping centers, and other locations miles distant from bank offices. Conceivably, even arrangements for a loan could be made by telephone and remote video screen. Rapidly rising energy costs suggest that future banking needs will be met mainly by transferring information rather than by requiring people to move from one location to another. The banker's principal function will be one of providing the necessary equipment and letting customers conduct their own financial transactions. This development implies fewer bank employees but more equipment per dollar of deposits. A heavy investment of bank funds in computers and money machines will result in substantial fixed costs, requiring a large volume of transactions and favoring the largest banking organizations in the nation. The new technology of banking should further intensify pressures for consolidation of the industry into banks smaller in number but much larger in average size.

THE REGULATORY FRAMEWORK FOR BANKS

Commercial banks, due to their dominant importance in the financial system, are closely regulated. Moreover, in the United States banking is more heavily regulated than is true in most other industrialized countries. From this nation's earliest history there has been a fear of concentrated power in banking, since bank credit is so vital to the economic well-being of businesses and households. During the colonial period of U.S. history several banks were burned to the ground because of public mistrust and misunderstanding of their basic function in the economy. During the 19th century and again early in this century severe restrictions were placed on the growth of banks through branching and holding companies.

Another significant restriction on banking's growth and development occurred in 1934 when Congress passed the Glass-Steagall Act, forbidding commercial banks from acquiring or underwriting corporate stock. This step effectively prevented banks from gaining control of nonfinancial corporations through purchases of stock. When banks skirted this prohibition in the late 1960s through the formation of holding companies, Congress again applied the brakes by passing the 1970 amendments to the Bank Holding Company Act.

Responsibility for regulating U.S. banks is divided among three federal banking agencies and the state banking commissions of each of the 50 states. These regulatory agencies have overlapping responsibilities, so that most banks are subject to multiple jurisdictions. This division of authority and responsibility has stimulated a number of reform proposals in recent years to consolidate the regulatory process and make it more efficient.[2]

Commercial bank regulation today encompasses all of the following activities: (1) chartering new banks; (2) issuance and enforcement of laws and regulations; (3) periodic examinations of bank records; (4) approval of changes in banking powers, such as the offering of trust services or the acquisition of nonbank subsidiaries; (5) authorization of new branch offices; (6) approval of mergers and consolidations; (7) approval of acquisitions by existing bank holding companies and the formation of new holding companies; and (8) liquidation of banks.

The regulatory agencies responsible for enforcing banking's ground rules include the Federal Reserve System, the Comptroller of the Currency, and the Federal Deposit Insurance Corporation—all at the federal level—and the state banking commissions of the 50 states. Figure 3–1 provides a brief summary of the principal regulatory powers exercised by these federal and state agencies.

The Federal Reserve System

The Federal Reserve System is responsible for examining and supervising the activities of all its member banks. When a member wishes to merge with another bank or establish a branch office, it must seek Fed approval. The Fed must review and approve the formation of all bank holding companies active in the United States and approve the acquisition of nonbank businesses by holding companies. The Federal Reserve is responsible for certain U.S.-based international banking corporations (known as Edge Act subsidiaries) and for supervising member bank operations in foreign countries. It is responsible for regulating credit extended by banks and by security brokers and dealers for the purchasing or carrying of corporate stocks or convertible securities.

The Fed sets reserve requirements on both transactions deposits (such as checking accounts and NOW accounts) and time and savings deposits for all

---

[2] An important step was taken toward reform and consolidation of bank regulatory authority at the federal level in March 1980, when the Depository Institutions Deregulation and Monetary Control Act (DIDMCA) was passed. As we will see in more detail later on, DIDMCA brought all depository financial institutions under the same reserve requirements administered by the Federal Reserve System and created a new regulatory body to set maximum legal interest rates on checking and savings accounts for all depository institutions.

FIGURE 3-1
Principal Bank Regulatory Agencies

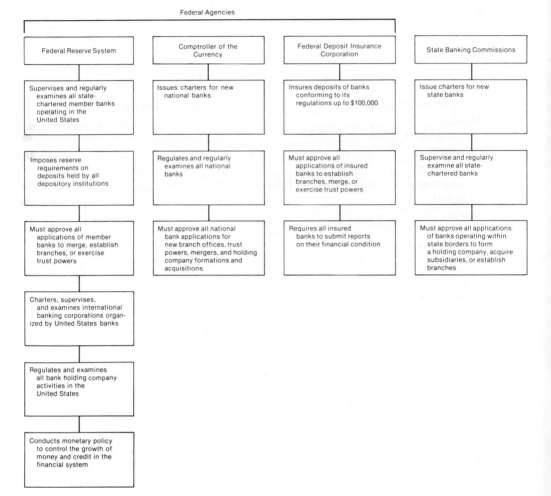

depository institutions, including commercial and savings banks, savings and loan associations, and credit unions. Moreover, the chairman of the Federal Reserve Board is a voting member of the Depository Institutions Deregulation Committee, which sets the maximum legal interest rates depository institutions can pay on their time and savings deposits.[3]

The Federal Reserve has the power to regulate consumer installment and real estate credit, although this power is not exercised currently. As we will see in Chapter 21, the Fed's most important power is that of carrying out

---

[3] See Chapter 22 for a discussion of legal interest-rate ceilings on deposits and the role of the Depository Institutions Deregulation Committee in setting those rate ceilings.

monetary policy to regulate the cost and availability of credit in the financial markets, all for the purpose of pursuing the nation's economic goals.

The Comptroller of the Currency

The Comptroller of the Currency—also known as the Administrator of National Banks—is a division of the United States Treasury, established under the National Banking Act of 1863. The Comptroller has the power to issue federal charters for the creation of *national banks*. These banks are subject to an impressive array of regulations, most of which pertain to the kinds of loans and investments that may be made and the amount and types of capital which each bank must hold. All national banks are examined at least once each year by the Comptroller's staff.

In chartering new national banks the Comptroller reviews all charter applications for the adequacy of their capital, the earnings potential of the proposed bank, the character of its management, and the convenience and needs of the community to be served. Similar criteria are applied to applications from existing national banks to open new branch offices, merge, or form holding companies.

Federal Deposit Insurance Corporation

The Federal Deposit Insurance Corporation insures deposits of U.S. commercial banks which meet its regulations; the coverage provides up to $100,000 per depositor. Roughly 98 percent of all U.S. banks are insured, and approximately 62 percent of all commercial bank deposits are covered by the FDIC's insurance program. Each participating bank is assessed annually an amount equal to about $1/10$ of 1 percent of its eligible deposits to build and maintain a national insurance fund.

One of the most important functions of the FDIC is to act as a check on the state banking commissions, because few banks today—even those with state charters—will open their doors without FDIC insurance. The FDIC reviews the adequacy of capital, earnings prospects, the character of management, and the public convenience and needs aspects of each application before granting deposit insurance. This agency is also charged with examining insured banks that are not members of the Federal Reserve System, and it must approve applications for branches, changes in location, or mergers involving federally insured banks. The FDIC is empowered to close a bank when it can no longer meet its obligations. In most cases an insolvent bank will be merged with or absorbed by a healthy one; the FDIC often purchases some of the bankrupt institution's weaker assets to support such a merger.

State Banking Commissions

The regulatory powers of the federal banking agencies overlap with those of the state banking agencies, which rule upon charter applications in their respective states and regularly examine all state-chartered banks. The states also have rules prescribing the minimum amount of equity capital for individual banks and frequently place interest-rate ceilings on deposits and loans. Many states in recent years have imposed restrictions on the growth and formation of bank holding companies, requiring state approval before a holding company may be formed or, once formed, before it can acquire additional subsidiaries. In chartering a new bank the state authorities, like the federal authorities, consider the new bank's prospects for earnings, the convenience and needs of the public in the area to be served, and the potential for damage to existing financial institutions if a new charter is granted.

One of the areas in which state banking law currently is supreme is that concerning branch banking. Since the McFadden Act of 1927, the federal government has allowed the states to determine whether commercial banks operating within their borders will be permitted to establish any branch offices and, if so, under what circumstances. Today, 15 states forbid full-service branch offices. These so-called *unit-banking states* are situated mainly in the Midwest and South and include Texas, Kansas, Nebraska, and Colorado. However, as we saw earlier, there is a definite trend toward greater use of branching and holding company activity in most parts of the United States. Recent examples include Florida, which until 1978 was a unit-banking state and now permits limited branching on a countywide basis. The state of New York converted to statewide branching in 1976 following an experiment with limited branching in designated regions. Most experts predict that in future years branch banking in one form or another will spread across the United States as needs for larger banking organizations and new financial services increase.

PORTFOLIO CHARACTERISTICS OF COMMERCIAL BANKS

Commercial banks are the "financial department stores" of the nation's financial system. They offer a wider array of financial services than any other form of institution, meeting the credit, payments, and savings needs of individuals, businesses, and governments. This characteristic of *financial diversity* is reflected in the basic financial statement of the industry—its balance sheet (or statement of condition). Exhibit 3–3 provides a list of the major sources of funds (liabilities and capital) and uses of funds (assets) for all FDIC-insured commercial banks.

Primary Reserves

All commercial banks hold a substantial part of their assets in *primary reserves*, consisting of *cash and deposits due from other banks*. These reserves are the banker's first line of defense against withdrawals by depositors, customer demand for loans, and immediate cash needs to cover expenses. Banks generally hold no more in cash than is absolutely required to meet

EXHIBIT 3–3
Assets, Liabilities and Capital of Insured Commercial Banks in the United States, 1980
($ millions)

Assets	
Cash and due from banks (primary reserves)	$ 331,909.3
Security holdings:	
U.S. Treasury securities	104,466.2
Federal agency securities	59,078.3
Municipal securities	146,263.4
Other securities	24,637.3
Federal funds sold and securities purchased under agreements to resell	70,321.8
Loans:	
Real estate loans	269,111.6
Loans to farmers	32,259.8
Commercial and industrial loans	390,930.8
Loans to individuals	187,375.7
All other loans	48,940.8
Less: Unearned income on loans	21,031.7
Less: Allowance for possible loan losses	13,993.2
Direct lease financing	13,993.2
Real estate owned	2,208.4
Other assets	110,394.6
Total assets	$1,855,687.8
Liabilities	
Demand deposits	$ 431,539.4
Savings deposits	200,869.8
Time deposits	554,740.0
Deposits in foreign offices	294,011.6
Total deposits	1,481,160.7
Federal funds purchased and securities sold under agreements to repurchase	133,290.7
Other liabilities	127,086.3
Total liabilities	1,741,537.7
Subordinated notes and debentures	6,553.6
Equity Capital	
Preferred stock—par value	134.6
Common stock—par value	21,672.0
Undivided profits, surplus, and reserves	85,789.9
Total equity capital	107,596.5
Total liabilities and capital	$1,855,687.8

Note: Figures may not add to totals due to rounding.
SOURCE: Federal Deposit Insurance Corporation, Bank Operating Statistics, 1980.

short-run contingencies, however, since the yield on cash assets is minimal or nonexistent. The deposits held with other banks do provide an implicit return, though, since they are a means of "paying" for correspondent banking services. In return for the deposits of smaller banks, the larger U.S. correspondent banks provide such important services as clearing of checks, management of security portfolios, tax advice, and computer processing of records. Thousands of smaller banks across the United States invest their excess cash reserves in loans to other banks (usually called federal funds) with the help of their larger correspondents.[4] Primary reserves also include reserves held behind deposits as required by the Federal Reserve System.

Investments and Secondary Reserves

Commercial banks hold *securities* acquired in the open market as a long-term investment and also as a secondary reserve to help meet short-run cash needs. For most banks municipal securities—bonds and notes issued by state, city, and other local governments—represent the largest portion of security investments. Commercial banks are subject to the same tax rates as most nonfinancial corporations and therefore find the tax-exempt interest income paid by municipal securities to be extremely attractive. In fact, banks today hold more than half of the total volume of state and local government debt outstanding.[5]

Close behind municipals in amount are bank holdings of U.S. Treasury obligations (including bills, notes, and bonds). Banks generally favor Treasury bills (which must mature within one year) and shorter-term Treasury notes and bonds because these securities can be marketed readily to cover short-run cash needs. Moreover, Treasury securities are free of default risk.

A closely related form of federal debt—securities issued by federal agencies such as the Federal Land Banks—has rapidly increased its share of bank portfolios. These securities carry yields slightly above those on direct Treasury obligations; yet they appear to involve little additional risk. Commercial banks also hold small amounts of corporate bonds, notes, and debentures, though they generally prefer to make direct loans to businesses as opposed to purchasing their securities in the open market. Under existing regulations, commercial banks are forbidden to purchase corporate stock. However, bands do hold small amounts of corporate stock as collateral for loans.

Loans

The principal business of commercial banks is to make *loans* to qualified borrowers. Loans are among the highest-yielding assets a bank can add to its portfolio, and they provide the largest portion of operating revenues.

Banks make loans of reserves to other banks through the federal funds market and to securities dealers through repurchase agreements. Far more

---

[4] A more complete discussion of the operations of the federal funds market is presented in Chapter 13.

[5] Purchases of tax-exempt state and local government bonds are the most important method used by banks today to tax shelter their earnings. Banks also tax shelter their income through the purchase and leasing of equipment to business firms. Equipment leasing enables a bank to secure a federal investment tax credit and write off the annual depreciation cost as a tax-deductible expense. Another bank tax shelter consists of setting aside a portion of current income as an operating expense for protection against possible losses on loans.

important in dollar volume, however, are *direct loans* to both businesses and individuals. These loans arise from negotiation between the bank and its customer and result in a written agreement designed to meet the specific credit needs of the customer and the requirements of the bank for adequate security and income.

As shown in Exhibit 3–3, most bank credit is extended to commercial and industrial customers. Historically, commercial banks have preferred to make short-term loans to businesses, principally to support purchases of inventory. In recent years, however, banks have substantially lengthened the maturity of their business loans. Today at least a third of bank business loans are *term loans* (which have maturities over one year) to finance the purchase of buildings, machinery, and equipment.[6] Most term loans are secured by liens against capital and equipment or even short-term assets, such as inventory or accounts receivable, and are amortized through monthly or quarterly installment payments.[7]

Longer-term loans to business have been supplanted to some extent in recent years by equipment leasing plans available from larger banks and the subsidiaries of bank holding companies. These leases are the functional equivalent of a loan: the customer not only makes the required lease payments for using the equipment but is responsible for repairs and maintenance and for any taxes due. Lease financing carries not only significant cost and tax advantages for the customer but also substantial tax advantages for the bank, since it can depreciate the equipment and write off a portion of the cost as an investment tax credit.

Commercial banks are also important lenders in the real estate field, supporting the construction of residential and commercial structures and even carrying out a limited volume of permanent mortgage financing for higher-priced residential and commercial ventures. Major types of loans in the real estate category include farm real estate credit, conventional and government-guaranteed (FHA and VA) single-family residential loans, conventional and government-guaranteed loans on multifamily residences, and

---

[6] Bank term loans are discussed in more detail in Chapter 19.

[7] There is evidence that more-volatile interest rates in recent years have caused banks to make a number of adjustments in their lending programs to protect profit margins. As the 1980s began, the proportion of long-term loans bearing floating as opposed to fixed interest rates rose significantly. At the same time the average maturity of loans (particularly commercial loans) shortened somewhat. The margin between loan rates and expected funding costs widened as well in order to reduce interest-rate risks.

These changes were motivated by the fact that banks carry a large volume of rate-sensitive liabilities (especially CDs). In an era when interest rates rise and fall rapidly, bank profit margins will be severely squeezed unless their assets (especially loans) can be made interest rate sensitive as well.

Loan terms are becoming more and more complicated, especially on commercial loans. Banks increasingly are using specific pricing of the different kinds of risk encountered in a credit agreement. Where possible, interest-rate risk is shifted to the borrower. The use of collateral is becoming more common on longer-term loans, and loans carrying the highest interest rates usually are fully collateralized.

mortgage loans on nonfarm commercial properties. Commercial banks are the most important source of construction financing in the U.S. economy.

Probably the most dynamic area in bank lending today is the making of installment loans to individuals and families. The number of new households has expanded rapidly in recent years, and commercial banks have moved aggressively to capture a larger share of the consumer credit market by offering longer maturities on installment loans and new types of credit arrangements, especially credit card plans. As a result the commercial banking industry has become the major consumer installment lending institution in the United States, taking over the number one position once held by finance companies. Banks finance the purchase of automobiles, mobile homes, recreational vehicles, home furnishings, and appliances and provide funds to modernize homes and other properties.

Deposits

In order to carry out their extensive lending and investing operations, banks draw upon a wide variety of deposit and nondeposit sources of funds. The bulk of commercial bank funds (80 percent or more) comes from deposits. There are three main types. *Demand deposits,* more commonly known as checking accounts, are the principal means of making payments because they are safer than cash and widely accepted. *Savings deposits* generally are in small dollar amounts; they bear a relatively low interest rate but may be withdrawn by the depositor with little or no notice. *Time deposits* carry a fixed maturity and offer the highest interest rates a bank can pay. Time deposits may be divided into nonnegotiable certificates of deposit (CDs), which are usually small, consumer-type accounts, and negotiable CDs that may be traded in the open market and are purchased principally by corporations.

During the 1970s new forms of checkable deposits appeared, combining the essential features of both demand and savings deposits. These *transaction accounts* include negotiable orders of withdrawal (NOWs) and automatic transfer services (ATS).[8] NOWs may be drafted to pay bills but also earn interest up to a maximum legal rate of 5¼ percent. ATS is a preauthorized payments service in which the bank transfers funds from an interest-bearing savings account to a checking account as necessary to cover checks written by the customer. Interest-bearing transaction accounts were authorized nationwide for banks and other depository institutions on December 31, 1980, following passage of the Depository Institutions Deregulation and Monetary Control Act.

---

[8] Transaction accounts include all deposits on which the account holder is permitted to make withdrawals by negotiable or transferable instruments, by telephone, or through preauthorized transfers for the purpose of making payments to others. NOWs, ATS, share drafts, telephone transfers, and ordinary checking accounts are all transaction accounts, but regular time and savings deposits are not.

The mix of bank deposits has changed dramatically in recent years. Demand deposits and other transaction accounts have declined as a percentage of bank funds, while the more costly interest-bearing time and savings deposits have grown rapidly. This shift toward more expensive deposits reflects, in part, the growing sophistication of bank customers, especially large corporations, who have developed efficient cash management practices and insist on maximum returns on their time accounts.

Banks have become increasingly dependent on the *consumer* for funds. Many new deposit programs have been developed in recent years to appeal to individuals and families. One example is the interest-bearing NOW account. While commercial banks did not invent the NOW, they readily seized upon the opportunity to use it in those states permitting this new consumer service, and today banks have become the dominant issuer of these transaction accounts. The 6-month money market CD and the 30-month CD developed recently are two other examples of banking innovations aimed squarely at the consumer.

The nonnegotiable money market CD, issued in a minimum denomination of $10,000, carries a yield tied to the average auction rate on six-month U.S. Treasury bills, permitting the customer to earn higher returns on short-term funds. In 1980 commercial and savings banks were authorized to offer small-saver CDs, whose rate is tied to the yield on 2½-year U.S. Treasury securities. These CDs carry no minimum denomination but must have maturities of 2½ years or more. Both money market and small-saver CDs grew rapidly in bank portfolios following their introduction, reflecting the increasing financial sophistication of consumers and a greater tendency for bank customers today to "shop around" for the highest returns available.

Nondeposit Sources of Funds

One of the most marked trends in banking in recent years is greater use of nondeposit funds to meet cash needs. Historically, when a bank needed additional funds beyond those supplied by deposits, it would usually liquidate its holdings of U.S. Treasury bills or other marketable securities. Today, however, under the pressure of higher interest rates, inflation, and increased competition, cash and other liquid assets have declined sharply as a percentage of total bank assets. Commercial banks have been forced to rely increasingly upon *liability management* to satisfy their demands for liquidity.

Principal nondeposit sources of funds for banks today include purchases of reserves (federal funds) from other banks, security repurchase agreements, mortgage borrowings, and the issuance of capital notes and debentures. Capital notes and debentures are of particular interest since these securities are eligible under federal regulations and the laws of most states to be counted as equity capital for purposes of determining a bank's loan limit. Both state and federal law limits the amount of money a commercial bank can lend to any one borrower to a fraction of the bank's equity capital (net worth).[9] In order to be counted as equity capital, however, capital notes and debentures must be *subordinated* to deposits, so that if a bank is liquidated the depositors have a first claim on its assets.

Equity Capital

Equity capital (or net worth) supplied by a bank's stockholders provides less than 10 percent of total funds for most banks today. In fact, the ratio of equity capital to bank loans and deposits has been falling for several decades. This development has many financial experts concerned, since one of the most important functions of stockholder equity capital is to keep a bank open even in the face of operating losses until management can correct the problem.

Revenues and Expenses

The majority of bank revenues come from interest and fees on loans, as shown in Exhibit 3–4. Interest and dividends on security holdings are the second-most-important source of bank revenue after loans. Other minor sources of income include earnings from trust (fiduciary) activities and service charges on deposit accounts (mainly checking accounts).

Bank expenses have risen rapidly in recent years, putting a "squeeze" on operating income. Greater competition from bank and nonbank financial institutions for sources of funds, especially consumer savings deposits and transaction accounts, has resulted in dramatic increases in the cost of raising funds. Interest on deposits is now the principal expense item for commercial banks, followed by the salaries and wages of their employees. Rising rapidly in importance is the interest cost on nondeposit sources of funds, such as borrowing in the federal funds market or long-term borrowing in the form of mortgages, notes, and debentures. Commercial banks must be more conscious of expense control and tax management in future years if they are to protect their profit margins, generate sufficient capital to grow, and provide a greater array of financial services to the public.

MONEY CREATION AND DESTRUCTION BY BANKS

Commercial banks differ from most other financial institutions in one critical respect: *banks have the power to create money.* The banking system creates and destroys billions of dollars in money each year at the stroke of a pen. As we will see in this section of the text, an individual bank cannot create any more money than the volume of excess reserves it holds. However, the banking system as a whole can create a volume of money equal to a

---

[9] For national banks the limit is a maximum of 10 percent of equity capital and surplus. Most states are more lenient, allowing loans to a single borrower up to a larger maximum percentage—25 percent is common—of net worth.

EXHIBIT 3–4
Earnings and Expenses of Insured Commercial Banks in the United States, 1980 ($ millions)

Sources of revenue:

Interest and fees on loans	$126,953.5
Interest on balances with depository institutions	16,256.3
Income on federal funds sold and securities purchased under agreement to resell	8,763.4
Interest on U.S. Treasury and federal agency securities	13,463.8
Interest on municipal securities	8,170.1
Income from other securities	1,442.6
Income from direct lease financing	1,370.6
Income from fiduciary activities	2,739.2
Service charges on deposit accounts	3,186.9
Other operating income	8,422.2
Total operating income	$190,768.3

Expenses:

Salaries and employee benefits	24,673.2
Interest on deposits	98,419.4
Expense of federal funds purchased and securities sold under agreements to resell	16,770.6
Interest on other nondeposit borrowings	4,932.7
Occupancy, furniture and fixture expenses	7,353.6
Provision for possible loan losses	4,478.6
Other operating expenses	14,635.5
Total operating expenses	$171,263.8

Income before taxes and security transactions	19,504.6
Applicable income taxes	5,019.7
Income before securities gains or losses	14,484.9
Securities gains, gross	−854.4
Applicable income taxes	−362.1
Securities gains, net	−492.0
Net income before extraordinary items	13,992.8
Extraordinary items, net of tax	16.8
Net income	14,009.6

Note: Figures may not add to totals due to rounding.
SOURCE: Federal Deposit Insurance Corporation, *Bank Operating Statistics*, 1980.

multiple of any excess reserves deposited with it simply by extending credit (i.e., making loans and purchasing securities).

Reserve Requirements and Excess Reserves

Money creation by banks is made possible because the public readily accepts claims on bank deposits (mainly checks) in payment for goods and services. In addition, the law requires individual banks to hold only a fraction of the amount of deposits received from the public in cash or near-cash reserves, thus freeing up a majority of incoming funds for the making of loans and the purchasing of securities. We need to look more closely at these so-called reserve requirements banks must meet, since they play a key role in the money-creation process.

Under current federal law, banks and other depository institutions must hold reserves in cash or in deposit form behind their transaction accounts and time and savings deposits. These reserve requirements are linked to the size of the depository institution and require that a specified percentage of all incoming deposits must be placed either in an account at the Federal Reserve bank in the region or as cash in the bank's vault.[10] Vault cash and deposits at the Fed constitute a bank's holdings of *legal reserves*—those assets acceptable for meeting reserve requirements behind the public's deposits. In 1980, following passage of the Depository Institutions Deregulation and Monetary Control Act, *all* deposit-type financial institutions (including commercial banks, mutual savings banks, savings and loan associations, and credit unions) were required to hold legal reserves equal to 3 percent of that portion of their transaction accounts (principally checking and NOW accounts) below $25 million and 12 percent for that portion over $25 million.[11]

Each bank's legal reserves may be divided into two categories—required reserves and excess reserves. *Required reserves* are equal to the legal reserve requirement ratio times the volume of deposits subject to reserve requirements. For example, if a bank holds $20 million in checking and other transaction accounts and $30 million in savings deposits and the law requires it to hold 3 percent of its transaction accounts and 3 percent of its savings deposits in legal reserves, then required reserves for this bank are $20 million $\times$ 3% + $30 million $\times$ 3%, or $1.5 million.

Excess reserves equal the difference between the total legal reserves actually held by a bank and the amount of its required reserves. For example, if a bank is required to hold legal reserves equal to $1.5 million but finds on a given date that it has $500,000 in cash on the premises and $1.5 million on deposit with the Federal Reserve bank in its region, this bank clearly holds $500,000 in excess reserves. Since legal reserve assets earn little or no interest income, most commercial banks try to keep their holdings of excess reserves as close to zero as possible. Indeed, the larger banks frequently run deficits in their required reserve position and must borrow additional legal reserves from other banks or attract more funds from their customers to cover the deficit.

---

[10] As a practical matter, banks hold most of their reserves in the form of deposits with the regional Federal Reserve banks. Vault cash holdings are kept at a minimum since insurance rates increase significantly when large amounts of vault cash are held on bank premises. The current reserve requirements of commercial banks and the important role which reserve requirements play in government monetary policy are discussed in Chapter 22.

[11] A reserve requirement of 3 percent was also imposed upon nonpersonal time deposits held by these financial institutions. Under the 1980 law the Federal Reserve Board was empowered to vary the transaction accounts' reserve requirement between 8 and 14 percent and the time deposit requirement between 0 and 9 percent.

The Creation of Money and Credit

The distinction between excess and required reserves is important because it plays a key role in the growth of credit in the economy and the creation of money by the commercial banking system. To understand why, we need to make certain assumptions concerning how banks behave and the rules and regulations they face. To simplify the arithmetic, assume that the Federal Reserve has set a basic reserve requirement of 20 percent behind the public's deposits. Therefore, for every dollar which the public deposits in the banking system, each commercial bank must put aside in either vault cash or deposits at the Federal Reserve 20 cents as required reserves. Assume also that, initially, the banking system is "loaned up." This means that bankers in attempting to increase their profits have loaned out all excess legal reserves available to them. No additional loans can be made until new deposits are received from the public or additional reserves are made available to the banking system from some external source. In addition, assume that all bankers are profit maximizers and will attempt to loan out immediately any excess funds available to them in order to earn the maximum interest income possible.

Suppose that a deposit of $1,000 is made from some source outside the banking system. Perhaps the Federal Reserve has purchased securities from a dealer and paid for its purchase by providing $1,000 in additional reserves to the dealer's bank. Alternatively, the public may have decided to convert a portion of its currency and coin holdings ("pocket money") into bank deposits for greater convenience and safety. Either way, a deposit of $1,000 appears at Bank A as shown in Exhibit 3–5. This exhibit contains an abbreviated balance sheet (T-account) for Bank A with changes in assets shown on the left-hand side and changes in liabilities and net worth shown on the right-hand side.

Under the assumed Federal Reserve regulations, Bank A would be required to place $200 aside as required reserves (i.e., 20 percent of the $1,000 deposit), leaving excess legal reserves of $800. Because the $800 in cash earns no interest income, the banker will immediately try to loan out these excess reserves. Banks make loans today by bookkeeping entry. The borrower signs a note indicating how much is borrowed at what rate of interest and when the note will come due. In return, the banker creates a checking account in the borrower's name. In our example, assume that Bank A has received a loan request from one of its customers and decides to grant the customer a loan of $800—exactly the amount of excess legal reserves it holds.

Commercial banks find that, when they make loans, the borrowed funds are withdrawn rapidly as borrowers spend the proceeds of their loans. Moreover, it is likely that most of the borrowed funds will wind up as deposits in other banks as loan customers writes checks against their accounts. For this reason, Bank A will not loan out any more than the $800 in

EXHIBIT 3-5
The Creation of Credit and Deposits by the Banking System

Bank A Receives New Deposit				Loan Made by Bank B		
Assets		Liabilities		Assets		Liabilities
Required		Deposits	1,000	Required		Deposits 800
reserves	200			reserves	160	
Cash	800			Loans	640	

Loan Made by Bank A				Deposit of Loan Funds in Bank C		
Assets		Liabilities		Assets		Liabilities
Required		Deposits	1,000	Required		Deposits 640
reserves	200			reserves	128	
Loans	800			Cash	512	

Deposit of Loan Funds in Bank B				Loan Made by Bank C		
Assets		Liabilities		Assets		Liabilities
Required		Deposits	800	Required		Deposits 640
reserves	160			reserves	128	
Cash	640			Loans	512	

By making loans whenever there are excess reserves, the banking system will ultimately generate a volume of deposits several times larger than the amount of the initial deposit received by Bank A.

Transactions within the Banking System:

Name of Bank	Deposits Received	Loans Made	Required Reserves
A	$1,000	$ 800	$ 200
B	800	640	160
C	640	512	128
D	512	410	102
—	—	—	—
—	—	—	—
Final amounts for all banks in the system	$5,000	$4,000	$1,000

excess legal reserves it currently holds. This way, when the borrower spends the funds and the money flows to other banks, Bank A will have sufficient funds in reserve to cover the cash letters demanding payment which it will receive from other banks.

Assume that the $800 loaned by Bank A eventually winds up as a deposit in Bank B. As indicated in Exhibit 3-5, Bank B must place $160 of this deposit in required reserves and then has excess reserves of $640, which are quickly loaned out. As this borrower spends the funds, the $640 loan finds its way into deposits at Bank C. After setting aside required reserves of $128, Bank C has excess reserves of $512. It too will move rapidly to loan out these funds if a suitable borrower can be found.

The pattern of these changes in deposits, loans, and required reserves should now be fairly clear. The results are summarized in the bottom portion of Exhibit 3–5. Note that the total volume of bank deposits has been considerably expanded by the time it reaches the third or fourth bank. Similarly, the total volume of new loans grows rapidly as funds flow from bank to bank within the system. If the credit-creation process works through the entire banking system and there are no leakages, then, with a 20 percent reserve requirement, the banking system ultimately will hold $5,000 in deposits and will have created loans in the amount of $4,000. Clearly, by making loans whenever and wherever excess reserves appear, the banking system eventually creates total deposits and total loans several times larger than the original volume of funds received.[12]

Destruction of Deposits and Reserves

Not only can the money supply expand by a multiple amount as a result of the injection of new reserves, but it can also *contract* by a multiple amount when reserves are withdrawn from the banking system. This is illustrated in Exhibit 3–6, where a depositer has decided to withdraw $1,000 from a transaction account at Bank A. Recall that behind the $1,000 deposit Bank A holds only $200 in required reserves. This means that when the deposit is withdrawn, that bank will have a deficiency of $800. If Bank A is loaned up and has used all of its cash in making loans and investments, it will have to raise the necessary funds through the sale of securities or through borrowing.

Suppose Bank A decides to sell securities in the amount of $800. As indicated in Exhibit 3–6, the sale of securities increases Bank A's required reserves by the necessary amount. However, the individuals and institutions who purchase those securities pay for them by writing checks against their deposits in other banks, reducing the legal reserves of those institutions.

For example, assume that Bank B loses deposits of $800 and required reserves of $800 as Bank A gains these funds. Considering Bank A and Bank B together, total deposits have fallen by $1,800. This deposit contraction has freed up about $360 ($200 + $160) in required reserves. However, if Bank B is also loaned up and has no excess reserves, the $800 lost to Bank A means Bank B has a net reserve deficiency of $640. Further contraction of

---

[12] In the foregoing example each dollar of required reserves supports five dollars in deposits, due to the fact that the legal reserve requirement is 20 percent. That is, total deposits created by the banking system are equal to the initial amount of legal reserves deposited in the system—in this example $1,000—times the reciprocal of the reserve requirement ratio—in this case, 1/0.20, or 5. The reciprocal of the reserve requirement ratio is known as the *deposit multiplier,* a concept we will discuss more fully in Chapter 22.

In the real world, leakages from the banking system greatly reduce the size of the deposit multiplier—probably to no more than two. Among the most important leakages are the public's desire to convert some portion of new demand deposits into currency and coin (pocket money) or into time and savings deposits, and the presence of unutilized lending capacity, which results because banks either cannot find qualified borrowers or wish to hold a protective "cushion" of reserves.

EXHIBIT 3–6
Deposit and Credit Destruction in the Banking System

Depositor withdraws funds:

Federal Reserve Bank		Bank A	
Assets	Liabilities	Assets	Liabilities
	Member bank reserves −1,000	Required reserves −1,000	Deposits −1,000

If Bank A was loaned up when the withdrawal occurred, it will now have a reserve deficiency of $800 as indicated below.

Total reserves lost at Bank A when depositor withdrew funds $1,000
Required reserves no longer needed due to deposit withdrawal . . . .   −200
Total reserve deficit at Bank A . . . . $ 800

Bank A sells securities to acquire additional reserves:

Bank A		Bank B	
Assets	Liabilities	Assets	Liabilities
Securities −800		Required	Deposits −800
Required		reserves −800	
reserves +800			

The sale of securities in the amount of $800 enables Bank A to cover its reserve deficit. However, customers of Bank B bought those securities and that bank was already loaned up. Therefore, Bank B now has a reserve deficiency of $640. Thus:

Total reserves lost at Bank B after deposit withdrawals to purchase
Bank A's securities $800
Required reserves no longer needed due to deposit withdrawals . . . . −160
Total reserve deficit at Bank B $640

The actions taken by Bank B to cover its reserve deficit will cause other banks to lose reserves and incur deficits. Deposits will continue to contract until total reserves available to the banking system are sufficient for all banks to meet their legal reserve requirements.

deposits will occur as Bank B attempts to cover its reserve deficiency by drawing reserves from other banks. In fact, with a 20 percent reserve requirement and no other leakages from the banking system, deposits will contract by a full $5,000 as banks try to cover their reserve deficits by raising funds at the expense of other banks.

Implications of Money Creation and Destruction

This unique ability of banks to create and destroy money has a number of important implications for the financial system and for the economy. Creation of money by banks is one of the most important sources of credit flows in the economy—an important supplement to the supply of savings in providing funds for investment so the economy can grow faster. Money created by banks is instantly available for spending and therefore, unless carefully controlled by government action, can fuel inflation. That is why the Federal Reserve System, the nation's central bank, regulates the growth of the money supply principally through controlling the growth of bank reserves—a subject dealt with at length in Chapter 22.

SUMMARY AND CONCLUSIONS

It is clear that the banking industry has undergone significant financial and structural changes in recent years. These changes have been brought about by shifts in regulations and by strong economic and financial pressures. Rising interest rates, soaring operating costs, and intense competition from nonbank financial institutions have propelled bankers into a new scenario in which the character of their loans, investments and sources of funds has changed markedly. Moreover, there is no end in sight to many of these trends. Costs of labor and funds continue to rise. Indeed, many experts looking at the age composition of the U.S. population and the expected rate of family formations in the decade ahead expect relatively high interest rates and continued pressure on bankers to find higher-yielding uses for their funds in order to offset rapidly rising costs. A key factor in the industry's response to these demand and cost pressures, of course, will be the willingness of federal and state regulatory authorities and the Congress to permit an expansion of banking services.

The drive toward larger and larger banking organizations centered around branch banks and bank holding companies appears to be a continuing trend for the future. Again, a key issue is whether the Congress and the states will readily permit greater branching and holding-company activity. One area of growing concern to the banking industry is the rise of "near-banks" which offer credit services and recently have begun to attract the public's funds through sales of depositlike IOUs. These organizations include such well-known names as Sears Roebuck, Prudential Insurance Company, American Express, and various stock brokerage firms. These organizations offer financial services to customers and yet are not subject to the extensive regulations which commercial banks must satisfy. The future, therefore, promises to foster intense competition not only within the banking industry but from without. In line with economic theory, stronger competition should mean lower profit margins and a more efficient use of financial resources within the banking sector.

STUDY QUESTIONS

1. Why are commercial banks frequently labeled "financial department stores"?
2. In what ways are commercial banks of special importance to the functioning of the money and capital markets and the economy?

3. Why are banks so heavily regulated? List the principal bank regulatory agencies. What areas of bank operations are subject to regulation?

4. What are the principal uses of commercial bank funds? Major sources of funds?

5. What has happened in recent years to bank liquidity? Capital adequacy? The composition of loans and deposits? What forces have brought about these changes?

6. Two dominant postwar movements in the structure of U.S. banking have been the spread of branch banking and the growth of bank holding companies. Explain what has happened in these two areas and why.

7. Why have the number and average size of failing banks increased in recent years?

8. Why and how are banks able to create money? Does the ability of banks to create money have implications for public policy? Please explain.

SELECTED REFERENCES

1. American Bankers Association. *The Commercial Banking Industry*. Englewood Cliffs, N.J.: Prentice-Hall, 1962. Monograph written for the Commission on Money and Credit.

2. Baughn, William H., and Charles E. Walker, eds. *The Bankers' Handbook*. Homewood, Ill.: Richard D. Irwin, 1966.

3. Bell, R. W., and Neil B. Murphy. *Costs in Commercial Banking: A Quantitative Analysis of Bank Behavior and Its Relation to Bank Regulations*. Research Report No. 41, Federal Reserve Bank of Boston, 1968.

4. Benston, George J. "Economies of Scale and Marginal Costs in Banking Operations." *The National Banking Review*, June 1965, pp. 507–49.

5. _____. "The Optimal Banking Structure: Theory and Evidence." *Journal of Bank Research*, Winter 1973, pp. 220–37.

6. Board of Governors of the Federal Reserve System. *The Federal Reserve System: Purposes and Functions*. 6th ed. Washington, D.C., 1973.

7. Boltz, Paul W., and Tim S. Campbell. *Innovations in Bank Loan Contracting: Recent Evidence*. Staff Study 104, Board of Governors of the Federal Reserve System, May 1979.

8. Boorman, John T., and Thomas M. Havrilesky. *Money Supply, Money Demand, and Macroeconomic Models*. Arlington Heights, Ill.: AHM, 1972.

9. Bowsher, Norman T. "Have Multibank Holding Companies Affected Commercial Bank Performance?" *Review*, Federal Reserve Bank of St. Louis, April 1978, pp. 8–15.

10. Buser, Stephen A. "Efficient Risk-Return Management in Commercial Banking." *Journal of Bank Research*, Winter 1980, pp. 235–47.

11. Chandler, Lester V. *The Economics of Money and Banking*. 6th ed. New York: Harper & Row, 1973.

12. Chase, Samuel, and John Mingo. "The Regulation of Bank Holding Companies." *Journal of Finance*, May 1975, pp. 282–92.

13. Daniel, Donnie L., William A. Longbrake, and Neil B. Murphy. "The Effects of Technology on Bank Economies of Scale for Demand Deposits." *Journal of Finance*, March 1973, pp. 131–46.

14. Fischer, Gerald C. *American Banking Structure*. New York: Columbia University Press, 1968.

15. _____. "The Commercial Bank Balance Sheet, 1960–1985." *Journal of Commercial Bank Lending*, November 1979, pp. 50–64.

16. Havrilesky, Thomas M., and John T. Boorman, eds. *Current Perspectives in Banking*. Arlington Heights, Ill.: AHM, 1976.

17. Horvitz, Paul M. *Monetary Policy and the Financial System*. Englewood Cliffs, N.J.: Prentice-Hall, 1974.

18. Kroos, H. E., and M. R. Blyn. *A History of Financial Institutions*. New York: Random House, 1971.

19. Merris, Randall C. "Business Loans at Large Commercial Banks: Policies and Practices." *Economic Perspectives*, Federal Reserve Bank of Chicago, November-December 1979, pp. 15–23.

20. Nadler, Paul S. "What Happened to Traditional Banking?" *The Bankers Magazine*, Spring 1971, pp. 32–40.

21. Nichols, Dorothy M. *Modern Money Mechanics: A Workbook on Deposits, Currency, and Bank Reserves*. Federal Reserve Bank of Chicago, June 1975.

22. Rose, John T. "An Analysis of Federal Reserve System Attrition since 1960." *Federal Reserve Bulletin*, January 1978, pp. 12–13.

23. Rose, Peter S. "People, Machines and the Future of Banking." *The Canadian Banker and ICB Review*, December 1980, pp. 56–61.

24. Rose, Peter S., and Donald R. Fraser. *Financial Institutions*. Dallas, Texas: Business Publications, Inc., 1980.

25. Sinkey, Joseph F., and David A. Walker. "Problem Banks: Identification and Characteristics." *Journal of Bank Research*, Winter 1975, pp. 208–17.

26. Snellings, Aubrey N. "The Financial Services Industry: Recent Trends and Future Prospects." *Economic Review*, Federal Reserve Bank of Richmond, January-February 1980, pp. 3–8.

27. White, George C. "Electronic Banking and Its Impact on the Future." *The Magazine of Bank Administration*, December 1979, pp. 39–42.

4

Nonbank Thrift Institutions: Credit Unions, Savings and Loan Associations, and Mutual Savings Banks

There is a tendency in discussions of the financial system to minimize the role of nonbank financial institutions and emphasize the part played by commercial banks in the flow of money and credit. Furthermore, until recently most analysts did not consider the liabilities of nonbank financial institutions, including deposits in savings and loan associations, mutual savings banks, and credit unions, as really close substitutes for bank deposits. It was argued that interindustry competition between commercial banks and other financial institutions was slight and, for all practical purposes, could be ignored. Beginning in the 1960s and continuing to the present day, however, a new view has emerged concerning the relative importance of nonbank financial institutions. We now recognize that these institutions play a *vital* role in the flow of money and credit within the financial system and are particularly important in selected markets, such as the mortgage market and the markets for corporate bonds, stocks, and consumer savings.

This new awareness of the critical importance of nonbank financial institutions in the economy and financial system stems from a number of sources. One is the rapid growth of selected nonbank financial intermediaries in recent years: some have outstripped commercial banks in the growth of their loans and total resources. For example, credit unions, money market mutual funds, and pension plans have been the fastest-growing financial institutions in the United States over the past three decades.

Still another factor is the increasing penetration of traditional banking markets by nonbank institutions. For example, credit unions, mutual savings banks, and savings and loan associations offer NOW accounts and other interest-bearing payments services that compete head-to-head with bank checking-account plans. For a number of years credit unions have marketed credit card plans, many of which have carried lower interest charges than those levied by banks. Moreover, the Depository Institutions Deregulation and Monetary Control Act of 1980 authorized federally chartered savings and loan associations to issue credit cards and make credit card loans. Insurance companies, savings banks, and credit unions today are offering new savings plans with fixed or floating interest rates that compete directly with commercial bank certificates of deposit and other savings plans.

On both the asset and liability side of the balance sheet, then, nonbank financial institutions are becoming increasingly like commercial banks and competing for the same set of customers. This is why financial analysts today stress the importance of studying the whole sector of financial institutions—bank and nonbank financial intermediaries—in order to understand how the financial system works. In this chapter and the next we examine the major types of nonbank financial institutions that channel savings into loans and investments.

CREDIT UNIONS

Growth of Credit Unions

The characteristics and operations of credit unions have been a neglected area of research in the financial system. Recently, however, there has been a strong revival of interest in credit union behavior and growth. One reason is the extremely rapid growth of this financial intermediary, making it one of the leading growth sectors in the American economy. For example, credit union assets have quadrupled since 1970 (see Exhibit 4–1). U.S. credit associations today are the third-largest institutional supplier of consumer installment credit, behind commercial banks and finance companies, and account for about one sixth of all consumer installment loans in the United States. These institutions are exclusively household-oriented inter-

EXHIBIT 4–1
Credit Unions in the United States

Years	Number of Credit Unions	Number of Members	Total Assets ($ millions)
1940	9,023	2,826,612	$ 253
1950	10,591	4,610,278	1,005
1960	20,456	12,037,533	5,653
1970	23,699	22,797,193	17,960
1980	21,930	45,420,000	72,250

SOURCE: Credit Union National Association, Inc., *Credit Union Statistical Report 1980* (Madison, Wis., 1980).

mediaries—offering their deposit plans and credit resources only to individuals and families.

Credit unions are really cooperative, self-help associations of individuals rather than profit-motivated financial institutions.[1] Savings deposits and loans are offered only to members of the association, and the members are technically the owners, receiving dividends and sharing in any losses that occur. Credit unions were first begun early in the 20th century to serve low-income individuals and families by providing inexpensive credit and an outlet for savings. The early growth of credit unions was modest until the decade of the 1950s, when these institutions broadened their appeal to middle-income individuals by offering many new financial services and engaging in aggressive advertising campaigns.

The credit union sector remains relatively small compared to other major financial institutions. However, the industry's potential for future growth appears excellent due to its innovative character and growing public acceptance. For both savings deposits and consumer installment loans, the credit union has become an aggressive competitor with commercial banks, savings and loan associations, and mutual savings banks. Beginning in 1978 credit unions were authorized to offer six-month money market certificates (MMCs) which can carry the same terms as the MMCs sold by commercial banks, savings and loans, and savings banks. In addition, many credit unions offer payroll savings plans where employees of a company can conveniently set aside a portion of their salary in a savings account.

Credit union loans have kept pace with the growth of their deposits. Consumer loan rates charged by credit unions are fully competitive with rates charged by the other two major consumer lenders—commercial banks and finance companies. For example, a recent study found that both banks and credit unions were then charging approximately 10½ percent on new car loans. However, credit unions granted their borrowing members interest refunds up to 20 percent of the amount of the loan.[2] In addition, many associations provide credit life insurance free to their customers—a service charged for by most other lending institutions.

Data released by the Federal Reserve Board show that credit unions accounted for only 4 percent of total consumer installment loans outstanding in 1950 but that by 1980 this figure had risen to 14 percent. In contrast, finance companies saw their share of consumer installment credit decline from about 36 percent in 1950 to 24 percent in 1980. Both commercial banks and credit unions have gained a larger share of the consumer credit market at the expense of other lenders.

Chartering and Regulation

In the United States credit unions are chartered and regulated at both state and federal levels. Today about 55 percent of all credit unions are

---

[1] See especially Harless (8).

[2] See, for example, Flannery (6) and Cargill (4).

chartered by the federal government and the remainder by the states. Federal credit unions have been regulated since 1970 by the National Credit Union Administration (NCUA), an independent agency within the federal government. Deposits are insured by the National Credit Union Share Insurance Fund (NCUSIF) up to $100,000. State-chartered credit unions may qualify for federal insurance if they conform to NCUA's regulations.

Credit Union Membership

Credit unions are organized around a common affiliation or common bond among their members. Most credit union members work for the same employer or for one of a group of related employers. In most cases if one family belongs to a credit union, other family members are eligible as well. Occupation-related credit unions account for about four fifths of all U.S. credit unions. About one sixth of American credit unions are organized around a nonprofit association, such as a labor union, a church, or a fraternal or social organization. Common area of residence, such as a city or state, has also been used in recent years as a base from which to get credit unions started.

Size of Credit Unions

There is a strong shift today toward smaller numbers of credit unions. For example, the number of associations reached an all-time high in 1969 at almost 24,000 and now totals less than 22,000 (see Exhibit 4–1). Meanwhile, the average credit union has increased significantly in size. For example, in 1970 only about one sixth of the nation's credit unions held more than $1 million in assets, but today that figure exceeds 40 percent.

The average-size credit union remains relatively small compared with other depository financial institutions, however. Nevertheless, credit union membership continues to grow rapidly, increasing about 3 million a year. There were fewer than 5 million U.S. credit union members in 1950, but this total exceeded 45 million in 1980. Worldwide, there are more than 55 million members associated with 45,000 credit unions operating in 69 countries.

New Services Offered

Credit unions are rapidly expanding the number of services they offer. Some sell life insurance today, while others act as brokers for group insurance plans where state law allows. Many credit unions are active in offering 24–hour teller services, traveler's checks, travel-planning services, and money orders. Larger credit unions compete directly with commercial banks for transaction accounts by offering *share drafts*—interest-bearing checkbook deposits. The share draft was first authorized by several states in 1974 and made legal for all federally insured credit unions when the Depository Institutions and Monetary Control Act was passed in 1980 (see Exhibit

EXHIBIT 4–2
Provisions of the Depository Institutions Deregulation and Monetary Control Act of 1980 Applying to Credit Unions, Savings and Loan Associations, and Mutual Savings Banks

New Deposit Powers
1. Interest rate ceilings on deposits will be phased out over a six-year period, permitting rates offered the public to respond to competition in the marketplace.
2. NOW accounts which bear interest and can be used to make payments may be offered to individuals and nonprofit organizations by all federally insured depository institutions beginning December 31, 1980.
3. Federally insured credit unions are authorized to offer share drafts (i.e., interest-bearing checking accounts) beginning March 31, 1980.
4. Mutual savings banks are empowered to offer demand deposits to their business customers.

New Loan and Investment Powers
1. Federally insured credit unions can offer real estate loans.
2. Federally chartered savings and loan associations may issue credit cards, offer trust services, and make investments in consumer loans, commercial paper, and corporate bonds up to 20 percent of their assets.
3. Mutual savings banks with federal charters may invest up to 5 percent of their total assets in commercial, corporate, and business loans within the home state of the bank or within 75 miles of the bank's home office.

4–2). About 3,500 credit unions across the nation now offer share-draft services.

U.S. credit unions have been under intense pressure to develop new services and penetrate new markets, due to increasing competition from other financial institutions and a decline in the demand for their most important credit service—automobile loans. The auto loan accounted for about a third of the volume of credit-union loans until recently, when consumers began buying smaller new cars and more used cars. In addition, a substantially larger proportion of family income today is spent on food, fuel, and other necessities; credit unions have begun shifting their loan programs into these areas. One innovative credit union in Baytown, Texas, offers notes to qualifying members that can be used in a manner similar to personal checks in purchasing goods and services. Each note is, in effect, a line of credit up to a maximum of $5,000. Credit-line services are more convenient than direct personal loans and reduce operating costs because the consumer avoids the necessity of filling out a loan application each time credit is needed. Revolving credit lines, long popular with business borrowers, are likely to become increasingly popular with consumers in the years ahead.

Government Regulation of Loans, Investments, and Dividends

Credit unions, like commercial banks, are heavily regulated in the services they are permitted to offer, the rates charged for credit, and dividends paid on deposits. Under current federal regulations, these institutions are permitted to make unsecured loans, including credit-card loans, not exceeding 5 years to maturity or secured loans out to 30 years. However, the interest rates on these loans cannot exceed 21 percent annually on the unpaid balance. Loans to officers and directors of the credit union cannot exceed $2,500 without approval of each association's board of directors.

Associations' permissible investments are limited to a list prescribed by either state or federal regulations. In the main, credit unions are permitted to acquire U.S. government securities; make loans to other credit unions not exceeding 25 percent of their capital and surplus; hold savings deposits at savings and loan associations, mutual savings banks, and federally insured credit unions; and purchase selected federal agency securities. Credit unions rely heavily on U.S. government securities and on savings deposits in other financial institutions to provide liquidity in order to meet deposit withdrawals and accommodate member credit needs.

Credit unions pay dividends to their members, who are technically owners rather than creditors of the association. These dividend payments may be paid only if sufficient revenues are available after all expenses are met. The maximum annual dividend payable by an association is 7 percent. Credit unions are labeled nonprofit associations doing business only with their owners and therefore are classified as tax-exempt mutual organizations. To qualify for tax exemption, however, all earnings except those flowing to equity reserves must be paid out to members.

A Strong Competitive Force

Credit unions today represent stiffer competition for commercial banks, savings banks, finance companies, and other financial institutions serving the consumer than was true in the past. Today, one out of every six Americans belongs to a credit union—roughly double the proportion a decade earlier. During the 1960s and 1970s the industry repeatedly demonstrated its capacity for innovation and the ability to compete successfully for both installment loans and small savings accounts. With the authority recently granted associations by the Depository Institutions Deregulation and Monetary Control Act and by other federal and state laws to make long-term mortgage loans and offer credit cards, transaction accounts, and higher-yielding savings certificates, the credit union is likely to be an even more significant competitive force in offering consumer credit and savings plans in the years ahead.

SAVINGS AND LOAN ASSOCIATIONS

Savings and loan associations are similar to credit unions because they extend financial services to households. They differ from credit unions, however, in their heavy emphasis on long-term rather than short-term lending. In particular, savings and loans are the major source in the United States of mortgage loans to finance the purchase of single-family homes and multifamily dwellings. And, like credit unions, savings and loans today are developing many new financial services to attract new deposit and credit accounts and protect their earnings.

The first savings and loans were started early in the 19th century as "building and loan associations." Money was solicited from individuals and families so that certain members of the group could finance the building of new homes. The same individuals and families who provided the funds were also borrowers from the association. Today, however, savers and borrowers from S&Ls are frequently different individuals.

Savings and loan associations began as basically a single-product industry—accepting savings deposits from middle-income individuals and families and lending those funds to home buyers—and this persisted until the 1970s. More recently, however, competition from commercial banks and credit unions, coupled with high and unstable interest rates, have forced savings and loans to diversify their operations and aggressively advertise for new accounts. Favorable regulatory decisions at federal and state levels have aided the industry recently in developing new services, though more progress is needed in this direction.

Chartering and Regulation

Currently savings associations receive their charters either from the states or from the federal government. Today, about two fifths of all S&Ls have federal charters, and these associations are insured (up to maximum of $100,000 per deposit) by the Federal Savings and Loan Insurance Corporation (FSLIC). S&Ls chartered by the states also may qualify for FSLIC insurance and, in fact, three quarters of the state associations have done so. Both federally chartered and federally insured state associations are supervised and examined by the Federal Home Loan Bank System—the principal regulator of the industry.

Most savings and loans are mutual organizations and therefore have no stockholders. Technically, they are owned by their depositors. However, a growing number of associations are converting to stock form. Stockholder-owned S&Ls can issue capital shares to increase their net worth—a privilege that is particularly important when deposits are growing rapidly. Nationwide, there are about 870 stock associations out of an industry population of about 4,600 S&Ls. The stockholder-owned associations held a quarter of the industry's $630 billion in assets at year-end 1980.

How Funds Are Raised and Allocated

Savings and loans, like credit unions, are gradually broadening their role and may eventually offer a full line of financial services for individuals and families. Nevertheless, home mortgage loans still dominate the asset side of the business. Exhibit 4–3, showing the industry's balance sheet for year-end 1980, indicates that mortgage credit accounted for four fifths of total assets. But, the current era has brought rapid growth in other housing-related

EXHIBIT 4–3
Assets and Liabilities of All Savings and Loan Associations in the United States, December 31, 1980

Item	Amount Outstanding ($ billions)	Percent of Total Assets
Assets		
Mortgage loans outstanding	$502.8	79.8%
Insured mortgages and mortgage-backed securities	27.5	4.4
Mobile home loans	2.8	0.4
Home improvement loans	5.6	0.9
Loans on savings accounts	7.1	1.1
Education loans	1.3	0.2
Cash and investments eligible for liquidity	49.6	7.9
Investments in service corporations	3.1	0.5
All other assets	30.0	4.8
Total assets	$629.8	100.0%
Liabilities and Net Worth		
Savings deposits	$511.0	81.1%
Federal Home Loan Bank advances	47.0	7.5
Other liabilities	38.5	6.1
Net worth	33.3	5.3
Total liabilities and net worth	$629.8	100.0%

SOURCE: United States League of Savings Associations, *'81 Savings and Loan Sourcebook* (Chicago, 1981).

investments, such as mortgage-backed securities, mobile home loans, and investments in service corporations which provide funds for land development, mobile home parks, and housing-rehabilitation projects.

Mortgage-backed securities include pass-throughs issued by the Government National Mortgage Association and participation certificates (PCs) issued by the Federal Home Loan Mortgage Corporation. Both pass-throughs and PCs are investor shares in a pool of mortgages and are backed by the issuing agency.[3]

In certain states, savings and loans are allowed to extend consumer credit for nonhousing purposes, such as to purchase automobiles and home appliances. In addition, as shown in Exhibit 4–2, the Depository Institutions Deregulation and Monetary Control Act granted federally chartered savings

---

[3] See Chapter 18 for a more complete discussion of mortgage-backed securities and their role in the nation's mortgage market.

and loans the power to issue credit cards and invest up to 20 percent of their assets in consumer loans, commercial paper, and corporate debt securities.[4]

Savings deposits provide the bulk of funds available to the savings and loan industry. However, there has been a significant shift in deposit mix from those savings accounts earning the low passbook interest rate to deposits earning much higher and more flexible returns. Particularly important among the new higher-rate savings deposit plans offered by the industry are 6-month money market CDs (MMCs), 30-month and longer-term small-saver certificates (SSCs), and Keogh and IRA-plan retirement accounts. MMCs, first authorized in June 1978, carry an interest rate tied to the yield on new six-month U.S. Treasury bills and are sold in minimum denominations of $10,000. Money market certificates have been the fastest-growing savings plan since their introduction and by 1980 accounted for about 30 percent of savings and loan deposits. SSCs, authorized in January 1980, carry no minimum legal size but offer a rate tied to the latest yield on 2½-year U.S. Treasury notes.

The federal regulatory authorities authorized these new savings plans in order to make savings and loans more competitive and to provide the industry with more-stable sources of funds. Mandatory penalties—the forfeiture of interest earnings—were imposed to discourage early withdrawals by depositors. Experience has shown, however, that savings and loan deposits are highly volatile in a period of rapidly rising interest rates. Many savers are quite willing to pay the penalty for early withdrawal if higher, more flexible interest returns are available elsewhere. The result is that savings and loans today are faced with *both* a more costly and a more volatile deposit base.

Savings and loans also rely upon several *nondeposit* sources of funds to support their loans and investments. One of the most important consists of advances (loans) from the Federal Home Loan Bank System, which provides extra liquidity in periods when deposit withdrawals are heavy or when loan demand exceeds incoming deposits.[5] Equity capital or net worth—the retained earnings and the general reserves held by individual associations—makes up about 5 percent of total funds sources, but is very important to the public. It is the net worth account which absorbs operating losses and keeps the doors open until management can correct any problems. Many savings and loans are thinly capitalized today, and the number of outright failures appears to have accelerated under the pressure of rising costs and increased competition.

---

[4] Savings and loan associations hold a substantial volume of liquid assets in the form of cash and marketable securities in order to meet deposit withdrawals and satisfy reserve requirements set by the Federal Home Loan Bank (FHLB) System.

[5] In recent years, savings associations have turned in growing numbers to the secondary mortgage market for funds, especially in periods when loan demand is high and deposit growth is impaired. Older, lower-yielding mortgages are sold to other investors during such periods, generating additional funds which may be invested in new, higher-yielding mortgages.

Trends in Revenues and Costs

As the 1980s began, savings and loans were experiencing one of the darkest periods in their history. In fact, 1980 was the least-profitable year for S&Ls since World War II. More than 30 percent of insured S&Ls reported operating losses for the year, while dozens of ailing associations were helped into mergers by the FSLIC, which purchased over a billion dollars in unprofitable or questionable industry assets. Some observers feared that a continuation of this adverse trend would eventually swamp the FSLIC's $6.5 billion insurance fund, perhaps bringing on a congressional bailout.[6]

What circumstances put the industry in such a dismal state? One cause is the fact that S&Ls historically have issued mortgage loans with fixed interest rates while accepting deposits whose interest rates are sensitive to changing market conditions. In short, the bulk of their assets are rate insensitive, while a growing portion of their liabilities are highly rate sensitive. In periods of rapidly rising interest rates, the industry's *net interest margin*—the difference between its interest earnings on assets and its interest costs on borrowed funds—has been severely squeezed. Indeed, in several recent periods, short-term interest rates paid on deposits have exceeded interest rates earned on long-term loans; the industry's net interest margin turned negative.

Other recent trends have also hurt the industry's profitability. The individuals and families whose savings provide the bulk of association funds have become more financially sophisticated, withdrawing their deposits whenever higher returns are available elsewhere. The savings and loan industry was damaged severely in the late 1970s and early 1980s by the rapid growth of money market mutual funds. These investment companies offer small savers shares in a pool of money market securities (principally U.S. Treasury bills and bank CDs) which carry higher and more-flexible yields than the returns on savings and loan deposits.[7] Money market funds expanded at a phenomenal rate between 1975 and 1980, attracting well over $100 billion in savings. A substantial portion of this massive inflow of dollars came from deposit withdrawals at savings and loan associations.

Legal Interest-Rate Ceilings

Added to this is the problem of legal interest-rate ceilings. As Exhibit 4–4 indicates, deposits at commercial banks, mutual savings banks, and savings

---

[6] In 1981 Congress permitted savings and loans to issue *tax-exempt* savings certificates that would pay 70 percent of the rate on one-year U.S. Treasury bills. Individual savers would be able to exclude from taxable income up to $1,000 in interest earnings from these certificates (up to $2,000 on a joint tax return). First offered in October 1981, these certificates attracted a substantial volume of new funds for the industry. The new tax-exempt certificates, coupled with lower interest rates as 1981 drew to a close, appeared to ease somewhat the severe financial pressures which many savings and loans had experienced up to that time.

[7] See Chapter 5 for a discussion of money market mutual funds.

EXHIBIT 4–4
Federal Interest-Rate Ceilings on Time and Savings Deposits at Federally Insured Institutions, July 1981 (percent per annum)

Type of Deposit	Commercial Banks	Savings and Loan Associations and Mutual Savings Banks
Ordinary savings deposits	5¼%	5½%
Negotiable orders of withdrawal	5¼	5¼
Time accounts:		
Fixed ceiling rates by maturity:		
14–89 days	5¼	*
90 days to 1 year	5¾	6
1 to 2½ years	6	6½
2½ to 4 years	6½	6¾
4 to 6 years	7¼	7½
6 to 8 years	7½	7¾
8 years or more	7¾	8
Issued to governmental units (all maturities)	8	8
IRA and Keogh plans (3 years or more)	8	8
Special variable ceiling rates:		
6-month money market CDs	†	†
2½-year or more small-saver CDs	‡	‡

* No separate account category.
† The rate on these certificates is tied to the discount rate (auction average) on the most recently issued six-month U.S. Treasury bills. For commercial banks the ceiling rate is 0.25 percent over the Treasury bill rate prevailing at time of issue, provided the bill rate is 7.5 percent or higher. When the bill rate is below 7.5, the legal ceiling for commercial banks is 7.75 percent. The maximum rate payable by savings and loan associations and mutual savings banks equals the bill rate plus 0.25 percent when the bill rate is 8.75 percent or higher, 9 percent when the bill rate is 8.5 to 8.75 percent, the bill rate plus 0.5 percent when the bill rate is 7.25 to 8.50 percent, and 7.75 percent when the bill rate is less than 7.25 percent.
‡ The maximum legal rates on these certificates are tied to the yield on 2½-year U.S. Treasury securities. When the Treasury yield is 12 percent and above, the bank ceiling is 11.75 percent, while savings and loans and mutual savings banks have a 12 percent ceiling. If the Treasury yield is 9.5 to 12 percent, the commercial bank ceiling equals the Treasury yield minus 0.25 percent, while the savings and loan and mutual savings bank maximum rate is equal to the Treasury yield. When the Treasury yield is below 9.5 percent the bank ceiling is 9.25 percent, while nonbank thrifts may offer up to 9.5 percent.
SOURCE: Board of Governors of the Federal Reserve System, *Federal Reserve Bulletin,* May 1981, Table 1.16.

and loan associations are subject to legal ceilings which specify the maximum rate that can be paid on each type of deposit. The ceiling rates are set by the Depository Institutions Deregulation Committee (DIDC), composed of the heads of the major federal financial regulatory agencies.[8] Negotiable certificates of deposit of $100,000 and over are the only deposits offered by banks and nonbank thrifts that are exempt from these legal rate ceilings. However, shares offered by money market funds and other securities sold in

[8] This committee was created as a result of passage of the Depository Institutions Deregulation and Monetary Control Act of 1980. Its membership consists of the chairmen of the Federal Home Loan Bank Board, Federal Reserve Board, Federal Deposit Insurance Corporation, and National Credit Union Administration, and the secretary of the Treasury. The Comptroller of the Currency is a nonvoting member. Any changes in legal rate ceilings on deposits must be made by majority vote of the committee. See Chapter 22 for a more-complete discussion of legal interest-rate ceilings and the reasons for them.

the open market are not subject to the legal ceilings. When interest rates on these alternative investments rise above the ceilings, many savers practice *disintermediation,* withdrawing their funds from banks and savings and loans.[9]

Like most regulations, the interest-rate ceilings usually lag well behind market conditions. Under the terms of the Depository Institutions and Monetary Control Act, these maximum legal rates are due to be phased out over a six-year period ending in 1987. Until then, the rate ceilings will continue to pose a problem for savings and loan associations.

Trends in Industry Structure

The pressure of rising costs and the resulting squeeze on earnings have caused many savings and loans to merge or be absorbed by larger associations. As a result, the number of associations in the United States has been declining for the past two decades. The S&L population decreased from about 6,300 in 1960 to only about 4,600 in 1980. Not surprisingly, with declining numbers, the average size of S&Ls has increased tremendously in recent years—from about $11 million in assets in 1960 to $136 million by year-end 1980. Still, the large majority of associations are relatively small. Three quarters of all savings and loans hold assets of under $100 million each. With large numbers of relatively small S&Ls, continuing increases in costs and competition, and downward pressure on earnings, more savings and loans will be absorbed into larger financial institutions in the future.

Remedies for the Industry's Problems

If savings and loans are to be viable institutions in the future, they will need help from at least two sources: (1) sound decision making by management to diversify their operations, identifying innovative new services to offer the public; and (2) a relaxation of government regulations to permit the offering of new services and the merging of smaller associations into larger ones. The classical model of a savings and loan association—investing the bulk of its assets in fixed-rate mortgages and offering relatively low-yielding savings accounts to the public—cannot survive in today's volatile economic environment.

More-aggressive associations are branching out in at least three different directions today. Some have followed a *real estate* model, literally becoming mortgage banking firms. These savings associations are selling off their long-term mortgages and converting into real estate service organizations, managing and developing property and brokering mortgages. Many have become *family financial centers,* offering a full range of retail banking services to the consumer. Services offered range from NOW accounts and credit cards to

---

[9] See Chapter 2 for a discussion of the causes and effects of disintermediation.

financial counseling and even assistance in preparing income tax returns. Other S&Ls have adopted a *diversified* model, becoming holding company organizations with ownership and control over commercial banks, retail-oriented consumer banks, and mortgage banking firms. Only time will tell which of these models can adapt successfully to the changing character of the nation's financial system.

Whatever the future of the industry, government will play a crucial role in that future. If the savings and loan association is to continue to fulfill its historic role of providing mortgage credit for single-family homes and for apartments and other multifamily dwellings, it must be allowed to offer more-flexible terms on mortgages. A significant step has been taken in this direction by permitting S&Ls to offer variable-rate and renegotiable-rate mortgages with shorter maturities and adjustable interest rates. Unfortunately, too many restrictions have been imposed upon the issue of these new financial instruments to date, limiting their usefulness to the industry.[10]

The Depository Institutions Deregulation and Monetary Control Act of 1980 granted the industry a number of new services. As Exhibit 4–2 indicates, S&Ls can offer NOW accounts nationwide and therefore participate fully in the nation's payments system. The consumer can now do "one-stop" banking—checking and savings—at those savings and loans willing to offer the new service. Federally chartered associations can issue credit cards and make credit card loans, operate trust departments, and invest up to 20 percent of their assets in consumer loans and corporate debt securities. Legal interest-rate ceilings on deposits are gradually being phased out, allowing savings and loans to offer more-competitive rates on their principal source of funds—time and savings deposits.

All these regulatory changes were long overdue. If this industry is to remain viable, more regulatory adjustments will be needed in the future as economic and financial conditions change. Laws and regulations in tune with the varying realities of the financial marketplace coupled with creative management and a willingness to compete are the keys to success in the financial sector today.

MUTUAL SAVINGS BANKS

Like savings and loan associations, mutual savings banks were started in the United States approximately 150 years ago to meet the financial needs of the small saver. However, unlike savings and loans, which have spread nationwide, mutuals have remained essentially rooted along the eastern seaboard of the United States, where they began. These institutions play an active role in the residential mortgage market, as do savings and loans, but are much more diversified in their investments, purchasing corporate bonds and common stock, making consumer loans, and investing in commercial mortgages.

---

[10] Chapter 18 discusses the features of variable-rate, renegotiable-rate, and other mortgages and regulations applying to them.

From their earliest origins mutual savings banks have designed their financial services to appeal to individuals and families. Deposit accounts can be opened for amounts as small as one dollar, with transactions carried out by mail or, in many instances, through 24–hour automated tellers in convenient locations. Mutual savings banks in Massachusetts and New Hampshire were the first to develop the interest-bearing NOW account, perhaps the most important new consumer financial service of the past decade. Many savings banks advertise the availability of family financial counseling services, low-cost insurance, and travel planning as well as a wide variety of savings instruments.

Number and Distribution of Savings Banks

The number of mutuals operating today is small—less than 500. Moreover, the savings bank population has been on the decline through most of this century. For example, in 1900 there were 626 mutuals operating in the United States, and the total number rose to a peak of 637 in 1910. Thereafter, a progressive decline set in until the number of savings banks totaled only 463 at year-end 1979.

Nevertheless, industry assets and deposits have grown quite rapidly. In 1950 total assets of all mutuals stood at $22 billion, but at year-end 1980, industry assets had reached almost $172 billion. Of course, with declining numbers and rapidly expanding assets, the average size of mutual savings banks has grown tremendously and now exceeds $300 million in total assets. Thus, the average mutual savings bank is far larger than most credit unions, savings and loan associations, or even commercial banks. This increase in average size has aided mutuals in offering a greater variety of services and in keeping their operating costs low.

Mutual savings banks are not evenly distributed across the United States but rather are located primarily in New England and the Middle Atlantic states. For example, Massachusetts leads the list with 163 mutuals operating as of year-end 1979, followed by New York with 112. Other states which have mutuals headquartered within their borders include Alaska, Connecticut, Delaware, Indiana, Maine, Maryland, Minnesota, New Hampshire, New Jersey, Oregon, Pennsylvania, Rhode Island, Vermont, Washington, and Wisconsin.

Charters and Regulations

Mutuals can be chartered by either the states or the federal government. Moreover, state and federal governments also share responsibility for insuring their deposits. About 70 percent of all savings banks have their deposits insured by the Federal Deposit Insurance Corporation (up to $100,000); the remainder are covered by state insurance programs. Today, only 17 states permit the chartering of mutuals within their borders, but these institutions are not bound by geography in raising funds or making loans and investments. Their mortgage-lending activities reach nationwide and occasionally even abroad to support the building of commercial and residential projects.

The largest mutual savings bank in the United States is the Philadelphia Savings Fund Society of Pennsylvania, which at year-end 1979 reported total deposits of almost $5.9 billion. Close behind was Bowery Savings Bank of New York City, with $4.7 billion in total deposits. Of the 10 largest mutuals in the United States, all but 3 are headquartered in the state of New York.

How Funds Are Raised and Allocated

Technically, mutual savings banks are owned by their depositors. All net earnings available after funds are set aside to provide adequate reserves must be paid to the depositors as owners' dividends. Regulations exercised primarily by the states are designed to insure maximum safety of deposits. This is accomplished principally through close control over the types of assets which a savings bank is permitted to acquire. For example, state law and the "prudent man" rule enforced by the courts generally limit mutuals' investments to first-mortgage loans (the majority of which must come from the home state), U.S. government and federal agency securities, high-grade corporate bonds and stocks, and municipal bonds.

The industry's role in the financial system can be seen by looking at its balance sheet. On the asset side, the key investment is mortgages and mortgage-related instruments (see Exhibit 4–5). For example, at year-end 1980, mutual savings banks had invested $128 billion in mortgage loans and mortgage-related securities, accounting for almost exactly two thirds of their total assets. Most of the mortgage total represented direct mortgage loans to build single-family homes, apartments, shopping centers, office facilities, and other commercial and residential structures. The remainder (about 8 percent of total assets) was devoted to Government National Mortgage Association (GNMA) pass-through securities (also known as Ginnie Maes), backed by a government-guaranteed pool of mortgages.[11]

A distant second in importance to mortgages are savings bank investments in corporate bonds and stock. These securities represented almost 15 percent of industry assets at year-end 1980, with the volume of corporate bonds outnumbering investments in stock about five to one. Due to the pressures of inflation and higher deposit costs, however, many states have liberalized their regulations to allow more purchases of common and preferred stock. Another factor favoring investments in stock has been the industry's increasing federal tax burden, especially following the Tax Reform Act of 1969. Since 85 percent of stock-dividend income is exempt from federal taxation, mutuals have taken a greater interest in the stock market. By year-end 1980 they held about $4 billion in equities. State law and tradi-

---

[11] See Chapter 18 for a discussion of GNMA pass-through securities.

EXHIBIT 4–5
The Balance Sheet of the Mutual Savings Bank Industry, December 31, 1980

Balance Sheet Item	Billions of Dollars	Percent of Total Assets
Assets		
Cash and deposits due from banks	$ 4.3	2.5%
U.S. Treasury and federal agency obligations	8.9	5.2
State and local government securities	2.4	1.4
Mortgage instruments:		
Mortgage loans	113.8	58.2
GNMA mortgage-backed securities	13.9	8.1
Corporate and other bonds	21.2	12.4
Corporate stock....................................	4.2	2.5
Other assets	16.8	9.8
Total assets	$171.6	100.0%
Liabilities and Reserves		
Time and savings deposits	$151.5	88.3%
Other deposits	2.1	1.2
Borrowings and mortgage warehousing	4.5	2.6
Other liabilities...................................	2.2	1.3
Capital notes and debentures	0.4	0.2
Other general reserves	11.0	6.4
Total liabilities and general reserve accounts	$171.6	100.0%

SOURCE: National Association of Mutual Savings Banks, *Mutual Savings Banking: Annual Report of the President,* May 1981.

tion, however, severely limit the growth potential of savings bank invest-ments in the stock market. Savings banks also make loans for the support of education, to fund home improvements, and to cover personal expenses.

The principal source of funds for savings banks is *deposits.* As shown in Exhibit 4–5, the industry held nearly $152 billion in time and savings de-posits as of year-end 1980, representing about 90 percent of total funds available. Savings deposits carry no specific maturity but may be withdrawn at any time by the customer and carry the lowest rate of interest. Time deposits, on the other hand, have fixed maturities, and savings banks are allowed to pay higher maximum rates on these accounts depending on their maturity date.

Industry deposits have grown rapidly over the past three decades, reflect-ing the ability of mutual savings banks to appeal to the financial needs of individuals and families. The larger savings banks have established extensive branch office systems and have been highly innovative in offering new ser-vices. Nearly all savings banks today offer money orders, Christmas club accounts, loans against passbook savings accounts, traveler's checks, and home-improvement loans. About 300 of the nation's 463 mutuals offer NOW accounts. Many savings banks also offer life insurance policies to their cus-tomers where pemitted by state law.

Like savings and loan associations, mutuals have discovered that the customers they serve have become more financially sophisticated in recent years. The highest-yielding time deposit accounts have grown much faster than lower-yielding savings plans. The most pronounced shift has been out of regular passbook savings accounts (which generally carry annual yields of 5½ percent) to fixed-maturity time deposits which, in some instances, carry contract rates that float with conditions in the money market (see Exhibit 4–4). Nondeposit borrowings also have grown rapidly.

The net result of all these changes has been to push interest costs higher, put pressure on earnings, and increase the volatility of funds flows. Savings banks today must be more concerned with their liquidity (cash) position than has been true in the past. Their NOW accounts and checking accounts in particular are more volatile than savings deposits and require an increased investment in liquid assets to back them up.

Current Trends and Future Problems

The savings bank industry faces a number of problems which will significantly affect its future growth and viability as a conduit for savings and investment. One factor is increasing competition with credit unions, savings and loan associations, and commercial banks offering similar services. Because of the heavy concentration of savings bank assets in mortgage-related investments, mutuals are less flexible than commercial banks in adjusting to changing financial conditions and to the changing service needs of their customers.

On the other hand, savings banks counter this relative inflexibility in their asset structure with aggressive competition for funds and innovative new services. For example, mutuals have been among the leading institutions in developing new types of variable-rate mortgages, such as the Canadian rollover mortgage, in order to introduce greater flexibility into their revenue flows.[12] The future growth of this industry, like that of most other financial institutions, will depend heavily upon the ability of savings banks to gain the necessary changes in federal and state regulations to allow them to expand their services on both the credit and the deposit side of their business.

SUMMARY AND CONCLUSIONS

Nonbank depository institutions, especially credit unions, are expected to grow rapidly in the coming years. But it will not be an era of trouble-free growth and expansion. The volatility in deposit flows experienced by non-bank thrifts during the late 1960s and throughout the 1970s may be accentuated in the years ahead by another powerful force—competition. An in-

---

[12] Canadian rollover mortgages are short-term real property loans in which the borrower must renegotiate the terms of a loan periodically (once every five years is common). See Chapter 18 for a discussion of rollover and other new mortgage instruments.

tense competitive battle for savings deposits, transaction accounts, and consumer loans is now under way between commercial banks and the nonbank thrifts in thousands of local markets across the United States.

This competitive struggle was reinforced when Congress passed the Depository Institutions Deregulation and Monetary Control Act in 1980. The new law authorizes bank and nonbank deposit-type financial institutions in all 50 states to offer NOW accounts—interest-bearing checkable deposits, once the exclusive province of commercial bankers. The Monetary Control Act also calls for a six-year phaseout of legal interest-rate ceilings on deposits, which historically have given nonbank thrift institutions a slight interest-rate advantage over commercial banks.[13] In the future all deposit-type financial institutions will be able to compete on equal "price" terms for savings funds.

This fierce competitive battle for deposits is not likely to end in the near future; it should in fact intensify as systems are developed for the electronic transfer of funds (EFTS). Savings and loans along with credit unions are determined to be a part of the growing "electronic money" network which will move funds almost instantly nationwide via computer tape and terminal. In fact, savings and loans in the Midwest have taken the lead in developing point-of-sale (POS) terminals in retail stores, automated tellers in shopping centers, and branch offices to service their customers' financial needs. Investment in these devices is motivated by the desire to bid transaction accounts away from commercial banks. As Professor Nadler (12) has observed,

> The savings organizations recognize that the days when they could survive as specialized thrift institutions are gone, and that for them to survive they must also offer the variety of services that banks can offer. They expect that in a few years there will be full-service banks for families, and they have the motive of fear of not surviving otherwise to spur them on to newer and newer innovation.

In this competitive battle, nonbank thrift institutions still retain certain advantages over commercial banks. They are allowed to set up branch offices in many states which prohibit or restrict commercial bank branching. In the case of savings and loans, favorable rulings by the Federal Home Loan Bank Board—the industry's chief regulator at the federal level— permit savings associations to operate mini-branches in shopping centers and retail stores, and mobile branches in outlying areas. Beginning in January 1981, federally chartered savings associations were permitted to set up new branch offices without the necessity to prove that a new branch is needed in a given location or is likely to be profitable. Moreover, even though legal interest-rate ceilings will be phased out in a few years, nonbank thrifts may be able to take advantage of the higher deposit interest rates they are now

---

[13] As shown in Exhibit 4–4, under current regulations mutuals and savings and loans are permitted to pay a one-quarter-point higher maximum rate than commercial banks on most types of time and savings deposits.

allowed to offer compared to banks in order to gain a solid foothold in the most-desirable consumer markets. Finally, federal and state authorities which oversee nonbank thrift institutions have shown a willingness in recent years, however belatedly, to liberalize operating rules so that these institutions can expand and improve their services to the public.

STUDY QUESTIONS

1. Credit unions are one of the fastest-growing financial intermediaries in the United States. What are the factors that have contributed to this rapid growth?

2. What are the principal differences between savings and loan associations and mutual savings banks? How are these institutions similar to each other?

3. Competition between commercial banks, credit unions, mutual savings banks, and savings and loan associations is increasing rapidly, especially in the markets for savings deposits, payments accounts, and consumer credit. Explain the reasons for this trend toward increasing competition. What are the probable consequences for the consumer? For these thrift institutions?

4. Discuss the factors which are most likely to affect the future growth of nonbank deposit-type financial institutions. Explain how each of these factors is related to the types of services and viability of these institutions in future years.

5. Why is the savings and loan industry in trouble? What solutions have been offered to deal with the problem?

6. What has happened in recent years to the number of nonbank thrift institutions in operation? Can you explain why?

7. What effect would you expect NOW accounts and share drafts to have on the loan and investment policies of nonbank thrift institutions? Please explain the reasoning behind your answer.

SELECTED REFERENCES

1. Arcelus, Francisco, and Allan H. Meltzer. "The Markets for Housing and Housing Services." *Journal of Money, Credit, and Banking.* February 1973, pp. 78–99.

2. Benston, George J. "Savings Banking and the Public Interest." *Journal of Money, Credit, and Banking,* February 1972, pp. 133–226.

3. Board of Governors of the Federal Reserve System, "Nonbank Thrift Institutions in 1975, 1976, and 1977." *Federal Reserve Bulletin,* December 1978, pp. 979–85.

4. Cargill, Thomas F. "Recent Research on Credit Unions: A Survey." *Journal of Economics and Business,* Winter 1977, pp. 155–62.

5. Credit Union National Association, *1979 Yearbook,* Madison, Wis.

6. Flannery, Mark J. "Credit Unions as Consumer Lenders in the United States." *New England Economic Review,* Federal Reserve Bank of Boston, July-August 1974, pp. 3–12.

7. Friend, Irwin. *Study of the Savings and Loan Industry.* Federal Home Loan Bank Board, Washington, D.C., July 1969.

8. Harless, Doris E. *Nonbank Financial Institutions.* Federal Reserve Bank of Richmond, October 1975.

9. Jaffee, Dwight M. "What to Do about Savings and Loan Associations?" *Journal of Money, Credit, and Banking,* November 1974, pp. 537–49.

10. Kroos, H. E., and M. R. Blyn. *A History of Financial Institutions.* New York: Random House, 1971.

11. Melvin, D. J., et al. *Credit Unions and the Credit Union Industry.* New York: New York Institute of Finance, 1977.

12. Nadler, Paul S. "As Savings and Loans Fight for Survival." *Banker's Monthly,* April 15, 1974, pp. 11–13 and 39.

13. National Association of Mutual Savings Banks. *Mutual Savings Fact Book.* New York, 1978.

14. _____. *1979 National Fact Book of Mutual Savings Banking.* New York, 1979.

15. National Credit Union Administration. *Annual Report 1977.* Washington, D.C., 1977.

16. Rose, Peter S., and Donald R. Fraser, *Financial Institutions.* Dallas, Texas: Business Publications, Inc., 1980.

17. Thomas R. Saving. "Toward a Competitive Financial Sector." *Journal of Money, Credit, and Banking,* November 1972, pp. 897–914.

18. United States League of Savings Associations, *Savings and Loan Fact Book, 1978.* Chicago, 1978.

19. _____. *Savings and Loan Fact Book, 1979.* Chicago, 1979.

20. _____. *'81 Savings and Loan Sourcebook.* Chicago, 1981.

5

Insurance Companies, Pension Funds, and Other Financial Institutions

We now turn to a highly diverse group of financial institutions which attract savings mainly from individuals and families and, for the most part, make long-term loans in the capital market. Included in this group are life insurance companies, pension funds, and property-casualty insurance companies, which today are leading institutional buyers of bonds and stocks. Finance companies, another member of the group, are active lenders to both business firms and consumers and borrow heavily in the nation's money market from commercial banks, insurance companies, and other financial institutions. While not generally providing *new* capital to businesses and other borrowers, investment companies (often called *mutual funds*) are active traders in corporate stocks and bonds and state and local government securities. Recently a new form of investment company has appeared—the money market fund—which actively buys short-term private and U.S. government securities. As we will soon see, all of these financial institutions provide important services to participants in the markets for business and consumer credit.

LIFE INSURANCE COMPANIES

Life insurance companies were present early in the history of the United States. In fact, they were one of the first financial institutions founded in the American colonies. The Corporation for Relief of Poor and Distressed Presbyterian Ministers and of the Poor and Distressed Widows and Children of Presbyterian Ministers, established in 1760, was the first life insurance company in the United States. Life insurance companies offer their customers a hedge against the risk of earnings loss which often follows death, disability, or retirement. Policyholders receive risk protection in return for the payment of policy premiums which are set high enough to cover estimated benefit claims against the company, operating expenses, and a target profit margin. Additional funds to cover claims and expenses are provided by investments made by life companies in bonds, stocks, mortgages, and other assets approved by law and government regulation. For figures on the volume of insurance in force in the United States, see Exhibit 5–1.

EXHIBIT 5–1
Life Insurance in Force in the United States, 1970–80*

Category	1970	1980
Total amount ($ billions):		
Ordinary	$ 735	$ 1,760
Group...........................	551	1,579
Industrial	39	36
Credit	77	165
	$ 1,402	$ 3,541
Average amount:		
Per family	$20,700	$41,500
Per insured family	24,400	48,300

* Columns may not add to totals due to rounding.
SOURCE: American Council of Life Insurance, *1981 Life Insurance Fact Book.*

The Insurance Principle

The insurance business is founded upon the Law of Large Numbers. This mathematical principle states that a risk—especially the risk of dying—which is not predictable for one person can be forecasted accurately for a substantial number of people. No insurance company can accurately forecast when any one person will die, but its actuarial estimates of the total number of policyholders who will die in a given year are usually quite accurate.

Life insurance companies today insure against three basic kinds of risk: (1) premature death; (2) the danger of living too long and outlasting one's accumulated assets; and (3) serious illness or accident. Actually, most of their benefit payments are made to living, rather than decreased, policyholders who receive annuities, disability checks, and other health insurance benefits. Insurance companies are heavily regulated by the states to guarantee adequate compensation to the companies themselves and to insure that the public is not overcharged or poorly served.

Investments of Life Insurance Companies

Life companies invest the bulk of their funds in long-term capital market securities, particularly bonds, stocks, and mortgages. They are able to commit their funds long term due to the high predictability of their cash inflows and outflows.[1] Moreover, this high cash-flow predictability normally would permit a life insurance company to accept considerable risk in the securities it acquires. However, both law and tradition require a life insurer to act as a "prudent man." This restriction is imposed to insure that sufficient funds are available to meet all legitimate claims from policyholders or their beneficiaries at precisely the time those claims mature.

Life companies pursue income certainty and safety of principal in their investments. In most years at least 90 percent of the corporate securities they purchase are in the top four credit-rating categories.[2] Moreover, life insurers frequently follow a "buy and hold" strategy, acting as long-term holders of securities rather than rapidly turning over their portfolios. This investment approach reduces the risk of fluctuations in income.

Exhibit 5–2 illustrates the kinds of investments made by U.S. life insur-

EXHIBIT 5–2
Assets of U.S. Life Insurance Companies, 1980

Item	Amounts ($ billions)	Percent of Total Assets
Government securities:		
U.S. Treasury obligations	$ 5.8	
Federal agency securities	11.1	
State and local debt obligations	6.7	
Debt of foreign governments and international agencies	9.3	
Total government securities	$ 33.0	6.9%
Corporate securities:		
Bonds	$179.6	
Common stocks	35.6	
Preferred stocks	11.8	
Total corporate securities	$227.0	47.4
Mortgages:		
Farm	$ 13.0	
Nonfarm	118.1	
Total mortgages	$131.1	27.4
Loans to policyholders	41.4	8.6
Miscellaneous assets	46.7	9.7
Total assets	$479.2	100.0%

SOURCE: American Council of Life Insurance, *1981 Life Insurance Fact Book.*

---

[1] While life insurance companies have the reputation of being "permanent" holders of bonds, mortgages, and other securities, they have become more-active traders and speculators in securities in recent years. Emphasizing performance more than permanency in their investments, the larger life companies have set up trading rooms to more closely monitor the performance of their investment holdings, selling out and reinvesting in higher-yielding alternatives when circumstances warrant.

[2] See Chapter 8 and Appendix A for an explanation of security ratings.

ance companies. The principal investment is corporate bonds, representing about 40 percent of the industry's total assets. The large majority of these bonds were issued by domestic companies, though purchases of foreign bonds (principally from Canada) are also important. Holdings of common and preferred stock were nearly $50 billion at year-end 1980, about 10 percent of total assets. Late in the 1970s life companies showed renewed interest in corporate stock due to rapid inflation and the growing importance of variable annuity policies and variable life insurance plans.

The second-most-important asset held by life insurance companies comprises mortgages on farm, residential, and commercial properties. At year-end 1980 industry investments in mortgages totaled $131 billion—roughly a quarter of industry resources. Substantial changes have occurred in life company mortgage investments in recent years. The industry has reduced its holdings of single-family and multifamily residential mortgages and increased its holdings of farm and commercial mortgages. For example, commercial mortgage loans on retail stores, shopping centers, office buildings, hospitals, and factories accounted for about 60 percent of all domestic mortgage investments. The higher yields and absence of legal rate restrictions on nonresidential mortgages explain much of the rapid growth of commercial mortgage lending by the life insurance industry.[3]

Government securities play a minor but still important role in the portfolios of life insurance companies. In total, the proportion of industry assets represented by federal, state and local, and foreign government debt obligations is only about 7 percent. However, these securities serve the important function of providing a reservoir of liquidity, since they may be sold with little difficulty when funds are required. Recently investments in government securities have been rising as industry cash flows have become more volatile, increasing demands for liquid reserves. Life insurance companies buy mostly federal government securities rather than state and local government obligations. The industry has only a limited need for the tax-exempt income provided by state and local bonds because its tax rate is still relatively low. When life companies do purchase local government securities, they generally prefer revenue bonds, which carry the highest yields.

One asset whose importance has increased dramatically during the past two decades is *loans to policyholders*. The holder of an ordinary life insurance policy usually is entitled to borrow against the accumulated cash value of the policy, which increases every year. The interest rate on such loans is stated in the contract accompanying the policy and is usually quite low. For

---

[3] In granting mortgage credit, life insurance companies usually employ *advance commitments*. These consist of promises to provide long-term mortgage funds to a real estate developer before a residential or commercial construction project begins. The developer will use that financing commitment as an aid in obtaining short-term cash (usually from commercial banks) to complete construction. Later, when the project is completed, the insurance company will loan the funds promised and the proceeds of that long-term loan will be used to repay any short-term borrowings. Recently, pressured by inflation and high interest rates, insurance companies have been insisting on shorter-term advance commitments, floating rather than fixed rates on mortgage loans, and a share in any net earnings from a residential or commercial project.

example, many policies issued not long ago carry an 8 percent loan rate.

Policy loans tend to follow the business cycle, rising rapidly in periods when economic activity and interest rates are on the upswing and declining when the economy and interest rates are headed down. For example, in 1979—a year of rising interest rates and economic activity—policyholders borrowed a record $35 billion against their life insurance policies. In 1980, another record was set when policy loans jumped to over $41 billion—almost one quarter of all borrowable funds held by life companies for their policyholders. Because of this cyclical characteristic, policy loans are a volatile claim on the industry's resources. When loan demand is high, life insurance companies frequently are forced to reduce their purchases of bonds and stocks.[4]

Sources of Life Insurance Company Funds

The industry's principal sources of funds have changed little since World War II. The principal income source is premium receipts from sales of life insurance policies, annuity contracts, and health and liability insurance policies. During 1980 the industry's premium receipts totaled nearly $94 billion, of which $41 billion came from sales of life insurance, $24 billion from annuity contracts, and about $29 billion from health and liability policies. Annual net income from investments in bonds, stocks, and other securities averages only about a third of premium receipts and totaled almost $34 billion in 1980. The industry's net earnings after expenses roughly equal its investment income each year, since virtually all premiums from sale of policies are ultimately returned to policyholders or their beneficiaries. This means that, on balance, the industry hopes to break even from its insurance-underwriting operations, with premiums flowing in balanced by benefits paid out.

Regulating the Industry

The life insurance business has been heavily regulated by the states since its inception. It is generally thought to be "vested with the public interest," and therefore its activities are carefully monitored by state insurance commissions and the courts. Field representatives must be licensed, and policy forms and premium rates approved by state agencies. All funds must be invested in accordance with court decisions and with state laws and regulations. Only commercial banking appears to be as heavily regulated as the life insurance business.

---

[4] Policy loans represent a form of *disintermediation* for life insurance companies as policyholders withdraw their funds and invest them elsewhere. (See Chapter 2 for a discussion of disintermediation.) Recently some companies have encouraged their policyholders to "roll over" old, low-interest policies into new ones carrying higher loan rates but with lower annual premiums and other attractive terms. They have also requested state regulatory authorities to permit higher fixed or even floating rates on the loans available from new policies.

EXHIBIT 5–3
The U.S. Life Insurance Company Dollar: Sources and Uses of Funds in 1980

Sources of income:

Policyholder premiums	73.0¢
Earnings from investments and other income	27.0¢
	100.0¢

How used:

Benefit payments	49.4¢
Additions to policy reserve funds	28.0
Additions to special reserves and surplus funds	2.9
	80.3¢

Operating expenses:

Commissions to agents	5.7¢
Home and field office expenses	9.5
	15.2¢
Taxes	3.4*
Dividends to stockholders of stock insurance companies	1.1†
	100.0¢

* Direct investment taxes (such as real estate) are excluded from taxes and are deducted, with other investment expenses, from investment income. Federal income taxes, however, are included in taxes.
† If only stockholder-owned companies are included, then the dividend ratio becomes 2.2 cents per dollar.
SOURCE: Adopted from the American Council of Life Insurance, *1981 Life Insurance Fact Book.*

Structure and Growth of the Life Insurance Industry

Most life insurance companies (more than 90 percent in the United States) are corporations owned by their stockholders. The rest are *mutuals,* which issue ownership shares to policyholders. However, mutual firms are much bigger on average and generally were established much earlier. In total, mutual life insurers hold about three fifths of industry assets, with stock companies accounting for the remaining 40 percent. Most new companies in recent years have been stockholder owned, and a few mutuals have become stockholder organizations to gain greater financial flexibility.

Until recently, the number of life insurance companies had been declining. Many smaller companies were absorbed by other insurers to counteract growing expenses and provide a broader range of services. However, as the 1970s drew to a close many new companies were formed to meet specialized local and regional insurance needs, leaving the older and larger companies to cover the national and international market for insurance. By year-end 1980 a record 1,948 life insurance companies were operating in the United States.

New Services

Life insurers are under increasing pressure to originate and market new services to the public. Increasing competition from other financial intermediaries, rising costs, and lagging growth have all played a part in encouraging development of new services. Among the most important new developments are the creation of separate accounts, universal and variable life insurance, mutual funds, tax shelters, venture-capital loans, and corporate cash-management systems.

A *separate account* is an asset account which a life insurance company holds on behalf of a customer (usually a pension fund) apart from its others assets. Funds stored in the account are subject to more-liberal investment rules, permitting a larger portion of these monies to be placed in common stock and other more-risky investments. *Universal life insurance* allows the customer to change the face amount of his or her policy and the size and timing of its premium payments. *Variable life insurance* pays benefits according to the value of assets pledged behind the policy (often common stock) rather than paying a fixed amount of money. It is a form of inflation-hedged life insurance now authorized in all but three states, though the number of variable policies issued is still relatively small. New services offered by life insurance companies in future years will depend heavily on changes in government laws and regulations, as is also true of other financial intermediaries.

PROPERTY-CASUALTY INSURANCE COMPANIES

Property-casualty insurers offer protection against fire, theft, bad weather, negligence, and other acts and events which result in injury to persons or property. So broad is the range of risks for which these companies provide protection that property-casualty insurers are sometimes referred to as today's "insurance supermarkets." In addition to their traditional insurance lines—automobile, fire, marine, personal liability, and property coverage—many of these firms have branched into the health and medical insurance fields, clashing head-on with life insurance companies offering the same services. (See Exhibit 5–4 for a list of the principal types of policies written by property-casualty insurers.)

Makeup of the Property-Casualty Insurance Industry

The property-casualty business has grown rapidly in recent years due to the effects of inflation, rising crime rates, and a growing volume of lawsuits arising from product liability and professional negligence claims. There were an estimated 2,900 property-casualty companies in the United States in 1979, holding nearly $175 billion in assets. Stockholder-owned companies are dominant, holding three fourths of the industry's total resources. Mutual companies—owned by their policyholders—hold roughly a fourth of all industry resources.

Changing Risk Patterns in Property-Liability Coverage

Property-casualty insurance is riskier business than life insurance. The risk of policyholder claims arising from crime, fire, bad weather, personal

EXHIBIT 5-4
Principal Lines of Insurance Coverage Provided by Property-Casualty Companies, 1979

Insurance Line	Net Premiums Written ($ millions)*	Insurance Line	Net Premiums Written ($ millions)*
Auto liability	$22,102	Workers' Compensation	$13,164
Auto physical damage	14,538	Inland Marine	2,061
Medical malpractice	1,204	Ocean Marine	1,009
Other Nonauto liability insurance	6,612	Surety and Fidelity	1,009
Fire insurance and allied lines	4,781	Burglary and Theft	1,155
Homeowners multiple peril insurance	8,792	Crop-Hail Protection	396
Commercial multiple peril insurance	7,185	Boilers and Machinery	283
		Credit Insurance	58
		Aircraft Insurance	147

* Net premiums written represent premium income returned by insurance companies, direct or through reinsurance, less payments made for business reinsured.
SOURCE: Insurance Information Institute, *Insurance Facts, 1980–81.*

negligence, and similar causes is much less predictable than is the risk of death. Moreover, inflation has had a potent impact upon the cost of property and services for which this form of insurance pays. For example, the cost of medical care more than doubled during the decade of the 1970s, while auto-repair costs increased an average of 10 percent a year.

Equally important, basic changes now seem to be underway in the risk patterns of many large insurance programs, creating problems in forecasting policyholder claims and new premium rates. Examples include much greater settlements awarded by the courts on policyholder claims, a rapid rise in medical malpractice suits, and a virtual explosion in product liability claims against manufacturers of automobiles, tires, home appliances, and other goods and services. In order to reduce risk, most property-casualty insurers have become *multiple-line companies,* diversifying into many different lines of insurance.

Investments by Property-Casualty Companies

The majority of funds received by property-casualty companies are invested in state and local government bonds and common stock. Property-casualty companies, unlike most financial institutions, must conform to the full federal corporate income tax rate (except that policyholder dividends are tax deductible). Faced with a heavy tax burden, these companies find tax-exempt state and local government bonds an attractive investment. As shown in Exhibit 5–5, industry holdings of state and local bonds represented close to half of total financial assets. Corporate stock, held as a hedge against inflation, accounted for about 15 percent of all assets. Other important investments included U.S. government securities, federal agency securities, and corporate bonds.

EXHIBIT 5–5
Financial Assets and Liabilities of U.S. Property-Casualty Insurance Companies,
December 31, 1979

Asset and Liability Items	Amounts ($ billions)	Percent of Total Assets or Liabilities
Demand deposits and currency	$ 2.3	1.5%
Corporate stock	25.6	15.3
U.S. government securities	11.9	7.6
Federal agency obligations	6.8	4.3
State and local government securities	74.7	47.7
Corporate bonds	22.2	14.2
Mortgages	0.3	0.2
Trade credit	12.9	8.2
Total financial assets	$156.7	100.0%
Policy payables	$100.6	99.1%
Profit taxes payable	1.0	0.0
Total liabilities	$111.6	100.0%

SOURCE: Board of Governors of the Federal Reserve System, *Flow of Funds Accounts: Assets and Liabilities Outstanding, 1969–79.*

It is interesting to compare the distribution of the assets held by life insurance companies and by property-casualty companies. The net cash flows of the two industries—their annual premium income—are roughly comparable. Yet, life insurers hold about three times the assets of property-casualty insurers. Much of the difference is explained by the fact that life insurance is a highly predictable business, while property and personal injury risks are not. Most life insurance policies are long-term contracts, and claims against the insurer are not normally expected for several years. In contrast, property-casualty claims are payable from the day the policy is written, since an accident or injury may occur at any time. Therefore, while life insurance companies can stay almost fully invested, property-casualty insurers must be ready at all times to meet policyholder claims. In addition, claims against property-casualty companies are directly affected by inflation, which drives up repair costs. However, most life insurance policies pay the policyholder or the designated beneficiary a fixed sum of money.

Sources of Income

Like life insurance firms, property-casualty insurers plan to break even on their insurance product lines and earn most of their net return from investments. Achieving the break-even point in insurance underwriting has been difficult in recent years, however, due to rising costs, increased litigation, and new forms of risk. For example, in 1979 the industry ran a net underwriting loss of $1.3 billion. Investment income, however, usually more than offsets underwriting losses. For example, during 1979 U.S. property-casualty insurers reported investment income of $10 billion, resulting in net income before taxes of $8.7 billion. This represented a return on net worth of about 15 percent for the year. Industry profits are highly volatile from year to year, however, due to unexpected losses, growing litigation expenses, and the refusal of many state insurance commissions to let policy premiums rise as fast as industry expenses.

Business Cycles, Inflation, and Competition

This is an industry whose earnings and sales revenue reflect the ups and downs of the business cycle. This cyclical sensitivity, coupled with the vulnerability of property-casualty insurers to inflation, has created a difficult environment for insurance managers. Inflation has pushed up claims costs, while intense competition holds premium rates down. Foreign insurance underwriters are more active in domestic markets today, and many U.S. corporations recently have started their own "captive" insurance companies. In order to improve their situation in future years, property-casualty insurers must become more innovative in developing new services and more determined to eliminate those services which have resulted in underwriting losses. This will not be easy due to extensive state government regulations and public pressure for lower insurance rates.

PENSION FUNDS

Pension funds protect individuals and families against loss of income in their retirement years by allowing workers to set aside and invest a portion of their current income. A pension plan will place current savings in a portfolio of stocks, bonds, real estate, and other assets in the expectation of building an even larger pool of funds in the future. In this way, the pension plan member can balance his or her planned consumption after retirement with the amount of savings set aside today.

One problem with this whole arrangement, of course, is estimating the rate of inflation. Any member of a pension fund can estimate his or her future retirement funds in *total dollars* based on the amount of current savings and the rate of interest. However, unless an individual accurately predicts the future course of inflation, the real purchasing power of his or her retirement income remains uncertain. Many pension recipients have discovered, quite tragically, that when the retirement years are reached, the real purchasing power of assets painstakingly accumulated over many years is simply inadequate to sustain their normal standard of living. The remedy for this problem is to place savings in those assets whose value increases along with the rate of inflation. The dilemma faced by pension funds today, however, is that many inflation-sensitive assets carry greatly increased risks or stringent legal restrictions against their use.

Growth of Pension Funds

Pension funds have been among the most rapidly growing of all American financial intermediaries. For example, between 1970 and 1979 the assets of all private and public pension funds more than doubled, rising from about $260 billion to almost $600 billion (see Exhibit 5–6). Approximately one half

EXHIBIT 5–6
Total Assets of U.S. Private and Public Pension Funds, Selected Years ($ billions)

Type of Plan	1940	1950	1960	1970	1979
Private pension programs	$2.0	$12.1	$ 52.0	$138.2	$362.6
Insured plans	0.6	5.6	18.8	41.2	139.2
Noninsured plans	1.4	6.5	33.1	97.0	223.5
Government pension programs	$2.3	$12.1	$ 33.6	$ 85.7	$230.1
State-local retirement systems	1.6	5.3	19.3	60.3	161.6
Federal civilian programs	0.6	4.2	10.5	23.1	65.9
Railroad retirement program	0.1	2.6	3.7	4.4	2.6
Military retirement plan	—	—	—	—	—
Social security program (OASDI)	$2.0	$13.7	$ 22.6	$ 38.1	$ 30.3
Total assets of all funds	$6.3	$37.9	$108.2	$262.0	$592.7

SOURCES: Securities and Exchange Commission; Railroad Retirement Board; U.S. Department of Health and Human Services; and the American Council of Life Insurance.

of all workers in commerce and industry and three quarters of all government civilian employees are protected by pension plans other than the social security program (OASDI). About 147 million persons are insured under social security.

Pension fund growth in the United States has been spurred on by the relatively few retirees drawing pensions compared to the number of people working and contributing to a pension program. That situation is changing rapidly, however; individuals over 65 years of age now represent 12 percent of the U.S. population, and analysts project that this percentage will rise much higher. The growing proportion of retired individuals will threaten the solvency of many private pension funds and has, in fact, already created major funding problems for the social security program.[5]

Intense competition among employers for skilled management personnel has also spurred pension fund growth as firms have tried to attract top-notch

---

[5] The present ratio of working adults to retired persons in the U.S. population is about three to one. This ratio will shrink to two to one by 1995. When the Social Security Act was passed in 1935, there were 11 working adults for each retired individual. Substantial changes will be needed in the way in which social security is funded, in its promised benefits to retirees, or more likely in *both* if this social insurance program is to remain actuarially sound. Current proposals to reform the system include increasing the eligible age for full retirement benefits from 65 to 68, federal taxation of at least a portion of social security benefits, and encouraging retired persons to stay in the labor force.

employees by offering attractive fringe benefits. This growth factor is likely to persist in the 1980s and beyond due to a developing shortage of young, skilled entry-level personnel. Some experts foresee a real problem in this area, however, stemming from the recent difficulties pension plans have had in keeping up with inflation. Workers in the future are likely to demand both better performance from their pension plans and greater control over how their long-term savings are invested.

Investment Strategies of Pension Funds

Pension funds are long-term investors with little need for liquidity. Their incoming cash receipts are known with great accuracy since a fixed percentage of each employee's salary is usually contributed to the fund. At the same time, cash outflows are relatively easy to forecast because benefit payments are stipulated in the contract between the fund and its members. This situation encourages pensions to purchase common stock, long-term bonds, and real estate and hold these assets on a more-or-less-permanent basis. In addition, interest income and capital gains from investments are exempt from federal income taxes, while pension plan members are not taxed on their contributions unless cash benefits are paid out.

While favorable taxation and predictable cash flows favor longer-term, somewhat riskier investments, the pension fund industry is closely regulated in all of its activities, including the investing of funds. The Employee Retirement Income Security Act of 1974 (ERISA) requires all private plans to be *funded*, which means that any assets held plus anticipated investment income must be adequate to cover all promised benefits. ERISA also requires that investments must be made in a "prudent" manner, which is usually interpreted to mean highly diversified holdings of high-grade common stock, corporate bonds, and government securities with only limited real estate investments.

While existing regulations do emphasize caution and conservatism in pension fund investments, the private plans have been under intense pressure in recent years by both management of the sponsoring company and employees to be more *liberal* in their investment policies. The sponsoring employer has a strong incentive to encourage its affiliated pension plan to reduce operating expenses and earn the highest possible returns on its investments. This permits the company to minimize its contributions to the plan. Both sponsoring employers and employees have a keen interest in seeing that the pension plan earns a high enough return on its investments to at least keep pace with inflation. Otherwise, the employees will tend to seek other jobs whose pension programs offer more lucrative returns.

Pension Fund Assets

The particular assets held as investments by pension funds depend heavily upon whether the fund is government controlled or private. As shown in

EXHIBIT 5-7
Financial Assets Held by Private, Noninsured Pension Funds and State and Local Government Employee Retirement Funds, December 31, 1979 ($ billions at year-end)*

Asset Items	Private, Noninsured Pension Funds		State and Local Government Employee Retirement Funds	
	Amount	Percent	Amount	Percent
Cash assets	$ 1.9	0.8%	$ 3.7	2.1%
Time deposits	8.7	3.7	—	—
Corporate stock	136.4	57.6	43.6	24.4
U.S. government securities	18.4	7.8	15.0	8.4
Federal agency securities	7.0	3.0	17.1	9.6
State and local government securities	—	—	4.0	2.2
Corporate bonds	55.2	23.3	86.2	48.2
Mortgages	3.5	1.5	9.4	5.3
Miscellaneous assets	5.8	2.4	—	—
Totals	$236.8	100.0%	$178.9	100.0%

* Columns may not add to totals due to rounding.
SOURCE: Board of Governors of the Federal Reserve System, *Flow of Funds Account—Assets and Liabilities Outstanding, 1969–79.*

Exhibit 5-7, private funds emphasize investments in corporate stock, which represented about three fifths of their assets at year-end 1979. Corporate bonds ranked a distant second, accounting for almost one fourth of all financial investments. With few liquidity needs, private pensions held relatively small amounts of cash, time deposits, or government securities.

Corporate stock is far less important in the portfolios of government pension funds. As Exhibit 5-7 shows, state and local government pension programs held almost $44 billion in corporate stock at year-end 1979, which represented about one quarter of their financial assets. However, stock investments were far outweighed by corporate bonds, which amounted to $86 billion—close to half the assets of public pensions.

Under the pressure of strict regulations and more-frequent benefit claims, public plans hold a larger proportion of cash and liquid government securities than do private plans. For example, investments in U.S. Treasury and federal agency securities, demand deposits, and currency represented a full 20 percent of total financial investments at year-end 1979. Government pensions also place moderate amounts of funds in state and local government securities—often IOUs issued by their own governmental unit.

Factors Affecting the Growth of Pension Funds

Most experts feel that pension fund growth is likely to slow significantly in future years. One reason is the rising proportion of pension beneficiaries to working contributors, related to the gradual aging of the general population.

At the same time, the cost of maintaining pension programs has increased dramatically. The full funding of a plan to cover all promised benefits places extreme pressure on corporate profits, while the recent mediocre performance of the stock and bond markets has diminished investment returns.

Even more significant is the rapidly rising cost of government regulation. The Employee Retirement Income Security Act (ERISA), passed by Congress in 1974, imposed costly reporting requirements on the industry and granted employees the right to join a pension program, in most cases, after only one year on the job. More-rapid vesting of benefits was also required so that employees can recover a higher proportion of their past contributions should they decide to retire early or move on to another job. Trying to eliminate the danger that pensions may not have adequate funds to pay future claims against them, Congress now requires employers to eventually cover any past liabilities not fully covered at present. In addition, a federal agency—the Pension Benefit Guaranty Corporation (PBGC)—was created in 1974 to *insure* some part of all vested employee benefits. PBGC is supported by premiums contributed annually by participating employers and can borrow up to $100 million from the U.S. Treasury in an emergency.

These new government regulations have forced many private pension plans to close. The control of others has been turned over to a financial institution—typically a bank trust department or life insurance company— better able to deal with the current rules. Without question, the pension sector faces troubled times and considerable uncertainty in the period ahead.

FINANCE COMPANIES

Finance companies are sometimes called "department stores of consumer and business credit." These institutions grant credit to businesses and consumers for a wide variety of purposes, including the purchase of inventories, business equipment, automobiles, home repairs, vacations, medical care, mobile homes, and home applicances. Most authorities divide firms in the industry into one of three groups—consumer finance companies, sales finance companies, and commercial finance companies.

Different Finance Companies for Different Purposes

Consumer finance companies, also known as small-loan companies, make personal cash loans available to many customers. The majority of their loans support the purchase of passenger cars, home appliances, recreational vehicles, and mobile homes. However, a growing proportion of consumer finance company loans center on aiding customers with medical and hospital expenses, educational costs, vacations, home repair and maintenance, and energy bills. Loans made by small-loan companies are considered to be more risky than other consumer installment loans and therefore generally carry steeper finance charges than those assessed by banks, credit unions, savings and loan associations, and other installment lenders.

Sales finance companies make indirect loans to consumers by purchasing installment paper from dealers selling automobiles and other consumer durables. Many of these firms are "captive" finance companies controlled by a dealer or manufacturer. Their principal function is to promote sales of the sponsoring firm's goods and services by providing credit. Companies having finance affiliates include General Electric, Motorola, Sears, Wards, and International Harvester. Generally, sales, finance companies will specify in advance to retail dealers the terms (i.e., maturities, minimum down payments, and finance charges) of installment contracts they are willing to accept. Frequently they will give the retail dealer a supply of contract forms which the dealer will fill out when the sale is made. The contract is then sold immediately to the finance company.

Commercial finance companies, as their name implies, focus principally on extending credit to business firms. Most of these companies provide "accounts receivable financing" or "factoring" services to small or medium-sized manufacturers and wholesalers. With accounts receivable financing, the commercial finance company may extend credit against the borrower's receivables in the form of a direct cash loan. Alternatively, a factoring arrangement may be used in which the finance company acquires the borrowing firm's credit accounts at an appropriate discount rate to cover the risk of loss. Most commercial finance companies today do not confine their credit-granting activities to the financing of receivables but also make loans secured by business inventories, machinery, and other fixed assets. In addition, they offer lease financing for the purchase of capital equipment and rolling stock (such as airplanes and railroad cars) and make short-term unsecured cash loans.

We should not overdramatize the differences between these three types of finance companies. The larger companies are active in all three areas. In addition, most finance companies today are extremely diversified in their credit-granting activities, offering a wide range of installment and working-capital loans, leasing plans, and long-term credit to support capital investment. Exhibit 5–8 shows that consumer loans were the most important financial asset held by finance companies at year-end 1979, accounting for almost half of total assets. Business loans were also significant at 42 percent of all assets. Additional funds were committed to real estate mortgages or held in cash to provide liquidity.

Growth of Finance Companies

Finance companies have been profoundly affected by recent changes in the character of competition among financial intermediaries. Their lack of an extensive network of branch offices has put them at a disadvantage in reaching the household borrower who values convenience. As a result, both com-

EXHIBIT 5–8
Financial Assets and Liabilities Held by Finance Companies, December 31, 1979

Asset and Liability Items	Amount ($ billions)	Percent of Total
Assets:		
Demand deposits and currency	$ 4.6	2.7%
Mortgages	11.4	6.7
Consumer credit	82.6	48.9
Loans to businesses	70.3	41.6
Total financial assets	$168.9	100.0%
Liabilities:		
Corporate bonds	$ 57.0	35.3%
Bank loans, NEC	20.8	12.9
Open-market paper	61.2	37.9
Profit taxes payable	0.9	0.6
Miscellaneous liabilities	21.5	13.3
Total liabilities	$161.5	100.0%

SOURCE: Board of Governors of the Federal Reserve System, *Flow of Funds Accounts—Assets and Liabilities Outstanding, 1969–79.*

mercial banks and credit unions have been able to capture a larger piece of the consumer installment loan market at the expense of finance companies. For example, data compiled by the Federal Reserve Board show that finance companies held about 45 percent of all consumer installment loans extended by financial institutions in 1950, but only 27 percent in 1980. Over the same interval of time, credit unions tripled their share of the consumer installment loan market.

While finance companies dominated the auto-loan market for many years, this service line may be "drying up" due to rising energy costs, higher prices of both new and used automobiles, and intense competition from banks and credit unions. Many experts now feel that the fastest-growing market for finance companies in future years will be business-oriented rather than consumer-oriented financial services. Revolving credit, second mortgages on real property, and equipment leasing are among the fastest-growing forms of credit extended by finance companies today.

Methods of Industry Financing

Finance companies are heavy users of debt in financing their operations. Principal sources of borrowed funds include bank loans, commercial paper, and long-term debentures sold primarily to banks, insurance companies, and nonfinancial corporations. Which source of funds these companies emphasize most heavily at any given time depends essentially on the structure of interest rates. When long-term rates are high, these companies tend to emphasize commercial paper and shorter-term bank loans as sources of funds. On the other hand, in years when long-term rates are relatively low, usually during a business recession, long-term debt will be drawn upon more heavily.

Recent Changes in the Character of the Finance Company Industry

The structure of the finance industry has changed markedly in recent years. As in the case of credit unions, savings and loans, and savings banks, the number of finance companies has been trending downward, although the average size of such companies has grown considerably. A survey by the Federal Reserve Board revealed that in 1960 there were more than 6,400 finance companies operating in the United States, but by 1980 only about 2,000 independent companies could be found. A modest rise in the number of new firms occurred during the 1970s, however, as bank holding companies centered around some of the nation's largest banks organized new finance company subsidiaries.

This long-term downtrend in the industry's population reflects a number of powerful economic forces at work. Rising cost pressures, the broadening of markets, the need to innovate, and intensified competition from other financial institutions have encouraged finance companies to strive for larger size and greater efficiency. Many smaller companies have sold out to larger conglomerates as high interest rates squeezed earnings. Despite their declining numbers, however, finance companies rank among the fastest-growing financial intermediaries in the United States and continue to be a potent force in the markets for business and consumer credit.

INVESTMENT COMPANIES

Investment companies provide an outlet for the savings of thousands of individual investors, directing their funds into bonds, stocks, and money market securities. These companies are especially attractive to the small investor to whom they offer continuous management services for a large and highly varied security portfolio. By purchasing shares offered by an investment company, the small saver gains greater price stability and reduced risk, opportunities for capital gains, and indirect access to higher-yielding securities which can only be purchased in large blocks. In addition, most investment company stock is highly liquid, since many companies stand ready at all times to repurchase their outstanding shares at current market prices.

The Background of Investment Companies

Investment companies made their appearance in the United States after World War I as a vehicle for buying up and often monitoring subsidiary corporations. Many were unsuccessful in the early years, and the Great Depression of the 1930s forced scores of these new firms into bankruptcy. New life was breathed into the industry after World War II, however, when investment companies began to appeal to a rapidly growing middle class of savers. They were also buoyed by rising stock prices which attracted millions of investors, most of whom had only modest amounts to invest and little knowledge of how the financial markets work. The industry launched an aggressive advertising campaign which ultimately attracted more than 40 million shareholders during the 1960s.

Then the roof fell in. The long postwar bull market in stocks collapsed in the late 1960s, and common stock price-earnings ratios plummeted. During the 1970s the market staged modest recoveries, only to be thrown back each time as it neared highs set during the 60s. Small investors began to pull out of the market in droves. Total assets of open-end investment companies reached nearly $48 billion in 1970 but five years later had dropped to less than $46 billion. In all but three years during the 1970s, *redemptions* of mutual fund shares exceeded sales.

Many investment companies disappeared in this shakeout period, most of them consolidated into larger firms. The future of the industry seemed very much in doubt until a new element appeared—*innovation*. Owners and managers began to develop new types of investment companies designed to appeal to groups of investors with specialized financial needs. By custom and tradition, investment companies had stressed investments in common stock, offering investors capital appreciation as well as current income. With the stock market performing poorly, however, these firms turned their focus increasingly to other markets, especially bonds and money market instruments.

The new *bond funds,* which first became prominent in the 1960s, today direct the majority of their funds into either corporate debt obligations or tax-exempt municipal bonds. Their principal objectives are to generate current income and, in the case of the municipal bond funds, a higher after-tax rate of return for the investor. Capital appreciation is normally a secondary consideration to these particular investment companies.

Money market funds began in 1972 with the announced intent of holding money market securities—mainly bank certificates of deposit (CDs), commercial paper, and U.S. Treasury bills.[6] They were created in response to record-high interest rates in U.S. money markets and the desire of the small investor to skirt federal interest-rate ceilings on time and savings deposits offered by banks and nonbank thrift institutions. The money market funds attracted millions of consumer and small business accounts, and total assets expanded, rising from $100 million in 1973 to $130 billion in June 1981. While their growth ebbs and flows with changes in open-market interest rates, money market funds are likely to retain a substantial share of the small-saver

---

[6] Each of these money market instruments is discussed in detail in Chapters 12, 13, and 14.

market in future years due to the many products and conveniences they offer. These include a low minimum investment (typically $500 to $5,000), redemption of funds by telephone or by wire, and the free transfer of the investor's money into another mutual fund (such as a bond or stock fund) operated by the same investment firm.

Regulation of Investment Companies

Investment companies are heavily regulated at the federal level through such laws as the Investment Company Act and the Investment Advisers Act, both passed by Congress in 1940. Registration of investment company securities and periodic reports to the Securities and Exchange Commission (SEC) are mandatory. Policies for investing funds are determined by the investment company's shareholders, who also elect at least two thirds of the company's directors. The portfolio held by an investment company is managed by a separate management company or investment advisory service, which levies a substantial fee for its services. The management fee is typically a percentage of the fund's total assets (normally in the 1 to 2 percent range) and is not based on the fund's performance. Any contractual arrangements between the investment advisory service and the investment company must be approved by the latter's stockholders and must come up for renewal or revision every two years. Most investment advisory services are provided by either life insurance firms or securities specialists.

Tax Status of the Industry

Investment companies have a highly favorable tax situation. Provided they conform to certain rules to qualify as an investment company, they do not pay federal taxes on income generated by their security holdings. However, no less than half their resources must be devoted to securities and cash assets. Investment companies must maintain a highly diversified portfolio—a maximum of one quarter of their total resources can be devoted to securities issued by any single firm. Only a small portion of their net income (no more than 10 percent) can be retained in the business. The rest must be distributed to the shareholders.

Open-End and Closed-End Investment Companies

There are two basic kinds of investment companies. *Open-end* companies—often called mutual funds—will buy back (redeem) their shares any time the customer wishes and sell open shares in any quantity demanded. Thus, the amount of their outstanding shares changes continually in response to public demand. The price of each open-end company share is equal to the net asset value of the fund—i.e., the difference between the value of its assets and its liabilities divided by the volume of shares issued.

Open-end companies may be either load or no-load funds. Load funds, which are in the majority, offer their shares to the public at net asset value plus a commission to brokers marketing all the shares. No-load funds sell their shares purely at net asset value. The investor must contact the no-load company himself, however. Whether load or no load, open-end investment companies are heavily invested in common stocks, with corporate bonds running a distant second. As Exhibit 5–9 shows, corporate stock represented

EXHIBIT 5–9
Financial Assets Held by Open-End Investment Companies, December 31, 1979

Asset Items	Amount ($ billions)	Percent of Total
Demand deposits and currency	$ 0.7	1.5%
Corporate stock	33.7	72.0
Credit instruments:		
U.S. government securities	1.4	3.0
Corporate bonds	6.5	14.0
Open-end market paper	3.8	8.0
Total financial assets	$46.2	100.0%

SOURCE: Board of Governors of the Federal Reserve System, *Flow of Funds Accounts—Assets and Liabilities Outstanding, 1969–79.*

nearly three quarters of their total financial assets at year-end 1979, and corporate bonds only about 15 percent.

Closed-end investment companies sell only a specific number of ownership shares. An investor wanting to acquire closed-end shares must find another investor who wishes to sell. The investment company does not take part in the transaction. In addition to selling equity shares, closed-end companies issue a variety of debt and equity securities to raise funds, including preferred stock, regular and convertible bonds, and stock warrants. In contrast, open-end companies rely almost exclusively on the sale of equity shares to the public to raise the funds they require.

Goals and Earnings of Investment Companies

Investment companies adopt many different goals. *Growth funds* are interested primarily in long-term capital appreciation and tend to invest mainly in common stocks offering strong growth potential. *Income funds* stress current income in their portfolio choices rather than growth of capital, and they typically purchase stocks and bonds paying high dividends and interest. *Balanced funds* attempt to bridge the gap between growth and income, acquiring bonds, preferred stock, and common stock which offer both capital gain (growth) and adequate current income. On average, balanced funds place about two thirds of their resources in stocks and about one third in bonds.

The majority of investment companies give priority to growth in capital over current income due to the tax advantages of capital gains to their investors.[7] However, the industry's growth in recent years has centered primarily in funds which stress current income. Prominent examples include bond funds, money market funds, and option income funds (which issue options against a portfolio of common stocks). While most investment companies hold a highly diversified portfolio of securities, a few specialize in stocks or bonds from a single industry or sector (such as precious metals or oil and natural gas).

It is not at all clear that investment companies hold a significant advantage over other investors in seeking out the highest returns available in the financial marketplace. Moreover, there is evidence that these companies may roll over their portfolios too rapidly, which runs up the cost of managing the fund and reduces net earnings. Less-frequent trading activity on the part of investment companies might well result in greater long-run benefits for the saver. Research evidence has been mounting for a number of years that security markets are highly efficient. Overvaluation or undervaluation of securities is, at most, a temporary phenomenon.[8] In this kind of environment it is doubtful that investment companies are of significant benefit to the large investor, though they may indeed aid the small investor in reducing information and transactions costs and opening up investment opportunities not otherwise available.

SUMMARY AND CONCLUSIONS

Financial institutions today face a number of pressures which have caused them to change significantly their methods of operation and the services they offer the public. The pressures of rising costs and intense competition in the financial sector have, as we have seen, led financial institutions to innovate in developing many new financial services in order to attract funds. These pressures are likely to intensify in the period ahead due to fundamental changes now occurring in the makeup of the nation's population. Large numbers of new families are being formed who will have heavy credit demands for housing, transportation, and other consumer goods and services. To survive in tomorrow's economic environment, financial institutions must be flexible, innovative, and highly competitive.

Social pressures will buffet the financial institutions' sector in the 1980s. Profit taking must be tempered by concern for the quality of the environment and human welfare. During the 1970s Congress recognized that access to

---

[7] See Chapter 9 for a discussion of the favorable federal tax rates applicable to capital gains.

[8] See especially the studies by Friend, Blum, and Crockett (8) and Malkiel (12), listed in the references at the end of this chapter, and the discussion of efficient markets in Chapter 20.

credit is one of the essential elements of modern living. Today lenders of funds are required to explain why certain customers are turned down for a loan or a lease and are forbidden to discriminate in providing credit on the basis of age, sex, race, religion, or national origin. The confluence of all these forces—competition, innovation, and regulation—is likely to have profound effects on the structure and growth of financial institutions in the years ahead.

STUDY QUESTIONS

1. Against what kinds of risk do life insurance companies protect their policyholders? How about property-casualty insurers?
2. What is the "Law of Large Numbers"? What is its relationship to the insurance business?
3. Compare and contrast the asset portfolios of life insurance companies and property-casualty insurers. Try to explain any differences you observe.
4. What are the principal lines of insurance offered by property-casualty insurance companies? Have the risks faced by this industry changed in recent years? Why?
5. What is the principal function of pension funds? Explain why these institutions have been among the most rapidly growing financial institutions in recent years. Do you expect their growth to be faster or slower in the future? Why?
6. What are the principal assets acquired by pension funds? What factors guide their selection of securities?
7. What role do finance companies play in providing funds to the financial markets? How many different kinds of finance companies are there?
8. Major changes have occurred in the structure of the finance company industry in recent years. Explain how these changes resemble those going on in other financial industries, such as credit unions and savings banks, and what the principal causes appear to be.
9. What advantages do investment companies offer the small saver? Why has their growth been so erratic in recent years?
10. Define the following terms:
    a. Open-end company.
    b. Closed-end company.
    c. Bond fund.
    d. Money market fund.
    e. Growth fund.
    f. Balanced fund.

SELECTED REFERENCES

1. American Council of Life Insurance, *1979 Life Insurance Fact Book.*
2. Blume, Marshall E., Jean Crockett, and Irwin Friend. "Stock Ownership in the United States: Characteristics and Trends." *Survey of Current Business,* Department of Commerce, November 1974.

3. Board of Governors of the Federal Reserve System. "Survey of Finance Companies, 1975." *Federal Reserve Bulletin,* March 1976, pp. 179–207.

4. Cook, Timothy, and Jeremy G. Duffield. "Average Cost of Money Market Mutual Funds." *Economic Review,* Federal Reserve Bank of Richmond, July-August 1979.

5. ____. "Short-Term Investment Pools." *Economic Review,* Federal Reserve Bank of Richmond, September-October 1980.

6. Dougall, Herbert E., and Jack E. Gaumnitz. *Capital Markets and Institutions.* Englewood Cliffs, N.J.: Prentice-Hall, 1975).

7. Friend, Irwin, Marshall Blum, and Jean Crockett. *Mutual Funds and Other Institutional Investors.* New York: McGraw-Hill, 1970.

8. Harless, Doris, *Nonbank Financial Institutions.* Federal Reserve Bank of Richmond, 1975.

9. Insurance Information Institute. *Insurance Facts,* 1978 and 1979.

10. Jacobs, Donald P., Loring C. Farwell, and Edwin H. Neave. *Financial Institutions.* 5th ed. Homewood, Ill.: Richard D. Irwin, 1972).

11. Burton G. Malkiel. *A Random Walk down Wall Street.* New York: W. W. Norton, 1975.

12. *The Private Pension Controversy.* New York: Bankers Trust Co., 1973.

13. Rose, Peter S. and Donald R. Fraser, *Financial Institutions,* Dallas, Texas: Business Publications, Inc., 1980.

14. Snellings, Aubrey N. "The Financial Services Industry: Recent Trends and Future Prospects." *Economic Review,* Federal Reserve Bank of Richmond, January-February 1980.

15. "Survey of Finance Companies, 1980." *Federal Reserve Bulletin,* May 1981, pp. 398–409.

part three

Interest Rates and Security Prices

6

Interest Rates in the
Financial System

In the opening chapter we described the money and capital markets as one vast pool of funds, depleted by the borrowing activities of households, businesses, and governments and replenished by the savings which these sectors of the economy also provide. The financial markets make saving possible by offering the individual saver a wide menu of choices where funds may be placed at attractive rates of return. By committing funds to one or more securities, the saver, in effect, becomes a lender of funds. The financial markets also make borrowing possible by giving the borrower a channel through which securities can be issued to lenders. And the financial markets make investment and economic growth possible by providing the funds needed for the purchase of machinery and equipment and the construction of buildings, highways, and other productive facilities.

Clearly then, the acts of saving and lending, borrowing and investment are intimately linked with each other through the financial system. And one factor which significantly influences all of them is the *rate of interest*. The rate of interest is the "price" a borrower must pay to secure scarce loanable funds from a lender for an agreed-upon period. It is the price of credit. But unlike other prices in the economy, the rate of interest is really a *ratio* of two quantities—the money cost of borrowing funds to the amount of money actually borrowed, usually expressed on an annual percentage basis.

Interest rates send *price signals* to borrowers, lenders, savers, and investors. For example, higher interest rates generally bring forth a greater volume of savings and stimulate the lending of funds. Lower rates, on the other hand, tend to dampen the flow of savings and reduce lending activity. Higher interest rates tend to reduce the volume of borrowing and capital investment, while lower rates stimulate borrowing and investment spending. In the ensuing sections of this chapter we will discuss in more detail the forces which determine rates of interest in the financial system.

FUNCTIONS OF THE RATE OF INTEREST IN THE ECONOMY

The rate of interest performs several different and highly important roles in the economy:

It helps guarantee that current savings will flow into investment to promote economic growth.

The rate of interest rations the available supply of credit, generally providing loanable funds to those projects with the highest expected returns.

It brings into balance the nation's supply of money with the demand for money.

The rate of interest is also an important tool of government policy through its influence upon the volume of saving and investment. If the economy is growing too slowly and unemployment is rising, the government can use its policy tools to lower interest rates in order to stimulate borrowing and investment. On the other hand, an overheated economy experiencing rapid inflation has traditionally called for a government policy of higher interest rates to slow both borrowing and spending.

In the pages of the financial press, the phrase "the interest rate" is frequently used. In truth, there is no such thing as "the interest rate," for there are thousands of different rates in the financial system. Even securities issued by the same borrower will often carry a variety of interest rates. In Chapters 8 and 9, the most important factors which cause rates to vary among different securities and over time are examined in detail. In this chapter, our focus is upon those basic forces that influence the level of *all* interest rates.

To uncover these general and pervasive rate-determining forces, however, we must make a simplifying assumption. We will assume there is *one* fundamental interest rate in the economy known as the *pure* or *risk-free rate of interest,* which is a component of all rates. The closest approximation to this pure rate in the real world is the yield to maturity on long-term U.S. government bonds. It is a rate of return presenting no risk of financial loss to the investor and represents the true "opportunity cost" of holding idle money because the investor can always invest in riskless securities and earn this minimum rate of return.

Once the pure rate of interest is determined, all other interest rates may be determined from it by examining the special characteristics of the securities issued by individual borrowers. For example, only the government can borrow at the pure, risk-free interest rate; other borrowers pay higher rates than this due, in part, to the greater risk of loss attached to their securities. Differences in liquidity, marketability, and maturity are other important factors causing various interest rates to differ from the pure, risk-free rate. First, however, we must examine the forces which determine the risk-free rate itself.

THE CLASSICAL THEORY OF INTEREST RATES

One of the oldest theories concerning the determinants of the risk-free interest rate is the classical theory, developed originally during the 18th and 19th centuries by a number of British economists, refined by the Austrian economist Bohm-Bawerk, and elaborated by Irving Fisher early in this century.[1] The classical theory argues that the rate of interest is determined by two forces—the supply of saving, derived mainly from households, and the demand for investment capital from the business sector. Let us examine these rate-determining forces of saving and investment demand in more detail.

Saving by Households

What is the relationship between the rate of interest and the volume of saving in the economy? Most saving in modern industrialized economies is carried out by individuals and families. For these households, saving is simply abstinence from consumption spending. *Current saving, therefore, is equal to the difference between current income and current consumption expenditures.*

In making the decision on the timing and amount of saving to be done, households typically consider several factors—the size of current and long-run income, the desired savings target, and the desired proportion of income to be put aside in the form of savings (i.e., the propensity to save). Generally, the volume of household saving rises with income. Higher-income families and individuals tend to save more and consume less relative to their total income than families with lower incomes do.

While income levels probably dominate savings decisions, interest rates also play an important role. For interest rates affect an individual's choice between current consumption and saving for future consumption. The classical theory of interest assumed that individuals have a definite *time preference* for current consumption over future consumption. A rational individual, it was assumed, would always prefer current enjoyment of goods and services over future enjoyment. Therefore, the only way to encourage an individual or family to consume less now and *save* more was to offer a higher rate of interest on current savings. If more were saved in the current period at a higher rate of return, future consumption and future enjoyment would be

---

[1] See especially Bohm-Bawerk (3) and Fisher (10) in the list of references at the conclusion of this chapter.

increased. For example, if the current rate of interest is 10 percent and a household saves $100 instead of spending it on current consumption, it will be able to consume $110 in goods and services a year from now.

The classical theory thus considers the payment of interest a *reward for waiting*—for the postponement of current consumption in favor of greater future consumption. Higher interest rates presumably increase the attractiveness of saving relative to consumption spending, encouraging more individuals to substitute savings (and future consumption) for some quantity of current consumption. On the other hand, lower rates increase the attractiveness of current consumption relative to saving. This so-called *substitution effect* calls for a *positive* relationship between interest rates and the volume of saving. Higher interest rates bring forth a greater volume of saving. Figure 6–1 illustrates the substitution effect: if the rate of interest in the financial

FIGURE 6–1
The Substitution Effect Relating Saving and Interest Rates

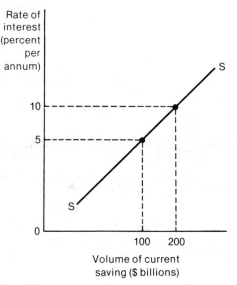

markets rises from 5 percent to 10 percent, the volume of current saving by households is assumed to increase from $100 billion to $200 billion.

Saving by Business Firms

Our principal focus to this point has been upon the determinants of saving by households. Businesses also save, however, and direct a portion of their savings into the financial markets to purchase securities and make loans.

Most business firms have temporary cash surpluses from week to week or month to month, and these frequently will be invested in money market instruments, such as U.S. Treasury bills or bank certificates of deposit. Many businesses also hold long-run savings balances in the form of retained earnings (as reflected in their equity, or net worth accounts.) The increase in retained earnings reported by business corporations each year is a key measure of the volume of current business saving. And these retained funds account for the majority of annual investment spending by business.

The volume of business saving depends upon two key factors—the level of business profits and the dividend policies of corporations. These two factors are summarized in the retention ratio—the ratio of retained earnings to net income after taxes. This ratio indicates the proportion of corporate profits retained in the business for investment purposes rather than paid out as stockholder dividends. Experience has shown that corporate dividend policies change infrequently. Many corporations prefer to keep their dividend payments level or increase them slightly each year, regardless of current earnings. Any shortfalls in earnings needed for dividend payments are made up through borrowing or by drawing upon previously accumulated funds. *The critical element in determining the amount of business saving is, therefore, the level of business profits.*

If profits are expected to rise, businesses will be able to draw more heavily upon earnings retained in the firm and less heavily upon the money and capital markets for funds. The result is a reduction in the demand for credit and a tendency toward lower interest rates. On the other hand, when profits fall but firms do not cut back on their investment plans, they are forced to make heavier use of the money and capital markets for investment funds. The demand for credit rises, and interest rates usually increase as well.

While the principal determinant of business saving is profits, interest rates also play a role, especially in the decision of what proportion of a firm's current operating costs and long-term investment expenditures should be financed internally and what proportion externally. Higher rates in the money and capital markets typically encourage firms to use internally generated funds (i.e., accumulated savings) more heavily in financing their projects. Conversely, lower interest rates encourage greater use of external funds from the financial marketplace.

Saving by Government

Governments also save, though less frequently and generally in smaller amounts than the household and business sectors. In fact, most government saving appears to be *unintended saving* which arises when government receipts unexpectedly exceed the actual amount of government expenditures. Such a condition—a budget surplus—usually reflects larger tax collections or a lesser need for government funds than was first anticipated. Income flows in the economy (out of which government tax revenues arise) and the pacing of government spending programs are the dominant factors affecting government saving; interest rates are probably not a key factor here.

The Demand for Investment Funds

Business, household, and government saving are important determinants of interest rates according to the classical theory of interest, but not the only ones. The other critical rate-determining factor in the classical theory is *investment spending* by business firms.

Businesses require huge amounts of funds each year for the purchase of equipment, machinery, and inventories and to support the construction of new buildings and other physical facilities. The majority of business expenditures for these purposes consists of what economists call *replacement investment*—expenditures to replace equipment and facilities which are wearing out or are technologically obsolete. A smaller, but more dynamic, form of business capital spending is labeled *net investment*—expenditures to acquire additional equipment and facilities in order to increase output. The sum of replacement investment plus net investment equals *gross investment.*

Replacement investment usually is more predictable and grows at a more even rate than does net investment. This is due to the fact that such expenditures are financed almost exclusively from *inside* the firm and frequently follow a routine pattern based upon depreciation formulas. Expenditures for *new* equipment and facilities (net investment), on the other hand, depend upon the business community's outlook regarding future sales, changes in technology, industrial capacity, and the cost of raising funds. Because these factors are subject to frequent changes, it is not surprising that net investment (particularly inventory investment) is highly variable.

Net investment, because of its total size and volatility, is a driving force in the economy. *Changes in net investment are closely linked to fluctuations in the nation's output of goods and services, employment, and prices.* A significant decline in net investment frequently leads to a business recession, a decline in productivity, and a rise in unemployment unless offset by increased consumer or government spending. In fact, substantial cutbacks in inventory investment and long-term capital spending occur, on average, every three to four years in the United States, usually precipitating a recession. Two recent examples occurred in 1975 and 1980 when soaring energy costs, sharply higher interest rates, and other factors combined to slow the pace of domestic net investment, leading to significant declines in industrial production and a sharp rise in the U.S. unemployment rate.

The Investment Decision-Making Process. The process of investment decision making by business firms is complex and depends upon a host of qualitative and quantitative factors. The firm must compare its current level of production with the capacity of its existing facilities and decide whether it has sufficient excess capacity to handle anticipated demand for its product. If expected future demand will strain the firm's existing facilities, it will consider expanding operating capacity.

Most business firms have several investment projects under consideration at any one time. While the investment decision making process varies from firm to firm, each business generally makes some estimate of *net cash flows* (i.e., revenues minus all expenses including taxes) which each project will generate over its useful life. From this information plus knowledge of each investment project's acquisition cost, management can calculate its *expected rate of return* and compare that projected return with anticipated returns from alternative projects.

One of the more popular methods for performing this calculation is the *internal rate of return* method, which equates the total cost of an investment project with the future net cash flows (NCF) expected from that project discounted back to their present values. Thus,

$$\text{Cost of project} = \frac{\text{NCF}_1}{(1 + r)^1} + \frac{\text{NCF}_2}{(1 + r)^2} + \cdots + \frac{\text{NCF}_n}{(1 + r)^n} \quad (6\text{--}1)$$

where each NCF represents the expected annual net cash flow from the project and r is its expected internal rate of return. The internal rate performs two functions: (1) it measures the annual yield the firm expects from an investment project; and (2) it reduces the value of all future cash flows expected over the useful economic life of the project down to their present value to the firm. In general, if the firm must choose among several mutually exclusive projects, it will choose the one with the highest expected internal rate of return.

While the internal rate of return provides a yardstick for selecting potentially profitable investment projects, how does a businessman decide how much to spend on investment at any point in time? How many projects should be chosen? It is here that the financial markets play a key role in the investment decision making process.

Suppose a business firm is considering the following projects with their associated expected rates of return:

Project	Expected Annual Rate of Return (internal)
A	15%
B	12
C	10
D	9
E	8

How many of these projects will be adopted? The firm must compare each project's expected rate of return with the cost of raising capital to finance the project.

Assume that funds must be borrowed in the financial marketplace to complete any of the above projects and the current cost of borrowing is 10 percent. Then, which projects are acceptable from an economic standpoint?

FIGURE 6–2
The Cost of Capital and the Investment Decision

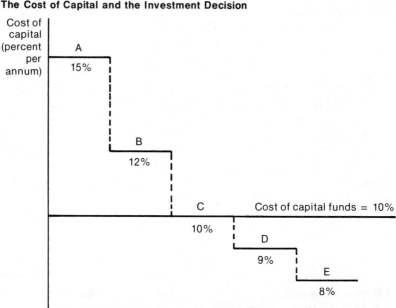

Dollar cost of investment projects

As shown in Figure 6–2, projects A and B clearly are acceptable because their expected returns exceed the cost of borrowing capital to finance them. The firm would be indifferent about project C since its expected return is no more than the cost of borrowed funds. Projects D and E, on the other hand, are unprofitable at this time.[2]

It is through changes in the cost of raising funds that the financial markets can exert a powerful influence on the investment decisions of business firms. As credit becomes scarcer and more expensive, the cost of capital rises, eliminating some investment projects from consideration. For example, if the cost of borrowed funds rises from 10 percent to 13 percent, it is obvious that

---

[2] The internal-rate-of-return method for evaluating investment projects is only one of several capital-budgeting techniques in use today. Another popular technique is net present value (NPV), which determines the net contribution in total after-tax dollars of a project by discounting all expected cash flows back to their present value using the individual firm's minimum required rate of return.

The payback period (PP) approach determines the number of years required for the firm to recover fully the cost of a project. If expected cash flows from a project pay the firm back more rapidly than the minimum length of time acceptable to management, the project is likely to be adopted.

Recent studies indicate that major corporations use a wide variety of capital-budgeting techniques and may apply several different methods to the same project. There is clearly a trend, however, toward greater use of discounted cash-flow techniques (such as net present value and internal rate of return), especially among larger firms. See, for example, the study by Petty, Scott, and Bird (19) and Klammer (14).

only project A in our earlier example would then be economically viable. On the other hand, if credit becomes more abundant and less costly, the cost of capital for the individual firm will tend to decline and more projects will become profitable. In our example, a decline in the cost of borrowed funds from 10 percent to 8½ percent would make all but project E economically viable and probably acceptable to the firm.

Investment Demand and the Rate of Interest. This reasoning explains, in part, why the demand for investment capital by business firms was regarded by the classical economists as *negatively* related to the rate of interest. Figure 6–3 depicts the business investment demand curve as drawn in the classical

FIGURE 6–3
The Investment Demand Schedule in the Classical Theory of Interest Rates

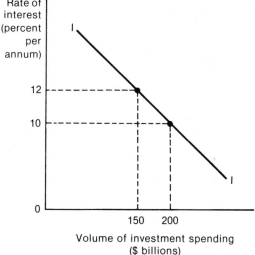

theory. This demand curve slopes downward and to the right, reflecting the declining net marginal productivity of capital as more and more capital funds are invested by firms.[3] At low rates of interest more investment projects become economically viable and firms require more funds to finance a longer list of projects. On the other hand, if the rate of interest rises to high levels, fewer investment projects will be pursued and less funds will be required

---

[3] As the quantity of investment capital is increased relative to land, labor, and other productive factors, the laws of production in economics suggest that output will increase at a decreasing rate. Therefore, with technology held constant, the marginal cost of capital rises as more of it is employed by the individual firm and the *net* marginal productivity of additional capital declines. As a firm spends more funds for investment purposes, it expects its return to capital to decline. For this reason the investment demand schedule shown in Figure 6–3 slopes downward with an increasing volume of investment spending.

from the financial markets. For example, at a 12 percent rate of interest only $150 billion in funds for investment spending might be demanded by business firms in the economy. If the rate of interest drops to 10 percent, however, the volume of desired investment by firms might rise to $200 billion.

The Equilibrium Rate of Interest in the Classical Theory of Interest

The classical economists believed that interest rates in the financial markets were determined by the interplay of the supply of saving and the demand for investment. Specifically, the equilibrium rate of interest is determined at the point where the quantity of savings supplied to the market is exactly equal to the quantity of funds demanded for investment. As shown in Figure 6–4, this occurs at point E, where the equilibrium rate of interest is i_E

FIGURE 6–4
The Equilibrium Rate of Interest in the Classical Theory

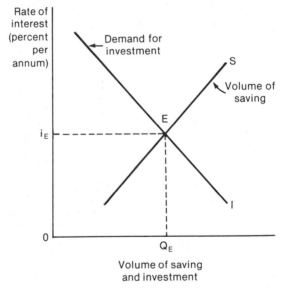

and the equilibrium quantity of capital funds traded in the financial markets and invested is Q_E.

The market rate of interest moves *toward* equilibrium, though the forces of demand and supply are continually changing and may prevent the interest rate from actually settling at the equilibrium level. If the market rate is temporarily *above* equilibrium, then the volume of saving exceeds the demand for investment capital, creating an excess supply of savings. Savers will offer their funds at lower and lower rates until the market interest rate approaches equilibrium. Similarly, if the market rate lies temporarily *below* equilibrium, investment demand exceeds the quantity of savings available. Business firms bid up the interest rate until it approaches the level at which the quantity saved equals the quantity of funds demanded for investment purposes.

Limitations of the Classical Theory of Interest.   The classical theory sheds considerable light on the factors affecting interest rates. However, it has some serious limitations.

The central problem is that the theory ignores several factors other than saving and investment which affect interest rates. For example, commercial banks have the power to create money by making loans to the public. When borrowers repay their bank loans, money is destroyed.[4] The amount of money created or destroyed affects the total amount of credit available in the financial marketplace and therefore must be considered in any explanation of the factors determining interest rates. In addition, the classical theory assumes that interest rates are the principal determinant of the quantity of savings available. Today, economists recognize that *income* is far more important in determining the volume of saving. Finally, the classical theory contends that the demand for borrowed funds comes principally from the business sector. Today, however, both consumers and governments are important borrowers, significantly affecting credit availability and cost. As we will see in the balance of this chapter, two more recent theories of the interest rate—liquidity preference and loanable funds—address a number of these limitations of the classical theory.

THE LIQUIDITY PREFERENCE THEORY

The classical theory of interest has been called a long-run explanation of interest rates since it focuses upon the public's thrift habits and the productivity of capital—factors which tend to change slowly. During the 1930s British economist John Maynard Keynes developed a short-run theory of the rate of interest which, he argued, was more relevant for policymakers and for explaining near-term changes in interest rates. This theory of interest-rate determination is known as liquidity preference.[5]

The Demand for Liquidity

Keynes argued that the rate of interest is really a payment for the use of a scarce resource—money. Businesses and individuals prefer to hold money for carrying out daily transactions and also as a precaution against future cash needs even though its yield is low or nonexistent. Investors in fixed-income securities, such as corporate and government bonds, frequently desire to

---

[4] For an explanation of how commercial banks create and destroy money, see Chapter 3 on the commercial banking system.

[5] See especially J. M. Keynes (13). Other discussions of liquidity preference are found in Ackley (1), Conrad (5), and Due and Clower (6).

hold money as a haven against declining security prices. Interest rates, therefore, are the "price" that must be paid to induce money holders to surrender a perfectly liquid asset and hold other assets which carry more risk. At times the preference for liquidity grows very strong. Unless the government expands the nation's money supply, interest rates will rise.

In the theory of liquidity preference, only two outlets for investor funds are considered—bonds and money (including bank deposits). Money provides perfect liquidity—instant spending power—while bonds pay interest but cannot be spent until converted into cash. If interest rates rise, the market value of bonds paying a fixed rate of interest will fall; the investor would suffer a capital loss if those bonds were converted into cash. On the other hand, a fall in interest rates results in higher bond prices; the bondholder will experience a capital gain if his bonds are sold for cash. To the classical theorists it was irrational to hold money because it provided little or no return. To Keynes, however, the holding of money could be a perfectly rational step if interest rates were expected to rise because increasing rates could result in substantial losses from investing in bonds.

Motives for Holding Money. Keynes observed that the public demands money for three different purposes (motives). The *transactions motive* represents the demand for money in order to purchase goods and services. Because inflows and outflows of money are not perfectly synchronized in either timing or amount, businesses, households, and governments must keep some cash in the till or in demand accounts simply to meet daily expenses. Some money also must be held as a reserve for future emergencies and to cover extraordinary expenses. This *precautionary motive* for holding money arises because we live in a world of uncertainty and cannot predict exactly what expenses will arise in the future.

Keynes assumed that money demanded for transactions and precautionary purposes was dependent upon the level of national income, business sales, and prices. Higher levels of income, sales, or prices increased the need for money to carry out transactions and protect against future emergencies. However, neither the precautionary nor the transactions demand for money was assumed to be affected by changes in interest rates. In fact, Keynes assumed money demand for precautionary and transactions purposes to be *fixed* in the short run. In a longer-run period, however, transactions and precautionary demands change as national income changes.

Short-run changes in interest rates were attributed by Keynes to a third motive for holding money—*the speculative motive.* As noted earlier, rising interest rates result in falling prices for bonds. To illustrate, suppose an investor has recently purchased a corporate bond for $1,000. The company issuing the bond promises to pay $100 a year in interest income. In order to simplify matters, assume the bond is a perpetual security. This means the investor will receive $100 a year for as long as he or she wishes to hold the security. The annual rate of return (or yield) on the bond, then, is 10 percent

($100/$1,000). Suppose now that the interest rate on bonds of similar quality rises to 12 percent. What happens to the price of the 10 percent bond? Obviously, its price in the marketplace will fall because its annual yield is less than 12 percent.

How far will the bond's price fall? It will approach $833 because at this price the $100 annual interest payment gives the investor an approximate yield of 12 percent ($100/$833). In the reverse situation, if interest rates were to decline—say, to 9 percent—the 10 percent bond would become more attractive and its market price would rise.[6]

If investors expect rising interest rates, many of them will demand money instead of bonds. As the expectation that interest rates will rise grows stronger and stronger in the marketplace, the demand for money increases. We may represent this speculative demand for money by a curve which slopes downward and to the right, as shown in Figure 6–5. At low rates of interest, many investors feel that interest rates are soon to rise (bond prices are going to fall), and therefore more money is demanded. At high rates of interest, on the other hand, many investors will conclude that rates soon will fall and bond prices rise. In this instance, the demand for money decreases, while the demand for bonds increases. Also, when interest rates are high, the opportunity cost of holding idle cash increases, encouraging investors to economize on their cash balances and buy bonds.

Total Demand for Money.   The total demand for money in the economy is simply the sum of transactions, precautionary, and speculative demands. Because the principal determinant of transactions and precautionary demands is income, not interest rates, these money demands are fixed at a certain level of national income. Let this demand be represented by the quantity OK shown along the horizontal axis in Figure 6–6. Then, any amount of money demanded in excess of OK represents speculative demand. The *total* demand for money is represented along curve D_T. Therefore, if the rate of interest at the moment is at i, Figure 6–6 shows that the speculative demand for money is KJ and the total demand for money is OJ.

---

[6] As we will see in Chapter 7, the same inverse relationship between the price and interest yield on a fixed-income security holds, even if we assume that the security is not perpetual but has a fixed maturity. This can be seen by comparing two formulas. The price of a *perpetual bond* (P) is related to its market interest rate (r) by the formula

$$P = R/r$$

where R is the annual income in dollars paid by the security. Clearly, as interest rate r increases, market price P falls.

In the case of a bond which matures in n years and is held to maturity by the investor, its market price is related to its interest rate by the formula

$$P = M/(1 + r)^n$$

where M is the maturity value of the bond. Once again, it is clear that a rise in rate r lowers the market value (price) of the bond, while a decline in r results in a higher market value for the bond.

FIGURE 6–5
Speculative Demand for Money

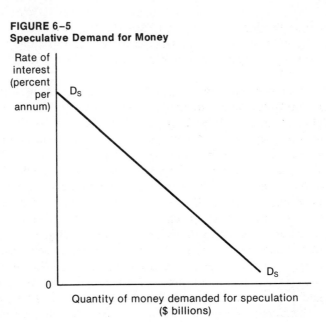

Rate of interest (percent per annum)

D_S

D_S

0

Quantity of money demanded for speculation
($ billions)

FIGURE 6–6
The Total Demand for Money in the Economy

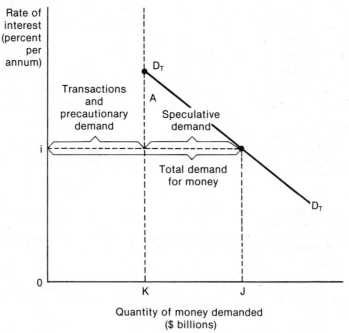

Rate of interest (percent per annum)

D_T

Transactions and precautionary demand

A

Speculative demand

i

Total demand for money

D_T

0

K

J

Quantity of money demanded
($ billions)

The Supply of Money

The other major element determining interest rates in liquidity preference theory is the supply of money. In modern economies the money supply is controlled or at least closely regulated by government. Because government decisions concerning the size of the nation's money supply are guided by the public welfare and not by the level of interest rates, we assume that the supply of money is inelastic with respect to the rate of interest. Such a money-supply curve is represented in Figure 6–7 by the vertical line M_S.

The Equilibrium Rate of Interest in Liquidity Preference Theory

The interplay of the total demand for money and the supply of money determines the equilibrium rate of interest in the short run. As shown in Figure 6–7, the equilibrium rate of interest is found at point i_E where the

FIGURE 6–7
The Equilibrium Rate of Interest in the Liquidity Preference Theory

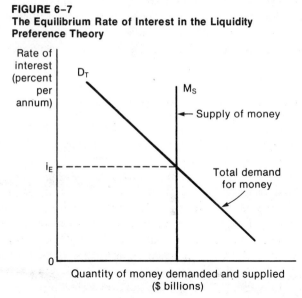

quantity of money demanded by the public equals the quantity of money supplied. *Above* this equilibrium rate, the supply of money exceeds the quantity demanded, and some businesses, households, and units of government will try to dispose of their unwanted money balances by purchasing bonds. The prices of bonds will rise, driving interest rates down toward equilibrium at i_E. On the other hand, at rates *below* equilibrium, the quantity of money demanded exceeds the supply. Some decision makers in the economy will sell their bonds to raise additional cash, driving bond prices down and interest rates up toward equilibrium.

Liquidity preference theory provides some useful insights into investor behavior and the influence of government policy upon the economy and financial system. For example, it suggests that it is rational at certain times for the public to hoard money and at other times to "dishoard" (spend away) unwanted cash. If the public disposes of some of its cash balances by purchasing securities, this action increases the quantity of loanable funds available in the nation's financial markets. Other things equal, interest rates will fall. On the other hand, if the public tries to hoard more money, expanding its cash balances by selling securities, less money will be available for loans. Interest rates will rise, *ceteris peribus*.

Liquidity preference illustrates how central banks such as the Federal Reserve System can influence interest rates in the financial markets, at least in the short run. For example, if higher interest rates are desired, the central bank can contract the size of the nation's money supply and rates will tend to rise, assuming the demand for money is unchanged. If the demand for money is increasing, then the central bank can bring about higher interest rates by ensuring that the money supply grows more slowly than money demands. In contrast, if the central bank expands the nation's money supply, interest rates will decline in the short run if the demand for money does not increase as well.

Limitations of the Liquidity Preference Theory

Still, liquidity preference theory has important limitations. It is only a *short-run* approach to interest-rate determination because it assumes that income levels remain constant. In the longer run, interest rates are affected by changes in the level of income. Indeed, it is impossible to have a stable-equilibrium interest rate without also reaching an equilibrium level of income, saving, and investment. Then, too, liquidity preference considers only the supply and demand for money, whereas business, consumer, and government demands for credit clearly have an impact upon the cost of credit to these borrowers. A more comprehensive view of interest rates is needed which considers the important roles played by *all* actors in the financial system—businesses, households, and governments.

THE LOANABLE FUNDS THEORY

An explanation of interest rates which overcomes many of the limitations of earlier theories is the *loanable funds* approach. This view argues that the risk-free interest rate is determined by the interplay of two forces—the demand for and the supply of loanable funds. The demand for loanable funds consists of credit demands from businesses, consumers, and units of government. The supply of loanable funds stems from three sources—saving, hoarding demand for money, and money creation by the banking system. We consider each of these demand and supply factors in turn.

Consumer Demand for Loanable Funds

Consumers demand loanable funds in order to purchase a wide variety of goods and services. Recent research indicates that consumers are not particularly responsive to the rate of interest when they borrow but focus instead principally upon the "nonprice" terms of a loan, such as the down payment, maturity, and size of installment payments. This implies that consumer demand for credit is relatively *inelastic* with respect to the rate of interest. Certainly a rise in interest rates leads to some reduction in consumer demand for loanable funds, while a decline in rates stimulates some additional consumer borrowing. However, along the consumer's relatively inelastic demand schedule, a substantial change in the rate of interest must occur before consumer demand for funds changes significantly.

Business Demand for Loanable Funds

The credit demands of business generally are more responsive to changes in the rate of interest than is consumer borrowing. Most business credit is for such investment purposes as purchases of inventories and new plant and equipment. As noted earlier in our discussion of the classical theory of interest, a higher interest rate eliminates some business investment projects from consideration because their expected rate of return is lower than the cost of funds. On the other hand, at lower rates of interest, many investment projects will be profitable, with their expected returns exceeding the cost of funds. Therefore, the demand for loanable funds from the business sector increases as the rate of interest falls.

Government Demand for Loanable Funds

Government demand for loanable funds is a growing factor in the nation's financial markets but does not depend significantly upon the level of interest rates. This is especially true of borrowing by the federal government. Federal decisions on spending and borrowing are made by Congress in response to social needs and the public welfare, not the rate of interest. Moreover, the federal government has the power both to tax and to create money in order to pay its debts. State and local government demand, on the other hand, is slightly interest elastic since many local governments are limited in their borrowing activities by legal interest-rate ceilings. When open-market rates rise above these legal ceilings, some state and local units of government are prevented from offering their securities to the public.

Total Demand for Loanable Funds

The total demand for loanable funds is the *sum* of consumer, business, and government credit demands. This demand curve slopes downward and to the

FIGURE 6–8
Total Demand for Loanable Funds

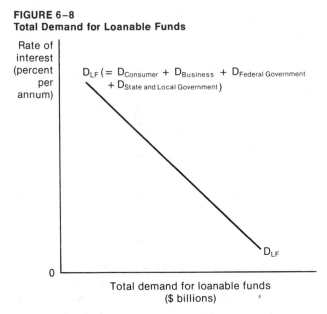

Total demand for loanable funds
($ billions)

right with respect to the rate of interest, as shown in Figure 6–8. Higher rates of interest lead some businesses, consumers, and governments to curtail their borrowing plans, while lower rates bring forth more credit demand. However, the demand for loanable funds does not determine the rate of interest by itself. The supply of loanable funds must be added to complete the picture.

The Supply of Loanable Funds

Loanable funds flow into the money and capital markets from at least three different sources: (1) saving by businesses, consumers, and governments; (2) dishoarding (spending down) of money balances; and (3) money created by the banking system. We consider each of these sources of funds in turn.

Saving. The supply of savings is the principal source of loanable funds. As noted earlier, most saving is done by households and is simply the difference between current income and current consumption. Businesses, however, also save by retaining a portion of current earnings and by adding to their depreciation reserves. Government saving, while relatively rare, occurs when current revenues exceed current expenditures.

Today, most economists believe that *income levels,* rather than interest rates, are the dominant factor in the decision of how much and when to save.[7] There is also evidence that business and household saving may be *goal oriented*. That is, some business firms and households set target levels of total savings as a long-run goal. For example, suppose an individual wishes to accumulate $100,000 in anticipation of his or her retirement. Interest rates subsequently rise from 5 percent to 10 percent. Will this individual save more out of each period's income or less? Probably *less,* because the higher interest rate will enable the saver to reach his or her goal with less sacrifice of current income. On the other hand, a lower interest rate might lead to a *greater* volume of saving because a business or household must accumulate more funds to achieve its savings goal.

This so-called *income effect* clearly has the opposite effect on the volume of saving from the *substitution effect,* described earlier in our discussion of the classical theory of interest. The two effects pull aggregate saving in opposite directions as interest rates change. It should not be surprising, therefore, that the annual volume of saving in the economy is an extremely difficult quantity to forecast.

Recent research using econometric models of the U.S. economy has suggested the importance of another factor—the *wealth effect*—in influencing savings decisions.[8] Individuals accumulate wealth in many different forms—real assets (automobiles, furniture, houses, land, etc.) and financial assets (stocks, bonds, etc.). What happens to the value of financial assets as interest rates change? If rates rise, the market value of financial assets will fall until their yield approaches market-determined levels. On the other hand, a decline in interest rates tends to increase the value of financial assets, especially long-term bonds. In general, then, a rise in interest rates will result in decreases in the value of wealth held in financial assets, forcing the individual to save more to protect his or her wealth position. Conversely, a decrease in interest rates will increase the value of financial assets, increasing wealth and perhaps necessitating a lower volume of current saving.

For businesses and individuals heavily in debt, however, the opposite effects may ensue. When interest rates rise, debt contracted in earlier periods, when interest rates were lower, seems less of a burden now. For example, a home mortgage taken on by a family when rates in the mortgage market were 10 percent seems a less-burdensome drain on family income when rates on new mortgages have risen to 15 percent. Therefore, a rise in interest rates tends to make those economic units carrying a large volume of debt relative to their financial assets feel better off, and they may tend to save *less* as a result. A decrease in interest rates, on the other hand, may result in more savings due to the wealth effect.

---

[7] There is, however, considerable controversy as to just what *measure* of income determines the annual volume of savings. Some economists argue that current saving is determined, not by current income levels, but by a long-run view of income, perhaps adjusted for the stage of life of the income recipient. See, for example, Ando and Modligiani (2) and Friedman (11).

[8] See especially Boskin (4), Feber (8), and Justen and Taylor (12).

The net effect of income, substitution, and wealth effects leads to a relatively interest-inelastic supply-of-savings curve. Substantial changes in interest rates usually are required to bring about any significant change in the volume of aggregate saving in the economy.

Dishoarding of Money Balances. Still another source of loanable funds is centered in the public's changing demands for money. As noted in our earlier discussion of liquidity preference theory, the public's demand for money varies with interest rates and income levels. The supply of money, on the other hand, is closely controlled by government. When the public's demand for money exceeds the supply, *hoarding* of money takes place as individuals and businesses attempt to increase their money holdings at the expense of others. Hoarding reduces the volume of loanable funds available in the financial markets. On the other hand, when the public's demand for money is less than the supply available, *dishoarding* occurs. Some individuals and businesses will dispose of their excess money holdings, increasing the supply of loanable funds available in the financial system.

Creation of Money by the Banking System. Commercial banks and nonbank thrift institutions offering demand deposits and other transaction accounts have the unique ability to create money. This capacity for money creation arises because transaction deposits are the principal means for making payments in the economy. Money created by the banking system represents an additional source of loanable funds, which must be added to the amount of savings and dishoarding of money balances (or minus the amount of hoarding demand) to derive the total supply of loanable funds in the economy. The total supply-of-loanable-funds curve is depicted in Figure 6–9. This curve rises with higher rates of interest, indicating that a greater

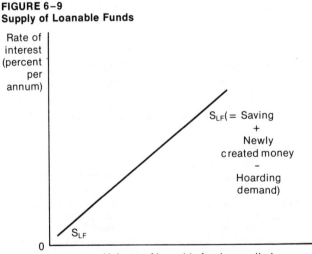

FIGURE 6–9
Supply of Loanable Funds

supply of loanable funds will flow into the financial marketplace when the returns from lending increase.

The Equilibrium Rate of Interest in the Loanable Funds Theory

The two forces of supply and demand for loanable funds determine, not only the volume of lending and borrowing going on in the economy, but also the rate of interest. The interest rate tends toward that equilibrium point at which the supply of loanable funds equals the demand for loanable funds. This point of equilibrium is shown in Figure 6–10 at i_E.

FIGURE 6–10
The Equilibrium Rate of Interest in the Loanable Funds Theory

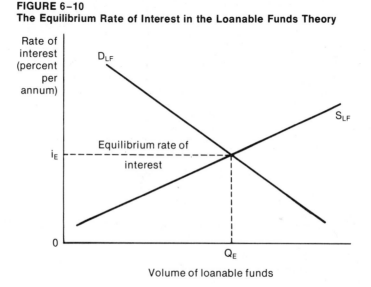

Volume of loanable funds

If the interest rate is temporarily *above* equilibrium, the quantity of loanable funds supplied by savers, by the banking system, and from the dishoarding of money balances (or minus hoarding demand) exceeds the total demand for loanable funds, and the rate of interest will be bid down. On the other hand, if the interest rate is temporarily *below* equilibrium, loanable funds demand from businesses, consumers, and governments will exceed the supply. The interest rate will be bid up by borrowers until it settles at equilibrium once again.[9]

---

[9] The equilibrium depicted in Figure 6–10 is only a *partial equilibrium* position. This is due to the fact that interest rates are affected by conditions in the economy as a whole. For the economy to be in equilibrium, planned saving must equal planned investment. For example, if planned investment exceeds planned saving at the equilibrium interest rate shown in Figure 6–10, investment demands will push interest rates higher in the short run. However, as additional investment spending occurs, incomes will rise, generating a greater volume of savings. Eventually, interest rates will fall. Only when the economy, the money market, and the loanable funds market are simultaneously in equilibrium will interest rates remain stable.

FIGURE 6–11
Changes in the Demand for and Supply of Loanable Funds

A. Effects of increased supply of loanable funds with demand unchanged

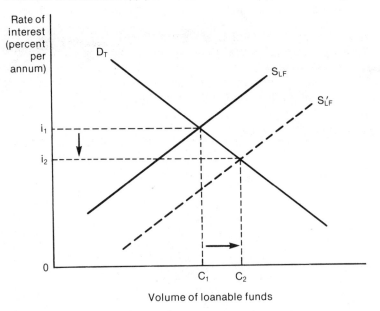

Volume of loanable funds

B. Effects of increased demand for loanable funds with supply unchanged

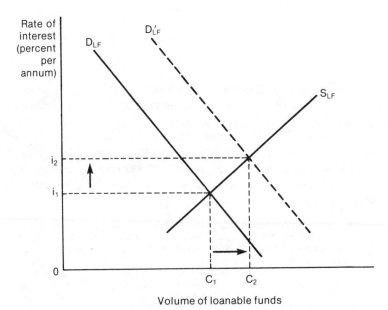

Volume of loanable funds

This simple demand-supply framework is useful for analyzing broad movements in interest rates. For example, if the supply of loanable funds from savings and other sources is increasing and the demand for loanable funds remains unchanged or rises more slowly, the volume of credit extended in the financial markets must increase, and interest rates will fall. This is illustrated in Figure 6–11A, which shows the supply curve sliding downward and to the right when S_{LF} increases to S'_{LF}, resulting in a decline in the equilibrium rate of interest from i_1 to i_2. The equilibrium quantity of loanable funds traded in the financial system increases from C_1 to C_2.

What happens when the demand for loanable funds increases with no change in the supply of funds available? In this instance, the volume of credit extended will increase, but loans will be made at higher interest rates. Figure 6–11B illustrates this. The loanable funds demand curve rises from D_{LF} to D'_{LF}, driving the interest rate upward from i_1 to i_2.

CONCLUSION

Each theory of the determinants of interest rates reviewed in this chapter offers useful insights into the functioning of the financial system. Collectively, the various views of interest-rate determination point to those forces in the economy which should be studied carefully if we are to understand current trends in interest rates and anticipate future trends. In the next chapter we consider several different methods for calculating interest rates to determine the "price" of credit actually paid by borrowers and the yields earned by investors in the financial system.

STUDY QUESTIONS

1. What are the different roles of the rate of interest in the economy?
2. What is the risk-free, or pure, interest rate? Explain its relationship to other interest rates in the economy.
3. What factors determine the rate of interest in the classical theory? Explain why the supply-of-savings curve has a positive slope. What determines the shape of the demand curve in this theory?
4. Compare and contrast the liquidity preference and classical theories of interest. What are the principal limitations of each?
5. Define the following: transactions motive, precautionary motive, and speculative motive. How is the total demand for money determined in liquidity preference theory? Why does the demand-for-money curve slope downward and to the right?
6. What factors make up the demand for loanable funds? The supply of loanable funds? How is the equilibrium rate of interest determined in the loanable funds theory?
7. Trace through what happens to the equilibrium rate of interest when the demand for loanable funds increases with supply unchanged. What happens to the

equilibrium rate if the supply of loanable funds expands with demand unchanged?

8. Of what possible use are interest rate theories in predicting future changes in rates?

SELECTED REFERENCES

1. Ackley, Gardner. *Macroeconomic Theory*. New York: Macmillan, 1961.

2. Ando, A., and Franco Modigliani. "The Life Cycle Hypothesis of Saving." *American Economic Review*, March 1963, pp. 55–84.

3. Bohm-Bawerk, Eugen von. *The Positive Theory of Capital*. New York: Macmillan, 1891.

4. Boskin, M. J. "Taxation, Savings and the Rate of Interest." *Journal of Political Economy*, April 1978, pp. S3–S27.

5. Conrad, Joseph W. *An Introduction to the Theory of Interest*. Berkeley and Los Angeles: University of California Press, 1959.

6. Due, John F., and Robert W. Clower. *Intermediate Economic Analysis*. 4th ed. Homewood, Ill.: Richard D. Irwin, 1961.

7. Fama, Eugene F., and Merton H. Miller. *The Theory of Finance*. New York: Holt, Rinehart & Winston, 1972.

8. Feber, R. "Consumer Economics: A Survey." *Journal of Economic Literature*, December 1973, pp. 1303–42.

9. Feldstein, Martin, and Otto Eckstein. "The Fundamental Determinants of the Interest Rate." *Review of Economics and Statistics*, November 1970, pp. 363–75.

10. Fisher, Irving. *The Theory of Interest*. New York: Macmillan, 1930.

11. Friedman, Milton. *A Theory of the Consumption Function*. Princeton, N.J.: Princeton University Press, 1957.

12. Justen F. T., and L. D. Taylor. "Towards a Theory of Saving Behavior." *American Economic Review*, May 1975, pp. 203–9.

13. Keynes, John M. *The General Theory of Employment, Interest and Money*. New York: Harcourt Brace Jovanovich, 1936.

14. Klammer, Thomas. "Empirical Evidence of the Adoption of Sophisticated Capital Budgeting Techniques." *Journal of Business*, July 1972, pp. 387–97.

15. Lutz, Friedrich A. *The Theory of Interest*. Dordrecht, Holland: D. Reidel Publishing, 1967.

16. Mishkin, Frederick. "Monetary Policy and Long-Term Interest Rates: An Efficient-Markets Approach." *Journal of Monetary Economics*, January 1981, pp. 29–55.

17. Mullineaux, Donald J. "Efficient Markets, Interest Rates, and Monetary Policy." *Business Review*, Federal Reserve Bank of Philadelphia, May-June 1981, pp. 3–10.

18. Pesando, James E. "On the Efficiency of the Bond Market: Some Canadian Evidence," *Journal of Political Economy*, LXXXVI (1978), pp. 1057–76.

19. Petty, J. William, David F. Scott, and Monroe M. Bird. "The Capital Expenditure Decision-Making Process of Large Corporations." *Engineering Economist*, Spring 1975, pp. 159–72.

20. Poole, William. "Rational Expectations in the Macro Model." *Brookings Papers on Economic Activity*, 2 (1976).

21. Protopapadakis, Avis. "Supply-Side Economics: What Chance for Success?" *Business Review*, Federal Reserve Bank of Philadelphia, May-June 1981, pp. 11–23.

22. Robinson, Roland I. and Dwayne Wrightsman. *Financial Markets: The Accumulation and Allocation of Wealth.* New York: McGraw-Hill, Inc., 1974.

23. Schiller, Robert. "The Volatility of Long-Term Interest Rates and Expectations Models of the Term Structure." *Journal of Political Economy*, October 1979, pp. 1190–1219.

7

Relationships between Interest Rates and Security Prices

Theories of the rate of interest help us to understand the forces that cause interest rates and the prices of securities to change. They provide clues on the future direction of interest rates. However, these theories provide little or no information on how interest rates should be *measured* in the real world. As a result, many different measures of interest rates on securities and loans have been developed, leading to some confusion, especially for small borrowers and investors. In this chapter the methods most frequently used to measure interest rates and security prices in today's financial markets are examined. We also consider the relationships between security prices and interest rates and how they influence each other.

UNITS OF MEASUREMENT FOR INTEREST RATES AND SECURITY PRICES

Definition of Interest Rates

The interest rate is, of course, the price charged a borrower for the loan of money. As noted in Chapter 6, this "price" is unique because it is really a *ratio* of two quantities—the cash benefits promised to a lender of funds over a specified period of time and the total amount of money loaned. By convention, the interest rate is usually expressed in percent per annum. Thus:

$$\text{Annual rate of interest on a loan (in percent)} = \frac{\text{Annual cash benefits promised to a lender}}{\text{Amount of money loaned}} \times 100 \qquad (7\text{-}1)$$

For example, an interest rate of 10 percent per annum on a new-car loan implies that the lender of funds has received a promise of annual cash benefits equal to 10 percent of the total amount of funds committed to the borrower. These promised cash benefits are in addition to any repayments of loan principal which may occur during the year.

This concept of annualized yield is used even for investments that are shorter than a year. For example, in the federal funds market commercial banks frequently loan reserves to each other overnight, with the loan being repaid the next day. Even in this market the interest rate quoted daily by lenders is expressed in percent per annum as though the loan were for a year's time. As we will soon see, however, various types of loans and securities have important differences in how cash benefits and cash outlays are valued or accounted for, leading to several different methods for determining interest rates. In addition, some interest-rate measures use a 360-day year and others, a 365-day year. Some employ compound rates of return, with interest income earned on accumulated interest, and some do not use compounding.[1]

Basis Points

Interest rates on securities traded in the open market rarely are quoted in whole percentage points, such as 5 percent or 8 percent. The typical case is a rate expressed in hundredths of a percent—e.g., 5.36 percent or 7.60 percent. Moreover, most interest rates change by only fractions of a whole percentage point in a single day or week. To deal with this situation the concept of the *basis point* was developed. A basis point equals 1/100 of a percent. Thus an interest rate of 10.5 percent may be expressed as 10 percent plus 50 basis points, or 1,050 basis points. Similarly an increase in a loan or security rate from 5.25 percent to 5.30 percent represents an increase of 5 basis points.

Security Prices

The prices of common and preferred stock in the United States are measured in dollars and eighths of a dollar. Thus, a stock price of 5⅛ is a quote of $5.125 (since one eighth of a dollar = $0.125), while 40¼ means each share of stock is selling for $40.25.

Bond prices are expressed in points and fractions of a point, with each point equal to $1 on a $100 basis. Thus, a U.S. government bond with a price quotation of 97 points is selling for $97 for each $100 in par (face) value. A $1,000-par-value bond, therefore, would be selling for $970. Fractions of

---

[1] Interest rates on U.S. Treasury bills, commercial paper, and few other short-term financial instruments are based on a 360-day year and do not compound interest. See Part 4, on the money market, for a discussion of these instruments and the basis for calculating their rates of return to the investor.

points are typically measured in 32d's, eighths, quarters, or halves, and occasionally even 64ths. Note that one-half point equals $0.50, while $1/32$ equals $0.03125 on a $100 basis. Thus a price quote on a bond of $97^4/32$ (sometimes expressed as 97.4 or 97-4) is $97.125 for each $100 or $971.25 for a $1,000 bond. Quotations expressed in 64ths usually will be indicated by a plus (+) sign added to the nearest 32nd. Thus, 100.2+ means $100^5/64$.

Security dealers quote two prices for a security rather than one. The higher of the two is the *asked* price, which indicates what the dealer will *sell* the security for. The *bid* price is the price at which the dealer is willing to purchase the security. The difference between bid and asked prices provides the dealer's commission for creating a market for the security. Generally, the longer the maturity of a security, the greater the *spread* between its bid and asked price. This is due to the added risks associated with trading in long-term securities. Short-term securities may trade with a spread between bid and asked prices as low as $1/32$ (equal to $312.50 for a sale of $1 million in securities). Purchases and sales of intermediate maturities may carry spreads of $4/32$ (equal to $1,250 on a $1 million trade), while long-term bonds may be trading on spreads of $8/32$ (or about $2,500 for every $1 million sold). On very large sales the dealer may forego a commission and quote a "net price." For small transactions, however, a commission fee is nearly always charged.

MEASURES OF THE RATE OF RETURN, OR YIELD, ON A SECURITY

The interest rate on a loan is the annual rate of return *promised* by the borrower to the lender as a condition for obtaining a loan. However, that rate is not necessarily a true reflection of the yield or rate of return actually earned by the lender during the life of the loan. Some borrowers will default on all or a portion of their promised payments. The market value of the security evidencing the loan may rise or fall, adding to or subtracting from the lender's total rate of return on the transaction. Thus, while the interest rate measures the "price" the borrower has agreed to pay for a loan, the yield or rate of return on the loan, from the lender's viewpoint, may be quite different. In this section a number of the most widely used measures of the yield or rate of return on a loan or security are discussed.

Coupon Rate

One of the best-known measures of the rate of return on a debt security is the *coupon rate* which appears on corporate, U.S. government, and munici-pal bonds. The coupon rate is the contracted rate which the bond issuer agrees to pay at the time a security is issued. If, for example, a company issues a bond with a coupon rate printed on its face of 9 percent, the bor-rower has promised the investor an annual interest payment of 9 percent of the bond's par value. Most bonds are issued with $1,000 par values, and interest payments are semiannual.

The amount of annual interest income paid by a bond is called its *coupon*. The annual coupon may be determined from the formula

$$\text{Coupon rate} \times \text{Par value} = \text{Coupon} \qquad (7\text{--}2)$$

Thus a bond with par value of $1,000 bearing a coupon rate of 9 percent pays an annual coupon of $90.

The coupon rate is not an adequate measure of the return on a bond or other debt security unless the investor purchases the security at a price equal to its par value, the borrower meets all of the promised payments, and the investor sells or redeems the bond at its par value. However, the prices of bonds fluctuate with market conditions, and rarely will a bond trade exactly at par.

Current Yield

Another popular measure of the return on a loan or security is its current yield. This is simply the ratio of the annual income (dividends or interest) generated by the loan or security to its current market value. Thus a share of common stock selling in the market for $30 and paying an annual dividend to the shareholder of $3 would have a current yield calculated as follows:

$$\text{Current yield} = \frac{\text{Annual income}}{\begin{array}{c}\text{Market price}\\ \text{of security}\end{array}} = \frac{\$3}{\$30} = 0.10, \text{ or } 10\% \qquad (7\text{--}3)$$

Frequently, the yields reported on stocks and bonds in the financial press are current yields. Like the coupon rate, the current yield is usually a poor reflection of the rate of return actually received by the lender or investor. It ignores the stream of actual and anticipated cash flows associated with a loan or security and the price for which the investor will be able to sell or redeem it.

Yield to Maturity

The most widely accepted measure of the rate of return on a loan or security is its yield to maturity. It is the rate of interest which the market is prepared to pay for a financial asset in order to exchange present dollars for future dollars. Specifically, the yield to maturity is the rate which equates the purchase price of a security or other financial asset (P) with the present value of all its expected annual net cash inflows (income). In general terms,

$$P = \frac{I_1}{(1 + y)^1} + \frac{I_2}{(1 + y)^2} + \cdots + \frac{I_n}{(1 + y)^n} \qquad (7\text{--}4)$$

where y is the yield to maturity and each I represents the expected annual income from the security, presumed to last for n years and terminate when the financial asset is retired. The I terms in the above formula include both receipts of income and repayments of principal.

To illustrate the use of this formula, assume the investor is considering the purchase of a bond due to mature in 20 years, carrying a 10 percent coupon. This security is available for purchase at a current market price of $850. If the bond has a par value of $1,000, which will be paid to the investor when the security reaches maturity, its yield to maturity, y, may be found by solving

$$\$850 = \frac{\$100}{(1+y)^1} + \frac{\$100}{(1+y)^2} + \cdots + \frac{\$100}{(1+y)^{20}} + \frac{\$1,000}{(1+y)^{20}} \quad (7-5)$$

In this instance y equals 12 percent.

The yield to maturity carries a number of significant advantages as a measure of the rate of return or yield on a financial asset. Unlike the coupon rate, it is based upon market values rather than par or book values. Unlike the current yield, this return measure considers the time distribution of expected cash flows from a security or other financial asset. Dealers and brokers typically use the yield to maturity in quoting rates of return to investors. Of course, this return measure does assume that the investor will hold a security until it reaches final maturity. It is an inappropriate measure for stocks, which are usually perpetual instruments, and even for some bonds, since the investor may sell them prior to their termination date. Another problem is that this yield measure assumes all cash flowing to the lender or investor can be reinvested at the computed yield to maturity.

Holding-Period Yield

A slight modification of the yield-to-maturity formula results in a return measure for those situations where an investor holds a security or other financial asset for a time and then sells it to another investor in advance of maturity. This so-called *holding-period yield* is simply

$$P = \frac{I_1}{(1+h)^1} + \frac{I_2}{(1+h)^2} + \cdots + \frac{I_m}{(1+h)^m} + \frac{P_m}{(1+h)^m} \quad (7-6)$$

where h is the holding-period yield, and the total length of the investor's holding period covers m time periods. Thus, the holding-period yield is simply that rate of discount (h) equalizing the market price of a financial asset (P) with all net cash flows expected between the time the asset is purchased and the time it is sold (including the selling price, P_m). If the asset is held to maturity, its holding-period yield equals its yield to maturity.

Calculating Yields to Maturity and Holding-Period Yields

Holding-period yields and yields to maturity can be calculated in several different ways. One method is to employ *present-value tables* identical to those presented in most basic finance and accounting texts.

Suppose, for example, that an investor is contemplating the purchase of a corporate bond, $1,000 par value with a coupon rate of 10 percent, currently selling for $900. The investor plans to hold the bond to maturity, which occurs in five years. We have:

$$\$900 = \frac{\$100}{(1 + y)^1} + \frac{\$100}{(1 + y)^2} + \frac{\$100}{(1 + y)^3}$$
$$+ \frac{\$100}{(1 + y)^4} + \frac{\$100}{(1 + y)^5} + \frac{\$1,000}{(1 + y)^5} \tag{7-7}$$

It is useful at this point to consider what each term in Equation 7–7 means. Both the yield-to-maturity and holding-period-yield formulas are based upon the concept of *present value*—funds to be received in the future are worth less than funds received today. Present dollars may be used to purchase and enjoy goods and services today, but dollars to be received in the future are only *promises* to pay and force us to postpone consumption until the funds actually are received. Equation 7–7 indicates that a bond promising to pay $100 for five successive years in the future plus a lump sum of $1,000 at maturity is worth only $900 in present-value dollars. The yield, y, serves as a rate of discount reducing each payment of future dollars back to its present value in today's market. The farther in the future that payment is to be made, the larger the discount factor, $(1 + y)^n$, becomes.

Turning the concept around, the purchase of a security in today's market represents the investment of present-value dollars in the expectation of a greater return in the form of future dollars. The familiar *compound interest formula* applies here. This formula,

$$A_n = P(1 + y)^n \tag{7-8}$$

indicates that the amount of funds accumulated n years from now, A_n, depends upon the principal originally invested, P, the expected rate of return or yield, y, and the number of years the funds are invested, n. Thus, a principal of $1,000 invested today at a 10 percent annual rate will amount to $1,100 a year from now (i.e., $1,000 \times (1 + 0.10)$). Rearrangement of the compound interest formula gives

$$P = \frac{A_n}{(1 + y)^n} \tag{7-9}$$

Equation 7–9 states that the present value of A_n dollars to be received in the future is P if the promised interest rate is y. If we expect to receive $1,100 one year from now and the promised interest rate is 10 percent, the present value of that $1,100 must be $1,000.

Each term on the right-hand side of the yield-to-maturity and holding-period-yield formulas is a form of Equation 7–9. Solving Equation 7–7 for the yield to maturity of a bond simply means finding a value for y which brings both right- and left-hand sides of the yield formula into balance, equating the current price (P) of a security or other financial asset with the stream of future dollars it will generate for the investor. When all expected annual cash flows are not the same in amount, trial and error may be used to find the solution. Fortunately, in the case of the bond represented in Equation 7–7, the solution is not complicated. Rewrite Equation 7–7 in the following form:

$$\$900 = \$100 \left[\frac{1}{(1 + y)^1} + \frac{1}{(1 + y)^2} + \cdots + \frac{1}{(1 + y)^5} \right]$$
$$+ \$1,000 \left[\frac{1}{(1 + y)^5} \right] \quad (7–10)$$

This indicates that the bond will pay an *annuity* of $1 per year (multiplied by $100) for five years, plus a lump-sum payment of $1 (multiplied by $1,000) at the end of the fifth year.

Use of Present-Value Tables. What is the yield on this bond? A reasonable initial guess is 10 percent. To determine how accurate a guess it is we need to consult the present-value and annuity tables in Appendix B. The annuity table in Appendix B indicates that the present value of $1.00 received annually for five years at a discount yield of 10 percent is $3.791. The present-value table in Appendix A shows that the present value of $1 to be received five years from today at 10 percent is $0.621. Inserting these figures into Equation 7–10 yields

$$\$100[3.791] + \$1,000[0.621] = \$1,000.1 > \$900 \quad (7–11)$$

An annual yield of 10 percent is obviously too small because it results in a present value for the bond far in excess of $900. A 12 percent yield gives a present value of $927.50, while a 14 percent yield results in a present value for the bond of $862.30. Clearly, the true yield to maturity of the $900 bond lies between 12 percent and 14 percent, but closer to 12 percent. Linear interpolation fixes this yield at 12.84 percent.[2] The investor interested in maximizing return would compare this yield to maturity with the yields available on other assets of comparable risk.

Present-value tables may also be used to calculate the holding-period yield

---

[2] The present-value tables in Appendix B provide the following information:

Difference in Yield to Maturity	Difference in Present Value of Bond
14%	862.3
12	927.5
2%	−65.2

There is a difference of $27.5 between the current $900 price of the bond and its present value at a yield of 12 percent, which is $927.50. Therefore, the bond's actual yield to maturity may be found from:

$$12\% + \frac{27.5}{65.2} \times 2\% = 12\% + 0.8436\% \approx 12.84\%$$

Linear interpolation of this sort must be used with care, especially where yield differentials are substantial, because the yield-value relationship is not linear.

on corporate stock. To illustrate, suppose an investor is considering the purchase of common stock issued by Gulf Oil Corporation currently selling for $40 per share. He plans to hold the stock for two years and sell out at an expected price of $50 per share. If dividends of two dollars per share are expected each year, what holding-period yield does the investor expect to earn? Following the form of Equation 7–6 we have

$$\$40 = \frac{\$2}{(1 + h)^1} + \frac{\$2}{(1 + h)^2} + \frac{\$50}{(1 + h)^2} \qquad (7-12)$$

The reader may wish to verify from the present-value and annuity tables that the holding period yield on Gulf Oil's stock is 16.54 percent.

Bond Yield Tables.   Present-value tables provide an accurate method for calculating maturity and holding-period yields. However, use of the tables is a trial-and-error process and can be quite time consuming. To save time, securities dealers and experienced investors use bond yield tables, which give the appropriate yield for bonds of a given coupon rate, maturity, and price. An example of a page from a bond yield table is shown in Exhibit 7–1.

EXHIBIT 7–1
Bond Yield Table (prices of a bond with a 10 percent coupon rate)*

Yield to Maturity in Percent	Maturity of a Bond in Years				
	5 Years	10 Years	15 Years	20 Years	25 Years
5%	121.88	138.97	152.33	162.76	170.91
6	117.06	129.75	139.20	146.23	151.46
7	112.47	121.32	127.59	132.03	135.18
8	108.11	113.59	117.29	119.79	121.48
9	103.96	106.50	108.14	109.20	109.88
10	100.00	100.00	100.00	100.00	100.00
11	96.23	94.02	92.73	91.98	91.53
12	92.64	88.53	86.24	84.95	84.24
13	89.22	83.47	80.41	78.78	77.91
14	85.95	78.81	75.18	73.34	72.40
15	82.84	74.51	70.47	68.51	67.56

* Prices expressed on the basis of $100 par value.

To illustrate, suppose the investor holds a corporate bond, bearing a 10 percent coupon rate, with 10 years remaining until maturity. The bond's purchase price may be found in the table under the correct number of years (or, for more detailed bond-yield tables, number of months and years) to maturity. The correct yield to maturity will then be found along the same line as the price in the extreme left-hand column of the table. For example, if the bond's purchase price was $88.53 (on a $100 basis), then its yield to maturity is 12 percent.

The Yield Approximation Formula. When tables are unavailable, the yield approximation formula can be used to estimate the rate of return on a security. This formula simply assumes that

$$\frac{\text{Average annual}}{\text{yield on a security}} = \frac{\text{Average annual income from the security}}{\text{Average amount of funds invested in the security}} \tag{7-13}$$

In the case of a bond, for example, the yield would be composed of annual interest income plus the average amount of price appreciation (or minus price depreciation) which occurs each year. The average amount of funds invested can be represented by the simple arithmetic average of the purchase price and the expected selling price of the security. That is,

$$\text{Average annual yield} = \frac{\text{Annual interest income} \pm \dfrac{\text{Capital gain or loss}}{\text{Years remaining until sold or redeemed}}}{\dfrac{\text{Purchase price} + \text{Selling price}}{2}} \tag{7-14}$$

To illustrate the use of this formula, suppose an investor is considering the purchase of a bond with a current market price of $900, a coupon rate of 10 percent, and the bond will be sold or redeemed in 10 years at an expected price of $1,000. The approximate expected yield would be:

$$\frac{\text{Average annual}}{\text{yield on bond}} = \frac{\$100 + \dfrac{(\$1,000 - 900)}{10}}{\dfrac{\$900 + \$1,000}{2}} = \frac{\$110}{\$950} \simeq 11.58\% \tag{7-15}$$

Note that the investor expects a capital gain of $100 over the remaining life of this bond because it sells currently for $900 and will be redeemed in 10 years for $1,000. The average annual gain in price, therefore, is $10.

The same formula may be used in the case of a security which is expected to experience a capital *loss* between time of purchase and time of sale or redemption. Suppose, for example, the investor wishes to purchase a $1,000-par-value bond currently selling for $1,200 with a coupon rate of 10 percent. If the bond matures in 10 years and is held to maturity,

$$\frac{\text{Average annual}}{\text{yield on bond}} = \frac{\$100 + \dfrac{(\$1,000 - \$1,200)}{10}}{\dfrac{\$1,200 + \$1,000}{2}} = \frac{\$100 - \$20}{\$1,100} \simeq 7.27\% \tag{7-16}$$

The expected capital loss on the bond partially offsets the annual interest income, reducing the investor's average yield.

YIELD-PRICE RELATIONSHIPS

The yield-to-maturity and holding-period-yield formulas indicate some important relationships between security prices and yields or interest rates which prevail in the financial system. One of these important relationships is:

The price of a security and its yield or rate of return are *inversely* related—a rise in yield implies a decline in price; conversely, a fall in yield is associated with a rise in the security's price.

Recall that investing funds in financial assets can be viewed from two different perspectives—the borrowing and lending of money or the buying and selling of securities. As noted in Chapter 6, the rate of interest from lending funds is determined by the interaction of the supply of loanable funds and the demand for loanable funds. Demanders of loanable funds (borrowers) supply securities to the financial marketplace, while suppliers of loanable funds (lenders) demand securities as an investment. Therefore, the rate of return or yield on a security and the price of that security are determined at one and the same instant and are simply different aspects of the same phenomenon—the borrowing and lending of loanable funds.

This point is depicted in Figure 7–1, which shows demand and supply curves for both the rate of interest (yield) and the price of securities. The supply-of-loanable-funds curve (representing lending) in the interest-rate diagram (Figure 7–1A) is analogous to the demand-for-securities curve (also representing lending) in the price-of-securities diagram (Figure 7–1B). Simi-

FIGURE 7–1
Equilibrium Security Prices and Interest Rates (Yields)

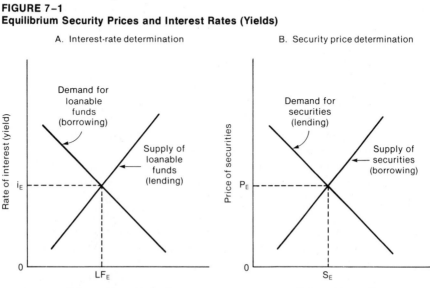

A. Interest-rate determination

B. Security price determination

larly, the demand-for-loanable-funds curve (representing borrowing) in the interest-rate diagram is analogous to the supply-of-securities curve (also representing borrowing) in the price-of-securities diagram. We note in Figure 7–1B that borrowers are assumed to issue a larger volume of securities at a higher price and that lenders will demand more securities at a lower price. The equilibrium interest rate in Figure 7–1A is determined, as discussed in Chapter 6, at point i_E, where the demand for loanable funds equals the supply of loanable funds. Similarly, in Figure 7–1B the equilibrium price for securities lies at point P_E, where the demand for and supply of securities are equal.

The *inverse* relationship between interest rates and security prices can be seen quite clearly when we allow the demand and supply curves depicted in Figure 7–1 to change. This is illustrated in Figure 7–2. For example, suppose that, in the face of continuing inflation, consumers and business firms accelerate their borrowing, increasing the demand for loanable funds. As shown in the upper left-hand portion of Figure 7–2, the demand-for-loanable-funds curve slides upward and to the right. With the supply of loanable funds unchanged, the rate of interest rises. However, the increasing demand for loanable funds also means that the supply of securities must expand, shown in the upper right-hand portion of Figure 7–2 by a shift of the supply curve from S to S′. A new *lower* equilibrium price for securities results.

Conversely, suppose consumers decide to save more, expanding the supply of loanable funds. As shown in the lower left-hand panel of Figure 7–2, the supply-of-loanable-funds curve slides downward and to the right from S to S′, leading to a lower interest rate. But with more saving, the demand-for-securities curve must rise, sliding upward and to the right from D to D′. The prices of securities rise as interest rates fall.

INTEREST RATES AND THE BUSINESS CYCLE

In the real world many factors cause interest rates and security prices to change. Political developments at home and abroad, changes in government economic policy, news reports of changes in corporate earnings or business conditions, announcements of new security offerings, and thousands of other bits of information flood the financial markets daily and bring about fluctuations in rates and prices. In fact, for actively traded securities (such as stocks listed on the New York Stock Exchange, or U.S. government bonds) demand and supply forces are continually shifting, minute by minute, so that investors interested in these securities must constantly stay abreast of the latest developments in the financial marketplace. Prices and rates sometimes change so fast that even a few minutes' delay in receiving market data can mean substantial losses for the uninformed investor.

Still, it is interesting that certain *long-run factors,* especially the condition of the nation's economy, are also important in influencing security rates and

FIGURE 7-2
Effects of Changing Supply and Demand on Security Rates (Yields) and Prices

A. Effects of an increase in the demand for loanable funds:
higher interest rates and lower security prices

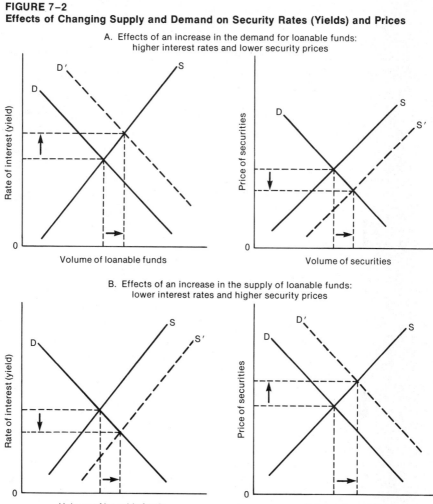

B. Effects of an increase in the supply of loanable funds:
lower interest rates and higher security prices

prices. These long-run demand and supply forces result in broad, sweeping price and rate trends which may last for many months or years. In particular:

The demand for and supply of loanable funds changes with the business cycle. Interest rates tend to fall (and the prices of bonds and other debt securities to rise) during a business recession, while rates typically rise (and debt security prices fall) during a period of economic expansion.

None of this should be particularly surprising. A boom period encourages both businesses and consumers to borrow more, and the resulting expansion in the demand for credit drives up interest rates. In contrast, business recessions are accompanied by declining sales and rising unemployment. Both businesses and consumers become more cautious during such periods, reducing their borrowings and building up savings as a precaution against loss of income. Interest rates usually fall under the combined pressure of reduced credit demands and a larger supply of savings.

This typical cyclical movement in interest rates is illustrated quite well in Exhibit 7–3, which tracks changes in yields on long-term U.S. Treasury, corporate, and municipal bonds. The U.S. economy entered a recession in 1969–70, and bond yields declined sharply after mid-1970, reaching a low point in late 1971. As business sales and employment recovered after the 1969–70 recession, interest rates climbed to new highs, peaking in mid-1974 just after the oil embargo. There followed in 1975 the worst business recession since World War II. Declining industrial production and a sharp rise in unemployment were accompanied by a long-term decline in interest rates, which did not cease until late in 1976 in the corporate and U.S. government bond markets and until the latter half of 1977 in the market for municipal bonds. A sharp rebound in economic activity during 1978 and 1979, accompanied by soaring, double-digit inflation, sent interest rates to unprecedented highs early in 1980. However, reflecting once again the powerful influence of the business cycle upon interest rates and security prices, bond yields plummeted rapidly beginning in the spring of 1980 as the economy entered the next business recession.

Relative Movements in Short-Term and Long-Term Interest Rates and Security Prices

The cyclical movements in the economy do not fall evenly across the broad spectrum of interest rates and security prices. In general, short-term interest rates (especially those attached to money market securities) are more volatile and sensitive to business cycle changes than long-term interest rates on bonds and other capital-market securities. Figure 7–4 depicts the typical pattern displayed by long- and short-term interest rates during the course of the business cycle.

During a boom period, when the economy is expanding at a rapid pace, *all* interest rates—both long-term and short-term—tend to rise. However, short-term interest rates typically rise faster than long-term rates and at some point, in the later stages of the boom, may climb above long-term rates. This means, of course, that at certain phases of the business cycle, especially around cyclical peaks, borrowers negotiating a loan for, say, six months will actually pay a higher annual interest rate than were the same loan to be stretched over 5 or 10 years. Once the expansion phase of the cycle is over and the economy starts down into a recession, however, all rates begin to fall. Short-term interest rates typically drop faster than long-term rates and fall below long-term rates as the recession deepens. Once the trough of the

FIGURE 7–3
Average Yields of Long-Term Treasury, Corporate, and Municipal Bonds

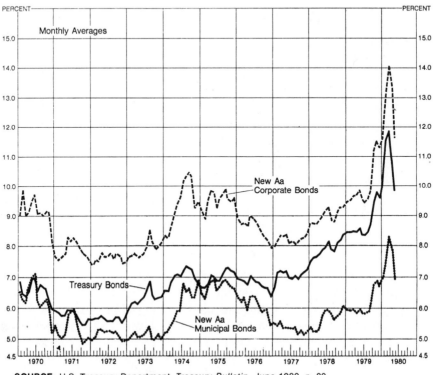

SOURCE: U.S. Treasury Department, *Treasury Bulletin,* June 1980, p. 80.

recession is reached, the process is repeated again, with short-term interest rates again rising more rapidly than long-term rates.

Why do long-term and short-term interest rates behave this way? Their behavior reflects another important relationship which exists between security prices and interest rates in the financial system:

> Long-term security prices tend to be more volatile than the prices of short-term securities. In contrast, short-term interest rates tend to be more volatile than long-term interest rates.

This important, somewhat paradoxical, relationship can be seen clearly by examining the yield approximation formula discussed earlier:

$$\begin{array}{l}\text{Average} \\ \text{annual} \\ \text{yield on} \\ \text{a security}\end{array} = \dfrac{\text{Annual income} \pm \dfrac{\text{Capital gain or loss}}{\begin{array}{c}\text{Years remaining until security} \\ \text{is sold or redeemed}\end{array}}}{\dfrac{\text{Purchase price} + \text{Selling price}}{2}} \quad (7\text{--}17)$$

FIGURE 7–4
Interest Rates over the Course of a Business Cycle

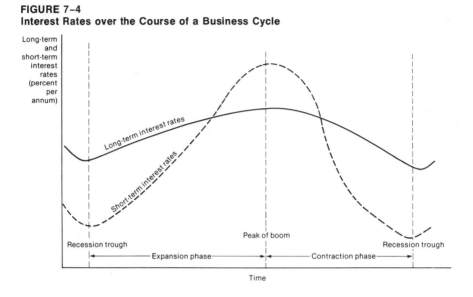

Note that for the *same* gain (or loss) in price, the yield on a long-term security changes by a smaller amount than the yield on a short-term security. This is true because the gain or loss is divided by a greater number of years in the case of the long-term security. Similarly, for the *same* change in interest rate or yield, the price change (gain or loss) on a long-term security has to be greater than the price change on a short-term financial instrument because, again, the gain or loss is spread over a longer period with the long-term security.

Fluctuations in market prices, then, will tend to be greater the longer is the maturity of a security. This conclusion also follows logically if we examine closely the yield-to-maturity formula shown in Equation 7–4. This formula indicates that the market price of any security equals the present value of all promised future payments, but each future payment is discounted by the security's yield. With a long-term security there are more future payments affected by any change in yield than is true for a short-term security. Therefore, a given increase in the interest rate will bring about a greater decrease in the price (present value) of a long-term security than in the price of a short-term security. Similarly, for the same decrease in interest rate, the price (present value) of the short-term security will be less affected than the price of the long-term security.

The greater volatility of long-term security prices means that investors in bonds and other long-term financial instruments face a greater risk of capital loss (i.e., increased *principal risk*) than investors in short-term securities. Partly as a result, interest rates charged on long-term loans are usually higher than those charged for short-term credit, other things being equal. Lenders must be compensated for the added risk of price fluctuations with long-term financial instruments. Of course, the long-term investor has the advantage of receiving a more-stable rate of return (i.e., reduced *income risk*) than the short-term investor. Long-term securities provide a stable cash flow over an extended period until the securities are sold or redeemed.

INTEREST RATES CHARGED BY INSTITUTIONAL LENDERS

Just as there are different measures of the rate of return, or yield, on bonds and other securities traded in the open market, institutional lenders of funds—commercial banks, credit unions, savings banks, insurance companies, and finance companies, to name the most important—employ a variety of different methods to calculate the rate of interest charged on loans. Four commonly used methods for calculating loan rates are discussed below.

The Simple-Interest Method

The widely used simple-interest method assesses interest charges on a loan only for the period of time the borrower actually has use of borrowed funds. The total interest bill actually *decreases* the more frequently a borrower must make payments on a loan.

For example, suppose you borrow $1,000 for a year at simple interest. If the interest rate is 10 percent, your interest bill will be $100 for the year. This figure is derived from the formula

$$I = P \times r \times t \qquad\qquad (7\text{--}18)$$

where I represents the interest charge (in dollars), P is the principal amount of the loan, r is the annual rate of interest, and t is the term (maturity) of the loan expressed in years or fractions of a year. (In this example, $1,000 \times 0.10 \times 1 = $100).

If the $1,000 loan is repaid in one lump sum at the end of the year, you will pay a total of

$$\frac{\text{Principal} + \text{Interest}}{\$1,000 + \$100} = \frac{\text{Total payment}}{\$1,100}$$

Suppose, however, that this loan is paid off in two equal installments of $500 each. Then, you will pay

	Principal + Interest	= Total payment
First installment:	$500 + $50 (i.e., 6 months' interest on $1,000 at 10%)	= $550
Second installment:	$500 + $25 (i.e., 6 months' interest on $500 at 10%)	= $525
		$1,075

Clearly, you pay a lower interest bill ($75 versus $100) with two installment payments instead of one. This happens because you effectively have use of the full $1,000 for only six months. For the remaining six months of the year, you have use of only $500. The simple-interest method is still popular with mortgage lenders, credit unions, and some commercial banks.

Add-On Rate of Interest

A method of calculating loan interest rates often used by finance companies and commercial banks is the add-on approach. In this instance, interest is calculated on the full principal of the loan, and the sum of interest and principal payments is divided by the number of payments to determine the dollar amount of each payment. For example, suppose you borrow $1,000 for one year at a rate of 10 percent. You agree to make two equal installment payments, six months apart. The total amount to be repaid is, then, $1,100 ($1,000 principal + $100 interest). At the end of the first six months you will pay half ($550), and the remaining half will be paid at the end of the year.

If money is borrowed and repaid in one lump sum (i.e., a single-payment loan), the simple interest and add-on methods give the same interest rate. However, as the number of installment payments increases, the borrower pays a higher effective interest rate under the add-on method. This happens because the average amount of money borrowed for the term of the loan declines with the greater frequency of installment payments, yet the borrower pays the same total interest bill. In fact, the effective rate of interest nearly doubles when monthly installment payments are required. For example, if you borrow $1,000 for a year at 10 percent simple interest but repay the loan in 12 equal monthly installments, you have only about $500 available for use, on average, over the course of the year. Because the total interest bill is $100, the interest rate exceeds 18 percent.

Discount Method

Many commercial loans, especially for working capital, are extended on a discount basis. This means the total interest bill is calculated on the basis of the amount to be repaid, and the borrower receives as proceeds of the loan the *difference* between the total amount owed and the interest bill. For example, suppose you borrow $1,000 at 10 percent, for a total interest bill of $100. Using the discount method, you actually receive $900 ($1,000 − $100) in net loan proceeds. The effective interest rate, then, is

$$\frac{\text{Interest paid}}{\text{Net loan proceeds}} = \frac{\$100}{\$900} \times 100 = 11.11\% \qquad (7\text{--}19)$$

Some lenders will grant the borrower the full amount of money required but add the amount of discount to the face amount of the borrower's note.

For example, if you need the full $1,000, the lender under this method will multiply the effective interest rate (11.11 percent) times $1,000 to derive the total interest bill of $111.11. The face value of the borrower's note and, therefore, the amount that must be repaid becomes $1,111.11. However, the borrower actually receives only $1,000 for use during the year. Most add-on loans are for terms of one year or less and usually do not require installment payments. These loans generally are settled in lump sum when the note comes due.

Annual Percentage Rate (APR)

The wide diversity of rates quoted by lenders is often confusing and discourages "shopping around" for credit. With this in mind, Congress passed the Consumer Credit Protection Act in 1968. More popularly known as Truth in Lending, this law requires institutions regularly extending credit to consumers to tell the borrower what interest rate he or she is actually paying and to use a prescribed method for calculating that rate.[3] Specifically, banks, credit unions, and other lending institutions are required to calculate an annual percentage rate (APR) and inform the loan customer what this rate is before the loan contract is signed. The *actuarial* method is used to determine the APR, and loan officers usually have tables at hand to translate simple interest or add-on rates into the APR.

The constant ratio formula, shown below, usually gives a good approximation to the true APR:

$$\text{APR} = \frac{\begin{array}{c}2 \times \text{Number of payment periods in a year}\\ \times \text{ Annual interest cost in dollars}\end{array}}{\begin{array}{c}(\text{Total number of loan payments} + 1)\\ \times \text{ Principal of the loan}\end{array}} \times 100$$

$$(7\text{--}20)$$

To illustrate, suppose you borrow $1,000 at 10 percent simple interest but must repay your loan in 12 equal monthly installments. The APR for this loan is calculated as follows:

$$\text{APR} = \frac{2(12)(\$100)}{(12 + 1)(\$1,000)} \times 100 = 18.46\% \qquad (7\text{--}21)$$

This computational formula slightly overstates the true APR. The actual rate on this loan is closer to 18 percent.

Congress anticipated that introduction of the APR would encourage consumers to exercise greater care in the use of credit and do more "shopping around." It is not at all clear that either goal has been realized, however. Most consumers continue to give primary weight to the size of their installment payments in deciding how much, when, and where to borrow. If their

---

[3] See Chapter 17 for a discussion of consumer credit laws.

budget can afford the principal and interest charges on a loan, most consumers seem little influenced by the reported size of the APR and are not usually inclined to ask other lenders for their rates on the same loan. While consumer education is vital to intelligent financial decision making, progress in that direction has been slow in coming.

CONCLUSIONS

Interest rates and security prices are among the most important ingredients of financial decisions. Over the years a number of methods have been developed for measuring interest rates and security prices. The intelligent investor must learn to distinguish one method from another. From a conceptual point of view the yield-to-maturity and holding-period-yield methods are among the best ones for measuring the true return from lending and investing funds because both consider the time value of money. From the borrower's point of view, the annual percentage rate (APR) is an effective technique for measuring the true cost of credit.

In this chapter we have highlighted two fundamental principles of finance. One is the mandatory *inverse* relationship between the prices of debt securities and interest rates. Falling security prices are generally associated with rising interest rates, while rising security prices imply falling interest rates. We also observed that long-term security prices are more unstable and volatile than short-term security prices. Thus, investors in long-term financial instruments usually face greater risk of capital losses but also greater opportunities for capital gains.

In the next two chapters various factors which influence the interest rate attached to a loan are reviewed. These factors, which include maturity, default risk, taxation, inflation, and other influences, have a significant impact on the price of credit in the nation's money and capital markets.

STUDY QUESTIONS

1. What is a basis point? How are stock and bond prices measured?
2. Suppose a bond is issued with a coupon rate of 8 percent when the market rate of interest is also 8 percent. If the market rate rises to 9 percent, what happens to the price of this bond? What happens to the bond's price if the market falls to 6 percent? Explain why.
3. An issue of preferred stock for XYZ corporation is issued at par for $50 per share. If stockholders are promised an 8 percent annual dividend, what was the stock's current yield at time of issue? If the stock's market price has risen to $60 per share, what is its new current yield?
4. Do you think the coupon rate and the current yield are good measures of the true rate of return on a bond? Why?
5. What is the difference between yield to maturity and holding-period yield? Why are bond yields typically quoted on a yield-to-maturity basis? Why are stock yields usually expressed in terms of current yield?

6. A AAA corporate bond has a current market price of $800 and will pay $100 in interest for 10 years. If its par value is $1,000, what is its yield to maturity? Suppose the investor plans to sell it in five years for $900. What would his holding-period yield be?

7. Using the yield-approximation formula, calculate the average annual yield on a $1,000 bond six years from final maturity with a 12 percent coupon rate, selling today for $1,100. What would the bond's yield be if it were selling for $940?

8. You plan to borrow $2,000 in order to take a vacation and want to repay the loan in a year. The banker offers you a simple-interest rate of 12 percent with repayment in two equal installments 6 months and 12 months from now. What is your total interest bill? What is the APR? Would you prefer an add-on interest rate with one payment at the end of the year? If the bank applies the discount method to your loan, what are the net proceeds of the loan? What is your effective rate of interest?

9. Explain why the business cycle of expansions and recessions influences interest rates and security prices. When are rising rates most likely? Falling rates?

10. Why are the prices of long-term securities generally more volatile than the prices of short-term securities? What is true of short- versus long-term interest rates? Explain why.

SELECTED REFERENCES

1. Cook, Timothy Q. "Some Factors Affecting Long-Term Yield Spreads in Recent Years." *Monthly Review*, Federal Reserve Bank of Richmond, September 1973, pp. 2–14.

2. The First Boston Corporation, *Handbook of Securities of the U.S. Government and Federal Agencies*. 30th ed. New York: The First Boston Corporation, 1978.

3. Freund, William C. *Investment Fundamentals*. American Bankers Association, Washington, D.C., 1970.

4. Homer, Sidney. *A History of Interest Rates*. New Brunswick, N.J.: Rutgers University Press, 1963.

5. Homer, Sidney, and Martin L. Leibowitz. *Inside the Yield Book*. Englewood Cliffs, N.J.: Prentice-Hall, 1972.

6. LaPorte, Anne Marie. "ABCs of Figuring Interest." *Business Conditions*, Federal Reserve Bank of Chicago, September 1973, pp. 3–11.

8

Yield Curves, Risk, and Inflation

In Chapter 6 we examined the demand and supply forces which determine the rate of interest. We know, however, that there is not one interest rate in the economy—there are thousands. And many of these rates differ substantially from one another. For example, in August 1981 the going market rate on one-year U.S. Treasury bills averaged 14.70 percent, while the market rate on seasoned corporate bonds was 15.60 percent. At the same time, major U.S. commercial banks were quoting average loan rates to their largest and most financially sound customers of 20 to 21 percent. Meanwhile, investors in the market for high-grade state and local government bonds were receiving an annual rate of return of about 12 percent.

Why are all these rates so different from one another? Are these rate differences purely random, or can we attribute them to a limited number of factors which can be studied and perhaps predicted? Understanding the factors which cause interest rates to differ among themselves is an indispensable aid to the investor in choosing securities for a portfolio. It is not always advisable, for example, to reach for the highest rates available in the marketplace. The investor who does so may assume unacceptable levels of risk, have the securities called in by the issuer in advance of their maturity, pay an unacceptably high tax bill, accept a rate of return whose value is seriously eroded by inflation, or suffer other undesirable consequences. Without question, the intelligent investor must have a working knowledge of the factors affecting interest rates and be able to anticipate future changes in those factors.

For example, what influence do changes in the maturity (term) of a loan or security have upon the rate of return which that financial instrument pays to the investor? Why are default risk and marketability important determinants of relative interest rates? What is call risk, and how does it influence the interest rate on callable securities? What roles do inflation, taxation, and convertibility play in accounting for differences between one rate and another? In this chapter and the next we address each of these important questions.

THE MATURITY OF A LOAN

One of the most important factors causing interest rates to differ from one another is differences in the maturity (or term) of securities and loans. Financial assets traded today in the nation's financial markets have a wide variety of maturities. In the federal funds and U.S. government securities markets, for example, some loans are overnight or over-the-weekend transactions, with the borrower repaying the loan in a matter of hours. At the other end of the spectrum, many mortgages used to finance the purchase of new homes extend out to 25 or 30 years. Corporate stocks are perpetual securities and will be traded as long as the issuing corporation continues to operate or until the stock is repurchased by the issuer and retired. In between these extremes lie thousands of securities issued by large and small borrowers with a tremendous variety of maturities.

The Yield Curve and the Term Structure of Interest Rates

The relationship between the rates of return (or yield) on financial instruments and their maturity is labeled the *term structure of interest rates*. The term structure of rates may be represented visually by drawing a *yield curve* for all securities of equivalent grade or quality. An example of a yield curve for United States government securities as it appeared in a recent issue of the *Treasury Bulletin* is shown in Figure 8–1. We note that yield to maturity (measured by the annual percentage rate of return) is plotted along the vertical axis, while the horizontal axis shows term to maturity (measured in months and years).

The yield curve considers only the relationship between the maturity or term of a loan and its yield at one moment in time, with all other factors held constant. For example, we cannot draw a yield curve for securities bearing different degrees of risk or subject to different tax laws because both risk and tax rates affect relative yields along with maturity. We may, however, draw a yield curve for United States government securities of varying maturities because they all have minimal default risk, the same tax status, and so on. Similarly, yield curves could be constructed for all corporate bonds or municipal bonds having the same credit rating.

FIGURE 8-1
Yields of Treasury Securities, March 31, 1980 (based on closing bid quotations)

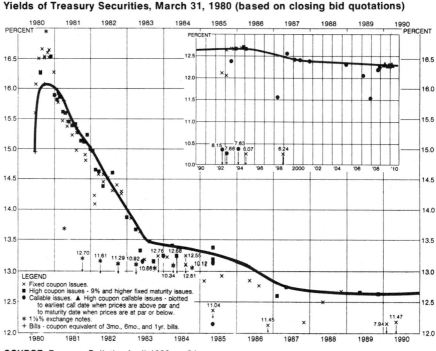

SOURCE: *Treasury Bulletin,* April 1980, p. 84.

Types of Yield Curves

Yield curves change their shape over time in response to changes in the public's interest-rate expectations, fluctuations in the demand for liquidity in the economy, and other factors. Several different shapes have been observed, but most yield curves may be described as upward sloping, downward sloping, or horizontal (flat). An upward-sloping yield curve, of course, indicates that borrowers must pay higher interest rates for longer-term loans than for shorter-term loans. A downward sloping yield curve means that long-term loans and securities presently carry lower interest rates than shorter-term financial assets. Figure 8-1 illustrates a downward-sloping yield curve, while Figure 8-3 pictures an upward-sloping curve. Figure 8-2 depicts a recent horizontal or flat yield curve. Each shape of the yield curve has important implications for lenders and savers, borrowers and investors, and the financial institutions that serve them.

The Expectations Hypothesis

What determines the shape or slope of the yield curve? One view (with considerable research evidence to support it) is the *expectations hypothesis,* which argues that investor expectations regarding future changes in short-

FIGURE 8-2
Yields of Treasury Securities, April 30, 1980 (based on closing bid quotations)

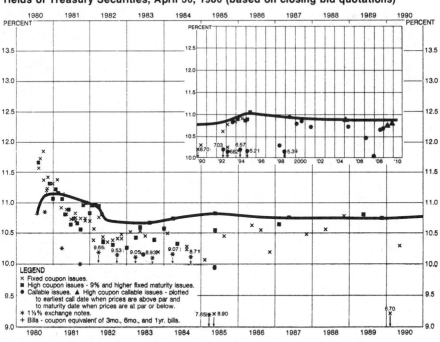

SOURCE: *Treasury Bulletin,* May 1980, p. 86.

FIGURE 8-3
Yields of Treasury Securities, May 30, 1980 (based on closing bid quotations)

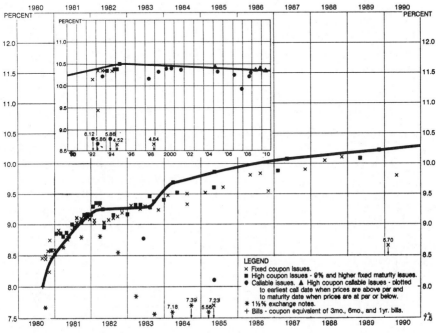

SOURCE: *Treasury Bulletin,* June 1980, p. 78.

term interest rates determine the shape of the curve.[1] For example, a rising yield curve is presumed to be an indication that investors expect short-term interest rates to *rise* above their current levels in the future. A declining yield curve suggests declining short-term rates in the future. Finally, a horizontal yield curve implies that investors in the market expect interest rates to remain essentially unchanged from their present levels. If the expectations hypothesis is true, then the yield curve becomes an important forecasting tool for the investor because it suggests the direction of future movements in short-term interest rates.

The unbiased expectations hypothesis assumes that investors act as *profit maximizers* over their planned holding periods and have no maturity preferences. All securities in a given risk class, regardless of their maturity, are perfect substitutes for each other. Each investor will seek those individual securities or combinations of securities offering the highest rates of return. For example, it is immaterial to investors with a planned 10-year investment horizon whether they buy a 10-year security, two 5-year securities, or a series of 1-year securities until the 10-year holding period terminates. Each investor will pursue that investment strategy which offers the greatest rate of return or yield over the length of the planned holding period.

Profit-maximizing behavior on the part of many thousands of investors interacting in the marketplace ensures that holding-period yields on all securities move toward equality. Once equilibrium *is* achieved, and assuming no transactions costs, *the investor should earn the same yield from buying a long-term security as from purchasing a series of short-term securities whose combined maturities equal that of the long-term security.* If the rate of return on long-term securities rises above or falls below the return the investor would receive from buying and selling several short-term securities, forces are quickly set in motion to restore equilibrium. Investors at the margin will practice *arbitrage*—moving funds from one security market to another—until long-term yields once again are brought into balance with short-term yields.

The Role of Expectations in Shaping the Yield Curve

How can a factor as intangible as expectations determine the shape of the yield curve? Expectations are a potent force in the financial marketplace because investors *act* on their expectations. For example, if interest rates are expected to rise in the future, this is disturbing news to investors in long-term bonds. As noted in Chapter 7, rising interest rates mean falling prices for bonds and other debt securities. Moreover, the longer the term of a bond, the more sensitive its price is to changes in rates. Faced with the possibility of falling bond prices, many investors will sell their long-term bonds and buy shorter-term securities or hold cash. As a result, the prices of long-term

---

[1] The expectations hypothesis was first stated by Irving Fisher (12) and further developed by Hicks (19) and Lutz (26).

bonds will plummet, driving their rates (yields) higher. At the same time, increased investor purchases of short-term securities will send the prices of these securities higher and their yields lower. With rising long-term rates and falling short-term rates, the yield curve will gradually assume an upward slope. The yield curve's prophecy of rising interest rates will have come true simply because investors responded to their expectations by making changes in their security portfolios.

Relative Changes in Long-Term and Short-Term Interest Rates

The expectations theory does help to explain an interesting phenomenon in the financial markets. As noted in Chapter 7, long-term interest rates tend to change slowly over time, while short-term interest rates are highly volatile and often move over wide ranges. The expectations hypothesis argues that the long-term interest rate is the *geometric* average of a series of rates on short-term loans whose combined maturities equal that of the long-term loan. The rate of interest on a 20-year bond, for example, is equivalent to the geometric average of the rates on a current 1-year loan plus the rates attached to series of 19 future (forward) 1-year loans, adding to 20 years. Experience teaches us that averages change much more slowly than the individual components making up an average. If the long-term interest rate is a geometric average of current and future short-term rates, it is not at all surprising that long-term rates tend to lag behind short-term rates and are less volatile.

Policy Implications of the Expectations Hypothesis

The expectations hypothesis has important implications for public policy. The theory clearly implies that changes in the relative amounts available of long-term versus short-term securities do *not* influence the shape of the yield curve unless investor expectations also are affected. For example, suppose the U.S. Treasury decided to refinance $100 billion of its maturing short-term IOUs by issuing $100 billion in long-term bonds. Would this government action affect the shape of the yield curve? Certainly, the *supply* of long-term bonds would be significantly increased, while the *supply* of short-term securities would be sharply reduced. However, according to the expectations theory, the yield curve itself would be *unchanged* unless investors altered their expectations about the future course of short-term interest rates.

To cite one more example, the Federal Reserve System buys and sells U.S. government and federal agency securities almost daily in the money and capital markets in order to promote the nation's economic goals.[2] Can the Fed influence the shape of the yield curve by buying one maturity of securities and selling another? Once again, the answer is no, unless the

---

[2] Federal Reserve open market operations are discussed at length in Chapter 22.

Federal Reserve can influence the interest-rate expectations of investors.[3] Why? The reason lies in the underlying assumption of the unbiased expectations hypothesis: *investors regard all securities, whatever their maturity, as perfect substitutes.* Therefore, the relative amounts of long-term bonds versus short-term securities simply should not matter to investors.

The Liquidity Premium View of the Yield Curve

The strong assumptions underlying the unbiased expectations theory coupled with the real-world behavior of investors have caused many financial analysts to question the theory's veracity. Securities dealers and analysts who trade actively in the financial markets frequently argue that other factors besides rate expectations also exert a significant impact on the character of the yield curve.

For example, in recent years most yield curves have sloped upward. Is there a built-in *bias* toward positively sloped yield curves due to factors other than interest-rate expectations? The *liquidity premium* view of the yield curve suggests that such a bias exists.

As noted in Chapter 7, longer-term securities tend to have more volatile market prices than short-term securities. Therefore, the investor faces greater risk of capital loss when buying long-term financial instruments. To overcome this risk, it is argued, investors must be paid an extra return in the form of an interest-rate premium to encourage them to purchase long-term securities. This rate premium for the surrender of liquidity on longer-term issues, if it exists, would tend to give yield curves a bias toward an upward slope.

Why then do some yield curves slope downward? In such instances, expectations of declining interest rates plus other factors simply overcome the liquidity premium effect. The liquidity premium view does not preclude the important role of interest-rate expectations in influencing the shape of the yield curve. Even though expectations may be the dominant factor influencing the yield curve, however, other factors such as liquidity play an important role as well.

---

[3] There is evidence that the Federal Reserve and the Treasury occasionally have attempted to significantly change the shape of the yield curve by selective buying and selling of different maturities of securities. The best-known example occurred during the early 1960s when the Fed and the Treasury pursued Operation Nudge. At that time the U.S. economy was recovering slowly from a recession in 1961, and unemployment remained high. At the same time, the United States was experiencing substantial balance-of-payments deficits as massive amounts of capital flowed overseas in search of higher interest rates. Government officials reasoned that, if the yield curve could be "twisted" so that long-term rates were held down to encourage more domestic investment while short-term rates were pushed higher to encourage short-term capital to stay at home, both problems could be solved. The Fed accelerated its purchases of long-term Treasury bonds, while the Treasury and the Fed collaborated to increase the supply of short-term government securities. After several months of little apparent effect, the project was abandoned.

Moreover, the liquidity argument may help explain why yield curves tend to "flatten out" at the longest maturities. (Note that this flattening out at the long-term end of the maturity spectrum is characteristic of all three yield curves shown in Figures 8–1, 8–2, and 8–3.) There are obvious differences in liquidity between a 1-year and 10-year bond, but it is not clear that major differences in liquidity exist between a 10-year bond and a 20-year bond, for example. Therefore, the size of the required liquidity premium paid to long-term investors may decrease for securities of the longest maturities.

The Segmented Markets Argument

A strong theoretical and empirical challenge to the expectations theory of the yield curve appeared in the 1950s, developed by economist John M. Culbertson and others.[4] This view is known alternatively as the *market segmentation* argument or the *hedging-pressure* theory of the term structure of interest rates. The underlying assumption is that all securities are *not* perfect substitutes in the minds of investors. Maturity preferences exist among major investor groups. Moreover, these groups will not stray from their "preferred habitats" along the maturity spectrum unless induced to do so by higher yields or other favorable terms on longer- or shorter-term securities.

Why would certain investors strongly prefer one maturity of security over another? Market segmentation theorists find the answer in a fundamental assumption concerning investor behavior, especially the investment behavior of such institutions as commercial banks, savings and loan associations, insurance companies, and pension funds. These investor groups, it is argued, often act as *risk minimizers* rather than the profit maximizers assumed in the expectations hypothesis. They prefer to hedge against the risk of fluctuations in the prices and yields of securities by balancing the maturity structure of their assets with the maturity structure of their liabilities.

For example, life insurance companies and pension funds have stable and predictable long-term liabilities. Therefore, these intermediaries prefer to invest in bonds, stocks, and other long-term assets. Commercial banks, on the other hand, with volatile deposits and short-term money market liabilities, prefer to confine the majority of their investments to short-term loans and securities. These important investor groups use the *hedging principle* of portfolio management—correlating the maturity of their liabilities with the expected cash flow generated by their assets.[5] This portfolio strategy reduces the risks of fluctuating income and loss of principal.

---

[4] See especially Culbertson (8). Later development and discussion of the segmented-markets theory may be found in Kessel (24), Malkiel (27), Meiselman (29), Struble (38), Modigliani and Sutch (31), Phillips and Pippenger (33), Elliott and Echols (10), and Dobson, Sutch, and Vanderford (9).

[5] See Chapter 19 for a discussion of the hedging principle applied to financial decision making.

The existence of maturity preferences among important investor groups implies that the financial markets are *not* one large pool of loanable funds but rather are segmented or divided into a series of submarkets. Thus, the market for securities of medium maturity (e.g., 5-to-10-year securities) attracts different investor groups than the market for long-term (e.g., over-10-year) securities. And *demand and supply conditions within each maturity range are held to be the dominant factors shaping the structure of interest rates within that range.* However, interest rates prevailing in one maturity range are little influenced by demand and supply conditions or rates in other maturity ranges. The segmented-markets theory does *not* rule out the possible influence of expectations in shaping the term structure of interest rates, but it argues that other factors related to maturity-specific demand and supply conditions are of dominant importance.

Policy Implications of the Segmented-Markets Theory

The segmented-markets theory, like the expectations theory, has significant implications for public policy. If markets along the maturity spectrum are relatively isolated from each other due to investor preferences, government policymakers can alter the shape of the yield curve merely by influencing supply and demand conditions in one or more market segments.

For example, if a positively sloped yield curve were desired, with long-term interest rates higher than short-term rates, the Treasury and the central bank could flood the market with long-term bonds. Simultaneously, the government could purchase large quantities of short-term securities. The expanded supply of bonds would drive long-term rates higher, while purchases of short-term securities would push short-term rates down, other factors held equal. Therefore, government monetary and debt-management policies could alter the shape of the yield curve.

Research Evidence

Which view of the yield curve is correct? Existing research evidence tends to support the *expectations* view. Studies by Sargent (37), Meiselman (29), Buse (1), and others find rate expectations to be a significant factor in shaping the maturity structure of interest rates. While all investors clearly do not regard all maturities of securities as perfect substitutes, there are sufficient numbers of traders in the financial marketplace who do *not* have specific maturity preferences. These investors are guided principally by relative interest rates on different securities. They bring about the results generally predicted by the expectations theory.

Nevertheless, there is evidence that other factors, especially the demand for liquidity, do affect the shape of the yield curve. Studies by Kessel (24), Van Horne (41), and others suggest the existence of a liquidity premium attached to the yields on longer-term securities, compensating investors for the risks associated with all but the shortest-term investments. The size of the liquidity premium does appear to decline with increasing maturity, however. There is also evidence that changes in the supply of securities in any particular maturity range can, at least temporarily, alter the shape of the yield curve, offering some support for the segmented-markets argument.[6] For example, at certain phases of the business cycle, commercial banks become heavy sellers of medium-term U.S. government and federal agency securities in order to raise cash and make more loans. During these periods, the yield curve frequently has a bowed or "humped" shape, with the highest yields offered by medium-term securities. In this instance, a sudden and massive increase in the supply of medium-term bonds appears to change the yield curve's overall shape.

Uses of the Yield Curve

The controversy surrounding the determinants of the yield curve should not obscure the fact that this curve can be an extremely useful tool for investors.

Forecasting Interest Rates.   First, if the expectations hypothesis is correct, the yield curve gives the investor a clue concerning the future course of interest rates. If the curve has an upward slope, the investor may be well advised to look for opportunities to move away from bonds and other long-term securities into investments whose market price is less sensitive to interest-rate changes. A downward-sloping yield curve, on the other hand, suggests the likelihood of near-term declines in interest rates and a rally in bond prices if the market's forecast of lower rates turns out to be true.

Uses for Financial Intermediaries.   The slope of the yield curve is critical for financial intermediaries, especially commercial banks, savings and loan associations, and savings banks. A rising yield curve is generally favorable for these institutions because they borrow most of their funds by selling short-term deposits and lend a major portion of those funds long term. The more steeply the yield curve slopes upward, the wider the spread between borrowing and lending rates and the greater the potential profit for a financial intermediary. However, if the yield curve begins to flatten out or slope downward, this should serve as a warning signal to portfolio managers of these institutions.

A flattening or downward-sloping yield curve squeezes the earnings of financial intermediaries and calls for an entirely different portfolio-management strategy than an upward-sloping curve. For example, if an upward-sloping yield curve starts to flatten out, portfolio managers of financial institutions might try to "lock in" relatively cheap sources of funds by getting long-term commitments from depositors and other funds-supplying

---

[6] Among the more important studies finding elements of market segmentation at work are those by Elliott and Echols (10), Modigliani and Sutch (31), and Terrell and Frazer (39).

customers. Borrowers, on the other hand, might be encouraged to take out long-term loans at fixed rates of interest. Of course, the financial institution's customers also may be aware of impending changes in the yield curve and resist taking on long-term loans or deposit contracts at potentially unfavorable interest rates.

Detecting Overpriced and Underpriced Securities. Yield curves can be used as an aid to investors in deciding which securities are temporarily overpriced or underpriced. This use of the curve derives from the fact that, in equilibrium, the yields on all securities of comparable risk should come to rest along the yield curve at their appropriate maturity levels. In an efficiently functioning market, however, any deviations of individual securities from the yield curve will be short-lived; so the investor must move quickly upon spotting a security whose yield lies temporarily above or below the curve.

If a security's rate of return lies *above* the yield curve, this sends a signal to investors that that particular security is temporarily *underpriced* relative to other securities of the same maturity. Other things equal, this is a buy signal which some investors will take advantage of, driving the price of the purchased security upward and its yield back down toward the yield curve. On the other hand, if a security's rate of return is temporarily *below* the yield curve, this indicates a temporarily *overpriced* financial instrument, because its yield is below that of securities bearing the same maturity. Some investors holding this security will sell it, pushing its price down and its yield back up toward the curve.

Indicating Trade-Offs between Maturity and Yield. Still another use of the yield curve is to indicate the current trade-off between maturity and yield confronting the investor. If the investor wishes to alter the maturity of a portfolio, the yield curve indicates what gain or loss in rate of return may be expected for each change in the portfolio's average maturity.

With an upward-sloping yield curve, for example, an investor may be able to increase a bond portfolio's expected annual yield from 9 percent to 11 percent by extending the portfolio's average maturity from six to eight years. However, the prices of longer-term bonds are more volatile, creating greater risk of capital loss. Moreover, longer-term securities tend to be less liquid and less marketable than shorter-term securities. Therefore, the investor must weigh the gain in yield from extending the maturity of his or her portfolio against added price, liquidity, and marketability risk. Because yield curves tend to flatten out for the longest maturities, the investor bent on lengthening the average maturity of a portfolio eventually discovers that gains in yield get smaller and smaller for each additional unit of maturity. At some point along the yield curve it clearly does not pay to further extend the maturity of a portfolio.

Riding the Yield Curve. Finally, some active security investors, especially dealers in United States government securities, have learned to "ride" the yield curve for profit. If the curve is positively sloped, with a slope steep enough to offset transactions costs from buying and selling securities, the investor may gain by timely portfolio switching.

For example, if a securities dealer purchases U.S. Treasury bills six months from maturity, holds them for three months, converts the bills into cash, and buys *new* six-month bills, he or she can profit in two ways from a positively sloped yield curve. Because the yield is lower on three-month than on six-month bills, the dealer experiences a capital gain on the sale. Second, the purchase of new six-month bills replaces a lower-yielding security with a higher-yielding one at a lower price. Riding the yield curve can be risky, however, since yield curves are constantly changing their shape. If the curve gets flatter or turns down, a potential gain can be turned into a realized loss. Experience and good judgment are indispensable in using the yield curve for investment decision making.

DEFAULT RISK AND INTEREST RATES

Another important factor causing one interest rate to differ from another is the degree of default risk carried by individual securities. Investors face many different kinds of risk,[7] of course, but one of the most important is *default risk*—the risk that a borrower will not meet all promised payments at the times agreed upon. All securities except U.S. government securities are subject to varying degrees of default risk. If you purchase a 10-year corporate bond with a $1,000 par value and a coupon rate of 9 percent, the issuing company promises in the indenture (i.e., bond contract) that it will pay you $90 a year (or more commonly, $45 every six months) for 10 years plus $1,000 at the end of the 10-year period. Failure to meet *any* of these promised payments on time puts the borrower in default, and the investor may have to go to court to recover at least some of the monies owed.

The Premium for Default Risk

The market yield on a security is *positively* related to the risk of borrower default as perceived by investors. Specifically, the market yield on a risky security is composed of at least two elements:

$$\begin{matrix} \text{Market} \\ \text{yield on} \\ \text{risky} \\ \text{security} \end{matrix} = \begin{matrix} \text{Risk-free} \\ \text{interest} \\ \text{rate} \end{matrix} + \begin{matrix} \text{Risk} \\ \text{premium} \end{matrix} \qquad (8-1)$$

where:

$$\begin{matrix} \text{Risk} \\ \text{premium} \end{matrix} = \begin{matrix} \text{Promised} \\ \text{yield on a} \\ \text{risky} \\ \text{security} \end{matrix} - \begin{matrix} \text{Risk-free} \\ \text{interest} \\ \text{rate} \end{matrix} \qquad (8-2)$$

---

[7] See Chapter 11 for a discussion of the principal types of risk confronting investors in financial instruments.

The *promised yield* on a risky security is the yield to maturity that will be earned by the investor if the borrower makes all the payments that are pledged, when they are due. The higher the degree of default risk associated with a security, the higher the *risk premium* on that security and the greater the required rate of return (yield) attached to that instrument in the marketplace. Any adverse development—a downturn in the economy, natural disaster, ill health, serious financial difficulties, etc—which makes a borrower appear more risky will lead the market to assign a higher risk premium to his or her security. And, if the risk-free rate remains unchanged, the security's market yield must rise and its price must decline.

The Expected Rate of Return or Yield

Increasingly in recent years, some of the nation's largest firms (such as the Penn Central Transportation Company, W. T. Grant, and Franklin National Bank of New York) have been forced into bankruptcy, while others, like Chrysler Corporation, have experienced highly publicized financial problems. Volatile changes in business and consumer spending, interest rates, and commodity prices frequently have led to serious miscalculations by both large and small firms, with sometimes fatal results. For this reason, many investors today have learned to look at the *expected rate of return,* or yield, on a security as well as its promised yield.

The expected yield is simply the weighted average of all possible yields to maturity from a security. Each possible yield is weighted by the probability that it will occur. Thus, if there are m possible yields from a given risky security,

$$\text{Expected yield} = \sum_{i=1}^{m} P_i Y_i \qquad (8\text{--}3)$$

where Y_i represents the ith possible yield and P_i is the probability that yield will be obtained.

Expected Default Loss and Market Risk Premiums

For a risk-free security held to maturity, the expected yield equals the promised yield. However, in the case of a risky security, the promised yield may be greater than the expected yield, and the difference between them is usually labeled the anticipated loss due to default. That is,

$$\begin{matrix}\text{Anticipated} \\ \text{loss on a risky} \\ \text{security}\end{matrix} = \begin{matrix}\text{Promised} \\ \text{yield}\end{matrix} - \begin{matrix}\text{Expected} \\ \text{yield}\end{matrix} \qquad (8\text{--}4)$$

The concept of *anticipated loss* is important because it represents each investor's view of what the appropriate risk premium on a security should be. To illustrate, let's suppose that an investor carries out a careful financial analysis of a company in preparation for purchasing its bonds and decides that the firm is a less-risky borrower than perceived by the market as a whole. Perhaps the market has assigned the firm's bonds a risk premium of 4 percent; however, the investor feels the true anticipated loss due to default is only 3 percent. Because the market-risk premium exceeds this investor's anticipated loss, he would be inclined to *buy* the security. As he sees it, the security's market yield (including its risk premium) is too high, and therefore its price is too low.

Consider the opposite case. An investor calculates the anticipated loss on bonds issued by a state toll road project. She concludes that a risk premium of 5 percent is justified because of a significant number of uncertainties associated with the future success of the project. However, the current yield on the security is only 10 percent, and the risk-free interest rate is 6 percent. Because the market has assigned only a 4 percent risk premium, while the investor prefers a 5 percent premium, it is unlikely that she will purchase the toll road bond. As the investor views this bond, its market yield is too low, and therefore its price is too high.

Major financial institutions, especially insurance companies and commercial banks, employ large numbers of credit analysts for the express purpose of assessing the anticipated loss on a wide range of securities they would like to acquire. These institutions feel they have a definite advantage over the average investor in assessing the true degree of default risk associated with any particular security. This high level of technical expertise may permit major institutional investors to take advantage of underpriced securities where, in their judgment, the market has overestimated the true level of default risk.

Factors Influencing Risk Premiums

What factors influence the risk premiums assigned by the market to different securities? For many years in the United States, *investment rating companies* have exercised a dominant influence on investor perceptions of the riskiness of individual security issues. The two most widely consulted investment rating companies are Moody's Investor Service and Standard & Poor's Corporation. Both companies rate individual security issues according to their perceived probability of default and publish the ratings as letter grades. A summary of the letter grades used by these companies for rating corporate and municipal bonds is shown in Exhibit 8–1.[8]

Moody's investment ratings range from Aaa for the highest-quality securities, with negligible default risk, to C for those securities deemed to be speculative and carrying a significant prospect of default. Quality ratings assigned by Standard & Poor's range from AAA for high-grade ("gilt-

---

[8] A more-detailed listing of the security rating scales used by Moody's and Standard & Poor's is provided in Appendix A.

EXHIBIT 8-1
Bond-Rating Categories Employed by Moody's Investors Service and
Standard & Poor's Corporation

Quality Level of Bonds	Moody's Rating Category	Standard & Poor's Rating Category	Risk Premium
High-quality or High-grade bonds	Aaa	AAA	Lowest
	Aa	AA	
	A	A	
Medium-quality or medium-grade bonds	Baa	BBB	
	Ba	BB	
	B	B	
Lowest grade, speculative, or poor-quality bonds	Caa	CCC	
	Ca	CC	
	C	C	
Defaulted bonds and bonds issued by bankrupt companies......................	—	DDD	Highest
	—	DD	
	—	D	

edged'') securities to those financial instruments actually in default (D) or issued by bankrupt firms. Bonds falling in the top four rating categories—Aaa to Baa for Moody's and AAA to BBB for Standard & Poor's—are called investment grade issues. State and federal laws frequently require commercial banks, insurance companies, and other financial institutions to purchase only those securities rated in these four categories. Lower-rated securities are referred to as speculative issues.

Figure 8-4 illustrates how the yields on bonds in two different Moody's categories—Aaa and Baa—have fluctuated in recent years, and it highlights the spread between the yields on these risky securities and those on riskless long-term U.S. government bonds. Exhibit 8-2 compares market yields on 20-year U.S. Treasury bonds with those on corporate bonds in the four top rating categories—Aaa to Baa. It is interesting to note that these yield relationships are all in the direction that theory would lead us to expect. For example, the yield on Aaa corporate bonds—the least risky of the securities rated by Moody's and Standard & Poor's—is consistently lower than yields attached to lower-rated bonds. Moreover, the graph lines representing Aaa and Baa bonds in Figure 8-4 never cross each other, and this phenomenon suggests that investors in the marketplace tend to rank securities in the same relative order as the rating agencies do. This is perhaps an appropriate strategy. A study by Hickman (18) covering the period from 1900 to 1943 found a high correlation between the ratings assigned by the agencies and actual default experience with corporate bonds.

FIGURE 8–4
Long-Term Bond Yields (quarterly averages)

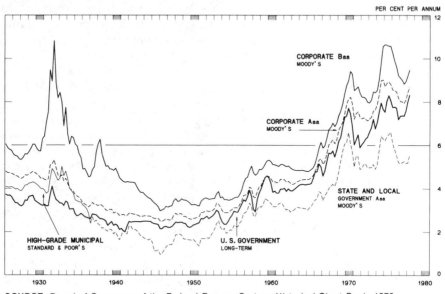

PER CENT PER ANNUM

CORPORATE Baa
MOODY'S

CORPORATE Aaa
MOODY'S

STATE AND LOCAL
GOVERNMENT Aaa
MOODY'S

HIGH-GRADE MUNICIPAL
STANDARD & POOR'S

U. S. GOVERNMENT
LONG-TERM

1930   1940   1950   1960   1970   1980

SOURCE: Board of Governors of the Federal Reserve System, *Historical Chart Book,* 1978.

EXHIBIT 8–2
Market Yields on Rated Corporate Bonds and 20-Year U.S. Treasury Bonds, 1977–1980

Type of Bond*	Average Yields (percent per annum)			
	1977	1978	1979	1980
20-year U.S. Treasury	7.67%	8.48%	9.33%	11.39%
Aaa corporate	8.02	8.73	9.63	11.94
Aa corporate	8.24	8.92	9.94	12.50
A corporate	8.49	9.12	10.20	12.89
Baa corporate	8.97	9.45	10.69	13.67

* Corporate bond ratings are from Moody's Investors Service.
SOURCE: Board of Governors of the Federal Reserve System, *Federal Reserve Bulletin,* selected issues.

We note, however, that the spreads between yields in different rating categories vary significantly over time. There is, for example, a pronounced association between risk premiums and *stage of the business cycle.* The yield spread between Aaa- and Baa-rated securities shown in Figure 8–4 increases during recessions and tends to decrease during periods of economic expansion. Note, for example, the marked increase in the yield spread between Aaa and Baa corporate bonds at the time of the 1969–70 and 1974–75 recessions and the narrowing of that spread following these economic downturns. The correlation is not perfect, of course. Fluctuations in the nation's output, employment, and income do not always influence the risk premium on one security versus another in the same way or to the same degree. But it is evident that, when economic and financial conditions suggest to investors that uncertainty has increased and that business prospects are less robust, the market translates these opinions into higher default-risk premiums.[9]

Several studies in recent years have addressed the question of what factors influence risk premiums on securities (especially corporate bonds) and the factors which security rating companies use to evaluate default risk. Among the factors identified for corporate securities are variability in company earnings, the period of time a firm has been in operation, and the amount of leverage employed (i.e., the amount of debt relative to equity).[10] A company with volatile earnings runs a greater risk of experiencing periods when losses will exceed the firm's ability to raise funds. Moreover, the longer a firm has been operating without default, the more investors come to expect continued successful performance. Greater use of financial leverage (debt) in the capital structure of a firm offers the potential for greater earnings per share of stock, because debt is a relatively cheap source of funds (measured on an aftertax basis). However, financial leverage is a two-edged sword. As the proportion of borrowed funds rises relative to equity, the risk of significant declines in earnings is increased.

In summary, careful study of the relationship between default risk and interest rates points to a fundamental principle in the field of finance: *risk and expected return are positively related*. The investor seeking higher expected returns must also be willing to accept greater risk of ruin. Moreover, default risk is correlated with both *internal* (or borrower-specific) factors associated with a loan and *external* factors, especially the state of the economy and changing demands for a particular industry's product or service.

INFLATION AND INTEREST RATES

The most serious problem confronting the U.S. economy and, indeed, most economies in the Western world today is *inflation*. Inflation is defined as a rise in the average level of prices for all goods and services. Some prices of individual goods and services are always rising, while others are declining. However, inflation occurs when the *average* level of all prices in the economy rises.[11] Interest rates represent the "price" of credit. Are they also affected by inflation? The answer is yes, though there is considerable debate as to exactly *how* inflation affects interest rates.

---

[9] This conclusion is supported by research studies prepared by Hickman (18) and Jaffe (20).

[10] See especially the studies by Fisher (13) and West (42).

[11] See Chapter 23 for a discussion of the nature and causes of, and recent public policy responses to, inflation.

The Correlation between Inflation and Interest Rates

To be sure, the apparent correlation in recent years between the rate of inflation in the United States and both long- and short-term interest rates is high. Exhibit 8–3, which tracks two popular measures of the rate of

EXHIBIT 8–3
Inflation and Interest Rates (annual rates)

Year	Rate of Inflation Measured by Percentage Change in		Interest Rate on Prime Commercial Paper (6-month maturities)
	Consumer Price Index	GNP Deflator	
1960	1.60%	1.70%	3.85%
1961	1.01	0.01	2.97
1962	1.12	1.83	3.26
1963	1.21	1.47	3.55
1964	1.31	1.56	3.97
1965	1.72	2.21	4.38
1966	2.86	3.28	5.55
1967	2.88	2.94	5.10
1968	4.20	4.49	5.90
1969	5.37	5.03	7.83
1970	5.92	5.35	7.72
1971	4.30	5.10	5.11
1972	3.30	4.14	4.69
1973	6.23	5.92	8.15
1974	10.74	9.71	9.84
1975	9.36	9.45	6.32
1976	5.77	5.27	5.35
1977	6.45	5.84	5.60
1978	7.60	7.30	7.99
1979	11.47	8.82	10.91
1980	13.52	8.79	12.29

SOURCES: U.S. Department of Commerce, *Survey of Current Business,* selected issues; and Board of Governors of the Federal Reserve System, *Federal Reserve Bulletin,* selected issues.

inflation—the consumer price index and the GNP deflator—and a money market interest rate—the yield on six-month prime commercial paper—suggests a close association between inflation and interest rates, especially during the 1970s. Note, for example, the sharp run-up in the rate of inflation between 1971 and 1974 and the parallel upward surge in the commercial paper rate, which reached an average yield of nearly 10 percent in 1974. Similarly, between 1974 and 1980 the inflation rate soared into double digits and interest rates did the same.

In reality, however, the correlation between these two data series has not always been so high. For example, a recent study by Cox (7) finds the following simple correlations between selected interest rates and the rate of inflation (measured by the GNP deflator):

	Correlation Coefficients	
	1952–65	1966–79
Prime bank rate and inflation rate.....................	0.11	0.70
Commercial paper rate and inflation rate..............	−0.06	0.81

During the 1950s and early 1960s a relatively calm economic environment prevailed, with modest annual price increases. Interest rates, too, were more stable, and the simple correlation between inflation and interest rates was not statistically significant. Late in the 1960s and during the 1970s, however,. spurred by the Vietnam War and rising price expectations, inflation soared and interest rates responded. The correlation between the two data series became highly significant in statistical terms.

The Nominal and Real Interest Rate

To examine the relationship between inflation and interest rates, several key terms must be defined. First, we must distinguish between nominal and real interest rates. The *nominal rate* is the published or quoted interest rate on a security or loan. For example, an announcement in the financial press that major commercial banks have raised their prime lending rate to 15 percent per annum indicates what nominal interest rate is now being quoted by banks to their most credit-worthy customers. In contrast, the *real rate* of interest is the return to the lender or investor measured in terms of its actual purchasing power. In a period of inflation, of course, the real rate will be lower than the nominal rate. Another important concept is the *inflation premium*, which measures the rate of inflation *expected* by investors in the marketplace during the life of a financial instrument.

These three concepts are all related to each other. Obviously, a lender of funds is most interested in the real rate of return on a loan—that is, the purchasing power of any interest earned. For example, suppose you loan $1,000 to a business firm or individual for a year and expect prices of goods and services to rise 10 percent during the year. If you charge a nominal interest rate of 12 percent on the loan, your real rate of return on the $1,000 face amount of the loan is only 2 percent, or $20. However, if the actual rate of inflation during the period of the loan turns out to be 13 percent, you have actually suffered a real decline in the purchasing power of the monies loaned. In general, lenders will attempt to charge nominal rates of interest which give them desired real rates of return on their loanable funds. And nominal interest rates will change as frequently as lenders alter their expectations regarding inflation.

The Fisher Effect

In a classic article written just before the turn of the century, economist Irving Fisher (12) argued that the nominal interest rate was related to the real rate by the following equation:

$$\begin{array}{c}\text{Nominal} \\ \text{interest} \\ \text{rate}\end{array} = \begin{array}{c}\text{Real} \\ \text{rate}\end{array} + \begin{array}{c}\text{Inflation} \\ \text{premium}\end{array} + \begin{array}{c}\text{Real} \\ \text{rate}\end{array} \times \begin{array}{c}\text{Inflation} \\ \text{premium}\end{array} \qquad (8\text{--}5)$$

The cross-product term in this equation is normally ignored because it is usually quite small.

Does the above equation suggest that an increase in expected inflation automatically increases nominal interest rates? Not necessarily. There are at least two different views on the matter. Fisher (12) argues that the real rate of return tends to be stable over time because it depends on such long-run factors as the productivity of capital and the volume of savings in the economy. Therefore, a change in the inflation premium is likely to influence only the nominal interest rate. The nominal rate will rise as the expected rate of inflation increases and decline with a drop in expected inflation. For example, suppose the real rate is 3 percent and the expected rate of inflation is 10 percent. Then the nominal rate will be calculated as follows:

$$\begin{array}{c}\text{Nominal} \\ \text{interest} \\ \text{rate}\end{array} = 3\% + 10\% = 13\% \qquad (8\text{--}6)$$

According to Fisher's hypothesis, if the expected rate of inflation now rises to 12 percent, the real rate will remain unchanged at 3 percent, but the nominal rate will rise to 15 percent.

If this view (known today as the Fisher effect) is correct, it suggests a method of judging the *direction* of future interest-rate changes. To the extent that rise in the actual rate of inflation causes investors to expect greater inflation in the future, higher nominal interest rates will soon result. Conversely, a decline in the actual rate of inflation may cause investors to revise downward their expectations of future inflation, leading to lower nominal interest rates.

An Alternative View

The Fisher effect conflicts with another view of the inflation-interest rate phenomenon, developed originally by the British economist Sir Roy Harrod.[12] It is based upon the liquidity preference theory of interest discussed in Chapter 6. Harrod argues that the *real* rate will be affected by inflation, but the nominal rate need not be. Following the liquidity preference theory, the nominal interest rate is determined by the demand for and supply of money. Therefore, unless inflation affects either the demand for or supply of money, the nominal rate must remain unchanged regardless of what happens to inflationary expectations.

What, then, is the link between inflation and interest rates according to this view? Harrod argues that a rise in inflationary expectations will lower the

---

[12] The Harrod view of inflation and interest rates is outlined by Clayton, Gilbert, and Sedgwick (3), Kennedy (23), and Mundell (32).

real rate of interest. In liquidity preference theory, the real rate measures the inflation-adjusted return on bonds. However, conventional bonds, like money, are not a hedge against inflation, because their rate of return is fixed by contract. Therefore, a rise in the expected rate of inflation lowers investors' real return from holding bonds. While the nominal rate of return on bonds remains unchanged, the real rate is squeezed by expectations of rising prices.

This so-called Harrod effect does not stop with bonds, however. There are two other groups of assets in the economy which, unlike bonds, often provide a hedge against inflation—common stocks and real estate. Inflationary expectations often lead to rapidly rising prices for homes, farmland, and commercial structures and to rallies in the stock market. Allegedly, an increase in the rate of inflation causes the demand for these inflation-hedged assets to increase as well. Real estate and stock prices rise and, of course, their nominal rates of return fall until an equilibrium set of returns on stocks, bonds, real estate, and other assets is achieved.

The Research Evidence

What does research evidence have to say regarding these two views of the relationship between inflation and interest rates? The evidence is decidedly mixed. As LeRoy (25) observes, during the 1950s and early 1960s the correlation between the inflation rate and nominal interest rates was positive but very low, providing some support for the Harrod effect. During the late 1960s and 1970s, however, there was a relatively high positive correlation between the inflation rate and nominal rates of return, tending to support Fisher's view. At the same time there has been a tendency for the prices of inflation-hedged assets, including common stocks and real estate, to respond to changes in inflationary expectations. It seems likely that a combination of the two views best describes the true impact of inflation upon rates of interest for both loans and securities.

SUMMARY AND CONCLUSIONS

While theories of interest-rate determination typically assume there is a single interest rate in the economy, in point of fact there are thousands of different interest rates confronting investors at any one time. This chapter has focused upon several factors—the maturity or term of a loan, the risk of borrower default, and inflationary expectations—which cause rates to vary on different types of securities. Knowledge of each of these factors is of critical importance to security investors in making intelligent portfolio decisions.

This chapter emphasizes the key importance of the yield curve in explaining and predicting interest-rate movements. The yield curve expresses the relationship between the annual rate of return on a financial instrument and its maturity when all other factors are held constant. Yield curves reflect the interest-rate expectations of the marketplace and hint at the direction, if not the magnitude, of future rate movements. They are a key tool in the management of financial intermediaries who borrow a substantial proportion of their funds at the short end of the maturity spectrum and lend heavily at the long-term end. Knowledge of what and how the yield curve is determined is vital, therefore, to the long-term profitability of financial institutions.

Differences in the yields attached to securities also arise from differences in the risk of borrower default. An increase in the risk of default on an individual security increases its risk premium, which is the difference between the promised yield on a risky security and the risk-free rate of interest. Other factors held constant, the market yield on the security must also rise. Risk premiums on securities appear to widen in periods of recession and increased economic uncertainty. Moreover, the more volatile are the net earnings of individual firms and the higher their proportions of debt to equity capital, the larger risk premiums tend to be on any securities issued by these firms. The linkage between default risk and risk premiums on securities reflects one of the fundamental principles of finance—investors seeking higher expected returns must be willing to accept greater risk. Research evidence to date shows quite clearly that this risk is closely correlated with both internal factors reflecting the financial status and condition of the borrower and external factors, such as political developments and the state of the economy.

The final factor affecting interest rates considered in this chapter is inflation. Increases in the general level of prices for all goods and services affect interest rates because lenders are unwilling to commit their funds to borrowers unless they are adequately protected against future losses in purchasing power. If lenders of funds expect a higher rate of inflation during the life of a credit contract, they will adjust upward the nominal rate on a loan in order to achieve their desired real rate of return. Modern financial theory argues that the nominal (published) rate on a loan or security equals the sum of the real rate of return (measured in terms of the real purchasing power of any income earned from the financial instrument) and the inflation premium (or expected rate of inflation). According to the so-called Fisher effect, if the expected inflation rate rises, the nominal interest rate on a loan or security must also rise. A lesser-known view developed by Harrod contends that, at least in the short run, a rise in the expected inflation premium squeezes the real rate of return to lenders but leaves nominal interest rates unchanged. Existing research tends to give greater support to the Fisher effect, though certain aspects of the Harrod argument appear to be correct as well. An accurate assessment of the true linkages between inflation and interest rates must await further research.

STUDY QUESTIONS

1. Explain the meaning of the phrase "term structure of interest rates." What is a yield curve? What assumptions are necessary to construct a yield curve?

2. Explain the differences between the expectations, market-segmentation, and liquidity-premium views of the yield curve. Depending upon which of these views is correct, what are the implications of each for investors? For public policy?

3. Define default risk. What factors appear to influence the degree of default risk possessed by a security? In what ways are security ratings designed to reflect default risk?

4. Explain how inflation affects interest rates. What is the Fisher effect? The Harrod effect?

5. The correlation between the inflation rate and market interest rates appears to have increased considerably in recent years. Can you explain why?

SELECTED REFERENCES

1. Buse, A. "The Expectations Hypothesis, Yield Curves, and Monetary Policy." *Quarterly Journal of Economics,* November 1965, pp. 666–68.

2. _____. "Interest Rates, the Meiselman Model and Random Numbers." *Journal of Political Economy,* February 1967, pp. 49–62.

3. Clayton, G., J. C. Gilbert, and R. Sedgwick. *Monetary Theory and Monetary Policy in the 1970's.* Oxford: Oxford University Press, 1971.

4. Cohan, Avery B. *The Risk Structure of Interest Rates.* Morristown, N.J.: General Learning Press, 1973.

5. _____. *Yields on Corporate Debt Directly Placed.* New York: National Bureau of Economic Research, 1967.

6. Conrad, Joseph W. *The Behavior of Interest Rates.* New York: National Bureau of Economic Research, 1966.

7. Cox, III. William N., "Interest Rates and Inflation: What Drives What?" *Economic Review,* Federal Reserve Bank of Atlanta, May-June 1980, pp. 20–23.

8. Culbertson, John M. "The Term Structure of Interest Rates." *Quarterly Journal of Economics,* November 1957, pp. 485–517.

9. Dobson, Steven W., Richard C. Sutch, and David E. Vanderford. "An Evaluation of Alternative Empirical Models of the Term Structure of Interest Rates." *Journal of Finance,* September 1976, pp. 1035–65.

10. Elliott, J. W., and M. E. Echols. "Market Segmentation, Speculative Behavior, and the Term Structure of Interest Rates." *Review of Economics and Statistics,* February 1976, pp. 40–49.

11. Fand, David. "High Interest Rates and Inflation in the United States: Cause or Effect?" *Banca Nazionale del Lavoro Quarterly Review,* March 1972, pp. 23–64.

12. Fisher, Irving. "Appreciation and Interest." *Publications of the American Economic Association,* August 1896.

13. Fisher, Lawrence. "Determinants of Risk Premiums on Corporate Bonds." *Journal of Political Economy,* June 1959, pp. 217–37.

14. Gibson, William E. "Interest Rates and Inflationary Expectations: New Evidence." *American Economic Review,* December 1972, pp. 854–65.

15. _____. "Price Expectations Effects on Interest Rates." *Journal of Finance,* March 1970, pp. 19–34.

16. Grier, Paul, and Steven Katz. "The Differential Effects of Bond Rating Changes among Industrial and Public Utility Bonds by Maturity." *Journal of Business,* April 1976, pp. 226–39.

17. Hamburger, Michael J., and Elliott N. Platt. "The Expectations Hypothesis and the Efficiency of the Treasury Bill Market." *Review of Economics and Statistics,* May 1975, pp. 190–99.

18. Hickman, W. Braddock. *Corporate Bond Quality and Investor Experience.* New York: National Bureau of Economic Research, 1958.

19. Hicks, John R. *Value and Capital.* 2d ed. London: Oxford University Press, 1946).

20. Jaffe, Dwight M. "Cyclical Variations in the Risk Structure of Interest Rates." *Journal of Monetary Economics,* July 1975, pp. 309–25.

21. Joehnk, Michael D., and James F. Nielsen. "Return and Risk Characteristics of Speculative Grade Bonds." *Quarterly Review of Economics and Business,* Spring 1975, pp. 27–46.

22. Johnson, Ramon E. "Term Structures of Corporate Bond Yields as a Function of Risk of Default." *Journal of Finance,* May 1967, pp. 318–21.

23. C. Kennedy. "Inflation and the Bond Rate." *Oxford Economic Papers,* October 1960, pp. 269–73.

24. Kessel, Reuben H. *The Cyclical Behavior of the Term Structure of Interest Rates.* New York: National Bureau of Economic Research, 1965.

25. LeRoy, Stephen F. "Inflation and Interest Rates." *Monthly Review,* Federal Reserve Bank of Kansas City, May 1973, pp. 11–18.

26. Lutz, Friedrich A. "The Structure of Interest Rates." *Quarterly Journal of Economics,* November 1940, pp. 36–63.

27. Burton G. Malkiel. *The Term Structure of Interest Rates.* Princeton, N.J.: Princeton University Press, 1966.

28. McCulloch, J. Huston. "An Estimate of the Liquidity Premium." *Journal of Political Economy,* January–February 1975, pp. 95–119.

29. Meiselman, David A. *The Term Structure of Interest Rates.* Englewood Cliffs, N.J.: Prentice-Hall, 1962.

30. Merton, Robert C. "On the Pricing of Corporate Debt: The Risk Structure of Interest Rates." *Journal of Finance,* May 1974, pp. 449–470.

31. Modigliani, Franco, and Richard Sutch. "Innovations in Interest Rate Policy." *American Economic Review,* May 1966, pp. 178–97.

32. Mundell, Robert. "Inflation and Real Interest." *Journal of Political Economy,* June 1963.

33. Phillips, Llad, and John Pippenger. "Preferred Habitat vs. Efficient Market: A Test of Alternative Hypotheses." *Review,* Federal Reserve Bank of St. Louis, May 1976, pp. 11–19.

34. Pyle, David. "Observed Price Expectations and Interest Rates." *Review of Economics and Statistics,* August 1972.

35. Sargent, Thomas J. "Anticipated Inflation and Nominal Interest," *Quarterly Journal of Economics,* May 1972.

36. _____. "Commodity Price Expectations and Interest Rates." *Quarterly Journal of Economics,* February 1969.

37. _____. "Interest Rates in the Nineteen Fifties." *Review of Economics and Statistics,* May 1968, pp. 164–72.

38. Struble, Frederick. "The Term Structure of Interest Rates." *Monthly Review,* Federal Reserve Bank of Kansas City, January-February 1966, pp. 10–16.

39. Terrell, William T., and William J. Frazer, Jr. "Interest Rates, Portfolio Behavior, and Marketable Government Securities." *Journal of Finance,* March 1972, pp. 1–35.

40. Turnovsky, J. "Empirical Evidence on the Formation of Price Expectations." *Journal of the American Statistical Association,* December 1970.

41. Van Horne, James. "Interest-Rate Risk and the Term Structure of Interest Rates." *Journal of Political Economy,* August 1965, pp. 344–51.

42. West, Richard R. "Bond Ratings, Bond Yields and Financial Regulation: Some Findings." *Journal of Law and Economics,* April 1973, pp. 159–68.

43. Yohe, William P., and Dennis S. Karnosky. "Interest Rates and Price Level Changes, 1952–69." *Review,* Federal Reserve Bank of St. Louis, December 1969.

9

Marketability, Call Privileges, Taxes, and Other Factors Affecting Interest Rates

In the preceding chapter we examined several factors which cause the interest rate or yield on one security to be different from the rate or yield on another security. These factors included the maturity or term of a loan, the risk of borrower default, and expected inflation. In this chapter our focus is upon a different collection of elements influencing relative interest rates: (1) marketability, (2) call privileges, (3) taxation of income from securities, and (4) convertibility. While the impact of each of these factors is analyzed separately, it should be noted that yields on securities typically are influenced by several factors acting *simultaneously*. For example, the market yield on a 20-year corporate bond may be 12 percent, while the yield on a 10-year municipal bond may be 7 percent. The difference in yield between these two securities reflects, not only the difference in their maturities, but also any differences in their degree of default risk, callability prior to maturity, and tax status. To analyze yield differentials between securities, therefore, we must understand thoroughly *all* the factors which shape and direct interest rates in the economy.

MARKETABILITY

One of the most important considerations for an investor is, Does a market exist for those assets he or she would like to acquire? Can an asset be sold quickly, or must the investor wait some time before suitable buyers can be found? This is the question of *marketability*, and financial instruments vary widely in terms of the ease and speed with which they can be sold and converted into cash.

For example, U.S. Treasury bills, notes, and bonds have one of the most-active and deepest markets in the world. Large lots of marketable Treasury securities in multiples of a million dollars are bought and sold daily, with the trades taking place in a matter of minutes. Small lots (under $1 million) of these same securities are more difficult to sell. However, there is usually no difficulty in marketing even a handful of Treasury securities provided the seller can wait a few hours or a few days. Similarly, common stock actively traded on the New York and American exchanges typically can be moved in minutes, hours, or overnight, depending on the number of shares being sold and how far removed the investor is from the center of trading activity. In active markets like these, negotiations are usually conducted by telephone and confirmed by wire, and frequently payment for any securities purchased is made the same day by wire or within one or two days by check.

For the thousands of lesser-known securities not actively traded each day, however, marketability is frequently a problem. For example, stocks, bonds, and notes issued by smaller companies usually have a narrow market, often confined to the local community or region. Trades occur infrequently, and it is difficult to establish a consistent market price. A seller may have to wait weeks or months to secure a desired price or, if the security must be sold immediately, its price may have to be discounted substantially from the expected figure. Marketability is *positively* related to the size (total sales or total assets) and reputation of the institution issuing the securities and to the number of similar securities outstanding. Not surprisingly, stocks and bonds issued in large blocks by the largest corporations or governmental units tend to find more ready acceptance in the market. With a greater number of similar securities available, buy-sell transactions are more frequent, and a consistent market price can be established.

Marketability is a decided advantage to the *investor*. In contrast, the *issuer* of securities is not particularly concerned about any difficulties the investor may encounter in the resale (secondary) market unless lack of marketability significantly influences security sales in the primary market. And where marketability *is* a problem, it does influence the yield the issuer must pay in the primary market. In fact, there is a *negative,* or inverse, relationship between marketability and yield. More-marketable securities generally carry a *lower* expected return, other things equal. Investors in securities which can be sold in the secondary market only with difficulty must be compensated for this inconvenience by a higher promised rate of return.

An interesting example of the impact of marketability on relative yields is provided by U.S. Treasury securities and the debt obligations of federal government agencies. Exhibit 9–1 contains some recent annual market yields on U.S. Treasury notes and bonds and on securities issued by federal agencies.[1] These agencies bear such well-known names as the Federal Land

---

[1] See Chapter 14 for a more complete discussion of federal agency securities.

EXHIBIT 9–1
Yields on U.S. Treasury and Federal Agency Securities of Varying Maturities, Week Ending December 28, 1979

Time to Maturity	Annual Yields to Maturity		
	Federal Agency Securities	U.S. Treasury Notes and Bonds	Yield Spread (basis points)
1 year	12.50%	11.90%	+60
2 years	11.45	11.35	+10
3 years	10.80	10.62	+18
5 years	10.70	10.51	+19
7 years	10.75	10.45	+30
10 years	10.65	10.43	+22
20 years	10.40	10.21	+19

SOURCE: Salomon Brothers, *Bond Market Roundup.*

Banks, Small Business Administration, Farmers Home Administration, and the Federal National Mortgage Association ("Fannie Mae"). While the market for federal agency securities has been growing rapidly in recent years, the agency market is still much less active and deep than that for U.S. Treasury securities. Consequently, agency securities nearly always carry higher yields than Treasury IOU's for instruments of the same maturity.

For example, as shown in Exhibit 9–1, one-year agency securities carried an annual yield of 12.50 percent at year-end 1979, a full 60 basis points (i.e., three fifths of a percentage point) higher than the annual yield on Treasury securities also maturing in one year. At the long-term end of the maturity spectrum, 20-year federal agencies were paying an annual yield of 10.40 percent, 19 basis points (i.e., about one fifth of a percentage point) higher than on comparable-maturity Treasury issues. Of course, not all of this particular yield differential is due to differences in marketability. While most investors consider federal agency securities to be as riskless as direct U.S. Treasury obligations, the majority of agency securities are not guaranteed by the federal government. Thus, the yield differences shown in Exhibit 9–1 probably reflect a small default risk premium as well as a premium for the lower marketability of agency securities. However, most financial analysts feel that Congress would quickly come to the rescue of any federal agency in serious financial trouble.

THE CALL PRIVILEGE

Nearly all corporate bonds and mortgages and some U.S. government bonds issued in today's financial markets carry a call privilege. This provision of the bond contract, or indenture, permits the borrower to retire all or a portion of a bond issue by buying back the securities in advance of their maturity. Bondholders usually are informed of a call through a notice in a newspaper of general circulation, while holders of record of registered bonds are notified directly. Normally, when the call privilege is exercised, the security issuer will pay the investor the *call price*, which equals the securities' face value plus a *call penalty*. The size of the call penalty is set forth in the indenture (contract) and generally varies with the number of years remaining to maturity. In the case of a bond, one year's worth of coupon income is often the minimum call penalty required.

Calculating Yields on Called Securities

Bonds may be callable immediately or the privilege may be deferred (postponed) for a time. In the corporate sector, bonds usually are not eligible for call for a period of 5 to 10 years after issue in order to give investors at least some protection against early redemption. Of course, calling a security at *any* point in advance of its final maturity has an impact on the investor's effective yield.

To demonstrate this, we recall from Chapter 7 that the *yield to maturity* of any security is that discount rate, y, which equates the security's price, P, with the present value of all future cash flows, I_i, expected from holding the security. In symbols,

$$P = \frac{I_1}{(1 + y)^1} + \frac{I_2}{(1 + y)^2} + \cdots + \frac{I_n}{(1 + y)^n} \qquad (9\text{--}1)$$

where n is the number of periods until maturity. Suppose that after k periods (with $k < n$) the borrower exercises the call option and redeems the security. The investor will receive the call price (C) for the security, which can be reinvested at the current market interest rate, i. If the investor's planned holding period ends in time period n, the expected holding-period yield (h) can be calculated by the following formula:

$$P = \frac{I_1}{(1 + h)^1} + \frac{I_2}{(1 + h)^2} + \cdots + \frac{I_k}{(1 + h)^k} + \frac{i \times C_{k+1}}{(1 + h)^{k+1}}$$
$$+ \frac{i \times C_{k+2}}{(1 + h)^{k+2}} + \cdots + \frac{i \times C_n}{(1 + h)^n} + \frac{C}{(1 + h)^n} \qquad (9\text{--}2)$$

Using summation signs, this reduces to:

$$P = \sum_{j=1}^{k} \frac{I_j}{(1 + h)^j} + \sum_{j=k+1}^{n} \frac{i \times C_j}{(1 + h)^j} + \frac{C}{(1 + h)^n} \qquad (9\text{--}3)$$

The first term in Equation 9–3 gives the present value of all cash flows (I) from the security until it is called in time period k. The second term captures the present value of income received by the investor after he or she reinvests at interest rate i the call price (C) received from the security's issuer. The third and final term in the equation shows the current discounted value of the call price which the investor expects to receive when the holding period ends in time period n.

Equation 9–3 shows quite clearly that the investor in callable securities encounters two major uncertainties:

1. The investor does not know if or when the securities might be called (i.e., the value of k).
2. The investor does not know the market yield (reinvestment rate i) which might prevail at the time the security is called.

Therefore, how aggressively the investor chooses to bid for a callable instrument will depend upon:

1. The investor's expectations regarding future changes in interest rates, especially decreases in market rates, during the term of the security.
2. The length of the deferment period before the security is eligible to be called.
3. The call price (face value plus call penalty) the issuer is willing to pay to redeem the security.

Advantages and Disadvantages of the Call Privilege

Clearly, the call privilege is an *advantage* to the security issuer because it grants him greater financial flexibility and the potential for reducing future interest costs. On the other hand, the call privilege is a distinct disadvantage to the security buyer, who may suffer a decline in the expected holding-period yield if the security is, in fact, called. The issuer will call in a security if the market rate of interest falls far enough so that the savings from issuing a new security at lower interest rates more than offset the call penalty plus flotation costs of a new security issue. This means, however, that an investor who is paid off will be forced to reinvest the call price in lower-yielding securities.

Another disadvantage for the investor is that call privileges limit the potential increase in a security's market price. In general, the market price of a security will not rise significantly above its call price, even when interest rates fall. The reason is that the issuer can call in a security at the call price, presenting the investor with a loss equal to the difference between the prevailing market price and the call price. Thus, callable securities have a more-limited potential for capital gains than noncallable securities.

The Call Premium and Interest-Rate Expectations

For all of the foregoing reasons, securities that carry a call privilege generally sell at lower prices and higher interest rates than noncallable securities. Moreover, there is an inverse relationship between the length of the call deferment period and the required rate of interest on callable securities. The longer the period of deferment and, therefore, the longer the investor is protected against early redemption, the *lower* the interest rate which the borrower must pay. Issuers of callable securities must pay a *call premium* in the form of a higher rate of interest for the option of early redemption and for a shorter period of deferment.

The key determinant of the size of the call premium is the interest-rate expectations of investors in the marketplace. If interest rates are expected to *rise* over the term of a security, the risk that the security will be called is low. Borrowers are very unlikely to call in their securities and issue new ones at higher interest rates. As a result, the yield differential between callable and noncallable securities normally will be minimal. Moreover, in this case call deferments will be of limited value to investors, and yields will be roughly equivalent for securities with varying call features. The same conclusions apply even if interest rates are expected to decline moderately but not enough to entice borrowers to call in their securities and issue new ones.

It is when interest rates are expected to *fall* substantially that securities are most likely to be called. In this instance security issuers can save large amounts of money—more than enough to cover the call penalty plus flotation costs of new securities—by exercising the call privilege. Thus, the call premium is likely to be significant as investors demand a higher yield on callable issues to compensate them for *call risk*. Moreover, the yield spreads between bonds with long call deferments versus those with short or no call deferments widen during such periods as investors come to value more highly the deferment feature.

Research Evidence

Is there evidence of an inverse relationship between interest-rate expectations and the value of the call privilege? Recent research answers in the affirmative. For example, Cook (4) finds that, when interest rates are high, the call premium rises because investors expect interest rates to fall in the future. Moreover, he points out that call provisions also influence yield *spreads* between corporate bonds, nearly all of which have the call privilege attached, and municipal and U.S. government bonds, which generally are not subject to call. For example, when interest rates are expected to fall, the spread between corporate and U.S. government bond rates tends to widen. Pye (11 and 12) and Jen and Wert (5, 6, and 7) find additional evidence that bonds carrying a call deferment have lower rates of return than bonds which are callable immediately.

Effect of Coupon Rates on Call Risk

Finally, we should note that the *coupon rate* on a bond is closely related to the investor's call risk. We recall from Chapter 7 that a bond's coupon rate is the rate of return against the security's par value promised by the borrower. High coupon rates mean that a bond issuer is forced to pay high interest costs as long as the bond is outstanding. Therefore, there is a strong incentive to call in such bonds and replace them with lower-coupon securities.

Another problem is that bonds bearing high coupons have less opportunity for capital gains than bonds carrying lower coupon rates. This is true because the market value of a high-coupon security is usually close to its call-price ceiling. In contrast, bonds with more-modest coupon rates sell at lower prices and carry considerably more potential for capital gains before hitting the call price. This means there is more risk of call and less potential capital gain to the investor who chooses high-coupon securities. As a result, the issuer of such securities must pay a higher yield to induce investors to buy them and accept greater call risk.

TAXATION OF SECURITY RETURNS

Taxes imposed by federal, state, and local governments have a profound effect on the returns earned by investors in financial assets. The income from most securities—interest or dividends and capital gains—is subject to taxation at the federal level and by many state and local governments as well.

Government uses its taxing power to encourage purchases of certain financial assets and thereby redirect the flow of savings and investment toward areas of critical social need. Today U.S. tax laws heavily favor two kinds of financial transactions: (1) long-term lending and investing of funds, as opposed to short-term lending and investing; and (2) fund raising by those sectors of the economy considered to be disadvantaged in the competition for loanable funds. Prominent among these "disadvantaged" groups are state and local governments and buyers and sellers of real estate, especially residential properties.

The Tax Treatment of Capital Gains

Short-Term Capital Gains. Governments frequently use tax laws to encourage greater long-term investment in capital goods in order to accelerate the economy's rate of growth. For example, the federal government imposes lower tax rates on long-term capital gains than on short-term capital gains.

Under current tax rules administered by the Internal Revenue Service, an increase in the value of a capital asset (including stocks and bonds) which the taxpayer converts into cash is subject to federal income taxation. For example, if you had purchased stock in XYZ Corporation for $1,900 and then sold it at a later date for $3,100, you would have experienced a capital gain of $1,200. Under current law, if you held the stock for one year or less before selling it, the $1,200 increase in value would be defined as a *short-term* capital gain. Such gains are taxable as ordinary income at your current income-tax rate. Thus, a $1,200 short-term capital gain for an investor in the 50 percent tax bracket would result in a tax liability of $600 ($1,200 × 0.50).

Long-Term Capital Gains.   Current tax policy calls for much lower tax rates, however, if XYZ Corporation's stock is held for a longer period before it is sold. For example, if the investor holds the stock for at least a year and a day before selling it, the result is a *long-term* capital gain of $1,200. For individual taxpayers, only 40 percent of this long-term gain ($480) is taxable. A taxpayer in the top 50 percent federal tax bracket, for example, would have a resulting tax liability of just $240 ($480 × 0.50). Under the terms of the Economic Recovery Tax Act of 1981, the maximum tax rate on long-term capital gains is 20 percent.

Treatment of Capital Losses.   Net *losses* on security investments are deductible for tax purposes within well-defined limits. For the individual taxpayer, a net *short-term* capital loss is deductible up to the amount of the capital loss, the size of ordinary income, or $3,000, whichever is smaller. For example, suppose an investor experiences a net loss on securities held for less than one year of $8,000. By definition, this is a short-term capital loss. Suppose this person receives other taxable income of $20,000. How much of the short-term loss can be deducted? What is this taxpayer's total taxable income? The maximum loss deduction in this case is $3,000, and therefore the taxpayer's net taxable income is $17,000 (i.e., $20,000 minus the $3,000 in deductible losses). Current federal law does allow the taxpayer to carry forward into subsequent years the remaining portion of the loss (i.e., $5,000 in this example) until all of the short-term loss has been deducted from ordinary income, but the loss cannot be carried backward.

In the case of net *long-term* capital losses, federal tax rules allow the individual taxpayer to recognize only 50 percent of the loss as a deduction from current taxable income. For example, suppose an investor purchased securities at a cost of $5,000 and sold them two years later in a declining market for $3,000. Then only $1,000 of the $2,000 long-term capital loss could be charged against other income in the current year. But the other $1,000 could be carried forward into future years' deductions. As in the case of short-term losses, a maximum amount of $3,000 in long-term losses can be deducted in any one year. Losses over $3,000 can be carried forward into future years but not backward into past years.

Netting Out Losses and Gains.   What happens when the taxpayer has a mixture of short- and long-term capital gains and losses? First, the long-term losses must be deducted from the long-term gains to yield the taxpayer's *net* long-term capital gain or loss. Next, short-term losses must be deducted from any short-term gains to derive the taxpayer's *net* short-term gain or loss.

When both net figures are *positive*, the investor pays the ordinary marginal income tax rate appropriate for his or her income bracket (see Exhibit 9–2) on the net short-term gain. In contrast the lower capital gains rate applies to the long-term net gain.

When both the net long- and short-term gains are *negative*, 50 percent of

EXHIBIT 9–2
Examples of Marginal Federal Income-Tax Rates (tax brackets) Applicable to Married Taxpayers Filing a Joint Return, 1980 and 1984

Taxable Income	Applicable Marginal Tax Rate (bracket)	
	1980	1984
$ 15,000	21%	16%
25,000	32	25
35,000	37	28
50,000	49	38
75,000	54	42
100,000	59	45
150,000	64	49
200,000	70	50

Note: Marginal tax rates for 1980 are as specified in the Revenue Act of 1978, while those for 1984 reflect changes brought about by the Economic Recovery Tax Act of 1981. The 1981 law provides for a gradual reduction of individual tax rates over a period of 33 months.

the long-term loss can be used to offset ordinary income up to $3,000. In contrast, all of the net short-term loss may be used to offset ordinary income up to $3,000. If the combined sum of a short-term loss and 50 percent of a long-term capital loss for a particular year exceeds $3,000, the taxpayer may carry the loss forward until all of it is written off.

When there is a net short-term capital loss and a long-term gain, the two are netted out. Any excess long-term gain over short-term loss is taxed at the lower capital gains rate. If there is a short-term gain exceeding a long-term capital loss, however, the net gain is taxed at the individual's marginal income tax rate.

The Capital Gains Effect. The low capital gains tax rate clearly favors those securities with the strongest capital gains potential. In particular, bonds have less appeal than common stock, especially growth stocks which often pay limited dividends but offer the prospect of significant capital appreciation. Capital gains tax rules also favor bonds bearing low coupon rates over those with high coupon rates. This is true because in a period of relatively high interest rates low-coupon bonds would be selling at a substantial discount from their par values. As a low-coupon security approaches maturity, its price rises toward par. Therefore, the investor will earn interest income as determined by the coupon rate on the bond and a capital gain.

An excellent example of this so-called capital gains effect occurred recently in the U.S. Treasury bond market. For example, U.S. Treasury bonds bearing a 4 percent coupon were issued in 1961 to mature in 1981. With interest rates during 1978, 1979, and into early 1980 rising to record double-digit levels, these low-coupon bonds were selling for about 60 percent of their face value. However, demand for these Treasury bonds was extremely heavy due to their expected capital gain at maturity. The Treasury must redeem its bonds at full face value on the maturity date. As a result, while other interest rates in the economy were climbing rapidly, market yields on the low-coupon Treasuries moved up much more slowly than those on higher-coupon securities. Investors were willing to accept lower yields on these securities in return for the prospect of significant capital gains, taxable at a highly favorable rate.

Planning for Capital Gains and Losses.   The favorable tax treatment of long-term capital gains and short-term capital losses encourages investors to carefully plan their purchases and sales of financial instruments. For example, many investors today hold securities for periods longer than normally desired in order to take advantage of the lower tax rate on long-term capital gains. Often capital gains are taken in years of depressed income, while capital losses are sought in high-income years in order to avoid reaching a higher tax bracket and to even out fluctuations in annual income. Capital losses may be taken early in order to offset capital gains earned later on.[2] Frequently, securities are sold via the "installment method" to defer realized capital gains in a given year and keep the investor out of a higher tax bracket. Due to the extreme complexity and constantly changing character of modern tax laws, the wise investor today seeks professional advice from competent tax attorneys and accountants when planning future security sales and purchases.

Tax-Exempt Securities

One of the most controversial tax rules affecting securities is the tax-exemption privilege granted investors in state and local government (municipal) bonds. The interest income earned on municipal bonds is exempt from federal income taxes, and most states exempt interest on their own securities

---

[2] The fact that long-term capital gains are more favorably taxed than short-term gains creates a dilemma for the investor when the market price of a security has made a short-term gain but is now declining. Should he or she sell now and take the short-term gain, which will be taxed as ordinary income (like salary, interest, and dividends), or hold the security for the required one year and one day to secure a long-term gain? As we noted above, 60 percent of a long-term capital gain is excluded from taxable income. If the security's price is dropping, when should the investor sell out to maximize his or her aftertax return?

A formula which has proved useful to many investors is:

$$\begin{array}{ll} \text{Aftertax} & \text{Long-term} & \text{Investor's} \\ \text{short-term} = \text{capital} - 0.40(\text{Long-term capital gain}) \times \text{marginal tax} \\ \text{capital gain} & \text{gain} & \text{rate} \end{array}$$

The investor knows what the short-term capital gain will be if he sells now and knows his current marginal tax rate. It is, then, a relatively simple matter to solve for the long-term gain which will make the above equation balance. The investor will benefit by holding the security as long as the gain does not drop below the calculated long-term capital gain.

from state income taxes.[3] Municipal bonds carry a federal tax-exemption privilege because the U.S. Constitution forbids levying federal taxes against the states and their political subdivisions. In addition, the tax-exempt privilege is a subsidy to induce investors to support local government by financing the construction of schools, highways, bridges, airports, and other needed public projects. The exemption privilege shifts the burden of federal taxation from buyers of municipal bonds to other taxpayers.

What investors benefit from buying municipals? The critical factor here is the *marginal tax rate* (or tax bracket) of the investor—the rate he or she must pay on the last dollar of income received during the tax year. For individual investors, these marginal tax rates range from zero for nontaxpayers to as high as 50 percent for the highest income earners. (See Exhibit 9–2 for an example of marginal tax rates applying to married taxpayers filing a joint tax return.) The marginal rate for corporations is 16 percent on the first $25,000 in taxable profits, 19 percent for taxable profits over $25,000 but less than $50,000, 30 percent for taxable corporate earnings over $50,000 but less than $75,000, 40 percent for earnings exceeding $75,000 but below $100,000, and 46 percent for all taxable profits in excess of $100,000.[4] In recent years, marginal tax rates in the 30 to 40 percent range have represented a break-even level for investors interested in municipal bonds. Investors carrying marginal tax rates above this range generally receive higher after-tax yields from buying tax-exempt securities instead of taxable securities. Below this range, taxable securities generally yield a better after-tax return.

The Effect of Marginal Tax Rates on After-Tax Yields. To illustrate the importance of knowing the investor's marginal tax rate in deciding whether to purchase tax-exempt securities, consider the following example. Assume the current yield to maturity on taxable corporate bonds is 12 percent, while the current tax-exempt yield on municipal bonds of comparable quality and rating is 7 percent. The after-tax yield on these two securities can be compared by using the following formula:

Before-tax yield (1 − Investor's marginal tax rate) = After-tax yield   (9–4)

For an investor in the 28 percent tax bracket (see Exhibit 9–2), the *after-tax* yields on these bonds are:

Taxable Corporate Bond	**Tax-Exempt Municipal Bond**
12% (1 − 0.28) = 8.64%	7% before and after taxes

---

[3] Capital gains earned on municipals are taxable at the capital gains rate. An exception to this rule occurs if a municipal bond is issued at a price below its par value. The appreciation between the original purchase price and par is tax exempt. However, if the price of the bond rises above par, that portion of the gain is fully taxable.

[4] In 1983 and subsequently, the tax rate on corporate taxable income of less than $25,000 decreases to 15 percent, while the tax rate applicable to the $25,000 to $50,000 corporate income bracket drops to 18 percent.

On the basis of yield alone, the investor in the 28 percent tax bracket would prefer the taxable corporate bond.[5]

At what tax rate would an investor be indifferent to whether securities are taxable or tax exempt? In other words, what is the break-even point between these two types of financial instruments?

This point is easily calculated from the formula

$$\text{Tax-exempt yield} = (1 - t) \times \text{Taxable yield} \qquad (9–5)$$

where t is the investor's marginal tax rate. Solving for the break-even tax rate gives

$$t = 1 - \frac{\text{Tax-exempt yield}}{\text{Taxable yield}} \qquad (9–6)$$

Clearly, if the current yield on tax-exempt securities is 6 percent and it is 10 percent on taxable issues, the break-even tax rate is $1 - 0.60$, or 40 percent. An investor in a marginal tax bracket above 40 percent would prefer a tax-exempt security to a taxable one, other factors held equal.

Comparing Taxable and Tax-Exempt Securities. The existence of both taxable and tax-exempt securities complicates the investor's task in trying to choose a suitable portfolio to buy and hold. In order to make valid comparisons between taxable and tax-exempt issues the investor must convert all expected security yields to an *after-tax basis*.

In the case of the yield to maturity on a security, this can be done by using the following formula.

$$P_o = \sum_{i=1}^{n} \frac{I_i(1 - t)}{(1 + a)^i} + \frac{(P_n - P_o)(1 - cg)}{(1 + a)^n} + \frac{P_o}{(1 + a)^n} \qquad (9–7)$$

which equates the current market value (P_o) of the security to the present value of all *after-tax* returns promised in the future. If the security is to be held for n years, I_i is the amount of interest or other income expected each year and t is the marginal income tax rate of the investor. If we assume the security will be sold or redeemed for price P_o at maturity, then $(P_n - P_o)$ measures the expected capital gain on the instrument which, of course, will be taxed at the appropriate capital gains rate, cg. Provided investors know their marginal income tax rate, the capital-gains tax rate, the current price of the security, and the expected distribution of future income from the security, they can easily calculate discount rate a, the after-tax yield to maturity.

As we will note in Chapter 25, the tax-exemption feature has limited the market for municipals essentially to top-income-bracket individuals, commercial banks, and property-casualty insurance companies. These groups all face high tax exposure under current federal rules and therefore generally find municipals an effective tax shelter. It is highly debatable, however, as to whether the exemption feature has aided either state and local governments or local taxpayers.

---

[5] It is important to note that the particular tax brackets favoring the purchase of municipals versus taxable securities change over time due to changes in tax laws and variations in the yield spread between taxable and tax-exempt securities.

Certainly the exemption privilege has lowered the interest rates at which municipals can be sold in the open market relative to taxable bonds, and therefore the amount of interest cost borne by local taxpayers. For example, during 1980 Aaa-rated municipal bonds carried an average yield to maturity of 7.85 percent compared to 11.94 percent on comparable-quality seasoned corporate bonds—a yield spread of more than 4 full percentage points. However, the primary beneficiaries of the exemption privilege are investors who can profitably purchase municipals and escape some portion of the federal tax burden. Other taxpayers must pay higher federal taxes in order to make up for these lost tax revenues. Moreover, by limiting the municipal market to high-tax-bracket investors, the exemption feature has increased the volatility and unpredictability of municipal interest rates and made the job of state and local government fiscal management more difficult.

CONVERTIBLE SECURITIES

Another factor which affects relative rates of return on different securities is *convertibility*. Convertible securities consist of special issues of corporate bonds or preferred stock which entitle the holder to exchange these securities for a specific number of shares of the issuing firm's common stock. Convertibles are frequently called "hybrid securities" because they offer the investor the prospect of both stable income in the form of interest or dividends plus capital gains on common stock, once conversion takes place. The timing of a conversion is purely at the option of the investor; however, the contract agreed to at time of purchase specifies the terms under which conversion may take place. An issuing firm often can "force" conversion of its securities by bringing about a rise in the price of its common stock, because conversion is most likely to occur in a rising market. Conversion is a one-way transaction—once convertibles are exchanged for common stock there is no way back for the investor.

Investors generally pay a *premium* for convertible securities over nonconvertible securities in the form of a higher price and reduced yield. Thus, convertibles will carry a lower rate of return than other securities of comparable quality and maturity issued by the same company. This occurs because the investor in convertibles is granted a hedge against future risk. If security prices fall, the investor still earns a fixed rate of return in the form of interest income from a convertible bond or dividend income from each share of convertible preferred stock. On the other hand, if stock prices rise, the investor can exercise the conversion option and share in any capital gains earned on the company's common stock.

Convertible Bonds

Bonds with the convertible feature are nearly always issued as debentures. A *debenture* is a long-term corporate IOU that is unsecured in the sense that no specific collateral is pledged to support the security in the event of financial problems. Instead, the debenture is backed by the general earning power of the issuing corporation, which promises to pay interest at specified times and return the principal (par) value of the security at maturity. The interest and principal amount owed on a convertible bond must be paid before any dividends are paid on the issuing company's preferred and common stock. Most convertibles are callable bonds and, like other callable bonds, are worth no more than their call price on the day of redemption.

Convertible bonds offer several significant advantages to the issuing company. Due to the conversion feature they can be issued at a lower net interest cost than conventional bonds. Convertibles offer an alternative to issuing more common stock, which a firm may wish to avoid because the additional stock could dilute the equity interest of current stockholders and reduce earnings per share. Moreover, dividends on stock are not deductible from federal income taxes but interest on convertible bonds *is* a deductible expense. Key advantages to the investor include the fact that convertible bonds guarantee the payment of interest (as long as the issuing company remains solvent) and generally appreciate in value when the company's common stock is rising in price. Moreover, there is a floor under the price of a convertible bond—known as its *investment value*—below which its price normally will not fall. This is the price which would produce a yield on the convertible equal to the yield on nonconvertible bonds of the same quality and rating.

In order to understand more fully the advantages and disadvantages of the convertibility feature, several terms need to be mentioned. These terms include the following:

A. *Conversion ratio*—the number of shares the investor receives from exchanging a convertible bond for common stock. For example, it may be stipulated in the bond contract that each $1,000 bond can be converted at the option of the holder into 20 shares of the company's common stock. While the conversion ratio is usually fixed for the life of the bond, some convertibles have a declining conversion ratio over time. And sometimes conversion may be made into either preferred or common stock or into the stock of a firm other than the issuing corporation (such as a parent company).

B. *Conversion price*—that price of the company's stock which, when multiplied by the number of shares of common stock available on conversion, gives the par value of the convertible bond. For example, if each $1,000 bond can be converted into 20 shares of stock, the conversion price must be $50, since 50×20 shares $= $1,000. Obviously, then, the conversion price equals the ratio of the convertible bond's par value to the number of shares of common stock available on conversion.

C. *Conversion value*—the current market value of the total amount of stock available from converting each bond. For example, if 20 shares are available for each $1,000 bond and the company's stock is selling today for $30 per share, the conversion value must be $600.

D. *Conversion premium*—the differential between the conversion value of the company's stock and the current market value of its convertible bond, expressed as a percent of conversion value. For example, suppose the conversion value of the stock is $600 while the bond's market value is $900. Then the conversion premium is clearly 50 percent (i.e., [$900 − $600]/$600 × 100).

E. *Investment value*—as defined previously, the price at which the yield on a convertible bond matches the yield on nonconvertible bonds of the same rating, expressed as a percentage of the bond's par value.

F. *Investment premium*—the differential between the investment value and the current market value of a convertible bond, expressed as a percentage of investment value. For example, if the bond's estimated investment value is $800 and its current market price is $1,000, the investment premium must be 25 percent (i.e., [$1,000 − $800]/$800 × 100).

With these terms in mind, a number of general observations can be made about the conversion and value of convertible bonds:

1. When the market price of a convertible bond exceeds its conversion value, investors are not inclined to convert their bonds into common stock but rather will probably hold the bonds in anticipation of future gains or sell them to another investor. For example, a convertible bond selling today in the market for $900 with a conversion value of $850 will not likely be converted by the investor since that would mean exchanging more value for less at today's price.

2. When the market price of common stock from a company that has issued convertible bonds goes up, the convertible bond's price usually goes up as well. However, the bond's price usually rises more slowly than the stock price due to increasing risk and decreasing yield.

3. When a convertible bond's conversion value equals its market value, conversion of the bond into common stock is more likely. At this point of equality the conversion premium is zero.

4. It is highly unlikely that a convertible bond will sell for less in the market than its conversion value, which acts in the nature of a price floor for the bond. If the market price of the bond temporarily drops below its conversion value, securities dealers will probably purchase the bond and sell the company's stock short.[6]

5. Declining stock prices usually are accompanied by decreasing prices of convertible bonds. However, the bond's price generally declines by a smaller percentage due to its increasing yield.

---

[6] In a *short sale* the seller agrees to deliver securities to a buyer at a specified price but does not presently own the securities sold. Therefore, when delivery must be made, the seller will be forced to buy or borrow the securities in order to fill the buyer's order. Naturally, the seller hopes the securities will fall in price so they can be purchased at a lower price when the delivery date arrives. A seller who can acquire the securities at a cheaper price than that agreed upon by the buyer makes a short-sale profit. However, if the price of securities sold short rises, then a short-sale loss will occur.

Convertible bonds have been exceedingly popular securities in recent years. The number of convertibles listed on the New York Stock Exchange nearly doubled during the 1970s. Firms issuing convertible bonds in recent years number among the largest corporations in the United States, including such firms as Alcoa, American Motors, Chase Manhattan Corporation, General Telephone, RCA, U.S. Steel Corporation, and United Airlines. Convertibles are generally regarded as a more conservative investment than purchasing the stock of the same company because they offer less risk than the stock. They also provide less potential return than the stock, of course; nevertheless, convertibles permit an investor to get "a piece of the action" in the stock market without actually holding stock.

Convertible Preferred Stock

Convertible preferred stock is similar in conversion features and market behavior to convertible bonds. Each share of convertible preferred is usually exchangeable for a fixed number of shares (or fractional shares) of common stock issued by the same company. Unlike convertible bonds, convertible preferred represents an ownership share in a company and will earn nothing if the firm's board of directors decides not to vote a dividend. Moreover, in the event of liquidation, preferred stockholders have a lower-priority claim on the issuing company's assets than do bondholders and general creditors. Therefore, convertible preferred stock is generally regarded as a more risky investment than convertible bonds.

Nevertheless, preferred shares offer the potential for greater price appreciation than do most convertible bonds and a greater guarantee of annual income than is available with common stock issued by the same company. Issues of convertible preferred have grown quite rapidly in recent years, and more than 200 issues are now listed on the New York Stock Exchange. Among the more prominent companies which have issued convertible preferred in the recent past are American Telephone & Telegraph, the Columbia Broadcasting System, Household Finance Corporation, Occidental Petroleum, RCA, and Union Oil of California.

SUMMARY AND CONCLUSIONS

As we conclude this chapter, it is important to gain some perspective on the fundamental purpose of this section of the book. In reality, Chapters 6, 7, 8, and 9 should be viewed as a unit, tied together by a common subject— what determines the level of and changes in interest rates and security yields. In Chapter 6 we argued that there is one interest rate which underlies all interest rates and is a component of all rates. This is the risk-free (or pure) rate of interest, which is a measure of the opportunity cost of holding money. All other interest rates are scaled upward by varying degrees from the risk-free rate, depending upon such factors as the term (maturity) of a loan, the risk of borrower default, and the marketability, callability, convertibility, and tax status of the security which evidences a loan. One interest rate differs from another because the securities to which those rates apply do differ in terms of maturity, risk, taxability, and other factors. However, the interest rates attached to all securities have the risk-free rate in common.

The risk-free interest rate itself may change in response to fluctuations in economic conditions, inflation, or government policy. And, when that happens, *all* interest rates will tend to move in the same direction, though by varying degrees due to differences in callability, convertibility, maturity, tax status, etc. The risk-free rate of interest is really an *anchor* for the entire structure of interest rates in the financial markets. Changes in the risk-free rate set the tone and the trend in credit market conditions faced daily by borrowers and lenders. In the next chapter we examine the sources of information used by many participants in the financial markets today to follow short- and long-term movements in interest rates and credit conditions.

STUDY QUESTIONS

1. Define the term *marketability*. Explain its importance to the securities investor and its relationship to the yield on a financial instrument.

2. What is a call privilege? Why is this privilege an advantage to the security issuer and a disadvantage to the investor?

3. What types of risk are encountered by the investor in callable securities? Does the coupon rate on a bond influence its call risk?

4. What is the principal determinant of the size of the call premium on callable securities?

5. Which kinds of securities are favored by current U.S. tax laws? Explain why these particular financial instruments are given favorable tax treatment.

6. What is a capital gain, and how exactly is it treated for tax purposes? How are net losses on security investments treated for tax purposes?

7. What portion of the income generated by municipal bonds is tax exempt, and what portion is taxable under federal law? Why do you think the law is structured this way? Should it be?

8. Explain the relationship between the investor's marginal tax rate and after-tax yields on corporate and municipal bonds. Would municipal bonds be a worthwhile investment for you today? Why?

9. Define the term *convertibility*. Why are convertibles sometimes called "hybrid securities"? Convertible bonds typically carry lower yields than nonconvertible bonds of the same maturity and risk class. Explain why this is true.

10. Define the following terms: *conversion ratio, conversion price, conversion value, conversion premium, investment value,* and *investment premium*. Explain their relationship to the decision of an investor to exchange a convertible security for common stock.

SELECTED REFERENCES

1. Bowlin, Oswald D. "The Refunding Decision: Another Special Case in Capital Budgeting." *Journal of Finance,* March 1966, pp. 55–68.
2. Caks, John. "The Coupon Effect on Yield to Maturity." *Journal of Finance,* March 1977, pp. 103–16.
3. Colin, J. W., and Richard S. Bayer. "Calculation of Tax Effective Yields for Discount Instruments." *Journal of Financial and Quantitative Analysis,* June 1970, pp. 265–73.
4. Cook, Timothy Q. "Some Factors Affecting Long-Term Yield Spreads in Recent Years." *Monthly Review,* Federal Reserve Bank of Richmond, September 1973, pp. 2–14.
5. Jen, Frank C., and James E. Wert. "The Deferred Call Provision and Corporate Bond Yields." *Journal of Financial and Quantitative Analysis,* June 1968, pp. 157–69.
6. ———. "The Effect of Call Risk on Corporate Bond Yields." *Journal of Finance,* December 1967, pp. 637–51.
7. ———. "The Value of the Deferred Call Privilege." *The National Banking Review,* March 1966, pp. 369–78.
8. McCollum, John S. "The Impact of the Capital Gains Tax on Bond Yields." *National Tax Journal,* December 1973, pp. 575–83.
9. McCulloch, J. Huston. "The Tax-Adjusted Yield Curve." *Journal of Finance,* June 1975, pp. 811–30.
10. Pye, Gordon. "On the Tax Structure of Interest Rates." *Quarterly Journal of Economics,* November 1969, pp. 562–79.
11. ———. "The Value of Call Deferment on a Bond: Some Empirical Results." *Journal of Finance,* December 1967, pp. 623–36.
12. ———. "The Value of the Call Option on a Bond." *Journal of Political Economy,* April 1966, pp. 200–205.

10

Sources of Information for Financial Decision Making

Every day in the money and capital markets, individuals and institutions must make important financial decisions. For those who plan to borrow funds, for example, key decisions must be made concerning the timing of a request for credit and exactly where the necessary funds should be raised. Lenders of funds must make decisions on when and where to invest their limited resources, considering such factors as the risk, marketability, and expected return on securities available in the financial marketplace. Government policymakers also are intimately involved in the financial decision-making process. It is the responsibility of government to ensure that the financial markets function smoothly in channeling savings into investment and in creating a volume of credit sufficient to support business and commerce. Government financial policy is aimed at stabilizing the financial system while, at the same time, promoting full employment, price stability, satisfactory economic growth, and a sustainable balance of payments position with the rest of the world. Central banks around the world, including the Federal Reserve System in the United States, must make decisions each day on whether to enter the marketplace and buy or sell securities in order to influence interest rates and credit availability.[1]

Sound financial decisions require adequate financial information. Borrowers, lenders, and those who make financial policy require data on the prices and yields attached to individual securities today and those likely to prevail in the future. A borrower, for example, may decide to postpone the taking

---

[1] We discuss central banking and the operations of the Federal Reserve System in Chapters 21 through 23.

out of a loan or to shorten the maturity of current borrowings if it appears that the cost of credit will be significantly lower six months from now than it is today. Those who wish to forecast future interest rates and security prices need information concerning the projected supply of new securities brought to market and the expected demand for those securities. Since economic conditions exert a profound impact upon the financial markets, the financial decision maker must also be aware of vital economic data series which reflect employment, prices, industrial output, spending on goods and services, the volume of savings flows, changes in business inventories, business capital expansion plans, and related types of information.

What are the principal sources of financial information? Where do financial decision makers go to find the data they need? Obviously, different sources must be consulted depending upon the needs of each decision maker. Certain sources specialize in providing data on security prices and interest rates, while others are more relevant for information concerning general credit conditions and the health of the nation's economy. We may divide the sources of information relied upon by financial decision makers into five broad groups: (1) bond prices and yields, (2) stock prices and dividend yields, (3) the financial condition of individual issuers of securities, (4) general economic and financial conditions, and (5) social accounting data. In the following sections we discuss some of the most important sources of these kinds of financial and economic information.

BOND PRICES AND YIELDS

One of the most important securities traded in the financial system is the *bond*. As noted in previous chapters, bonds are debt obligations issued by governments and corporations, usually in units (par values) of $1,000. While bonds generally pay a fixed rate of return to the investor in the form of coupon income, bond prices fluctuate widely as interest rates change. Therefore, while bonds are often referred to as fixed-income securities, the investor may experience significant capital gains or losses on these securities as their prices change. All bonds issued in the United States today carry a set maturity date, at which time the issuer must pay the bondholder the security's par value. Bonds are generally identified by the name of the issuing company or governmental unit, their coupon rate, and the maturity date.

Quotations of prices and yields on bonds actively traded in the financial markets are available from a wide variety of published sources. Major securities dealers trading in bonds publish *quote sheets* showing the market prices, yields, and amounts of bonds outstanding. A sample page from a major bond dealer's quote sheet is shown in Exhibit 10–1. This particular exhibit presents price quotations on U.S. Treasury bonds and notes posted by First Boston Corporation, one of the nation's leading securities dealers.[2]

---

[2] As we will see in Chapter 24, Treasury notes carry original-issue maturities of 1 to 10 years, while bills must mature within 1 year. Treasury bonds can carry any maturity, but usually exceed 10 years.

The prices shown for each security issue—identified by its coupon rate and date of maturity—are quoted in terms of $100 par value.

As noted in Chapter 7, the market prices of bonds generally are expressed in 32nds of a dollar and sometimes in 64ths, indicated by a plus (+) sign. Both bid and asked prices are posted by the dealer, who will purchase securities at the bid price but sell to customers at the asked price.[3] Yields are computed against the asked price and are generally figured to maturity when the security is selling at a discount. When the security is selling at a premium over par and has various possible maturity dates, the yield is generally figured to the nearest maturity date.[4] New prices and yields must be posted daily by dealers because demand and supply factors continually alter the price and return on individual securities.

To illustrate the kinds of information displayed in a dealer's quote sheet, let us examine the first entry in Exhibit 10–1. The security represented there is a U.S. Treasury note bearing an 8½ percent coupon rate. It was issued July 31, 1978, and matured July 31, 1980. However, on June 30, 1980, when this security was a month away from reaching final maturity, the dealer was willing to buy (bid) the note at $100^2/_{32}$ and sell it at $100^4/_{32}$. Because each 32nd equals $0.03125 per $100, this coupon security would sell for $100.125 assuming a par value of $100, or $1,001.25 for a $1,000 par-value security. Its yield to maturity at that price would be 6.68 percent before federal income taxes and 3.61 percent after taxes for a corporation subject to maximum federal tax rates. A total of about $3,337 million of these Treasury notes was held by the public at the time these quotations were published. An investor interested in this particular note would, of course, want to compare one dealer's asked price with the prices posted by other dealers.

Financial newspapers report daily quotations on the most actively traded bonds and other securities. Most daily newspapers contain a list of prices for bonds traded on the New York and American stock exchanges. One of the most complete listings of daily price and yield quotations appears in *The Wall Street Journal* (*WSJ*), published by Dow Jones. *WSJ* reports the prices of securities traded on the major securities exchanges and also issues sold over the counter (OTC). Exhibit 10–2 shows the prices of corporate bonds traded on the New York Stock Exchange on August 15, 1980, as reported in *The Wall Street Journal*. In these quotations, bonds are priced in dollars and fractions of a dollar (in this case, down to one eighth of a dollar, or $0.125), assuming a $100 par value. For example, we note that bonds issued by AMF Corporation, carrying a coupon rate of 10 percent and due to mature in 1985, traded the previous business day at a high and low price of 91½ and closed at that price. This means that, when trading ended on the date indicated, the

---

[3] Dealer quotations like those shown in Exhibit 10–1 are generally for purchases and sales of *round lots,* consisting of at least 100 securities. Additional service charges or price adjustments are made for smaller (odd-lot) transactions.

[4] The yield-to-maturity concept assumes the investor will hold the security until final maturity. (See Chapter 7 for a discussion of yield to maturity.) After-tax yields generally are figured using a 46 percent corporate profits tax rate on coupon income and a 28 percent corporate tax rate on long-term capital gains.

EXHIBIT 10–1
Dealer Quotation Sheet for U.S. Treasury Securities

United States Treasury Securities

First Boston

20 Exchange Place New York N.Y 10005

NEW YORK	ATLANTA	BOSTON	CHICAGO	CLEVELAND	DALLAS	LOS ANGELES	PHILADELPHIA	SAN FRANCISCO
(212) 825-2000	(404) 658-9000	(617) 542-7200	(312) 372-8840	(216) 696-8822	(214) 742-2900	(213) 485-9898	(215) 972-1700	(415) 981-0700

U.S. TREASURY NOTES AND BONDS

Coupon	Maturity	Bid	Asked	Chg.	Yield to Mat. *	Yield After Tax ⊕	Corp. Tax Equiv	Yield Value Per 1/32	1979 Range High	1979 Range Low	Amt. Pub Held	Dated Date
N 8 1/2	7-31-80	100- 2	100- 4	.....	6.68	3.61	6.68	.1803	100- 4	96-30	5337	7-31-78
N 6 3/4	8-15-80	99-25	99-27	.....	7.85	4.24	7.85	.2549	99-30	95-30	3445	8-15-77
N 9	8-15-80	99-31	100- 3	- 3	7.95	4.29	7.95	.2522	100- 8	96-28	1612	8-15-74
N 8 3/8	8-31-80	99-29	99-31	- 3	8.33	4.50	8.33	.1900	100- 6	96- 8	2993	8-31-78
N 6 7/8	9-30-80	99-18	99-20	- 4	8.29	4.46	8.29	.1286	99-28	94- 2	1988	9-14-76
N 8 5/8	9-30-80	99-30	100- 0	- 2	8.44	4.56	8.44	.1270	100-13	95-20	3180	10- 2-78
N 8 7/8	10-31-80	100- 2	100- 4	.....	8.36	4.51	8.36	.0961	100-19	95-12	3373	1-31-78
B 3 1/2	11-15-80	98- 8	98-16	.....	7.64	4.13	7.64	.0873	98-16	92-10	1129	10- 3-60
N 7 1/8	11-15-80	99-12	99-16	- 2	8.44	4.56	8.44	.0868	99-28	94- 0	1840	11-15-77
N 9 1/4	11-30-80	100- 8	100-12	- 7	8.24	4.45	8.24	.0778	100-28	95- 6	2872	11-30-78
N 5 7/8	12-31-80	98-26	98-30	- 2	8.11	4.38	8.11	.0664	99- 9	92- 8	2654	12- 7-76
N 9 7/8	12-31-80	100-18	100-22	-10	8.42	4.55	8.42	.0653	101-11	95-12	3005	1- 2-79
N 9 3/4	1-31-81	100-22	100-26	- 6	8.26	4.46	8.26	.0550	101-10	94-28	2725	1-31-79
N 7	2-15-81	99- 0	99- 4	- 5	8.45	4.56	8.45	.0528	99-23	92-24	1281	2-15-74
N 7 3/8	2-15-81	99- 5	99- 9	- 3	8.56	4.62	8.56	.0528	99-30	92-21	3696	2-18-75
N 9 3/4	2-28-81	100-25	100-29	- 3	8.28	4.47	8.28	.0489	101-14	94-16	2483	2-28-79
N 6 7/8	3-31-81	98-27	98-31	- 4	8.31	4.49	8.31	.0444	99-15	91-26	2590	3- 8-77
N 8 5/8	3-31-81	100-24	100-28	- 2	8.35	4.51	8.35	.0406	101-18	94- 6	2810	4- 9-79
N 9 3/4	4-30-81	100-28	101- 1	- 7	8.40	4.54	8.40	.0393	101-31	93-27	2834	4-30-79
N 7 3/8	5-15-81	99- 2	99- 6	- 5	8.35	4.51	8.35	.0382	99-28	91-13	1829	1-26-76
N 7 1/2	5-15-81	99- 4	99- 8	- 4	8.39	4.53	8.39	.0382	99-30	91-13	2826	2-15-78
N 9 3/4	5-31-81	100-30	101- 2	- 7	8.50	4.59	8.50	.0359	102- 2	93-18	2178	5-31-79
N 6 3/4	6-30-81	99-12	99-16	- 5	8.35	4.51	8.35	.0337	99- 4	89-22	2434	6- 5-77
N 9 1/8	6-30-81	99-18	99-22	- 6	9.46	5.11	9.46	.0337	101-13	92- 9	2726	7- 2-79
N 9 3/8	7-31-81	100-24	100-28	- 8	8.62	4.65	8.62	.0307	101-22	92-16	2911	7-31-79
N 7	8-15-81	98-20	98-28	-16	8.06	4.54	8.41	.0299	99-12	89- 8	397	8-15-71
N 7 5/8	8-15-81	98-26	98-30	- 6	8.63	4.84	8.96	.0300	99-24	90- 8	2230	7- 9-76
N 8 3/8	8-15-81	99-26	99-30	- 3	8.42	4.55	8.43	.0298	100-26	91- 2	2748	8-15-78
N 9 5/8	8-31-81	100-26	101- 0	- 4	8.68	4.69	8.68	.0285	102- 2	92-19	3165	8-31-79
N 6 3/4	9-30-81	97-24	97-24	-10	8.68	5.03	9.32	.0274	98-26	88- 4	2837	9- 7-77
N10	9-30-81	101-16	101-30	- 3	8.43	4.55	8.63	.0265	102-22	93- 2	3290	1- 9-79
N12 5/8	10-15-81	104-15	104-19	- 7	8.86	4.78	8.86	.0245	105-28	95-19	5891	10-31-79
N 7	11-15-81	97-20	97-24	-10	8.77	5.05	9.36	.0250	98-22	88- 0	2427	10-12-76
N 7 3/4	11-15-81	98-20	98-24	-10	8.72	4.89	9.05	.0248	99-22	88-12	2609	11-15-74
N12 1/8	11-30-81	104- 9	104-13	- 5	8.72	4.71	8.72	.0232	105-16	94-17	4268	11-30-79
N 7 1/4	12-31-81	97-24	97-28	- 9	8.80	5.03	9.31	.0231	99- 0	87-12	3275	12- 7-77
N11 3/8	12-31-81	103-10	103-14	- 4	8.74	4.79	8.87	.0222	104-23	93-12	3736	12-31-79
N11 1/2	1-31-82	103-13	103-17	- 7	9.09	4.88	9.04	.0211	105- 0	93-12	4046	1-31-80
N 6 1/8	2-15-82	96- 6	96-10	- 7	8.64	5.12	9.48	.0215	97- 8	85-30	2638	1- 6-77
B 6 3/8	2-15-82	96- 4	96-12	-12	8.81	5.20	9.63	.0216	97-10	86-16	1669	2-15-72
N13 7/8	2-28-82	106-30	106-34	-14	9.25	5.09	9.25	.0197	108-22	97-12	3972	2-29-80
N 7 7/8	3-31-82	98- 0	98- 4	-14	9.05	5.10	9.44	.0199	99- 6	87- 6	2608	3- 6-76
N15	3-31-82	108-28	109- 1	-13	9.25	4.99	9.25	.0186	110-18	99-12	3513	3-31-80
11 3/8	4-30-82	103-13	103-17	-10	9.21	4.98	9.21	.0184	105- 7	99-27	4095	4-30-80
N 7	5-15-82	96-22	96-26	- 6	8.88	5.13	9.51	.0189	98-10	85-24	2560	4- 4-77
N 8	5-15-82	98-12	98-20	-14	8.80	4.90	9.07	.0186	99-24	87-12	1297	5-15-75
N 9 1/4	5-15-82	100-12	100-20	- 6	8.87	4.79	8.87	.0184	101-30	90- 0	2537	11-15-78
N 9 3/8	5-15-82	100- 8	100-12	- 9	9.15	4.94	9.15	.0181	102- 1	100- 6	4000	6- 4-80
N 8 1/8	6-30-82	98-20	98-28	-14	8.88	4.91	9.09	.0175	100- 8	87-28	2478	6- 7-78
W1 5/8	6-30-82	99- 4	99- 8	- 9	9.04	4.96	9.18	.0175	100-11	99- 4	N/A	6-30-80
N 8 1/8	8-15-82	98- 8	98-16	-14	8.91	4.89	9.17	.0166	99-20	86-24	1754	8-15-75
N 9	8-15-82	99-28	100- 4	- 8	8.92	4.82	8.92	.0165	101-14	87-22	2516	8-15-79
N 8 3/8	9-30-82	98- 4	98-12	- 8	9.15	5.10	9.45	.0158	100- 1	86-12	2432	9- 6-78
N 7 1/8	11-15-82	95-16	95-24	-20	9.15	5.31	9.93	.0153	97-20	84- 0	2509	10-17-77
N 7 7/8	11-15-82	97- 6	97-14	- 2	9.09	5.13	9.50	.0151	99- 4	85- 8	2122	11-17-75
N 9 3/8	12-31-82	100-16	100-16	-10	9.14	4.94	9.14	.0142	102- 0	88-12	2746	1- 2-79
N 8	2-15-83	96-28	97- 4	- 4	9.25	5.22	9.67	.0139	99- 2	84-16	5820	2-17-76
N 9 1/4	5-15-83	99-26	100- 2	- 6	9.21	4.97	9.21	.0131	102- 4	88- 0	2921	5- 5-79
N 7 7/8	5-15-83	96-18	96-26	-10	9.16	5.17	9.58	.0128	98-20	84- 0	2466	4- 5-78

SOURCE: The First Boston Corporation, *Handbook of Securities of the United States Government and Federal Agencies*, 29th ed., 1980, p. 220.

CLOSING QUOTATIONS— MON., JUNE 30, 1980   YIELDS FOR DELIVERY— WEDS., JULY 2, 1980

U.S. Treasury Notes and Bonds are exempt from state and local income taxes. They are subject to all federal income taxes.

*Yield to first call for callable issues quoted at a premium.

As of 11/30/79 Issue Date if Later
* Amounts in millions.

Yield after corporate tax of 48%. For obligations selling at a discount from par and which are more than twelve months from maturity, effect is given to the corporate capital gains tax of 28%.

EXHIBIT 10–2
Bond Price and Yield Quotations from *The Wall Street Journal*

CORPORATION BONDS
Volume, $16,130,000

Bonds	Cur Yld	Vol	High	Low	Close	Net Chg
AMF 10s85	11.	20	91½	91½	91½	+ ⅜
APL 10¾97	14.	20	75	75	75	– ½
ARA 4⅝s96	cv	14	57	57	57	– ½
AbbtL 6¼93	8.6	23	73	72⅞	72⅞	+1¾
AetnCr 8¾83	9.2	1	95	95	95	+1½
AetnCr 9¾86	11.	2	90	90	90	–3
AlaP 8½s01	13.	28	68	66¼	68	+1¼
AlaP 8⅞s03	13.	65	66¾	66¼	66¾	+ ¼
AlaP 8¼s03	13.	25	66	66	66	+3½
AlaP 9¾s04	13.	20	73	72¼	73	+ ⅞
AlaP 10½05	13.	3	78⅛	78⅛	78⅛	–3½
AlaP 8⅞06	13.	3	67⅞	67⅞	67⅞	+2⅞
AlaP 9¼07	13.	6	70	69½	69½	– ½
AlaP 9⅝08	13.	13	72	72	72	– ½
AlaP 12⅝10	14.	40	92⅜	92⅛	92¼	+ ¼
Alexn 5½96	cv	20	50	49½	49½	– ½
AllgL 4s81	cv	5	101¼	101¼	101¼	–2¼
Allen 11½94	cv	17	170	170	170	+1¾
AlsCha 12s90	12.	1	98½	98½	98½	–1⅜
AllstF 9⅝86	11.	6	91	91	91	.....
Alcoa 5¼s91	cv	7	122¼	122¼	122¼	–1
Alcoa 6s92	9.2	3	65	65	65	+2⅜
Alcoa 9s95	11.	5	83¾	83¾	83¾	.....
Alcoa 9.45s00	12.	10	82	82	82	–6¾
AluCa 9½95	11.	9	85½	85½	85½	+2½
AMAX 8s86	9.0	11	89⅜	88½	88½	.....
AHes 6¾96	9.3	10	72½	72½	72½	– ½
AFoP 4.8s87	7.0	5	68¾	68¾	68¾	– ¼
AAirl 4¼92	8.5	59	50	48⅛	50	– ½
ACeM 6¾91	cv	20	64	63½	63½	– ½
ACyan 7⅜01	11.	3	68	68	68	–3
AExC 9½s82	9.6	20	98¾	98¾	98¾	– ½
AExC 7.7s87	9.5	27	81	80⅝	81	+1
AHosp 5¾99	cv	63	138	137	137⅞	+1⅜
AmMed 8s00	cv	3	127	126	127	+3⅞
AmMot 6s88	cv	1	70	70	70	– ½
ATT 2¾s82	3.0	31	91½	91⅛	91½	– ½
ATT 3¼s84	4.0	7	81¼	81¼	81¼	+ ½
ATT 4⅜s85	5.5	5	79⅞	79⅞	79⅞	– ⅛
ATT 3⅞s90	6.4	65	60⅞	60½	60⅞	+ ⅛
ATT 8¾00	11.	129	80⅞	80⅛	80⅛	– ⅝
ATT 7s01	11.	90	67	66	66½	–1⅛
ATT 7⅛s03	11.	49	67⅝	66¾	66¾	– ¾
ATT 8.80s05	11.	130	79⅝	78⅞	79⅝	+ ⅜
ATT 7¾s82	8.0	16	96½	96⅜	96⅜	–1
ATT 8⅝s07	11.	18	78⅜	77½	78⅜	+ ⅜
ATT 10⅜90	11.	108	95¾	95⅛	95¾	+ ¼
Amfac 5¼94	cv	3	81⅝	81⅝	81⅝	– ⅜
AMP 8⅝s85	9.9	5	86¾	86¾	86¾	– ¼
Ampx 5½94	cv	55	71½	70½	71½	+1½
AppP 11⅛83	11.	4	100⅛	100⅛	100⅛	– ⅜
AppP 11s82	11.	5	100	100	100	– ½
AppP 11s87	12.	2	95	95	95	–3
Arco 8.70s81	8.9	11	98½	97⅞	97⅞	– ⅝
Arco 8s82	8.3	20	96¾	96⅜	96⅜	– ⅝
Arco 8⅜s83	8.9	1	94	94	94	.....
Arco 8s84	8.6	10	93	93	93	+ ½
Arco 7½82	8.0	37	93¾	93¼	93⅝	+ ⅜
Arco 7¾86	9.2	45	84⅝	84	84	–2½
ArizP 9½s82	9.6	38	98⅞	97¾	98⅞	+ ⅜
ArCk 8.45s84	9.3	5	91	91	91	+ ⅜
AshO 8.2s02	12.	30	70	70	70	– ⅝
AsCp 8⅝81	8.7	25	98¾	98¾	98¾	.....
Atchsn 4s95	6.9	20	58	54	58	+2
AvcoC 5½93	cv	16	63½	63¼	63¼	– ¼
AvcoC 7½93	12.	4	62¾	62¾	62¾	– ½
AvcoC 12s90	13.	5	92	92	92	– ¾
AvcoF 7⅞89	10.	4	76⅝	76⅝	76⅝	.....
AvcoF 8½s84	9.4	10	90¼	90¼	90¼	+ ¼
AvcoF 8⅞91	12.	2	75⅛	75⅛	75⅛	+1⅞
BldwU 10s09	13.	10	76	76	76	+1
Bally 6s98	cv	46	102½	100½	100½	–2
BalGE 10s82	10.	13	99⅞	99⅞	99⅞	+ ⅛
BalGE 9⅞05	12.	1	84	84	84	– ½
BkCal 6½96	cv	30	102	100¾	102	+2¼
BkNY 6¼94	cv	15	95	94	95	+1
Banka 7⅞03	12.	9	64	64	64	–6
Banka 8⅞05	12.	18	75¾	75¼	75¾	+ ½
Banka 8¾01	11.	7	77	75	77	+1
BnkTr 8⅛99	11.	5	71	69	71	+2
BnkTr 8⅝02	12.	25	74½	74½	74½	+1⅞
BecD 4⅛s88	cv	10	85¼	85¼	85¼	– ¼
Belco 4¾s88	cv	5	130	130	130	+7

New York Exchange Bonds

Friday, Aug. 15, 1980

Total Volume $16,320,000

	Domestic Fri	Domestic Thurs	All Issues Fri	All Issues Thurs
Issues traded	800	752	812	764
Advances	315	282	318	288
Declines	326	292	331	298
Unchanged ..	159	178	163	178
New highs ...	22	19	22	19
New lows	13	9	14	9

SALES SINCE JANUARY 1

1980	1979	1978
$3,089,286,000	$2,204,429,000	$2,940,487,000

Dow Jones Bond Averages

–1978– High	–1978– Low	–1979– High	–1979– Low	–1980– High	–1980– Low		FRIDAY –1980–	FRIDAY –1979–	FRIDAY –1978–
90.86	84.54	86.10	73.35	76.61	63.87	20 Bonds	70.24 – .20	86.01 + .15	88.85 – .05
95.00	86.27	88.60	72.40	78.63	61.37	10 Utilities	70.92 + .06	88.21 + .24	92.33 – .17
86.79	82.78	84.28	74.25	74.92	66.03	10 Industrial	69.57 – .46	83.82 + .07	85.37 + .06

Bonds	Cur Yld	Vol	High	Low	Close	Net Chg
ElPas 6s93A	cv	4	123	123	123	–1
Ens 9¾s95	11.	2	88	88	88	+2½
EqutG 9s96	12.	30	76⅝	75½	75½	–1
EssxC 11⅜98	14.	17	83½	83½	83½	+1½
Exxon 6s97	9.5	113	63¼	63	63⅛	+ ⅛
ExxP 7.65s83	8.1	15	95	95	95	+1½
ExxP 8¼01	11.	7	76	76	76	.....
FMC 4¼92	cv	2	69⅛	69⅛	69⅛	– ⅛
FMCF 9½83	10.	5	93⅛	93⅛	93⅛	– ⅞
Farah 5s94	cv	1	42	42	42	+1
Feddr 5s96	cv	2	38½	38	38	.....
Feddr 8⅞94	14.	3	62⅜	61⅝	62⅜	+ ¾
FedN 4⅜s96	cv	2	78	78	78	– ¾
Filmwy 11s98	16.	1	70	70	70	– ¼
Filmwy 10s99	16.	6	64⅜	64⅜	64⅜	–1⅛
Finan 10¼90	11.	4	89½	89½	89½	– ⅛
FinCpA 6s88	9.2	2	65½	65½	65½	.....
Firest 8½83	9.5	25	89⅝	89⅝	89⅝	– ⅞
FBkSy 8¾83	9.4	15	94	93½	93½	–1½
FstChi 6¾80	6.8	50	99⅜	99⅜	99⅜	.....
FstChi 7¾86	9.2	8	83⅞	83⅞	83⅞	+2⅞
FtNBo 8s82	8.5	5	94½	94½	94½	– ¾
FtNBo 10.65s87	11.	3	98½	98½	98½	– ½
FishF 6½94	cv	10	62¼	62¼	62¼	.....
FlaPL 8⅞82	9.1	5	97	97	97	.....
FlaPL 10¾81	11.	5	101	101	101	.....
FlyTigr 9s91	11.	4	80	80	80	+1¾
Ford 8⅛90	11.	15	75½	75½	75½	+1½
Ford 9¼94	13.	11	75¾	73½	73½	–1¼
Ford 14¼90	13.	10	106	106	106	– ½
FrdC 8⅞90N	11.	5	79	79	79	–1
FrdC 4⅞98	cv	29	60	60	60	–1
FrdC 8⅜82	8.9	35	94½	94	94½	+1¾
FrdC 9¾81	9.8	45	100¼	99¾	100	+ ¼
FrdC 8⅝83	9.3	15	94⅝	93	93	– ¾
FrdC 9.7s00	12.	6	79½	79½	79½	.....
FrdC 8⅝86	10.	30	84½	83	83	.....
FrdC 9⅛01	12.	10	73½	73½	73½	–1¼
FrdC 8.1s84	9.5	21	87	85⅝	85⅝	– ½
FrdC 7⅞89	11.	49	72½	71	72½	+2⅜
FrdC 8⅜84	9.9	11	85½	84⅜	84⅜	–5⅛
FrdC 8½88	11.	9	78⅞	78⅞	78⅞	+2⅛
FrdC 9½85	11.	44	89½	89¼	89½	– ½
FrdC 9.55s89	12.	25	79	79	79	–3
FoMcK 6s94	cv	40	95½	95	95	.....
Fruf 5½94	cv	2	68	68	68	.....
Fuqua 9½98	14.	14	70⅛	69¼	69¼	– ⅛
Gamb 10s89	11.	2	88	88	88	–1⅞
Gelco 14⅝99	15.	76	97	96⅞	96⅞	+ ⅝
GnEl 5.3s92	7.9	4	67	67	67	.....
GnEl 7½96	9.8	5	76¾	76¾	76¾	+2
GnEl 8½04	11.	5	79	79	79	.....
GElCr 8.6s85	9.5	21	91	91	91	

Bonds	Cur Yld	Vol	High	Low	Close	Net Chg
MohD 5½94	cv	7	59½	59½	59½	+ ½
Mons 9⅛00	11.	2	79½	79½	79½	+ ½
MntWC 9s89	11.	2	80¾	80¾	80¾	– ¼
Morgn 4¾98	cv	27	65¾	65	65	– ⅜
Morgn 8s86	9.1	15	88	88	88	+1
MtSTl 7⅜11	12.	5	65½	64	64	–3¾
MtSTl 9⅝15	12.	5	81⅝	81⅝	81⅝	+ ⅝
MtSTl 8.7s81	8.9	15	98¼	98¼	98¼	+ ⅛
MtSTl 8⅝18	12.	20	73⅛	73	73⅛	–1⅜
MtStTl 11¼19	12.	10	96	96	96	–1¼
Murph 7⅜97	12.	10	62	62	62	–4½
NCNB 8.495	12.	10	73	73	73	+3½
NCNB 8⅜99	12.	3	71½	71½	71½	–1
NCity 5½88	cv	16	65¼	65	65¼	+ ¼
NHom 4¾96	cv	1	36½	36½	36½	+ ⅛
NtMed 12¾00	14.	5	92	92	92	+1
NRUt 9⅛s85	9.7	10	94	94	94	.....
NStl 8⅜06	12.	6	68	67½	67½	–1½
NEnT 8⅝09	12.	39	74¼	73¼	73¼	–1
NEnT 7⅜07	11.	13	64¼	62½	64¼	+ ¼
NEnT 8s03	11.	115	70⅜	68⅜	70⅜	+1⅜
NEnT 12.20s17	12.	111	98⅝	98	98⅝	+ ⅛
NJBTl 7¼11	11.	3	63⅝	63⅝	63⅝	+ ⅝
NJBTl 7⅜12	11.	2	65	65	65	–3¾
NJBTl 8¾18	12.	1	76	76	76	.....
NYBS 11.30s81	11.	26	100⅛	100⅛	100⅛	.
vjNYH 4s07f	..	66	92	91¾	92	+ ½
NYEG 7⅝81	7.9	10	97	97	97	.....
NYEG 9⅜05	13.	13	75½	75	75	– ¾
NYTl 4½91	7.8	3	58	58	58	+ ⅜
NYTl 4⅛93	7.6	2	54½	54½	54½	+1½
NYTl 3⅜96	7.6	10	44¼	44¼	44¼	+ ⅜
NYTl 7¾06	12.	5	67⅜	67⅜	67⅜	+ ⅜
NYTl 8s08	11.	15	71	70	71	+2⅛
NYTl 7⅜11	12.	10	64	64	64	–1¼
NYTl 8.3s12	12.	10	72⅛	72⅛	72⅛	.....
NYTel 9s14	12.	10	77	77	77	+ ⅛
NYTel 8s83	8.6	10	93	93	93	.....
NiMP 4⅞87	7.5	5	65	65	65	–3
NiMP 12.6s81	12.	13	102⅝	101½	101⅝	–1⅛
NoAPh 4s92	cv	12	70	70	70	.....
NoIllG 8½83	9.0	8	94¾	94	94	–2
NoNG 9s85	9.8	20	91⅜	91⅜	91⅜	– ⅝
NoPac 4s97	9.2	1	43½	43½	43½	.....
NoPac 3s47	9.2	2	32½	32½	32½	.....
NoSP 3⅛s84	4.1	3	75⅜	75⅜	75⅜	.....
NwBn 6¾03	cv	1	91	91	91	+2
NwBn 16.05s89	17.	20	93	93	93	– ¼
NwnBl 7⅞11	12.	10	68¼	68¼	68¼	+ ¼
NwnBl 10s14	12.	8	85	85	85	– ⅛
NwnBl 9½16	12.	40	82⅜	81	81½	+ ¼
NwnMu 6s91	cv	8	64	64	64	+ ¼

SOURCE: *The Wall Street Journal,* August 18, 1980.

AMF bonds were selling for $915 for a $1,000 par-value security. This closing price was ⅜ higher than the closing price the previous business day, which was 91⅛, or $911.25 per bond. The AMF bond's current yield—or ratio of coupon income to its current price—was 11 percent.[5]

The bulk of bond trades on the major securities exchanges, such as the New York Stock Exchange, are small-volume, odd-lot transactions. Purchases and sales of large quantities of bonds between dealers and major institutional investors generally take place off the major exchanges through direct negotiation or with the aid of security brokers. Prices and yields on such large transactions (round lots) must be gathered from other sources of information, including dealer quote sheets such as the one shown in Exhibit 10–1.

Several other sources of information on bond yields and prices are readily available to investors in published form. The *Daily Bond Buyer,* for example, gives a detailed breakdown of daily prices and yields for a large number of actively traded bond issues, as does the *Commercial and Financial Chronicle,* a financially oriented newspaper. Moreover, a number of bond-yield indices have been compiled in recent years; they pool several bond issues of similar quality and report the average rate of return (yield) to the investor for the entire pool of bonds. In this way bond market investors and companies planning to issue new bonds can read the "drift" of recent price and yield changes and decide if their plans need to be altered to reflect the latest developments.

Among the most popular bond-yield indices are those compiled by Moody's Investor Service and the *Bond Buyer* newspaper for both corporate and state and local government bonds. In addition, the United States Treasury makes available estimated average yields for its notes and bonds, arrayed by maturity (e.g., 1-year, 2-year, 3-year, 5-year, 10-year, and 20-year Treasury securities). Dow Jones publishes a daily index of prices for some of the most actively traded corporate bonds, including 10 utility and 10 industrial issues. The Dow bond averages date back to 1915.

These various bond yield indicators appear in numerous publications, including both private and governmental sources. The *Federal Reserve Bulletin,* published by the Board of Governors of the Federal Reserve System, and the *Survey of Current Business,* published by the U.S. Department of Commerce, report weekly, monthly, and annual average bond yields. Recent changes in various bond-yield indices as reported in the *Federal Reserve Bulletin* are shown in Exhibit 10–3. We note the strong upward trend in bond yields between 1977 and 1980, reflecting the rapid inflation and heavy demands for credit which characterized these years.

---

[5] Current yields are not shown in the case of convertible bonds. These are designated cv. See Chapter 9 for a description of convertible bonds.

EXHIBIT 10-3
Indicators of Average Bond Yields (average annual yields in percent)

Yield Series	1977	1978	1979	1980
State and local government notes and bonds:				
Aaa—Moody's Series	5.20	5.52	5.92	7.85
Bond Buyer Series	5.68	6.03	6.52	8.59
Corporate bonds:				
Seasoned issues, all industries—Moody's	8.43	9.07	10.12	12.75
Classified by rating:				
Aaa	8.02	8.73	9.63	11.94
Aa	8.24	8.92	9.94	12.50
A	8.49	9.12	10.20	12.89
Baa	8.97	9.45	10.69	13.67

SOURCE: Board of Governors of the Federal Reserve System, *Federal Reserve Bulletin,* June 1981.

STOCK PRICES AND DIVIDEND YIELDS

Of all securities traded in the money and capital markets, stocks are among the most popular with investors. Stock prices can be extremely volatile, offering the prospect of substantial capital gains if prices rise but also significant capital losses if prices fall. Most corporations issuing stock pay dividends regularly, thus giving the investor a reasonably steady source of income as well as the opportunity to achieve "windfall" gains if the value of the stock rises. Unlike a bond, however, a share of stock is a certificate of ownership in a corporation and not a debt obligation. No corporation need pay dividends to its stockholders, and some never do, preferring to retain any after-tax earnings in the business.

As in the case of bonds, price and yield data on the most actively traded stocks are reported daily in the financial press. Most daily newspapers list current stock prices, especially for those equities traded on the New York and American stock exchanges. *The Wall Street Journal* contains an extensive list of the daily prices and dividend yields of major stocks sold over the counter and on the major securities exchanges, including the New York, American, Midwest, Pacific, Philadelphia, Boston, and Cincinnati stock exchanges. An example of *WSJ* stock-price quotations is shown in Exhibit 10-4.

We note that each stock-price quotation is identified by the abbreviated name of the company using it. High and low prices at which the stock has been traded during the past year and the most recent annual dividend declared by the issuing company are given.[6] The dividend yield, or ratio of dividends to current price, appears next, along with the ratio of the stock's current price to the past 12 months of company earnings, or the P-E ratio. All

---

[6] The occasional letters which appear beside certain stocks in the list of quotations refer to footnotes which give information regarding special or extra dividends paid by the stock in question. All stocks shown are common equity shares unless the symbol pf appears, indicating an issue of preferred stock.

EXHIBIT 10–4
Stock Price Quotations from *The Wall Street Journal*

NYSE-Composite Transactions

Friday, Aug. 15, 1980

Quotations include trades on the American, Midwest, Pacific, Philadelphia, Boston and Cincinnati stock exchanges and reported by the National Association of Securities Dealers and Instinet

52 Weeks High	52 Weeks Low	Stock	Div.	Yld %	P-E Ratio	Sales 100s	High	low	Close	Net Chg.
27	19	CrckN	pf2.18	8.8	..	21	25¼	24⅞	24⅞	−⅛
24⅞	14	CrmpK	1.20	5.1	6	13	24	23½	23½	−⅜
29⅞	17⅝	CrouHi	s .92	3.2	12	384	29	27¾	29	+1¼
35¼	22⅞	CrwnCk		..	6	209	30⅜	30⅛	30⅜	+¼
54⅝	33½	CrwZel	2.30	4.4	11	1024	53⅛	51⅞	52½	−½
63½	43¾	CrZel	pf4.63	7.3	..	9	63⅜	63⅛	63⅜	+⅛
28¾	25¾	CrumF	s1.44	5.1	5	86	28½	28	28	−⅜
11	6	Culbro		..	..	270	9⅝	9⅜	9½	+⅛
37½	27¼	CumEn	1.80	5.2	17	50	34½	34⅛	34½	.....
12⅞	8⅜	CunnDrg	.40	3.7	10	3	10⅞	10¾	10⅞	−⅛
11	7⅝	CurrInc	1.10	12.	..	11	9¼	9¼	9¼	−½
31	15⅛	CurtW	1	4.0	5	99	25⅛	24⅞	24⅞	+⅛
38½	22¾	CurtW A	2	6.6	..	11	31	30½	30½	−½
29⅞	18¾	Cyclops	.88	3.5	17	145	25½	24¾	25½	+¾
		– D–D–D –								
10⅞	4½	DPF		..	6	93	8⅜	8¼	8⅜	+⅛
10	3⅝	Damon	.20	2.0	30	570	u10¼	10	10	.....
20	12	DanRiv	1.12	6.6	4	273	17¼	16¼	16⅞	+⅝
30¼	17⅞	DanaCp	1.60	6.7	6	153	24⅜	23½	24	+¼
43⅞	16⅜	Daniel	.30b	.7	19	215	u44	42⅜	44	+1⅞
49⅝	35⅛	DartInd	2	4.6	6	261	44	43⅜	43½	−½
49¼	35⅛	Dart pf	2	4.6	..	32	43½	42¾	43½	.....
86½	46	DataGen		..	17	39	83¾	83	83¼	.....
47¾	16⅜	DataTer	.30	.9	20	68	31⅞	31⅝	31⅞	+¼
75½	44¼	Datpnt	s	..	21	224	75⅜	74½	75⅜	−⅛
18½	9¾	Dayco	.56b	4.4	4	23	12⅞	12⅝	12¾	+⅛
50½	36½	DaytHd	1.80	3.7	7	163	48⅞	48¼	48⅜	−⅛
16⅞	12½	DaytPL	1.74	12.	7	102	14⅛	13⅞	14	+⅛
41½	28½	Deere	1.90	5.1	8	2854	37¼	37	37	.....
14⅛	10¼	DelmP	1.48	11.	8	77	13	12¾	13	+⅛
50¾	31⅛	DeltaA	1.20	2.5	10	283	48	47½	47½	−½
10⅜	2⅜	Deltec	8c	..	..	38	3	3	3	.....
17	8	Deltona		..	..	90	13½	13⅛	13½	+⅛
45⅞	35½	DeluxC	n1.56	3.5	12	118	44⅜	44	44	−¼
20½	15¾	DenMfg	1.16	6.4	7	22	18¼	18	18	+¼
21⅝	11⅞	Dennys	.88	4.2	11	1002	21	20½	21	+⅜
21⅜	13	Dentsply	.88	4.8	14	239	18⅜	17⅝	18⅜	+⅝
14⅞	10¼	DeSoto	1	7.3	7	18	13¾	13½	13⅝	.....
15⅞	10⅞	DetEd	1.60	13.	8	402	12¾	12⅜	12½	.....
88	62	DetE	pf9.32	13.	..	z350	73	73	73	−1
76	49	DetE	pf7.68	13.	..	z10	58	58	58	−1
25¾	19	DE	pfF 2.75	12.	..	5	22⅛	22	22⅛	+⅛
25⅝	19¼	DE	pfB 2.75	12.	..	4	22¾	22¾	22¾	−⅛
21½	14½	DetE	pr2.28	13.	..	10	17½	17½	17½	.....
30	19⅞	Dexter	1	3.4	10	43	29	28⅝	29	.....
15⅛	7	DiGior	.56	5.7	8	97	10	9⅞	9⅞	.....
24	13¾	DiGior	pf.88	5.9	..	z180	15	15	15	+½
27	16½	DiGior	pf2.25	9.8	..	2	22⅞	22⅞	22⅞	+½
22¾	14⅛	DialCp	1.20	6.4	6	18	18⅞	18¾	18⅞	+⅜
50	28¼	DiaInt	2.20	6.0	10	32	36⅞	36⅝	36⅝	−⅛
36¾	23⅛	DiamS	1.60	4.9	8	620	32⅞	32⅜	32½	−⅜
41¼	24⅞	Diebold	.80	2.0	10	366	40⅝	39¾	39⅞	−⅝
90⅛	56¾	DigitalEq		..	16	1147	87⅝	86⅜	87	−⅝
15⅜	8¼	Dillingm	.70	4.4	6	1139	u16⅛	15⅛	15¾	+1⅛
28	20¾	Dillngm	pf2	6.9	..	21	u29½	28½	29⅛	+1⅛
23¼	14	Dillon	1.08	5.8	11	19	18½	18¼	18½	+⅜
53⅞	35½	Disney	.72	1.4	13	368	53¼	52¾	53	+½
8¾	3⅞	DivrsfdIn		..	9	510	7½	6⅞	7⅜	+¼
6⅞	2⅝	DivrsMtg		..	..	193	4⅝	4⅜	4½	.....
16⅞	9½	DrPeppr	.76	5.8	11	294	13¼	13	13⅛	.....
25¾	6¾	Documat		..	..	228	16¼	15¾	15⅞	−⅛
115	36¼	Dome g	.50	.5	..	180	109	105¼	105¼	−2⅜
24	16⅛	Donald	n.60	2.5	11	49	23⅞	23½	23⅝	+¼
8⅛	3½	DonLJ	.16	2.0	11	569	8⅛	7¾	8⅛	+¼
35¼	23¾	Donnly	1.14	3.3	10	19	34⅞	34½	34½	−⅜
20	12⅜	Dorsey	.80	5.4	5	28	15	14¾	14⅞	−⅛
49¾	27¾	Dover	s 1.04	2.2	13	53	47¾	47	47	−⅛
39¼	27⅛	DowCh	1.60	4.2	9	2007	37¾	37	37¾	+⅝
49½	34⅞	DowJn	1.60	3.3	15	40	49	48½	48⅞	+⅜
39⅝	25⅝	Dravo	1.36	3.5	14	53	38⅞	38⅝	38⅞	+¼
72¾	47⅝	Dressr	1.10	1.5	11	300	u72⅞	72¼	72¼	.....
17½	13	DrexB	1.90e	12.	..	5	16⅜	16⅛	16⅜	+¼
36⅜	16¾	Dreyfs	.80	2.3	7	54	35¾	35¼	35½	−¼
49	31⅛	duPont	2a	4.0	8	889	u49½	48¼	49½	+1
42⅞	31⅝	duPnt	pf3.50	9.5	..	5	36¾	36¼	36¾	−¼

52 Weeks High	52 Weeks Low	Stock	Div.	Yld %	P-E Ratio	Sales 100s	High	low	Close	Net Chg
60¾	38	GnInstr	pf 3	4.9	..	27	60⅝	60	60⅝	+⅝
30¼	19	GnMills	1.32	4.3	9	800	u30⅝	29¾	30½	+½
65⅞	39½	GMot	3.85e	6.7	95	3348	57⅞	55¾	57⅞	+1¾
45⅞	32	GMot	pf3.75	9.6	..	3	38⅞	38⅞	38⅞	+½
61½	43¼	GMot	pf 5	9.9	..	8	50⅝	50¼	50⅝	+⅜
22⅞	12⅛	GnPort	.80	3.6	5	360	22½	21⅝	22⅜	+½
10⅛	3⅜	GPU		..	7	590	5⅞	5¾	5¾	.....
13½	6¾	GnRefr		..	6	9	9⅛	9	9	−⅛
43⅜	28¼	GnSignl	1.28	3.1	11	206	41¾	41	41⅜	+⅜
10⅜	6¾	GnSteel	.44	4.5	8	57	9¾	9⅝	9¾	.....
30⅝	23	GTE	2.72	10.	8	903	27⅜	27⅛	27¼	.....
29⅞	22⅛	GTE	pf 2.50	9.3	..	3	26¾	26¾	26¾	.....
26	17¾	GTE	pf 2.48	11.	..	12	22⅜	22⅛	22⅛	.....
90	64¼	GTFI	pf8.16	12.	..	z100	70	70	70	.....
23⅞	12¼	GTire	1.50	7.3	17	457	20¾	19⅞	20½	+¼
5⅛	2¾	Genesco		..	22	245	4⅜	4¼	4⅜	.....
34	17¼	Genst	g 1.60	..	8	354	32⅝	32¼	32½	+½
30	18	Gst pf	1.68	5.9	..	2	28¾	28⅜	28⅜	−⅝
29	18¾	GenuPt	1.04	4.0	11	170	26½	26	26⅛	+¼
34⅞	21½	GaPac	1.20	4.1	12	598	29¾	29¼	29½	+¼
36⅜	27⅛	GaPac	pf2.24	6.5	..	1	34¼	34¼	34¼	+¼
24½	16¼	GaPw	pf2.56	12.	..	2	20½	20½	20½	−¼
24⅛	16½	GaPw	pf2.52	12.	..	6	20½	20⅜	20½	+⅛
26⅝	19¾	GaPw	pf2.75	12.	..	2	23⅛	23⅛	23⅛	−⅛
72⅛	50	GaPw	pf7.72	13.	..	z250	60	59½	60	+1
81	35⅞	Geosrc	.92	1.1	16	39	u82	80¼	82	+2
30¾	17⅞	GerbPd	1.74	7.5	7	58	23¼	22⅞	23⅛	.....
97¾	52	Getty	1.80e	2.2	8	187	83⅛	82¼	82½	−½
18¼	12½	Getty	pf1.20	7.7	..	1	15½	15½	15½	−¼
11⅞	4⅝	GiantPC		..	..	30	6½	6⅜	6½	.....
16⅝	6¼	GibrFn	.60	5.5	27	429	10⅞	10⅝	10⅞	+¼
33⅞	18½	GidLew	s 1	3.0	6	243	33⅞	32⅜	33¼	+1
20¾	12	GiffHill	.92	4.6	8	51	20⅜	20	20⅛	−¼
29⅝	17⅝	Gillette	1.90	6.4	7	1375	u29⅞	29⅛	29½	+¼
13¼	7¼	GinosInc	.44	4.3	..	47	10⅜	10⅛	10¼	+⅛
25¾	15¼	GleasW	.80	3.7	7	112	22	21½	21¾	+½
42⅜	26½	GlobM	s .20	.5	14	745	42¼	40⅝	42¼	+1⅝
19	11⅛	GldWFn	.54	3.0	7	99	18⅜	18⅛	18¼	.....
24	16⅜	Gdrich	1.56	7.0	6	241	22½	22¼	22⅜	+⅜
9⅞	7¼	Gdrich	pf.97	11.	..	z200	8½	8½	8½	.....
16⅜	10¾	Goodyr	1.30	8.1	7	2082	16⅛	15⅞	16⅛	+⅛
29	17	GordJw	.72	2.8	5	23	25⅞	25½	25½	−⅜
29¼	19¼	Gould	1.72	6.3	8	176	27¾	27	27¼	−⅜
27	19	Gould	pf1.35	5.1	..	1	26½	26½	26½	−⅜
45⅞	30½	Grace	2.30	5.1	8	1478	45½	45	45⅛	+¼
40¼	25	Graingr	1	2.9	11	174	34⅝	34¼	34⅜	.....
14⅛	9¾	Granitvl	1	7.6	5	43	13⅜	13	13⅛	−⅛
13½	9	GrayDr	.80	6.8	6	71	11⅞	11⅝	11¾	+⅛
10¼	4⅝	GtAtPc		..	..	414	5⅞	5⅝	5¾	−⅛
32¼	17⅞	GtLkInt	.68a	2.6	6	43	26½	26⅛	26⅛	.....
32	23½	GNIrn	3.75e	13.	10	15	28	27⅝	27⅞	−¼
40⅜	27¾	GtNoNk	1.60	4.2	7	165	38¼	37¼	38¼	+1¼
27¾	14	GtWFin	.88	4.2	7	654	21⅜	21	21	−⅛
18⅝	11⅞	Greyh	1.20	7.6	6	989	16⅛	15⅞	15⅞	−⅛
4¼	⅞	Greyhnd	wt	..	..	21	2¾	2⅝	2¾	.....
16½	8⅛	GrowG	.44b	3.1	9	129	14⅜	14⅛	14¼	+⅛
7	3¾	GthRty		..	..	81	5¾	5⅜	5½	.....
32½	16¼	Grumm	1.20	5.0	10	605	24⅜	23⅞	24	.....
24⅞	18¼	Grum	pf2.80	12.	..	24	23	22⅝	22⅞	−⅛
18⅜	10	GuardIn	.40	2.2	8	196	18¼	17⅝	17⅞	+⅜
18¾	13½	GlfWst	s .75	3.9	4	9278	u19⅜	18⅞	19⅛	+⅜
72½	61¼	GlfW	pf 5.75	9.1	..	1	63	63	63	.....
111½	69¾	GlfW	pf 3.87	3.4	..	3	u114	113	114	+2½
47½	30¾	GlfW	pf 2.50	5.2	..	69	u49	48	48½	+1
54½	27½	GulfOil	2.50	5.8	5	3539	43⅝	42⅝	42¾	−⅝
37⅞	13¾	GulfRes	.50	2.2	10	391	23⅝	22¾	22¾	−½
47½	19	GulfR	pf1.30	4.4	..	2	29⅞	29⅞	29⅞	+1⅝
43½	19⅝	GulfR	pf1.60	5.9	..	2	27	27	27	+½
13½	9	GlfStUt	1.36	12.	5	940	11¾	11½	11½	+⅛
100¼	71	GlfSU	pf8.80	12.	..	z30	76	76	76	−1¼
27¼	13½	GulfUtd	1.24	5.6	8	214	22¼	21½	22⅛	+½
54½	38	GlfU	pf 3.78	7.9	..	3	48	48	48	−¼
17¾	10⅛	Gulton	.60	3.6	8	68	17⅛	16¾	16¾	−¼

SOURCE: *The Wall Street Journal*, August 18, 1980.

remaining entries provide a summary of the previous business day's transactions in the markets where that particular stock is bought and sold. The one-day sales volume, expressed in hundreds of shares, is shown, as well as the highest and lowest prices at which the stock was exchanged that day. The closing price for which the stock was traded in the last sale of the day is reported, expressed in dollars and fractions of a dollar down to eighths. The final entry gives the net change between yesterday's closing price and the closing price one business day earlier.

Stock prices for individual companies, covering a period of several years, are provided by *The Value Line Investment Survey,* published weekly by Arnold Bernhard & Company of New York. Each company's business is described, and basic financial information, such as sales, net earnings, long-term indebtedness, and return on invested capital, is provided for at least a decade. Similar financial and price data for more than 1,100 actively traded stocks are published in the monthly series *3-Trend Security Charts* and in the quarterly series *3-Trend Cycli-Graphs,* both published by Securities Research Company of Boston. Extensive charts showing weekly stock price ranges, earnings, dividends, and number of shares traded appear in each issue.

Stock prices and basic internal financial data for individual companies are also presented in comprehensive reports compiled by Standard and Poor's Corporation (S&P) and published as *Stock Reports.* This monthly S&P series covers shares traded on the New York and American stock exchanges and over the counter. Information is provided subscribers on dividends paid by each company, its principal products, significant income and balance-sheet items, and an analysis of management performance. Daily and weekly stock price movements are also reported in S&P's quarterly publication, the *Daily Stock Price Record.*

The stock market is watched closely by investors as a barometer of expectations in the business community. A rising trend in stock prices generally signals an optimistic assessment of future business prospects and expectations of higher corporate earnings. A declining market, on the other hand, is often a harbinger of adverse economic news and may signal a cutback in business investment and lower corporate earnings.

Many students of the financial markets follow several broad stock-price indices which reflect price movements in groups of similar-quality securities. One of the most popular indices is the Dow-Jones Industrial Average of 30 stocks, including such major companies as American Telephone & Telegraph, Exxon, General Motors, Sears Roebuck, and U.S. Steel. Dow Jones also reports a Transportation Average of 20 stocks (including such industry leaders as American Airlines and Southern Pacific Company) and a Utility Average of the shares of 15 leading utility companies (such as Consolidated Edison and Pacific Gas and Electric). The Utility Average is of special importance to many investors because it appears to be highly sensitive to interest-rate fluctuations, and some analysts regard it as a barometer of interest-rate expectations. Recent movements in the Dow Jones Industrial

FIGURE 10–1
The Dow-Jones Industrial Stock-Price Averages

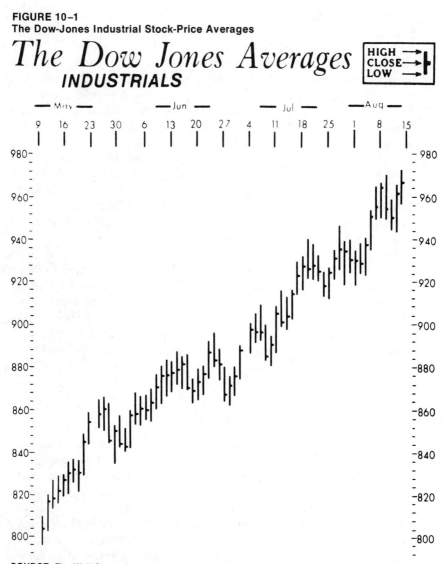

The Dow Jones Averages [HIGH → / CLOSE → / LOW →]

INDUSTRIALS

SOURCE: *The Wall Street Journal,* August 18, 1980.

Average reported in *The Wall Street Journal* are shown in Figure 10–1. Daily reports on the performance of all the Dow series also may be found in local newspapers as well as in Standard and Poor's *Daily Stock Price Record.*[7]

[7] The Dow Industrial, Transportation, and Utility averages are combined to form a fourth market indicator—the 65 Stock Composite Average. The Dow Industrial Average is the oldest of the four series, dating back to 1897, when it contained share prices for just 12 major industrial firms. Probably the most widely followed stock market index in the world, the Dow Industrial

Two of the most comprehensive stock market indicators available are Standard and Poor's 400 Industrial Stock Price Index and 500 Composite Stock Price Index, both including the most actively traded U.S. corporate equity shares. The S&P 500 includes the shares of 40 utility companies, 20 transportation firms, and 40 financial stocks not present in the S&P 400 industrial index. All five S&P stock series—the 400 Index, Utility Index, Transportation Index, Financial Stock Index, and the 500 Composite Index—are widely followed and regarded as sensitive barometers of general stock price movements in the United States.[8] An even broader price index than the S&P 500 Composite is the NYSE Composite, which includes over 2,000 shares traded on the New York Stock Exchange. The NYSE Composite, which gives greatest weight to stocks having the highest market values, is considered a useful indicator of total market performance. Many analysts use it to compare the performance of major institutional investors, such as investment companies and pension funds, against the market as a whole.[9]

Many newspapers, including *The Wall Street Journal,* and financially oriented magazines contain a daily stock market diary similar to that shown in Exhibit 10–5. Such summaries of recent market developments indicate both price movements and the volume of trading on the major exchanges. Market diaries usually report the total number of shares traded on a given day or week, the number of stocks advancing or declining in price, and those whose price remains unchanged after recent trading. Many stock analysts chart movements in the ratio of advances to declines as an indicator of "oversold" or "overbought" conditions in the market.

INFORMATION ON SECURITY ISSUERS

Lenders of funds have a pressing need to secure accurate financial information on those individuals and institutions who seek to borrow funds or sell their stock. Those who lend short-term funds are especially concerned about the *liquidity* of borrowers—their ability to raise cash quickly to cover interest and principal payments. In contrast, lenders of long-term funds pay special attention to the long-run viability of the individuals and institutions to whom they grant funds. Those providing long-term credit typically examine the ratio of a borrower's aggregate financial charges (interest payments and leasing fees) to earnings, the volume of debt incurred relative to owner's

Average is constructed by adding up the current prices of the 30 industrial stocks represented and dividing by an adjustment factor designed to account for stock splits and changes in the list of companies represented in the average. (For example, in June 1979, IBM and Merck were substituted for Esmark and Chrysler.) The current adjustment factor for all four Dow stock-price averages may be found in the latest issue of *Barron's* magazine.

[8] See Chapter 20 for a discussion of the market for corporate stocks and the factors which influence stock prices.

[9] Two other broad market indicators are the AMEX Index, a weighted average of all stocks traded on the American Stock Exchange, and the NASDAQ OTC Composite, which measures price movements in stocks sold over the counter.

EXHIBIT 10–5
Daily Stock Market Diary

MARKET DIARY

	Mon.	Fri.	Thu.	Wed.	Tue.	Mon.
Issues traded	1,893	1,864	1,873	1,905	1,893	1,874
Advances	298	794	761	901	524	767
Declines	1,302	621	689	604	957	708
Unchanged	293	649	423	400	412	399
New highs	8	19	19	18	9	13
New lows	41	15	32	22	39	20

DOW JONES CLOSING AVERAGES

			– – – – –Monday– – – – –		Yr. Ago		– –Since – –	
		1981	Change	%	1980	% Chg.	Dec. 31	%
Ind		940.54	–18.36	–1.91	928.67	+ 1.28	– 23.45	2.43
Trn		403.16	– 8.24	–2.00	312.43	+28.63	+ 5.06	+ 1.27
Uti		107.15	– 1.24	–1.14	114.17	– 6.15	7.27	6.35
Cmp		366.91	– 6.82	–1.82	339.39	+ 8.11	6.53	1.75

Ex-dividends of Procter & Gamble Co. 95 cents lowered the industrial average by 0.76.
The above ex-dividends lowered the composite average by 0.16.

OTHER MARKET INDICATORS

		1981	– Change –		1980
N.Y.S.E.	Composite	74.84	– 1.12	–1.47%	70.10
	Industrial	86.56	– 1.25	–1.42%	80.70
	Utility	38.78	– 0.53	–1.45%	38.89
	Transp.	74.78	– 1.27	–1.67%	61.92
	Financial	74.09	– 1.60	–2.11%	67.88
Am. Ex. Mkt Val Index		363.65	– 6.37	–1.72%	312.04
Nasdaq OTC	Composite	209.27	– 3.49	–1.64%	170.48
	Industrial	255.90	– 4.73	–1.81%	204.43
	Insurance	191.30	– 3.65	–3.84%	168.12
	Banks	138.08	– 1.23	–0.88%	113.65
Standard & Poor's	500	128.72	– 2.04	–1.56%	122.51
	400 Industrial	145.01	– 2.23	–1.51%	138.40

TRADING ACTIVITY

Volume of advancing stocks on N.Y.S.E., 4,787,800 shares; volume of declining stocks, 32,997,900. On American S.E., volume of advancing stocks, 408,400; volume of declining stocks, 2,781,200. Nasdaq volume of advancing stocks, 3,679,300; volume of declining stocks, 12,970,800.

SOURCE: *The Wall Street Journal*, July 21, 1981.

equity, and the efficiency with which the borrower manages resources and collects amounts owed. Many lenders prepare "spread sheets" on individual borrowers; these list key balance-sheet and income-statement items covering a period of several years in order to reveal significant trends in a security issuer's financial condition.

Financial information on individual companies and other security issuers comes from a wide variety of published sources. Two of the most respected sources of information on major security issuers are Moody's Investors Service, Inc., and Standard & Poor's Corporation, both headquartered in New York City. In a series of annual volumes, Moody's provides financial data on industrial corporations, commercial banks, insurance companies, investment funds, real estate companies, utilities, and state and local units of government. The most widely known Moody's volumes include the *Industrial Manual, Bank and Finance Manual, Public Utility Manual, Transportation Manual,* and *Municipal and Government Manual.* In the case of individual corporations, Moody's provides information on the history of each firm, including any recent acquisitions or mergers, names of key officers, and recent financial statements. In addition, Moody's assigns credit ratings to selected issuers of corporate and municipal bonds, commercial paper, and preferred stock as a guide for investors. These ratings are published monthly in Moody's *Bond Record*. Standard & Poor's provides similar credit ratings for corporate and municipal bonds, assessing the likelihood of default on a security issue and the degree of protection afforded the investor. The S&P *Bond Guide*, containing relevant financial information on more than 6,000 bond issues, appears once a month.[10]

Even more extensive financial data are provided by the reports and registration statements which corporations must file with the Securities and Exchange Commission (SEC). These SEC reports and statements are available in many libraries on microfiche or microfilm. One company, Disclosure Incorporated, which is under contract with the SEC, provides its subscribers with microfiche copies of more than 100,000 corporate documents filed each year by approximately 11,000 U.S. companies.

The most important of these corporate documents is the SEC's *10-K Report*—an annual business and financial report which must be filed by most companies within 90 days after their fiscal year-end. 10-K reports identify the principal products or services and markets served by a firm, provide a summary of its operations for the past five years, note any securities outstanding, include complete audited financial statements, and list the names of key officers. SEC regulations pursuant to the Securities Act of 1933 and the Securities Exchange Act of 1934 also require corporations offering securities for public sale to file *registration statements*. While these statements vary in content with the type of organization selling the securities, registration statements generally include a prospectus outlining the terms of sale of new securities, marketing arrangements, issue and distribution expenses, and company financial reports.

Another useful source of data on business firms seeking credit is the Business Information Report prepared by Dun & Bradstreet, Inc. This credit-rating company collects information on approximately 3 million Canadian and U.S. firms, making detailed financial reports available to its subscribers. A sample page from a Dun & Bradstreet Business Information Report is presented in Exhibit 10–6. Dun & Bradstreet also provides industrywide financial data so that the financial condition of an individual business borrower can be compared with that of other firms in the same industry.

Information on individuals and families who seek credit is assembled and disseminated to institutional lenders such as banks and finance companies by nearly 2,000 credit bureaus in the United States. The files of these bureaus include such information as the individual's place of residence and occupation, marital status, loans and credit charges outstanding, and the promptness with which the individual pays his or her bills. A typical credit file for an individual will indicate whether he or she has filed for bankruptcy or has

---

[10] Moody's and Standard & Poor's investment ratings are discussed in Chapter 8 and presented in detail in Appendix A.

EXHIBIT 10-6
The Dun & Bradstreet Business Information Report

		This report has been prepared for:
Dun & Bradstreet, Inc.		
BE SURE NAME, BUSINESS AND ADDRESS MATCH YOUR FILE	ANSWERING INQUIRY	SUBSCRIBER: 008-001042

THIS REPORT MAY NOT BE REPRODUCED IN WHOLE OR IN PART IN ANY MANNER WHATEVER

CONSOLIDATED REPORT		{FULL REVISION}

```
DUNS:  06-647-3261              DATE PRINTED              SUMMARY
RETTINGER PAINT CORP.           AUG 13, 197-       RATING      CC2

727 WHITMAN WAY                 WHOL PAINTS &       STARTED     1950
BENSON, MI  48232               VARNISHES           PAYMENTS    DISC-PPT
     TEL 313 961-0720                               SALES     $ 424,612
                                SIC NO.             WORTH     $ 101,867
CARL RETTINGER, PRES.           51 98               EMPLOYS     5
                                                    HISTORY     CLEAR
                                                    CONDITION   GOOD
                                                    TREND       STEADY
```

SPECIAL EVENTS   Business burglarized July 3 but $18,000 loss is fully insured.

PAYMENTS   {Amounts may be rounded to nearest figure in prescribed ranges}

REPORTED	PAYING RECORD	HIGH CREDIT	NOW OWES	PAST DUE	SELLING TERMS	LAST SALE WITHIN
07/7-	Disc	30000	17000	-0-	2 10 30	1-2 mos.
	Disc	27000	14000	-0-	1 10 30	2-3 mos.
	Disc-Ppt	12000	4400	200	2 10 30	1 mo.
	Ppt	9000	8000	-0-	30	1 mo.
06/7-	Disc	16000	7500	-0-	2 10 30	2-3 mos.
05/7-	Disc	9000	3800	-0-	2 10 30	1 mo.
	Ppt	1500	-0-	-0-	30	1-2 mos.

```
FINANCE
06/22/7-      Fiscal statement dated May 31, 197-:
           Cash            $  20,623      Accts Payable       $  47,246
           Accts Rec          55,777      Owing Bank             34,000
           Merchandise        92,103      Notes Pay {Trucks}      7,020
                           ---------                          ---------
           Current           168,503      Current                88,266
           Fixts. & Equip.    13,630      Common Stock           35,000
           Trucks              8,000      Earned Surplus         66,867
                           -------                            ---------
           Total Assets      190,133      Total                 190,133
           SALES {Yr}: $424,612.  Net profit $17,105.  Fire ins. mdse $95,000;
    equipt $20,000.  Mo. rent: $3500.  Prepared by Steige Co., CPAs, Detroit, MI.
                              --0--
           06/22/7- Lawson defined monthly payments: $3000 to bank, $400 on notes.
    Admitted collections slow but losses insignificant.  Said inventory will drop
    to $60,000 by December.  Expects 5% sales increase this year.
PUBLIC FILINGS
03/25/7-        March 17, 197- financing statement #741170 named subject as debtor and
           NCR Corp., Dayton, O. as secured party.  Collateral: equipment.
05/28/7-        May 21, 197- suit for $200 entered by Henry Assoc., Atlanta, Ga. Docket
           #27519.  Involves merchandise which Lawson says was defective.
BANKING
06/25/7-        Account, long maintained, carries average balances low to moderate five
           figures.  Unsecured loans to moderate five extended and now open.
HISTORY
06/22/7-  CARL RETTINGER, PRES.            JOHN J. LAWSON, V PRES.
          DIRECTORS:  The Officers
                Incorporated Michigan February 2, 1950.  Authorized capital 3500 shares,
           no par common.  Paid in capital $35,000, officers sharing equally.
                RETTINGER, born 1920, married.  Employed by E-Z Paints, Detroit 12 yrs,
           five as manager until starting subject early 1950.
                LAWSON, born 1925, married.  Obtained accounting degree 1946 and then
           employed by Union Carbide, Chicago until joining Rettinger at inception.
OPERATION
06/22/7-        Wholesales paints and varnishes {85%}, wallpaper and supplies.  500
           local accounts include retailers {75%} and contractors.  Terms: 2 10 30.  Peak
           season spring thru summer.  EMPLOYEES:  Officers active with three others.
           LOCATION: Rents 7500 sq ft. one-story block structure, good repair.
```

SOURCE: Dun & Bradstreet.

judgments or liens against either assets or income. Most credit bureaus maintain files on an individual's bill-paying records for up to seven years and may release that information only to those lenders, debt collectors, employers, or licensing agencies who have a legitimate right to know the individual's credit standing. As discussed in Chapter 17, the Fair Credit Reporting Act, passed in 1971, gives individuals access to their credit files and the right to dispute information contained therein.

GENERAL ECONOMIC AND FINANCIAL CONDITIONS

A number of different sources provide market participants with information on developments in the economy, prevailing trends in the money and capital markets, and actions by the government which may affect economic and financial conditions. For example, many of the nation's major commercial banks publish monthly and weekly newsletters for the benefit of their smaller correspondent banks and customers. These newsletters frequently contain discussions of recent changes in employment, prices, industrial output, the nation's money supply, security prices, and interest rates.

The Federal Reserve System releases large quantities of financial information to the public upon request. Statistical releases available on a weekly or monthly basis cover such items as interest rates, money supply measures, assets and liabilities held by commercial banks and nonbank thrift institutions, the federal government's fiscal and debt-financing operations, and reports on corporate earnings, consumer borrowing, industrial output, and international transactions. Information of this sort is summarized each month in the *Federal Reserve Bulletin,* published by the Board of Governors of the Federal Reserve System in Washington, D.C. The board also publishes the results of internal staff studies which examine in detail recent financial trends or address major issues of public policy.

Within the Federal Reserve System, the Federal Reserve Bank of St. Louis publishes large quantities of financial data in its weekly, monthly, and quarterly news releases. One of the most popular is *U.S. Financial Data,* which appears weekly and contains a summary of week-to-week changes in interest rates and in the components of the nation's money supply. Another regular St. Louis Fed publication is *Monetary Trends,* summarizing monthly changes in the money supply and bank reserves. These data series are watched closely by many investors because they often foreshadow broad movements in interest rates, security prices, and national economic conditions.

A number of published sources regularly report on the status of the national economy, particularly as reflected in employment, prices, and production. Newsletters published by banks in major money centers, and daily financial newsheets such as *The Wall Street Journal,* nearly always include important economic data. The Federal Reserve Bank of St. Louis publishes a monthly news release, *National Economic Trends,* which tracks changes in

U.S. employment, consumer and wholesale prices, industrial production, productivity, and labor costs. The *Survey of Current Business,* published by the U.S. Department of Commerce, contains one of the most up-to-date and comprehensive collections of U.S. economic data available anywhere. The *Survey* reports the latest available information on industrial production and income flows, including consumer spending, government expenditures at all levels, changes in business inventories, business capital spending, and exports and imports. The *Survey* contains a detailed breakdown of U.S. production volume by market and industry groupings, and it tracks movements in manufacturers' sales, inventories, and new orders. Other economic data series found in the *Survey* cover residential and commercial construction, mortgage lending, wholesale and retail trade, employment, and prices of consumer, farm, and producer goods.

SOCIAL ACCOUNTING DATA

Students of the economy and the financial markets also make use of *social accounting systems* to keep track of broad trends in national economic and financial conditions. *Social accounting* refers to a system of recordkeeping which reports transactions between the principal sectors of the economy, such as households, financial institutions, corporations, and units of government. The two most widely accepted and closely followed social accounting systems in the United States today are the National Income Accounts (NIA) and the Flow of Funds Accounts.

National Income Accounts

The National Income Accounts are compiled and released quarterly by the U.S. Department of Commerce. The NIA accounting system presents data on the nation's production of goods and services, income flows, investment spending, consumption, and total savings. Probably the best-known account in the NIA series is Gross National Product (GNP), which is a measure of the market value of all goods and services newly produced in the U.S. economy within a year's time. GNP may be broken down into the *uses* to which the nation's output of goods and services is put—consumption spending, investment in capital goods and inventories, net exports of goods and services, and government purchases of goods and services. For example, Exhibit 10–7, drawn from the *Survey of Current Business,* indicates that the U.S. GNP reached $2.6 trillion in 1980, of which consumer spending for new goods and services accounted for almost $1.7 trillion. Purchases by federal, state, and local governments totaled nearly $535 billion in the same year, while businesses spent another $395 billion on investments in fixed assets and stockpiling of inventories. The NIA accounts also show that imports of goods and services into the United States reached a total of more

EXHIBIT 10–7
National Income and Product Accounts: The Components of U.S. GNP, 1980 (billions of current dollars)

Personal consumption expenditures		$1,672.8
Durable goods	$211.9	
Nondurable goods	675.5	
Services	785.2	
Gross private domestic investment		395.3
Fixed investment	401.2	
Change in business inventories	−5.9	
Net exports of goods and services		23.3
Exports	339.8	
Imports	316.5	
Government purchases of goods and services		534.7
Federal	198.9	
State and local	335.8	
Gross National Product of the United States		$2,626.1

SOURCE: U.S. Department of Commerce, *Survey of Current Business,* July 1981.

than $316 billion in 1980, spurred by sharp increases in the price of imported oil, but were exceeded by exports of nearly $340 billion.

Clearly, the National Income Accounts provide valuable information on the level and growth of the nation's economic activity. However, these accounts provide little or no information on financial transactions and the money and capital markets. For example, one component of the NIA system reports the annual amount of personal savings, but it does not show how those savings are *allocated* among purchases of bonds, bank deposits, stocks, and other financial assets. This task is left to the Flow of Funds Accounts, prepared by the Board of Governors of the Federal Reserve System.

The Flow of Funds Accounts

Flow of funds data have been prepared and published quarterly by the Federal Reserve System since 1955, and some data series go back to 1945. Monthly issues of the *Federal Reserve Bulletin* contain the latest summary reports of flow of funds transactions, while detailed breakdowns of financial transactions among major sectors of the economy are readily available on both a quarterly and an annual basis from the Federal Reserve Board in Washington, D.C.

Purposes of the Flow of Funds Accounts. The basic purposes of the Flow of Funds Accounts are to (1) trace the flow of savings by businesses, households, and governments into purchases of financial assets; (2) show how the various parts of the financial system are related to and interact with each other; and (3) and highlight the interconnections between the financial sector and the rest of the economy.

Flow of Funds Construction and Sector Balance Sheets. Construction of the Flow of Funds Accounts takes place in four basic steps. First, the economy is divided into several broad *sectors,* each consisting of economic units (transactors) with similar balance sheets. The 13 major sectors in the current account series include:

Households, including personal trusts, foundations, private schools and hospitals, labor unions, churches, and charitable organizations.

Farm Businesses.

Nonfarm Noncorporate Businesses, including partnerships and proprietorships engaged in nonfinancial activities.

Corporations.

State and Local Governments.

U.S. Government, including government-owned agencies.

Federally Sponsored Credit Agencies, such as the Federal Land Banks and Federal National Mortgage Association.

Monetary Authorities, including the Federal Reserve System and certain monetary accounts of the U.S. Treasury.

Commercial Banks.

Foreign Banking Agencies.

Savings Institutions, including savings and loan associations, mutual savings banks, and credit unions.

Insurance Intermediaries, including life insurance and property-casualty insurers and private and government pension funds.

Other Financial Institutions, such as finance companies, investment companies, and security brokers and dealers.

The second step in assembling the Flow of Funds Accounts is to construct *balance sheets* for each of the sectors listed above at the end of each quarter. Like any balance sheet prepared for a business firm or household, sector balance sheets contain estimates of the total assets, liabilities, and net worth held by each sector as of a single point in time. Assets are divided into financial assets and real (nonfinancial) assets. Detailed breakdowns of total financial assets and liabilities outstanding for each sector are made available to the public once a year.

An example of such a partial balance sheet containing financial assets and liabilities for the household sector during the 1969–79 period is shown in Exhibit 10–8. We note, for example, that households (including personal trusts and nonprofit organizations) held total financial assets of more than $3.8 trillion at year-end 1979 (shown in line 1). A substantial part of this total was represented by holdings of demand deposits, currency, and time and savings deposits at commercial banks and nonbank savings institutions. These liquid financial assets totaled $2.6 trillion (lines 3 and 5), or more than half of all household sector financial assets. The next-most-important finan-

EXHIBIT 10–8

Statement of Financial Assets and Liabilities for the Household Sector, 1969–79 ($ billions)

		Year-End Outstandings									
	1969	1970	1971	1972	1973	1974	1975	1976	1977	1978	1979
1 Total financial assets:	1863.6	1926.6	2152.7	2387.1	2300.5	2200.6	2551.5	2944.4	3118.0	3422.0	3827.1
2 Deposits + credit market instruments	744.0	796.5	872.5	970.6	1087.0	1194.6	1314.5	1461.9	1628.7	1815.2	2007.1
3 Deposits	492.1	544.5	624.3	711.0	788.7	853.9	943.2	1067.4	1198.7	1329.1	1454.6
4 Demand deposits + currency	109.0	117.8	129.8	142.2	156.1	163.0	166.9	181.9	203.7	222.1	228.4
5 Time + savings accounts	383.1	426.7	494.5	568.8	632.6	688.5	772.6	881.9	991.1	1096.3	1181.0
6 At commercial banks	168.4	195.4	223.5	252.4	287.7	322.6	347.2	387.4	427.6	471.7	512.6
7 At savings institutions	214.7	231.4	271.0	316.4	344.9	365.9	425.4	494.5	563.4	624.6	668.4
8 Money market fund shares	—	—	—	—	—	2.4	3.7	3.7	3.9	10.8	45.2
9 Credit market instruments	251.9	252.0	248.2	259.7	298.3	340.7	371.3	394.5	430.0	486.0	552.5
10 U.S. government securities	113.5	107.2	97.0	96.6	115.4	136.0	152.8	162.8	177.2	203.8	243.0
11 Treasury issues	95.9	84.9	76.5	79.6	96.7	113.6	133.4	139.6	149.4	166.7	189.4
12 Savings bonds	51.8	52.1	54.4	57.7	60.4	63.3	67.4	72.0	76.8	80.7	79.9
13 Other treasury	44.1	32.8	22.1	21.9	36.4	50.3	66.0	67.6	72.7	86.0	109.5
14 Agency issues	17.7	22.3	20.5	17.0	18.6	22.4	19.4	23.2	27.7	37.1	53.6
15 State + local obligations	46.9	46.0	46.1	48.4	53.7	61.9	68.1	70.6	73.2	75.0	74.3
16 Corporate + foreign bonds	24.8	34.3	43.1	48.0	50.1	55.2	63.5	69.3	66.3	64.8	71.6
17 Mortgages	51.3	52.9	54.1	60.5	62.9	68.2	70.9	79.8	91.8	106.2	123.0
18 Open-market paper	15.4	11.7	7.9	6.2	15.3	19.5	15.1	11.9	21.6	36.1	40.6
19 Corporate equities	746.9	729.4	834.1	914.1	712.7	504.8	659.7	827.2	777.0	808.5	906.9
20 Investment company shares	48.3	47.6	56.7	59.8	46.5	34.1	42.2	47.0	42.8	42.6	46.2
21 Other corporate equities	698.6	681.8	777.4	654.3	666.1	470.7	617.5	780.2	734.2	765.9	860.7
22 Life insurance reserves	125.0	130.5	136.8	143.7	151.3	158.0	166.6	175.0	186.5	198.5	210.7
23 Pension fund reserves	218.7	239.4	275.8	322.3	310.6	302.5	365.7	427.9	465.5	530.5	622.1
24 Security credit	5.2	4.4	4.9	5.0	4.9	3.9	4.5	6.3	7.3	8.8	11.3
25 Miscellaneous assets	23.8	26.3	28.7	31.3	34.1	36.8	40.6	46.0	52.9	60.5	69.0

26	Total liabilities:	477.7	502.0	550.9	621.5	698.3	749.3	801.2	899.3	1044.8	1210.0	1375.8	26
27	Credit-market instruments	456.1	481.2	526.6	591.5	671.7	722.8	772.3	863.3	1003.4	1164.8	1326.9	27
28	Home mortgages	276.5	290.7	317.1	358.6	405.7	440.9	479.0	540.6	634.0	738.2	847.0	28
29	Other mortgages	17.9	19.0	20.3	21.5	22.6	23.7	24.8	25.8	26.9	27.9	28.9	29
30	Installment consumer credit	101.2	105.5	118.3	133.2	155.1	164.6	172.4	194.0	230.8	275.6	311.3	30
31	Other consumer credit	36.6	37.6	39.5	44.5	48.6	49.0	50.9	54.8	58.6	64.3	70.9	31
32	Bank loans NEC	5.7	7.5	9.2	10.1	13.5	15.2	13.7	14.6	17.4	19.2	23.2	32
33	Other loans	18.3	20.9	22.3	23.6	26.2	29.4	31.5	33.4	35.7	39.5	45.5	33
34	Security credit	12.2	10.4	13.1	17.5	13.2	11.4	12.1	17.2	20.3	21.7	22.9	34
35	Trade credit	4.7	5.3	5.8	6.5	7.1	0.0	9.1	10.5	11.8	13.2	14.6	35
	Deferred and unpaid life												
36	Insurance premiums	4.7	5.1	5.4	6.0	6.4	7.1	7.7	8.4	9.3	10.3	11.4	36

* Excludes corporate equities.

SOURCE: Board of Governors of the Federal Reserve System, Flow of Funds Accounts—Assets and Liabilities Outstanding, 1969–79, August 1980.

cial asset held by households was corporate stock (equities), totaling about $907 billion in 1979 (line 19), or about one quarter of the sector's financial resources. Debt security holdings, including U.S. Treasury issues, federal agency securities, state and local government bonds, mortgages and similar assets, amounted to $552 billion (line 9). It is interesting that the total indebtedness of individuals and families in the United States is far less than their holdings of financial assets.[11] Exhibit 10–8 indicates that the household sector's liabilities totaled close to $1.4 trillion in 1979 (line 26)—roughly a third of its financial assets. Most of the household sector's indebtedness was in the form of home mortgages (line 28) and installment debt (line 30).

Sources of Data. Data needed to construct sector balance sheets in the Flow of Funds Accounts come from a wide variety of public and private sources. For example, the U.S. Treasury provides monthly statements of its receipts and expenditures and selected data on state and local government financial activity. Information on lending, borrowing, and acquisition of securities by nonfinancial businesses is derived from the Securities and Exchange Commission, the Internal Revenue Service, the U.S. Department of Agriculture, the Commerce Department, the Bureau of the Census, and the Federal Reserve itself. The National Association of Mutual Savings Banks, the Institute of Life Insurance, the Investment Company Institute, the National Association of Real Estate Investment Trusts, and the National Credit Union Administration provide financial data on their respective industries, while the Securities Industry Association provides selected information on gross offerings of securities.

As the Federal Reserve Board observed recently:

> Flow of funds accounting consists of absorbing and digesting a wide variety of financial information, both flows and balances, each part of which has been constructed in isolation from the others with its own accounting procedures, timing classifications, and institutional coverage.[12]

Inevitably, inconsistencies arise in classifying financial transactions due to differences in accounting procedures used by those agencies and groups contributing data to the accounts. Moreover, in an economy as vast and complex as that of the United States, some financial transactions are lost "between the cracks." To deal with these problems of consistency and coverage, the Federal Reserve includes a Statistical Discrepancy account which brings each sector into balance.

Preparation of Sources and Uses of Funds Statements. After balance sheets are constructed for each sector of the economy, the third step in the construction of the Flow of Funds Accounts is to prepare a sources and uses of funds statement for each sector. The sources and uses statement shows

---

[11] The relationship between household debt and holdings of financial assets is examined in more detail in Chapter 17.

[12] See Board of Governors of the Federal Reserve System, *Introduction to the Flow of Funds*, February 1975, p. 51.

changes in net worth and *changes* in holdings of financial assets and liabilities taken from each sector's balance sheet at the beginning and end of a calendar quarter or year. Thus:

Sources and Uses of Funds Statement

Uses of Funds	Sources of Funds
Change in real assets (or net real investment)	Change in liabilities outstanding (or net borrowing)
Change in financial assets (or net financial investment)	Change in net worth (or net current savings)
Change in total assets = Total uses of funds	Change in liabilities and net worth = Total sources of funds

An example of such a statement for the commercial banking sector, covering the years 1975–79, is shown in Exhibit 10–9. The top portion of the sources and uses statement (lines 1–10) shows changes in the banking sector's net worth (i.e., current surplus, representing net current savings), real assets (plant and equipment), and net acquisitions of financial assets. The lower portion of the statement (lines 11–38) reflects net borrowing as reflected in an increase in the liabilities carried by U.S. commercial banks and their affiliates.[13] We note, for example, that U.S. commercial banks added net $126 billion in various kinds of financial assets to their portfolios during 1979 (line 3). The bulk of this addition came in the form of loans to consumers, businesses, and other borrowers totaling $101.1 billion (line 11). Banks also acquired $9.7 billion of state and local government debt obligations in 1979 (line 9). Commercial bank holdings of U.S. government securities rose $9.1 billion (line 6).

Where did the banking sector get the funds it needed to make loans, purchase securities, and increase its investment in plant and equipment? A small portion of the necessary funds came from retained earnings as reflected in the current surplus account (line 1), which rose $4.3 billion during 1979. Most of the required funds, however, were derived from issuing liabilities. Liabilities of the banking sector rose $117.9 billion during 1979 (line 20), net of repayments of outstanding debt. Exhibit 10–9 shows that the bulk of the borrowed funds were derived by selling time deposits to the public in the form of CDs, passbook savings accounts, and other attractive savings instruments. Time deposits outstanding rose $52 billion during 1979 (line 24). In contrast, checking accounts (demand deposits) increased net only $12.5 billion (line 21). Banks also raised funds by selling stocks and bonds (lines 33 and 34), borrowing reserves from other banks and selling securities under

---

[13] All changes on a sources and uses of funds statement are shown *net* of purchases and sales. When purchases of an asset exceed sales of that asset, the resulting figure is reported as a positive increase in the asset. When sales exceed purchases, an asset item will carry a negative sign. A nonnegative liability item on the sources and uses statement indicates that *net* borrowing (i.e., total borrowings minus debt repayments) has occurred during the period under study. If a liability item is negative, debt repayments exceeded new borrowings during the period of the statement.

EXHIBIT 10-9
Sources and Uses of Funds Statement for the Banking Sector ($ billions)

	Seasonally Adjusted Annual Rates					1978			1979				
	1975	1976	1977	1978	1979	III	IV	I	I	II	III	IV*	
1 Current surplus	2.8	3.4	3.2	3.4	4.3	3.4	3.6	3.8	4.0	4.6	4.9		1
2 Plant + equipment	4.6	4.6	4.4	4.2	4.1	3.5	4.1	4.1	4.0	4.1	4.3		2
3 Net acquisition of financial assets	31.0	64.8	98.0	141.2	126.0	140.8	146.9	116.3	169.5	169.5	48.5		3
4 Demand deposits + currency	.1	-.2	.5	.3	.3	.2	.3	.3	.2	.3	.2		4
5 Total bank credit	31.5	66.3	89.9	125.9	120.2	126.6	112.1	128.3	146.0	168.6	37.8		5
6 U.S. government securities	30.0	20.2	-1.1	-.5	9.1	6.5	-24.2	10.5	13.6	13.3	-.9		6
7 Treasury issues	28.6	18.7	-1.9	-6.5	2.0	-3.0	-29.8	5.5	8.6	1.5	-7.6		7
8 Agency issues	1.4	1.5	.8	7.0	7.1	9.5	5.6	5.0	5.0	11.8	6.7		8
9 State + local obligations	1.8	3.0	9.2	9.6	9.7	9.6	14.8	12.1	2.5	12.1	12.2		9
10 Corporate bonds	1.8	-.6	*	-.3	.3	.4	-.6	1.2	-.3	1.0	-.9		10
11 Total loans	-2.1	43.7	81.9	116.1	101.1	110.1	122.0	104.5	130.2	142.2	27.4		11
12 Mortgages	3.8	14.3	27.4	35.0	32.8	38.9	35.4	32.7	34.0	33.5	31.0		12
13 Consumer credit	3.1	12.0	22.3	26.9	17.0	25.6	25.4	24.1	21.5	16.7	6.1		13
14 Bank loans NEC	-12.2	7.0	29.8	58.4	49.5	48.2	75.4	35.5	64.1	95.8	2.2		14
15 Open-market paper	1.1	3.7	.3	-1.3	2.2	1.5	-6.9	5.1	4.0	2.0	-2.3		15
16 Security credit	2.1	6.6	2.2	-2.9	-.4	-4.1	-7.3	7.1	6.5	-5.9	-9.5		16
17 Corporate equities	*	*	*	*	*	*	*	*	*	*	*		17
18 Vault cash + member bank reserve	.8	-1.0	3.5	5.9	1.7	.3	19.9	-7.0	2.7	4.8	6.2		18
19 Miscellaneous assets	-1.4	-.3	4.1	9.1	3.8	13.7	14.7	-5.3	20.5	-4.2	4.3		19

20	Net increase in liabilities	29.2	63.0	93.3	135.8	117.9	132.8	140.7	110.3	160.2	161.9	39.2
21	Demand deposits, net	5.0	12.6	26.1	22.0	12.5	20.9	36.8	−48.0	61.1	55.0	−18.1
22	U.S. government	−1.7	−.1	4.3	6.8	.1	−2.5	25.7	−28.5	39.5	12.0	−23.2
23	Other	6.7	12.7	21.8	15.2	12.5	23.5	11.1	−19.5	21.6	43.0	5.1
24	Time deposits	30.3	40.3	54.7	65.0	52.4	66.3	69.4	26.0	30.3	101.0	52.5
25	Large negotiable CDs	−10.1	−17.5	12.0	22.6	−2.2	13.3	37.1	−13.4	−47.6	37.6	14.8
26	Other at commercial banks	37.1	57.4	40.5	36.0	50.9	45.0	23.0	36.7	69.8	53.8	43.5
27	At foreign banking offices	3.4	.4	2.2	6.4	3.7	8.1	9.2	2.8	8.2	9.6	−5.8
28	Fed funds + security RPs	1.5	13.9	10.6	18.8	18.6	14.8	10.6	60.2	20.1	1.8	−7.5
29	Net interbank claims	−9.8	−8.2	−6.9	9.7	19.7	18.2	−.6	66.3	20.8	−7.4	−1.1
30	To monetary authorities	1.6	−1.3	1.4	3.6	.5	3.5	7.2	−3.9	−3.9	−2.5	12.4
31	To foreign banks	−9.9	−5.9	−.8	5.4	21.4	17.0	−3.6	75.6	23.9	.1	−13.9
32	To domestic banks (2)	−1.5	−1.0	−7.6	.7	−2.3	−2.4	−4.2	−5.4	.8	−5.0	.5
33	Corporate equity issues	1.0	1.6	.6	1.1	.9	1.0	1.0	1.0	.9	.9	.8
34	Credit market debt	.5	−.1	1.8	6.9	4.8	4.1	11.5	2.7	10.2	6.1	.1
35	Corporate bonds	.2	.7	.6	.2	.2	.2	.1	.3	.2		.2
36	Open-market paper	.3	−.8	1.3	6.7	4.5	3.9	11.3	2.4	10.1	5.8	−.1
37	Profit taxes payable	−.3	—	.3	.3	.5	.5	.4	.5	.5	.5	.5
38	Miscellaneous liabilities	1.0	2.9	6.5	11.9	8.6	7.0	11.7	1.6	16.5	4.0	12.0
39	Discrepancy	−3.7	−2.9	−6.0	−6.3	−7.8	−8.1	−6.7	−6.3	−9.2	−7.1	−8.8
40	Memo: credit market funds advanced	29.4	59.6	87.6	128.7	120.6	130.7	119.3	121.1	139.5	174.5	47.3

* IV/79 based on incomplete information.
† Consists of U.S.-chartered commercial banks, their domestic affiliates, Edge Act corporations, agencies and branches of foreign banks, and banks in U.S. possessions. Edge Act corporations and offices of foreign banks appear together in these tables as "foreign banking offices."
‡ Floats and discrepancies in interbank deposits and loans.

SOURCE: Board of Governors of the Federal Reserve System, *Flow of Funds Accounts*, Fourth Quarter 1979, February 11, 1980.

agreements to repurchase them at a future date (line 28), and borrowing from the Federal Reserve banks and foreign banking organizations (lines 30 and 31).

Balancing Out a Sources and Uses Statement. As we have seen, sources and uses of funds statements in the Flow of Funds Accounts are derived from the aggregated balance sheets of each sector of the economy. Because balance sheets must always balance out, with total assets equal to total liabilities plus net worth, we would also expect a sources and uses of funds statement to balance out (except, of course, for discrepancies due to gaps or inaccuracies in the underlying data). In a sources and uses statement,

$$\begin{array}{c} \text{Net investment} \\ \text{in plant} \\ \text{and equipment} \end{array} + \begin{array}{c} \text{Net acquisitions} \\ \text{of financial} \\ \text{assets} \end{array} = \begin{array}{c} \text{Net increase in} \\ \text{liabilities} + \text{Change} \\ \text{in current surplus account} \end{array} \quad (10\text{--}1)$$

Net acquisitions of financial assets are frequently referred to as financial investment, while net purchases of plant and equipment may be labeled real investment. Both are *uses* of funds for a sector or economic unit. Net increases in liabilities represent "borrowing" in the current period. And changes in the current surplus account reflect current saving. Both of these latter items are *sources* of funds. Therefore, the relationship shown above may be written simply as

$$\begin{array}{c} \text{Net real investment} + \text{Net financial investment} \\ = \text{Net borrowing} + \text{Net current saving} \end{array} \quad (10\text{--}2)$$

or,

$$\text{Total uses of funds} = \text{Total sources of funds} \quad (10\text{--}3)$$

For all units—businesses, households, and governments—and for all sectors of the economy, the above statements must hold true. For example, in the commercial banking sector during 1979 we have, as shown in Exhibit 10–9:

Uses of Funds ($ billions)		Sources of Funds ($ billions)	
Net real investment in plant and equipment (line 2)	$ 4.1	Net borrowing (line 20)	$117.9
Net financial investment (line 3)	126.0	Net current saving (line 1)	4.3
			$122.2
		Statistical discrepancy (line 39)	7.8
Total uses	$130.1	Total sources	$130.0

Once the statistical discrepancy is taken into account, total uses and sources of funds should be equal for this and all other sectors in the financial system. In this instance, rounding of the figures still produces a slight statistical discrepancy in the totals of $0.1 billion.

EXHIBIT 10–10
Flow of Funds Matrix for the U.S. Economy ($ billions)

	Seasonally Adjusted Annual Rates					1978		1979				
	1975	1976	1977	1978	1979	III	IV	I	II	III	IV*	
1 Total funds raised	223.5	296.0	392.5	481.7	481.5	471.5	525.0	456.5	487.7	548.1	433.5	1
2 Investment company shares	-.1	-1.0	-.9	-1.0	-.9	-1.7	-1.3	*	-.6	-2.7	-.6	2
3 Other corporate equities	10.8	12.9	4.9	4.7	6.6	10.1	8.6	5.6	5.4	6.9	8.4	3
4 Debt instruments	212.8	284.1	388.5	478.0	475.8	463.1	517.7	450.8	482.9	543.8	425.7	4
5 U.S. government securities	98.2	88.1	84.3	95.2	89.9	93.3	87.5	72.5	74.3	92.6	120.3	5
6 State + local obligations	16.1	15.7	23.7	28.3	21.3	33.0	24.4	22.3	12.5	25.2	25.1	6
7 Corporate + foreign bonds	36.4	37.2	36.1	31.6	33.7	26.4	31.7	35.4	35.9	34.9	28.7	7
8 Mortgages	57.2	87.1	134.0	149.0	159.5	154.2	158.7	158.3	164.5	159.3	155.8	8
9 Consumer credit	9.7	25.6	40.6	50.6	42.3	48.8	53.3	51.1	45.3	43.0	30.0	9
10 Bank loans, NEC	-12.2	7.0	29.8	58.4	49.5	48.2	75.4	35.5	64.1	95.8	2.2	10
11 Open-market paper	-1.2	8.1	15.0	26.4	40.5	20.3	40.6	37.7	44.9	55.4	24.1	11
12 Other loans	8.7	15.3	25.2	38.6	39.2	39.0	46.1	38.2	41.4	37.6	39.6	12

* Based on incomplete information.
SOURCE: Board of Governors of the Federal Reserve System, *Flow of Funds Accounts,* Fourth Quarter, 1979, February 1980.

EXHIBIT 10–11
Credit Market Funds Raised by Financial and Nonfinancial Sectors of the U.S. Economy ($ billions)

	Seasonally Adjusted Annual Rates					1978		1979			
	1975	1976	1977	1978	1979	III	IV	I	II	III	IV
Credit market funds raised by nonfinancial sectors											
Total funds raised											
1 By nonfinancial sectors	210.8	271.9	338.5	400.3	394.6	398.7	433.6	374.5	394.1	460.9	348.0
2 Excluding equities	200.7	261.1	335.4	398.2	390.5	391.0	427.6	371.6	391.6	456.1	342.0
3 U.S. government	85.4	69.0	56.8	53.7	37.4	52.8	39.2	24.7	29.9	40.4	54.5
4 Treasury issues	85.8	69.1	57.6	55.1	38.8	55.1	40.7	27.3	31.9	40.8	55.2
5 Agency issues + mortgages	-.4	-.1	-.9	-1.4	-1.4	-2.3	-1.5	-2.6	-2.0	-.4	-.6
6 All other nonfinancial sectors	125.4	202.9	281.8	346.6	357.2	345.9	394.4	349.8	364.2	420.6	293.5
7 Corporate equities	10.1	10.8	3.1	2.1	4.1	7.7	5.9	2.9	2.5	4.8	6.1
8 Debt instruments	115.3	192.0	278.6	344.5	353.1	338.3	388.5	346.9	361.7	415.7	287.4
Private domestic											
9 Nonfinancial sectors	112.1	182.0	267.9	314.4	334.4	319.2	333.3	340.2	340.1	361.1	295.3
10 Corporate equities	9.9	10.5	2.7	2.6	3.2	7.6	6.4	2.9	2.8	2.9	4.4
11 Debt instruments	102.1	171.5	265.1	311.8	331.1	311.6	326.9	337.3	337.4	358.2	290.9
12 Debt capital instruments	98.4	123.5	175.6	196.6	203.8	205.6	204.7	202.6	202.6	203.4	206.4
13 State + local obligations	16.1	15.7	23.7	28.3	21.3	33.0	24.4	22.3	12.5	25.2	25.1
14 Corporate bonds	27.2	22.8	21.0	20.1	21.8	17.9	21.3	21.1	25.4	18.5	21.8
15 Mortgages	55.0	85.0	131.0	148.2	160.8	154.7	159.0	159.2	164.7	159.6	159.5
16 Home mortgages	39.5	63.7	96.4	104.5	106.1	104.9	113.6	111.0	111.1	102.0	100.4
17 Multi-family resid.	*	1.8	7.4	10.2	10.1	11.8	10.5	9.0	7.2	12.4	11.9

18	Commercial	11.0	13.4	18.4	23.3	27.2	26.3	24.4	22.9	28.5	29.5	28.1	18
19	Farm	4.6	6.1	8.8	10.2	17.2	11.6	10.5	16.2	17.9	15.7	19.1	19
20	Other debt instruments	3.8	48.0	89.5	115.2	127.3	106.0	122.2	134.8	134.7	154.8	84.4	20
21	Consumer credit	9.7	25.6	40.6	50.6	42.3	48.8	53.3	51.1	45.3	43.0	30.0	21
22	Bank loans NEC	-12.3	4.0	27.0	37.3	47.1	26.1	36.8	41.4	52.4	65.7	28.6	22
23	Open-market paper	-2.6	4.0	2.9	5.2	10.9	9.9	.3	12.7	8.8	23.0	-1.1	23
24	Other	9.0	14.4	19.0	22.2	27.0	21.3	31.8	29.6	28.3	23.1	27.0	24
25	By borrowing sector:	112.1	182.0	267.9	314.4	334.4	319.2	333.3	340.2	340.1	361.0	295.3	25
26	State + local governments	13.7	15.2	20.4	23.6	18.0	30.5	21.7	18.9	10.0	21.0	22.2	26
27	Households	49.7	90.5	139.9	162.6	160.4	162.3	176.0	167.2	167.9	159.4	147.3	27
28	Nonfinancial business	48.6	76.3	107.6	128.2	156.0	126.4	135.7	154.1	162.3	180.7	125.8	28
29	Farm	8.8	10.9	14.7	18.1	26.8	19.6	22.0	24.6	22.7	27.8	32.0	29
30	Nonfarm noncorporate	2.0	4.7	12.9	15.4	16.1	16.4	12.6	17.5	12.8	23.6	10.5	30
31	Corporate	37.9	60.7	79.9	94.7	113.1	90.4	101.1	112.1	126.8	129.4	83.2	31
32	Debt instruments	28.0	50.2	77.2	92.2	109.8	82.8	94.7	109.2	124.0	126.5	78.8	32
33	Equities	9.9	10.5	2.7	2.6	3.2	7.6	6.4	2.9	2.8	2.9	4.4	33
34	Foreign	13.3	20.8	13.9	32.3	22.9	26.7	61.1	9.6	24.1	59.5	-1.8	34
35	Corporate equities	.2	.3	.4	-.5	.9	.1	-.5	.1	-.2	2.0	1.6	35
36	Debt instruments	13.2	20.5	13.5	32.8	22.0	26.7	61.6	9.6	24.3	57.5	-3.4	36
37	Bonds	6.2	8.6	5.1	4.0	5.0	1.9	4.2	4.2	2.8	6.5	6.5	37
38	Bank loans NEC	3.9	6.8	3.1	18.3	2.8	20.4	34.1	.5	8.0	26.9	-24.2	38
39	Open-market paper	.3	1.9	2.4	6.6	11.2	-.7	19.9	1.7	10.5	21.5	11.1	39
40	U.S. government loans	2.8	3.3	3.0	3.9	3.0	5.1	3.3	3.2	3.1	2.7	3.1	40
41	Memo: U.S. govt. cash balance / Totals net of changes in U.S. government cash balances—	2.9	3.2	1.1	3.8	.1	6.9	-2.0	-14.0	8.1	12.5	-6.3	41
42	Total funds raised	207.9	268.8	337.4	396.6	394.5	391.8	435.6	388.5	386.1	448.4	354.3	42
43	By U.S. government	82.5	65.9	55.7	49.9	37.3	45.9	41.2	38.7	21.8	27.9	60.8	43

EXHIBIT 10-11 (concluded)

Credit market funds raised by financial sectors

	Seasonally Adjusted Annual Rates					1978		1979				
	1975	1976	1977	1978	1979	III	IV	I	II	III	IV	
Total funds raised												
By financial sectors	12.7	24.1	54.0	81.4	86.9	72.8	91.4	82.0	93.6	87.2	85.5	1
U.S. govt. related	13.5	18.6	26.3	41.4	52.4	40.4	48.3	47.7	44.2	52.2	65.7	2
Sponsored cr. ag. sec.	2.3	3.3	7.0	23.1	24.6	23.9	24.7	25.3	18.1	18.6	36.4	3
Mortgage pool securities	10.3	15.7	20.5	18.3	27.8	16.5	23.6	22.4	26.1	33.6	29.3	4
Loans from U.S. government	.9	-.4	-1.2	—	—	—	—	—	—	—	—	5
Private financial sectors	-.8	5.5	27.7	40.0	34.5	32.4	43.1	34.3	49.4	35.0	19.8	6
Corporate equities	.6	1.0	.9	1.7	1.6	.8	1.4	2.7	2.3	-.6	1.7	7
Debt instruments	-1.4	4.4	26.9	38.3	32.9	31.6	41.8	31.6	47.1	35.6	18.1	8
Corporate bonds	2.9	5.8	10.1	7.5	7.0	6.6	6.2	10.1	7.7	9.9	.4	9
Mortgages	2.3	2.1	3.1	.9	-1.2	-.4	-.3	-.8	-.1	-.2	-3.7	10
Bank loans NEC	-3.7	-3.7	-.3	2.8	-.5	1.7	4.5	-6.4	3.7	3.3	-2.2	11
Open-market paper	1.1	2.2	9.6	14.6	18.4	11.1	20.4	23.2	25.7	10.9	14.1	12
Loans from FHLBs	-4.0	-2.0	4.3	12.5	9.2	12.6	11.0	5.4	10.0	11.7	9.5	13
Total, by sector	12.7	24.1	54.0	81.4	86.9	72.8	91.4	82.0	93.6	87.2	85.5	14
Sponsored credit agencies	3.2	2.9	5.8	23.1	24.6	23.9	24.7	25.3	18.1	18.6	36.4	15
Mortgage pools	10.3	15.7	20.5	18.3	27.8	16.5	23.6	22.4	26.1	33.6	29.3	16
Private financial sectors	-.8	5.5	27.7	40.0	34.5	32.4	43.1	34.3	49.4	35.0	19.8	17
Commercial banks	1.2	2.3	1.1	1.3	1.1	1.1	1.1	1.3	1.0	1.1	1.0	18
Bank affiliates	.3	-.8	1.3	6.7	4.5	3.9	11.3	2.4	10.1	5.8	-.1	19
Savings + loan associations	-2.3	.1	9.9	14.3	9.8	13.3	11.1	5.1	14.6	15.9	3.7	20
Other insurance companies	1.0	.9	.9	1.1	1.0	1.1	1.2	1.0	1.0	1.0	.9	21
Finance companies	.5	6.4	17.6	18.6	19.5	15.4	21.1	25.1	23.7	14.5	15.5	22
REITs	-1.4	-2.4	-2.2	-1.0	-.6	-.7	-1.4	-.6	-.4	-.8	-.5	23
Open-end investment companies	-.1	-1.0	-.9	-1.0	-.9	-1.7	-1.3	*	-.6	-2.7	-.6	24

Constructing a Flow of Funds Matrix for the Economy as a Whole. The final step in the construction of the Federal Reserve's Flow of Funds Accounts is to combine the sources and uses of funds statement for each sector into a Flow of Funds Matrix for the whole economy. An example of such a matrix is provided in Exhibit 10–10, which shows the total amount of funds raised by all sectors in the American economy during the 1975–79 period. This exhibit indicates that $481.5 billion net was raised in U.S. money and capital markets during 1979 alone (line 1). The majority of funds sought by businesses, consumers, and governments in the nation's financial markets were raised by issuing debt instruments which totaled a net $475.8 billion (line 4). Residential and commercial mortgages were the most heavily used borrowing instrument, totaling $159.5 billion (line 8). The U.S. Treasury and various federal agencies were also heavy borrowers of funds, issuing about $90 billion in debt instruments (line 5). State and local governments borrowed $21.3 billion (line 6), while U.S. corporations and foreign borrowers issued $33.7 billion net in bonds during 1979 (line 7). Installment credit extended to consumers totaled more than $42 billion (line 9).

What sectors of the economy were the heaviest borrowers in the financial system during 1979? Exhibit 10–11, illustrating another component of the Flow of Funds Matrix, shows that households led all other sectors, raising $160.4 billion in credit market funds (line 27), followed closely by nonfinancial businesses, which borrowed $156 billion (line 28). Within the business sector, corporations accounted for the bulk of fund-raising activity, issuing nearly $110 billion in debt (line 32) and $3.2 billion in stock (line 33). Foreign businesses and agencies drew upon U.S. money and capital markets for almost $23 billion in debt and equity funds (line 34) during 1979.

Limitations and Uses of the Flow of Funds Accounts. It should be clear by now that the Flow of Funds Accounts provide a vast amount of information on current and past trends in the financial system. They are an indispensable aid in tracing the flow of savings and other funds through the nation's money and capital markets. However, these social accounts contain a number of limitations which must be kept in mind.

First, the Flow of Funds Accounts present no information on transactions among economic units *within* each sector. If a household sells stock to another household, this transaction will not be picked up in the accounts since both units are in the same sector. However, if a household sells stock to a business firm, this transaction will be captured by the flow of funds bookkeeping system. Moreover, the accounts show only *net* flows over the period under study, not changes or fluctuations which occurred between beginning and ending points of the study period.

Finally, all flow of funds data are expressed in terms of current market values. Therefore, these accounts measure not only the flow of saving in the economy but also fluctuations in the prices of stocks, bonds, and other financial assets (i.e., capital gains and losses). This market-value bias distorts estimates of the amount of saving and investment activity occurring from quarter to quarter and from year to year.

Despite these limitations, however, the Flow of Funds Accounts are one of the most comprehensive sources of information available to students of the financial system. They provide vital clues on the demand and supply forces which shape movements in interest rates and security prices. The Flow of Funds Accounts indicate which types of securities are growing or declining in volume and which sectors finance other sectors within the economic system. One of the principal uses of flow of funds data today is to forecast interest rates and build econometric models to simulate future conditions in the credit markets. Coupled with the National Income Accounts and other sources of information, flow of funds accounting provides us with the raw material out of which financial decisions can be made.

CONCLUSIONS

An unimpeded flow of relevant information is vital to the functioning of the financial system. If the scarce resource of credit is to be allocated efficiently and an ample flow of savings made available for investment, financial information must be easily and instantly accessible to market participants. There are really two types of markets within the financial system—an information market and a market for financial claims, evidencing loans and investments. The two markets must work together in coordinated fashion to accomplish the desired end result—a smooth flow of scarce loanable funds toward their most profitable and beneficial uses.

In this chapter we have examined the information market in some detail. Our principal focus has been upon five broad categories of financial information available today—bond prices and yields, stock prices and dividend yields, the financial condition of security issuers, general conditions in the nation's economy and financial system, and social accounting data. The purpose of this chapter has been to give the student of the financial system a broad overview of the kinds and quality of information currently available. Knowing where to find relevant and up-to-date information is an essential ingredient in the process of solving economic and financial problems.

STUDY QUESTIONS

1. Why is the availability of financial information important to borrowers and lenders of funds? Government policymakers?
2. List several major sources of financial information, and discuss what types of information each contains.
3. If you needed to gather information for a possible stock or bond purchase, where would you look? What information is available on the financial condition of major U.S. companies?

4. What is *social accounting?* Compare and contrast the Flow of Funds Accounts with the National Income Accounts. What types of information does each provide that might be useful for financial decisions?

5. Explain how the Flow of Funds Accounts are constructed. What is a sources and uses of funds statement?

6. Discuss the principal limitations of flow of funds data and the implications of those limitations.

SELECTED REFERENCES

1. Cohen, J. "Copeland's Moneyflows After Twenty-Five Years: A Survey." *Journal of Economic Literature*, March 1972, pp. 1–25.

2. Freund, William C., and Edward D. Zinbarg. "Application of Flow of Funds to Interest-Rate Forecasting." *Journal of Finance*, May 1963, pp. 231–48.

3. Goldsmith, Raymond W. *Capital Market Analysis and the Financial Accounts of the Nation*. Morristown, N.J.: General Learning Press, 1972.

4. National Bureau of Economic Research. *The Flow-of-Funds Approach to Social Accounting*. New York, 1962.

5. Lawrence S. Ritter. *The Flow of Funds Accounts: A Framework for Financial Analysis*. New York: Institute of Finance, New York University, 1968.

part four

The Money Market

11

Characteristics of the Money Market

To the casual observer, the nation's financial markets appear to be one vast cauldron of borrowing and lending activity in which some individuals and institutions are seeking credit while others supply the funds needed to make lending possible. All transactions carried out in the financial markets seem to be basically the same—borrowers issue securities which lenders purchase. When the loan is repaid, the borrower retrieves the securities and returns funds to the lender. Closer examination of our financial institutions reveals, however, that beyond the simple act of exchanging securities for funds, there are major differences between one financial transaction and another. For example, you may borrow $100,000 for 30 years to purchase a new home, whereas my financing need may be for a six-month loan of $3,000 to cover my federal-income-tax obligation. A corporation may enter the financial markets this week to offer a new issue of 20-year bonds to finance the construction of an office building and next week find itself in need of funds for 60 days to purchase raw materials so that production can continue without interruption.

Clearly, then, the *purposes* for which money is borrowed within the financial system vary greatly from person to person, institution to institution, and transaction to transaction. And the different purposes for which money is borrowed result in the creation of different kinds of financial assets, having different maturities, yields, default risks, and other features. In this chapter and the others in this section of the book we will be focusing upon a collection of financial markets which share common purposes in their trading activity and deal in financial instruments with similar features. Our particular focus is upon the *money market*—the market for short-term credit.

In the nation's money market, loans have an original maturity of one year or less. Money market loans are used to help corporations and governments pay the wages and salaries of their workers, make repairs, purchase inventories, pay dividends and taxes, and satisfy other short-term working-capital needs. In this respect the *money market* stands in sharp contrast to the *capital market*. The capital market deals in long-term credit that has over a year to maturity and is usually used to finance capital investment projects. There are important similarities between the money and capital markets, as we will see in subsequent chapters, but also important differences which make these two markets unique.

CHARACTERISTICS OF THE MONEY MARKET

The money market, like all financial markets, provides a channel for the exchange of financial assets for money. However, it differs from other parts of the financial system in its emphasis upon loans to meet purely short-term cash needs. *The money market is the mechanism through which holders of temporary cash surpluses meet holders of temporary cash deficits.* It is designed, on the one hand, to meet the short-run cash requirements of corporations, financial institutions, and governments, providing a mechanism for granting loans as short as overnight and as long as one year to maturity. At the same time, the money market provides an investment outlet for those spending units (also principally corporations, financial institutions, and governments) who hold surplus cash for short periods of time and wish to earn at least some return on temporarily idle funds. The essential function of the money market, of course, is to bring these two groups into contact with each other in order to make borrowing and lending possible.

The Need for a Money Market

Why is such a market needed? There are two basic reasons. First, inflows of cash and outflows of cash are rarely in perfect harmony with each other. Governments, for example, collect taxes from the public only at certain times of the year, such as in April, when personal and corporate income tax payments are due. Disbursements of cash must be made throughout the year, however, in order to cover such items as wages and salaries of government employees, office supplies, repairs, and fuel costs as well as unexpected expenses. When taxes are collected, governments usually are flush with funds which far exceed their immediate cash needs. At these times they frequently enter the money market as lenders and purchase U.S. Treasury bills, bank deposits, and other attractive financial assets. Later on, however, as cash runs low relative to current expenditures, these same governmental units must once again enter the money market to sell securities, cash in deposits, and even borrow short-term money.

Business firms, too, collect sales revenue from their customers at one point in time and dispense cash at other points in time to cover wages and salaries, make repairs, and meet other operating expenses. The checking account of an active business firm fluctuates daily between large surpluses and low or nonexistent balances. A surplus cash position frequently brings such a firm into the money market as a net lender of funds, investing idle funds in the hope of earning at least a modest rate of return. Cash deficits force it onto the borrowing side of the market, however, seeking other institutions with temporary cash surpluses. Clearly, then, the money market serves to bridge the gap between receipts and expenditures of funds, covering cash deficits with short-term borrowings when current expenses exceed receipts and providing an investment outlet to earn some interest income for those units whose current receipts exceed their expenditures.

To fully appreciate the workings of the money market, we must remember that *money* is one of the most perishable of all commodities. The holding of idle surplus cash is expensive, since cash balances earn little or no income for the owner. When idle cash is not invested, the holder incurs an opportunity cost in the form of interest income which is foregone.[1] Moreover, each day that idle funds are not invested is a day's income lost forever. When large amounts of funds are involved, the income lost from not profitably investing idle funds for even 24 hours can be substantial. For example, the interest income from a loan of $1 million for one day at a 10 percent annual rate of interest amounts to nearly $280.[2] In a week's time close to $2,000 in interest would be lost from not investing a million dollars of idle funds. Many students of the financial system find it hard to believe that investment outlets exist for loans as short as one day or even two or three days. In fact, however, billions of dollars in credit are extended in the American money market each day to securities dealers, commercial banks, and nonfinancial corporations to cover such temporary shortfalls of cash. As we will see in Chapter 13, one important money market instrument—the federal funds loan—is designed mainly for extending credit overnight or over a weekend.

---

[1] The nationwide spread of interest-bearing checking accounts (such as NOW accounts) has reduced the opportunity cost of holding cash balances for some units in the economy. However, the yields on these balances are still among the lowest available in the financial system. For example, the maximum legal interest rate on NOWs is 5¼ percent, and these accounts may be held only by individuals and nonprofit institutions.

[2] As we saw in Chapter 7, the amount of interest income from a loan may be calculated from the formula:

$$I = P \times r \times t$$

where I is interest income, P is the principal amount loaned, r is the annual rate of interest, and t is the maturity of the loan. In the example given above, we have:

$$I = (\$1,000,000)(0.10)(^1/_{360}) = \$277.78$$

Note that for purposes of simplifying the calculation we have assumed a 360-day year—a common assumption made in determining the yields on money market instruments.

Borrowers and Lenders in the Money Market

Who are the principal lenders of funds in the money market? And, who are the principal borrowers? These questions are difficult to answer since the same institutions frequently operate on *both sides* of the market. For example, a large commercial bank operating in the New York money market, such as Chase Manhattan or Manufacturers Hanover, will be borrowing short-term funds aggressively in the market through CDs, federal funds, and Eurodollars while simultaneously lending short-term funds to corporations who have temporary cash shortages. Frequently, large nonfinancial corporations borrow millions of dollars on a single day only to come back into the money market later in the week as a lender of funds due to a sudden upsurge in cash receipts. Institutions which typically play both sides of the money market include commercial banks, major nonfinancial corporations, state and local units of government, finance companies, and savings banks. Even the nation's central bank, the Federal Reserve System, may be an aggressive supplier of funds to the money market on one day and reverse itself the day following, demanding funds through the sale of securities in the open market. One institution which is virtually always on the demand side of the market, however, is the U.S. Treasury, which borrows billions of dollars every week through the issuance of Treasury bills.

The Goals of Money Market Investors

Investors in the money market seek mainly *safety* and *liquidity* plus the opportunity to earn some interest income. This is because funds invested in the money market represent only temporary cash surpluses and are usually needed in the near future to meet tax obligations, cover wage and salary costs, pay stockholder dividends, and so on. For this reason money market investors are especially *sensitive to risk*.

The strong aversion to risk among money market investors is especially evident when there is even a hint of trouble concerning the financial condition of a major money market borrower. For example, when the huge Penn Central Transportation Company collapsed in 1970 and defaulted on its short-term commercial notes, the commercial paper market virtually ground to a halt because many investors refused to buy even the notes offered by top-grade companies. Similarly, in 1974 when Franklin National Bank of New York, holding nearly $4 billion in assets, closed its doors, the rates on short-term certificates of deposit (CDs) issued by other big New York banks surged upward due to fears on the part of money market investors that *all* large-bank CDs had become more risky.

Types of Investment Risk

What kinds of risk do investors face in the financial markets? And how do money market instruments rank in terms of these different kinds of risk?

First, all securities, including money market instruments, carry *market risk*, which refers to the danger that their prices will fall, subjecting the investor to a capital loss. Even U.S. Treasury notes and bonds decline in price when interest rates rise. Only the dollar bill (i.e., a Federal Reserve note) escapes market risk in the domestic economy because, of course, a dollar always exchanges for a dollar.

Securities issued by private firms and state and local governments also carry *default risk*. For such securities there is always some positive probability that the borrower will fail to meet some or all of the promised principal and/or interest payments.

Lenders of funds face the possibility that increases in the average level of prices for all goods and services will reduce the purchasing power of their income; this is known as *inflation risk*. Of course, lenders usually attempt to offset anticipated inflation by charging higher contract rates on their loans.[3]

International investors also face *currency risk*—possible loss due to unfavorable changes in the value of foreign currencies. For example, if an American investor purchases British treasury bills in the London money market, the return from these bills may be severely reduced if the value of the British pound falls relative to the dollar during the life of the investment.[4]

Finally, *political risk* refers to the possibility that changes in government laws or regulations will result in a diminished rate of return to the investor or, in the extreme case, a total loss of invested capital. For example, the windfall profits tax on U.S. petroleum companies levied by Congress in the Spring of 1980 has reduced the earnings of petroleum stockholders. Investors in industries that are closely regulated, such as banking, insurance, and public utilities, continually run the risk that new price controls, output or service quotas, or other restrictions will be imposed, reducing their earnings potential. In some foreign countries, facilities and equipment owned by U.S. corporations have been expropriated by national governments, resulting in a complete loss for investors.

A summary of each of the foregoing kinds of risk is shown in Exhibit 11–1. Money market instruments generally offer more protection against such risks than most other investments. For example, the prices of money market securities tend to be remarkably stable over time compared to the prices of bonds, stocks, real estate, and actively traded commodities, such as wheat, corn, gold, and silver. Money market instruments generally do not offer the prospect of significant capital gains for the investor, but neither do they normally raise the specter of substantial capital losses. Similarly, default risk is minimal in the money market. In fact, money market borrowers must be well-established institutions with impeccable credit ratings before their securities can even be offered for sale in this market.

Few investments today adequately protect the investor against inflation

---

[3] Default risk and inflation risk are discussed in greater detail in Chapter 8.

[4] See Chapters 26 and 27 for a further examination of currency or exchange-rate risk.

EXHIBIT 11–1
Types of Risks Confronting Investors in the Financial Markets

Type of Risk	Definition
Market risk	The risk that the market price (value) of an asset will decline, resulting in a capital loss when sold. Sometimes referred to as interest-rate risk.
Default risk	The probability that a borrower will fail to meet one or more promised principal or interest payments on a loan or security.
Inflation risk	The risk that increases in the general price level will reduce the purchasing power of investor earnings from a loan or security investment.
Currency risk	The risk that adverse movements in the price of one national currency vis-à-vis another will reduce the net rate of return from a foreign investment. Sometimes called exchange-rate risk.
Political risk	The probability that changes in government laws or regulations will reduce the investor's return from an investment.

risk. While fine china, oil properties, single-family homes, diamonds, and even rare postage stamps have been rising rapidly in value, many security investments have lagged well behind. For example, a recent study by Salomon Brothers, a prestigious New York securities dealer and investment advisor, reveals that, over the 1968–78 period, common stocks, on average, rose in value only 2.8 percent a year, and high-grade corporate bonds, about 6 percent—both below the annual rate of inflation measured by the consumer price index.[5] In contrast, gold prices increased at an average annual rate of about 16 percent, while prices for farmland climbed almost 11 percent annually over the same period. Money market securities usually are not an effective hedge against inflation, but they do offer the investor superior liquidity, allowing him to quickly cash them in when a promising inflation-hedged investment opportunity comes along.

Currency risk concerns the international investor who frequently must convert one currency into another. This risk has dramatically increased in recent years due to the advent of foreign exchange rates which float with market conditions. Investors who purchase securities in foreign markets cannot completely escape currency risk, but they are probably less prone to such losses when buying money market instruments, due to the short-term nature of these securities. Money market instruments also provide some hedge against political risk because they are short-term investments and fewer changes in government policy are likely over brief intervals of time.

---

[5] See Salomon Brothers, "Ten-Year Compound Growth," from *Stocks Are Still the Only Bargain Left,* July 3, 1978, p. 1.

Money Market Maturities

Despite the fact that money market securities cover a narrow range of maturities—one year or less—there are maturities available within this range to meet just about every short-term cash and investment need. We must distinguish here between *original maturity* and *actual maturity,* however. The interval of time between the issue date of a security and the date on which the borrower promises to redeem it is the security's original maturity. Actual maturity, on the other hand, refers to the number of days, months, or years between today and the date the security is actually redeemed or retired.

Original maturities on money market instruments range from as short as one day on many federal funds transactions and loans to security dealers, out to a full year on some Eurodollar deposits, bankers' acceptances, bank certificates of deposit, and U.S. Treasury bills. Obviously, once a money market instrument is issued, it grows shorter in actual maturity every day. Because there are thousands of money market securities outstanding, some of which reach maturity each day, investors have a wide menu from which to select the precise number of days they need to invest cash.

Depth and Breadth of the Money Market

The money market is extremely *broad* and *deep,* meaning it can absorb a large volume of transactions with only small effects on security prices and interest rates. Investors can easily sell most money market instruments on short notice, often in a matter of minutes. This is one of the most efficient markets in the world, containing a vast network of securities dealers, major banks, and funds brokers in constant touch with one another and alert to any "bargains." The slightest hint that a security is underpriced (i.e., carries an exceptionally high yield) usually brings forth a flood of buy orders, while money market traders are quick to dump or avoid overpriced securities. This market is dominated by active traders who constantly search their video display screens and tote boards for opportunities to *arbitage* funds—i.e., move money from a corner of the market with relatively low yields to investments offering the highest returns available. And overseeing the whole market is the Federal Reserve System, which tries to ensure that trading is orderly and prices are reasonably stable.

There is no centralized trading arena in the money market as there is on a stock exchange, for example. The money market is a *telephone market,* in which participants arrange trades over the phone and usually confirm by wire. Speed is of the essence in this market because, as we observed earlier, money is a highly perishable commodity. Each day that passes may mean thousands of dollars in lost interest income from uninvested funds. Most business between traders, therefore, is conducted in seconds or minutes, and payment is made almost instantaneously.

Federal Funds versus Clearinghouse Funds

How can funds move so fast in the money market? The reason is that money market traders usually deal in federal funds. These funds are mainly deposit balances of commercial banks held at the regional Federal Reserve banks and at larger correspondent banks across the nation. When a dealer firm buys securities from an investor, for example, it immediately contacts its bank and requests that funds be transferred from its account to the investor's account at another bank. Many of these transactions move through the Federal Reserve's wire transfer network. In this case the Fed removes funds from the reserve account of the buyer's bank and transfers these reserves to the seller's bank. The transaction is so quick that the seller of securities has funds available to make new investments, pay bills, or for other purposes the same day the trade is carried out. Federal funds are often called "immediately available funds" because of the speed with which money moves from one bank's reserve account to that of another.

Contrast this method of payment with that used generally in the capital market and by most businesses and households. When most of us purchase goods and services—especially those involving large amounts of money— the *check* is the most desirable means of paying the bill. Funds transferred by check are known as *clearinghouse funds*. This is because, once the buyer writes a check, it goes to the seller's bank, which forwards that check eventually to the bank upon which it was drawn. If the two banks are in the same community, they exchange bundles of checks drawn against each other every day through the local *clearinghouse*—an agreed-upon location where checks and other cash items are delivered and passed from one bank to another.

Clearinghouse funds are an acceptable means of payment for most purposes, but not in the money market, where speed is of the essence. It takes at least a day to clear local checks and two to three days for checks moving between cities. For money market transactions, this is far too slow, because no interest can be earned until the check is collected. Clearinghouse funds also have an element of risk because a check may be returned as fraudulent or for insufficient funds. Federal funds transactions, however, are not only speedy but safe.

A Market of Large Borrowers and Lenders

The money market of the United States is dominated by a relatively small number of large financial institutions. No more than a hundred commercial banks in New York, Chicago, San Francisco, Dallas, and a handful of other money centers are at the heart of the market. These large banks account for the bulk of federal funds trading through which money market transactions are carried out. In addition, securities move readily from sellers to buyers through the market-making activities of about three dozen major government security dealers and a handful of dealers and brokers in commercial paper, bankers' acceptances, certificates of deposit, and federal funds. And, of course, the U.S. government plays a major role in this market as the largest borrower and as regulator, setting the "rules of the game." The Federal Reserve System, operating principally through the trading desk at the Federal Reserve Bank of New York, is in the market nearly every day, either supplying funds to banks and securities dealers through purchases of securities or absorbing funds through security sales.

Individual transactions in the money market involve huge amounts of funds. Most trading occurs in multiples of a million dollars. For this reason the money market is often referred to as a "wholesale" market for funds, as opposed to the "retail" market where consumers and small businesses borrow.

PRINCIPAL INSTRUMENTS OF THE MONEY MARKET

The principal financial instruments traded in the money market are U.S. Treasury bills, federal agency securities, dealer loans and repurchase agreements, bank certificates of deposit (CDs), federal funds, commercial paper, bankers acceptances, financial futures, and Eurodollar deposits. Because each of these instruments is discussed in more detail in the next several chapters, we will give only a brief overview of the major money market instruments here.

Treasury Bills

Treasury bills are direct obligations of the United States government which must have an original maturity of one year or less. Most bills are issued in three-month, six-month, and one-year maturities and are auctioned every week in the money market. Treasury bills are discussed at length in Chapter 12.

Federal Agency Securities

Another popular government IOU traded in the money market is the federal agency security, issued by several different agencies and administrative units within the federal government. Examples of such agencies include the Federal Land Banks, the Federal Home Loan Banks, the Banks for Cooperatives, the Tennessee Valley Authority, and the Federal National Mortgage Association. The majority of federal agencies issuing open-market securities are not officially a part of the federal government but are semiprivate institutions operated to aid certain sectors of the economy, such as small businesses and home buyers. As a result, most federal agency securities are not guaranteed by the federal government as are U.S. Treasury bills. Nevertheless, these securities are regarded by most investors as virtually free of default risk. Federal agency securities are examined in greater detail in Chapter 14.

Dealer Loans and Repurchase Agreements

Securities dealers who make a daily market in U.S. Treasury and federal agency securities must depend heavily upon the money market for borrowed funds. These dealer houses carry hundreds of millions of dollars in government and private securities to offer their customers, deriving the bulk of their operating capital by floating short-term loans with commercial banks, nonfinancial corporations, and other lenders. The two most heavily used sources of dealer funds are demand loans from major-money-center banks and security repurchase agreements (RPs) with banks and cash-rich nonfinancial corporations. These dealer credits are among the safest and most liquid investments in the money market because they are usually backed by U.S. government securities. Dealer loans and repurchase agreements are discussed in Chapter 12.

Bank-Related Money Market Instruments: Acceptances, CDs, Federal Funds, and Eurodollars

Commercial banks are the direct issuers of four major types of money market instruments—bankers' acceptances, certificates of deposit, federal funds loans, and Eurodollars. Bankers' acceptances are short-term instruments issued by the largest commercial banks and used primarily to assist in the financing of international trade. These time drafts, representing a bank's promise to pay, are discussed in Chapter 15.

Certificates of deposit—better known as CDs—are a receipt for funds deposited in a bank for a set period of time at a set interest rate. While banks issue CDs of many different sizes, including small, nonnegotiable consumer-type instruments with denominations as low as $500 or $1,000, the true money market CDs are negotiable instruments issued in minimum denominations of $100,000. There is an active secondary market for these large CDs, served by half a dozen major securities dealers in New York City. The characteristics of large, negotiable CDs are examined in Chapter 13.

Federal funds transactions are loans of reserves between banks, often as short as overnight, with the transaction being reversed the next day. There is a trend, however, toward longer-term federal funds transactions where banks have a more-permanent need for borrowed reserves. As we observed earlier, federal funds are the principal means of making payments in the American money market. The federal funds market is discussed in more detail in Chapter 13.

Deposits denominated in dollars but held in bank offices outside the United States are known as Eurodollars. As we will see in Chapter 15, the volume of Eurodollars grew rapidly during the 1960s and 1970s due to heavy lending and borrowing overseas by American banks and the investment of huge amounts of funds in Europe, Japan, and the Middle East by large U.S. manufacturing corporations. Foreign business activities by U.S. companies have created a need for dollar deposits abroad which can readily be bought and sold to provide working capital. In addition, the largest U.S. banks have come to rely upon the Eurodollar market as a supplementary source of reserves when domestic funds are scarce.

Commercial Paper

Another segment of the money market dominated by large corporations is the commercial paper market. Commercial paper consists of short-term notes (generally with maturities of nine months or less) issued by companies with the highest credit ratings. Paper issues are used, in most cases, to meet business working-capital needs, especially to purchase inventories of goods and raw materials. Because the secondary market for commercial paper is not well developed, issuers try to tailor paper maturities to match the needs of key investors in this market. Commercial paper is analyzed in greater detail in Chapter 14.

Financial Futures

One of the most innovative and rapidly growing short-term financial markets in recent years involves trading in financial futures. Futures trading is designed to protect the investor against market risk by transferring that risk to someone else willing to bear it. As we will see in Chapter 16, traders in the financial futures market enter into short-term contracts for the delivery of certain securities (mainly Treasury bills, long-term Treasury bonds, GNMA mortgage-backed securities, and commercial paper) at a specific location, time, and price. These markets enable investors to "lock in" a particular yield on a security and, therefore, protect the return from a financial investment.

VOLUME OF MONEY MARKET SECURITIES

The volume of money market securities has grown rapidly in recent years. One reason is the economy's growing need for liquid, readily marketable investment securities. Another factor in the money market's growth has been the attractive yields offered investors. Frequently in recent years money market yields have risen above rates available on longer-term securities, causing many investors to shift their savings into the money market. In May 1981, for example, market rates on three-month Treasury bills averaged 16.3 percent, while the average yield on 20-year Treasury bonds was only 13.8 percent. Then, too, in a period of severe inflation, such as characterized the late 1970s and early 1980s, many investors are hesitant to commit their funds to long-term securities, particularly those with fixed rates of return. In an inflationary environment, investors often prefer the marketability and liquidity of money market securities.

As shown in Exhibit 11–2, two of the most important money market instruments (measured by dollar volume) are U.S. Treasury bills and bank

EXHIBIT 11–2
Volume of Selected Money Market Instruments, 1977–1980

Financial Instrument	Billions of Dollars at Year-End			
	1977	1978	1979	1980
U.S. Treasury bills	$161.1	$161.7	$172.6	$216.1
Federal agency securities	112.5	137.1	—	193.2
Commercial paper	65.1	83.4	112.8	125.1
Bankers' acceptances	25.5	33.7	45.3	54.7
Federal funds borrowings and repurchase agreements	58.4	80.7	90.0	109.6
Eurodollar borrowings by domestic banks from own foreign branches	8.6	14.7	29.3	22.8
Certificates of deposit ($100,000 or more)	145.4	194.7	219.0	247.0

SOURCE: Board of Governors of the Federal Reserve System, *Federal Reserve Bulletin,* selected issues.

certificates of deposit (CDs). At the close of 1980, $216 billion in Treasury bills were outstanding, representing almost one quarter of the federal government's debt. During 1980 alone the volume of Treasury bills rose almost $44 billion. Somewhat larger in total amount were $100,000-plus certificates of deposit issued by U.S. banks and thrift institutions. These large-denomination CDs totaled close to $250 billion at the end of 1980. We should note, however, that the volume of CDs fluctuates widely with credit-market conditions, corporate earnings, and changes in interest rates available on other securities.

Nearly as large as Treasury bills and CDs is the total volume of securities issued by federal agencies. These high-quality securities, nearly half of which fall due within a year and therefore are true money market instruments, exceeded $190 billion at year-end 1980. Three quarters of all agency IOUs are issued by just three federally sponsored organizations—the Federal Home Loan Banks, the Federal National Mortgage Association, and the Farm Credit Banks. The remaining agency issues come from a variety of government-related enterprises and organizations, including the Department of Defense, Export-Import Bank, Postal Service, Tennessee Valley Authority, and Student Loan Marketing Association.

Commercial paper issued by topflight U.S. corporations totaled $125 billion in 1980 and represented one of the most rapidly growing money market instruments. Many large corporations have found the commercial paper market a cheaper and more flexible place to obtain credit than borrowing from banks. Bankers' acceptances—time drafts against large multinational banks—have grown even more rapidly, paralleling the spiraling growth of world trade. Acceptances more than doubled between 1977 and 1980, reaching nearly $55 billion in the latter year.

The volume of federal funds loans is difficult to estimate because thousands of U.S. banks are active in this market every day and not all transactions are reported. Moreover, the federal funds market is extremely volatile, reflecting wide swings in the flow of funds through the banking system. Estimates by the Federal Reserve System indicate that fed funds loans outstanding (including repurchase agreements) totaled nearly $110 billion in December 1980, compared to only $58 billion three years before.

The true size of the Eurodollar market is also unknown, principally because this market spans so many nations and is not regulated. The amount shown in Exhibit 11–2 of $22.8 billion includes only the net amount of Eurodollar borrowings by U.S. banks from their foreign branches. Conservative estimates of total Eurodollar deposits worldwide place the net figure between $480 and $670 billion.[6]

THE PATTERN OF INTEREST RATES IN THE MONEY MARKET

The rates of return on money market securities vary over time and among different securities. The foundation of the market's rate structure is the level of yields on U.S. Treasury bills. These securities are considered to have zero default risk and minimal market risk as well. Moreover, the resale market for Treasury bills is the most active and deep of all securities markets, making bills readily marketable should the investor need cash in a hurry. Because of this combination of low risk and ready marketability, Treasury bills carry the lowest yields in the American money market.

Other yields in the money market are scaled upward from Treasury bill rates. One set of yields which hovers very close to T-bill rates is the yield on federal agency securities, considered virtually riskless by many investors. Nevertheless, agency securities are less marketable than bills, and their quantity has increased rapidly in recent years. As a result, the yield spread between agencies and bills in recent periods averages at least a full percentage point in favor of agency securities.

Another yield in the money market which stays fairly close to the Treasury bill rate is the rate charged on federal funds loans. The low risk of these loans coupled with their short maturities helps to explain their relatively low yields. As shown in Exhibit 11–3, the fed funds rate in May 1981 was about three percentage points (or 300 basis points) above the rate of return on three-month Treasury bills.

---

[6] See Chapter 15 for a discussion of size estimates of the Eurodollar and Eurocurrency markets.

EXHIBIT 11–3
Yield Relationships in the Money Market, Week of May 29, 1981

Security	Yield (percent per annum)	Yield Spread with 3-Month U.S. Treasury Bills (basis points)
U.S. Treasury bills:*		
3-month	15.61%	—
6-month	14.55	−106
1-year	13.67	−194
Federal funds rate	18.71	+310
Commercial paper (prime):		
1-month	17.13	+152
3-month	16.77	+116
6-month	15.79	+ 18
Bank certificates of deposit:† ($100,000 or more):		
1-month	17.44	+183
3-month	17.57	+196
6-month	16.70	+109
Bankers' acceptances, 3-month	16.68	+107
Eurodollar deposits, 3-month	19.16	+355
Prime bank lending rate‡	19.61	+400
Federal Reserve discount rate	13	−261

* Based on daily closing bid prices in the secondary market and the bank discount method.
† Secondary market.
‡ Average for May 1981.
SOURCE: Board of Governors of the Federal Reserve System, *Federal Reserve Bulletin,* June 1981.

The interest rates on two bank-related financial instruments—negotiable CDs and bankers' acceptances—also tend to follow changes in the market yield on Treasury bills and hover close to prevailing bill rates for the same maturities. As shown in Exhibit 11–3, the secondary market yield on three-month CDs was almost two percentage points (or about 200 basis points) higher than the three-month T-bill rate, while the spread between this bill rate and the rate of return on three-month bankers' acceptances was only about one percentage point. CDs issued by the largest U.S. banks are rated prime and carry the lowest yields in the CD market. The same is true of prime-rated bankers' acceptances. Acceptances are considered to be a high-quality investment nearly as riskless as U.S. Treasury bills. However, the resale market for acceptances is not as active or as deep as the T-bill market, which helps to explain why acceptances must carry a slightly higher yield.

Large, well-established corporations in need of credit can, of course, draw upon many different sources of funds. However, when short-term credit is needed, two of the most popular funds sources are borrowing from commercial banks and issuing marketable IOUs in the commercial paper market. The largest and best-known corporations generally qualify for the prime bank lending rate. Thus, the market for prime-rate bank loans is a direct competitor with the commercial paper market. As shown in Exhibit 11–3, for those corporations able to tap either market, it is generally cheaper to borrow in the commercial paper market. The gap between commercial paper and prime rates is even wider than indicated in the exhibit because commercial banks usually require borrowing corporations to hold minimum cash balances on deposit with them equal to a specified percentage (usually 15 to 20 percent) of the loan. This spread in rates on short-term corporate loans favoring commercial paper explains why the commercial paper market has been one of the most rapidly growing segments of the U.S. money market in recent years.

The final money market interest rate shown in Exhibit 11–3 is the discount rate charged member banks when they borrow from the Federal Reserve banks. In contrast to the other yields discussed to this point, the discount rate is not determined by demand and supply forces in the marketplace but is set by the Federal Reserve banks with the approval of the Board of Governors of the Federal Reserve System. The level of the discount rate is governed by the Federal Reserve's assessment of the state of the economy and credit market conditions. Where possible, however, the Fed tries to keep the discount rate reasonably close to rates on U.S. Treasury bills (as illustrated in Figure 11–1). An unusually low discount rate may result in excessive bor-

FIGURE 11–1
Short-Term Interest Rates, Money Market (discount rate, effective date of change; all others, quarterly averages)

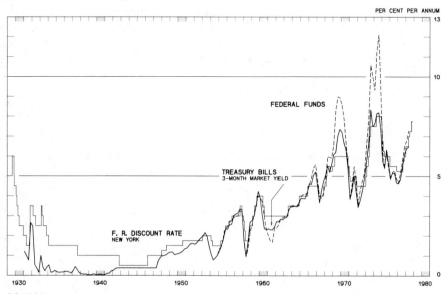

SOURCE: Board of Governors of the Federal Reserve System, *Historical Charts Book,* 1978.

rowing at the Fed's "discount window." In contrast, an excessively high discount rate forces banks to borrow heavily in the open market, increasing the volatility of interest rates and sometimes creating unstable market conditions.

SUMMARY AND CONCLUSIONS

In this chapter we have presented a broad overview of one of the most important components of any financial system—the money market. By convention, money markets are defined as the collection of institutions and trading relationships that move short-term funds from lenders to borrowers. All money market loans have an original maturity of one year or less. Most loans extended in the money market are designed to provide short-term working capital to businesses and governments so that they can purchase inventories, meet payrolls, pay dividends and taxes, and deal with other immediate needs for cash. These short-run cash needs arise from the fact the inflows and outflows of cash are not perfectly synchronized. In the real world, even with the best of planning, temporary cash deficits and temporary cash surpluses are more the rule rather than the exception.

The money market at one and the same time answers the needs of borrowers for short-term credit and the needs of lenders for temporary interest-bearing outlets for their surplus funds. In a period of rapid inflation and high interest rates, it is too costly to let cash lie idle for even a few days. At the same time, however, money market investors are extremely conservative when it comes to investing their funds. They will accept little or no risk of borrower default, prefer financial instruments whose prices are stable, and usually require an investment where their funds can be recaptured quickly as the need arises. For this reason nearly all money market instruments are of prime quality—among the safest, most liquid, and most readily marketable in the financial system. In the remaining chapters of this section we examine in detail the characteristics of each of the money market's key financial instruments.

STUDY QUESTIONS

1. What is the money market? Explain why there is a critical need for money market instruments.
2. Who are the principal lenders and borrowers active in the U.S. money market?
3. Define the following:
    a. Money risk.
    b. Credit risk.
    c. Inflation risk.
    d. Currency risk.
    e. Political risk.

Which of these risks are minimized by investing in money market instruments? Does a money market investor avoid *all* of the above risk factors? Why or why not?

4. Why do interest rates on the various money market instruments tend to move together in the same direction at approximately the same time?

5. What are federal funds? Clearinghouse funds? Explain which is more important in the money market and why.

6. Who is the principal borrower in the money market? What is the role of the Federal Reserve System in the money market?

7. Describe the structure of interest rates in the U.S. money market. Which instrument anchors the market and appears to be the foundation for other interest rates? Can you explain why this is so?

SELECTED REFERENCES

1. Banks, Lois. "The Market for Agency Securities." *Quarterly Review,* Federal Reserve Bank of New York, Spring 1978.

2. Federal Reserve Bank of Richmond, *Instruments of the Money Market,* 1977.

3. Lucas, Charles M., Marcos T. Jones, and Thom B. Thurston. "Federal Funds and Repurchase Agreements." *Quarterly Review,* Federal Reserve Bank of New York, Summer 1977, pp. 33–48.

4. McCurdy, Christopher J. "The Dealer Market for U.S. Government Securities." *Quarterly Review,* Federal Reserve Bank of New York, Winter 1977–78.

5. Melton, William C. "The Market for Large Negotiable CD's." *Quarterly Review,* Federal Reserve Bank of New York, Winter 1977–78, pp. 22–34.

6. Polakoff, Murray E. and others. *Financial Institutions and Markets.* Boston: Houghton Mifflin Co., 1970.

7. Robinson, Roland I. and Dwayne Wrightsman. *Financial Markets: The Accumulation and Allocation of Wealth.* New York: McGraw-Hill, 1974.

12

U.S. Treasury Bills,
Dealer Loans, and
Repurchase Agreements

As we noted in the previous chapter, the money market is an institution designed to supply the cash needs of short-term borrowers and provide investors who hold temporary cash surpluses with an outlet for their funds. In this chapter we focus upon one of the most important of all money market instruments—the U.S. Treasury bill. Purchases and sales of Treasury bills represent the largest volume of daily transactions in the money market. Interest rates on bills are the anchor for all other money market interest rates. Trading in T-bills, as these instruments are usually called "on the street," is one component of a vast domestic and international market for securities issued by the United States government. These government IOUs, which include bills, notes, and long-term bonds, carry great weight in the financial system due to their risklessness, ready marketability, and high liquidity. At the heart of the market for Treasury bills, notes, and bonds is a handful of securities dealers who make the market "go" and aid the federal government in selling billions of dollars in new securities each year. In this chapter, we examine the activities of these securities dealers and how they finance their daily trading operations in T-bills and other financial instruments.

U.S. TREASURY BILLS

Treasury bills are direct obligations of the United States government. By law, they must have an original maturity of one year or less. T-bills were first issued by the U.S. Treasury in 1929 in order to cover the federal government's frequent short-term cash deficits.

The federal government's fiscal year runs from October 1 to September 30. However, the largest single source of federal revenue, individual income taxes, is not fully collected until April of each year.[1] Therefore, even in those rare years when a sizable federal budget surplus is expected, the government is likely to be short of cash during the fall and winter months and often in the summer as well. During the spring, personal and corporate tax collections are usually at high levels, and the resulting inflow of funds can be used to retire some portion of those securities issued earlier in the fiscal year. T-bills are well suited to this seasonal ebb and flow of Treasury cash since their maturities are short, they find a ready market among banks and other investors, and their prices adjust readily to changing market conditions.

Volume of Bills Outstanding

The volume of U.S. Treasury bills outstanding has grown rapidly in recent years, especially since the mid-1960s. As shown in Exhibit 12–1, the total

EXHIBIT 12–1
U.S. Treasury Bills: Total Amount Outstanding and their Proportion of the Marketable Public Debt

End of Year	Volume of Bills Outstanding ($ billions)	Total Marketable Public Debt of the United States ($ billions)	T-Bills as a Percent of the Marketable Public Debt
1960	$ 39.4	$189.0	20.8%
1965	60.2	214.6	28.1
1970	87.9	247.7	35.5
1975	157.5	363.2	43.4
1976	164.0	421.3	38.9
1977	161.1	459.9	35.0
1978	161.7	487.5	33.2
1979	172.6	530.7	32.5
1980	216.1	623.2	34.7
1981*	224.5	656.2	34.2

* As of May 31, 1981.
SOURCE: Board of Governors of the Federal Reserve System, *Federal Reserve Bulletin*, selected issues.

volume of bills outstanding climbed to more than $220 billion in 1981, compared to only $88 billion in 1970 and less than $40 billion in 1960. The major

---

[1] In fiscal 1980, individual income taxes provided an estimated 43 percent of all federal revenues. Corporate income taxes added 13 percent; social security taxes, 30 percent; borrowing, 5 percent; and excise taxes and other sources, 9 percent. Individual income taxes are, for the most part, collected once a year in April, while most corporations pay estimated taxes quarterly. See *The Budget of the United States, Fiscal 1980* (Washington, D.C.: U.S. Government Printing Office), p. 2; and Chapter 24 of this text.

factors behind the recent growth of T-bills have been record federal budget deficits; deep recessions which reduced government tax revenues; and the rapid expansion of federal government programs for welfare and national defense.

At the same time, issues of longer-term Treasury notes and bonds have been restrained by adverse movements in interest rates and bond prices. Treasury bonds are subject to a 4¼ percent interest-rate ceiling imposed by Congress during World War I. This low interest-rate ceiling has made it difficult, often impossible, for the Treasury to issue substantial quantities of bonds.[2] Moreover, the U.S. economy has grown rapidly in recent years, creating a greater need for liquid assets such as bills to aid commercial banks and other investors in the efficient management of their cash positions. These factors have all combined to increase gradually the relative share of bills in the total marketable public debt, as shown in Exhibit 12–1. T-bills represented only one fifth of all marketable U.S. government securities in 1960, but they accounted for more than a third of that debt in 1981. While the T-bill share of government marketable securities declined in the late 1970s, it appeared to be on the rise again as the 1980s began.

Types of Treasury Bills

There are several different types of Treasury bills. *Regular-series* bills are issued routinely every week or month in competitive auctions. Bills issued in the regular series have original maturities of three months, six months, and one year. New three- and six-month bills are auctioned weekly, while one-year bills normally are sold once each month. Of these three bill maturities, the six-month bill provides the largest amount of revenue for the Treasury.

On the other hand, *irregular-series* bills are issued only when the Treasury has a special cash need. These instruments include tax-anticipation bills (TABs), strip bills, and cash management bills. *Tax-anticipation* bills were issued a number of years ago in an effort to attract the money set aside by corporations to pay their federal taxes. TABs were set up to mature one week after the quarterly date when corporate taxes came due; however, a corporation could redeem TABs at the Treasury for their full face value in payment of its taxes.

A package offering of bills requires investors to bid for an entire series of different maturities, known as *strip bills*. Investors who bid successfully must

---

[2] Because interest rates have been well above the 4¼ percent legal ceiling since the early 1960s, the Treasury would be forced to issue its bonds at a deep discount from par, something it has been very hesitant to do. Congress has allowed limited amounts of bonds to be issued without regard to this rate ceiling in order to prevent further shortening in the average maturity of the public debt. While these limited-issue bonds have helped somewhat, the average length (or term) of the U.S marketable public debt has shortened drastically in recent years, as discussed in Chapter 24.

accept bills at their bid price each week for several weeks running. *Cash-management* bills consist simply of reopened issues of bills that were sold in prior weeks. The reopening of a bill issue normally occurs when there is an unusual or unexpected need for Treasury cash.

How Bills Are Sold

Treasury bills are sold using the *auction* technique. The marketplace, not the U.S. Treasury, sets bill prices and yields. A new regular bill issue is announced by the Treasury on Thursday of each week, with bids from investors due the following Monday at 1:30 P. M., Eastern Standard Time (unless a federal holiday intervenes). Interested investors fill out a form tendering an offer to the Treasury for a specific bill issue at a specific price. These forms must be filed by the Monday deadline with one of the 37 regional Federal Reserve banks or branches. The interested investor can appear in person at a Federal Reserve bank or branch to fill out a tender form, submit the form by mail, or place an order through a security broker or bank.

The Treasury will entertain both competitive and noncompetitive tenders for bills. *Competitive* tenders typically are submitted by large investors, including commercial banks and government securities dealers, who buy several million dollars worth at one time. Institutions submitting competitive tenders bid aggressively for bills, trying to offer the Treasury a price high enough to win an allotment of bills but not too high, because the higher the price bid, the lower the rate of return.[3] *Noncompetitive* tenders (normally less than $500,000 each) are submitted by small investors who agree to accept the average price set in the weekly or monthly bill auction. Generally, the Treasury fills all noncompetitive tenders for bills.

In the typical bill auction, Federal Reserve officials open all the bids at the designated time and array them from the highest down to the lowest price. For example, a typical series of bids in a Treasury bill auction might appear as follows:

Hypothetical Bid Prices
for Three-Month U.S. Treasury Bills

$99.115
99.113
98.985
98.982
.

.
.

97.729
97.664
97.657

---

[3] Recall the inverse relationship between price and yield discussed in Chapter 7.

Note that all bids are expressed on a $100 basis as though T-bills have a $100 par value.[4] In fact, the minimum denomination for bills is $10,000, and they are issued in multiples of $5,000 above that minimum. The highest bidder (in this case the one offering to pay $99.115) receives his bills, and those who bid successively lower prices also receive their bills, until all available securities have been allocated.

The lowest price at which at least some bills are awarded is called the *stop-out price*. Let's suppose that this is a price of $97.729, the third price from the bottom in the array of prices shown above. No one bidding less than the stop-out price will receive any bills in this particular auction. However, once bills are acquired by successful bidders, many of them will be sold right away in the secondary market, giving the unsuccessful bidders a chance to add to their T-bill portfolios. Payment for bills won in the auction must be made in Federal funds, cash, by redeeming maturing bills, or, when permitted by the Treasury, through crediting tax and loan accounts at banks.[5] All bills today are issued only in book-entry form.

Results of a Recent Bill Auction

A summary of the results from each T-bill auction is published in *The Wall Street Journal*. The results from a recent auction are presented in Exhibit 12–2. We note that in this particular auction, held during August 1980, two maturities of bills—13 and 26 weeks—were offered to the public, and both issues were heavily oversubscribed. More than $7.1 billion in 13-week bills and almost $6.5 billion in 26-week bills were requested; however, the Treasury awarded only $3.8 billion of each. Sixty-five percent of the bids offering the low (or stop-out) price on the 13-week issue received bills, while 93 percent of the bids offering the low price for the 26-week issue were awarded some bills. Noncompetitive tenders in the amount of $811 million for the 13-week issue and almost $438 million for the 26-week issue received their bills.

The dollar-weighted-average auction price for the 13-week bills was $97.795 per $100, or $9779.50 for a $10,000-denomination bill. The 26-week issue sold for an average price of $9550.50. This works out to an 8.72 percent rate of return on the 13-week bill and an 8.89 percent return on the 26-week issue.[6] On a yield-to-maturity (or coupon-equivalent) basis, the 13-week bill

---

[4] The Treasury requires that competitive tenders carry a price expressed on the basis of 100 and containing not more than three places to the right of the decimal point.

[5] These so-called T&L accounts are Treasury deposits kept in about 12,000 of the nation's 15,000 commercial banks. The purpose of these accounts is to minimize the impact on the financial system of Treasury tax collections and debt-financing operations. As taxes are collected or securities sold, the Treasury deposits the funds received in these T&L accounts and gradually withdraws money from them as needed into its checking accounts held at the Federal Reserve banks. (See Chapter 24 for further discussion of T&L accounts.)

[6] These rates of return are figured on a bank discount basis, as discussed below.

EXHIBIT 12–2
Report of Results from a Typical Weekly Auction of U.S. Treasury Bills, August 14, 1980

Item	13-Week Bill Issue	26-Week Bill Issue
Applications for bills	$7,140,370,000	$6,497,475,000
Accepted bids	3,800,465,000	3,800,885,000
Percent accepted at low price	65%	93%
Noncompetitive bids accepted	$ 811,115,000	$ 437,815,000
Average auction price (rate)	97.795(8.723%)	95.505(8.891%)
High price (rate)	97.810(8.664%)	95.554(8.794%)
Low price (rate)............................	97.785(8.763%)	95.480(8.941%)
Coupon equivalent yield	9.04%	9.44%

Notes: The 13-week bills mature November 13, 1980, and the 26-week bills mature February 12, 1981. The interest rates (yields) reported under each price are determined by the difference between the purchase price and the face value and assume a 360-day year. The coupon-equivalent yield is based upon a 365-day year.
SOURCE: *The Wall Street Journal,* August 12, 1980.

carried an average return of 9.04 percent, while the 26-week bill had an average return of 9.44 percent. The highest competitive bidders paid a price of $9,781.00 for the 13-week security and $9,555.40 for the 26-week instrument. The lowest successful bidders received their 13-week bills for only $9,778.50 and 26-week bills for $9,548.00. Those who bid less than these prices underbid in the auction and received no bills. If these unsuccessful bidders wish to purchase bills in this particular issue they must buy them in the secondary market, usually from a government securities dealer.

Calculating the Yield on Bills

Treasury bills do not carry a promised interest rate but instead are sold at a discount from par. Thus, their yield is based on their appreciation in price between the time the bills are issued and the time they mature or are sold by the investor. Any price gain actually realized by the investor is treated, not as a capital gain, but as ordinary income for federal tax purposes.[7] We saw in Chapter 7 that the rate, or yield, on most debt instruments is calculated as a yield to maturity. However, bill yields are determined by the bank discount method, which ignores the compounding of interest rates and uses a 360-day year for simplicity.

The bank discount rate (DR) on bills is given by the following formula:

$$DR = \frac{\text{Par value} - \text{Purchase price}}{\text{Par value}} \times \frac{360}{\text{Number of days to maturity}} \quad (12\text{–}1)$$

---

[7] While the income earned from investing in T-bills is not exempt from federal taxes, it *is* exempt from state and local income taxes.

For example, suppose you purchased a Treasury bill at auction for $97 on a $100 basis (par value) and the bill matured in 180 days. Then the discount rate on this bill would be:

$$DR = \frac{(100 - 97)}{100} \times \frac{360}{180} = 6\%$$

Because the rate of return on T-bills is figured in a different way than the rate of return on most other debt instruments, the investor must convert bill yields to an investment (or coupon-equivalent) yield in order to make realistic comparisons with other securities. The investment yield or rate (IR) on Treasury bills is given by the following formula:

$$IR = \frac{365 \times DR}{360 - (DR \times \text{Days to maturity})} \qquad (12\text{--}2)$$

For example, the investment yield of the bill discussed above, which had a discount rate (DR) of 6 percent, would be calculated as follows:

$$\frac{365 \times 0.06}{360 - (0.06 \times 180)} = 6.27\%$$

Because of the compounding of interest rates on longer-term securities and the use of a 365-day year, the investment yield on a bill will always be higher than its discount rate.

Several other formulas have become popular among investors for calculating yields on Treasury bills when the bills are not held to maturity. Both formulas 12–1 and 12–2 assume that the investor buys a T-bill and ultimately redeems it with the Treasury on its due date. But what if the investor needs cash right away and sells bills to a dealer or other investor in advance of their maturity? In this instance we may use the following formula:

Change in DR over the investor's holding period
$$= \frac{(\text{Days to maturity when purchased} - \text{Days held})}{\text{Days held}}$$
$$\times \text{ Difference in DR on date purchased and date sold} \qquad (12\text{--}3)$$

To calculate the actual yield to the investor on a bank discount basis over the holding period, we then use:

Holding-period yield on bill = DR when purchased
$$\pm \text{ Change in DR over the holding period} \qquad (12\text{--}4)$$

For example, suppose the investor buys a new six-month (or 180-day) bill at a price which results in a discount rate (DR) of 6 percent. As is typical, the bill's price begins to rise (and DR to fall) as the bill approaches maturity. Thirty days after purchase, the investor needs immediate cash and is forced to sell at a price which results in a DR of 5.80 percent. What is the investor's holding-period yield? Using formula 12–3,

$$\text{Change in DR over holding period} = \frac{(180 - 30)}{30}$$

$$\times \ (6.00\% - 5.80\%) = \frac{150}{30} \times 0.20\% = 1.00\%$$

Then, using formula 12–4,

$$\text{Holding-period yield on bill} = 6.00\% + 1.00\% = 7.00\%$$

Because this T-bill rose in price, the investor experienced a gain which increased the bill's yield by 1 percent over the original discount rate of 6 percent.

Consider another problem which frequently confronts the T-bill investor. Suppose a corporation has just purchased some bills to serve as a temporary reserve of liquidity, but it knows that sometime in the next few weeks it will need those funds to help finance a building project. However, the firm wants to hold the bills long enough to earn a specific *target yield*. How many days must the bills be held to hit the target yield? The correct formula is as follows:[8]

Number of days to hold bill for target yield

$$= \frac{\text{Days to maturity when purchased} \ \times \text{Difference in DR on date purchased and date sold}}{\text{Desired change in DR over holding period} \ + \text{Difference in DR on date purchased and date sold}} \quad (12\text{–}5)$$

To illustrate the use of this formula, we can draw upon the figures in the preceding example and assume the investor wants to achieve a 7 percent yield. We have:

$$\text{Number of days to hold bills} = \frac{180 \times (0.20\%)}{1.00\% + 0.20\%} = \frac{36\%}{1.20\%} = 30 \text{ days}$$

Therefore, a 180-day bill purchased at a discount rate of 6 percent must be held for 30 days if the investor desires a 7 percent annual yield and expects the bill's discount rate to decline by 20 basis points.

Market Interest Rates on Treasury Bills

Due to the absence of default risk and because of the superior marketability of T-bills, the yields on these popular financial instruments are typically the lowest in the money market. And because of the tremendous size of the bill market, conditions there tend to set the tone in all other segments of the money market. A rise in T-bill rates, for example, usually is quickly trans-

---

[8] Sometimes interest rates rise sharply after a Treasury bill auction, and the market price of bills falls below their original purchase price. An investor unloading bills in such a market will take a loss unless they can be held until prices rise again. Formula 12–5 can also be used to determine the number of days bills must be held to avoid a loss, provided the change in DR over the holding period is replaced by the DR on the date the bills were purchased.

lated into increases in interest rates attached to bankers' acceptances, commercial paper, CDs, and other money market instruments. Easier conditions in the bill market which lead to lower T-bill rates rapidly spread to other segments of the short-term market, and conditions there usually ease as well.

While the prices of Treasury bills, like those attached to all money market instruments, tend to be quite stable, yields on bills fluctuate widely in response to changes in economic conditions, government policy, the demand for credit, and a host of other factors. This can be seen quite clearly in Exhibit 12–3, which gives annual averages for the secondary market yields

EXHIBIT 12–3
Market Interest Rates on U.S. Treasury Bills, 3-, 6-, and 12-Month Maturities (annual percentage rates)

Year	3-Month	6-Month	12-Month	Year	3-Month	6-Month	12-Month
1960	2.87%	3.20%	3.41%	1971	4.33%	4.52%	4.67%
1961	2.36	2.59	2.81	1972	4.07	4.49	4.77
1962	2.77	2.90	3.01	1973	7.03	7.20	7.01
1963	3.16	3.25	3.30	1974	7.84	7.95	7.71
1964	3.54	3.68	3.74	1975	5.80	6.11	6.30
1965	3.95	4.05	4.06	1976	4.98	5.26	5.52
1966	4.86	5.06	5.07	1977	5.27	5.53	5.71
1967	4.29	4.61	4.71	1978	7.19	7.58	7.74
1968	5.34	5.47	5.46	1979	10.07	10.06	9.75
1969	6.67	6.86	6.79	1980	11.43	11.37	10.89
1970	6.39	6.51	6.49	1981*	16.30	15.29	14.29

* Average for May 1981.
SOURCE: Board of Governors of the Federal Reserve System, *Federal Reserve Bulletin,* selected monthly issues.

on 3-, 6-, and 12-month bills. T-bill rates typically fall during periods of recession and sluggish economic activity as borrowing and spending sag. Note, for example, the decline in bill yields in 1960–61, 1969–71, and 1974–76, as shown in Exhibit 12–3. All of these years were periods in which the economy reached the peak of a boom period and then dropped into a recession. During periods of economic expansion, on the other hand, T-bill rates frequently surge upward, as happened between 1961 and 1966 and in 1967–69, 1972–74, and especially from 1976 to 1981. Inflationary expectations also appear to have a potent impact on bill market yields, as evidenced by the sharp run-up in T-bill rates in the late 1960s and again during the late 1970s and early 1980s—both periods when price increases accelerated rapidly and, in the latter case, soared to double-digit levels.

It is interesting to examine the shape of the yield curve for bills. As Exhibit 12–3 suggests, that curve generally slopes upward, with 12-month bill maturities carrying the highest yields, 6-month next highest, and 3-month maturities the lowest yields. This is not always the case, however. During certain periods—1974 and 1979–81 are good examples—the bill yield curve seems to signal the onset of a recession by sloping downward. Occasionally, too, the yield curve for bills assumes a pronounced "humped" or inverted U shape, with middle maturities carrying the highest rates of return. This happened during the 1968–70 and 1973–74 periods. It is difficult to assign any particular cause to this phenomenon. Sometimes the bend in the curve in the middle maturities appears to reflect heavy Treasury issues of new six-month bills or heavy commercial bank sales of T-bills as bankers try to accommodate customer loan demand by converting their bills into loanable funds. It is noteworthy that the "humped" curve has generally appeared near the end of a boom period and shortly before the onset of a recession. During these times, investors in the financial marketplace are especially uncertain as to which way interest rates are headed.

Investors in Treasury Bills

Principal holders of Treasury bills include commercial banks, nonfinancial corporations, state and local governments, and the Federal Reserve banks. Commercial banks and private corporations hold large quantities of bills as a reserve of liquidity until cash is needed. The most-attractive feature of bills to these institutions is their ready marketability and relatively stable price. The Federal Reserve banks conduct the bulk of their open-market operations in T-bills because of the depth and volume of activity in this market. In fact, bills play a crucial role in the conduct of monetary policy by the Federal Reserve System. The Fed purchases and sells bills in an effort to influence other money market interest rates and thereby alter the volume and growth of bank credit and ultimately the total amount of investment spending and borrowing in the economy.[9]

DEALER LOANS AND REPURCHASE AGREEMENTS

The money market depends heavily upon the buying and selling activities of securities dealers to move funds from cash-rich units to those with cash shortages. About three dozen primary dealers in United States government securities trade today in both new and previously issued Treasury bills, bonds, and notes. Many of these dealers also buy and sell other money market instruments, such as commercial paper, CDs, and bankers' acceptances. They are the principal points of contact with the money market for thousands of individual and institutional investors and are essential to the efficient functioning of that market.

While the dealers supply a huge volume of securities daily to the financial market, they also depend heavily upon the money market for borrowed funds. Most dealer houses invest little of their own equity in the business. The bulk of dealer operating capital is obtained through borrowings from

---

[9] We will examine Federal Reserve open-market operations and the role of Treasury bills in those operations in Chapter 22.

commercial banks, nonfinancial corporations, and other institutions. A major dealer firm carries hundreds of millions of dollars in securities in its trading portfolio, with 90 percent or more of that portfolio supported by short-term loans, some carrying only 24-hour maturities.

The two most heavily used sources of dealer funds are demand loans from the nation's largest banks and repurchase agreements (RPs) with banks and other lenders. Every day, the major New York banks post rates at which they are willing to make short-term loans to dealers. Generally, one rate is quoted on new loans and a second (lower) rate is posted for renewals of existing loans. A *demand loan* may be called in at any time if the banks need cash in a hurry. Such loans are virtually riskless, however, since they usually are collateralized by U.S. government securities, which may be transferred temporarily to the lending bank or its agent.

Repurchase Agreements

An increasingly popular alternative to the demand loan is the repuchase agreement (RP). Under this arrangement, the dealer sells securities to a lender but makes a commitment to buy back the securities at a later date at a fixed price plus interest. Some RPs are for a set length of time (term) while others carry no explicit maturity date but may be terminated by either party on short notice. Larger commercial banks provide *both* demand loans and RPs to the dealers, while nonfinancial corporations have provided an growing volume of funds to dealers through RPs in recent years. Other lenders active in the RP market include state and local governments, insurance companies, and foreign financial institutions who find the market a convenient, riskless way to invest temporary cash surpluses which may be retrieved quickly and easily when the need arises.

Until recently, RPs were principally overnight transactions or expired in a few days. Today, however, there is a substantial volume of one- to three-month agreements, and some carry even longer maturities. The interest rate on RPs is the return which a dealer must pay a lender of short-term funds for the temporary use of money and is closely related to other money market interest rates.[10] To determine the lender's total interest income from an RP transaction, the agreed-upon rate is multiplied by the value of the securities pledged as collateral behind the RP. Usually the securities pledged are valued at a discount from their current market prices, giving the lender added protection in case security prices fall. Most RP transactions involve at least a million dollars in marketable securities.

In order to promote a smoothly functioning market, the Federal Reserve System through its trading desk at the New York Fed frequently participates with the dealers in RPs. In a *straight* RP transaction, the Federal Reserve buys securities from a dealer on a short-term basis and then sells the securi-

---

[10] The interest rate attached to an RP transaction is figured on the basis of a 360-day year, like the yield on Treasury bills.

ties back at the end of the agreed-upon period. The Fed may also enter into a *reverse* RP transaction with one or more dealers. In this case the Federal Reserve Bank of New York will sell securities to a dealer with an agreement to buy them back after a short period of time, thus temporarily absorbing dealer funds and reducing the ability of the dealers' banks to make loans. Whereas the dealers use the RP to protect or increase their earnings from securities trading, the Federal Reserve uses RPs to steady the money market and to promote national economic goals.[11]

Sources of Dealer Income

Securities dealers take on substantial risk in order to make a market for Treasury bills and other financial instruments. To be sure, the securities they deal in are among the highest-quality instruments available in the financial marketplace. However, the prices of even top-quality securities can experience rapid declines if interest rates rise. Moreover, established dealer houses cannot "run and hide" but are obliged to stand ready at all times to buy and sell on customer demand, regardless of the condition of the market. In contrast to securities brokers, who merely bring buyers and sellers together, dealers take a "position of risk," which means that they act as principals in the buying and selling of securities. Dealers add any securities purchased to their own portfolios.

Dealers stand ready to buy specified types of securities at an announced bid price and to sell them at an announced asked price. This is called "making a market" in a particular financial instrument. The dealer hopes to earn a profit from such market-making activities—in part from the positive *spread* between bid and asked prices for the same security. This spread varies with market conditions but on U.S. government securities is generally about one thirty-second to four thirty-seconds of a point on short-term securities and will range higher on longer-term notes and bonds or on securities not actively traded.[12]

As we have seen, the dealers' holdings of securities are financed by loans, so their portfolio positions are extremely sensitive to fluctuations in interest rates. For this reason dealers frequently will shift from long positions to short positions, depending upon the outlook for interest rates. A *long* position means that dealers purchase securities outright, take title to them, and hold

---

[11] We will discuss Federal Reserve RP transactions in more detail in Chapter 22.

[12] We recall from Chapter 7 that $1/32$nd of a point is equal to $0.03125 for each $100. On a million-dollar trade in Treasury bills, the dealer's spread would normally be about $50. For shorter-term coupon issues the spread usually lies in the range of $312.50 to $1,250 for each million dollars in par value. However, dealer spreads are difficult to predict in advance because they vary with the nature and total size of each transaction and current demand and supply conditions in the marketplace.

Generally, dealers will deliver securities sold the next business day after a sale has been made (known as regular delivery), though smaller, odd-lot transactions are usually completed within five business days. Sometimes large customers or dealers themselves may demand same-day settlement (known as a cash delivery). Payment for all deliveries is usually made in federal funds.

them in their portfolios as an investment or until a customer comes along. A *short* position, on the other hand, means that dealers sell securities they do not presently own for future delivery to a customer. In so doing, they hope the prices of those securities will fall before they must be delivered to the buyer. Obviously, if interest rates fall (and security prices rise), the dealer will experience capital gains on a long position but losses on a short position. On the other hand, if interest rates rise (resulting in a drop in security prices), the dealer's long position will experience capital losses while the short position will post a gain.

In periods when interest rates are expected to rise, dealers typically reduce their long positions and go short. Conversely, expectations of falling rates lead the dealers to increase their long positions and avoid short sales. By correctly anticipating rate movements, the dealer can earn sizable *position profits*. Dealers also receive *carry income*, which is the difference between the yield on securities they hold and their cost of borrowing funds. Generally, dealers earn higher rates of return on the securities they hold than the interest rates paid for dealer loans, but this is not always so. Because most dealer borrowings are short term, securities dealers normally are better off if the yield curve is positively sloped.

Dealer Positions in Securities

As reflected in the first section of Exhibit 12–4, dealer holdings of U.S. government and other securities are both huge and subject to erratic fluctuations. For example, during 1979, the roughly three dozen U.S. government security dealers held average daily positions of $3.2 billion in U.S. government securities and nearly $1.5 billion in the IOUs of various federal agencies. Three years earlier, in 1976, however, average daily dealer positions in U.S. government securities were more than double the 1979 average at almost $7.6 billion.

Why was there such a tremendous difference in the size of dealer portfolios during those years? Interest rates fell in 1976, creating ample opportunities for sizable dealer profits on securities held in long positions as market prices rose. In 1979, however, interest rates increased sharply, sending security prices downward. Fearing substantial losses, the dealers shifted out of long positions, especially in longer-term notes and bonds, and held mostly Treasury bills, whose prices are relatively stable. In fact, as Exhibit 12–4 shows, the dealers actually went *short* on 1-to-5-year and under-1-year government securities and held only nominal amounts of maturities exceeding 10 years.

Sources of Dealer Financing

Where do government security dealers derive most of their funds to purchase and carry securities? As the second section of Exhibit 12–4 shows,

EXHIBIT 12–4
Positions and Sources of Financing for Dealers in U.S. Government Securities
(figures in millions of dollars)*

	1979	1978	1977	1976	1975	1974
Average daily dealer positions:						
U.S. government securities	$ 3,223	$ 2,656	$5,172	$7,592	$5,884	$2,580
Bills	3,813	2,452	4,772	6,290	4,297	1,932
Other within 1 year	−325	260	99	188	265	−6
1–5 years	−455	−92	60	515	886	265
5–10 years	160	40	92	402	300	302
Over 10 years	30	−4	149	198	136	88
Federal agency securities	1,471	606	693	729	943	1,212
Sources of dealer financing:†						
All sources	$16,003	$10,204	$9,877	$8,715	$6,666	$3,977
Commercial banks:						
New York City	1,396	599	1,313	1,896	1,621	1,032
Outside New York City	2,868	2,174	1,987	1,660	1,466	1,064
Corporations	3,373	2,379	2,358	1,479	842	459
All other lenders	4,104	5,052	4,155	3,681	2,738	1,423

* All security holdings are expressed in their par values and are averages of daily figures.
† Includes both borrowings and internally generated funds.
SOURCE: Board of Governors of the Federal Reserve System, *Federal Reserve Bulletin,* selected monthly issues.

commercial banks are the largest single source of dealer funds, year in and year out. Indeed, half a dozen of the largest dealers are really dealer departments housed in some of the nation's largest banks. However, nonfinancial business corporations are the most rapidly growing source of funds for major securities dealers. Many industrial corporations today find the dealer loan market a convenient and safe way to dispose of temporarily idle monies. With wire transfer of funds between banks readily available, a company can lend a dealer millions of dollars in idle cash and recover those funds in a matter of hours if a cash emergency rears its head.

Dealer Transactions

Trading among securities dealers and between dealers and their customers amounts to billions of dollars a day. As shown in Exhibit 12–5, average daily transactions in the U.S. government securities market were in excess of $13.1 billion in 1979. Indeed, so large is the government securities market that the volume of trading usually exceeds by four or five times the total volume of trading on the major U.S. stock exchanges. Exhibit 12–5 makes clear that the majority of trades by far are in Treasury bills. It is also clear that government securities dealers trade heavily among themselves, usually through brokers. Government security brokers do not take investment positions themselves but try to match bids and offers placed with them by dealers and other investors.

EXHIBIT 12–5
Average Daily Transactions Carried Out by U.S. Government Security Dealers ($ millions)*

	1979	1978	1977	1976	1975	1974
U.S. govt. securities	$13,183	$10,285	$10,838	$10,449	$6,027	$3,579
By maturity:						
Bills...........................	7,914	6,173	6,746	6,676	3,889	2,550
Other within 1 year	454	392	237	210	223	250
1–5 years......................	2,417	1,889	2,320	2,317	1,414	465
5–10 years	1,121	965	1,148	1,019	363	256
Over 10 years	1,276	867	388	224	138	58
By type of customer:						
Other U.S. government security						
dealers	1,448	1,135	1,268	1,360	885	652
U.S. government security						
brokers	5,170	3,838	3,709	3,407	1,750	965
Commercial banks	1,905	1,804	2,294	2,426	1,451	998
All others†	4,660	3,508	3,567	3,256	1,941	964
Transactions in federal agency						
securities	2,724	1,895	1,734	1,548	1,043	965

* All securities traded are expressed in par values and figures represent averages of daily reports submitted to the Federal Reserve Bank of New York. The figures exclude allotments of and exchanges for new U.S. Government securities, redemptions of called or matured securities, or purchases or sales of securities under repurchase, reverse repurchase, or similar contracts.
† Includes all other dealers and brokers in commodities and securities, foreign banking agencies, and the Federal Reserve System.
SOURCE: Board of Governors of the Federal Reserve System, *Federal Reserve Bulletin,* selected monthly issues.

Dealerships are a cutthroat business where each dealer firm is out to maximize its returns from trading even if gains must be made at the expense of competing dealers. Indeed, market analysts housed within each dealer firm study the daily price quotations of their competitors. If one dealer temporarily underprices some securities (i.e., offers excessively generous yields), other dealers are likely to rush in for a "hit" before the offering firm has a chance to correct its mistake. It is a business with little room for the inexperienced or slow-moving trader. Yet, as we have seen, the government securities dealers are essential to the smooth functioning of the financial markets and to the successful placement of billions of dollars in new U.S. government securities issued each year.

CONCLUSIONS

In this chapter we have examined in some detail one of the most important of all securities markets—the market for Treasury bills and other U.S. government securities. This market has grown rapidly in recent years in response to huge Treasury borrowing needs and the needs of investors for highly liquid, readily marketable financial instruments. It is difficult to over-

estimate the importance of the government securities market in the functioning of the American financial system. This market sets the tone for the whole
financial system in terms of interest rates, security prices, and the availability of credit. And it is in this market today that most government economic
policy measures begin in the form of U.S. Treasury issues of new securities
and Federal Reserve open-market operations. A thorough knowledge of the
workings of the market for government securities tells us much about the
how and why of the American financial system.

STUDY QUESTIONS

1. Why has the volume of U.S. Treasury bills grown so rapidly in recent years?
   Explain why the T-bill is so popular with money market investors.

2. List and define the various types of U.S. Treasury bills. Why are there so many
   different varieties?

3. Explain how the T-bill auction works. Can you cite some advantages of this
   method of sale? Disadvantages?

4. How are the yields on U.S. Treasury bills calculated? How does this method
   differ from the method used to calculate bond yields? Why is this difference
   important?

5. From the following sets of figures: (1) calculate the bank discount rate on each
   T-bill; and (2) convert that rate to the appropriate investment (or coupon-
   equivalent) yield.

   a. A new three-month T-bill sells for $98.25 on a $100 basis.

   b. The investor can buy a new 12-month T-bill for $96 on a $100 basis.

   c. A 30-day bill is available from a U.S. government securities dealer at a price
       of $97.50 (per $100).

6. Calculate the holding-period yield for the following situations:

   a. The investor buys a new 12-month T-bill at a discount rate of 7½ percent.
       Sixty days later the bill is sold at a price which results in a discount rate of 7
       percent.

   b. A large manufacturing corporation acquires a T-bill in the secondary market
       30 days from its maturity but is forced to sell the bill 15 days later. At time
       of purchase the bill carried a discount rate of 8 percent, but it was sold at a
       discount rate of 7¾ percent.

7. What is the normal, or typical, slope of the yield curve for T-bills? Why? What
   other slopes have been observed, and why do you think these occur?

8. Who are the principal investors in U.S. Treasury bills? What factors motivate
   these investors to buy bills?

9. Explain why dealers are essential to the smooth functioning of the securities
   markets. Where do most dealer funds come from?

10. What is a demand loan? An RP? Explain their role in dealer financing.

11. In what ways do dealers earn income and possibly make a profit? To what risks
    is each source of dealer income subject?

12. Are the majority of U.S. government security dealers' positions in short-term or
    long-term securities? What causes their positions to change?

13. Where do government securities dealers borrow most of the funds they need?
14. What types of securities dominate dealer trading? Why?

SELECTED REFERENCES

1. Bowsher, Norman H. "Repurchase Agreements." *Review*, Federal Reserve Bank of St. Louis, September 1979, pp. 17–22.
2. Federal Reserve Bank of New York. "Federal Funds and Repurchase Agreements." *Review*, Summer 1977, pp. 33–48.
3. Federal Reserve Bank of Richmond. *Instruments of the Money Market*. 4th ed. 1977.
4. The First Boston Corporation. *Handbook of Securities of the United States Government and Federal Agencies*. 25th ed. 1972.
5. McCurdy, Christopher J. "The Dealer Market for United States Government Securities." *Quarterly Review*, Federal Reserve Bank of New York, Winter 1977–78, pp. 35–47.
6. Simpson, Thomas D. *The Market for Federal Funds and Repurchase Agreements*. Staff Study, Board of Governors of the Federal Reserve System, July 1979.

13

Federal Funds, Negotiable CDs, and Loans from the Discount Window

The single most important financial institution in the money market is the commercial bank. Large money-center banks, such as those headquartered in New York City, Chicago, San Francisco, Philadelphia, and a handful of other major cities, provide billions of dollars in funds daily through the money market to governments and corporations in need of cash. For example, as we saw in the previous chapter, bank loans and repurchase agreements are a principal source of financing for dealers in U.S. government securities, while banks also make large direct purchases of U.S. Treasury bills and other money market securities. Commercial banks support private corporations borrowing in the money market, both by purchasing their securities and by granting lines of credit to backstop a new security issue.[1] Banks conduct acceptance financing to support the movement of goods in international trade, resulting in the creation of a high-grade money market instrument—the bankers' acceptance.[2] And both large and small banks today readily lend their cash reserves to other financial institutions and to industrial corporations overnight or for a few days to cover short-term liquidity needs.

---

[1] As we will note in Chapter 14, commercial paper sold by large corporations usually cannot be marketed unless prior arrangements are made to secure a bank line of credit in the amount of the issue. This step protects investors who, in today's uncertain markets, need to be reassured that a borrowing corporation can pay its bills either from current cash flow or by drawing upon an existing credit line.

[2] Bankers' acceptances are discussed in Chapter 15.

In order for commercial banks to lend huge amounts of funds daily in the money market, they must also *borrow* heavily in that market. As we saw in Chapter 3, the owners (stockholders) supply only a minor portion of a commercial bank's total resources; the bulk of bank funds must be borrowed. While the majority of those funds (at least 80 percent for most banks) come from deposits, a growing portion of the industry's financing needs are supplied by the money market. However, bank managers today are more cautious in their use of money market borrowings than was true even a few years ago. Such funds are relatively expensive to use, and their interest cost is more volatile than for most kinds of deposits. Many large banks today follow the strategy of maintaining a roughly equal balance between their lending and borrowing activities in the money market. The volume of short-term bank debt is counterbalanced by a nearly equal volume of short-term bank assets.[3]

In this chapter we examine three of the most important money market sources of funds for banks and other deposit-type financial institutions—federal funds, certificates of deposit (CDs), and loans from the Federal Reserve's discount window. In Chapter 15 we discuss still another important source of funds for many of the nation's largest depository institutions—Eurodollars.

FEDERAL FUNDS

As we saw in the introductory chapter on the money market, Federal funds are among the most important of all money market instruments for one key reason: *fed funds are the principal means of making payments in the money market.* By definition, Federal funds are any monies available for immediate payment. They are generally transferred from one depository institution to another by simple bookkeeping entries requested by wire or telephone after a purchase of securities is made or a loan is granted.

The Nature of Federal Funds

The name *federal funds* came about because early in the development of the market the principal source of immediately available money was the reserve balances which member banks keep at the Federal Reserve banks. If one member bank needs to transfer funds to another, it need only contact the Federal Reserve bank in its district, and money is transferred into the appropriate reserve account—a transaction accomplished in minutes or seconds by computer.

---

[3] The idea of maintaining a roughly equal balance between borrowing and lending in the money market follows one of the oldest concepts in the field of finance—the *hedging principle.* As discussed in Chapter 8, in a world of uncertainty, borrowers of funds can reduce risk by matching the maturity of their assets and liabilities. This approach reduces the risk of borrowing when funds are not needed and also lowers the risk of not having sufficient cash when interest payments and other bills come due.

Today, however, the Fed funds market is far broader in scope than just reserves on deposit with the Federal Reserve banks. For example, virtually all banks maintain deposits with large correspondent banks in the principal U.S. cities, and these deposits may be transferred readily by wire from the account of one bank to that of another. Savings and loan associations, credit unions, and mutual savings banks maintain deposits with commercial banks that also are available for immediate transfer to a customer or to another financial institution.[4] Business corporations and state and local governments can lend Federal funds by executing repurchase agreements with securities dealers, banks, or other funds traders. Securities dealers who have received payment for securities sold can turn around and make their funds immediately available to borrowers through the federal funds market. Borrowers of Federal funds include securities dealers, corporations, state and local governments, and nonbank financial intermediaries, such as savings and loan associations and insurance companies. Without question, however, the most important of all borrowers in the Fed funds market are commercial banks, who use this instrument as the principal way to adjust their legal reserve positions.

Commercial Banks in the Federal Funds Market

As we saw in Chapter 3, commercial banks and other depository institutions must hold liquid assets in a special reserve account, equal to a fraction of the funds deposited with them by the public. Only vault cash held on the premises and reserve balances kept with the Federal Reserve bank in the district count in meeting this legal reserve requirement. Frequently, commercial banks (especially small banks) hold more legal reserves than the law requires. Because these reserves earn little or no income, most bankers active in the money market try to dispose of any excess legal reserves in their possession, even if they can only lend the funds overnight.

Banks are aided greatly in this endeavor by the fact that their legal reserve requirement is calculated on an *average* basis over a week. The reserve requirement is stated as a daily average for the seven days stretching from Thursday to the following Wednesday. Moreover, Federal Reserve regulations allow the manager of the individual bank's money desk—the department responsible for keeping track of the bank's legal reserve position—to base the current week's legally required reserve holdings on the level of deposits prevailing two weeks earlier.[5] Current Federal Reserve regulations also permit the money desk manager to use the amount of vault cash held

---

[4] As we saw in Chapters 3 and 4, nonbank thrift institutions which offer transaction accounts must also keep reserve balances at the Federal Reserve banks under the terms of the Depository Institutions Deregulation and Monetary Control Act of 1980. These reserve balances are available for borrowing and lending in the Federal funds market.

[5] Existing regulations are even more lenient than this. A bank or other depository institution can fall up to 2 percent below its required reserve level in a given week provided it runs a corresponding excess reserve position the following week.

two weeks before to satisfy a portion of the current week's reserve requirement.

Because the amount of vault cash is known in advance, the money manager's key problem is to adjust the bank's reserve balances held at the Fed to the right level. That is,

$$\begin{array}{l} \text{Required reserves for a bank this week} \\ - \text{ Vault cash holdings of two weeks ago} \end{array} = \begin{array}{l} \text{Required average daily} \\ \text{deposits held at the Federal Reserve this week} \end{array} \quad (13-1)$$

Each week the money desk manager will try to make sure that the bank's average deposit balance at the Fed hits or comes close to this required level. The Federal funds market is an indispensable tool for this kind of daily reserve management, especially for the largest and most aggressive banks, which hold few reserves of their own. The majority of Federal funds transactions are 24-hour (overnight) loans to cover reserve deficiencies. There is a trend in the market, however, toward longer-term Fed funds loans for banks and other depository institutions with "permanent" reserve needs. Indeed, many large U.S. banks today borrow virtually their entire reserve requirement on a more-or-less-permanent basis from the Federal funds market.

Mechanics of Federal Funds Trading

The mechanics of Federal funds trading vary depending upon the locations of the buying (borrowing) and selling (lending) institutions. For example, suppose two commercial banks involved in a Federal funds transaction are located in the heart of the New York money market. These banks can simply exchange checks. The borrowing bank is given a check drawn on the lending bank's reserve account at the Federal Reserve Bank of New York or drawn on a correspondent balance held at some other bank in New York City. This check is payable immediately ("same day money"), and, therefore Fed funds are transferred to the borrower's reserve account before the close of business that same day. The lender, on the other hand, receives a check drawn on the borrower. This check is "one-day money" (i.e., payable the following day) because it must pass through the New York Clearing House for proper settlement. Thus, funds flow instantly to the borrowing bank's reserve account and are automatically returned to the lending bank's reserve account the next day or whenever the loan agreement terminates. Interest on the loan may be included when the funds are returned, paid by separate check, or settled by debiting and crediting correspondent balances.

If the transacting institutions are not both located within the New York Federal Reserve District, the loan transaction proceeds in much the same way except that two Federal Reserve banks are involved. Once borrower and lender agree on the terms of a Federal funds loan, the lending institution will directly, or indirectly through a major correspondent bank, contact the Federal Reserve bank in its district, requesting a wire transfer of funds. The

Federal Reserve bank then merely transfers reserves through the Fed's wire network to the Federal Reserve bank serving the region of the country where the borrowing institution is located. Funds travel the reverse route when the loan is terminated.

Volume of Borrowings in the Funds Market

Commercial banks borrow billions of dollars each day in the funds market. As shown in Exhibit 13–1, total federal funds sold (loans) by all U.S.

EXHIBIT 13–1
Federal Funds Sold and Purchased by Commercial Banks, Amounts Outstanding September 30, 1978 ($ millions)

| | | | Member Banks | | | | |
| | | | Large Banks | | | | |
Item	All Insured Com- mercial Banks	Total	New York City	Chi- cago	Other Large Cities	All Other	Non- mem- ber Banks
Federal funds sold by banks and securities resale agreements to:.....	$41,258	$31,999	$ 3,290	$1,784	$16,498	$10,427	$9,365
Commercial banks	34,256	25,272	1,987	1,294	12,279	9,717	9,090
Brokers and dealers	4,259	4,119	821	396	2,361	541	140
Other borrowers	2,753	2,608	482	94	1,863	169	135
Federal funds purchased by banks and agreements to repurchase securities from:	$91,981	$85,582	$21,149	$8,777	$41,799	$13,857	$6,398
Commercial banks	42,174	39,607	6,991	5,235	21,609	5,773	2,566
Brokers and dealers	12,787	11,849	2,130	1,616	6,381	1,722	939
Other lenders	37,020	34,126	12,028	1,926	13,809	6,362	2,894

Note: Data include consolidated reports, including figures for all bank-premises subsidiaries and other significant majority-owned domestic subsidiaries.
SOURCE: Board of Governors of the Federal Reserve System, *Federal Reserve Bulletin,* July 1980.

insured banks (including security resale agreements) stood at more than $41 billion in September 1978, while federal funds purchased (borrowings) and security resale agreements reached almost $92 billion on the same date. The large banks in New York City, by virtue of their strategic location at the heart of the money market, still account for a disproportionate share of Fed funds transactions. However, the market has broadened considerably in recent years to include banks in Atlanta, Chicago, Dallas, San Francisco, and other major U.S. cities, as well as thousands of smaller banks in outlying areas. Member banks of the Federal Reserve System, despite their smaller total numbers, are more important in this market than nonmember banks due to their greater average size and strategic locations.

Most Federal funds loans are either overnight (one-day) transactions or *continuing contracts* that have no specific maturity date and can be terminated without advance notice by either party (see Exhibit 13–2). One-day loans carry a fixed rate of interest, but continuing contracts often do not.

EXHIBIT 13–2
Federal Funds and Repurchase Agreements of Large U.S. Member Banks
(averages of daily figures, $ millions)*

By Maturity and Source	1981 Week Ending on Wednesday			
	May 6	May 13	May 20	May 27
One-day and continuing contract:				
Commercial banks in the United States	$52,324	$49,016	$45,222	$44,399
Other depository institutions, foreign banks and foreign official institutions, and U.S. government agencies	13,716	12,875	13,812	13,650
Nonbank securities dealers	3,265	2,816	2,561	2,782
All other..........................	19,992	19,090	19,403	19,708
All other maturities:				
Commercial banks in the United States..........................	3,524	3,639	3,788	3,467
Other depository institutions, foreign banks and foreign official institutions	7,064	7,365	7,591	7,434
Nonbank securities dealers	4,435	4,780	5,183	5,183
All other..........................	10,143	10,497	10,549	10,655

* Includes banks with assets of $1 billion or more as of December 31, 1977.
SOURCE: Board of Governors of the Federal Reserve System, *Federal Reserve Bulletin*, June 1981.

There is a growing volume of loans lasting beyond one day, often arising from security repurchase agreements. These interbank loans are usually called term Federal funds and are being supplied increasingly by foreign banks and domestic nonbank financial institutions (such as mutual savings banks and savings and loan associations) as a safe, easy, and profitable way to warehouse funds until they are needed for long-term loan commitments.

Rates on Federal Funds

The Federal funds interest rate is highly volatile from day to day and week to week, though on an annual basis it tends to move roughly in line with other money market rates (see Exhibit 13–3). The short-run volatility of the rate arises from substantial variations in the volume of funds made available by lenders each day and the size of daily cash deficits experienced by banks and other money market participants. The funds rate tends to be most volatile toward the close of the banker's reserve settlement week (especially on

EXHIBIT 13–3
Effective Interest Rates on Federal Funds Transactions, 1960–1981 (percent per annum)*

Year	Average Daily Rate on Federal Funds	Year	Average Daily Rate on Federal Funds
1960	3.22%	1971	4.67%
1961	1.96	1972	4.44
1962	2.68	1973	8.74
1963	3.18	1974	10.51
1964	3.50	1975	5.82
1965	4.07	1976	5.05
1966	5.11	1977	5.54
1967	4.22	1978	7.94
1968	5.66	1979	11.20
1969	8.22	1980	13.36
1970	7.17	1981†	19.10

* Figures in the table are averages of daily effective rates for each week ended on Wednesday during the indicated year. The daily effective rate is an average of the interest rates on a given day weighted by the volume of transactions at these rates.
† Average for the month of June.
SOURCE: Board of Governors of the Federal Reserve System, *Federal Reserve Bulletin,* selected monthly issues.

Wednesdays), depending on whether larger banks across the nation are flush with reserves or are coming up short. There are also definite seasonal patterns, with the funds rate tending to rise around holiday periods, when loan demand and deposit withdrawals are heavy.

Federal Funds and Government Policy

The Federal funds market is an easy and riskless way to invest excess reserves for short periods and still earn some interest income. It is essential to the daily management of bank reserves, since credit can be obtained in a matter of minutes to cover emergency situations. As we have seen, the Federal funds market is also critical to the whole money market, since these funds serve as the principal means of payment for securities and loans. Moreover, the funds market transmits the effects of Federal Reserve monetary policy quickly throughout the banking system. Today, the daily Federal funds rate is regarded as a key indicator of monetary policy because the Federal Reserve frequently sets daily and weekly funds-rate targets and then buys or sells securities to achieve the particular rate desired.

The Federal funds rate usually stays above the discount rate the Federal Reserve charges on loans of reserves to banks and other depository institutions. This is due to the fact that many banks prefer to borrow reserves directly from other institutions in the private sector rather than deal with the government agency (the Federal Reserve System) that regulates them. Many bankers fear that heavy use of direct loans from the Fed rather than from the impersonal Federal funds market will subject them to closer scrutiny by the regulatory authorities.

Until recently, Federal funds transactions were not subject to legal reserve requirements as deposits are. However, during the week of October 25, 1979, the Federal Reserve imposed a *marginal reserve requirement* of 8 percent on Federal funds borrowing by member banks from nonmember banks when these borrowings exceeded a certain base amount. Later, in April 1980, this reserve requirement was increased to 10 percent; it was lowered to 5 percent in June 1980 and then reduced to zero the following month. The purpose of this marginal reserve requirement was to "cool off" severe inflationary pressures building up in the U.S. economy. The marginal reserve requirement raised the effective cost of federal funds borrowed and therefore tended to discourage some bank lending and investing. It is clear that the Federal Reserve System will impose reserve requirements on Federal funds borrowings again if economic or financial conditions warrant them.

There are no legal interest-rate ceilings on Federal funds loans as there are on most deposits. Nevertheless, the regulatory authorities, especially the Federal Reserve, watch the funds market carefully in order to prevent excessive and reckless borrowing by individual banks. This market is a key one in the financial system. For this reason, government intervention and control is an ever present possibility.

NEGOTIABLE CERTIFICATES OF DEPOSIT

One of the largest of all money market instruments, measured by dollar volume, is the negotiable certificate of deposit (CD). A CD is an interest-bearing receipt for funds deposited in a bank or other depository institution for a set period of time.[6] While banks, savings and loan associations, and other deposit-type institutions issue many types of CDs, the true money market CDs are *negotiable* instruments that may be sold any number of times before reaching maturity and carry minimum denominations of $100,000. The usual round-lot trading unit for CDs bought and sold in the money market is $1 million.

The interest rate on a large, negotiable CD is set by negotiation between the issuing institution and its customer and generally reflects prevailing credit conditions. Therefore, like the rates on other money market securities, CD rates rise in periods of tight money when loanable funds are scarce and fall in periods of easy money when loanable funds are more abundant.

The negotiable CD is one of the youngest of all American money market instruments. It dates from 1961, when First National City Bank of New York began offering the instrument to its largest corporate customers. Simulta-

---

[6] The minimum maturity permitted for CDs under federal regulations is 14 days. There is no legal upper limit on maturities, however. CDs must be issued at par and trade on an interest-bearing basis, unlike Treasury bills.

neously, a small group of securities dealers agreed to make a secondary (resale) market for CDs of $100,000 or more. Other money-center banks soon entered the competition for corporate funds and began to offer their own CDs.

The decision to offer this new money market instrument was agonizing for the nation's major banks, because CDs have sharply raised the average cost of bank funds. However, bankers had little choice but to offer the new instrument or face the loss of billions of dollars in interest-sensitive deposits. The cash management departments of major corporations have become increasingly aware of the many profitable ways available today to invest their short-term funds. Prior to the introduction of the negotiable CD, many bankers found that their biggest customers were reducing their deposits (especially demand deposits) and buying U.S. Treasury bills, bankers' acceptances, RPs, and other money market instruments. The CD was developed to attract these lost deposits back into the banking system.

Growth of CDs

Negotiable CDs are a real success story for American banks. By year-end 1980, large ($100,000 +) CDs outstanding totaled $257 billion, or about $40 billion more than the amount of Treasury bills outstanding on the same date. This compares with only $93 billion in large CDs as recently as December 1974 and $24 billion in December 1968.

Until the Penn Central crisis in 1970, large negotiable CDs were subject to legal interest-rate ceilings as specified in the Federal Reserve Board's Regulation Q. However, the bankruptcy of the huge Penn Central Transportation Company rocked the money market, and many large corporations could not sell their commercial notes to raise short-term funds. To ease this serious liquidity crunch, the Fed suspended interest-rate ceilings on large short-term (30–89 day) CDs in June 1970 and lifted the ceilings on longer-term CDs in May 1973. Freed from legal interest-rate ceilings, the volume of large CDs has soared during periods of rapid economic growth. Trading of CDs by dealers in the secondary market now approaches $2 billion a day.

Terms Attached to CDs

Negotiable CDs may be registered with the issuing bank or other depository institution or issued in bearer form. CDs issued in bearer form are more convenient for resale in the secondary market. Denominations range from $25,000 to $10 million, though, as we noted previously, CDs traded in the money market carry minimum denominations of $100,000. Maturities range from 1 to about 18 months, depending upon the customer's needs. However, most money market CDs have maturities of six months or less.

Interest rates in the CD market are computed as a yield to maturity but figured on a 360-day basis. Therefore, to convert the yield on CDs to a coupon-equivalent basis, we must multiply their yield by the ratio 365/360. The market yield on CDs normally is slightly above the U.S. Treasury bill rate. For example, as shown in Exhibit 13–4, in May 1981 the market yield on three-month CDs was about two percentage points above the three-month

EXHIBIT 13–4
Recent Interest Rates on Money Market CDs ($100,000 or more) and U.S. Treasury Bills

Instrument	Period				
	1977	1978	1979	1980	1981*
Certificates of deposit:†					
1-month	5.48%	7.88%	11.03%	12.91%	18.16%
3-month	5.64	8.22	11.22	13.07	18.27
6-month	5.92	8.61	11.44	12.99	17.66
U.S. Treasury bills:‡					
3-month	5.27	7.19	10.07	11.43	16.30
6-month	5.53	7.58	10.06	11.37	15.29

* Rates as of May 1981.
† Based upon five-day average rates for each week of the period as quoted by five dealers in CDs. All rates expressed in percent per annum.
‡ Bill yields in the secondary market are quoted on a bank discount basis from daily closing bid prices.
SOURCE: Board of Governors of the Federal Reserve System, *Federal Reserve Bulletin,* selected issues.

Treasury bill rate. However, the yield spread between CDs and other money market instruments varies over time, depending upon investor preferences, the supply of CDs and other money market instruments, and the financial condition of issuing banks.

One of the most interesting developments in recent years is the appearance of a *multitier market* for CDs. Investors have grouped issuing banks into different risk categories, and yields in the market are scaled accordingly. This development is a legacy of the collapse of such banking giants as United States National Bank of San Diego in October 1973 and Franklin National Bank of New York in October 1974. Faced with the specter of major-bank failures, those banks viewed as less stable by investors were forced to issue their CDs at significantly higher interest rates. CDs from the largest and most financially sound banks are rated prime, while smaller banks or those viewed as less stable issue nonprime CDs at higher interest rates.

Buyers of CDs

The principal buyers of large, negotiable CDs include nonfinancial corporations, state and local governments, foreign central banks and governments, wealthy individuals, and a wide variety of financial institutions. The latter include insurance companies, pension funds, investment companies, savings banks, and credit unions. Large CDs appeal to these investors because they are readily marketable at low risk, may be issued in any desired maturity, and carry a somewhat higher yield than on U.S. Treasury bills. However, the investor gives up some marketability in comparison with T-bills since the resale market for CDs averages only around $2 billion dollars a day—well below the average daily volume of trading in bills.

Most buyers hold CDs until they mature. However, prime-rated CDs issued by the nation's billion-dollar banks are actively traded in the secondary market, which is centered in New York City. The purpose of the secondary market is principally to accommodate corporations that need cash quickly or see profitable opportunities from the sale of their deposits. Also, buyers of CDs who desire shorter maturities or higher yields than are available on new issues will enter the secondary market. No bank is allowed to purchase its own CDs in the secondary market or redeem them in advance of maturity, except under special circumstances. Moreover, banks usually will not lend money using their own CDs as collateral because, in the event of borrower default, the bank may be forced to redeem the pledged CD in advance of its maturity.

CDs in Liability Management

Commercial banks and other depository institutions use the CD as a supplement to Federal funds when additional reserves are needed. A depository institution in need of funds simply raises the rate it is currently offering on CDs to attract new deposits. Financial institutions may also trade CDs (not their own) in the secondary market to raise funds, much as they might sell U.S. Treasury bills for cash. Today the negotiable CD plays a prominent role in the strategy of liability management, where banks control their funds sources as well as their funds uses to achieve both long- and short-range objectives.

New Types of CDs

Bankers are becoming increasingly innovative in packaging CDs to meet the needs of their customers. One notable innovation occurred in 1975 when the *variable-rate CD* was introduced. Variable-rate CDs issued by major banks today generally carry maturities of one year or less, with an interest rate that is adjusted every 30 to 90 days. The rate is usually based on a fixed premium over the secondary market rate for major bank CDs. Variable-rate CDs give the investor a higher return than could be obtained by continually renewing shorter-term CDs.

Another interesting development occurred in 1976 when Morgan Guaranty Trust in New York City introduced the *rollover CD* (also known as the roly-poly CD). Because six-month CDs are the maximum maturity traded in the secondary market, Morgan offered its customers longer-term CDs with higher rates, but in packages composed of a series of six-month CDs. Thus, the roly-poly CD promised higher returns plus the ability to market some CDs in the package in advance of maturity to meet emergency cash needs. However, the bank's customer is still obligated to purchase the remaining certificates at each six-month anniversary date until the contract expires. Some roly-poly CDs are issued with fixed rates, while others carry floating rates which change every six months.

Another variation on the CD theme is the *Eurodollar CD,* developed in 1966. Eurodollar CDs are negotiable, dollar-denominated time deposits issued by the foreign branches of major U.S. banks and some foreign-owned banks. These instruments generally carry higher yields than comparable domestic CDs because there are no legal reserve requirements overseas. Most Eurodollar CDs carry fixed rates, but floating-rate instruments were introduced in 1977. These CDs carry maturities over one year with a rate adjusted every three to six months to match changes in the London Interbank Offer Rate (LIBOR). There is now an active secondary market for Eurodollar CDs centered in New York City and London. Further innovations in CDs are likely in the future as banks face increasingly stiff competition for funds.

LOANS FROM THE FEDERAL RESERVE'S DISCOUNT WINDOW

A money market source of funds available to commercial banks and other depository institutions is the Federal Reserve's discount window. Each of the 12 Federal Reserve banks has a department where banks and other qualified borrowers can come to borrow reserves for short periods.[7] Indeed, most discount-window loans are for a maximum of 15 days, though longer-term credit can be arranged upon presentation of acceptable collateral and adequate reasons for the request. The mechanics of borrowing from the discount window are relatively simple. A depository institution granted a loan merely receives an increase in its reserve account at the Federal Reserve Bank in its district. When the loan comes due, the Fed merely removes the amount owed from the borrowing institution's reserve account.[8]

Causes and Effects of Borrowing from the Discount Window

Borrowing from the Fed increases the total volume of reserves available in the banking system until the loan is repaid. Many banks and other depository institutions come to the Federal Reserve near the end of their re-

---

[7] Until 1980 only member banks could borrow from the Federal Reserve Banks except under special circumstances. However, with passage of the Monetary Control Act of 1980, mutual savings banks, savings and loan associations, and credit unions offering transaction accounts or nonpersonal time deposits were authorized to borrow from the Fed's discount window on the same basis as member banks.

[8] See Chapter 22 for a more complete discussion of the methods used by depository institutions to borrow from the Federal Reserve.

serve settlement week, when they find themselves short of legal reserves. Frequently, the funds available from the Federal Reserve carry a lower interest rate than prevails in the Federal funds market, on CDs, or on other money market sources. This is especially true in periods of rapidly rising interest rates because the Fed changes its loan rate rather infrequently.[9] As the gap between open-market rates (especially on Federal funds) and the Fed's rate widens, demands on the discount window increase. In contrast, a period of falling rates usually brings about a decline in borrowings from the Fed.

This last point is illustrated by the figures shown in Exhibit 13–5. Money market interest rates rose to record levels in 1979 and 1980, spurred on by

EXHIBIT 13–5
Volume of Borrowings from the Federal Reserve Banks, 1960–81 ($ millions at year-end)

Year	Discount Window Loans to Depository Institutions	Year	Discount Window Loans to Depository Institutions
1960	$ 33	1971	$ 39
1961	130	1972	1,981
1962	38	1973	1,258
1963	63	1974	299
1964	186	1975	211
1965	137	1976	25
1966	173	1977	265
1967	141	1978	1,174
1968	186	1979	1,454
1969	183	1980	1,617
1970	335	1981*	2,038

* As of June 1981.
SOURCE: Board of Governors of the Federal Reserve System, *Federal Reserve Bulletin*, selected issues.

high rates of inflation. For example, the Federal funds rate averaged just over 11 percent in 1979 and more than 13 percent in 1980, rising to a high of almost 20 percent in December 1980. Nevertheless, the Federal Reserve kept the rate on its loans around 10 percent until late 1979 and held it in the 10 to 12 percent range through most of 1980. With discount-window loans much cheaper than other money market sources of funds, borrowers predictably turned to the Federal Reserve banks for huge amounts of funds. Discount-window loans averaged more than $1.5 billion during the 1979–80 period and climbed to well over $2 billion in the fall of 1980.

Collateral for Discount Window Loans

Most loans granted through the Fed's discount window are secured by United States government securities. However, the Federal Reserve also

---

[9] For example, the discount rate was changed only seven times in 1980 and only four times in 1979.

will make loans against commercial or farm paper, bankers' acceptances, and bills of exchange. Discount-window loans may be for terms as long as 90 days if the collateral used consists of U.S. government securities or eligible paper, and up to four months on other forms of collateral. However, as we noted earlier, most loans from the discount window are for a maximum of 15 days. To make the borrowing process as simple as possible, many depository institutions keep U.S. government securities in the vaults of the Federal Reserve banks and sign loan authorization agreements with the Fed's discount department in advance so that they can borrow over the telephone. Such requests must be confirmed in writing, however.

Restrictions on Federal Reserve Credit

Large money-center banks are the heaviest users of the discount window since they incur reserve deficits most frequently. However, less than 10 percent of all institutions eligible regularly borrow from the Federal Reserve System, despite the fact that it is often the cheapest source of reserves. In part, this is due to an uneasy feeling experienced by most bankers about being in debt to a government regulatory agency. Then too, the Fed's own regulations discourage heavy and frequent use of the window. For example, Federal Reserve officials stress that borrowing is a "privilege, not a right" and that no depository institution should come to rely upon Federal Reserve credit. Borrowing institutions are required to alternate between the window and other money market sources, especially Federal funds.

The Federal Reserve's Discount Rate

The *discount rate* is the interest rate charged by the Fed on loans of reserves secured by U.S. government securities or other acceptable collateral. In reality, there are four different discount rates. The cheapest rate applies to loans (advances) for short-term liquidity adjustment or seasonal needs, secured by U.S. government securities or high-grade commercial ("eligible") paper. In the summer of 1981 this rate was 14 percent. A slightly higher interest rate is levied against discount window loans secured by collateral of lesser quality. In times of national emergency, the Fed may also extend credit to individuals, partnerships, and even nonfinancial corporations, but the interest rate is much higher on such loans.[10]

An interesting development occurred in 1981 when the Fed imposed a *penalty rate* on borrowing by the nation's largest depository institutions. Effective May 5, 1981, a 4 percent surcharge was applied to short-term borrowings by financial institutions holding total deposits of $500 million or more when these institutions attempted to borrow in successive weeks or in more than four weeks in a calendar quarter. Because the discount rate was

---

[10] See Chapter 22 for a schedule of rates charged on various types of discount-window loans.

well below interest rates on federal funds, CDs, and other popular sources of reserves, many large banks were using the window to support their lending operations, contributing (in the Federal Reserve's opinion) to inflationary pressures. The 4 percent surcharge brought the cost of Fed loans closer to open-market rates and encouraged larger banks to look elsewhere for funds.

The individual Federal Reserve banks often recommend that the discount rate be changed; however, a change in that rate must be approved by the Federal Reserve Board in Washington, D.C. In recent years the Fed has levied a higher interest rate for emergency borrowings when a bank is in serious financial trouble. Large, continuous borrowings over a prolonged period of time may be approved at a rate of 1 to 2 percent above the regular Federal Reserve discount rate.

A CONCLUDING COMMENT ON BANK ACTIVITY IN THE MONEY MARKET

In this chapter we have focused our attention upon the major money market sources of funds used by commercial banks and other depository institutions. As we have seen, banks operate on *both sides* of the money market, supplying billions of dollars in credit to governments, corporations, securities dealers, and financial intermediaries each day while also borrowing huge amounts daily from many of the same institutions.

The money market has not always been as important a source of funds for banks and other depository institutions as it is today. Prior to the 1960s even many of the largest money-center banks in the United States regarded short-term deposits and nondeposit borrowings from the money market as a secondary, supplementary source of funds. Bankers were aware that heavy dependence on money market borrowings would make their earnings more sensitive to fluctuations in interest rates. When interest rates rose rapidly, bank profit margins would be squeezed. However, the force of competition intervened in the 1960s and 1970s, and many banks were compelled to draw more heavily upon the money market simply to protect their share of credit and deposit markets.

The real catalyst for growing money market borrowing by U.S. banks and other depository institutions has been the growing financial sophistication of their largest customers. When major corporations began to seek alternative investments for their short-term funds, especially the purchase of commercial paper and U.S. Treasury bills, rather than holding most of their money in bank deposits, bankers were forced to turn to the money market for additional funds. As we have seen in this chapter, the banking community approached the problem in two ways. One was to offer a new financial instrument—the negotiable certificate of deposit—to compete directly for short-term corporate funds. The other approach to the problem was to draw more intensively upon *existing* sources of money market funds, especially the Federal funds market.

Prior to the 1960s and 1970s, the Federal funds market was confined principally to the nation's largest banks, who swapped reserves with each other. As bankers turned more and more to the funds market, however, it broadened tremendously. Thousands of small banks and other nonbank financial institutions in cities, towns, and rural areas across the United States began supplying their excess reserves to larger banks in the central cities, hoping to boost their earnings. In turn, the greater supply of Fed funds encouraged the nation's largest banks to rely even more heavily upon the money market and less upon customer deposits as a source of reserves. The Federal funds market had become an accepted institution for both the smallest and the largest financial institutions in the nation.

As we will see in later chapters, the rapid expansion of the CD and Federal funds markets was just the beginning of banking's *money market strategy.* When the Federal Reserve became concerned over the rapid growth of CDs and Federal funds, especially in periods of severe inflation, it clamped down with tight-money policies and a slower growth in available reserves. Innovative financial managers were forced to find new sources of reserves or face a real cutback in their lending activities. Many turned to the Eurodollar market, borrowing deposits from abroad, or organized holding companies and issued commercial paper through subsidiary corporations. Still others found innovative ways to use repurchase agreements backed by Treasury bills and other government securities to raise additional funds.

All of these clever manuevers form part of what has been called the technique of *liability management.* For decades prior to the 1960s and 1970s, bankers devoted most of their time and attention to the management of their assets—mainly loans and security investments—and assumed their deposits and other liabilities would take care of themselves. Many financial analysts argued that deposits were essentially beyond management's control, determined by such external factors as interest rates, economic conditions, and government policy. Heavier dependence upon the money market for funds changed all that, however. Bankers very quickly came to realize that, simply by varying the daily interest rates (yields) they were willing to offer on CDs, Federal funds, Eurodollars, commercial paper, and other funds sources, they could gain a measure of control over the volume of incoming funds. If more funds were needed on a given day to accommodate customer loan demand, for example, a bank active in the money market would simply offer a higher yield on the particular money market instrument it desired to use. If a smaller volume of funds were required at another time, the institution might simply lower, or at least not increase, its offer rate on money market borrowings.

What is especially fascinating about the growth of liability-management strategies is that they have had precisely the effects many financial analysts predicted from the start. The earnings of banks and other financial institutions have become more sensitive to fluctuations in interest rates; and, in periods of rapidly escalating rates, profit margins have been squeezed. The use of liability-management strategies appears to have fundamentally altered the earnings-size relationship in banking. Until the 1970s the largest U.S. banks generally reported the highest earnings rates, but no more! Today the most-profitable banks are generally those of only moderate size. The heavier use of expensive and often highly volatile money market borrowings has contributed in many instances to more-rapid increases in bank expenses than in revenues.

Whether this adverse impact on the earnings of major banks will continue into the future remains to be seen. The great innovative abilities of these institutions and their willingness to accept new challenges and open up new markets will do much to shape their earnings performance in the years ahead. But whatever the future holds, bankers have transformed the money market into a far larger, more dynamic, and more vital institution than at any other time in history. The future rapid growth of money market transactions, with banks at the very center of trading activity, seems assured.

STUDY QUESTIONS

1. Define the term *federal funds*. Why are federal funds so important to the functioning of the money market?

2. Who are the principal borrowers in the federal funds market? Principal lenders?

3. Describe the process of reserve position adjustment for commercial banks and other depository institutions. What role does the federal funds market play in the management of a bank's money (reserve) position?

4. How does federal funds trading take place?

5. Describe the different types of federal funds loans. What factors explain why the daily rate on federal funds is one of the most-volatile interest rates in the U.S. financial system?

6. Why do you suppose the funds market is so important to the Federal Reserve in the conduct of monetary policy?

7. What is a large, negotiable CD? When and why were CDs first offered in the U.S. money market?

8. What factors appear to influence the interest rate offered on the CDs issued by any particular depository institution? Explain the meaning of the term *multitier market*.

9. Who are the principal buyers of money market CDs? Why?

10. What role do large, negotiable CDs play in liability management?

11. What is a variable-rate CD? Roly-poly CD? Eurodollar CD? Many financial experts expect banks and other deposit institutions to continue to develop new and more-innovative forms of CDs in the future. Can you explain why?

12. What is a discount-window loan, and how is the loan made and repaid?

13. What role does the discount window play in managing the reserves of depository institutions?

SELECTED REFERENCES

1. Federal Reserve Bank of Boston. *Controlling Monetary Aggregates.* 1968.
2. Federal Reserve Bank of Richmond. *Instruments of the Money Market.* 4th ed. 1977.
3. Lucas, Charles M., Marcos T. Jones, and Thom B. Thurston. "Federal Funds and Repurchase Agreements." *Quarterly Review,* Federal Reserve Bank of New York, Summer 1977, pp. 33–48.
4. Melton, William C. "The Market for Large Negotiable CDs." *Quarterly Review,* Federal Reserve Bank of New York, Winter 1977–78, pp. 22–24.
5. Poole, William. "The Making of Monetary Policy: Description and Analysis." *New England Economic Review,* Federal Reserve Bank of Boston, March-April 1974, pp. 21–30.
6. Simpson, Thomas D. *The Market for Federal Funds and Repurchase Agreements.* Staff Study, Board of Governors of the Federal Reserve System, July 1979.

14

Commercial Paper and Federal Agency Securities

In the previous chapter we discussed the vital role played by banks as major borrowers and lenders in the money market. However, banks have had to share the limelight in recent years with two other groups of money market borrowers—federal government agencies and large corporations. Indeed, the largest of all borrowers in the American money market is not a bank, but a unit of government—the U.S. Treasury Department. Moreover, in the 1960s and 70s, other units within the federal government's huge structure, known as federal agencies, come to be major demanders of money market funds. Many of these agencies, such as the Federal Land Banks, Small Business Administration, and Federal National Mortgage Association, have become familiar names to investors who are regularly offered a menu of attractive notes and bonds so that these agencies can carry out their mission of assisting the so-called disadvantaged sectors of the economy.

The ranks of *private* money market participants have also grown rapidly in recent years due to the borrowing and lending activities of some of the nation's largest corporations. Each year companies like American Telephone & Telegraph, General Motors, and Philip Morris borrow billions of dollars in the money market through the sale of unsecured promissory notes, known as commercial paper. A recent study by the Federal Reserve Board found that more than 300 industrial corporations, approximately 170 public utilities, and more than 200 other firms were regularly selling their commercial notes to money market investors.[1] Commercial paper issued by large corporations

---

[1] See reference 6 at the end of this chapter.

and bought principally by other large corporations has become one of the most dynamic and rapidly growing segments of the American money market. In this chapter we take a close look at both commercial paper and federal agency securities and their important roles within the financial system.

COMMERCIAL PAPER

What Is Commercial Paper?

Commercial paper is one of the oldest of all money market instruments, dating back to the 18th century in the United States. By definition, commercial paper consists of short-term, unsecured promissory notes issued by well-known companies that are financially strong and carry high credit ratings.[2] The funds raised from a paper issue normally are used for *current transactions*—i.e., to purchase inventories, pay taxes, meet payrolls, and cover other short-term obligations. However, a growing number of paper issues today are used to provide interim financing for construction projects, such as the building of pipelines, ships, office buildings, nuclear power plants, and manufacturing assembly lines.

Commercial paper is generally issued in multiples of $1,000 and is traded mainly in the *primary* market. Opportunities for resale in the secondary market are limited, though some dealers will redeem the notes they sell in advance of maturity. Because of the limited resale possibilities, investors are usually quite careful to purchase those paper issues whose maturity matches their planned holding period.

Types of Commercial Paper

There are two major types of commercial paper—direct paper and dealer paper.

The main issuers of *direct paper* are large finance companies and bank holding companies, who deal directly with the investor rather than using a securities dealer as an intermediary. These companies, which regularly extend installment credit to consumers and large working-capital loans and leases to business firms, announce the rates they are currently paying for various maturities. Investors then select those maturities which most closely approximate their expected holding periods and buy the securities directly from the issuer.

Leading finance-company borrowers in the direct paper market include General Motors Acceptance Corporation, CIT Financial Corporation,

---

[2] As a further backstop to reduce investor risk, borrowers in the commercial paper market nearly always secure a line of credit at a commercial bank. However, because the line of credit cannot be used to directly guarantee payment if the company goes bankrupt, many commercial note issuers today also take out irrevocable letters of credit prepared by their banks. Such a letter makes the bank responsible for repayment if the corporation defaults on its commercial paper.

Commercial Credit Corporation, and General Electric Credit Corporation. The leading bank holding companies which issue commercial paper are centered around the largest banks in New York, Chicago, San Francisco, and other major U.S. cities.[3] Today, about 80 financially oriented U.S. companies account for nearly all the directly placed paper, with finance companies issuing approximately three fourths of the total. All of these firms have an ongoing need for huge amounts of short-term money, possess top credit ratings, and have established working relationships with major institutional investors in order to rapidly place their new note issues.

Directly placed paper must be sold in large volume to cover the substantial costs of its distribution and marketing. On average, each direct issuer has between $600 and $700 million outstanding at any one time and will usually borrow at least $100 million per month. While issuers of direct paper do not have to pay dealers' commissions and fees, these companies must operate a marketing division to maintain constant contact with active investors. Sometimes direct issuers must sell their paper even when they have no need for funds. This is the price of maintaining a good working relationship with active investor groups. These companies also cannot escape paying fees to banks for supporting lines of credit, to rating agencies who rate their paper issues, and to agents (usually banks) who dispense required payments and collect funds.

The other major variety of commercial paper is *dealer paper,* issued by securities dealers on behalf of their corporate customers. Also known as industrial paper, dealer paper is issued mainly by nonfinancial companies as well as by smaller bank holding companies and finance companies. The issuing company may sell the paper directly to the dealer, who buys it less discount and commission and then attempts to sell it at the highest possible price in the market. Alternatively, the issuing company may carry all the risk, with the dealer agreeing only to sell the issue at the best price available less commission (often referred to as a best efforts basis). Finally, the open-rate method may be used, in which the borrowing company receives some money in advance but the balance depends upon how well the issue sells in the open market.

Recent Growth of Commercial Paper

As Exhibit 14–1 indicates, the volume of both directly placed and dealer paper more than doubled between 1976 and 1981. By May 1981 more than 700 companies had over $134 billion in commercial notes outstanding.

---

[3] Bank holding companies issue both direct and dealer paper, with the largest companies going the direct placement route. Much of this so-called bank-related paper comes from finance-company subsidiaries of large bank holding companies. Frequently, a holding company will issue paper through a nonbank subsidiary and then funnel the proceeds to one or more of its subsidiary banks by purchasing some of the bank's assets. This transaction gives the bank additional funds to lend and may be especially helpful when that bank is having difficulty attracting deposits through the normal channels.

EXHIBIT 14–1
Volume of Commercial Paper Outstanding ($ billions, end of period)

Instrument	1976	1977	1978	1979	1980	1981*
All issuers	$53.0	$65.0	$83.4	$112.8	$125.1	$134.2
Finance companies:						
Dealer-placed paper						
Total	7.3	8.9	12.3	17.6	19.6	24.2
Bank-related	1.9	2.1	3.5	2.8	3.6	4.4
Directly-placed paper						
Total	32.6	40.6	51.8	64.9	67.9	69.5
Bank-related	6.0	7.1	12.3	17.6	22.4	22.9
Nonfinancial companies†	13.1	15.5	19.4	30.3	37.6	40.5

* Through April 1981.
† Includes public utilities and firms engaged primarily in communications, construction, manufacturing, mining, wholesale and retail trade, transportation, and similar activities.
SOURCE: Board of Governors of the Federal Reserve System, *Federal Reserve Bulletin,* selected issues.

Slightly more than half the total was placed directly with investors by larger finance companies and bank holding companies.

What factors explain the rapid growth in commercial paper? One key factor is the relative cost of other sources of credit compared to interest rates prevailing on current commercial paper issues. For the largest, best-known corporations, commercial paper is often an efficient, cost-effective substitute for bank loans and other forms of borrowing. This is especially true for nonfinancial companies issuing notes through dealers. These firms usually come to the commercial paper market when it is significantly cheaper to borrow there rather than tap bank lines of credit. Another reason for the market's rapid growth is the high quality of most commercial paper obligations. Many investors regard this instrument as a close substitute for Treasury bills, bank CDs, and other money market instruments. As a result, market yields on commercial notes tend to move in the same direction and by similar amounts as do the yields on other money market securities.

This fact is shown clearly in Exhibit 14–2, which compares the market yields on three-month maturities of commercial paper, Treasury bills, negotiable CDs, and bankers' acceptances. Rates on these four money market instruments tend to stay within a percentage point or two of each other. We note that commercial paper yields are always higher than market rates on comparable-maturity U.S. Treasury bills, due to greater risk and lower marketability.

Maturities of Commercial Paper

Maturities on commercial paper range from three days ("weekend paper") to nine months. Most commercial notes carry an original maturity of 60 days or less, with an average maturity ranging from 20 to 45 days. Commercial paper is generally not issued for longer maturities than 270 days

EXHIBIT 14–2
Market Yields on Commercial Paper Compared to Yields on Other Money Market Instruments (average yields on three-month maturities, percent per annum)

Instrument	1977	1978	1979	1980	1981*
Commercial paper	5.54%	7.94%	10.97%	12.66%	17.56%
U.S. Treasury bills	5.27	7.19	10.07	11.43	16.30
Certificates of deposit	5.64	8.22	11.22	13.07	18.27
Prime bankers' acceptances	5.59	8.11	11.04	12.78	17.56

Notes: Commercial paper yields are unweighted averages of rates quoted by at least five dealers. Treasury bill rates are secondary-market yields computed from daily closing bid prices. CD rates are secondary-market yields quoted as five-day averages by five dealers. Bankers' acceptance rates are on 90-day maturities and are an average of the midpoint of the range of daily dealer closing rates offered for domestic issues. All yields except CDs are quoted on a bank discount basis.
* As of May 1981.
SOURCE: Board of Governors of the Federal Reserve System, *Federal Reserve Bulletin,* selected issues.

since, under the provisions of the Securities Act of 1933, any security sold in the open market for a longer term must be registered with the Securities and Exchange Commission.

Yields to the investor are calculated by the *bank discount method* as in the case of Treasury bills. Like T-bills, most commercial paper is issued at a discount from par, and the investor's yield stems from the price appreciation of the security between purchase date and maturity date. However, coupon-bearing paper is also available. The minimum denomination is usually $25,000, and the notes typically are issued in bearer form. New issues generally average about $2 million each in total amount. Payment is made at maturity upon presentation to the particular bank listed as agent on the front of the note. Settlement in federal funds is usually made the same day the note is presented for payment.

Changing Yields on Paper Issues

Because yields on commercial paper are open-market rates, they fluctuate daily with the ebb and flow of supply and demand forces in the marketplace. In the wide swings between easy and tight money which characterized the 1970s and early 1980s, commercial paper rates fluctuated between extreme highs and lows. For example, in 1977—a year of modest economic growth and moderate credit demands—paper rates averaged only about 5.5 percent (see Exhibit 14–3). Early in 1981, however, when intense credit demands and rapid inflation characterized the economic situation, paper rates ranged upward to nearly 18 percent, or more than three times as high as in 1977.[4]

---

[4] It is interesting to note the variations in the shape of the yield curve for one-month, three-month, and six-month commercial paper, as shown in Exhibit 14–3. In most years, yields on longer-term note issues are higher than on the shortest-term notes, resulting in an upward-sloping yield curve. This is evident for the years 1977 and 1978. However, as interest rates rose to record highs in 1979, 1980, and 1981, investors came to expect that rates would soon decline, and the yield curve for commercial paper displayed a downward slope with advancing maturity.

EXHIBIT 14-3
Market Interest Rates on Commercial Paper Issues (averages, percent per annum)*

Instrument Maturity	1977	1978	1979	1980	1981†
Dealer paper:†					
1-month	5.42%	7.76%	10.86%	12.76%	17.91%
3-month	5.54	7.94	10.97	12.66	17.56
6-month	5.60	7.99	10.91	12.29	16.66
Direct paper:					
1-month	5.38%	7.73%	10.78%	12.44%	17.47%
3-month	5.49	7.80	10.47	11.49	15.56
6-month	5.50	7.78	10.25	11.28	14.97

Note: Commercial paper yields are quoted on a bank discount basis.
* Beginning November 1977, the rates reported are unweighted averages of offering rates quoted by at least five dealers or at least five finance companies.
† Rates are as of May 1981.
SOURCE: Board of Governors of the Federal Reserve System, *Federal Reserve Bulletin,* selected issues.

The commercial paper market is highly volatile and difficult to predict. This is why many corporations eligible to borrow there still maintain close working relationships with commercial banks and other institutional lenders.

Advantages of Issuing Commercial Paper

There are several financial advantages to a company able to tap the commercial paper market for funds. Generally, rates on paper are lower than on corporate loans extended by commercial banks. This is evident from the data shown in Exhibit 14–4. During 1979, for example, the bank prime rate was consistently at least a full percentage point and sometimes more than two percentage points higher than the rate on six-month dealer paper. This spread between the bank prime rate and the six-month paper rate widened to three or four percentage points in both 1980 and 1981.

Moreover, the *effective* rate on most commercial loans granted by banks is even higher than the quoted prime rate, due to the fact that corporate borrowers usually are required to keep a percentage of their loans in a bank deposit. This so-called compensating balance requirement is generally 15 to 20 percent of the amount of the loan. Suppose a corporation borrows $100,000 at a prime interest rate of 15 percent but must keep 20 percent of this amount on deposit with the bank granting the loan. Then the effective loan rate is 18.75 percent (or $15,000/$80,000).

Another advantage of borrowing in the commercial paper market is that rates there are more flexible than bank loan rates. Moreover, a company in need of funds can raise money quickly through either dealer or direct paper. Dealers maintain close contact with the market and generally know where

EXHIBIT 14–4
Spread between the Average Prime Rate Quoted by Major U.S. Banks and the Six-Month Commercial Paper Rate, 1979–81*

Month	Bank Prime Rate	Six-Month Commercial Paper Rate	Rate Spread
1979:			
September	12.90%	11.60%	1.30%
October	14.39	13.23	1.16
November	15.55	13.26	2.29
December	15.30	12.80	2.50
1980:			
April	19.77	14.93	4.84
May	16.57	9.29	7.28
June	12.63	8.03	4.60
July	11.48	8.29	3.19
1981:			
February	19.43	14.87	4.56
March	18.05	13.59	4.46
April	17.15	14.16	2.99
May	19.61	16.66	2.95

* The prime rate is the average of rates posted by major U.S. banks. The commercial paper rate is an unweighted average of offering rates quoted by at least five dealers. Both rates are measured on a bank discount basis.
SOURCE: Board of Governors of the Federal Reserve System, *Federal Reserve Bulletin,* selected issues.

cash may be found. Frequently, notes can be issued and funds raised the same day or within a day or two.

Generally, larger amounts of funds may be borrowed more conveniently through the paper market than from other sources, particularly bank loans. This situation arises due to federal and state regulations which limit the amount of money a bank can lend to any single borrower. For national banks, the maximum unsecured loan is 10 percent of the bank's capital and surplus account. Frequently, corporate credit needs exceed an individual bank's loan limit, and a group of banks (consortium) has to be assembled to make the loan. However, this takes time and requires lengthy and complicated negotiations. Using the paper market is generally much faster than trying to hammer out a loan agreement among several parties. Moreover, the ability to issue commercial paper gives a corporation considerable leverage when negotiating with banks. A banker who knows that the customer can draw upon the commercial paper market for funds is more likely to offer advantageous terms on a loan and be more receptive to future customer credit needs.

Possible Disadvantages of Issuing Commercial Paper

Despite the advantages, there are some risks for corporations that choose to borrow frequently in the commercial paper market. One of these is the risk of alienating banks whose loans might be needed when a real emergency develops. The paper market is highly volatile and sensitive to financial and economic problems. This fact was demonstrated quite convincingly in 1980 when Chrysler Financial, the finance-company subsidiary of Chrysler Corporation, was forced to drastically cut back its borrowings in the commercial paper market due to the widely publicized troubles of its parent company. At times, it is extremely difficult even for those companies in sound financial condition to raise funds in the paper market at reasonable rates of interest. It helps to have a loyal and friendly banker available to supply emergency credit when the market turns sour. Another problem lies in the fact that commercial paper cannot be paid off at the issuer's discretion but generally must remain outstanding until it reaches maturity. In contrast, many bank loans permit early retirement without penalty.

Principal Investors

The most important investors in the commercial paper market include nonfinancial corporations, money market funds, bank trust departments, smaller commercial banks, pension funds, and insurance companies. In effect, this is a market where corporations borrow from other corporations. These investor groups regard commercial paper as a low-risk outlet for their surplus funds.

A recent innovation in the direct paper market is the *master note,* most frequently issued to bank trust departments and other "permanent" money market investors. Under a master note agreement, the investing company notifies the issuing company how much paper it will purchase each day for immediate payment. The investor agrees to take some paper each day up to an agreed-upon maximum amount. Interest owed is figured on the average daily volume of paper taken on by the investor during the current month. The prevailing interest rate on six-month commercial paper generally is used to determine the appropriate rate of return.

Commercial Paper Ratings

Commercial paper is generally rated as prime, desirable, or satisfactory, depending on the credit standing of the issuing company. Firms desiring to issue paper generally will seek a credit rating from one or more of three rating services—Moody's Investor Service, Standard & Poor's Corporation, and Fitch Investor Service. Moody's assigns ratings of Prime-1 (P-1) for the highest-quality paper, with lower-quality issues designated as Prime-2 (P-2) or Prime-3 (P-3). Standard & Poor's assigns ratings of A-1, A-2, or A-3, while Fitch uses F-1, F-2, or F-3.

It is extremely difficult in today's volatile conditions to market unrated commercial paper. Indeed, paper available is mainly from top-quality issuers; about three quarters of the firms currently selling notes carry A-1 or P-1 ratings. Generally, commercial notes bearing credit ratings from at least two rating agencies are preferred by both investors and dealers.

Dealers in Paper

The market is relatively concentrated among a handful of dealers who account for the bulk of all trading activity. The top commercial paper dealers today include Goldman Sachs & Co.; A. G. Becker, Inc.; the First Boston Corporation, Lehman Brothers; Kuhn Loeb, Inc.; Salomon Brothers; and Merrill Lynch, Pierce, Fenner and Smith. Dealers maintain inventories of unsold new issues or repurchased paper but usually expect to turn over all their holdings within a week to 10 days. Like dealers in U.S. government securities, commercial-paper dealers draw upon repurchase agreements (RPs) and demand loans from banks to help finance their inventory positions. They pay interest rates which usually are only a few basis points higher than on RPs collateralized by U.S. Treasury securities.

FEDERAL AGENCY SECURITIES

For at least the past 50 years, the federal government has attempted to aid certain sectors of the economy which appear to have an unusually difficult time raising funds in the nation's money and capital markets. These so-called disadvantaged sectors include agriculture, housing, and small businesses. Dominated by smaller, less-credit-worthy borrowers, these sectors allegedly get "shoved aside" in the race for scarce funds by large corporate borrowers and governments, especially in periods of tight money. Beginning in the 1920s and 30s, the federal government created several federal agencies to make direct government loans to, or guarantee private loans for, disadvantaged borrowers. Today, these federal credit agencies are large enough and, with the government's blessing, financially sound enough to compete successfully for funds in the open market and channel those funds to areas of critical social need.

Types of Federal Credit Agencies

There are two types of federal credit agencies—government-sponsored agencies and the true federal agencies. *Government-sponsored* agencies are not officially a part of the federal government's structure, but are quasi-private institutions. Their borrowing and lending activities are not reflected in the federal government's budget. This has aroused the ire of many fiscal conservatives who regard the credit-granting operations of government-sponsored agencies as a disguised form of federal government spending. Because these agencies are omitted from the federal government's books, annual federal budget deficits look considerably smaller and conceal the full extent of federal deficit financing.[5] True *federal agencies,* on the other hand, are legally a part of the government structure, and their borrowing and lending activities *are* included in the federal budget. Exhibit 14–5 lists the

EXHIBIT 14–5
Principal Borrowers in the Federal Agency Market

Agencies Part of the Federal Government	
Export-Import Bank (EXIM)	Government National Mortgage Association (GNMA, or Ginnie Mae)
Farmers Home Administration (FmHA)	Postal Service (PS)
General Services Administration (GSA)	Tennessee Valley Authority (TVA)

Government-Sponsored Agencies	
Banks for Cooperatives (BC)	Federal Intermediate Credit Banks (FICB)
Federal Farm Credit Banks (FFCB)	Federal Land Banks (FLB)
Federal Home Loan Banks (FHLB)	Federal National Mortgage Association (FNMA, or Fannie Mae)
Federal Home Loan Mortgage Corporation (FHLMC, or Freddie Mac)	

principal federal and government-sponsored agencies that borrow in the money and capital markets.

In their borrowing and lending activities, federal and government-sponsored agencies act as true financial intermediaries. They issue attractively packaged certificates, notes, and bonds to capture funds from savers, and they direct the resulting flow of funds into loans and loan guarantees to farmers, ranchers, small-business owners, financial institutions, and mortgage borrowers. While the securities issued by these government agen-

---

[5] Public concern over the growth of federal agency activities has increased in recent years, perhaps with some justification. To the extent that agency borrowing and lending activities increase the total amount of credit available in the economy and add to aggregate spending for goods and services, they may add to inflationary pressures.

Moreover, there is a tendency to create a new agency each time a new financial problem rears its head, increasing the cost burden of government activities. A prominent example is the Chrysler Corporation Loan Guarantee Board established by Congress in 1979. This board, whose voting members consist of the secretary of the Treasury, the chairman of the Federal Reserve Board, and the comptroller general of the United States, is authorized to guarantee with the "full faith and credit of the United States" notes issued by financially troubled Chrysler Corporation and other eligible borrowers. While this board is presently limited to $1.5 billion in guarantees, its creation raises a number of significant issues concerning government involvement in the private sector of the economy. How many other firms should the federal government guarantee against failure in the future? Upon what basis are such guarantees to be made? What happens to the efficiency of the market system when some firms are not allowed to fail?

cies are usually not guaranteed by the federal government, most investors feel that the government is "only a step away" in the event any agency gets into trouble.[6]

Growth of the Agency Market

Armed with this implied government support, the agency market has grown rapidly, with the volume of outstanding securities climbing from about $2 billion during the 1950s to almost $200 billion today (see Exhibit 14–6). Agency debt today equals about one fifth of the huge U.S. public debt and is roughly one third the amount of corporate bonds outstanding.

EXHIBIT 14–6
Growth of Agency Market Debt ($ billions)

Year End	Total Agency Debt Outstanding
1961	$ 8.6
1966	22.7
1971	50.7
1976	103.8
1977	112.5
1978	137.1
1979	163.3
1980	193.2
1981*	198.8

* As of March 1981.
SOURCE: Board of Governors of the Federal Reserve System, *Federal Reserve Bulletin*, selected issues; and U.S. Treasury Department, *Treasury Bulletin*, selected issues.

The agency market is dominated by the government-sponsored agencies, which have restricted access to federal government coffers and must rely mainly on the open market to raise money. The federal agencies, in contrast, are financed through the Federal Financing Bank (FFB), which borrows money from the Treasury. The FFB is closely supervised by the Treasury Department and, in fact, is staffed by Treasury employees. If present trends continue, all outstanding federal agency debt will be FFB securities issued to

---

[6] The government-sponsored agencies are permitted to draw upon the U.S. Treasury for funds up to a specified limit with Treasury approval. However, neither the principal nor the interest on the debt of government-sponsored agencies is guaranteed by the federal government, though the issuing agency guarantees its own securities. In contrast, securities of those federal agencies operated by the government are fully guaranteed by the credit of the United States government.

the Treasury, and only the government-sponsored agencies, which cannot borrow through the FFB, will directly tap the open market for funds.[7]

Terms on Agency Securities

Agency securities are generally short- to medium-term (out to 10 years), and about 40 percent have original maturities under 1 year. Longer-term agency securities are available in denominations as small as $1,000, while the shorter-term notes traded actively in the money market generally come in minimum denominations of $50,000 or more. They are subject to federal income taxes, and most are subject to state and local taxes as well. Only the securities issued by the Federal Home Loan Banks (FHLB), the U.S. Postal Service, and the sponsored farm-credit agencies are exempt from state and local government income taxes. However, state and local government estate, gift, and inheritance taxes do apply to all agency obligations.

One of the most popular agency securities is the certificate of participation (PC) used by the Federal National Mortgage Association (FNMA) and the Government National Mortgage Association (GNMA). PCs represent an interest in a pool of securities which entitles the holder to receive a portion of any income earned by the pool. In addition, the agencies issue notes and debentures, some of these backed by security investments previously acquired by the issuing agency. The heaviest agency borrowers in recent years, as indicated in Exhibit 14–7, have been the Federal National Mortgage Association ("Fannie Mae"), the Federal Home Loan Banks (FHLB), and the Farm Credit Banks. These three agencies accounted for 75 percent of the outstanding debt issued by all federal and government-sponsored agencies at year-end 1980. Clearly, most agency borrowing goes to support the housing market and agriculture.

The securities of all government-sponsored agencies are regarded as highly similar to each other by investors, and therefore comparable maturities tend to have about the same yield regardless of the issuing agency. Each agency is able to borrow at interest rates below the average yield on its asset portfolio due to government support and control. Generally, the yield on agency securities is close to the yield on U.S. government securities of

---

[7] Due to FFB activities, the Treasury has to add a certain amount to its regular borrowings each year in order to cover any FFB drawings. As of April 1980 the Federal Financing Bank had borrowed a total of $74 billion from the Treasury to fund the federal agencies.

The FFB was created by Congress in 1973. Up to that time, each federal agency did its own borrowing. As a result, the number of different federal agency issues was proliferating at a rapid rate, creating some confusion among investors as to the terms and characteristics of each issue. There were also fears expressed in Congress that agency borrowing was growing out of control. Centralization of borrowing in one agency, it was hoped, would increase efficiency in the fund-raising process, improve the marketability of agency securities, and give Congress a more adequate measure of the growth of agency activities. All FFB obligations are fully guaranteed by the United States government. The FFB, in turn purchases only those securities fully guaranteed as to principal and interest by the issuing agency.

EXHIBIT 14–7
Total Debt Outstanding of Federal and Government-Sponsored Agencies,
December 1980 ($ billions)

Agency	Total Debt Outstanding
Federal agencies:	
Export-Import Bank	$ 11.3
Federal Housing Administration	0.5
Government National Mortgage Association	2.8
Postal Service	1.8
Tennessee Valley Authority	11.2
Other Agencies	1.0
Total federal agency debt	$ 28.6
Government-sponsored agencies:	
Federal Home Loan Banks	$ 41.3
Federal Home Loan Mortgage Corporation	2.5
Federal National Mortgage Association	55.2
Federal Land Banks	12.4
Federal Intermediate Credit Banks	1.8
Banks for Cooperatives	0.6
Farm Credit Banks*	48.2
Student Loan Marketing Association	2.7
Total government-sponsored agency debt	$164.7

* In January 1979 the Farm Credit Banks began issuing consolidated bonds to replace those securities previously issued by the Federal Land Banks, Federal Intermediate Credit Banks, and the Banks for Cooperatives.
SOURCE: Board of Governors of the Federal Reserve System, *Federal Reserve Bulletin,* June 1981.

comparable maturity, but slightly higher. Most of this small difference in yield is due to the fact that agency securities are less marketable than Treasury IOUs. The Treasury issues a security homogenous in quality and other financial characteristics, while the agency market is splintered into many small pieces due to differences among the agencies themselves. The yields on agency securities are lower than yields on private debt issues, however, due to their superior credit standing.

The Marketing of Agency Issues

Most agency issues are sold through a fiscal agent in New York City, who assembles groups of banks, dealers, and brokers to bring each issue to market. The agent sets the maturity, offering date, size, and price of each new issue.[8] The marketing syndicate of dealers and other participating institu-

---

[8] Approval of the U.S. Treasury Department usually is obtained before new agency securities come to market.

tions then distributes the securities on the street and receives a commission for its efforts.

Among the most-active buyers of agency securities are commercial banks, mutual savings banks, state and local governments, savings and loan associations, U.S. government trust funds, and the Federal Reserve System. The Federal Reserve has been authorized to conduct open-market operations in agency IOUs since 1966. Fed buying and selling of these securities has helped to improve their marketability and stature among private investors. Major securities dealers who handle U.S. government securities also generally trade in agency issues.

SUMMARY AND CONCLUSIONS

In this chapter we have looked at two of the most rapidly growing securities markets of the past decade—commercial paper and agency securities. Major industrial corporations, faced with rapidly growing demands for their products and services, have turned increasingly to the market for short-term commercial notes to meet pressing cash needs. The commercial-paper market, as we have seen, offers a flexible avenue for borrowing, often at lower interest rates than those available from commercial banks and other institutional lenders. At the same time, commercial banks and finance companies, faced with burgeoning demands for credit from households, business firms, and federal, state, and local governments, have found the commercial-paper market an excellent avenue for raising large amounts of short-term funds quickly, at minimum cost and with minimum inconvenience. The pressure of demand from these large groups of industrial and financial firms caused the volume of commercial paper outstanding to increase fivefold during the 1960s and to nearly quadruple during the 1970s. Further rapid expansion of this market is expected during the 1980s and beyond.

Equally impressive has been the growth of debt securities issued by agencies created by the U.S. government. Their extensive borrowing and lending activities in the financial markets channel billions of dollars in funds to farmers, ranchers, commercial fishers, small businesses, mortgage borrowers, and mortgage-lending institutions on more generous terms than the open market often provides. Many of these agencies, especially those aiding agriculture and the mortgage market, have been operating since the 1920s and 30s, but their growth in recent years has been unprecedented. As we saw in this chapter, federal agency debt increased more than threefold during the 1970s and now amounts to about 20 percent of the total public debt of the United States government.

All federal agencies are creatures of Congress and may be destroyed, in theory at least, at the stroke of a pen. In reality, however, with continuing rapid growth in the number of new families formed in the United States each year and the rising costs of energy, housing, and food, the role of the federal agencies in the nation's financial markets probably will continue to expand. Agency securities will continue to be an attractive investment for commercial banks, savings and loan associations, credit unions, industrial corporations, and other investors who seek competitive rates of return on their funds with minimal risk.

STUDY QUESTIONS

1. What is commercial paper? What features make it attractive to money market investors?
2. Distinguish between direct paper and dealer paper. Who are the principal issuers of each?
3. Describe the role that dealers play in the functioning of the commercial paper market.
4. What range of maturities is attached to newly issued commercial paper? Why?
5. How is the yield (or rate of return) on commercial paper calculated?
6. What are the principal advantages accruing to a company large enough to tap the commercial paper market for funds? Are there any disadvantages to issuing commercial paper?
7. Who are the principal investors in commercial paper? How and why is this paper rated?
8. What are "disadvantaged" sectors of the economy? Give some examples.
9. What is the difference between a government-sponsored agency and a federal agency? Give some examples of each.
10. Are federal or government-sponsored agencies really financial intermediaries? Why?
11. What are the principal investment characteristics of agency securities?
12. How are agency securities marketed?

SELECTED REFERENCES

1. Banks, Louis. "The Market for Agency Securities." *Quarterly Review,* Federal Reserve Bank of New York, Spring 1978.
2. Board of Governors of the Federal Reserve System. "Survey of Finance Companies, 1975." *Federal Reserve Bulletin,* March 1976.
3. Dill, Arnold. "Liability Management Banking: Its Growth and Impact." *Monthly Review,* Federal Reserve Bank of Atlanta, February 1971.
4. Federal Reserve Bank of Richmond. *Instruments of the Money Market.* 4th ed. 1979.
5. Federal Trade Commission. *Quarterly Financial Report for Manufacturing Mining, and Trade Corporations.* Selected quarterly issues.
6. Hurley, Evelyn M. "The Commercial Paper Market." *Federal Reserve Bulletin,* June 1977, pp. 525–36.

7. Jaffee, Dwight. "An Econometric Model of the Mortgage Market." In *Savings Deposits, Mortgages, and Housing,* edited by Edward Gramlich and Dwight Jaffee. Lexington, Mass.: D. C. Heath, 1972.

8. McCurdy, Christopher. "The Dealer Market for U.S. Government Securities." *Quarterly Review,* Federal Reserve Bank of New York, Winter 1977–78, pp. 35–47.

9. Zwick, Burton. "The Market for Corporate Bonds." *Quarterly Review,* Federal Reserve Bank of New York, Autumn 1977, pp. 27–36.

15

International Money Market Instruments: Bankers' Acceptances and Eurodollars

The money market today is not confined within the boundaries of a single nation. Money flows around the globe, seeking out those investments offering the highest expected returns for a given degree of risk. Moreover, world trade has expanded in recent years at a rapid pace, especially among the United States, Japan, Western Europe, and the Middle East. Further rapid increases in international trade and commerce are expected in the decade ahead, including a significant expansion of trade between East and West. China, the Soviet Union, and the Eastern European nations are developing close economic ties with several Western countries. The exporting of agricultural products and advanced technology by the United States, Japan, and Western Europe to Third World countries and, in some cases, to the Communist bloc constitutes one of the major avenues for international trade in the modern world.

And, of course, the growth and development of international commerce requires a concomitant expansion in both long-term and short-term sources of financing. Long-term capital is needed to build new factories, transport systems, dams, deep-water ports, and energy-producing and refining facilities. Short-term capital from the money market is needed to finance the annual export and import of goods, the carrying of inventories, and the payment of tax obligations, and to provide other working-capital needs. In this chapter we focus upon two of the most widely used international money market instruments—bankers' acceptances and Eurodollars.

BANKERS' ACCEPTANCES

A banker's acceptance is a *time draft* drawn on a bank by an exporter or an importer to pay for merchandise or to buy foreign currencies. If the bank honors the draft, it will stamp "accepted" on its face and endorse the instrument. By so doing, the issuing bank has unconditionally guaranteed to pay the face value of the acceptance at maturity. Acceptances carry maturities ranging from 30 to 180 days (with 90 days being the most common) and are considered prime-quality money market instruments. They are actively traded among bank and nonbank financial institutions, manufacturing and industrial corporations, and securities dealers as a high-quality investment and source of ready cash.

Why Acceptances Are Used in International Trade

Acceptances are used in the import and export trade because most exporters are uncertain of the credit standing of the importers to whom they ship goods. Exporters may also be concerned about business conditions or political developments in foreign countries. Nations experiencing terrorist violence or even civil war have serious problems in attracting financing for imports of goods and services because of the obvious risks carried by businesses extending credit to them. However, exporters usually are quite content to rely upon acceptance financing by a foreign bank.

How Acceptances Arise

Trade acceptances usually begin when an importer goes to a bank to secure a line of credit to pay for a shipment of goods from abroad. Once the line of credit is approved, the bank will issue an irrevocable letter of credit in favor of the foreign exporter. This document authorizes the exporter to draw a time draft for a specified amount against the issuing bank.

Because the letter of credit authorizes the drawing of a time draft and not a sight draft (which is payable immediately upon presentation), the exporter must wait until the draft matures (perhaps as long as six months) to be paid. However, such a delay is unacceptable for most export firms. They must meet payrolls, purchase inventories, pay taxes, and satisfy other near-term obligations. Moreover, the time draft will generally be redeemed in the home currency of the issuing bank, and this particular currency may not be needed by the exporter. A French exporter holding a time draft from a U.S. bank, for example, would be paid in dollars on its maturity date, even though the exporter probably needs francs to pay his employees and meet other expenses. Typically, then, exporters will discount the time draft with their own bank, negotiating a reasonable price for it. The exporters then receive immediate payment in local funds and avoid the risks of trading in foreign currencies.

The foreign bank which has now acquired the time draft from the exporter will forward it to the bank issuing the original letter of credit. The issuing bank checks to see that the draft is correctly drawn and then stamps "accepted" on its face. Two things happen as a result of this action: (1) a banker's acceptance—a high-quality, negotiable money market instrument—has been created; and (2) the issuing bank has acknowledged a debt which must be paid in full at maturity. Frequently, the issuing bank will discount the new acceptance for the foreign bank which sent it and credit that bank's correspondent account. The acceptance may then be held as an asset or sold to a dealer. Meanwhile, shipping documents are handed to the importer against a trust receipt, permitting the importer to pick up and distribute the goods. However, under the terms of the letter of credit, the importer must deposit the proceeds from selling these goods at the issuing bank in sufficient time to pay for the acceptance. When the time draft matures, the acceptance will be presented for payment by its holder.

It should be clear that all three principal parties to the acceptance transaction—the exporter, importer, and issuing bank—benefit from this method of financing international trade. The exporter receives funds with little or no delay. The importer, however, may delay payment for a time until the related bank line of credit expires. The issuing bank regards the acceptance as a readily marketable financial instrument which can be sold before maturity to an acceptance dealer in order to cover short-term cash needs. However, there are costs associated with all of these benefits. A discount fee is charged off the face value of the acceptance whenever it is discounted in advance of maturity. And the accepting bank earns a commission, which may be paid by either exporter or importer.

Recent Growth of Acceptance Financing

Reflecting the significant advantages of acceptance financing for exporters, importers, and banks, it is not surprising that the volume of bankers' acceptances outstanding has grown rapidly in recent years. As Exhibit 15–1 shows, the volume of acceptances increased from less than $400 million in 1950 to just over $2 billion in 1960 and then tripled by 1970 to slightly more than $7 billion outstanding. However, even these rapid rates of growth look pale when compared with the virtual explosion of acceptance financing during the decade of the 1970s. By December 1980 the volume of bankers' acceptances outstanding exceeded $54 billion—a sevenfold increase in a decade!

What factors account for this impressive growth in acceptances? Exhibit 15–2 helps us find the answer. The majority of acceptances created by U.S. banks arise from three types of financial transactions: (1) the financing of imports into the United States; (2) the financing of exports from the United States; and (3) the financing of goods stored in or transported between other countries. Acceptances arising from the last source are called third-country

EXHIBIT 15–1
The Growth of Bankers' Dollar Acceptances
($ millions)

Year-End	Volume Outstanding
1950	$ 394
1960	2,027
1970	7,058
1975	18,727
1976	22,532
1977	25,450
1978	33,700
1979	45,321
1980	54,744
1981*	62,320

* Figure as of April 1981.
SOURCES: Board of Governors of the Federal Reserve System, *Federal Reserve Bulletin* and *Banking and Monetary Statistics,* selected issues.

EXHIBIT 15–2
Uses of Acceptance Financing ($ millions)

Uses of Acceptance Financing	Year-End						
	1975	1976	1977	1978	1979	1980	1981*
Imports into the United States	$ 3,726	$ 4,992	$ 6,378	$ 8,574	$10,270	$11,536	$13,634
Exports from the United States	4,001	4,818	5,863	7,586	9,640	11,339	13,368
All other uses	11,000	12,713	13,209	17,540	25,411	31,480	35,319

* As of April 1981.
SOURCE: Board of Governors of the Federal Reserve System, *Federal Reserve Bulletin,* selected issues.

bills. While all three types of acceptances have grown rapidly in recent years, it is the third-country bills which have dominated the growth in acceptance financing, led by Japan and nations in the Middle East whose export and import trade have mushroomed during the past decade.

Despite their rapid growth abroad, however, acceptances are not widely used inside the United States for purely domestic trade. A small amount of domestic acceptance financing is carried out to support the storage of staple commodities such as cotton, grain, rice, wood, or tobacco. However, if a company can borrow from a bank at or close to the prime interest rate, that is generally a cheaper source of funds than acceptance financing. Moreover, it is usually much easier for a domestic firm to assess the financial condition of its domestic customer than to evaluate the credit standing of a foreign firm thousands of miles distant. For this reason suppliers of goods in the domestic market usually extend short-term credit (accounts receivable) directly to their customers rather than insisting on time drafts against a bank (acceptances). Moreover, in domestic commerce no exchange of foreign currencies is necessary, eliminating one important type of business risk.

Acceptance Rates

Acceptances do not carry a fixed rate of interest but are sold at a discount in the open market like Treasury bills. The prime borrower under an acceptance contract is charged a commitment fee for this line of credit, which is usually 1½ percent (i.e., ⅛ of 1 percent per month) for top-quality customers. If the bank wishes to sell the acceptance in advance of its maturity, the rate of discount it must pay is determined by the current bid rate on acceptances of similar maturity in the open market. The yield on acceptances is usually only slightly higher than on U.S. Treasury bills because banks who issue them are among the nation's largest and have solid international reputations (see Exhibit 15–3). Adding to the stature and marketability of accep-

EXHIBIT 15–3
Interest Rates on Bankers' Acceptances and U.S. Treasury Bills* (averages, percent per annum)

| | 1981 | | | | | | |
Instrument	March	April	May	1977	1978	1979	1980
Prime 90-day bankers' acceptances	13.88%	14.65%	17.56%	5.59%	8.11%	11.04%	12.78%
Three-month U.S. Treasury bills	13.36	13.69	16.30	5.27	7.22	10.04	11.43

* Both banker's acceptance and Treasury bill yields are quoted on a bank discount basis. Acceptance yields are averages of the midpoint of the range of daily dealer closing rates offered for domestic issues. Bill rates are auction averages for the week in which bills were issued.
SOURCE: Board of Governors of the Federal Reserve System, *Federal Reserve Bulletin*, selected issues.

tances is the fact that the Federal Reserve System occasionally conducts its open market operations in acceptances (often on behalf of foreign central banks) and holds a small portfolio of these instruments.[1] Depository institutions are permitted to borrow reserves from the Fed's discount window using eligible acceptances (90 days or less to maturity) as collateral.

---

[1] The banker's acceptance is one of the safest of all financial instruments. It is an irrevocable primary debt of the bank stamping "accepted" on its face as well as a contingent liability of the drawing firm and of any other bank, firm, or individual who endorses the document. At the same time the customer (usually an importer) who has requested the initiating letter of credit which gives rise to the acceptance has guaranteed payment by the maturity date. Then, too, any goods shipped under the letter of credit are nearly always insured and accompanied by trust and warehouse receipts and other documents specifying value and ownership. There is no record of a defaulted acceptance in the U.S. banking system, though, of course, the value of discounted acceptances does fluctuate with market conditions.

Investors in Acceptances

Commercial banks regard the acceptance as a high-grade negotiable instrument suitable for liquidity management purposes. In addition, the essential safety of acceptances is recognized by the U.S. Treasury, which permits banks to use acceptances as collateral to back the Treasury's tax and loan accounts held in a majority of the nation's commercial banks. As shown in Exhibit 15–4, in 1980 U.S. bank holdings of acceptances topped $10 billion

EXHIBIT 15–4
Holders of Bankers' Acceptances ($ millions)

Holders	Year-End						
	1975	1976	1977	1978	1979	1980	1981*
Accepting banks:	$7,333	$10,442	$10,434	$ 8,579	$ 9,865	$10,564	$10,781
Own bills	5,889	8,769	8,915	7,635	8,327	8,963	9,626
Bills bought	1,435	1,673	1,519	927	1,538	1,601	1,155
Federal Reserve banks:							
Own accounts	1,126	991	954	1	704	776	0
Foreign correspondents	293	375	362	664	1,382	1,791	1,383
Other holders	9,975	10,715	13,700	24,456	33,370	41,614	50,156

* As of April 1981.
SOURCE: Board of Governors of the Federal Reserve System, *Federal Reserve Bulletin,* selected issues.

(consisting mostly of their own drafts), which was about one fifth of the total amount of acceptances outstanding.

The majority of investors in this market, however, are *foreign* individuals and institutions. This is due to the fact that income earned on acceptances by American investors is subject to federal income tax, but the same income usually is tax-exempt to a foreign investor. Other important investors in the acceptance market include industrial corporations, savings banks, insurance companies, and individuals. To many investors, acceptances are a close substitute for U.S. Treasury bills, negotiable CDs, or commercial paper in terms of quality, though the acceptance market is far smaller in volume of trading.

Only a few dealers—today there are 15 major ones—regularly trade in acceptances, usually as an adjunct to their trading activities in Treasury bills and U.S. government notes and bonds. Trading is carried out purely on a negotiated basis, with most daily volume accounted for by swaps of holdings among accepting banks. Dealers' inventories of acceptances available for purchase are small. While a wide variety of denominations are available for both large and small investors, nonbank investors usually find the menu of fresh offerings very limited. Nevertheless, an investor who is willing to accept the odd-lot denominations in which most acceptances are issued will generally find the investment quite rewarding in terms of a competitive rate of return, low risk, and brisk resale demand, especially from bank and foreign nonbank investors.

EURODOLLARS

Comparable to the domestic money market, a chain of international money markets trading in the world's most convertible currencies stretches around the globe. This so-called *Eurocurrency market* has arisen because of a tremendous need worldwide for funds denominated in dollars, marks, pounds, francs, yen, and other relatively stable currencies. For example, as American corporations have expanded their operations in Europe and the Middle East, they have needed huge amounts of U.S. dollars to purchase machinery and other goods in the United States and to pay federal and state taxes. These same companies have also required huge amounts of other national currencies to carry out transactions in the countries where they are represented. To meet this kind of need, large international banks headquartered in the world's key financial centers—London, Paris, Zurich, Tokyo, New York, and other major cities—began in the 1950s to accept deposits denominated in currencies other than that of the host country and to make loans in those same foreign currencies. Thus, the Eurocurrency market was born.

What Is a Eurodollar?

Because the dollar is the chief international currency today, the market for Eurodollars dominates the Eurocurrency markets. What are Eurodollars? Eurodollars are deposits of U.S. dollars in banks located outside the United States. The banks in question record the deposits on their books in U.S. dollars, not in the home currency. While the large majority of Eurodollar (and other Eurocurrency) deposits are held in Europe, these deposits have spread worldwide, and Europe's share of the total is actually declining.[2]

Frequently, banks accepting Eurodollar deposits are foreign branches of American banks. For example, in the city of London—the center of the Eurocurrency market today—branches of American banks outnumber British banks and bid aggressively for deposits denominated in U.S. dollars.[3]

---

[2] Among the most important non-European centers for Eurocurrency trading are the Bahamas, Bahrain, Canada, the Cayman Islands, Hong Kong, Japan, Panama, and Singapore.

[3] U.S. banks are prohibited from accepting deposits or making loans in currencies other than U.S. dollars in the domestic market. However, banks in other countries and foreign branches of U.S. banks can accept foreign-currency-denominated accounts.

Many of these funds will then be loaned to the home office in the states to meet reserve requirements and other liquidity needs. The remaining funds will be loaned to private corporations and governments abroad who have need of U.S. dollars.

No one knows exactly how large the Eurodollar market is. One reason is that the market is almost completely unregulated. Moreover, many international banks refuse to disclose publicly their deposit balances in various currencies. Another reason for the relative lack of information on market activity is that Eurocurrencies are merely bookkeeping entries on a bank's ledger and not really currencies at all. You cannot put Eurodollars in your pocket like bank notes. Moreover, Eurodollar deposits are continually on the move in the form of loans. They are employed to finance the import and export of goods, to supplement government tax revenues, to provide working capital for the foreign operations of U.S. multinational corporations, and, as we noted earlier, to provide liquid reserves to the largest banks headquartered in the United States.

One recent estimate for mid-1980 drawn from figures compiled by Morgan Guaranty Trust Company in New York gave the *gross* size of the entire Eurocurrency market at $1,470 billion. The term *gross* in this instance means the sum of all foreign-currency-denominated liabilities outside the country of the currency's origin. The *net* size of the Eurocurrency market, netting out deposits owned by Eurocurrency banks, was estimated at close to $700 billion. Because Eurodollars represent about three quarters of all Eurocurrency liabilities, the gross size of the Eurodollar market would be about $1,100 billion, while the net total is probably close to $500 billion.[4] Figures of this magnitude would make the Eurodollar market the largest of all money markets.

The Creation of Eurodollars

To illustrate how Eurodollar deposits arise, we trace through a simple, but quite typical, example. While our discussion will be in terms of Eurodollars, the reader should be aware that the process being described really applies to any Eurocurrency.

Suppose a French exporter of fine wines ships cases of champagne to a New York importer, accompanied by a bill for $10,000. The importing firm pays for the champagne by issuing a check drawn on its local bank in the requested amount. Because the French exporter deals regularly in the United States, frequently buying American equipment and securities, it is happy to accept the importer's check denominated in dollars and deposits it right away in a U.S. bank—First American Bank—where the French firm

---

[4] See reference (14) at the conclusion of this chapter, December 1980 issue.

maintains a commercial checking account. After this check clears, the results of the transaction are shown below.

French Exporter			First American Bank	
Assets	Liabilities		Assets	Liabilities
Demand +$10,000 deposit in U.S. bank				Demand +$10,000 deposit owed French exporter

Is the deposit shown above a Eurodollar deposit? *No,* because the deposit of dollars occurred in the United States, where the dollar is the official monetary unit. Suppose now, however, that the French exporter is offered an attractive rate of return on its dollar deposit by its own local bank in Paris and decides to move the money there. The Paris bank wants to loan these dollars to other customers who need them to pay bills or make purchases in the United States. After the wine exporter and its Paris bank exchange letters setting out the terms of the deposit, the French exporter will receive a receipt for a dollar-denominated time deposit in its Paris bank. That bank will now hold claim to the original dollar deposit in the United States. The Paris bank will have at least one U.S. correspondent bank and will ask to have the original dollar deposit transferred there. We show these transactions as follows:

French Exporter			First American Bank	
Assets	Liabilities		Assets	Liabilities
Demand −$10,000 deposit in U.S. bank			Reserves −$10,000 transferred to U.S. correspondent bank	Demand −$10,000 deposit owed French exporter
Time +$10,000 deposit in Paris bank				

U.S. Correspondent Bank			Paris Bank	
Assets	Liabilities		Assets	Liabilities
Reserves +$10,000 received from First American Bank	Demand +$10,000 deposit owed Paris bank		Deposit +$10,000 with U.S. correspondent bank	Time +$10,000 deposit owed French exporter

Do we now have a Eurodollar deposit? *Yes,* in the form of a $10,000 time deposit in a Paris bank. The wine exporter's deposit has been accepted and recorded on the Paris bank's books in U.S. dollars, even though the official monetary unit in France is the franc.[5]

Let us follow this Eurodollar deposit through one more step. Assume now that the Paris bank makes a loan of $10,000 to a small oil company based in Manchester, England. The British company needs dollars to pay for a shipment of petroleum drilling equipment from Houston, Texas. By securing a dollar credit from the Paris bank, the British oil firm, in effect, receives a claim against dollars deposited in U.S. banks. The appropriate accounting entries would be:

Paris Bank		British Oil Company	
Assets	Liabilities	Assets	Liabilities
Loan to +$10,000 British oil company		Demand +$10,000 deposit in U.S. corre- spondent bank	Loan +$10,000 owed to Paris bank
Deposit −$10,000 in U.S. corre- spondent bank			

U.S. Correspondent Bank	
Assets	Liabilities
	Deposit −$10,000 owed to Paris bank
	Deposit +$10,000 owed to British oil company

Note that we have assumed the British oil company held a deposit account in the same U.S. bank where the Paris bank held its correspondent deposits. This, of course, is often not the case, but it was done here to reduce the number of accounting entries. If another U.S. bank were involved, we would simply transfer deposits and reserves to it from the U.S. correspondent that held the account of the Paris bank. The end result would be exactly the same as in our example: *the total amount of dollar deposits and U.S. bank reserves remains unchanged.* These funds are merely passed from U.S. bank to U.S. bank as loans are extended and deposits made in the Eurodollar market. Thus, Eurodollar activity does not alter the total reserves of the U.S. banking system. In fact, the workings of the Eurodollar market remind us of a fundamental principle of international finance: *money itself usually does not leave the country where it originates; only the ownership of money is transferred across international boundaries.*

---

[5] The $10,000 time deposit is used here for illustrative purposes only. The vast majority of Eurocurrency deposits are far larger. In fact, the normal trading unit in this market is 1 million currency units.

The chain of Eurodollar loans and deposits started in our example by the wine exporter's bank in Paris will go on unbroken as long as dollar loans are in demand and the funds are continually redeposited somewhere in the international banking system. Eurobanks, like domestic U.S. banks, can create a multiple volume of deposits and loans for each dollar of deposits they receive. Even though Eurobanks are not limited in their creation of deposits and loans by legal reserve requirements, most experts in the field believe there are more leakages of funds from the Eurocurrency system than there are from the U.S. banking system. Therefore, the size of the international deposit multiplier is probably smaller than the domestic deposit multiplier. [6]

Of course, just as Eurodollars are created by making loans, they are also destroyed as loans are repaid. In our example above, suppose the British oil company trades pounds for dollars with a foreign currency dealer and uses the dollars purchased to repay its loan from the Paris bank. At about the same time, the dollar time deposit held by the French exporter matures, and the exporter spends those dollars in the United States. As far as U.S. banks are concerned, total deposits and reserves remain unchanged. However, as a result of these transactions, all dollar deposits are now held in the United States and therefore have ceased to be Eurodollars.

Eurodollar Maturities

Most Eurodollar deposits are short term (ranging from overnight loans to call money loaned for a few days out to one year) and therefore are true money market instruments. However, a small percentage are long-term time deposits, extending in some instances out to about five years. However, most Eurodollar deposits carry one-month maturities to coincide with payments for shipments of goods. Other common maturities are 2, 3, 6, and 12 months. [7]

Even though Eurobanks do not issue demand deposits, funds move rapidly in the Eurocurrency market from bank to bank in response to the de-

---

[6] See Chapters 3 and 22 for a discussion of the deposit multiplier. The granting of a Eurodollar loan to a borrower does *not* give the borrower "money" in a strict sense. Eurodollars are not generally acceptable as a medium of exchange to pay for goods and services. They are more like time deposits rather than checking accounts. The holder of a Eurodollar deposit must convert that deposit into some national currency unit before using it for spending. Thus, Eurodollars and other Eurocurrency deposits are not negotiable instruments. The Eurocurrency system can create credit, but not money. A lender of Eurocurrencies who needs liquid funds before a deposit matures must go back into the market and negotiate a separate loan.

Interest usually is paid only at maturity unless the Eurodollar deposit has a term of more than one year. Most deposit interest rates are tied to the London Interbank Offer Rate (LIBOR) and are usually fixed for the life of the deposit, though floating rates tied to semiannual changes in LIBOR are not uncommon on longer-term deposits.

[7] Banks active in the Eurodollar market for liquidity-adjustment purposes use so-called short date deposits. Comparable to federal funds transactions in the domestic U.S. money market, short dates represent deposits available for as long as 14 days, though generally they are weekend or 2-day money, with some 7-day maturities as well. Short dates may carry fixed maturities or simply be payable on demand with minimal notice (such as 24 or 48 hours).

mand for short-term liquidity from corporations, governments, and Eurobanks themselves. There is no central trading location in the market. Traders may be thousands of miles distant from each other, conducting negotiations by cable, telephone, or telex with written confirmation coming later. Funds normally are transferred on the second business day after an agreement is reached through correspondent banks.

Eurocurrency deposits are known to be volatile and highly sensitive to fluctuations in interest rates. A slight difference in interest rates on currency values between two countries can cause a massive flow of Eurocurrencies across national boundaries. One of the most famous examples of this phenomenon occurred in West Germany in 1971, when speculation that the German mark would be upvalued brought an inflow into Germany of more than $5 billion in a few days, forcing the West German government to cut the mark loose from its official exchange value and allow that currency to float.

The Supply of Eurodollars

Where do Eurodollars come from? A major factor in the market's growth has been the enormous balance-of-payments deficits which the United States has run since the late 1950s.[8] American firms building factories and purchasing goods and services abroad have transferred ownership of dollar deposits to foreign companies, banks, and governments. Domestic shortages of oil and natural gas have forced the United States to import from a third to 40 percent of its petroleum needs, generating an enormous outflow of dollars to oil-producing nations. The OPEC countries, for example, accept dollars in payment for crude oil and use the dollar as a standard for valuing the oil they sell. American tourists visiting Europe, Japan, Singapore, and the Middle East frequently use dollar-denominated traveler's checks or take U.S. currency with them and convert it into local currency overseas. Dollar loans made by U.S. corporations and foreign-based firms have added to the vast Eurodollar pool. Many of these dollar deposits have gravitated to foreign central banks, such as the Bank of England and the Bundesbank in the Federal Republic of Germany, as these institutions have attempted to support the dollar and their own currencies in international markets.

Eurodollars in Domestic Bank Operations

Since the late 1960s American banks have drawn heavily upon Eurodollar deposits as a means of adjusting their domestic reserve positions. Thus, the manager of the money desk at a large U.S. bank, knowing the bank will need extra cash reserves in a few days, can contact foreign banks holding dollar deposits and arrange a loan. The manager can also contact other U.S. banks

---

[8] See Chapter 26 for a discussion of the causes and effects of U.S. balance-of-payments deficits.

with branches abroad and borrow Eurodollars from them. Alternatively, if the money manager's own bank operates foreign branches accepting dollar deposits, these can be placed at the disposal of the home office.

Eurodollar borrowing of bank reserves has been especially heavy during periods of rapidly rising interest rates in the United States. For example, during the "credit crunches" of 1966, 1969–70, 1973–74, and 1979–80, when domestic money market rates rose to record levels, major U.S. banks tapped the Eurodollar market for billions of dollars in short-term funds. In the midst of the 1969–70 credit crunch, U.S. bank dollar liabilities to their foreign branches reached $15 billion—a record not surpassed until 1979, when net Eurodollar borrowings by U.S. commercial banks totaled nearly $35 billion. Such borrowings are highly volatile, however, and extremely interest-rate sensitive. For example, when U.S. money market rates fell precipitously from all-time record highs in the spring of 1980 and domestic sources of reserves became much less expensive, American banks repaid their Eurodollar borrowings nearly as fast as they had borrowed these international deposits months earlier. The volume of U.S. bank net Eurodollar borrowings from foreign-related institutions, which totaled $28 billion in December 1979, stood at only about $8 billion by the end of 1980 (see Exhibit 15–5).

EXHIBIT 15–5
Eurodollar Borrowings by Commercial Banks Operating in the United States, Monthly Averages for December ($ billions)

Item	1976	1977	1978	1979	1980	1981*
Net balances due to foreign-related institutions	$3.7	−$1.3	$6.8	$28.1	$8.2	$0.3
Domestic chartered U.S. banks' net positions with their own foreign branches	−6.0	−12.5	−10.2	6.4	−14.7	−21.3
Gross due from balances	12.8	21.1	24.9	22.9	37.5	43.1
Gross due to balances	6.8	8.6	14.7	29.3	22.8	21.8

* Average for April 1981.
SOURCE: Board of Governors of the Federal Reserve System, *Federal Reserve Bulletin*, selected issues.

Eurodollars usually carry higher reported interest rates than other sources of bank reserves, such as the federal funds market or domestic deposits (see Exhibit 15–6). However, there are fewer legal and regulatory restrictions on the borrowing of Eurodollars. For example, Eurodollar deposits are not subject to Regulation Q interest-rate ceilings and, in most periods, have been free of reserve requirements. Moreover, U.S. banks must pay assessments to the Federal Deposit Insurance Corporation on domestic nonbank deposits to cover the costs of deposit insurance. Eurodollar deposits, however, are not insured.

EXHIBIT 15–6
Interest Rates on Eurodollar Deposits and Other Money Market Instruments

Period	Eurodollar Deposits		U.S. Treasury Bills		Federal Funds Rate
	3-Month	6-Month	3-Month	6-Month	
1969	11.44%	10.81%	6.68%	6.85%	8.22%
1970	6.50	6.75	6.46	6.56	7.17
1971	5.81	6.00	4.35	4.51	4.67
1972	5.81	6.14	4.07	4.47	4.44
1973	11.13	10.81	7.04	7.18	8.74
1974	10.00	10.00	7.89	7.93	10.51
1975	6.00	7.25	5.84	6.12	5.82
1976	5.00	5.19	4.99	5.27	5.05
1977	7.25	7.50	5.27	5.51	5.54
1978	11.69	12.38	7.22	7.57	7.94
1979	14.94	15.00	10.04	10.02	11.20
1980	14.00	n.a.	11.43	11.37	13.36

n.a. = not available.
SOURCE: U.S. Department of Commerce, *Business Statistics,* selected editions; and Board of Governors of the Federal Reserve System, *Federal Reserve Bulletin,* selected monthly issues.

In addition to meeting their own reserve needs from the Eurodollar market, U.S. banks have actively aided their corporate customers in acquiring and transmitting Eurocurrency deposits. Direct loans in Eurodollars and other Eurocurrencies are made by U.S. banks, and these banks will readily swap Eurocurrencies at the customer's request. While most Eurocurrency loans to nonbank customers are short-term credits to provide working capital, a sizable percentage in recent years have consisted of medium-term (one-to-five-year) loans for equipment purchases, frequently set up under a revolving credit agreement. The total amount of Eurodollar and other Eurocurrency loans is unknown, though fairly reliable estimates are available from branches of U.S. banks operating abroad. As shown in Exhibit 15–7, foreign branches of U.S. banks reported holding dollar claims of almost $290 billion in 1980, of which $116 billion represented claims on foreign banks, $23 billion were claims on public borrowers, and nearly $56 billion were claims on other nonbank foreign institutions.

Profit margins generally are very low on Eurodollar loans because the market is highly competitive, the cost of lending operations is low, and the risk is minimal. Borrowers are generally well-known institutions with substantial net worth and solid credit standing. Market transactions are usually carried out in large, even denominations, ranging from about $500,000 to $5 million or more.

Benefits and Costs of the Eurodollar Market

For the most part, the development of Eurodollar trading has resulted in substantial benefits to the international community and especially to U.S.

EXHIBIT 15–7
Total Claims Payable in U.S. Dollars Held by Foreign Branches of U.S. Banks, (end of period, $ billions)

Period	1976	1977	1978	1979	1980
Total dollar claims	$167.7	$193.8	$224.9	$267.6	$289.9
Claims on foreigners	156.9	178.9	203.5	229.1	253.5
Other branches of parent bank	37.9	44.3	55.4	61.5	58.3
Banks	66.3	70.8	78.7	96.2	116.0
Public borrowers	9.0	12.6	19.6	21.6	23.4
Nonbank foreigners	43.6	51.2	49.8	49.7	55.8
Claims on United States	7.6	11.0	16.4	31.2	27.2
Parent bank	4.3	7.7	12.6	25.6	19.9
other	3.3	3.4	3.8	5.5	7.3

SOURCE: Board of Governors of the Federal Reserve System, *Federal Reserve Bulletin*, August 1980.

banks and multinational corporations. The market ensures a high degree of funds mobility between international capital markets and provides a true international market for bank and nonbank liquidity adjustments. It has provided a mechanism for absorbing huge amounts of U.S. dollars flowing overseas and generally lessened international pressure to foresake the dollar for gold and other currencies.

The market reduces the costs of international trade by providing an efficient method of economizing on transactions balances in the world's most heavily traded currency, the dollar.[9] Moreover, it acts as a check on domestic monetary and fiscal policies, especially on the European continent, and encourages international cooperation in economic policies because interest-sensitive traders in the market will quickly spot interest rates that are out of line and move huge amounts of funds quickly to any point on the globe. Central banks, such as the Bank of England, the Bundesbank, and the Federal Reserve System, monitor the Eurodollar market continuously in order to moderate heavy inflows or outflows of funds which may damage their domestic economies.

The capacity of the Eurocurrency market to quickly mobilize massive amounts of funds has brought severe criticism of this market from central bankers in Europe and from certain government officials, economists, and financial analysts in the United States. They see the market as contributing to instability in currency values, particularly when Eurocurrency trading places severe downward pressure on the dollar and other key trading currencies. As noted above, the market can wreak havoc with monetary and fiscal policies designed to cure domestic economic problems. This is especially true if a nation is experiencing severe inflation and massive inflows of Eurocurrency occur at the same time. The net effect of Eurocurrency expan-

---

[9] See Balbach and Resler (2) on this point. In effect, the Eurodollar market lowers the cost of dollar-denominated financial intermediation.

sion, other things equal, is to push domestic interest rates down, stimulate credit expansion, and accelerate the rate of inflation. The ability of local authorities to deal with inflationary problems might be completely overwhelmed by a Eurocurrency glut. This danger is really the price of freedom, for an unregulated market will not always conform to the plans of government policymakers.[10]

It is not surprising that certain European central banks have for more than a decade called for controls on Eurocurrency trading. One of the most frequently heard proposals is to impose reserve requirements on Eurodollar deposits. For example, during the 1970s France levied a 9.5 percent reserve requirement on Eurodollar loans. But such controls have not really been effective because of lack of unanimity among foreign governments and central banks. Funds tend to flow away from areas employing controls and toward free and open markets. The key to the future of controls in this market probably rests with the Bank of England, because London is the heart of the Eurodollar market. And thus far, the Old Lady of Threadneedle Street, as that bank is often called, remains firmly against significant government restraints on Eurocurrency trading.

CONCLUDING COMMENTS

"The world is getting smaller all the time"—a familiar and trite phrase. It is also true. Travel time between distant cities and even across oceans is measured today in hours and minutes instead of days. The new supersonic jet transports, such as the British Concorde, have cut in half jet travel time between London and New York and between the major European and American financial centers and their counterparts in Asia, the Middle East, and the Far East.

However, the great speed at which people can travel today is far outclassed by the velocity of funds and information transfers worldwide. Communications satellites, orbiting thousands of miles above the earth's surface, speed financial and other data to their destination in minutes, seconds, and microseconds. On the ground telex and telegraph networks linking large and small financial centers permit the carrying out of financial transactions between traders separated by thousands of miles, oceans, mountain ranges, and deserts almost as conveniently as among those traders who meet face-to-face on the floor of the New York Stock Exchange. The financial world is shrinking rapidly in size, and it is becoming intensely more competitive, better informed, and more sensitive to the receipt of relevant information.

---

[10] There is little evidence that the rapid growth of the Eurodollar market has had any adverse effects on U.S. economic policies, however. For example, a recent study by Balbach and Resler (2) concludes: "Eurodollar flows . . . have only minor effects on the U.S. money stock. This evidence warrants the conclusion that the Eurodollar market does not pose a serious threat to the ability of the Federal Reserve to control the money supply." (See [2], p. 11.)

It is within this environment of change, which emphasizes speed and the availability of relevant information, that the international money market instruments we have discussed in this chapter—bankers' acceptances and Eurodollars—have grown to a position of dominance. The vast improvements in information flow and speed have broadened markets for the products and services of all businesses and linked national economies into an interdependent network—a multinational economic and financial system. That system requires a fluid market for the flow of loanable funds from those businesses and governments with cash surpluses, and therefore a need to invest idle funds, to those business and governmental institutions with cash deficits and a need to borrow money as briefly as overnight or for periods covering months and years.

And, as in any money market, there is great concern for risk within the multinational financial and economic system. Will the borrower be able to repay a loan and make the interest payments on it? What is the borrower's true credit position? These burgeoning international needs—for financial and credit information, for credit to support trade and commerce, and for low-risk investment outlets—have led to the development and growth of both bankers' acceptances and Eurodollars. Both instruments provide large amounts of credit to businesses engaged in international trade and commerce and, at the same time, offer an attractive, high-quality investment.[11] Moreover, both acceptances and Eurodollars are traded in largely unregulated and efficient markets where interest rates are highly responsive to changing demand and supply forces and investor expectations. This is why thousands of American corporations, including the nation's largest commercial banks, have entered these international markets as both borrowers and lenders of funds. And, in the absence of government regulation and control, markets linking financial systems should continue to grow in size and relative importance, exerting an ever widening influence upon the character of economic and political relationships in the international community.

There is one pressing need of today's money market investor that we have not fully addressed in this and the foregoing chapters—the need to protect trading and investing in securities against future changes in interest rates and security prices. All the money markets we have discussed to this point are *spot* markets, designed for the immediate delivery of credit and securities. However, today's financial markets are significantly more volatile—with

---

[11] As Goodfriend (8) observes, Eurodollars are not without risk. There is *political risk* because governments may restrict or prohibit the movement or repatriation of funds across national borders as the United States did for a time during the Iranian crisis. There may also be disputes between nations over the legal jurisdiction and control of deposits.

Default risk may also be a factor because banks in the Eurobanking system may fail, and Eurocurrency deposits usually are not insured. This problem is compounded by the fact that it is more difficult to secure information on the financial condition of foreign banks than on domestic banks. However, on the positive side, Eurobanks are among the largest and most-stable banking institutions in the world. Moreover, most foreign nations have tried to encourage the growth of the Eurocurrency markets through lenient regulation and taxation rather than restrict that growth.

wider swings in interest rates and security prices—than was true even a decade ago. This increased volatility and uncertainty have stimulated the development of a collection of financial markets where credit and securities are scheduled for future delivery with prices and rates set in advance. It is to these relatively new *futures markets* that we turn now in the next and final chapter on the money market.

STUDY QUESTIONS

1. What is a banker's acceptance? What does the word *accepted* mean?
2. Explain why acceptances are popular with exporters and importers of goods. Why are these instruments not as widely used within the United States as they are in financing international trade?
3. Evaluate bankers' acceptances as a security investment. What are their principal advantages and disadvantages from an investment point of view?
4. Who are the principal investors in the acceptance market? Why are they active in this market?
5. Describe the recent growth trend in acceptance financing. Which sector of the market has grown most rapidly? Why?
6. What is a Eurocurrency market? Why is it needed?
7. Define the term *Eurodollar*. Can a U.S. bank create Eurodollars? Why?
8. Describe the process by which Eurodollars are created. Explain what happens to the total volume of U.S. bank reserves and deposits in the creation process.
9. Can Eurodollars be destroyed? How?
10. List the sources of Eurodollar deposits. List their principal uses.
11. What role do Eurodollar deposits play in the reserve management operations of major U.S. banks? What are the advantages of Eurodollar borrowings over other sources of bank reserves?
12. Evaluate the Eurocurrency markets from a social point of view. What are the major benefits and costs of this rapidly growing institution? Would you support closer regulation of the Eurocurrency markets? Why or why not?

SELECTED REFERENCES

1. Ashby, David F. V. "Changing Patterns in the $800 Billion Super-Dollar Market." *The Banker*, March 1979, pp. 21–23.
2. Balbach, Anatol B., and David H. Resler. "Eurodollars and the U.S. Money Supply." *Review*, Federal Reserve Bank of St. Louis, June-July 1980, pp. 2–12.
3. Christelon, Dorothy B. "International Policies toward Foreign Direct Investment." *Quarterly Review*, Federal Reserve Bank of New York, Winter 1979–80, pp. 21–32.
4. Clarke, Stephen V. O. "Perspective on the United States External Position Since World War II." *Quarterly Review*, Federal Reserve Bank of New York, Summer 1980, pp. 21–38.

5. Dufey, Gunter, and Ian H. Giddy. *The International Money Market*. Englewood Cliffs, N.J.: Prentice-Hall, 1978.

6. Einzig, Paul. *The Eurodollar System*. 5th ed. New York: St. Martin's Press, 1973.

7. Federal Reserve Bank of Richmond. *Instruments of the Money Market*. 4th ed. 1977.

8. Goodfriend, Marvin. "Eurodollars." *Economic Review*, Federal Reserve Bank of Richmond, May-June 1981, pp. 12–18.

9. Goodman, Laurie S. "The Pricing of Syndicated Eurocurrency Credits." *Quarterly Review*, Federal Reserve Bank of New York, Summer 1980, pp. 39–49.

10. Helfrich, Ralph T. "Trading in Bankers' Acceptances: A View from the Acceptance Desk of the Federal Reserve Bank of New York." *Monthly Review*, Federal Reserve Bank of New York, February 1976.

11. Henson, John, and Eisuke Sakakibara. *The Eurocurrency Markets and Their Implications*. Lexington, Mass.: Lexington Books, 1975.

12. Lee, Boyden E. "The Eurodollar Multiplier." *Journal of Finance*, September 1973, pp. 867–74.

13. Makin, John H. "Identifying a Reserve Base for the Eurodollar System." *Journal of Finance*, June 1973, pp. 609–17.

14. Morgan Guaranty Trust Company of New York. *World Financial Markets*, selected issues.

15. Resler, David H. "Does Eurodollar Borrowing Improve the Dollar's Exchange Value?" *Review*, Federal Reserve Bank of St. Louis, August 1979, pp. 10–16.

16. "Stateless Money." *Business Week*, August 21, 1978, pp. 76–79.

17. Terrell, Henry, and Michael G. Martinson. "Market Practices in Syndicated Bank Eurocurrency Lending." *The Bankers Magazine*, November 1978.

18. Throop, Adrian W. "Eurobanking and World Inflation." *Voice*, Federal Reserve Bank of Dallas, August 1979, pp. 8–23.

16

The Financial
Futures Market

One of the most innovative markets to be developed in recent years and also one of the most rapidly growing is the market for financial futures. Futures trading is designed to protect the investor against market risk. In the financial futures markets, the risk of future changes in the prices of securities is transferred to someone—an individual or an institution—willing to bear that risk.

While relatively new in the field of finance, risk protection through futures trading is a very old concept in commodities trading. As far back as the Middle Ages, traders in farm commodities developed contracts calling for the future delivery of farm produce at a guaranteed price. Trading in rice futures began in Japan in 1697. In the United States, the Chicago Board of Trade established a futures market in grains in 1848. Later, the Board of Trade developed futures markets for metals and wood products; more recently, it has done so for selected kinds of financial instruments.[1]

The Nature of Futures Trading

In the futures market, buyers and sellers enter into contracts for the delivery of commodities, securities, or cash at a specific location and time

---
[1] The major commodities currently traded on various exchanges in the United States include wheat, corn, soybeans, soybean meal, soybean oil, cattle, hogs, pork bellies, barley, flaxseed, copper, platinum, oats, rye, eggs, iced broilers, lumber, plywood, sugar, coffee, orange juice, cotton, cocoa, potatoes, silver, and gold. As we will soon see, there is now an active futures market for U.S. Treasury bills, bonds, and notes; high-quality commercial paper; GNMA mortgage instruments; and commercial bank certificates of deposit (CDs).

and at a price which is set when the contract is made. The principal reason for the existence of a futures market is *hedging*—the act of buying or selling a commodity or claim in order to protect against the risk of future price fluctuations. Adverse movements in prices can result in increased costs and lower profits and, in the case of financial instruments, reduced value and yield. Many business firms and investors today find that even modest changes in prices, interest rates, and other costs can lead to magnified changes in their net earnings. Some investors see the futures markets as a means to ensure that their profits depend more upon planning and design rather than on the dictates of a treacherous and volatile market.

Hedging may be compared to *insurance*. Insurance protects an individual or business firm against risks to life and property. Hedging protects against the risk of fluctuations in market price. However, there is an important difference between insurance and hedging. Insurance rests upon the principal of sharing or *distributing* risk over a large group of policyholders. Through an insurance policy the risk to any one individual or institution is reduced. Moreover, the risks covered by most insurance plans are highly predictable, especially the risk of death.

In contrast, hedging does *not* reduce risk. It merely *transfers* that risk from one investor or institution to another. Ultimately, some investor must bear the risk of fluctuations in the prices of commodities or securities. Moreover, that risk is generally less predictable than would be true of most insurance claims. The hedger who successfully transfers risk through a futures contract can protect an acceptable selling price for a commodity or a desired yield on a security weeks or months ahead of the sale or purchase of that item. In the financial futures markets, the length of such contracts normally ranges from three months to two years.

GENERAL PRINCIPLES OF HEDGING

The basic principles of hedging may be described most easily through the use of a model. In this section we will examine the model of a *complete* or *perfect* hedge. Such a hedge contracts away *all* risk associated with fluctuations in the price of an asset. The hedger creates a situation in which *any* change in the market price of a commodity or security is exactly offset by a profit or loss on the futures contract. This enables the hedger to "lock in" the price or yield that he or she wishes to obtain.

Opening and Closing a Hedge

Suppose an agricultural firm produces a commodity such as wheat and is anticipating a decline in wheat prices. This unfavorable price movement can be hedged by *selling futures contracts* equal to the current value of the wheat. Sale of these contracts, which promise the future delivery of wheat days, weeks, or months from now, is called "opening a hedge."[2] When the firm does sell its wheat, it can buy back the same number of futures contracts as it sold originally and "close the hedge."

Of course, the firm could deliver the wheat as specified in the original futures contract. However, this is not usually done. If the price of wheat does decline as expected, then it costs the firm less to repurchase the futures contracts than it originally sold them for. Thus, the profit on the repurchase of wheat futures offsets the decrease in the price of wheat itself. The firm would have perfectly hedged itself against any adverse change in wheat prices over the life of the futures contract.

What would happen if wheat *rose* in price instead of declined? A perfect hedge would result in a profit on the sale of the wheat itself, but a loss on the futures contract. This happens because the firm must repurchase its futures contract at a higher price than its original cost due to the higher price for wheat. Figure 16–1 summarizes how a profit (or loss) on a futures contract can be used to offset a decrease (or increase) in the market price of an asset, helping the hedger to achieve a desired price.

Why Hedging Can Be Effective

The hedging process can be effective in transferring risk because prices in the *spot* (or cash) market for commodities and securities are generally correlated with prices in the futures (or forward) market. Indeed, the price of a futures contract in today's market represents an estimate of what the spot (or cash) market price will be on the contract's delivery date. Hedging essentially means adopting *equal* and *opposite* positions in the spot and futures markets for the same asset.

Risk Selection through Hedging

In the preceding paragraphs we have described a complete (perfect) hedge. Such a hedge is essentially a profitless hedging position. Many speculators and investors, however, are willing to take on added risk by not fully closing a hedge, believing they can guess correctly which way prices are going. Through the futures markets, the investor can literally "dial" the degree of risk he or she wishes to accept. If the investor wishes to take on *all* the risk of price fluctuations in the hope of achieving the maximum return, no hedging will take place. On the other hand, risk can be eliminated completely by using a perfect hedge.[3]

---

[2] Opening a hedge represents the forward sale of an asset.

[3] Hedging in the futures market is not a costless exercise, however. There are brokerage commissions with each transaction. Moreover, a complete hedge denies the investor the benefits of any unanticipated, but favorable movements in the price of a security or commodity. Reducing the risk of losses also limits potential gains.

FIGURE 16–1
Price Changes on Assets Can Be Offset by Profits or Losses on Futures Contracts

A. When assets decline in price

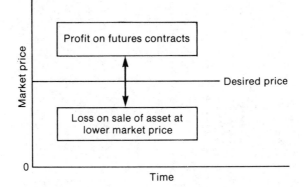

B. When assets rise in price

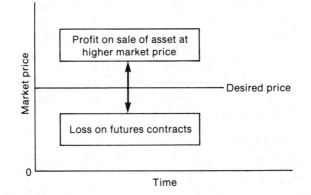

FINANCIAL FUTURES

Beginning in October 1975, the Chicago Board of Trade opened active trading in futures contracts for GNMA mortgage-backed certificates. In the ensuing months, futures contracts for U.S. Treasury securities and commercial paper appeared on the scene. Exhibit 16–1 provides a list of the most important financial instruments traded in the futures market today.

The development of future markets for these securities was motivated by the extremely volatile interest-rate movements which have characterized the financial markets for the past two decades. Repeatedly, interest rates have risen to record levels under the pressure of tight money policies and inflation, shutting out important groups of borrowers from ready access to credit.

EXHIBIT 16–1
The Most Important Interest-Rate Futures Contracts Currently Traded on U.S. Commodities Exchanges

Financial Instrument	Exchange Where Traded	Year Trading First Began	Maturity of Instrument	Contract Size	Stated Interest Rate	Basis of Price Quotations	Average Daily Trading Volume, (March 1979)
U.S. Treasury bonds	CBT	1977	15 years	$ 100,000	8%	Percent of par	4,351
U.S. Treasury notes	CBT	1979	4–6 years	100,000	8	Percent of par	—
U.S. Treasury bills	CME	1976	90 days	1,000,000	—	Complement of discount rate	4,719
U.S. Treasury bills	CME	1978	52 weeks	250,000	—	Complement of discount rate	79
GNMA mortgage-backed certificates, CDR	CBT	1975	12 years	100,000	8	Percent of par	3,093
GNMA mortgage-backed certificates, CD	CBT	1978	12 years	100,000	8	Percent of par	197
GNMA mortgage-backed certificates, CD	ACE	1978	12 years	100,000	8	Percent of par	309
Commercial paper	CBT	1977	90 days	1,000,000	—	Complement of discount rate	235
Bank certificates of deposit	CBT, CME NYFE	1981	90 days	1,000,000	—	—	—

SOURCE: Naomi L. Jaffee and Ronald B. Hodson, *Survey of Interest-Rate Futures Markets*: Division of Economics and Education, Commodity Futures Trading Commission, December 1979; and Board of Trade of the City of Chicago, *An Introduction to Financial Futures*, February, 1981.

These high and volatile rates have been a source of concern to regulatory authorities in the field of banking and financial institutions. Rising interest rates reduce the value of securities held by financial institutions, threatening them with a liquidity crisis and, in some cases, ultimate failure.[4] Some members of the regulatory community have favored the growth of financial futures as a way to reduce the risks associated with security investments. However, as we will soon see, other regulatory authorities feel that the development of the futures markets may have encouraged speculation and increased the riskiness of those financial institutions participating in futures trading. These regulatory agencies have placed tight restrictions on the use of the futures markets, especially by commercial banks.

Overall, the growth of trading in financial futures has been impressive. For example, the volume of trading in financial futures at the Chicago Board of Trade was less than 1 million contracts in 1977, topped 3 million in 1979, and soared to nearly 9 million in 1980. By August 1980, the third anniversary of trading in U.S. Treasury bond futures, more than 6 million T-bond contracts had exchanged hands, with a total par value of about $600 billion.[5]

The Purposes of Trading in Financial Futures

The basic principle behind trading in financial futures is the same as in the commodity markets. A securities dealer, commercial bank, or other investor may *sell* futures contracts on selected securities in order to protect against the risk of *falling* security prices (rising interest rates) and therefore a decline in the rate of return or yield from an investment. If the price of the security in question does fall, the investor can "lock in" the desired yield because a profit on the futures contract may fully offset the capital loss incurred when selling the security itself. On the other hand, a *rise* in the market price of a security (fall in interest rates) may be fully offset by a loss in the futures market. Either way, the investor is able to maintain the desired holding-period yield. These points are illustrated in Figure 16–2.

Financial futures may also be used by financial institutions and other investors to reduce the risk of interest-rate fluctuations when borrowing money. For example, suppose that a commercial bank is planning to raise funds by issuing certificates of deposit (CDs) and borrowing in the Eurodollar market one year from today. However, the bank's economics department forecasts that interest rates are likely to rise significantly by the time the borrowing takes place. The adverse impact of these expected higher

---

[4] A prime example of the damaging effects of rapid, sustained increases in interest rates is the savings and loan industry. As the discussion of this industry in Chapter 4 illustrates, rapidly rising interest rates have drastically reduced the value of fixed-rate mortgage loans, which make up the majority of savings and loan assets. The net worth of many associations has fallen to dangerously low levels, bringing on numerous bankruptcies or forced mergers with solvent institutions.

[5] See, in particular, Board of Trade of the City of Chicago (3), pp. 4–5.

FIGURE 16–2
Changes in the Yield on Securities Can Be Offset by
Profits or Losses on Futures Contracts

A. When interest rates rise and security prices fall

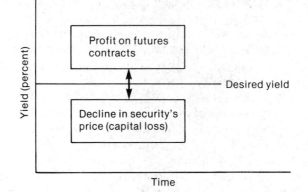

B. When interest rates fall and security prices rise

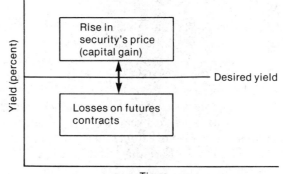

borrowing costs on the bank's profit position could be reduced by a sale and then a purchase of financial futures contracts. For example, management could sell one-year Treasury bill futures contracts now and then "zero out" this sale by purchasing a like amount of T-bill contracts when the delivery date arrives. Provided interest rates on Treasury bills, bank CDs, and Eurodollars increase by about the same magnitude, the added CD and Eurodollar borrowing costs would be offset by a profit on the futures position in T-bills. The bank could "lock in" its desired borrowing cost.[6]

_____
[6] Note that even if interest rates fall, thereby *reducing* the bank's borrowing costs, the use of financial futures still stabilizes the bank's position. In this instance, losses would be incurred on

Many financial analysts feel that the relationship between prices in the spot securities market and in the financial futures market is more stable and predictable than is true of prices in either market considered separately. This relatively stable relationship between spot and futures prices is what allows investors to reduce risk by hedging in financial futures.

Under a financial futures contract, the seller agrees to deliver a specific security at a specified price at a specific time in the future. Delivery under the shortest contracts is usually in 3 months from today's date, while a few contracts stretch out to 18 months or even two years. When the delivery date arrives, the security's seller can do one of three things: (1) make delivery of the security if he or she holds it; (2) buy the security in the spot (cash) market and deliver it as called for in the futures contract; or (3) purchase a futures contract for the same security with a delivery date exactly matching the first contract. This last option would result in a buy and a sell order maturing on the same day, which "zero out" and clear the market. In reality, settlement of contracts generally occurs exclusively in the futures market through offsetting buy and sell orders rather than by using spot (cash) transactions.

SECURITIES USED IN FINANCIAL FUTURES CONTRACTS

The number of futures markets and the types of securities and contracts traded in those markets have been expanding rapidly in recent years. In 1975 only one type of contract was traded at the Chicago Board of Trade. In 1981 25 different futures contracts were being traded on several different exchanges. However, most trading in financial futures today centers around five types of securities: (1) U.S. Treasury bills, (2) Treasury bonds and notes, (3) GNMA mortgage pass-through (or mortgage-backed) securities, (4) prime-quality commercial paper, and (5) bank certificates of deposit (CDs). The Chicago Board of Trade first offered interest-rate futures contracts for GNMA mortgage instruments in October 1975. Soon, other commodities exchanges—the International Monetary Market of the Chicago Mercantile Exchange (IMM), the Amex Commodities Exchange, Inc. (ACE), and the Commodity Exchange, Inc. (Comex)—began offering futures trading in T-bills and GNMA certificates. Then, in August 1980 the New York Stock Exchange opened its own futures floor. Known as the New York Futures Exchange, it has began to capture a larger share of the contract market, especially for trades in bank CDs.

Each of these exchanges completely controls which security contracts may be offered for sale, acceptable delivery dates, delivery methods, posting of prices, contract par values, and other essential terms of trade. Current

---

the sale and purchase of financial futures but could be fully offset by reduced borrowing costs. However, if interest rates do fall, the bank would have been better off without its position in financial futures because its profits would have been greater. In addition, gains or losses on futures contracts are taxable, and there are brokerage commissions to consider.

terms of trade for each of the four securities now represented on the exchanges are summarized below.[7]

U.S. Treasury Bonds and Notes

The futures market for U.S. Treasury bonds and notes is one of the most active markets for the forward delivery of an asset to be found anywhere in the world. As we will see in Chapter 24, Treasury bonds and notes are a popular investment medium for individuals and financial institutions because of their safety and liquidity. Nevertheless, there is substantial market risk involved with longer-term Treasury bonds and notes due to their lengthy maturities and relatively thin market. For example, Treasury bonds, which have original maturities stretching beyond 10 years, totaled only about $85 billion at year-end 1980, less than 10 percent of the total public debt of the United States and much less than half the volume of Treasury bills outstanding. Because the market for Treasury bonds is thinner than for bills, their price is more volatile, creating greater uncertainty for investors. Not surprisingly, then, Treasury bonds were among the first financial instruments for which a futures market developed to hedge against the risk of price fluctuations.

Only those Treasury bonds which either have maturities of at least 15 years or cannot be called for at least 15 to 20 years from their date of delivery (depending on the exchange selected) are eligible for futures contracts. Moreover, all Treasury bonds delivered under a futures contract must come from the same issue. The basic trading unit is $100,000 (measured at par) with a coupon rate of 8 percent. Bonds with coupon rates above or below 8 percent are deliverable at a premium or discount from their par values. Delivery of Treasury bonds is accomplished by book entry, and accrued interest is prorated. Price quotes in the market are expressed as a percentage of par value. The minimum price change which is recorded on published lists or in dealer quotations is one thirty-second of a point, or $31.25 per futures contract.[8]

Contracts for U.S. Treasury notes and noncallable bonds with maturities of four to six years also are traded today. Like Treasury bond contracts, T-note contracts are priced as a percentage of their par (or face) value, based on an 8 percent coupon rate. The basic trading unit is $100,000 face value.

---

[7] The contract exchanges carry a heavy burden of responsibility in preserving the integrity of futures trading and the orderliness of the markets. Each exchange stands behind the transactions conducted on its floor and imposes strict rules to minimize risk to the investor. For example, daily price fluctuations are not permitted to go beyond well-defined limits. Qualifications of floor traders and financial standards for member firms are set and monitored on a continuing basis by management and the governing board. The federal government also regulates futures trading through the Commodity Futures Trading Commission.

[8] See Chapter 7 for a discussion of the meaning of 32nds and points and how security prices are measured.

Trading in Treasury note futures began at the Chicago Board of Trade in June 1979, while Treasury bond contracts were first traded in August 1977.

U.S. Treasury Bills

In January 1976, U.S. Treasury bills were declared eligible for trading in the financial futures market. The International Monetary Market (IMM), a division of the Chicago Mercantile Exchange, announced that contracts for future delivery would be written on T-bills of 90-day and one-year maturities. Ninety-day T-bill contracts are for $1 million each, while single contracts on one-year bills carry denominations of $250,000.

Futures trading in the bill market has become extremely popular. For example, during 1979 daily average trading in T-bill contracts on the IMM was about $7.5 billion. This was almost as large as the daily volume of spot market trading in T-bills conducted by U.S. government securities dealers.

GNMA Mortgage Pass-Through or Mortgage-Backed Securities

During the 1970s the federal government became increasingly active in the secondary market for mortgages in order to expand the volume of funds available to the housing market. One of the most successful federal government programs in this area is carried out by the Government National Mortgage Association (GNMA or, more commonly, "Ginnie Mae"). Ginnie Mae purchases residential mortgages in the secondary market and adds them to an investment pool. All mortgages in the pool bear the same interest rate, carry similar maturities, and represent loans against similar types of residences. Then, Ginnie Mae issues its own securities (which it guarantees) as claims against the principal and interest earned by the mortgage pool. These Ginnie Mae IOUs—usually called passthroughs or mortgage-backed securities[9]—are standardized, readily marketable instruments with interest rates generally higher than on U.S. Treasury securities.

In October 1975 the Chicago Board of Trade opened trading activity in futures contracts for GNMA pass-through certificates. The basic trading unit was set at $100,000 for certificates with a stated interest rate of 8 percent ("Ginnie Mae 8's"). If the rate of interest on a Ginnie Mae issue is lower than 8 percent, then the basic trading unit will be greater than $100,000. On the other hand, if the interest rate is above 8 percent, the basic trading unit is scaled down below $100,000. For example, $107,816.70 is the basic trading unit at a 7 percent interest rate, while $93,167.70 is the basic trading unit for an interest rate of 9 percent. Prices on Ginnie Mae issues are quoted as a percent of par with minimum quotes in 32nds of a point. Delivery months on

---

[9] For a more-complete discussion of GNMA passthroughs and their role in the nation's mortgage market, see Chapter 18.

GNMA futures contracts are February, March, May, June, August, September, November, and December.

Two types of GNMA futures are traded today: (1) GNMA CDR (collateralized depositary receipt), and (2) GNMA CD (certificate delivery). The difference between these two contracts hinges on current market interest rates. As we noted above, GNMA certificates with an 8 percent coupon rate were chosen as the basis for GNMA futures contracts traded at the Chicago Board of Trade. The 8 percent figure was chosen because it was a common interest rate attached to GNMA certificates when trading first began. When interest rates rise above or fall below 8 percent, one of two types of adjustments are made in GNMA futures contracts. The dollar amount on the contract invoices can be adjusted with the principal balance unchanged—a GNMA CD. Alternatively, the amount of GNMA certificates actually delivered (known as the principal balance) can be altered to capture interest-rate changes with the dollar amount of the contract invoice remaining unchanged. This is known as a GNMA CDR contract. Also, a GNMA CD contract calls for delivery of the actual GNMA certificates, while a CDR contract requires the delivery of a receipt which evidences GNMA certificates held in safekeeping by an authorized depository.

90-Day Commercial Paper

As noted in Chapter 14, one of the most important and rapidly growing money market instruments today is the short-term marketable debt obligations issued by major corporations, known as commercial paper. Commercial paper ranges in original maturity from nine months to as short as three or four days. However, the Chicago Board of Trade has ruled that commercial paper traded in the futures market must mature either 30 or 90 days from date of delivery. It must be of the highest quality, rated either A-1 by Standard & Poor's Corporation or P-1 by Moody's Investor's Service,[10] and be approved by the Chicago Board of Trade. The basic trading unit for 90-day paper is a face value at maturity of $1 million, while contracts for 30-day paper are based on a $3 million face value. Prices are quoted on an annual discount basis, with minimum price fluctuations of one basis point or $25 per contract.

Futures trading in commercial paper is extremely light compared to the other securities represented on the major contract exchanges. For example, a survey by the Commodity Futures Trading Commission in March 1979 found that daily trading volume in 90-day commercial paper contracts was less than 5 percent of T-bill contract trading volume. One major problem with paper futures is that the contracts do not specify precisely what issue of commercial paper is to be delivered to fulfill each contract. Because paper issued by any number of firms may be used to satisfy the contractual agree-

---

[10] See Chapter 14 for a discussion of how commercial paper is rated.

ment, investors face an unusual degree of uncertainty in this market. In addition, a substantial volume of commercial paper is issued in original maturities of less than 90 days; so the supply of 90-day paper is often quite limited.

Bank Certificates of Deposit

Futures trading in bank certificates of deposit (CDs) began in 1981. Three exchanges in the United States—the Chicago Board of Trade, the Chicago Mercantile Exchange, and the New York Futures Exchange—are most active in this market today. In addition, the London International Financial Futures Exchange was set up to begin trading in London-dollar CDs in the spring of 1982. The CD futures market offers investors the opportunity to hedge against changing interest rates on commercial loans. CD futures contracts are obligations to deliver or receive a $1 million CD maturity in approximately 90 days.

TYPES OF HEDGING IN THE FINANCIAL FUTURES MARKET

There are basically three types of hedges used in the financial futures market today: (1) the long hedge, (2) the short hedge, and (3) the cross hedge. Cross hedges, as we will see, may be either long or short. Each type of hedge meets the unique trading needs of a particular group of investors. All three types have become increasingly popular as interest rates and security prices have become more volatile in recent years.

The Long (or Buying) Hedge

A *long hedge* involves the *purchase* of futures contracts today, before the investor must buy the actual securities desired at a later date. The purpose of the long hedge is to guarantee ("lock in") a desired yield in case interest rates decline before securities are actually purchased in the cash market.

As an example of a typical long-hedge transaction, suppose that a commercial bank, life insurance company, pension fund, or other institutional investor anticipates receiving $1 million 90 days from today.[11] Assume that today is April 1 and the funds are expected on July 2. The *current* yield to maturity on securities the investor hopes to purchase in July is 12.26 percent. We might imagine that these securities are long-term U.S. Treasury bonds, which appeal to this investor because of their high liquidity and zero default risk. Suppose, however, that interest rates are expected to decline over the next three months due to a recession. If the investor waits until the $1 million in cash is available 90 days from now, the yield on Treasury bonds may well

---

[11] This example of the long hedge and the subsequent examples of short and cross hedges are drawn from examples developed by the Chicago Board of Trade in its instructional pamphlet, *An Introduction to Financial Futures,* February 1981, and are used with CBT's permission.

be lower than 12.26 percent. Is there a way to lock in the higher yield available *now* even though funds will not be available for another three months?

Yes, if a suitable long hedge can be negotiated with another investor or trader. In this case the investor can purchase (''go long'') 10 September Treasury bond futures contracts at their current market price. (Recall that Treasury bond futures are sold in $100,000 denominations.) Cash payment on these contracts will not be due until September. Suppose their price currently is 68-10, or $68,312.50 on a $100,000 face-value contract. Assume too that, as expected, bond prices rise and interest rates fall. At some later point the investor may be able to *sell* the bond futures contracts at a profit, since prices on these contracts tend to rise along with rising bond prices in the cash market. Selling the bond futures contracts at a profit will help this investor offset the lower yields on Treasury bonds that will prevail in the cash market once the $1 million actually becomes available on July 2.

The details of this long hedge transaction are given in Exhibit 16–2. We note that on July 2 the investor goes into the spot market and buys $1 million

EXHIBIT 16–2
An Example of a Long Hedge Using U.S. Treasury Bonds

Spot (or cash) Market Transactions	Futures (or forward) Market Transactions
April 1: A portfolio manager for a financial institution wishes to "lock in" a yield of 12.26% on $1 million of 20-year, 8¼% U.S. Treasury bonds at 68-14.	April 1: The portfolio manager purchases 10 September Treasury bond futures contracts at 68-10.
July 2: The portfolio manager purchases $1 million of 20-year, 8¼-percent U.S. Treasury bonds at 82-13 for a yield of 10.14%.	July 2: The portfolio manager sells 10 September Treasury bond futures contracts at 80-07.
Results: Opportunity loss of $139,687.50 due to lower Treasury bond yields and higher bond prices.	Results: Gain of $119,062.50 on futures trading.

Note: No commissions or exchange service fees are included in these transactions which would reduce the investor's gain from that shown here.
SOURCE: Based on an example developed by the Chicago Board of Trade in *An Introduction to Financial Futures,* February 1981. Reprinted by permission of the Chicago Board of Trade.

in 8 percent, 20-year U.S. Treasury bonds at a price of 82-13. At the same time, the investor sells 10 September Treasury bond futures contracts at 80-07. Due to higher bond prices (lower yields) in July, the investor loses $139,687.50, because the market price of Treasury bonds has risen from 68-14 to 82-13. This represents an opportunity loss because the $1 million in investable funds was not available in April when interest rates were high and bond prices low. However, this loss is at least partially offset by a gain in the futures market of $119,062.50, because the 10 September bond futures purchased on April 1st were sold at a profit on July 2. Over this period, bond futures contracts rose in price from 68-10 to 80-07. In effect, the investor will pay only $705,000 for the Treasury bonds bought in the cash market on July 2. The market price of these bonds will be $824,062.50 (or 82-13) per bond, but the investor's *net* cost is lower by $119,062.50 due to a gain in the futures market.

The Short (or Selling) Hedge

A financial device of growing popularity is the *short hedge*. This hedge involves the immediate *sale* of financial futures contracts until the actual securities must be sold in the cash market at some later point. Short hedges are especially useful to investors who may hold a large portfolio of securities which they plan to sell in the future but, in the meantime, must be protected against the risk of declining security prices. We examine a typical situation where a securities dealer might employ the short hedge.

Suppose the dealer holds $1 million in U.S. Treasury bonds, carrying an 8¾ percent coupon and a maturity of 20 years. The current price of these bonds is 94-26 (or $948.125 per $1,000 par value), which amounts to a yield of 9.25 percent. However, the dealer is concerned because higher interest rates appear to be in the offing. Any upward climb in rates would bring about lower bond prices and therefore reduce the value of the dealer's portfolio. A possible remedy in this case is simply to *sell* bond futures contracts in order to counteract the anticipated decline in bond prices. For example, suppose the dealer decides to sell 10 Treasury bond futures contracts at 86-28, and 30 days later is able to sell $1 million of 20-year, 8¾ percent Treasury bonds at a price of 86-16 for a yield of 10.29 percent. At the same time the dealer goes into the futures market and buys 10 Treasury bond futures contracts at 79-26 to offset the previous forward sale of bond futures.

The financial consequences of these combined trades in the spot and futures markets are offsetting, as shown in Exhibit 16–3. The dealer has lost $83,125 in the cash market due to the price decline in the bonds held. However, a gain of about $70,625 (less fees, commissions, and any tax liability) has resulted from the gain in the futures price. This dealer has helped to insulate the value of the portfolio from the risk of price fluctuations through a short hedge.

Cross Hedging

Another approach to minimizing risk is the cross hedge—a combined transaction between the spot market and the futures market using different types of securities in each market. This device rests upon the assumption that the prices of most financial instruments tend to move in the same direction and by roughly the same proportion. Because this is only approximately

EXHIBIT 16-3
An Example of a Short Hedge Using U.S. Treasury Bonds

Spot (or cash) Market Transactions	Futures (or forward) Market Transactions
October 1: A securities dealer owns $1 million of 20-year, 8¾ percent U.S. Treasury bonds priced at 94-26 to yield 9.25%.	October 1: The dealer sells 10 Treasury bond futures contracts at 86-28.
October 31: The dealer sells $1 million of 20-year, 8¾ percent U.S. Treasury bonds at 86-16 to yield 10.29%.	October 31: The dealer purchases 10 Treasury bond futures contracts at 79-26.
Results: Loss of $83,125 in spot market.	Results: Gain of $70,625 on futures trading.

Note: No commissions or exchange service fees are included in these transactions; their inclusion would reduce the dealer's gain from that shown here.
SOURCE: Based on an example developed by the Chicago Board of Trade in *An Introduction to Financial Futures,* February 1981. Reprinted by permission of the Chicago Board of Trade.

true in any real-world situation, cross hedging does not usually result in forming a perfect hedge. Profits or losses in the cash market will not exactly offset losses or profits in the futures market. Nevertheless, if the investor's goal is to minimize risk, cross hedging is often preferable to a completely unhedged position.

As an example, consider the case of a commercial bank which holds good-quality corporate bonds carrying a face value of $5 million with an average maturity of 20 years. The bank's portfolio manager anticipates a rise in interest rates, which will reduce the value of the corporate bonds. Unfortunately, there is no futures market for corporate bonds, and therefore the portfolio manager cannot construct a perfect hedge involving these securities. However, futures contracts can be negotiated in U.S. Treasury bonds or even in Ginnie Mae passthroughs, providing either a long or a short hedge to offset the risk of a decline in the value of the corporate bonds.

To illustrate how such a cross-hedge transaction might take place, suppose that on January 2 the market value of the bank's corporate bonds is $3,673,437.50. This means that each $1,000 par value bond currently carries a market price of $734.6875 (or 73-15 on a $100 basis). The portfolio manager decides to sell 50 Treasury bond futures contracts at 81-20 (or $816.25 per $1,000 face value). About two and a half months later, on March 14, interest rates have risen significantly. The value of each corporate bond has fallen to 64-13 (or $644.0625 per $1,000 bond). At this point the bank's portfolio manager decides to sell the bonds, receiving $3,220,312.50 from the buyer. This represents a loss on the bonds of $453,125.00. At the same time, however, the portfolio manager buys back 50 U.S. Treasury bond futures contracts at 69-20. The result is a gain from futures trading of $600,000. In this

particular transaction the gain from futures trading more than offsets the loss
in the cash market. (See Exhibit 16–4 for a summary of this transaction.)

Of course, this example of a cross hedge and the preceding examples of
long and short hedges are simplified considerably to make the fundamental

EXHIBIT 16–4
An Example of a Short Cross Hedge Involving Corporate and U.S. Treasury Bonds

Spot (or cash) Market Transactions	Futures (or forward) Market Transactions
January 2: A commercial bank holds a diversified portfolio of $5 million in high-grade corporate bonds with an average maturity of 20 years and a current market value of 73-15 per bond. The market value of the total portfolio is, therefore, $3,673,437.50.	January 2: The bank's portfolio manager sells 50 U.S. Treasury bond futures contracts at 81-20.
March 14: The market price per bond falls to 64-13, for a total value of the portfolio of $3,220,312.50.	March 14: The portfolio manager purchases 50 U.S. Treasury bond futures contracts at 69-20.
Results: The total loss in value of the corporate bonds is $453,125.00.	Results: Gain of $600,000 on the Treasury bond futures contracts.

Note: No commissions or exchange service fees are included in these transactions; they would
reduce the investor's gain from that shown here.
SOURCE: Based on an example developed by the Chicago Board of Trade in *An Introduction to
Financial Futures*, February 1981. Reprinted by permission of the Chicago Board of Trade.

principle of futures trading easier to understand. In the real world the placing
and removal of hedges is an exercise requiring detailed study of the futures
market and, in most cases, a substantial amount of trading experience.

TRADERS ACTIVE IN THE FUTURES MARKET

A wide variety of financial institutions and individuals are active in futures
trading today. As shown in Exhibit 16–5, the principal traders in financial
futures are individuals and commodity pools. Commodity pools are like
mutual funds, offering shares to the individual investor who regularly purchases futures contracts. Commodity pools offer the advantage of diversifying risk by trading in many contracts with varied maturities; in addition, they
are professionally managed. The majority of commodity pools try to limit
losses to the investor's original investment, liquidating investor holdings
rather than issuing margin calls. Combined, individuals and commodity
pools held close to half of total open contract positions in 1979, and their
share has been growing over time.

Firms and individual traders representing the futures industry run a close
second to individual investors and commodity pools, with open positions

EXHIBIT 16–5
Traders Active in the Futures Markets, March 30, 1979 (number of contracts)

| | Instruments Specified in Futures Contracts | | | | | |
| | GNMA Passthroughs | | Treasury Bonds | | Three-Month Treasury Bills | |
Active Traders	Amount	Per-cent of Total	Amount	Per-cent of Total	Amount	Per-cent of Total
Commercial traders:						
Security dealers	4,270	7.2%	8,226	18.2%	5,596	12.5%
Commercial banks	655	1.1	1,472	3.3	1,581	3.5
Savings and loan associations ...	2,500	4.2	394	0.9	136	0.3
Mortgage bankers	1,472	2.5	330	0.7	· 974	2.2
Others	2,003	3.4	1,971	4.4	6,706	15.0
Totals	10,899	18.3%	12,393	27.4%	14,992	33.6%
Noncommercial traders:						
Futures industry	21,113	35.4%	12,924	28.6%	8,434	18.9%
Commodity pools	11,097	18.6	9,484	21.0	5,640	12.6
Individual traders	16,495	27.7	10,418	23.0	15,586	34.9
Totals	48,705	81.7%	32,826	72.6%	29,661	66.4%
Grand total—all active traders	59,604	100.0%	45,219	100.0%	44,654	100.0%

SOURCES: Commodity Futures Trading Commission Survey; Federal Reserve Bank of New York, "Interest Rate Futures," *Quarterly Review*, Winter 1979–80, pp. 33–46.

ranging from a fifth to about 35 percent of contracts outstanding, depending on the instrument being traded. Many of these industry personnel speculate on interest-rate movements or arbitrage between spot and futures markets, purchasing one contract and selling another in the expectation that interest rates on purchased contracts will decline more than (or rise less than) rates on contracts sold. Alternatively, futures firms and industry traders will buy or sell futures contracts simultaneously with a sell or buy move in the spot market.

Financial institutions also play a prominent role in futures trading, led by securities dealers, commercial banks, mortgage bankers, and savings and loan associations. Securities dealers appear to be less interested in risk reduction through hedging and more interested in profitable trades arising from correctly guessing the future course of interest rates and contract prices. Savings and loan associations and mortgage bankers, not surprisingly, are most involved in futures trading of GNMA mortgage-backed instruments. Rapid increases in long-term mortgage rates and volatile swings in the demand for new housing over the past two decades have brought substantial risk to the mortgage lending business, as we noted in Chapter 4. Under pressure from rising interest costs and deposit withdrawals, many savings and loan associations today have been forced to deeply discount and sell their old, low-yielding mortgage loans in the secondary market in order to raise funds. Losses incurred in the sale of old mortgages can be at least partially offset by trades executed in GNMA futures contracts. For their part, mortgage bankers frequently sell GNMA futures to hedge against interest-rate changes that may occur between the time mortgage loans are taken into their portfolios and the time they are sold in packages to other investors.

The participation of savings and loan associations in futures trading was given a substantial boost in July 1981. The Federal Home Loan Bank Board (FHLBB), the industry's chief regulator, loosened the old rules, which limited the total volume of futures contracts an S&L could have outstanding at any one time to no more than the association's net worth position (normally about 5 percent of total assets). The new rules permit a savings and loan to hedge *all* of its assets if it so chooses. Trading may be carried out in any securities which a savings association is legally entitled to hold. Many savings and loans sell GNMA futures to hedge the fixed-rate mortgages they hold on single-family homes. However, the new rules for futures trading set by the FHLBB allow savings associations to hedge on *both* the asset and liability side of the balance sheet and especially to offset the rapidly rising cost of deposits and nondeposit borrowings.

Participation by commercial banks in futures trading has been quite limited to date. As shown in Exhibit 16–5, banks accounted for no more than 4 percent of all positions in the three most-active futures markets, according to a survey taken in March 1979. The survey, conducted by the Commodity Futures Trading Commission, found that only 24 banks held open positions in Treasury bill futures and only 14 carried positions in bond futures at that time. One major factor limiting commercial bank participation in the futures market is uncertainty over the attitude of the regulatory authorities, especially the Federal Reserve System and the Comptroller of the Currency. Another problem centers on the required accounting treatment of gains and losses from futures trading. Losses must be recognized immediately for tax purposes, while gains can be deferred. The result is volatile fluctuations in reported income for those banks active in futures trading. However, it is anticipated that bank participation in the futures market will expand significantly as the regulatory community becomes more comfortable with the hedging concept.

POTENTIAL BENEFITS TO FINANCIAL INSTITUTIONS FROM THE FUTURES MARKET

Trading in security futures opens up several potential advantages for financial institutions and for individual investors. The prospect of hedging against changes in security prices offers the potential for reducing risk and offsetting losses stemming from adverse movements in interest rates. Financial futures contracts can be especially beneficial for those financial institutions and individual investors heavily leveraged with debt, which makes their net earnings particularly sensitive to changes in interest rates. This is certainly true of major commercial banks, savings and loan associations, mutual savings banks, securities dealers, and mortgage banking institutions. These financial intermediaries experience marked fluctuations in net income with changes in the differential between interest rates on borrowed funds and returns on loans and other assets. [12]

Moreover, if the futures market does lead to a reduction of risk, this will enable many financial institutions to extend greater amounts of credit. The result could be a more efficient allocation of scarce funds within each financial institution and within the financial system. Moreover, the futures markets provide for a freer flow of information concerning alternative uses and outlets for funds, permitting each financial institution to rapidly adjust its risk position to changes in interest rates and other costs. As noted by Stevens (12), the existence of a futures market may result in "increased market information, less search time, integration of markets and greater specialization of risk bearing."

SOCIAL CONSEQUENCES OF THE FUTURES MARKET

Not all observers agree that the futures market results in a net gain for society by helping financial institutions reduce risk and use scarce resources more efficiently. Some analysts believe that the futures markets are largely speculative and not really geared for the hedging of risks per se. They see these markets as aimed principally at providing wealthy investors with a speculative outlet for their funds, and resulting in unnecessary risks due to excessive speculation. Some have argued that the futures markets increase the price volatility of those securities whose contracts are actively traded. If this is true, it would tend to make the impact of government economic policy, aimed at promoting high employment and low inflation, more difficult to predict. There is evidence from the commodities field that trading in futures tends to smooth out seasonal fluctuations, but only limited evidence exists to date as to the overall impact on the securities markets of contract trading.

Certainly the mere existence of the futures market and its continuing growth creates additional problems for regulatory authorities, especially those concerned with the regulation of financial institutions. Another market must be supervised and additional regulations prepared to cover new forms of risk and new fiduciary relationships. Some observers have expressed the fear that the futures markets substitute "gambling" with securities for "in-

---

[12] It is certainly not true that every financial institution would benefit from trading in financial futures. The critical determining factor is the overall interest-rate sensitivity of each institution's asset and liability portfolio. If *both* liabilities and assets carry floating interest rates, for example, hedging may be unnecessary, even in a period of rising interest rates. Considering all costs, futures trading could increase the interest-sensitivity of a financial institution's earnings and do more harm than good.

vesting'' in securities.[13] If this view is correct, it suggests a withdrawal of some risk-taking activity from the traditional securities markets and a redirection of this activity towards the futures market. To the extent that risk taking by securities investors is curtailed, this limits the flow of funds into venture capital and decreases the aggregate volume of investment in the economy. Other things equal, the economy's rate of growth is reduced.

On balance, the financial futures market probably has resulted in a modest net benefit to the financial system and to the economy. Those who support the development of this market have certainly overdramatized its positive features, alleging, for example, that interest rates tend to be lower and less volatile with a well-functioning futures market. There is little evidence that this is, in fact, the case. Regardless, it seems clear that the futures market has separated the risk of changing security prices and interest rates from the lending of funds, at least for those institutions actively participating in this market. The risk of price and yield changes is transferred to investors quite willing to assume such risks. The futures market has helped to reduce search costs and expand the flow of information on market opportunities for those who seek risk reduction through hedging. In this sense, the market tends to promote greater efficiency in the use of scarce financial resources. Moreover, this developing institution has tended to unify many local markets into a national forward market, overcoming geographic and institutional rigities which tend to separate one market from another.

It should not be forgotten that futures trading is not without its own special risks. While the risk of price and yield fluctuations is reduced through negotiating a futures contract, the investor faces the risk of changing interest rates and security prices *between* the futures and spot markets. It is rare that gains and losses from simultaneous trading in spot and futures markets will exactly offset each other, resulting in a perfect hedge. Moreover, there are substantial brokerage fees for executing futures contracts, and required minimum deposits for margin accounts.[14] To the extent that the futures market encourages speculation, does not fully offset all price and interest-rate risks, and is characterized by substantial transactions costs, its net benefit to society will remain both limited and a subject of continuing controversy and close regulatory scrutiny.

SUMMARY AND CONCLUSIONS

The increasingly volatile interest rates of recent years have increased the risk sensitivity of many investors. With increased uncertainty concerning the

---

[13] See, in particular, Wallich (14), p. 11.

[14] Brokerage commissions and margin requirements in futures trading are not inconsequential. For example, a so-called round trip—buying and selling of contracts—in 90-day Treasury bill futures in the minimum denomination of $1 million will cost approximately $60. Margin accounts must be maintained above a specified minimum level. Each account is evaluated daily, and additional funds must be supplied when the account declines below the minimum level. Many traders pledge securities to their margin accounts to eliminate the necessity of repeatedly supplying new funds.

future course of interest rates, managers of security portfolios find that financial planning is a far more difficult task today than in years past. Financial institutions which both borrow and lend in the money and capital markets have found that both their earnings and their cost of funds have become less predictable and subject to wide swings. It is not surprising, therefore, that many individual and institutional investors have sought new and innovative ways to insulate their investments from fluctuations in interest rates and security prices. The financial futures market, inaugurated by the Chicago Board of Trade in 1975, has become an increasingly popular form of "insulation" against the risks of investing in debt securities.

Futures markets are based upon the notion of *hedging,* which is simply the act of contracting to buy or sell a security in the future but at a price agreed upon today. By setting the price and other terms of such a contract *now,* the investor is at least partially insulated against the risk of future changes in interest rates and security prices. Hedging, in effect, transfers risk from one investor to another willing to bear that risk in the hope of scoring a significant gain. The hedger contracts away all or a portion of the risk of security price fluctuations in order to "lock in" a targeted rate of return on an investment. This is accomplished by taking equal and opposite positions in the spot (or cash) market and in the forward (or futures) market. If interest rates are expected to fall and the investor desires to "lock in" a current high yield on a security, the thing to do is to buy a contract calling for the future delivery of the security at a set price. Then, if interest rates do fall, the investor will earn a profit on the futures contract which will wholly or partially offset the lower yields available from buying the security in the spot (cash) market. An opposite set of buy-sell transactions in futures would generally be used if interest rates were expected to rise.

Trading in financial futures is limited today to a short list of high-quality financial instruments—U.S. Treasury bonds, notes, and bills; GNMA mortgage-backed securities; commercial paper; and bank CDs. But the list is growing, and the volume of daily trading in these markets is rapidly expanding. Most observers expect continued growth in futures market activity due to increasingly volatile conditions in the financial markets and the increasing financial sophistication of investors.

STUDY QUESTIONS

1. What is the basic purpose of futures trading in commodities? in securities? Where is most futures trading carried out in the United States?
2. Explain the similarities and differences between hedging in the futures market and insurance.
3. What is a perfect or complete hedge? Define the terms *opening a hedge* and *closing a hedge.*
4. How do spot (cash) markets differ from futures (forward) markets?

5. For what specific kinds of securities is there now an active futures market in the United States? Who issues these securities? Describe the restrictions imposed on trading in futures contracts involving these securities.

6. Define and explain the use of the following:
   a. Long hedge.
   b. Short hedge.
   c. Cross hedge.

7. What are the principal benefits to financial institutions such as commercial banks, securities dealers, savings and loan associations, and mortgage bankers from the use of the futures market? Can you see any possible dangers?

8. What risks are inherent in futures trading? Costs? Evaluate the futures market from a social point of view.

SELECTED REFERENCES

1. Arak, Marelle, and Christopher J. McCurdy. "Interest Rate Futures." *Quarterly Review*, Federal Reserve Bank of New York, Winter 1979–80, pp. 33–46.

2. Board of Trade of the City of Chicago. *Hedging Interest Rate Risks*. 1st rev. ed. 1977.

3. _____. *An Introduction to Financial Futures*. 1981.

4. _____. *Introduction to Hedging*. 1972.

5. Chicago Mercantile Exchange. *Futures Trading in International Currencies*. 1977.

6. Comptroller of the Currency, Federal Deposit Insurance Corporation, and Federal Reserve Board. "Regulators Adopt Revisions to Policy on Futures, Forward and Standby Contracts." Joint news release, March 12, 1980.

7. Jaffe, Naomi L., and Ronald B. Hobson. *Survey of Interest-Rate Futures Markets*. Commodity Futures Trading Commission, 1979.

8. Kasriel, Paul L. "Hedging Interest Rate Fluctuations." *Business Conditions*, Federal Reserve Bank of Chicago, April 1976, pp. 3–10.

9. Menich, Judy Z. "Interest-Rate Futures." *Economic Commentary*, Federal Reserve Bank of Cleveland, June 16, 1980.

10. Polaris, Mark F., and David C. Fisher. "Banking on Interest Rate Futures." *The Magazine of Bank Administration*, August 1979, pp. 34–39.

11. Snider, Thomas E. "Using the Futures Market to Hedge." *Monthly Review*, Federal Reserve Bank of Richmond, August 1973, pp. 2–7.

12. Stevens, Neil A. "A Mortgage Futures Market: Its Development, Uses, Benefits and Costs." *Review*, Federal Reserve Bank of St. Louis, April 1976, pp. 12–19.

13. U.S. Treasury Department and the Federal Reserve System. *Treasury Futures Markets: A Study by the Staffs of the U.S. Treasury and Federal Reserve System*. Washington, D.C.: 1979.

14. Wallich, Henry C. member, Board of Governors of the Federal Reserve System. Speech before the Commodities and Financial Futures Conference, Federal Bar Association and Commerce Clearing House, Washington, D.C., November 1, 1979.

part five

The Consumer in the Financial Markets

17

Consumer Lending and Borrowing

One of the most important of all financial markets is the market providing credit to individuals and families. Many financial analysts have referred to the period since World War II as the "age of consumer finance" because individuals and families not only are the principal *source* of loanable funds flowing into the financial markets today but also are one of the largest groups of *borrowers* in the entire financial system.[1] Commercial bankers today point out that not only do consumers provide the bulk of the banking industry's deposits, but installment loans to consumers represent one of the fastest-growing forms of bank credit. Moreover, the market for consumer financial services is the one financial market that virtually everyone, regardless of income or social status, will enter at one time or another during their lifetime. In this chapter we examine the major characteristics of the consumer market for financial services, the principal lenders active in this market, and some of the more-important rules and regulations applying to consumer borrowing and lending today.

CONSUMERS AS LENDERS OF FUNDS

Each of us is a consumer of goods and services virtually every day of our lives. Scarcely a single day passes that we do not enter the marketplace to

---

[1] For a further analysis of the growing role of the consumer in the American financial system, see especially the studies by Goldsmith (10), Katona, Mandell, and Schiedeskamp (12), National Commission on Consumer Finance (17), O'Brien (18), and Rose (20, 21) in the list of references at the end of this chapter. Parts of this chapter are drawn from (21), (22), and (23).

purchase food, shelter, entertainment, books, newspapers, and thousands of other "essentials" of modern living. We are also well aware, perhaps from personal experience, that consumers often borrow heavily in the financial marketplace to achieve their desired standard of living. U.S. consumers borrowed more than $100 billion in 1980, for example, and by the end of that year owed almost $1.5 trillion to various lending institutions.

What is not nearly so well known or so often recognized, however, is the fact that consumers as a group are also the most important *lenders of funds* in the American economy. Loanable funds are supplied by consumers when they purchase financial assets from other units in the economy. In 1980 gross saving by U.S. households totaled over $400 billion, of which $280 billion flowed into commercial bank deposits, savings deposits at nonbank financial institutions, bonds, stocks, and direct cash loans made to individuals and businesses. By comparison, nonfinancial businesses recorded gross savings of only $257 billion, the federal government had negative savings (i.e., a deficit) of about $60 billion, and state and local governments racked up a paltry $29 billion in gross savings. Clearly, the consuming public is the chief source of the raw material—loanable funds—exchanged in the nation's financial markets.[2]

Financial Assets Purchased by Consumers

If consumers make loanable funds available to other units in the economy by purchasing financial assets, what kinds of financial assets do they buy? And what are the principal sources of borrowed funds for consumers? The Federal Reserve Board's Flow of Funds Accounts provide us with a wealth of information on the borrowing and lending habits of American households.[3]

Exhibit 17–1 summarizes information contained in recent Flow of Funds reports on the kinds of *financial assets* acquired by households. One fact immediately evident is the wide diversity of financial assets purchased by individuals and families, ranging from those of very low risk and short maturity (such as bank deposits and U.S. government securities) to long-term, high-risk investments (such as mortgages and corporate stock).

The most-important household financial asset today is *time and savings deposits,* held at commercial banks, savings and loan associations, credit unions, mutual savings banks, and other thrift institutions. These interest-bearing thrift accounts represented close to 30 percent of the total financial asset holdings of American consumers in 1980. Moreover, as Exhibit 17–1 reveals, the importance of thrift deposits in consumer financial investments has been increasing as bank and nonbank thrift institutions have offered higher returns and greater convenience to savers. As recently as 1960, for

---

[2] For a more-detailed discussion of the importance of households in providing loanable funds, see O'Brien (18) and Goldsmith (10).

[3] See Chapter 10 for a review of the sources of data and method of construction used in the Flow of Funds Accounts, compiled quarterly by the Federal Reserve System.

EXHIBIT 17-1
Principal Financial Assets of U.S. Households Outstanding, Year-End 1950, 1960, 1970, and 1980 ($ billions)

Financial Asset	1950 Amount	1950 Percent	1960 Amount	1960 Percent	1970 Amount	1970 Percent	1980 Amount	1980 Percent
Demand deposits and currency	$ 56.5	12.6%	$ 70.2	7.3%	$ 126.5	6.5%	$ 268.0	6.0%
Time and savings accounts:	67.3	15.0	165.3	17.1	422.4	21.7	1,294.4	28.8
At commercial banks	32.4	7.2	62.0	6.4	189.0	9.7	—	—
At nonbank thrift institutions	34.9	7.8	103.3	10.7	233.4	12.0	—	—
Shares in money market mutual funds	—	—	—	—	—	—	74.4	1.7
U.S. government securities	69.1	15.4	73.5	7.6	100.4	5.2	282.8	6.3
State and local government securities	10.0	2.2	30.8	3.2	47.4	2.4	74.2	1.7
Open-market paper	0.1	0.0	0.1	0.0	6.1	0.3	38.2	0.9
Corporate and foreign bonds	4.9	1.1	9.8	1.0	39.8	2.0	86.9	1.9
Mortgages	17.4	3.9	31.8	3.3	42.5	2.2	122.5	2.7
Corporate stock:	133.7	29.9	396.1	40.9	763.1	39.2	1,215.6	27.1
Investment companies	3.3	0.7	17.0	1.8	47.6	2.4	63.7	1.4
Other corp. shares	130.4	29.1	279.0	39.2	715.4	36.8	1,151.8	25.6
Life insurance reserves	55.0	12.3	85.2	8.8	130.3	6.7	222.5	5.0
Pension fund reserves	24.0	5.4	90.7	9.4	237.4	12.2	727.1	16.2
Security credit	0.9	0.2	1.1	0.1	2.2	0.1	12.6	0.3
Other assets	8.7	1.9	13.3	1.4	26.3	1.4	74.4	1.7
Total financial assets	$447.5	100.0%	$967.9	100.0%	$1,944.3	100.0%	$4,493.6	100.0%

SOURCE: Board of Governors of the Federal Reserve System, *Flow of Funds Accounts: Financial Assets and Liabilities Outstanding*, indicated years.

example, time and savings deposits represented less than 20 percent of consumer-held financial assets.

While household investments in thrift deposits are growing in both absolute and relative terms, purchases of *corporate stock* have declined drastically in relative terms. Exhibit 17–1 shows that individuals and families held as much as 40 percent of their financial investments in corporate stock in 1960 and a full 39 percent in 1970. However, the stock market's volatile and lackluster performance during the 1970s, coupled with attractive returns available elsewhere, have driven thousands of small investors out of that market. By year-end 1980 only about one quarter of household financial investments remained committed to corporate stock. Other financial assets—U.S. government securities, state and local government bonds, life insurance policies, and cash itself—also have fallen in favor with the average consumer. Faced with volatile economic conditions and rapid inflation, households have come to emphasize safety, liquidity, and long-term financial security in choosing their financial assets. This is evidenced by the growing importance of consumer investments in time and savings deposits, shares in money market mutual funds, and pension plans in recent years.

Government Regulation and Returns to the Small Saver

One serious problem that must be overcome in attracting savings from consumers is the restrictive impact of government regulation. During the 1930s, when thousands of banks and smaller thrift institutions were failing, Congress imposed maximum legal interest rates that commercial banks could pay on their deposits. These so-called Regulation Q interest-rate ceilings were designed to promote bank safety and soundness by restricting competition for savings deposits.[4] Later, in 1966, legal rate ceilings were imposed upon deposits at credit unions, savings and loan associations, and mutual savings banks. Because these rate ceilings are changed infrequently, they usually lag well behind interest rates available on securities sold in the open market and often compare poorly to yields on a number of popular nonfinancial investments (including gold, silver, and real estate). A good example of this phenomenon occurred in the summer of 1981, when interest rates offered on top-quality, seasoned corporate bonds climbed above 15 percent, while the maximum legal rates that could be offered to small savers on passbook accounts and fixed-rate, long-maturity certificates of deposit ranged from only 5¼ to 8 percent.

Despite Congress's good intentions during the Great Depression, we now know that interest-rate ceilings do not prevent failures of financial institutions. However, these legal ceilings clearly do injure the small saver. One device that many financial institutions have used to get around the damaging effects of interest-rate ceilings in attracting consumer funds is to develop

---

[4] See Chapters 4 and 22 for further discussions of the reasons for and effects of Regulation Q interest-rate ceilings on deposits.

interest-bearing checking accounts—NOWs. These accounts were first developed by a mutual savings bank in Massachusetts and spread rapidly throughout the New England area during the 1970s. They offer a return on transactions money, which was previously forbidden by federal law. Well over 90 percent of the NOWs presently offered pay a 5¼ percent interest rate—the maximum currently allowed by law—and most institutions pay interest from day of deposit to day of withdrawal.

NOWs are more convenient for the consumer because they minimize the need to shift funds from savings to checking accounts and back again. They increase competition between commercial banks and savings banks, which *may* benefit the consumer through lower interest rates on loans and higher rates on deposits. However, some observers fear that offering institutions will be forced to charge higher fees for checks, loans, and other services in order to offset the cost of NOWs. Moreover, a number of recent research studies indicate the consumer needs an average balance of at least $1,000 to reap any significant benefits from the NOW service.[5]

The Depository Institutions Deregulation Act of 1980 authorizes two services which compete directly with NOWs. One of these—Automatic Transfers (ATS)—permits the consumer to preauthorize a bank to move funds from a savings account to a checking account in order to cover overdrafts. The net effect is to pay interest on transactions balances. This particular service was first made legal for commercial banks in November 1978 but was subsequently struck down by federal court decisions until Congress acted in 1980. Credit unions are permitted to offer their own version of the NOW, known as the *share draft*. These interest-bearing checkbook plans, offered today by more than 1,600 U.S. credit unions, give the consumer the advantage of a duplicate record system for any checks written, extra float time, and potentially higher interest rates because federal regulations permit share draft accounts to earn up to 7 percent interest.[6]

Legal interest-rate ceilings were dealt what many hope was a death blow by the Depository Institutions Deregulation and Monetary Control Act of 1980. (See Exhibit 17–2 for a summary of major provisions of the Depository Institutions Act affecting the consumer.) Congress declared that interest-rate ceilings on deposits were "inequitable to the small saver" and discouraged savings. Accordingly, a six-year phaseout of the ceilings is planned, and a new committee—the Depository Institutions Deregulation Committee—has been set up to phase out the legal limits and to control ceiling rates until they are ultimately eliminated. Legal ceilings on certain loan rates were also eliminated or liberalized. For example, state usury laws on first-mortgage loans were dropped as of March 31, 1980, unless a state adopts a new ceiling before April 1983. State usury ceilings on business and agricultural loans

---

[5] A summary of research findings regarding NOWs is presented in Rose (20). For a further discussion of the possible impact of NOWs on depository institutions, see Chapters 3 and 4 of this text.

[6] See Chapter 4 for a more-detailed description of share drafts.

EXHIBIT 17-2
Summary of Major Provisions of the Depository Institutions Deregulation and Monetary Control Act of 1980 Affecting the Consumer

Item	The Law States
NOW accounts	After December 31, 1980, all depository institutions may offer NOWs (interest-bearing checking accounts) to individuals and nonprofit organizations.
Automatic transfers and share drafts	Effective April 1980, banks may provide automatic transfers of funds from savings to checking accounts; savings and loan associations may provide remote service units; and all federally insured credit unions can offer share draft accounts.
Deposit interest-rate ceilings	Federal interest-rate ceilings on deposits offered by commercial banks, credit unions, and savings banks will be phased out over a six-year period. A Depository Institutions Deregulation Committee (DIDC)* will set deposit interest-rate ceilings after March 31, 1980, and make plans for a phaseout of the ceilings.
State usury ceilings on loan rates	Ceiling interest rates imposed on first residential mortgage loans by the states are eliminated unless a state adopts a new ceiling before April 1, 1983. Credit unions may increase their maximum loan rate from 12 to 15 percent.
Deposit insurance	Federal deposit insurance at commercial banks, savings banks, savings and loan associations, and credit unions is increased from $40,000 to $100,000 per account, effective immediately.
Additional powers granted to nonbank thrift institutions	Federally chartered credit unions are authorized to grant residential real estate loans, while federally insured savings and loan associations may issue credit cards, offer trust services, and make consumer loans and investments in corporate debt securities up to 20 percent of their total assets.

* Voting members of the DIDC include the secretary of the Treasury, chairman of the Federal Reserve Board, chairman of the board of the Federal Deposit Insurance Corporation, chairman of the Federal Home Loan Bank Board, and chairman of the board of the National Credit Union Administration. The Comptroller of the Currency (administrator of national banks) is a nonvoting member.

above $25,000 were preempted by a new legal ceiling equal to the Federal Reserve's discount rate plus 5 percent. This step should promote greater availability of mortgage, agricultural, and business credit in the future. We have learned too slowly and painfully that while government interest-rate ceilings may hold down the cost of a loan, they frequently result in the customer's getting no loan at all.

CONSUMERS AS BORROWERS OF FUNDS

We have noted that consumers provide most of the savings out of which loans are made and financial assets created. However, it is also true that consumers are among the most important groups of borrowers in the U.S. financial system. For example, in 1979 households borrowed $170 billion in the nation's credit markets, while nonfinancial businesses raised $154 billion, financial institutions $86 billion, and governments (federal, state, and local) $55 billion (see Exhibit 17–3).

EXHIBIT 17–3
Credit Market Funds Raised by Major Sectors in the U.S. Economy ($ billions)

Sector	1975	1976	1977	1978	1979	1980
Households	$49.7	$90.5	$139.9	$162.6	$170.6	$101.7
Nonfinancial business:	48.6	76.3	107.6	128.2	153.7	136.5
Farm	8.8	10.9	14.7	18.1	24.6	14.5
Nonfarm noncorporate	2.0	4.7	12.9	15.4	15.5	15.8
Corporate:	37.9	60.7	79.9	94.7	113.6	106.1
Debt	28.0	50.2	77.2	92.2	110.1	93.2
Equities	9.9	10.5	2.7	2.6	3.5	12.9
Financial institutions	12.7	24.1	54.0	81.4	86.2	66.7
U.S. government	85.4	69.0	56.8	53.7	37.4	79.2
State and local governments ...	13.7	15.2	20.4	23.6	18.0	25.3
Foreign	13.3	20.8	13.9	32.3	22.0	29.2

SOURCE: Board of Governors of the Federal Reserve System, *Flow of Accounts* and *Federal Reserve Bulletin,* selected issues.

Equally impressive is the total amount of debt owed by households relative to other sectors of the economy. For example, as shown in Exhibit 17–4, the total outstanding debt owed by U.S. households reached nearly $1.5 trillion at year-end 1980. This was actually less than the total indebtedness of

EXHIBIT 17–4
Total Liabilities of Major Sectors of the U.S. Economy, Outstanding at Year-End ($ billions)

Sector	1975	1976	1977	1978	1979	1980
Households	$ 801.2	$ 899.3	$1,044.8	$1,210.0	$1,375.8	$1,493.5
Nonfinancial business	1,065.9	1,158.1	1,287.9	1,466.1	1,695.7	1,855.5
Farm	89.2	101.0	116.4	135.4	163.1	166.7
Nonfarm:						
noncorporate	124.8	131.6	144.5	157.9	174.6	195.0
corporate	851.9	925.5	1,027.0	1,172.9	1,358.0	1,493.9
U.S. government	511.6	590.9	655.7	719.5	767.6	857.9
State and local governments .	234.5	250.4	271.7	296.3	315.4	337.9

SOURCE: Board of Governors of the Federal Reserve System, *Flow of Funds Accounts: Assets and Liabilities Outstanding,* selected issues.

all nonfinancial businesses in the economy, which was more than $1.8 trillion, but exceeded the total amounts owed by the federal government and by all state and local governments. In fact, the aggregate indebtedness of individuals and families exceeded the combined debt of all U.S. governmental units (federal, state, and local) by nearly $300 billion in 1980.

Is Consumer Borrowing Excessive?

Are consumers too heavily in debt today? Have they jumped in over their heads? Certainly, the total volume of household debt outstanding is huge in both absolute terms and relative to most other sectors of the economy. However, to judge whether consumer borrowing is really excessive, that debt should be compared to the financial assets consumers hold. These assets, presumably, can be drawn upon to meet any interest and principal payments that come due on consumer borrowings. Exhibit 17–5 shows, that while the volume of consumer debt has increased rapidly in recent years, the volume of household financial assets also has grown rapidly. For example, in 1980 financial assets held by U.S. households exceeded their outstanding liabilities by about $3 trillion. Moreover, the absolute size of that financial asset cushion has increased dramatically over the past three decades. In 1970, for example, the spread between household financial assets and liabilities was $1.4 trillion and in 1960, only $742 billion.

When we measure the ratio of consumer liabilities to financial assets, however, the picture is not so optimistic. As shown in Exhibit 17–5, this ratio has nearly doubled since 1950, increasing from less than 20 percent to more than 30 percent. Whether the liability–financial asset ratio has reached an "excessive" level depends, of course, upon economic conditions and the educational level and degree of financial sophistication of individuals and families. If the average consumer today is better educated and more capable of managing a larger volume of debt, a higher ratio of liabilities to financial assets in household portfolios is probably not an alarming development. Moreover, the *total wealth* held by consumers includes not just their financial assets but also their real assets—homes, automobiles, furniture, etc. While we have no really reliable measure of the value of real assets held by consumers, it is obvious that the total wealth of individuals and families (including both real and financial assets) far exceeds their debt obligations.

Categories of Consumer Borrowing

The range of consumer borrowing needs is enormous. Loans to the household sector support a more diverse group of purchases of goods and services than is true of any other sector of the American economy. Consumers generally borrow long term to finance purchases of *durable* goods— single-family homes, automobiles, mobile homes, recreational vehicles, repair and modernization of existing homes, boats, and home appliances. They

EXHIBIT 17–5
The Household Sector as a Net Lender of Funds, Outstanding at Year-End ($ billions)

Item	1950	1960	1970	1975	1976	1977	1978	1979	1980
Total financial assets	$447.5	$967.9	$1,926.6	$2,551.5	$2,944.4	$3,118.0	$3,4422.0	$3,827.1	$4,493.6
Total financial liabilities	77.4	226.2	502.0	801.2	899.3	1,044.8	1,210.0	1,375.8	1,493.5
Difference: assets − liabilities	$370.1	$741.7	$1,424.6	$1,750.3	$2,045.1	$2,073.2	$2,212.0	$2,451.3	$3,000.1
Ratio of household liabilities to financial assets	17.3%	23.4%	26.1%	31.4%	30.5%	33.5%	35.4%	35.9%	33.2%

SOURCE: Board of Governors of the Federal Reserve System, *Flow of Funds Accounts: Financial Assets and Liabilities Outstanding*, indicated years.

usually borrow short term to cover purchases of *nondurable* goods and services—medical care, vacations, fuel, food, and clothing. Financial analysts frequently divide the credit extended to consumers into three broad categories: (1) residential mortgage credit to support the purchase of new or existing single-family homes, duplexes, and other permanent dwellings; (2) installment credit used primarily for long-term nonresidential purposes; and (3) noninstallment credit.

Which of these forms of consumer borrowing is most important? Exhibit 17–6 provides a clear answer. Far and away the dominant form of consumer borrowing is aimed at providing shelter for individuals and families through *mortgage loans*. Home mortgage indebtedness by U.S. households reached $940 billion at year-end 1980 and represented more than 60 percent of all household debt. Moreover, the volume of home mortgage credit flowing to households has grown rapidly in recent years with the increasing attractiveness of home ownership as a tax shelter. For example, residential mortgage loans taken on by households more than tripled during the 1970s. We will examine the huge residential mortgage market in much greater detail in Chapter 18.

Installment credit is the second major component of consumer debt in the United States. Installment debt consists of all consumer liabilities other than mortgages that are retired in two or more consecutive payments, usually made monthly or quarterly. Four major types of installment credit are extended by lenders in this field: (1) automobile credit, (2) revolving credit, (3) mobile homes, and (4) other consumer installment loans. An incredibly wide variety of consumer goods and services is financed by this kind of credit, including the purchase of furniture and appliances, payment of medical and dental expenses, vacations, the purchase of transportation and recreational vehicles, and the consolidation of outstanding debts.

As shown in Exhibit 17–6, consumer installment debt totaled nearly $313 billion at year-end 1980, or more than triple the amount of such debt in 1970. Consumer installment borrowing set a record for growth in a single year during 1978, when installment borrowing rose almost $45 billion (see Exhibit 17–7). However, when *all* forms of consumer borrowing—mortgage and nonmortgage—are combined, U.S. households borrowed more in 1979 than at any time in previous history—a record $168 billion.

For many years, the majority of installment loans extended to consumers in the United States were used to finance the purchase of *automobiles*. This is no longer the case, however, though auto paper still represents somewhat more than a third of all consumer installment debt outstanding (see Exhibit 17–8). The largest installment debt category today is a miscellaneous group of loans which cover household expenses, debt consolidation, and purchases of durable goods other than automobiles. The energy crisis and inflation have had a significant impact here. Rapidly rising gasoline and new car prices have encouraged the substitution of smaller, less-expensive cars for the heavy gas guzzlers. At the same time, faced with home heating and air conditioning

EXHIBIT 17–6
Principal Liabilities of U.S. Households Outstanding at Year-End 1950, 1960, 1970, and 1980 ($ billions)

Liabilities	1950 Amount	1950 Per-cent	1960 Amount	1960 Per-cent	1970 Amount	1970 Per-cent	1980 Amount	1980 Per-cent
Home mortgages	$42.6	55.0%	$136.8	60.5%	$273.1	56.5%	$ 940.4	63.0%
Other mortgages	2.4	3.1	9.2	4.1	20.5	4.2	30.9	2.1
Consumer installment credit	14.7	19.0	43.0	19.0	101.2	20.9	312.8	20.9
Other consumer credit	6.8	8.8	13.2	5.8	25.6	5.3	72.2	4.8
Banks loans N.E.C.*	3.8	4.9	7.2	3.2	21.9	4.5	28.8	1.9
Other loans	2.9	3.7	7.0	3.1	20.9	4.3	54.8	3.7
Security credit	2.5	3.2	5.4	2.4	10.0	2.1	23.7	1.6
Trade credit	0.9	1.2	2.1	0.9	5.3	1.1	16.9	1.1
Deferred and unpaid life insurance premiums	1.0	1.3	2.4	1.1	5.1	1.1	12.9	0.9
Total liabilities	$77.4	100.0%	$226.2	100.0%	$483.6	100.0%	$1,493.5	100.0%

* Not elsewhere classified.
SOURCE: Board of Governors of the Federal Reserve System, *Flow of Funds Accounts: Financial Assets and Liabilities Outstanding,* indicated years.

EXHIBIT 17–7
Recent Growth of Consumer Borrowing in the United States ($ billions)

Item	1970	1975	1976	1977	1978	1979	1980
Net annual increase in total liabilities of U.S. households	$22.5	$52.2	$97.3	$145.3	$166.4	$167.6	$110.1
Net annual increase in categories of consumer borrowing:							
Home mortgages	12.5	38.1	61.3	93.2	103.8	111.3	83.4
Other mortgages	1.4	1.0	1.1	1.0	1.0	1.0	1.5
Installment credit	5.0	7.8	21.6	34.3	44.8	35.7	1.4
Other consumer credit	1.1	1.9	3.9	6.2	5.8	6.6	0.9
Bank loans, N.E.C.	0.9	−1.2	0.8	2.8	3.4	3.3	5.6
Other loans	2.6	2.2	1.8	2.3	3.8	6.3	8.9
Security credit	−1.8	0.7	4.8	3.1	1.4	0.9	5.0
Trade debt	0.5	1.1	1.4	1.3	1.4	1.4	2.1
Miscellaneous borrowings	0.4	0.7	0.6	0.9	1.1	1.1	1.2

SOURCE: Board of Governors of the Federal Reserve System, *Flow of Funds Accounts,* selected issues.

EXHIBIT 17–8
Consumer Installment Debt Outstanding, 1980

Item	Amount Outstanding ($ Billions)	Percent of Total
Total installment credit	$313.4	100.0%
By major type of credit:		
Automobile	116.3	37.1
Revolving credit	59.9	19.1
Mobile home loans	17.3	5.5
Other forms of installment credit	119.9	38.8
By lender:		
Commercial banks	$145.8	46.5
Finance companies	76.8	24.5
Credit unions	44.0	14.0
Retailers*	29.4	9.4
Savings and loan associations	9.9	3.2
Mutual savings banks	2.8	0.9
Gasoline companies	4.7	1.5

* Includes auto dealers and excludes 30-day charge credit held by travel and entertainment companies.
SOURCE: Board of Governors of the Federal Reserve System, *Federal Reserve Bulletin,* June 1981.

bills which frequently exceed their home mortgage payments, more consumers today are borrowing simply to cover fuel bills, purchase energy-efficient appliances and insulation, make home repairs, and meet home operating expenses.

The final major category of consumer debt is *noninstallment credit,* which is normally paid off in a lump sum. This form of consumer credit includes single-payment loans, charge accounts, and credit for services, such as medical care and utilities. The total amount of noninstallment loans outstanding is difficult to estimate because many such loans are made by one individual to another or by department stores, oil and gas companies, and professional service firms who do not report their lending activities. Commercial banks, however, make a substantial volume of noninstallment loans to consumers. For example, as of September 30, 1978, U.S. commercial banks had extended $30 billion in single-payment loans to individuals, representing nearly 10 percent of all loans made by banks to consumers.

CREDIT AND DEBIT CARDS

One of the most popular forms of installment credit available to consumers today comes through the credit card. Through this encoded piece of plastic, the consumer has instant access to credit for any purchase up to a prespecified credit limit. More recently, another piece of plastic—the debit card—has made instant cash available and check cashing much easier. The growth of credit and debit cards has been truly phenomenal to date, and the future looks equally promising. Current estimates suggest that there are more than 800 million credit and debit cards in use worldwide.

In the United States today a major battle for credit-card customers is shaping up among some of that nation's largest banks, savings and loan associations, credit unions, and mutual savings banks. Many of these institutions have launched aggressive advertising campaigns, sending out millions of invitations to customers to join the nationwide VISA and Master Charge credit-card systems. Aggressive marketing of credit cards represents an attempt to change the whole competitive climate of consumer banking in the United States. In the future a wide array of new financial services is likely to be offered through plastic credit- and debit-card programs. Such services might include consumer revolving credit lines and preauthorized borrowing, interest paid on surplus credit-card balances, optional credit repayment plans, and the payment of other household bills.

Many of these consumer-oriented financial services are already offered on a limited basis in selected markets across the United States. In the future customers will need to make fewer trips to their bank or other financial institution because transactions will be handled mainly over the telephone or through a conveniently located computer terminal, either in the home or in easily accessible public locations. The hometown financial institution will lose much of its convenience advantage for local customers. It will be nearly as convenient for the customer to maintain a checking, savings, or loan account in a city hundreds of miles away as to keep it in a local financial institution. In short, the ticket to many, perhaps most, financial services will be a plastic credit card or debit card—and electronic processing of consumer financial data across great distances.

Growth of Credit Cards

The growth of credit extended through plastic cards has been extremely dynamic in recent years. At year-end 1980 receivables outstanding on bank credit cards in the United States totaled an estimated $30 billion, compared to roughly $1 billion in 1970. Since total consumer installment credit outstanding at U.S. commercial banks totaled $313 billion at year-end 1980, credit card receivables accounted for nearly 10 percent of the installment total.

Bank credit cards evolved from small, independent operations designed to finance local purchases of goods and services on a 30-day account. These early card programs were used primarily to charge travel and entertainment expenses and were similar to the well-known Diners Club, Carte Blanche, and American Express programs of today. The first bank credit card was issued in 1951 by the now-defunct Franklin National Bank of New York.

While the early growth and acceptance of the credit card brought forth many small card plans with little coordination, the 1970s ushered in the nationwide dominance of two systems—VISA (formerly National Bank-Americard, Inc.), headquartered in San Francisco, and Master Charge (formerly Interbank Card Association, Inc.), headquartered in New York City. Both systems maintain nationwide facilities for the processing of credit slips, encompassing approximately 1,200 card-issuing financial institutions and 8,500 agency institutions, which help distribute cards to new customers. At the same time about 200 small, independent card programs serve regional and local markets. The industry is now highly concentrated, however, with VISA and Master Charge holding better than 90 percent of all credit-card receivables.

The phenomenal growth of credit cards may be attributed to many factors. One is the profitability of many card plans which have grown and prospered after an initial period of loss. The availability of high-speed computers also is a contributing factor. The computer helps to reduce the administrative costs of charge-card operations and promotes high volume, which reduces total costs per unit.

Credit-Card Users

Credit cards are used for very different purposes depending upon the social class, education, income, and lifestyle of the user. Customers who use their credit cards merely as a substitute for cash are referred to as *convenience users*. These people tend to be in the upper-middle or top income-earning brackets and do not necessarily seek out stores accepting their cards. Customers who purchase large items (such as furniture, appliances, and gifts) or maintain large outstanding credit-card balances are referred to as *installment users* because they pay only a portion of their outstanding balances each month. These individuals frequently are in lower and middle-income brackets.

For both convenience and installment users, the principle advantage of credit cards is convenience. There is no minimum number of transactions for which the card must be used. Also, as two or three cards have become more widely accepted in thousands of stores, the number of different plastic cards needed by the customer has been reduced. The installment feature of the credit card is a major attraction because it functions as a revolving line of credit. In addition, the card itself serves to identify the customer and records pertinent information when the privilege of using the card is exercised.

To most merchants the credit card has been a positive financial innovation because it increases the potential number of customers and allows smaller firms to compete with larger ones. Banks and credit-card companies do collect a discount fee, however, on the dollar volume of a merchant's credit-card sales. This charge is designed to compensate the lender for the expenses of credit investigation, bookkeeping, and collections. The actual discount fee charged is negotiable but typically is inversely related to the volume of a merchant's sales and the average size of credit-card purchases. A store with membership in a credit-card plan deposits card sales slips along with other receipts in its account at a bank or other financial institution. If the receiving financial institution is merely an agency rather than a card-issuing institution, it forwards the credit slips through correspondents to the card issuer. It is the card-issuing firms who generally bear the full risk of buyer default or fraud, though some risk also may be shared with participating agency institutions.

Today, the largest credit-card programs generally operate at a profit. In the beginning, however, most card programs were confronted with substantial losses. Both credit delinquencies and losses due to fraud were high, due in large part to indiscriminate mass mailing of cards to customers. Moreover, the heavy cost of processing many small purchases of goods and services was not fully considered. Also, most banks and credit-card companies underestimated the problem of controlling bad-debt losses. Today, however, the major credit-card programs in the United States are at least 20 to 30 years old. This long-term experience with operating problems has paid off in recent years. Nationwide acceptance of cards and the card interchange program have pushed the volume of activity in the largest card programs beyond the break-even point.[7]

Operational Problems in Offering Credit Cards

Banks and other companies offering credit cards must solve several significant operational problems. First, the *break-even point* in card operations appears to be relatively high, placing pressure on credit card companies to

---

[7] One serious problem which has damaged the profitability of many credit card plans recently stems from the interest-rate ceilings on consumer loans imposed by a number of states. When the cost of acquiring loanable funds rises, profits from credit-card operations are squeezed because legal rate ceilings prevent card issuers from increasing their charges to card users. See Rose (23).

sign up enough merchants to accept the cards and enough individuals to use them. The two problems are, of course, interrelated. Merchants are willing to accept a card only if they believe there will be sufficient customers using it to make the program worthwhile. Similarly, individuals are willing to make use of their cards only if a large number of merchants will accept them in payment for goods and services. One problem that has plagued credit-card operations for many years is losses due to customer fraud. Recent estimates by the Federal Reserve System find that fraud losses represent 15 to 20 percent of total card charge-offs for most plans.[8]

During the late 1960s some U.S. banks tried to overcome the card-acceptance barrier by mass mailing of unsolicited cards, resulting in large-scale credit and fraud losses. Fearing that the safety and soundness of the banking system might be jeopardized and public confidence in banks shaken, Congress passed the Consumer Credit Protection Act, which prohibits unsolicited mailing of credit cards. Moreover, once the card-issuing company has been notified, the customer is no longer liable for any unauthorized use of his or her card. Prior to notification, the cardholder can only be held responsible for a maximum of $50 in unauthorized charges per card. Moreover, the customer cannot be held liable for unauthorized use of his or her credit card if the card was not requested or used, if it carries a means of identifying the authorized user (such as a signature or photograph), or if the customer was not notified of the $50 maximum liability. In addition, card issuers must provide the customer with a means of notifying them in case of card loss or theft.

Federal legislation has done much to enhance public acceptance of credit cards. Most cards are issued to customers today only after a careful analysis of their credit standing. That is why cardholders frequently are able to use their cards as a credit reference to aid in the cashing of checks or to obtain other forms of credit. Most merchants know that charge-card holders tend to have higher incomes and better payment records than the general population.

The most profitable credit-card accounts from the point of view of the issuing companies are those with high balances which are not paid off immediately (i.e., those held by installment users). However, less than half the sales volume experienced by most card programs winds up as carry-over balances subject to finance charges. Most card users are *convenience users,* who pay off their credit purchases within the normal billing cycle. Banks have found that they cannot make significant profits on their credit card operations when over half their cardholders are only convenience users. Moreover, card users with the highest incomes and best repayment records typically economize on their cash balances and delay payment as long as possible, which further reduces the earnings from card operations. However, the performance of credit-card programs does improve with experi-

---

[8] See, in particular, Seiders (25) and Rose (23).

ence. Card companies become more skillful at identifying profitable groups of customers and at minimizing fraud and bad-debt losses. In addition, credit card programs bring in customers who may purchase other financial services from the same institution, such as installment loans and savings plans.

Debit Cards

Until recently, commercial banks were the only major financial institutions actively involved in the plastic card field. Other than banks, the other major issuers of cards were retail department stores and oil companies. This situation changed rapidly during the 1970s, however, as nonbank financial institutions (principally credit unions, mutual savings banks, and savings and loan associations) successfully invaded the plastic card market using *debit cards*. While a credit card permits the customer to buy now and pay later, debit cards are merely a convenient way of paying now. A debit card enables its users to make deposits and withdrawals from an automated teller (''money machine'') and also to pay for purchases by direct electronic transfer of funds from their own account to the merchant's account. Debit cards are also used for identification and check-clearing purposes and to access remote computer terminals for information or for the transfer of funds.

An important feature of debit cards is their potential for the complete elimination of checkbook float. Electronic funds-transfer systems activated with a debit card will take only seconds instead of days (as checks now do) to move money from one account to another. Overall, the outlook for debit cards is excellent. The fact that many credit-card users do not take advantage of the credit feature but merely use their card for convenience in shopping suggests that there is a market for debit-card services.

Both the credit card and the debit card offer significant opportunities to financial institutions to develop new services and open up new markets. The overall cost of consumer lending can be reduced by encouraging small borrowers to use a revolving charge-card account rather than negotiating separate loans each time funds are needed. Credit and debit cards linked to money machines and point-of-sale terminals can provide the means for moving funds in many different directions—for purchases of goods and services, for additions to savings, and for investment. Most, if not all, consumer financial services—credit, savings, and checking—may be offered through card programs, offering the consumer greater speed, convenience, and accuracy in record keeping.

THE DETERMINANTS OF CONSUMER BORROWING

As we noted earlier, consumers represent one of the largest groups of borrowers in the financial system. Yet individual consumers differ widely in their use of credit and their attitudes toward borrowing money. What factors appear to influence the volume of borrowing carried out by households?

Recent research points to a number of factors which bear on the consumer's decision of when and how much to borrow.[9] Leading the list is the size of individual *family income*. Families with larger incomes use greater amounts of debt in both absolute dollar amounts and relative to income. In part, the debt-income relationship reflects the high correlation between income levels and education. Families whose principal breadwinners have made a significant investment in education are more often aware of the advantages (as well as the dangers) of using debt in order to supplement current income. Moreover, there is a high positive correlation between the level of education and the income-earning power of the principal breadwinners in a family. The result is a three-way interrelationship between income, education, and the use of household debt.

The *stage of life* in which adult income-earning members of a family find themselves is a major influence on household borrowing. The so-called life-cycle hypothesis contends that young families just starting out tend to be heavy users of debt.[10] The purchase of a new home, automobile, appliances, and furniture follow soon after a new family is formed. As children come along, living costs rise and a larger home may be necessary, resulting in additional borrowing. Research suggests families with children tend to borrow more heavily relative to current income than either singles or childless couples. Moreover, the more volatile a family's income, the more debt it tends to use relative to current income. Similarly, a family which holds a low proportion of liquid assets (such as insurance policies, stocks, bonds, and deposits) tends to use more debt per dollar of income than a household with a high proportion of liquid assets.

Consumer borrowing is correlated with the *business cycle*. During periods of economic expansion the number of jobs increases, and many households become more optimistic about their future financial situation. New borrowings usually outstrip repayments of outstanding loans, and the net volume of household debt rises. When an economic expansion ends and a recession begins, however, unemployment increases, and many households turn pessimistic about the future. Some, fearing a drop in income or even loss of their jobs, will attempt to build up their savings and cut back on borrowing. Loan repayments rise relative to new borrowings, and total household debt declines. During the deepest postwar recession in 1974–75, for example, household borrowing was cut in half as both home mortgage loans and installment credit dropped precipitously. However, during the expansion period which began late in 1975 and lasted until 1980, household borrowing rose to unprecedented levels.

One factor which accentuates the cyclical behavior of consumer borrow-

[9] Two excellent discussions of the factors influencing household borrowing are the studies by Katona, Mandell, and Schiediskamp (12) and the National Commission on Consumer Finance (17).

[10] See especially Ando and Modigliani (1).

ing is fluctuations in the *demand for durable goods*.[11] When the economy turns down into a recession, many households postpone replacement of worn-out furniture, home appliances, and automobiles. Repairing the old automobile, for example, is often viewed as a safer, less-expensive alternative than incurring additional debt and committing uncertain future income to buy a new one. Therefore consumers are likely to cut back on purchases of durables and the debt used to finance them when a recession hits. However, new furniture, appliances, and automobiles become more attractive in boom periods, and consumer debt used to buy these items usually increases.

In recent years *price expectations* have influenced consumer borrowing heavily; this has been especially the case since the late 1960s, when the rate of inflation accelerated. Postponing the purchase of an automobile, a new home, furniture, and appliances usually means these goods will simply cost more in the future. According to consumer price reports published monthly by the Bureau of Labor Statistics, the average cost of living for an urban family of four increased approximately 2.7 times between 1967 and 1981. It is interesting to note that U.S. household debt increased at roughly the same growth rate over this same 14-year period. If family incomes are not increasing at least as fast as consumer prices, it often pays to "buy now" through borrowing rather than postpone purchases of goods and services. This is especially true if funds can be borrowed either at fixed interest rates or at interest rates which change more slowly than consumer prices.

Fluctuations in *interest rates* also play a role in shaping the volume and direction of consumer borrowing. Interest rates rise as the economy expands and gathers momentum. At first, the rising rates are not high enough to offset strong consumer optimism, and household borrowing continues to increase. As the period of economic expansion reaches a peak, however, the rise in interest rates and the accompanying increase in monthly payments on installment loans become so significant that consumer borrowing begins to decline. The drop in borrowing also leads to a decline in consumer spending, which may worsen the impending recession. We should note, however, that consumer loan rates tend to be "sticky" over the course of the business cycle and change slowly compared to the majority of other interest rates.[12]

CONSUMER LENDING INSTITUTIONS

Financial intermediaries—commercial banks, savings banks and savings and loan associations, credit unions, and finance companies—account for most of the loans made to consumers in the American economy. For example, of the $313 billion in installment loans owed by consumers at year-end 1980,

---

[11] For a discussion of the factors influencing purchases of consumer durables, see Dunkleberg and Stevenson (5).

[12] See Chapter 7 for an explanation of the influence of the business cycle on both long- and short-term interest rates.

financial intermediaries accounted for $279 billion, or about 90 percent. Intermediaries also dominate the market for noninstallment credit and make the bulk of home-mortgage loans. While each type of financial institution prefers to specialize in one type or a few selected areas of consumer lending, there has been a tendency in recent years for these institutions to *diversify* their lending operations. One important result of this diversification has been to bring all major consumer lenders into direct competition with each other.

It is principally through financial intermediaries that consumers exert their impact upon the financial system. Consumers generally don't borrow directly in the open market, for a variety of reasons. The cost of credit investigation is substantial relative to the small size of most consumer loans. The majority of investors in open-market securities are unwilling to incur these costs, and it is more efficient for *local* financial institutions to process consumer loans. They can more readily investigate credit quality and, if necessary, repossess the property involved in the loan transaction. Then, too, consumer loans vary greatly in amount, purpose, maturity, and quality of the credit, whereas securities sold in the open market tend to be relatively homogenous in all of these features.

Commercial Banks

The single-most-important consumer lending institution is the commercial bank. Commercial banks approach the consumer in three different ways—by direct lending, through purchases of installment paper from merchants, and by making loans to other consumer lending institutions. As Exhibit 17–9 shows, commercial banks held nearly $380 billion in consumer mortgage and nonmortgage loans at year-end 1980.[13] About 40 percent of that total consisted of mortgages to support the purchase or construction of one-to-four-family residential dwellings, while the rest consisted of installment and noninstallment credit to cover purchases of goods and services and debt retirement. In the mortgage field, commercial banks usually prefer to provide short-term construction financing rather than long-term permanent loans for family housing. They usually leave the long-term lending in this field to savings and loan associations, mutual savings banks, and insurance companies.

Within the nonmortgage loan category, banks made a wider variety of consumer loans than any other lending institution and dominate most areas of consumer lending. Commercial banks grant about three fifths of all auto loans extended by financial institutions to consumers each year. However, most bank credit in the auto field is *indirect*—installment paper purchased from auto dealers—rather than being made directly to the auto-buying consumer. Starting out behind, commercial banks also have come to dominate

---

[13] For a comprehensive study of commercial bank lending procedures, see Hayes (11). Additional information on commercial bank lending policies is provided in Chapter 3 of this text.

EXHIBIT 17–9
Consumer-Related Loans Held by Commercial Banks, Year-End 1980
($ billions)

Type of Loan	Amount	Percent of Total
Residential mortgage loans:		
One-to-four family	$160.7	42.3%
Multifamily	12.3	3.2
Nonmortgage consumer loans:		
Automobile	61.0	16.1
Indirect paper	34.9	9.2
Direct loans	26.2	6.9
Revolving credit	30.0	7.9
Mobile homes	10.4	2.7
Other loans	44.4	11.7
Totals	$379.9	100.0%

SOURCE: Board of Governors of the Federal Reserve System, *Federal Reserve Bulletin*, June 1981.

lending to support the purchase of mobile homes. About 60 percent of all mobile home loans are held by banks, with finance companies and savings and loan associations accounting for the remainder. In other forms of consumer installment credit, however, the lead of commercial banks is narrower and the share of other consumer lending institutions is on the rise. Installment loans to cover consumer purchases of furniture, appliances, medical bills, vacations, and miscellaneous goods and services totaled $120 billion at year-end 1980. Commercial banks held $44 billion of these loans, or 37 percent of the total. But finance companies were a close second with $39 billion, followed by credit unions, which held $23 billion.

Finance Companies

Finance companies have a long history of active lending in the consumer installment field, providing funds directly to the consumer through thousands of small-loan offices and indirectly by purchasing installment paper from appliance dealers.[14] These active household lenders provide auto loans, credit for home improvements and for the purchase of appliances and furniture, and revolving credit arrangements. (See Exhibit 17–10.)

As we noted in Chapter 5, there are actually two different kinds of finance companies serving the consumer. *Sales finance companies* purchase consumer installment contracts from retail merchants. These companies loan monies to retail dealers to acquire inventories of consumer goods—mainly home furniture, appliances, and automobiles. As the goods are sold, the dealer repays the loan. *Consumer finance companies* make cash loans directly to individuals and families. These companies borrow through bank lines of

---

[14] See Matson (15) for a good discussion of finance-company lending practices.

EXHIBIT 17–10
Consumer-Related Loans Held by Finance Companies,
Year-End 1980 ($ billions)

Type of Loan	Amount	Percent of Total
Automobile	$34.2	44.6%
Mobile home	3.7	4.8
Other installment loans	38.8	50.6
Totals.....................	$76.7	100.0%

SOURCE: Board of Governors of the Federal Reserve System, *Federal Reserve Bulletin*, June 1981.

credit and frequently have large loan losses because they usually accept more-risky loans than other consumer lenders. Consumer finance companies have legal limits on the interest rates they can charge for household loans and the maximum size of such loans. These limits are set by each state; loan rates usually cannot exceed 3 percent per month on a loan's unpaid balance, and single loans normally cannot exceed $5,000.

Other Consumer Lending Institutions

The fastest-growing group of consumer installment lenders comprises credit unions, whose attractive interest rates on deposits and loans have swelled their membership greatly in recent years. Credit unions make a wide variety of loans for such diverse purposes as purchases of automobiles, vacations, medical expenses, home repair and modernization, and, more recently, mortgage credit for the purchase of new homes (see Exhibit 17–11).

EXHIBIT 17–11
Consumer-Related Loans Held by Credit Unions, Year-End
1980 ($ billions)

Type of Loan	Amount	Percent of Total
Automobile	$21.1	47.8%
Mobile home	0.5	1.1
Other installment loans	22.5	51.0
Totals.....................	$44.1	100.0%

SOURCE: Board of Governors of the Federal Reserve System, *Federal Reserve Bulletin*, June 1981.

Also making sizeable inroads into the consumer loan field in recent years have been savings and loan associations and mutual savings banks (see Exhibit 17–12). While these institutions have long been dominant in residential mortgage lending, they have aggressively expanded their portfolios of

EXHIBIT 17–12
**Consumer-Related Loans Held by Savings and Loan Associations
and Mutual Savings Banks, Year-End 1980 ($ billions)**

Type of Loan	Amount	Percent of Total
Mortgage loans:		
One-to-four family	$484.8	87.7%
Multifamily	55.3	10.0
Nonmortgage loans:		
Mobile home	2.7	0.5
Other installment loans	10.0	1.8
Totals	$552.8	100.0%

SOURCE: Board of Governors of the Federal Reserve System, *Federal Reserve Bulletin*, June 1981.

credit-card, education, home improvement, furniture, appliance, and mobile home loans over the past decade.[15]

FACTORS CONSIDERED IN MAKING CONSUMER LOANS

Consumer loans are considered one of the most profitable uses of funds for most financial institutions. There is evidence, however, that such loans usually carry greater risk than most other kinds of loans, and they are more costly to make per dollar of loan.[16] On the other hand, the lender often can offset these costs by charging higher interest rates. Consumer credit markets in many communities are less competitive than the market for business loans or for marketable securities, giving the lender something of an advantage.

The making of consumer loans is one of the most challenging aspects of modern financial management. It requires not only a thorough knowledge of household financial statements but also an ability to assess the *character* of the borrower and the likelihood that he or she will honor financial commitments in the future.[17] Over the years most loan officers have developed decision "rules of thumb" as an aid to processing and evaluating consumer loan applications. These decision rules often vary greatly with the financial institution doing the lending and the experience of each loan officer, but a few of the more common practices may be noted.

For example, many consumer loan officers insist that household debt (exclusive of housing costs) should not exceed a certain critical percentage of a family's monthly or annual gross income. A maximum of 15 to 20 percent of

---

[15] See Chapter 4 for a discussion of the lending policies and practices of credit unions, savings banks, and savings and loan associations.

[16] Credit investigations and record keeping are the principal costs associated with consumer lending. See, for example, Federal Reserve Bank of Boston, *Analysis of High-Earning Banks, 1978*, Functional Cost Analysis Program (7).

[17] For a discussion of the principal elements in the consumer lending decision, see Wood (25).

gross income is a common standard in this instance. For younger borrowers, without substantial assets to serve as collateral for a loan, a cosigner may be sought whose assets and financial standing represent more adequate security. The duration of employment of the borrower is often a critical factor, and many institutions will deny a loan request if the customer has been employed at his or her present job for less than a year.

The past payment record of a customer usually is the key indicator of character and the likelihood that the loan will be repaid in timely fashion. Many lenders refuse to make loans to those consumers who evidence "pyramiding of debt"—that is, borrowing from one financial institution to pay another. Evidence of sloppy money handling, such as unusually large balances carried on charge accounts or a heavy burden of installment payments, is regarded as a negative factor in the loan decision. Loan officers are particularly alert to evidence of a lack of credit integrity as reflected in frequent late payments or actual default on past loans. The *character* of the borrower is the single-most-important issue in the decision to grant or deny a consumer loan. Regardless of the strength of the borrower's financial position, if the customer lacks the willingness to repay his or her debt, then the lender has made a bad loan.

Most lenders feel that those who own valuable property such as land, buildings, or marketable securities are more reliable than those who do not own such property, especially if the property itself is pledged to secure the loan. For example, homeowners are usually considered to be better risks than those who rent. Moreover, a borrowers' chances of getting a loan usually are better if they do other business (such as maintain a deposit) with the lending institution. If more than one member of the family works, this is often viewed as a more-favorable factor than if the family depends upon one breadwinner who may become ill, die, or simply lose his or her job. Having a telephone at home is another positive factor in evaluating a loan application, since the telephone gives the lender an inexpensive way to contact the borrower. One way to lower the cost of a loan is for the consumer to pledge a bank deposit, marketable securities, or other liquid assets behind the loan. The disadvantage here is that such a pledge "ties up" the asset pledged as security until the loan is repaid.

FINANCIAL DISCLOSURE AND CONSUMER CREDIT

A number of important new laws have appeared in recent years designed to protect the consumer in dealings with lending institutions. One major area of emphasis in recent consumer legislation is *financial disclosure*—making all relevant information about the terms of a loan contract available to the borrower before a commitment is made. The basic assumption is that an informed borrower will be a wise user of credit. Moreover, if all important information is laid out "on the table" before a loan agreement is reached, this may encourage the consumer to shop around to find the cheapest and most-convenient sources of funds. However, there is considerable debate today on whether consumer-protection legislation has really accomplished its goals. Both lenders and borrowers are confronted with a confusing array of laws and regulations which encourage violations and may be of little benefit to the consumer.[18] (See Exhibit 17–13 for a summary of financial disclosure laws.)

EXHIBIT 17–13
Disclosure of Financial Information to the Consumer—a Summary of Recent Laws Affecting U.S. Consumer Lending Institutions

---

1. *Consumer Credit Protection Act* (Truth in Lending): banks and other lenders are required to tell the customer the true cost of a loan, indicated by the annual percentage rate (APR), and other essential terms of credit in simple, easily understood language.

2. *Fair Credit Billing Act:* The credit customer who feels a bill is wrong or desires more information may notify the creditor within 60 days and withhold payment of the contested amount until the dispute is settled. No finance charges may be levied on the disputed amount, and the creditor cannot report the account as delinquent. Payment for defective merchandise purchased on a credit card may be withheld provided the customer makes a good-faith effort to resolve the problem with the merchant. The creditor must acknowledge the customer's inquiry within 30 days.

3. *Consumer Leasing Act:* Personal property leased by an individual for more than four months for personal, family, or household use is subject to disclosure rules. Before agreeing to a lease, the customer must receive a written statement of costs (including the number and amount of regular payments, advance payments, maintenance costs, taxes, and other required fees) and be informed of any insurance required, terms for cancellation of the lease, penalties for late payment, and warranties.

4. *Fair Credit Reporting Act:* The consumer of credit is entitled to see his or her credit file, including his or her credit rating, and to dispute any items on it. When notified by a customer of an alleged inaccuracy in his or her credit file, the credit bureau involved must investigate the matter and modify or remove inaccurate data. The customer may include a statement of explanation of 100 words or less on any item in the credit file which he or she believes to be inaccurate, and sue if damaged by a violation of the law.

SOURCE: Peter S. Rose, "Social Responsibility in Banking: Pressures Intensify in the U.S.," *The Canadian Banker and ICB Review,* April 1979, pp. 62–67.

Truth in Lending

In 1968 Congress passed a watershed piece of legislation in the consumer-credit field—the Consumer Credit Protection Act, more widely known as "Truth in Lending." However, the Consumer Credit Protection Act covered more than just truthful disclosure by lenders of the terms of a loan. It defined and prohibited extortionate credit practices, limited garnishment of wages, and created a National Commission on Consumer Fi-

---

[18] Recent studies by Day and Brandt (4), Mandell (13, 14), and Parker and Shay (19) suggest that many of the goals sought by recent consumer-oriented financial legislation have not been achieved. Consumers rarely shop for credit and appear more concerned about the affordability of monthly payments on a loan than with how one lender's interest charge on a loan compares with that quoted by another. Survey evidence suggests that the majority of consumers are unaware of the rights and privileges granted them under recent federal financial legislation and see little practical benefit from these laws. See also Rose (21) and (22).

nance to oversee enforcement of the law. Shortly after the act was passed, federal regulatory agencies prepared new rules to implement and enforce the principles of truth in lending. The most famous of these is the Federal Reserve Board's Regulation Z.

Truth in Lending simply requires banks and other lenders to provide sufficient information about a credit contract, in easily understood terms, so that the consumer can make an intelligent decision about purchasing credit. The law does not tell the creditor how much to charge or to whom it may lend money. Rather, the lender is required to tell the customer the true cost of a loan and any other terms of the loan which might have an impact on the consumer's financial well-being.

At the same time the consumer was granted certain rights. For example, he or she has the right to sue the lender for failure to conform to the Consumer Credit Protection Act and its supporting regulations. Consumers have the right to cancel or rescind a credit agreement within three business days if their home is included as part of the collateral for a loan. This so-called right of rescission usually applies to the repair or remodeling of a home or the taking out of a second mortgage on an existing home. It does not cover an application for a first mortgage to make the initial purchase of a home, however.

Commercial banks, credit unions, finance companies, savings and loan associations, life insurance companies, mortgage bankers, retailers extending credit, auto dealers, and real estate brokers all fall under the provisions of Truth in Lending. Indeed, the law specifies that *anyone* providing or arranging credit in the ordinary course of their business must conform to its provisions. Still, some loans are exempted. The credit requested must be intended for personal, family, household, or agricultural purposes and result in a debt obligation repayable in more than four installments. Amounts in excess of $25,000 generally are not covered by the law unless real property is involved. Moreover, to receive protection under the law, the borrower must be a natural person rather than a corporation, partnership, estate, trust, or similar organization.

The most widely known provision of Truth in Lending is the requirement that a lender must tell the customer the annual percentage rate of interest (APR) charged on a loan. Lenders must disclose the total dollar cost associated with granting a loan—known as the *finance charge*—which is the sum of all charges the customer must pay as a condition for securing the loan. These charges may include credit investigation fees, insurance to protect the lender, and points on a mortgage loan. Once the finance charge is determined, it must then be converted into the APR by comparing it with the amount of the loan. The APR is really the ratio of the dollar finance charge to the declining unpaid balance of a loan, determined by the actuarial method.[19] Because all lenders must quote the APR, computed by the same method, this

---

[19] See Chapter 7 for a discussion of how the APR can be figured and Rose (21).

makes it easier (at least in theory) for the consumer to shop around and to purchase credit from the cheapest source available.

The concept of Truth in Lending has been extended in a number of directions in recent years. One important new dimension concerns *advertising*. A lender who advertises one attractive feature of a credit package to consumers must also disclose other relevant credit terms. For example, if a car dealer advertises its low down payments, it must also disclose other aspects of its loans, such as how many payments are required, what the amount of each payment is, and how many months or years are involved. One obvious weakness of the original Truth in Lending bill was its failure to protect the public against *discriminatory* advertising. That legal loophole was closed in the mid-1970s, as we will soon see.

Fair Credit Reporting Act

A further extension of Truth in Lending occurred when the Fair Credit Reporting Act was passed by Congress in 1970. This law entitles consumers to have access to their credit files, which are kept by thousands of credit bureaus active in the United States. These credit bureaus supply subscribing lenders with vital information on amounts owed and the payment records and credit ratings of individuals and families. They aid greatly in reducing the risks inherent in consumer lending. However, because the information credit bureaus supply has a substantial impact on the availability of credit to individuals and families, their activities and especially the accuracy of the information they provide have been brought under closer scrutiny in recent years by federal and state regulatory authorities.

Under the provisions of the Fair Credit Reporting Act, the consumer is entitled to review his or her credit file at any time. Moreover, he or she may challenge any items which appear in the file and demand an investigation. The credit bureau must respond and, if inaccuracies exist, remove or modify the incorrect information. If the consumer determines that an item in the credit file is damaging and requires clarification, he or she may insert a statement of 100 words or less explaining the consumer's version of the matter. Data in the file may be shown only to properly identified individuals for approved purposes or upon direct written request from the consumer. No information may be disclosed to anyone after a period of seven years unless the consumer is seeking a loan of $50,000 or more, purchasing life insurance, or applying for a job paying $20,000 or more per year, or has declared personal bankruptcy. The consumer may sue if damaged by incorrect information in his or her credit file.

Fair Credit Billing Act

In 1974 Congress passed the Fair Credit Billing Act, which amended the original Truth in Lending law. The new amendment came in response to a torrent of consumer complaints about credit billing errors, especially on credit cards. Many individuals found that they were being billed for items never purchased or received, that some merchants would not respond when contacted about billing errors, and that finance charges were frequently assessed even though the consumer claimed no responsibility for charges listed on the billing statement. Consumers seemed to have no effective way of resolving billing disputes without considerable cost, frustration, and inconvenience.

The Fair Credit Billing Act requires a creditor to respond to a customer's billing inquiry within 30 days. In most cases, the dispute must be resolved within 90 days. The customer may withhold payment of any amounts in dispute, though he or she must pay any portions of a bill which are not in dispute. However, no creditor can report a customer as "delinquent" over amounts of a bill which are the subject of disagreement. A creditor who fails to respond to the customer's inquiry or makes no effort to settle the dispute may forfeit the disputed sum up to $50.

Consumer Leasing Act

In 1976 Congress passed the Consumer Leasing Act, which requires disclosure by leasing companies of the essential terms of any lease involving personal property. Short-term leases are excluded, but all those with terms over four months are covered by the law. The leased property must be designed for personal, family, or household use. The applicant (or lessee) is entitled to a written statement of all charges, specifying the number and amount of payments, any property maintenance costs, taxes, or other fees. The customer must be told about any insurance required, the terms under which the lease may be cancelled, any penalties for late payments, and any express warranties which go with the property. The lease customer is entitled to sue for damages plus court costs if the requirements of the law are not met.

CREDIT DISCRIMINATION LAWS

The civil rights movement has also had an impact on the granting of consumer loans in recent years. Among the most important new civil rights laws involving consumer credit are the Equal Credit Opportunity Act of 1974 and its amendments in 1976, the Fair Housing Act of 1968, the Home Mortgage Disclosure Act of 1975, and the Community Reinvestment Act of 1977. The fundamental purpose of these laws is to outlaw discrimination in the granting of credit due to the age, color, marital status, national origin, race, religious affiliation, or sex of the borrower. They are motivated by growing public support for fair and equal treatment in both public and private transactions and a greater measure of social responsibility in the allocation of credit. These new laws represent a major shift of focus in the regulation of the financial marketplace. Heretofore, the laws and regulations governing the behavior of lenders have stressed safety and the making of sound loans. Today, however, the lender must be able to justify in terms of fairness and objectivity, not only the loans that are made, but also those that are not made.

Community Reinvestment Act

One of the most important and controversial pieces of financial legislation in recent years is the Community Reinvestment Act, signed into law by President Jimmy Carter on October 12, 1977. Under its terms financial institutions are required to make an "affirmative effort" to meet the credit needs of low- and middle-income customers, including households, small businesses, farms, and ranches. Moreover, the regulatory authorities are required to consider the performance of lending institutions in meeting these community credit needs when processing applications for mergers, new branch offices, corporate charters, and holding company acquisitions by these same lending institutions.

Each commercial and savings banks must define its own local "trade territory" and describe the services that it offers or is planning to offer in that local area. Once a year each institution must prepare an updated map which delineates the trade territory served, without deliberately excluding low- or moderate-income neighborhoods. The lending institution's board of directors must adopt a CRA Statement, which specifies that lender's trade territory and lists the principal types of credit offered in that territory. A notice must be posted in the lobby, alerting customers to their rights and where the institution's CRA Statement may be found. Customers are entitled to make written comments concerning the lender's performance in meeting local credit needs. These comments must be retained on the premises for at least two years and be available for public inspection. The basic purpose of the Community Reinvestment Act is to avoid "gerrymandering" out low-income neighborhoods and other areas that the lender may consider undesirable.

Equal Credit Opportunity Act

The Equal Credit Opportunity Act of 1974 forbids discrimination against credit applicants on the basis of age, sex, marital status, race, color, religion, national origin, receipt of public assistance, or good-faith exercise of rights under the federal consumer credit protection laws. Major beneficiaries of this law are women, who no longer can be denied credit solely on the basis of their sex, age, family plans, or the fact that they are or are not wage earners. Women may receive credit under their own signature, based on their own personal credit record and earnings, without having the husband's joint signature. Credit applicants must be notified of the approval or denial of their loan request within 30 days of filing a completed application. The reasons for denial of a loan application must be set forth in writing, and the lender may not request information on the borrower's race, color, religion, national origin, or sex, except in the case of residential mortgage loans.

Fair Housing and Home Mortgage Disclosure Acts

Two other important antidiscrimination laws are the Fair Housing Act, which forbids discrimination in lending for the purchase or renovation of residential property, and the Home Mortgage Disclosure Act (HMDA). The latter requires financial institutions to disclose to the public the amount and location of their home mortgage and home improvement loans. HMDA was designed to eliminate "redlining," in which some lenders would mark out areas of a community as unsuitable for mortgage loans because of low income, high crime rates, or other negative factors. Not only was the law supposed to increase home mortgage loans to low- and moderate-income neighborhoods, but it was also intended to encourage the public to divert its funds away from those institutions practicing redlining. Unfortunately, this law reveals information about the *supply* of mortgage credit but not the demand. Also, nondeposit mortgage lenders are exempted from its provisions even though they are often significant factors in the local real estate market.

Both HMDA and the Fair Housing Act require nondiscriminatory advertising by lenders. No longer can a consumer lending institution direct its advertisements solely to high-income neighborhoods to the exclusion of other potential customers. When loans to purchase, construct, improve, repair, or maintain a dwelling are advertised, the lender must state that such loans will be made without regard to race, color, religion, sex, or national origin. On written advertising, an "Equal Housing" symbol must be attached. Clearly, then, in advertising the availability of credit, in accepting and evaluating loan applications, and in the actual granting of credit, the principles of civil rights and nondiscrimination apply. Lenders are free to choose who will receive credit, but that decision must be made within the framework of the nation's social goals.

SUMMARY AND CONCLUSIONS

One of the most remarkable developments in the financial system over the past century is the awakening of the consumer as a borrower and lender of funds. Better educated and more aware of their financial opportunities today, householders have become the principal source of loanable funds flowing into the financial markets and also one of the most important borrowers. Consumer holdings of financial assets totaled almost $4.5 trillion at year-end 1980, with more than $2.5 trillion of this total held in the form of either corporate stock or as savings deposits at banks, savings and loan associations, credit unions, and other thrift institutions. On the other side of the balance sheet, consumer debt reached almost $1.5 trillion in 1980—a figure second only to the total borrowings of business firms and much larger than the combined debt of federal, state, and local governments.

There is some concern today that households have become too deeply mired in debt, that too high a proportion of family incomes is committed to mortgage payments on a home, installment contracts for autos, furniture, and appliances, and debt to cover living expenses. Those who see financial trouble ahead for the household sector point out, for example, that the ratio of household debt to financial assets has more than doubled over the past three decades. While consumer debt figures certainly bear close watching, especially in times of economic uncertainty, these fears must be gauged against the purposes for which consumers borrow today. Three fifths of all consumer debt consists of residential mortgages; for many families today, their residence is their most important asset. In fact, ownership of residential property has been one of the most-effective hedges against inflation open to individuals and families in recent years.

The growing role of the consumer in the financial system has brought with it greater political influence. The 1960s and 1970s ushered in landmark pieces of federal legislation to aid the consumer in borrowing and lending funds. On the borrowing side, such laws as the Consumer Credit Protection Act of 1968 (''Truth in Lending''), the Fair Credit Billing Act (1974), the Consumer Leasing Act (1976), and the Fair Credit Reporting Act (1971) have supported the rights of consumers to know what they are being charged for credit, that their credit complaints are heard and acted upon, and how their financial affairs are being monitored and evaluated by the financial community. As a result of such laws as the Community Reinvestment Act (1977), the Equal Credit Opportunity Act (1974), the Fair Housing Act (1968), and the Home Mortgage Disclosure Act (1975), lenders must make an ''affirmative effort'' to make credit available to all segments of their local communities without regard to the age, sex, marital status, race, color, religion, or national origin of the borrower. Consumers with the support of the federal government are asking today not only to be told more about the cost of credit but also why credit is denied to some and granted to others.

Until 1980, consumers were largely neglected on the financial-asset side of the ledger. Interest-rate ceilings (such as the Federal Reserve Board's Regulation Q) severely limited the yields banks and other deposit-type financial institutions could pay on consumer savings deposits. Federal banking laws have prohibited interest payments on checking accounts since the Great Depression of the 1930s. Consumers soon discovered that the returns they were earning on thrift deposits were so far below the rate of inflation that the purchasing power of their financial reserves was rapidly declining. Many switched their savings into gold, silver, precious stones, real estate, and other more-speculative investments. Moreover, due to restrictive interest-rate ceilings (usury laws) imposed by the states on installment and mortgage loans, consumers found that the credit they needed to supplement their incomes was simply not available.

A rising chorus of consumer complaints led to passage of the Depository Institutions Deregulation and Monetary Control Act of 1980. This sweeping piece of consumer-oriented financial legislation legalized interest-bearing checking accounts (NOWs), authorized automatic transfers of funds from savings to checking accounts, set up regulatory machinery for a phaseout of deposit interest-rate ceilings, lifted ceiling rates on home mortgage loans, and increased the amount of insurance behind the public's deposits held in commercial banks, savings banks, savings and loan associations, and credit unions.

Unquestionably, there is more to come. Consumers have awakened financially to an awareness, not only of the critical role credit and savings play in determining their own individual economic well-being, but to their powerful collective influence on the whole financial system. The consumer now seems well aware that decisions made in the financial sector help to determine how many and what kinds of jobs are available, the rate of inflation and economic growth, and even the outcome of the great social issues of modern-day society—better housing, improved educational facilities, equality and justice under the law, and freedom of economic opportunity. For the most part, modern governments have shown a strong determination to ensure that the individual consumer is treated fairly in the financial marketplace and that the financial system contributes to, rather than impedes, the progress of peaceful social change. Unfortunately, we cannot yet determine whether the recent plethora of consumer-oriented financial laws have brought the laudable benefits hoped for by their authors, or simply threaten to mire our financial system in a debilitating swamp of bureaucracy and red tape. If the new rules reduce incentives in the financial community to compete, to offer new services, and to price existing financial services commensurate with the dictates of the marketplace, then both the consumer and society as a whole may have lost more than they have gained. On that important issue, we must await the impartial verdict afforded by time.

STUDY QUESTIONS

1. Which sector of the economy provides the largest amount of loanable funds for borrowers to draw upon? Does this sector make primarily direct loans or indirect loans to borrowers?

2. What is the most important financial asset held by households? What proportion of total household financial investments does this asset represent? What financial asset is in second place in household portfolios?

3. What are Regulation Q interest-rate ceilings? In what ways do they discriminate against the small saver? Create problems for financial institutions whose deposits are subject to the rate ceilings? Lead to a misallocation of financial resources?

  4. Summarize the main provisions of the Depository Institutions Deregulation and Monetary Control Act of 1980 affecting consumers.

  5. Define the following terms:
  a. NOWs.
  b. ATS.
  c. Share drafts.
  In what ways do these financial services benefit the consumer? What kinds of problems might they create for financial institutions offering the service?

  6. How much money do U.S. households owe today? Do you believe American consumers are too heavily in debt? Why or why not?

  7. Into what broad categories is consumer borrowing normally divided? Which is most important, and why?

  8. Discuss the factors which influence the volume of borrowing by individuals and families. What role do you believe inflation plays in the borrowing and saving decisions of households today?

  9. List the principal consumer lending institutions in the United States. What types of consumer loans does each institution prefer to grant?

  10. What factors do consumer lending institutions usually look at when evaluating a loan application? Why?

  11. What is Truth in Lending? Describe the law's major features and explain why it was enacted.

  12. What protections are offered the consumer under the Fair Credit Billing Act? Consumer Leasing Act? Fair Credit Reporting Act? Why?

  13. What are the principal purposes of the Community Reinvestment Act? Equal Credit Opportunity Act? Fair Housing Act? Home Mortgage Disclosure Act? Assess the benefits and costs of these pieces of social responsibility legislation.

SELECTED REFERENCES

  1. Ando, Albert, and Franco Modigliani. "The 'Life Cycle' Hypothesis of Savings: Aggregate Implications and Tests." *American Economic Review*, March 1963, pp. 55–84.

  2. Board of Governors of the Federal Reserve System. *Consumer Handbook to Credit Protection Laws*. Washington, D.C.: 1978.

  3. Board of Governors of the Federal Reserve System. *1977 Consumer Credit Survey*. Washington, D.C.: 1978.

  4. Day, George S., and William K. Brandt. "Consumer Research and the Evaluation of Information Disclosure Requirements: The Case of Truth in Lending." *Journal of Consumer Research*, June 1974, pp. 21–32.

  5. Dunkelberg, William C., and James Stevenson. *Durable Goods Ownership and the Rate of Return*. Washington, D.C.: National Commission on Consumer Finance, 1972.

  6. Dyl, Edward A. "Prepayment Penalties Inherent in the Rule of 78s—A Truth-in-Lending Issue." *Journal of Bank Research*, Spring 1977, pp. 16–21.

  7. Federal Reserve Bank of Boston. *Analysis of High-Earning Banks, 1978*. Functional Cost Analysis Program.

8. Federal Reserve Bank of Chicago. "ABC's of Figuring Interest." *Business Conditions,* September 1973, pp. 3–11.

9. Godfrey, John M., and B. Frank Kind. "Money Market Certificates: An Innovation in Consumer Deposits." *Economic Review,* Federal Reserve Bank of Atlanta, May-June 1979, pp. 59–64.

10. Goldsmith, Raymond W. *A Study of Savings in the United States.* 3 vols. New York: National Bureau of Economic Research and Princeton University Press, 1955–56.

11. Hayes, Douglas A. *Bank Lending Policies: Domestic and International.* Ann Arbor: University of Michigan Bureau of Business Research, 1971.

12. Katona, George, Lewis Mandell, and Joy Schiedeskamp. *1970 Survey of Consumer Finances.* Ann Arbor: University of Michigan Press, 1971.

13. Mandell, Lewis. "Consumer Knowledge and Understanding of Consumer Credit." *Journal of Consumer Affairs,* Summer 1973, pp. 23–26.

14. _____. "Consumer Perception of Incurred Interest Rates: An Empirical Test of the Efficiency of the Truth-in-Lending Law." *Journal of Finance,* March 1974, pp. 217–25.

15. Matson, Ray H. "Finance Company Loans." In *The Bankers Handbook,* edited by William H. Baughn and Charles E. Walker. Homewood, Ill.: Richard D. Irwin, 1966.

16. McNees, Stephen K. "The 1979 Consumer Spending Spree: New Era or Last Gasp?" *New England Economic Review,* Federal Reserve Bank of Boston, May-June 1980, pp. 5–21.

17. National Commission on Consumer Finance. *Consumer Credit in the United States.* Washington, D.C., 1972.

18. O'Brien, James M. "The Household as a Saver." *Business Review,* Federal Reserve Bank of Philadelphia, June 1971, pp. 14–23.

19. Parker, George G. C., and Robert P. Shay. "Some Factors Affecting Awareness of Annual Percentage Rates in Consumer Installment Credit Transactions." *Journal of Finance,* March 1974, pp. 217–25.

20. Rose, Peter S. "The NOW Row." *The Canadian Banker and ICB Review,* June 1979, pp. 60–68.

21. _____. "Social Responsibility in Banking: Pressures Intensify in the U.S." *The Canadian Banker and the ICB Review,* April 1979, pp. 62–67.

22. _____. "Credit Discrimination Under Attack." *The Canadian Banker and ICB Review,* June 1979, pp. 70–75.

23. _____. "Bank Cards: The Promise and The Peril." *The Canadian Banker and ICB Review,* December 1978, pp. 62–67.

24. Saxon, Joyce, and Alonzo Sibert. "Proposed Guidelines for Truth in Lending Compliance." *Issues in Bank Regulation,* Autumn 1977, pp. 20–25.

25. Seiders, David. "Credit-Card and Check-Credit Plans at Commercial Banks." *Federal Reserve Bulletin,* September 1973, pp. 646–53.

26. Steinberg, Edward I. "Consumer Credit, 1960–80." *Survey of Current Business,* February 1981, pp. 14–18.

27. Wood, Oliver G., Jr. *Commercial Banking,* New York: D. Van Nostrand, 1978.

18

The Residential
Mortgage Market

One of the most important goals for many American families is to own their own home. Besides the psychic benefits of privacy and a feeling of belonging to the local community, home ownership has conferred important financial and economic benefits upon those families and individuals both able and willing to make the investment. The market value of single-family residences has risen substantially faster than the rate of inflation over the long term, offering individuals and families of even modest means one of the few effective long-term hedges against inflation.[1] Moreover, the interest cost on home mortgages is tax deductible, reducing significantly the after-tax interest rate levied on residential mortgage loans.

Unfortunately for those families seeking home ownership, the residential mortgage market has shifted from an accommodative posture to one of extreme credit restraint, with funds available only to a limited few over the past decade. Loan-value ratios have declined sharply, while mortgage interest rates repeatedly have broken through previous record highs to reach unprecedented levels. The resulting declines in residential construction and employment have reverberated throughout the economy. In this chapter we take a close look at this often troubled and most important sector of the consumer-related financial markets.

---

[1] A recent study by Salomon Brothers, the prestigious New York investment banking firm, indicated that single-family residences increased in value an average of 9.1 percent a year over the 1968–78 period. while the overall cost-of-living index (CPI) rose about 6.2 percent a year over the same period. See Chapter 11 for a discussion of this study and the implications of inflation for lenders and borrowers.

RECENT TRENDS IN NEW HOME PRICES AND THE TERMS OF MORTGAGE LOANS

We can get a glimpse of the tremendous pressures buffeting the market for residential mortgages today by looking at recent trends in the prices of new homes and the cost of financing them. Exhibit 18–1 provides us with recent data on the average prices of new single-family residences in the United States and the average terms quoted nationwide on *conventional* mortgage loans. A conventional mortgage loan is not guaranteed by the government but is purely a private loan contract between the home buyer and the lending institution. In this case, the lender of funds bears the risk that the home buyer will default on principal or interest payments associated with a mortgage loan, forcing foreclosure and resale of the home. In contrast, mortgage loans issued through the Federal Housing Administration (FHA) or Veterans Administration (VA) are partially guaranteed as to principal and interest by the federal government and are generally used to finance low-cost and moderately priced housing.

As shown in Exhibit 18–1, the average purchase price of a conventional single-family residence in the United States more than doubled between 1974 and 1980, climbing above $83,000 in the latter year. At the same time, lenders of funds, confronted with increased uncertainty regarding inflation, interest rates, and the economy, reduced the percentage of a new home's purchase price they were willing to lend. The loan-to-value (or loan/price) ratio rose from 74 percent in 1974 to 76 percent in 1977 but then fell to 73 percent in 1980. Thus home buyers were forced to come up with larger down payments both in total dollars and relative to the market value of a new home.

We note also from Exhibit 18–1 that mortgage lenders were willing to extend credit for longer periods as a partial offset to the sharply increased cost of new homes and declining loan-value ratios. The average maturity of conventional home-mortgage loans climbed from about 26 years in 1974 to 28 years in 1980. Extra fees and charges ("points") levied by lenders as a condition for making mortgage credit available also rose sharply, from about 1.3 percent of the amount of a conventional mortgage loan to 2.1 percent—an increase of more than 60 percent. The average contract interest rate on conventional mortgages climbed from an 8.7 percent average during 1974 to 12¼ percent in 1980. During the fall of 1981, conventional contract interest rates on conventional new-home loans climbed into the 16 to 17 percent range but then eased back slightly as the year drew to a close.

The combination of higher home-mortgage interest rates and higher market prices for new homes greatly increased monthly mortgage payments and shut many families out of the housing market. For example, a family putting 10 percent down on a $40,000 home in 1974, when conventional home-mortgage rates ranged from about 8½ to 9 percent, would have faced monthly payments (including taxes and insurance) in the $350 to $400 range. During 1980,

EXHIBIT 18–1
Prices and Yields of Conventional Home Mortgage Loans

	Terms and Yields						
Item	1974	1975	1976	1977	1978	1979	1980
Primary Market:							
Conventional mortgages on new homes:							
Purchase price ($ thousands)	$40.1	$44.6	$48.4	54.3	$62.6	$74.4	$83.5
Amount of loan ($ thousands)	29.8	33.3	35.9	40.5	45.9	59.3	59.3
Loan/price ratio (%)	74.3	74.7	74.2	76.3	75.3	73.3	73.3
Maturity (years)	26.3	26.8	27.2	27.9	28.0	28.2	28.2
Fees and charges (% of loan)	1.30	1.54	1.44	1.33	1.39	2.16	2.10
Contract interest rate (%)	8.71	8.75	8.76	8.80	9.30	10.48	12.25
Yield—FHLBB series	8.92	9.01	8.99	9.01	9.54	10.77	12.65
Yield—HUD series	9.22	9.10	8.99	8.95	9.68	11.15	13.95

SOURCE: Board of Governors of the Federal Reserve System, *Federal Reserve Bulletin*, June 1981.

however, the same house would have cost about $80,000 with mortgage rates in the 12 to 13 percent range, so that monthly home mortgage payments would have averaged $800 to $1,000, depending on the specific terms of the loan. There is also evidence that the prices of new single-family homes have risen faster than family incomes in recent years, making home ownership less affordable for the average American family.[2]

Several factors account for this dramatic escalation in the cost of home ownership. Certainly, inflation has played a key role in driving up building costs, especially the prices of lumber and other building materials, and this increase has been passed on to the consumer. On the demand side, a substantial rise in the number of new family formations occurred during the 1970s. Children born during the great postwar baby boom of the 1940s and 50s began to establish their own families during the latter 60s and the 70s. An estimated 32 million Americans reached 30 years of age during the 1970s alone. Therefore, while the U.S. birth rate dropped to the lowest level in history within the past decade, the sharp increase in new families and in numbers of children born into those new families dramatically increased the demand for housing, especially low- and medium-priced homes. At the same time, the proportion of the U.S. population represented by middle-aged Americans in their 40s and 50s began to decline. Yet, historically, this group has provided the bulk of savings out of which home-mortgage lenders can make new loans. In fact, during 1979 the ratio of savings to personal income in the United States fell to the lowest level since World War II. This combination of increased demand for new family residences and a smaller savings flow has sharply raised the cost of housing and diminished the financial attractiveness of single-family homes.

THE STRUCTURE OF THE MORTGAGE MARKET

Volume of Mortgage Loans

Mortgages are among the most important securities in the financial system. The total of all mortgages outstanding in the United States was close

---

[2] A study by Miller (16) finds that between 1965 and 1975 median prices of new single-family homes rose at just about the same rate as median family income. By 1978, however, housing prices were 2.4 times their 1967 levels, while income was only 2.2 times the 1967 figure. Even after adjustment for improvements in quality, rising new-home prices outstripped median family income by a substantial margin. However, Miller finds that the *total* cost of home ownership as measured by the consumer price index has increased at approximately the same rate as family income, with homeowners aided by the income-tax deductibility of mortgage-interest payments and property taxes.

Interestingly enough, as the 1980s began, there was evidence of a softening in home prices and, in some cases, an inflation-adjusted decline in real estate values, particularly in major metropolitan areas. The downward price adjustments were modest—about 2 to 5 percent on an annual basis—but broke a long-term uptrend in housing prices which prevailed for more than 30 years. Record-high mortgage-interest rates coupled with the sharply higher cost of commuting from remote suburban areas appear to be leading causes of the recent softening in housing prices.

EXHIBIT 18–2
Total Mortgage Debt
Outstanding in the United
States, Year-End ($ billions)

Year	Amount
1950	$ 72.8
1955	129.9
1960	206.8
1965	325.8
1970	451.7
1975	741.5
1980	1,451.8

SOURCES: Board of Governors
of the Federal Reserve System,
Annual Statistical Digest, 1971–
75 and *Federal Reserve Bulletin,*
selected issues.

to $1.5 trillion at year-end 1980 (see Exhibit 18–2). This total represented 55 percent of the nation's gross national product (GNP) and made the mortgage market the largest primary-security market in the United States. In fact, the sum of mortgage loans outstanding exceeded the combined total of all money market instruments. Moreover, the mortgage market has grown rapidly in recent years under the combined pressures of inflation and heavy credit demands. During the 1960s the volume of mortgages outstanding more than doubled, and it tripled during the 1970s. Thus, an enormously important market within the financial system became even more important as time progressed.

Residential versus Nonresidential Mortgage Loans

The mortgage market can be divided into two major segments: (1) *residential,* which encompasses all loans secured by single-family homes and other dwelling units; and (2) *nonresidential,* which includes loans against business and farm properties. Which of these two sectors is the most important? As Exhibit 18–3 shows, loans to finance the building and purchase of homes, apartments, and other residential units dominate the American mortgage market. In 1980 residential mortgage loans on one-to-four-family properties and multifamily structures represented three fourths of all mortgage loans outstanding. Mortgages on commercial and farm properties accounted for the remaining one fourth of all mortgages issued.

In recent years the residential portion of the market has grown faster than nonresidential mortgages. As shown in Exhibit 18–4, the most-dramatic growth occurred in loans on one-to-four-family properties, which rose from 61 percent of total mortgage debt outstanding in 1975 to 66 percent in 1980.

EXHIBIT 18–3
Mortgage Loans Outstanding, End of Period, 1980 ($ billions)

Property	Amount	Percent
Residential properties:		
1–4 family	$ 960.4	66.2%
Multifamily	136.6	9.4
Total residential	$1,097.0	75.6%
Nonresidential properties:		
Commercial	$ 258.3	17.8%
Farm	96.5	6.6
Total nonresidential	$ 354.8	24.4%
All properties	$1,451.8	100.0%

SOURCE: Board of Governors of the Federal Reserve System, *Federal Reserve Bulletin,* selected issues.

EXHIBIT 18–4
Recent Growth in Mortgage Loans

Property	1975	1976	1977	1978	1979	1980
In millions of dollars:						
1–4 family	$490,761	$555,657	$ 656,566	$ 765,217	$ 878,931	$ 960,422
Multifamily	100,601	104,516	111,841	121,138	128,852	136,580
Commercial	159,289	171,223	189,274	211,851	236,451	258,338
Farm	50,877	57,031	65,824	71,206	82,516	96,500
Total	$801,537	$888,427	$1,023,505	$1,169,412	$1,326,750	$1,451,840
Percent of total:						
1–4 family	61.0%	62.5%	64.2%	65.4%	66.2%	66.2%
Multifamily	12.6	11.8	10.9	10.4	9.7	9.4
Commercial	20.0	19.3	18.5	18.1	17.8	17.8
Farm	6.4	6.4	6.4	6.1	6.2	6.6
Total	100.0%	100.0%	100.0%	100.0%	100.0%	100.0%

SOURCE: Board of Governors of the Federal Reserve System, *Federal Reserve Bulletin,* selected issues.

This category of mortgages is dominated by single-family home loans, which increased significantly due to the rapid growth of new family formations and the effects of inflation.

The 1970s also ushered in a speculative investment boom in the building of condominiums, duplexes, triplexes, and smaller residential structures by wealthy investors. Much of this speculative construction activity has been aimed at the rental housing market, designed especially to appeal to college students and low- to middle-income families. Unlike owner-occupied residences, rental properties can be depreciated so that *both* mortgage-loan costs and annual depreciation expenses are legitimate income tax deductions for investors in such properties. As reflected in Exhibit 18–4, while one-to-four-family residential mortgages were capturing a larger share of the total market, both multifamily (apartment) and commercial mortgage loans were declining in relative importance.

Because residential mortgages dominate the market, it should not be surprising that households are the leading mortgage borrower, as shown in Exhibit 18–5. The next-largest group of borrowers—nonfinancial

EXHIBIT 18–5
Mortgage Debt Classified by Borrower

Borrower Group	1975	1976	1977	1978	1979	1980
In millions of dollars:						
Households	$749.0	$540.6	$ 634.0	$ 738.2	$ 847.0	$ 940.0
Nonprofit institutions	24.8	25.8	26.9	27.9	28.9	30.0
Nonfinancial corporations	152.0	165.4	184.5	207.3	233.9	248.9
Farms	50.9	57.0	65.7	76.0	93.4	92.0
Nonfarm noncorporate	86.7	90.2	99.2	109.0	117.8	123.0
Other	8.2	10.2	13.2	14.0	12.8	11.8
Totals	$801.6	$889.2	$1,023.5	$1,172.4	$1,333.8	$1,447.
Percent of total:						
Households	59.7%	60.8%	61.9%	63.0%	63.5%	65.0%
Nonprofit institutions	3.1	2.9	2.6	2.4	2.2	2.1
Nonfinancial corporations	19.0	18.6	18.1	17.7	17.5	17.0
Farms	6.4	6.4	6.4	6.5	7.0	6.0
Nonfarm noncorporate	10.8	10.1	9.7	9.3	8.8	8.0
Other	1.0	1.2	1.3	1.1	1.0	0.0
Totals	100.0%	100.0%	100.0%	100.0%	100.0%	100.0%

SOURCE: Federal Reserve Board, *Flow of Funds Accounts: Assets and Liabilities Outstanding*, September 1981.

corporations—is a distant second. Moreover, the share of the market represented by households has risen in recent years due to an upward surge in the demand for housing, while other mortgage borrowers have declined in relative importance.

MORTGAGE-LENDING INSTITUTIONS

In the years before World War II mortgages were one of the most widely held securities in the financial system, comparable to stock in the great diversity of investors who chose to add these loans to their portfolios. Individuals were then the dominant mortgage investors, with financial institutions in second place. However, the rapid growth of commercial banks, savings and loan associations, mutual savings banks, and insurance companies as major mortgage lenders during the past three decades has forced individual investors into the background. As we will see later in this chapter, however, the 1980s have ushered in more-creative types of mortgage financing, in which individuals are once again playing a larger role as lenders and investors in mortgages.

Exhibit 18–6 shows the total amounts of mortgage loans held by various investor groups in 1980. Clearly, savings and loan associations are the prin-

EXHIBIT 18–6
Major Lenders in the U.S. Mortgage Market, Year-End 1980

Lender Group	Volume of Mortgage Loans Held ($ billions)	Percent of Total
Savings and loan associations	$ 502.8	34.6%
Commercial banks	264.6	18.2
Life insurance companies.....................	131.1	9.0
Mutual savings banks	98.8	6.8
Mortgage pools or trusts.....................	142.2	9.8
Federal and related government agencies	114.3	7.9
Individuals and others*	198.0	13.6
Totals.................................	$1,451.8	100.0%

* Includes mortgage companies, REITs, state and local credit agencies, state and local government retirement funds, noninsured pension funds, credit unions, and U.S. government agencies for which amounts are small or separate data are not available.
SOURCE: Board of Governors of the Federal Reserve System, *Federal Reserve Bulletin*, June 1981.

cipal mortgage-lending institution in the United States, accounting for about 35 percent of all mortgage loans outstanding. Commercial banks rank a distant second, holding about half as many mortgage loans as S&L's, followed by life insurance companies and mutual savings banks. In general, the relative share of the mortgage market accounted for by commercial banks and savings and loan associations has risen, while life insurance companies and mutual savings banks have lost ground (see Exhibit 18–7). In part, these changes reflect the rapid growth of the southern and western regions of the United States, where commercial banks and savings and loans historically have dominated mortgage lending. They also reflect the upward surge in loans on single-family residences and small multifamily structures in recent years—areas where both commercial banks and savings and loan associations make a heavy volume of new mortgage credit available.

THE ROLES PLAYED BY FINANCIAL INSTITUTIONS IN THE MORTGAGE MARKET

Mortgage lenders tend to specialize in the types of loans they grant, and some are far more important to the residential market than in commercial

EXHIBIT 18–7
Changes in Mortgage Holdings of Four Major Lending Institutions

Financial Institution	1975	1976	1977	1978	1979	1980
In millions of dollars:						
Commercial banks	$136,186	$151,326	$178,979	$214,045	$245,187	$264,602
Mutual savings banks	77,249	81,639	88,104	95,157	98,908	99,827
Savings and loan associations	278,590	323,130	381,163	432,808	475,688	502,812
Life insurance companies	89,168	91,555	96,765	106,167	118,784	131,145
Totals	$581,193	$647,650	$745,011	$848,177	$938,567	$998,386
Percent of total:						
Commercial banks	23.4%	23.4%	24.0%	25.2%	26.1%	26.5%
Mutual savings banks	13.3	12.6	11.8	11.2	10.5	10.0
Savings and loan associations	47.9	49.9	51.2	51.0	50.7	50.4
Life insurance companies	15.4	14.1	13.0	12.5	12.7	13.1
Totals	100.0%	100.0%	100.0%	100.0%	100.0%	100.0%

SOURCE: Board of Governors of the Federal Reserve System, *Federal Reserve Bulletin*, June 1981.

mortgage lending. Moreover, even within the residential lending field, different institutional lenders will favor one type of mortgage—for example, conventional versus government guaranteed—over another and also desire a certain range of maturities. Some lenders are organized to deal with home-mortgage borrowers one at a time, while others may prefer to acquire large packages of mortgages associated with major residential building projects. In the sections that follow, the roles played by each of the principal residential mortgage-lending institutions are examined.

Savings and Loan Associations

Savings and loan associations are predominantly *local* lenders, making the majority of their mortgage loans in the communities where their offices are located. Moreover, S&Ls usually service the mortgage loans they make rather than turning that task over to a mortgage bank or trust company. Servicing a mortgage involves maintaining ownership and financial records on the mortgaged property, receiving installment payments from the borrower or an agent of the borrower, checking on the mortgaged property to ensure that its value is maintained, and, in the event of borrower default, foreclosing on the property to collect any unpaid balance on the loan. While, historically, S&Ls have preferred single-family home mortgages, they have diversified their portfolios in recent years to include many new kinds of assets, some mortgage related and some not (see Exhibit 18–8). Prominent

EXHIBIT 18–8
Mortgage Loans Held by Savings and Loan Associations, Year-End 1975, 1978, 1979, and 1980 ($ billions)

	1975		1978		1979		1980	
Property	Amount	Percent	Amount	Percent	Amount	Percent	Amount	Percent
1–4-family dwellings	$223.9	80.4%	$365.1	82.3%	$394.3	82.9%	$419.4	83.4%
Multifamily units	25.5	9.1	36.1	8.3	37.6	7.9	38.1	7.6
Commercial	27.1	10.5	40.5	9.4	43.8	9.2	45.3	9.0
Totals*	$278.6	100.0%	$432.8	100.0%	$475.7	100.0%	$502.8	100.0%

* Columns may not add to totals due to rounding.
SOURCE: Board of Governors of the Federal Reserve System, *Federal Reserve Bulletin,* selected issues.

on the list are mobile home loans, mortgage credit for the purchase of duplexes and other multifamily housing units, apartment loans, and consumer installment loans for the purchase of automobiles, furniture, and home appliances.

Savings and loans associations provide more residential mortgage credit than any other lender. For example, at year-end 1980 savings and loan associations held 44 percent of all mortgage loans outstanding on one-to-four-family dwellings and 28 percent of all loans secured by multifamily dwellings. In total, S&Ls accounted for 42 percent of the total volume of all residential mortgages outstanding in the United States. They were not only the largest single holder of mortgage loans against single-family homes, duplexes, triplexes, and similar dwellings, but also the largest single investor in apartment mortgages. The cost and availability of credit in the American mortgage market depends heavily upon the ability of savings and loans to attract deposits from the public and their willingness to make long-term financing available on reasonable terms.

Commercial Banks

In recent years commercial banks have expanded their market share of nearly every type of mortgage loan. Overall, they rank second to savings and loans among all mortgage lenders, holding nearly $265 billion in mortgage credit at year-end 1980 (see Exhibit 18–9). They hold more commercial

EXHIBIT 18–9
Mortgage Loans Held by Commercial Banks, Year-End 1975, 1978, 1979, and 1980 ($ billions)

Property	1975		1978		1979		1980	
	Amount	Percent	Amount	Percent	Amount	Percent	Amount	Percent
1–4-family dwellings	$ 77.0	56.6%	$129.2	60.4%	$149.5	61.0%	$160.7	60.7%
Multifamily units	5.9	4.3	10.3	4.8	11.2	4.6	12.3	4.6
Commercial	46.9	34.4	66.1	30.9	76.0	31.0	82.7	31.1
Farm	6.4	4.7	8.5	4.0	8.6	3.5	8.9	3.4
Totals*	$136.2	100.0%	$214.0	100.0%	$245.2	100.0%	$264.6	100.0%

* Columns may not add to totals due to rounding.
SOURCE: Board of Governors of the Federal Reserve System, *Federal Reserve Bulletin*, selected issues.

mortgages than any other lender, rank second among private lenders in farm mortgages, fourth in apartment loans, and second in loans to finance the purchase of one-to-four-family residences. In this last category their share has climbed from less than 14 percent of one-to-four-family loans in 1965 to 17 percent at year-end 1980. By any measure, commercial banks are a powerful competitive force in the mortgage market, known for their flexibility and innovativeness in developing new credit programs.

Life Insurance Companies

Life insurance companies make substantial investments in commercial as well as residential mortgage properties. As shown in Exhibit 18–10, com-

EXHIBIT 18-10
Mortgage Loans Held by Life Insurance Companies, Year-End 1975, 1978, 1979, and 1980
($ billions)

Property	1975 Amount	1975 Percent	1978 Amount	1978 Percent	1979 Amount	1979 Percent	1980 Amount	1980 Percent
1-4 family dwellings	$17.6	19.7%	$ 14.4	13.6%	$ 16.2	13.6%	$ 17.9	13.7%
Multifamily units	19.6	22.0	19.0	17.9	19.3	16.2	19.6	15.0
Commercial	45.2	50.7	62.2	58.6	71.1	59.8	80.8	61.6
Farm	6.8	7.6	10.5	9.9	12.2	10.3	12.8	9.8
Totals*	$89.2	100.0%	$106.2	100.0%	$118.8	100.0%	$131.1	100.0%

* Columns may not add to totals due to rounding.
SOURCE: Board of Governors of the Federal Reserve System, *Federal Reserve Bulletin*, selected issues.

mercial mortgages make up more than 60 percent of mortgage obligations held by life insurance companies, with residential units accounting for between a third and a quarter of their mortgage total. These companies will search national and international markets for good mortgage investments instead of focusing upon only one or a few local areas.

In the past, life companies strongly preferred government-guaranteed mortgages. In recent years, however, the higher yields available on conventional mortgages have caused some shift of emphasis toward these more risky loans. Despite the greater flexibility of conventional home mortgages, life insurance companies have been gradually reducing their holdings of home mortgages and emphasizing commercial and apartment mortgages. Commercial and apartment loans often carry "equity kickers," which permit the lender to receive a portion of project earnings as well as a guaranteed interest rate.[3]

At the end of 1980 life insurance companies held about 9 percent of total mortgage loans outstanding in the United States. This market share placed them third among private mortgage lenders, behind savings and loan associations and commercial banks. This high ranking is due in part to the fact that life insurers are the largest institutional holder of farm mortgages, stand second only to commercial banks in mortgage loans for commercial properties, and rank second to savings and loans in apartment loans. However, in making loans to finance one-to-four-family residential dwellings, life companies rank a distant fourth among all private lenders. For example, at year-end 1980 they held only $18 billion in one-to-four-family residential loans, compared to $65 billion for mutual savings banks, more than $160 billion

---

[3] See Chapter 19 for a discussion of equity kickers in commercial mortgage lending and Chapter 5 for an overview of the operations of the life insurance industry.

reported by commercial banks, and nearly $420 billion held by savings and loan associations.

Mutual Savings Banks

Another lender of great importance in the residential mortgage market is the mutual savings bank, headquartered mainly in the New England area and in the Middle Atlantic states of New York, New Jersey, and Pennsylvania.[4] These institutions invest in both government-guaranteed and conventional mortgage loans. While single-family homes constitute the bulk of savings bank mortgage loans, their loans supporting multifamily units (including large apartment projects) have grown rapidly in recent years.

Savings banks still provide most of their mortgage credit for the purchase of single-family homes and small multifamily dwellings, as shown in Exhibit 18–11. At year-end 1980, 65 percent of all mortgage obligations held by mutu-

EXHIBIT 18–11
Mortgage Loans Held by Mutual Savings Banks, Year-End 1975, 1978, 1979, and 1980
($ billions)

Property	1975 Amount	1975 Percent	1978 Amount	1978 Percent	1979 Amount	1979 Percent	1980 Amount	1980 Percent
1–4 family dwellings	$50.0	64.8%	$62.3	65.4%	$64.7	65.4%	$65.3	65.4%
Multifamily units	13.8	17.8	16.5	17.3	17.3	17.5	17.2	17.2
Commercial	13.4	17.3	16.3	17.1	17.0	17.2	17.1	17.1
Farm	0.1	0.1	0.1	0.1	0.1	0.1	0.1	0.1
Totals*	$77.2	100.0%	$95.2	100.0%	$98.9	100.0%	$99.8	100.0%

* Columns may not add to totals due to rounding.
SOURCE: Board of Governors of the Federal Reserve System, *Federal Reserve Bulletin,* selected issues.

als were secured by one-to-four-family residential properties. However, apartment financing and commercial mortgages on shopping centers, office buildings, and factories represented a respectable one third of mortgage loans granted by this financial intermediary. Among private mortgage lenders, mutuals rank fourth in total mortgages held, behind savings and loan associations, commercial banks, and life insurance companies. While the dollar total of mortgage loans held by mutuals has risen every year, their share of the market has declined significantly over the past two decades. Mortgage lending by savings and loans, commercial banks, and federal government agencies has grown much faster.

---

[4] See Chapter 4 for a more-complete discussion of the structure and characteristics of the mutual savings bank industry.

Mortgage Bankers

Mortgage banking houses act as a channel through which builders or contractors in need of long-term funds can find permanent mortgage financing. In providing this service mortgage bankers take on portfolios of mortgages from property developers, using mainly bank credit to carry their inventories of mortgages. Then within a relatively short time span these mortgages are placed with long-term institutional investors. Mortgage bankers supply important services to *both* institutional investors and property developers. The developers receive a commitment for permanent financing, which encourages them to proceed with planned real estate projects. Institutional investors, especially life insurance companies and mutual savings banks, receive mortgages appropriately packaged to match the timing of their cash flows and risk-return preferences.

GOVERNMENT ACTIVITY

Adequate housing for all U.S. citizens is a major goal of the federal government. One of the first steps taken by Congress to achieve this goal was the establishment of the Federal Housing Administration (FHA) in 1934. FHA has sought to promote home ownership by reducing the risk to private lenders of residential mortgage contracts. At the same time efforts have been made to encourage the development of an active secondary market for existing mortgage instruments. Such a market makes old mortgages liquid, enabling lenders to raise cash to make new loans, and attracts new investors into the mortgage business.

The combination of government guarantees (FHA-VA) and the development of a secondary market has led to greater participation in mortgage lending by so-called long-distance lenders—particularly insurance companies, pension funds, and savings banks. (Figure 18–1 provides an overall view of the role of private lenders and federal government agencies in the mortgage market.) Because of the predominantly localized nature of the housing industry and the wide variety of mortgage loans, the absence of an effective secondary market and government guarantees would make the home mortgage a long-term commitment of money with little flexibility for the lender.

The Impact of the Great Depression upon Government Involvement in the Mortgage Market

Any attempt to understand how the mortgage market operates today must begin with the Great Depression and the enormous impact that economic calamity had upon the market for property loans. The Great Depression generated massive, unprecedented unemployment; an estimated one quarter to one third of the civilian labor force was thrown out of work between 1929

FIGURE 18–1
The Structure of the Mortgage Market

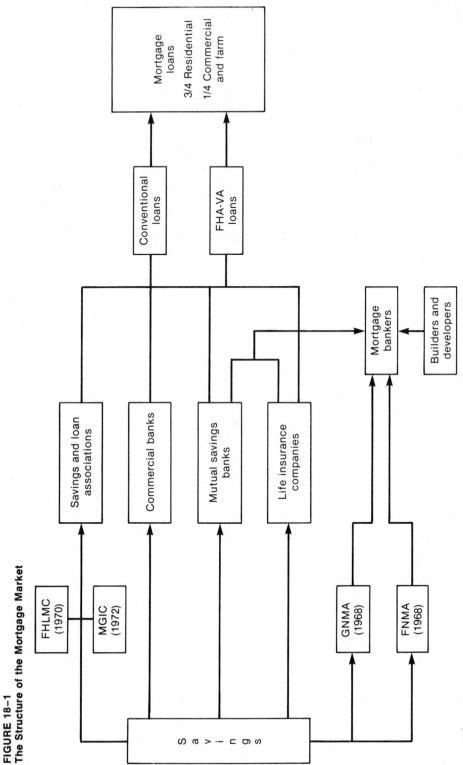

SOURCE: Based upon a diagram in "Structure of the Residential Mortgage Market," *Monthly Review*, Federal Reserve Bank of Richmond, September 1972.

and 1933. Moreover, the scarcity of jobs lasted not just a few months as in recent recessions, but for years. It was not until the United States began a military rearmament program in the late 1930s that the nation's employment picture really began to improve. Few new mortgage loans were made during this period, and thousands of existing mortgages were foreclosed. With so many forced sales, property values declined precipitously, endangering the financial solvency of thousands of mortgage lenders, particularly savings and loan associations and commercial banks. Indeed, scores of banks and S&Ls were forced either into bankruptcy or into mergers with larger institutions.

The federal government elected to tackle the mortgage market's problems by moving in several directions at once: (1) it provided mortgage insurance through FHA for low- and medium-priced homes; (2) it insured the deposits of mortgage-lending institutions through such agencies as the Federal Deposit Insurance Corporation and the Federal Savings and Loan Insurance Corporation; (3) it placed more-rigid controls on lending by banks, savings and loans, and other institutional lenders but also provided them with easier access to credit through direct government loans; and (4) it created several new federal agencies to buy and sell residential mortgages.

For example, in 1932 the Federal Home Loan Bank System (FHLB) was created to supervise the activities of savings and loan associations and make loans to those in trouble. A year later the Home Owner's Loan Corporation was set up to refinance those mortgages on one-to-four-family dwellings which were due to be canceled or foreclosed. By the time this agency ceased operations in 1954, it had made a major contribution toward reshaping the nation's mortgage market by popularizing the long-term amortized mortgage, thereby fostering the growth of private home ownership in the United States.

In 1934, the National Housing Act was passed, setting up a system of federal insurance for qualified home-mortgage loans. The Federal Housing Administration was authorized to guarantee repayment of up to 90 percent of acceptable home loans, encouraging private lenders to lend more of a home's market value, accept longer terms on home mortgages, and charge lower interest rates.

Shortly before the end of World War II, the Veterans Administration (VA) was created with passage of the Servicemen's Readjustment Act (1944). The VA was designed to aid military servicemen returning to civilian life in finding jobs and adequate housing. Like FHA, VA offered to insure residential mortgages. This program permitted mortgage lenders to commit their funds at low risk and reduced the required down payment on a new home.

The Creation of Fannie Mae (FNMA)

The FHA-VA insurance program was an almost instant success and home mortgage lending grew rapidly following its inception. Federal government efforts to create a resale (secondary) market for residential mortgages, however, were far less effective at first. An agency set up during the 1930s to purchase FHA-VA loans, the Reconstruction Finance Corporation, was dissolved in 1948. However, one federal agency committed to improving the secondary mortgage market did survive the turmoil of the Great Depression and World War II. This was the Federal National Mortgage Association (FNMA), better known as Fannie Mae, created in 1938.

Fannie Mae was established for the purpose of buying and selling FHA-guaranteed mortgages in the secondary market. Later, in 1948, it was authorized to trade in VA-guaranteed mortgages as well. Adjusting to the changing character of the mortgage market, FNMA began to exert a potent impact on mortgage trading in the 1950s. One reason was the launching of its standby commitment program.

Standby Commitments. Under the terms of a standby commitment, Fannie Mae agrees to purchase a specific mortgage within a stipulated period of time at a set price. The standby commitment aids builders and property developers because it provides a floor price for a mortgage and allows the holder to sell the instrument at a higher price if market conditions prove favorable. Such commitments usually are made for 4-month or 12-month periods and are sold at auction.

Following reorganization as a privately owned corporation in 1968, Fannie Mae announced that it would begin buying conventional mortgages as well as FHA- and VA-guaranteed loans. In recent years close to half of its purchases have been conventional mortgage loans, acquired mainly from mortgage bankers. A major factor in supplying funds to the mortgage market, FNMA noted recently that between 1968 and 1979 it had purchased a total of $65 billion in home mortgages, involving nearly 3 million housing units. Fannie Mae raises funds for its mortgage purchases by selling short-term discount notes and medium-term debentures in the open market.

Purchase Options. A second innovation developed by FNMA was the purchase option. The opposite of a standby commitment, a purchase option allows the seller of a mortgage to repurchase that mortgage from FNMA within nine months at the original price paid by the agency. FNMA now conducts biweekly auctions where mortgage lenders indicate the interest rates at which they are willing to sell various amounts of mortgages. Based on its cost of funds and market conditions, FNMA will issue both standby commitments and purchase options to those institutions offering the best terms.

The Mortgage Guarantee Insurance Corporation (MGIC)

Fannie Mae is the world's largest mortgage bank and, until recently, had a virtual monopoly in secondary market trading activities. Early in the 1970s, however, the Mortgage Guarantee Insurance Corporation (MGIC) was organized by a private group in Milwaukee, Wisconsin. Known as "Maggie Mae," this corporation insures conventional home mortgage loans carrying down payments as low as 5 percent. In contrast, Fannie Mae is permitted to acquire conventional mortgage loans with down payments only as low as 10 percent. Of course, Fannie Mae has a significant advantage over Maggie Mae because it operates as a federally sponsored agency with a privileged borrowing status and normally can raise funds at lower cost.

The Creation of Ginnie Mae (GNMA)

Efforts by Congress to make the federal government's budget "look better" resulted in the splitting of Fannie Mae into two agencies in 1968. Fannie Mae itself became a private, shareholder-owned corporation devoted to secondary-market trading. At the same time, those loan programs requiring government subsidies or direct government credit were handed over to a new corporation set up within the Department of Housing and Urban Development, known as the Government National Mortgage Association (GNMA) or "Ginnie Mae." This federal agency pursues a two-part program to aid the nation's mortgage market. Under one portion of its program Ginnie Mae purchases mortgages to finance housing for low-income families at below-market interest rates. These "assistance mortgages" are eventually sold to FNMA or to private investors at current market prices.

Far more important for the secondary market, however, is GNMA's mortgage-backed-securities program. Beginning in 1970, Ginnie Mae agreed to guarantee principal and interest payments on securities issued by private mortgage institutions if those securities were backed by pools of government-guaranteed mortgages. These so-called pass-throughs are popular with savings and loans associations, pension funds, commercial banks, and even individual investors as safe, readily marketable securities with attractive rates of return. They are issued mainly by mortgage bankers, but about a quarter of all pass-throughs issued each year come from savings and loan associations, mutual savings banks, and commercial banks. The issuing institutions can raise cash to make new loans by selling the pass-throughs and still continue to earn servicing income on the mortgages in the pool. By year-end 1979 there were more than 800 active issuers of GNMA pass-through securities and over 33,000 pools of mortgages.[5] Today more than 90 percent of all newly originated FHA-VA mortgages on single-family dwellings are either in mortgage pools supporting pass-throughs or are sold to Fannie Mae.

---

[5] See Sivesind (18) in the list of references at the end of this chapter. All mortgages placed in a pool against which GNMA pass-throughs are issued must carry the same interest rate and have issue dates no older than one year. The coupon rate on pass-through securities must be one half percentage point below the contract interest rate on the pooled mortgages with six hundreths of a percent (i.e., six basis points) paid to GNMA in return for its guarantee. Pass-throughs are registered securities with coupons, and pay interest and principal each month.

The Federal Home Loan Mortgage Corporation

Another federal agency created to aid the secondary mortgage market appeared in 1970. The Emergency Home Finance Act passed that year gave birth to the Federal Home Loan Mortgage Corporation (FHLMC), more popularly known as "Freddie Mac." FHLMC is a branch of the Federal Home Loan Bank System which, like Ginnie Mae, may combine the mortgages it buys into pools and issue bonds against them. Securities issued by Freddie Mac are guaranteed by GNMA and are very popular with individual and institutional investors, particularly savings and loan associations and mutual savings banks.

The creation of Freddie Mac reflected a desire by the federal government to develop a stronger secondary market for *conventional* home mortgages. As we have seen, Fannie Mae and Ginnie Mae have made major contributions to the marketability of government-guaranteed (FHA-VA) mortgages, but four fifths of all home mortgages today are conventional, nonguaranteed loans. Freddie Mac buys conventional mortgages, about 80 percent of which come from savings and loan associations; the remainder are supplied by mortgage banking houses, commercial banks, and mutual savings banks.

To raise funds to support these purchases, Freddie Mac sells mortgage participation certificates (PCs) and guaranteed mortgage certificates (GMCs). PCs represent an ownership interest in a pool of conventional mortgages bought and held by Freddie Mac.[6] PCs are sold through Freddie Mac directly and through major securities dealers, who also make an active resale market in these instruments. Freddie Mac guarantees the investor's monthly interest and principal payments passed through from the mortgage pool, but PCs are not guaranteed by the federal government. They are issued in minimum denominations of $100,000. More than $10 billion worth were outstanding at year-end 1979.

Guaranteed mortgage certificates (GMCs), like PCs, are claims against a pool of mortgages. They are similar to corporate bonds in that interest is paid semiannually to investors. Repayments of principal are made once a year. While not guaranteed by the federal government, GMCs are guaranteed as to principal and interest by Freddie Mac and are available in minimum denominations of $100,000. Freddie Mac agrees to repurchase any outstanding principal remaining after a period of 15 years.

Remaining Problems in Developing a Secondary Market for Mortgages

Though considerable progress has been made in the development of an active secondary mortgage market, there is still substantial room for improvement. Among the major obstacles are differences between one mortgage and another in the quality of property and borrower credit stand-

---

[6] As noted by Sivesind (18), the pool underlying an average PC issue includes approximately 5,000 mortgages amounting to between $100 million and $300 million.

ing, which crucially affect each instrument's risk and market value. In addition, different lenders have their own particular preferences for certain kinds of mortgage instruments. For example, savings and loan associations tend to prefer conventional, single-family home mortgages of relatively long maturities, while life insurance companies and mutual savings banks have a preference for FHA-VA home mortgages and are actively expanding their lending in the multifamily and commercial mortgage fields. Differences in foreclosure laws among the states complicate the picture as do different state rules concerning the taxation of mortgage-lending institutions.

Other securities traded in the open market typically carry larger denominations than residential mortgages, are usually more uniform in quality, and are not amortized through installment payments. Moreover, on-site inspection of mortgaged property is often necessary to adequately judge the quality of the mortgage instrument. Government guarantee programs serve to lower mortgage risk but of course do not aid the purchaser of conventional mortgages unless a private firm guarantees these. The packaging of individual mortgages into pools by Freddie Mac, Ginnie Mae, and some private lenders is a positive development which tends to standardize the mortgage instrument and make it more attractive to investors. However, the secondary market for mortgages is still far less well developed than the markets for corporate, municipal, and U.S. government securities. We have made great progress as a society in creating a resale market to improve the liquidity of mortgages, particularly home mortgages. However, substantially greater progress will be needed if we are to grapple effectively with the nation's enormous housing demands in the years ahead.

SENSITIVITY OF THE MORTGAGE MARKET TO MONETARY POLICY AND CREDIT CONDITIONS

The mortgage market is one of the most sensitive of all financial markets to changing interest rates and money and credit conditions. For example, as interest rates rise, the mortgage market is affected from two different directions. Lenders are forced to reduce their mortgage commitments in the face of rising interest rates due to usury laws in some states which impose maximum interest-rate ceilings.[7] In addition, commercial banks, savings and loan associations, and mutual savings banks lose deposits due to disintermediation as their more interest-sensitive depositors seek more-attractive investment opportunities elsewhere.[8] With fewer deposits coming in, a smaller volume of funds is available for mortgage loans, and what funds are available

---

[7] Title V of the Depository Institutions Deregulation and Monetary Control Act of 1980 overrode state-imposed usury provisions applying to first-mortgage loans on residential real property. However, this law gave the states until April 1, 1983, to reinstate usury ceilings on mortgage loans by either passing a new law or allowing each state's voters to adopt a provision stating explicit that the state does not want to be subject to the provisions of Title V.

[8] See Chapter 2 for a discussion of the causes and effects of disintermediation.

usually carry higher rates. Finally, the total cost of a home goes up as interest rates rise, and this depresses the demand for housing. In many ways the mortgage market is a "boom-and-bust" affair, growing rapidly in easy-money periods when interest rates are relatively low and contracting sharply in high-rate, tight-money periods.

Fannie Mae, Ginnie Mae, Freddie Mac, and other government mortgage agencies have helped to stabilize the market to some extent by purchasing mortgages in tight-money periods and selling them in times of easy money and rapid credit expansion. One obvious problem, however, is that this approach frequently goes against Federal Reserve monetary policy designed to stabilize the economy and fight inflation. In tight-money periods, for example, the Federal Reserve System attempts to reduce the volume of borrowing and spending in the economy through high interest rates and slower growth of the nation's money supply. However, because these developments would tend to depress the mortgage market and reduce the availability of mortgage funds, government mortgage agencies will respond by purchasing mortgages and making loans to private mortgage-lending institutions.

Conversely, when the Federal Reserve attempts to pull the economy out of a recession by promoting low interest rates and more rapid money-supply growth, the government mortgage-lending agencies tend to sell mortgages in the secondary market and cut back on loans to the housing sector. Thus, the activities of the government mortgage agencies probably contribute to economic instability to an indeterminate extent. This is a clear example of a conflict in the nation's economic and social goals—stabilizing the economy versus supporting the housing industry.

INNOVATIONS IN MORTGAGE INSTRUMENTS

To this point in the chapter we have described a number of problems which have impaired the functioning of the mortgage market and limited the availability of funds for housing. The extreme sensitivity of the mortgage market to monetary policy and changing credit conditions and the struggle to develop a viable and active secondary mortgage market represent major difficulties which decades of work have only partially resolved. Still another problem with mortgages reared its head in the tumultuous economic and financial environment of the 1960s and 70s. This problem centers on the *inflexibility* of the conventional fixed-rate mortgage in the face of inflation and rising interest rates.

Repeatedly over the past two decades interest rates have climbed to record levels, only to fall back during brief recessions and then to surge upward again. And each upward movement in interest rates forced mortgage lenders to cut back on the availability of funds for housing. In part, these cutbacks in mortgage funds are a response to the widespread use of fixed-rate mortgages. Since the 1930s most home mortgages have been long-term (20-to-30-year) loans with a contractual rate of interest fixed for the life of the loan. These fixed-rate mortgages (FRMs), therefore, return to the lender the same annual interest income (cash flow) regardless of what is happening to inflation or to interest rates in the open market. When savings and loan associations, commercial banks, and other depository institutions are forced to pay higher rates on their deposits to attract funds, their profits tend to be squeezed because their revenues from FRMs remain unchanged. Of course, these lending institutions are able to charge higher rates on *new* mortgage loans, but new loans are always a small fraction of each institution's total loan portfolio. The bulk of that portfolio is in *old* mortgages granted during an era when interest rates usually were much lower.

In short, the FRM amplifies the normal up-and-down cycle of earnings for a mortgage-lending institution, leading to low or even negative earnings in periods of rising interest rates and positive earnings in periods of falling rates. FRMs require the *lender* to bear the risk of interest-rate fluctuations. An alternative to the FRM is needed which both guarantees lenders a satisfactory real rate of return on mortgage loans and makes funds available to home buyers on reasonable terms. Various new and old types of mortgage instruments are described in Exhibit 18–12.

Graduated-Payment Mortgages

The problems created by fixed-rate mortgages have led to the development of several new mortgage instruments in recent years. One which may be of at least as much help to lower-income families as to mortgage lenders is the graduated-payment mortgage (GPM), which FHA began insuring in 1977. With the GPM, initial monthly payments on a new home are lower than they would be under a traditional FRM. Subsequently, payments rise, but they level off after several years. The idea is to tailor the debt-service payments on a home mortgage to the financial needs and improving financial position of the borrower. And GPMs have proven to be popular with young families who otherwise might be stymied by high mortgage payments until their earning power increased.[9] By the end of 1980 a quarter million new GPMs had been insured by FHA.

Of course, the total amount of interest paid by the borrower will be much larger with a GPM than it would be under a conventional FRM. In part, this occurs because the low initial monthly payments do not cover the full amount of interest owed each month, forcing the lender to actually increase the amount of the mortgage loan in the early years. Moreover, due to the delayed receipt of income, lenders generally raise the interest rate on GPMs above rates prevailing on level-payment mortgages.[10]

---

[9] A related type of mortgage instrument is the *pledged-account mortgage*, in which some fraction of the borrower's down payment is placed in a pledged savings account. This account is drawn down gradually to supplement monthly payments during the early years of the mortgage loan.

[10] In August 1980, FHA allowed lenders to charge a one-half percentage point higher rate on GPMs than on conventional fixed-rate mortgages.

EXHIBIT 18–12
Types of Mortgage Instruments

Fixed-Rate Mortgage (FRM): The contract interest rate is set at the time a mortgage loan is made and does not change over the life of the loan. The maturity (term) of the mortgage usually is fixed as well.

Variable-Rate Mortgage (VRM): The contract interest rate specified in the mortgage loan is tied to another interest rate which is sensitive to current supply and demand conditions in the open market. Higher interest rates usually result in higher monthly mortgage payments.

Adjustable Mortgage Loan (AML): Changes in the interest rate attached to the mortgage loan can be passed along to the borrower by changing the loan principal, loan maturity, or monthly payment or by varying some combination of these credit terms.

Graduated-Payment Mortgage (GPM): Installment payments required under a mortgage contract are set lower than those required under a comparable fixed-rate mortgage but rise over time with inflation, borrower income, or some other index.

Canadian Rollover Mortgage (CRM): This mortgage loan is of much shorter term than a conventional fixed-rate mortgage and usually requires the borrower to renegotiate and refinance the loan on the due date.

Renegotiated-Rate Mortgage (RRM): With this long-term residential mortgage loan, the interest rate is set for a period shorter than the term of the mortgage and must be re-negotiated between borrower and lender on a periodic basis.

Deferred-Interest Mortgage (DIM): This mortgage loan has interest rates that are generally lower than on conventional fixed-rate mortgages, but at a later point the borrower must reimburse the lender for accumulated interest not paid earlier.

Flexible-Payment Mortgage (FPM): The borrower pays only the interest on a mortgage loan for the first five years; subsequent payments must be high enough to fully amortize the loan, however.

Shared-Appreciation Mortgage (SAM): The borrower agrees to give the lender a portion of the profits from the sale of mortgaged property in return for a lower contractual interest rate and lower monthly payments.

Reverse-Annuity Mortgage (RAM): This is a device to raise money by borrowing against an existing home or other structure (usually a property whose original mortgage loan has been paid off), with the borrower receiving fixed annuity payments based on the value of the mortgaged property.

Variable-Rate and Other Adjustable Mortgages

Another new mortgage instrument used extensively on the West Coast and to a lesser extent in the New England area is the *variable rate mortgage* (VRM). A VRM permits the lender to vary the contractual interest rate on a mortgage loan as market conditions change. Generally, the mortgage rate is linked to a reference interest rate not determined by the lender. For example, the yield on long-term U.S. Treasury bonds may be used as a reference rate so that, if Treasury bond yields rise, the home owner pays a higher contractual interest rate and makes a higher monthly payment on the mortgage. Alternatively, under a broader *adjustable mortgage,* the maturity of the mortgage instrument may be lengthened (up to a maximum of 40 years) or a combination of rate increases and maturity changes may be made as interest rates rise. In some cases the loan principal can be increased, reducing the growth of the home owner's equity—a process known as "negative amortization.'' In effect, VRMs and other adjustable mortgage instruments shift the risk of interest-rate fluctuations partially or wholly from the lender to the borrower.

VRMs were first issued in California in 1975 and were authorized for other parts of the nation by the Federal Home Loan Bank Board in 1979. Many institutions offering VRMs have added ''sweeteners'' to induce borrowers to accept a variable rather than a fixed-rate mortgage contract. Examples of these special inducements include guaranteeing the borrower an open line of credit at the mortgage interest rate and collecting no prepayment penalty if the borrower can pay off the mortgage early.

The broader *adjustable mortgages* mentioned above are more flexible and have more-lenient regulations than pure VRMs. Under most state and federal laws, changes in the interest rates attached to VRMs are limited as to frequency and amount. However, adjustable mortgages, with their option of varying monthly payments, the maturity of a mortgage loan, or the loan principal as interest rates change, face few legal restrictions and are likely to grow rapidly in future years. For example, in 1981 the Federal Home Loan Bank Board freed federally chartered savings and loan associations from any significant regulatory restrictions on the offering of adjustable mortgages.

Canadian Rollover and Other Renegotiated Mortgage Loans

Recently, there has been considerable interest in the United States in Canadian rollover mortgages (CRMs). These instruments are usually issued for short to medium terms—5- and 10-year maturities are common—at the end of which the note falls due. The borrower must then either pay off the debt or negotiate a new loan. A related variety of loan is the *renegotiated rate mortgage* (RRM). Unlike the Canadian rollover mortgage, it carries a long maturity, but its interest rate must be renegotiated periodically—usually every three to five years.

Still another renegotiated-type property loan is the *deferred-interest mortgage* (DIM), in which the borrower pays a lower interest rate than with a conventional FRM and thus has lower mortgage payments. However, the borrower must reimburse the lender for any accumulated interest that is postponed during the life of the loan plus an additional fee. This reimbursement may occur through a refinancing of the loan at the end of a certain period or when the property is sold or transferred to another owner.[11]

---

[11] A new type of mortgage related to CRMs, RRMs, and DIMs is the *flexible-payment mortgage* (FPM). This instrument requires the borrower to pay only the interest on the loan and no principal during the first five years. After the initial five-year period, however, the mortgage loan must be fully amortized as to both principal and interest. However, since the bulk of the early payments on conventional mortgage instruments go to pay interest anyway, with very little reduction of principal, the monthly savings from FPMs are usually small—typically under $50.

Another new mortgage instrument developed in the western United States is the *shared-appreciation mortgage* (SAM). The borrower is offered substantially smaller monthly payments and a contractual interest rate well below rates prevailing on conventional mortgages in return

Reverse-Annuity Mortgages

A mortgage-financing device which may be of help to older families and retired individuals is the *Reverse-Annuity Mortgage* (RAM). This financial instrument is designed to provide additional income to those who may have already paid off their home mortgage but intend to keep their present home. The lender determines the current value of the home and pays the borrower a fixed monthly annuity, amounting to a specified percentage of the property's value. The loan is secured by a gradually increasing mortgage on the borrower's home. Repayment of the loan occurs either when the annuity holder dies, with the loan being discharged against the deceased's estate, or when the home is sold.

CREATIVE FINANCING TECHNIQUES

Soaring prices of new homes and record-high mortgage interest rates put a damper on the demand for single-family homes as the 1970s drew to a close and the 80s began. Home owners and real estate agents sought out innovative financing techniques to make single-family homes more affordable for the average home buyer. These innovative techniques, known collectively as "creative financing," accounted for close to half of all housing sales in the United States in 1980.

Second Mortgages

One of the most-popular creative financing techniques is the second, or junior, mortgage. A second mortgage is a claim against real property which is subordinated to a first mortgage claim and usually payable in monthly installments. Its maturity typically is much shorter than that of a first-mortgage loan—5-to-10-year terms are common. Because the second-mortgage holder has a subordinated claim, the interest rate is often significantly higher than on a first-mortgage loan.

The shorter maturities and higher interest rates attached to second mortgages have made them attractive to many lenders, particularly savings and loan associations, commercial banks, and finance companies. Historically, second mortgages have been used by homeowners to draw upon the growing equity investment in their home in order to pay for improvements (such as adding an extra bedroom) or to raise cash to make other investments. More recently, second mortgages have been used as a form of seller financing to speed up home sales.

---

for a commitment to turn over a fraction of any capital gain resulting from the sale of the mortgaged property. One popular SAM contract requires the borrower to pay one third of any profit earned on the sale of a home. At the time this book was being written, the Federal Home Loan Bank Board was considering approving SAMs for federally insured savings and loan associations.

For example, a homeowner who has placed his or her house on the market with an $80,000 price tag may find few buyers due to high interest rates. Buyers would prefer to assume the homeowner's old first mortgage which, let us say, has an unpaid balance of $50,000 and an attractive interest rate of 8½ percent. However, few families would be able to raise the $30,000 difference between the price of the home and the balance owed on the first mortgage. Increasingly, therefore, financial institutions and homeowners themselves are agreeing to take a second deed of trust in lieu of a portion of the required down payment. The home buyer benefits even though the interest rate is much higher on the second mortgage. This is true because the low interest rate on the first mortgage results in an *average* rate on both loans significantly lower than is usually obtainable on new first mortgages.

Home-Leasing Plans

In addition to second mortgages, *lease-purchase agreements* are now being used in certain markets. Under this arrangement the buyer leases a home while retaining the option to buy for a period of at least one year. The seller receives monthly lease payments plus option money, which the buyer may later apply towards a down payment on the home. The advantage of this financing technique is that it permits the buyer to move in right away and still have time to accumulate enough savings to make the required down payment. Meantime, the seller is receiving cash payments while still enjoying the tax advantages of owning a home.

Land-Leasing Plans and Property Exchanges

A related lease-financing option is the *land lease*. In this case the buyer acquires title only to the house and any improvements on the land, and the seller retains title to the land on which the house stands. In return for monthly lease payments, the buyer will receive a long-term lease (sometimes stretching out to 100 years) on the land, frequently with an option to buy. This creative financing technique reduces monthly payments and results also in a lower initial down payment.

A simpler but equally effective approach is a *property exchange* between buyer and seller. Any difference in value between the two houses exchanged can be handled by a promissory note issued by the owner of the cheaper property. Sometimes the difference in value will be made up by swapping personal property, such as savings deposits, stocks, bonds, jewelry, automobiles, etc.

Seller Financing through Wraparound Loans

Wraparound financing has become popular in many real estate markets, though state laws limit its use in some locations. Monthly payments on an old, low-interest mortgage continue to be the responsibility of the seller when an existing home is sold. However, the seller receives from the home buyer a new mortgage at a higher interest rate and therefore providing for larger monthly payments. The seller pockets the difference between the monthly payments on the old and new mortgages. However, a portion of the seller's gain is passed on to the buyer, who gets a new mortgage at a lower interest rate than is generally available from regular mortgage lenders.

The Future of Creative Financing Techniques

These and other creative financing techniques are growing in popularity and are likely to become even more important in the future. The new methods attempt to take advantage of the low rates on old mortgages, the tax advantages of home ownership, and the desire of sellers to avoid large capital gains taxes when a home is sold. They illustrate one favorable aspect of high interest rates and tight credit—such conditions frequently stimulate the invention of new financial instruments to better serve the public's needs and more efficiently utilize scarce funds. Creative home-financing techniques also serve as a reminder to those government agencies responsible for regulating the financial system: *Rules and regulations which ignore or try to suppress the basic forces of supply and demand in the marketplace soon will be outmoded by the ever changing technology of finance.*

SUMMARY AND CONCLUSIONS

In this chapter we have focused our attention upon one of the most important and also one of the most troubled markets in the American financial system—the residential mortgage market. Huge by almost any standard, the total volume of mortgage debt outstanding in the United States reached $1.4 trillion in 1980, or more than half the size of the United States GNP and far larger than any other financial instrument. Mortgages on one-to-four-family dwellings and apartments totaled just over $1 trillion, so that loans to support the building of residences for individuals and families accounted for three quarters of all mortgage debt in the United States. The health and vitality of this market has a powerful impact upon the nation's standard of living, social welfare, and public attitudes. It is inextricably intertwined with the political sphere and has been the object of government intervention, supervision, and regulation for decades.

Three major problems have affected the performance of the mortgage market in recent years. One concerns the relatively weak resale market for existing mortgages. When lenders have difficulty selling their old mortgages in order to make new loans, the availability of financing for the construction of new homes, apartments, shopping centers, office buildings, and other structures is curtailed. This is a particularly serious problem in view of the heavy demand for new housing expected during the 1980s and beyond. Between 1980 and 1990 an estimated 42 million Americans will reach age 30—considered a prime home-buying age. However, federal government efforts to deal with this problem through the creation of special agencies actively buying and selling mortgages in the open market have begun to bear fruit. An active and increasingly broad secondary market for both government-guaranteed and conventional mortgages appears to be developing slowly but surely.

Government and private efforts to deal with a second major problem—the redesigning of the basic mortgage instrument itself—also appear to be making progress. Years of rapid inflation and record-high interest rates have rendered the conventional fixed-rate mortgage inappropriate in today's financial environment. As a result, lenders have turned increasingly to new forms of mortgage credit whose cash flows vary with interest rates and general market conditions. Included in this list are graduated-payment mortgages, variable-rate mortgages, Canadian rollover mortgages, renegotiated-rate mortgages, deferred-interest mortgages, and reverse-annuity mortgages. Slow at first to authorize these newer and more-flexible mortgage loans, Congress and the federal regulatory authorities have begun to respond, initially allowing limited use of variable- and renegotiated-rate instruments. Further liberalization of mortgage-lending rules is expected in the future in response to the nation's growing demands for new and better housing.

The third major problem which marks mortgage-trading activity is the extreme volatility and sensitivity of this market. It tends to be a countercyclical market, expanding rapidly in periods when the economy is in a recession or experiencing a slow recovery and declining in expansion periods when the rest of the economy is buoyant. When the mortgage market is depressed, the building of new homes and other structures virtually grinds to a halt, and unemployment in the construction industry soars. In part, these difficulties are traceable to the nature of the conventional mortgage instrument itself, because its long maturity and fixed-contract interest rate make its market value highly sensitive to fluctuations in interest rates. Another problem is restrictive government regulations, particularly certain state usury, foreclosure, and property laws and federal deposit interest-rate ceilings. These legal restrictions limit the returns mortgage lenders can pay savers in order to attract loanable funds, and they restrict the cash flows from mortgage loans already made. These regulations serve to accentuate the normal cyclical movements in the supply and demand for mortgage funds.

The federal government's response to these problems has been to create federal agencies with the power to borrow money and buy mortgages in the open market or guarantee them against default. The buying and selling of mortgages has been carried out by such government agencies as the Federal National Mortgage Association (FNMA), the Government National Mortgage Association (GNMA), and the Federal Home Loan Mortgage Corporation (FHLMC). Government guarantees for residential mortgages are issued by the Federal Housing Administration (FHA) and the Veterans Administration (VA). Most recently, federal and state interest-rate ceilings which restrict both loan and deposit growth have been attacked. For example, passage of the Depository Institutions Deregulation and Monetary Control Act in 1980 marked the beginning of a planned six-year phaseout of interest-rate ceilings on deposits. At the same time, state usury laws on residential mortgages have been preempted unless reinstated by the individual states before April 1, 1983.

These serious problems in the mortgage market will not be solved overnight, as the record of the past several decades suggests. The best that can be said to date is that progress *is* being made. The residential mortgage market is slowly being released from the many artificial constraints which have limited the free interplay of demand and supply forces and prevented an optimal allocation of scarce resources. And none too soon, for the thousands of new families formed in the United States each year are placing unprecedented pressures on this huge and volatile market. Indeed, for many families seeking new homes the changes may be coming too late. Inflation, heavy tax burdens, and high interest rates have all but destroyed the dream of home ownership for families and individuals of modest means.

STUDY QUESTIONS

1. What has happened in recent years to the prices of new homes? To interest rates and other terms on conventional home-mortgage loans? What are the causes of these trends?

2. Mortgages may be classified in several different ways. Describe the structure of the mortgage market as it relates to:
   a. Type of mortgage contract—conventional versus government guaranteed.
   b. Residential versus nonresidential mortgages.
   c. Type of mortgage borrower.

3. List the principal mortgage-lending institutions in the United States. Which is most important? In what mortgage-lending areas?

4. Compare and contrast the mortgage-lending activities of savings and loan associations, mutual savings banks, insurance companies, commercial banks, and mortgage banking houses. How are these institutions alike, and how do they differ in their mortgage-lending activities?

5. Why is it important to have a viable and active secondary market for mortgages? Discuss the efforts of the federal government to develop a secondary mortgage market.

6. Identify the following federal agencies and describe their function:
   a. FHA.
   b. VA.
   c. FHLB.
   d. FNMA.
   e. GNMA.
   f. FHLMC.

7. Why is the mortgage market particularly sensitive to monetary policy and changing credit conditions?

8. A number of new mortgage instruments have been developed in recent years to replace the conventional fixed-rate mortgage (FRM). These new financial instruments include:

   a. Graduated-payment mortgages (GPM).
   b. Variable-rate mortgages (VRM).
   c. Canadian rollover mortgages (CRM).
   d. Renegotiated-rate mortgages (RRM).
   e. Flexible-payment mortgages (FPM).
   f. Shared-appreciation mortgages (SAM).
   g. Deferred-interest mortgages (DIM).
   h. Reverse-annuity mortgages (RAM).

   Describe how each of these mortgage instruments work. Why have these alternatives to the fixed-rate mortgage been developed?

9. What is "creative financing?" What factors have given rise to its growth and development?

10. Explain what the following terms mean:

    a. Second mortgage.
    b. Lease-purchase agreement.
    c. Land lease.
    d. Property exchange.
    e. Wraparound financing.

SELECTED REFERENCES

1. Berkman, Neil G. "Mortgage Finance and the Housing Cycle." *New England Economic Review,* Federal Reserve Bank of Boston, September-October 1979, pp. 54–76.

2. Bettner, Jill. "Projected Yields on Ginnie Maes Lure Savers, but the Mortgage Pools' True Yields Are Elusive." *The Wall Street Journal,* October 20, 1980, p. 44.

3. Brock, Bronwyn. "Regulatory Changes Bring New Challenge to S&L's, Other Depository Institutions." *Voice,* Federal Reserve Bank of Dallas, September 1980, pp. 5–9.

4. Brockschmidt, Peggy. "Multi-Family Housing in the 1970's." *Economic Review,* Federal Reserve Bank of Kansas City, July-August 1978.

5. _____. "The Secondary Market for Home Mortgages." *Monthly Review,* Federal Reserve Bank of Kansas City, September-October 1977.

6. _____. "Tax-Exempt Single-Family Mortgage Bonds." *Economic Review,* Federal Reserve Bank of Kansas City, May 1980, pp. 3–12.

7. Davidson, Philip H. "Structure of the Residential Mortgage Market." *Monthly Review,* Federal Reserve Bank of Richmond, September 1972, pp. 2–6.

8. DeLeeuw, Frank, and Larry Ozanne. "The Impact of the Federal Income Tax on Investment in Housing." *Survey of Current Business,* December 1979, pp. 50–61.

9. Federal Reserve Bank of Dallas. "The Deregulation and Monetary Control Act of 1980." *Voice,* September 1980, pp. 1–4.

10. Francis, Jack Clark. "Helping Americans Get Mortgages." *Business Review,* Federal Reserve Bank of Philadelphia, January 1974, pp. 14–21.

11. Gibson, William E. "Protecting Homebuilding from Restrictive Credit Conditions." *Brookings Papers on Economic Activity,* 1973, pp. 647–91.

12. Gillingham, Robert. "Estimating the User Cost of Owner-Occupied Housing." *Monthly Labor Review,* February 1980, pp. 31–35.

13. Hill, G. Christian. "Now May Finally Be the Time to Get a Variable-Rate Mortgage." *The Wall Street Journal,* October 22, 1980, p. 25.

14. Melton, William C. "Graduated Payment Mortgages." *Quarterly Review,* Federal Reserve Bank of New York, Spring 1980, pp. 21–28.

15. Melton, William C., and Diane L. Heidt. "Variable Rate Mortgages." *Quarterly Review,* Federal Reserve Bank of New York, Summer 1979, pp. 23–31.

16. Miller, Glenn H. "The Affordability of Home Ownership in the 1970's." *Economic Review,* Federal Reserve Bank of Kansas City, September-October 1980, pp. 17–23.

17. Rufolo, Anthony M. "What's Ahead for Housing Prices?" *Business Review,* Federal Reserve Bank of Philadelphia, July-August 1980, pp. 9–15.

18. Sivesind, Charles M. "Mortgage-Backed Securities: The Revolution in Real Estate Finance." *Quarterly Review,* Federal Reserve Bank of New York, Autumn 1979, pp. 1–10.

19. United States League of Savings Associations. *Homeownership: Coping with Inflation.* Chicago, 1980.

20. United States League of Savings Associations. *Savings and Loan Fact Book '80.* Chicago, 1980.

part six

Businesses in the Financial Markets

19

Business Borrowing in the Money and Capital Markets

Business firms in the United States draw upon a wide variety of sources of funds in order to finance their daily operations and to carry out long-term investment. In 1979, for example, nonfinancial business firms in the United States raised nearly $392 billion in funds to carry out long-term investment, purchase inventories of goods and raw materials, and acquire financial assets. Of this total, $192 billion (49 percent) were supplied directly from the financial markets through issues of bonds, stocks, notes, and other financial instruments and through trade credit extended by suppliers.

FACTORS AFFECTING BUSINESS ACTIVITY IN THE MONEY AND CAPITAL MARKETS

Many factors affect the extent to which business firms draw upon the money and capital markets for funds. One prominent factor is the *condition of the nation's economy* and the demand for goods and services. A booming economy will generate rapidly growing sales, encouraging businessmen to borrow to expand inventories and to issue stocks and bonds in order to purchase new plant and equipment. In contrast, a sagging economy normally will be accompanied by declining sales and a reduction in both inventory purchases and long-term investment. Other factors held equal, the need for external fund-raising declines when the economy grows more slowly or heads down into a recession. In contrast, rising demands for business goods and services are usually translated into rising demands for short- and long-term capital supplied from the financial markets.

Credit availability and *interest rates* also have powerful effects on the level of business activity in the financial markets. Rising interest rates, which typically accompany a period of economic prosperity or rapid inflation, eventually choke off business borrowing and spending plans because of the increasing cost of carrying inventories, floating new securities, and renewing existing credit lines. Moreover, rising interest rates are usually accompanied by reduced credit availability to many business firms because commercial banks and other institutional lenders frequently lose funds ("disintermediation") during such periods. Falling interest rates, on the other hand, can stimulate business borrowing and spending, leading to a restocking of inventories and an expansion of long-term capital investment financed by bonds, stocks, and direct loans.

Because the financial markets are largely a supplemental funds source for business firms, drawn upon to backstop internal cash flows when credit availability, interest rates, and economic conditions are favorable, it should not surprise us to learn that business fund-raising activity in the financial system is highly *volatile*. Heavy business borrowings and new stock issues in one year often are followed by a dearth of new offerings and even significant paydowns of outstanding loans and securities in succeeding years. A good example is provided by the experience of the U.S. economy during the middle and late 1970s.

In 1975, with the U.S. economy in the midst of a deep recession, corporations saw little need to borrow substantial amounts of funds to expand inventories or carry out long-term investment. Nonfinancial companies raised net only $37 billion in funds from the financial marketplace that year after a record $145 billion in borrowings and stock issues the previous year. In fact, during 1975 corporate treasurers actually paid off and retired a net $9.5 billion in loans outstanding and also redeemed nearly $3 billion in short-term commercial paper issues. During the 1976–78 period, however, the economy was booming. And, with interest rates at relatively moderate levels, business borrowing soared. Combined issues of corporate stocks, bonds, notes, and loans rose almost $61 billion in 1976, $80 billion in 1977, and $95 billion in 1978. Instead of paying down loans on balance as happened in 1975, corporate loans from banks rose a net $32 billion, business mortgages jumped $23 billion, and issues of new corporate bonds added another $20 billion during 1978 alone.

These marked fluctuations in business fund-raising activities in the financial markets result in wide savings in interest rates and security prices. Much of the volatility in stock and bond prices reported in the daily financial press may be attributed to the on-again-off-again character of financial market activity by the business sector. The key actors in this rapidly changing drama are, of course, the largest industrial and manufacturing corporations who have the reputation and financial stature to tap both the open market and negotiated-loan markets for debt and equity funds. Skillful security analysts often can read which way the wind is blowing as far as interest rates and security prices are concerned by watching what is happening to the current earnings and investment plans of the nation's major corporations.

CHARACTERISTICS OF CORPORATE NOTES AND BONDS

If a corporation decides to use long-term funds to finance its growth, the most popular form of long-term financing is the corporate bond or note. This is especially true for the largest corporations whose credit standing and reputation is so strong they can avoid dealing directly with an institutional lender such as a bank, finance company, or insurance company and sell their long-term IOUs in the open market. Smaller companies without the necessary "standing" in the eyes of security investors usually must confine their long-term financing operations to negotiated loans with an institutional lender, an occasional stock issue, and heavy use of internally generated cash.

Principal Features of Corporate Notes and Bonds

A distinction needs to be drawn here between notes and bonds. By convention, a *note* is corporate debt contract whose original maturity is five years or less; a *bond* carries an original maturity of more than five years. Both securities promise the investor an amount equal to the security's par value at maturity plus interest payments at specified intervals until maturity is reached. Since both securities have similar characteristics other than maturity, we will use the term *bond* to refer to both notes and bonds in the discussion that follows.

Corporate bonds are generally issued in units of $1,000 and earn income which, in most cases, is fully taxable to the investor. Each bond is accompanied by an *indenture* which is a contract listing the rights, privileges, and obligations of the borrower and the investor.

Term Bonds versus Serial Bonds

The majority of corporate bonds issued today are *term bonds,* which means that all the bonds in a particular issue mature on a single date. In contrast, most bonds issued by state and local governments (municipals) and a few corporate bonds are *serial bonds,* carrying a range of maturity dates.[1]

Recent Trends in Original Maturities of Bonds

There is a trend today toward shorter and shorter original maturities for corporate bonds due to inflation, rapid changes in technology, and heavy

---

[1] See Chapter 25 for a discussion of the serial feature of municipal bonds.

borrowing demands from other sectors of the economy. During the 1950s and 60s corporations usually found a ready market for 20- to 30-year bonds. Such long-term debt contracts were extremely desirable from the borrowing company's standpoint because they locked in relatively low interest costs for many years and made financial planning much simpler. Today, with inflation and other factors frequently sending market interest rates soaring to record levels, bonds and notes with 3- to 15-year maturities are becoming commonplace.

Some financial analysts expect to see a substantial number of corporate bonds issued in the future whose interest rates are indexed to commodity prices (especially silver and gold) or to the price of energy. These *commodity-indexed bonds* are designed to provide the investor a hedge against inflation and, as a result, carry substantially lower coupon rates than conventional bonds.[2] Another recent innovation is the issuance of *zero-coupon bonds* which carry no fixed rate of return but offer the investor the prospect of significant capital gains. Those bonds still issued with fixed interest rates may carry "openers" which call for periodic adjustments in the principal amount of the loan as interest rates change. In brief, the trend in corporate bonds today is toward shorter maturities and a more flexible rate of return for the investor.

Call Privileges

Nearly all corporate bonds issued today carry call privileges allowing early redemption of the bonds if market conditions prove favorable. As we saw in Chapter 9, the redemption (or "call") price decreases as a callable bond approaches maturity. Depending upon the call premium and market conditions, investors generally prefer that the redemption of a bond be deferred as long as possible to protect them against loss of income from lower interest rates. And most corporate bonds issued today defer the call privilege for 5 to 10 years. The call feature gives the firm greater flexibility in financing its operations but can be expensive to a company when interest rates are high and expected to fall. Investors realize that the bond will likely be called if rates fall far enough and demand a higher yield as compensation for call risk.

Sinking Fund and Refunding Provisions

Most corporate bonds issued in the U.S. carry sinking fund provisions designed to insure that the issuing company will be able to pay off the bonds

---

[2] A good example of commodity-indexed bonds appeared in April 1980 when Sunshine Mining Company issued $25 million in silver-indexed debt securities. Investors were promised a payment at maturity equal to the greater of the security's par value ($1,000) or the market value of 50 ounces of silver. These silver-indexed bonds carried a coupon rate of 8½ percent at a time when seasoned corporate bonds of comparable maturity and rating were posting yields in the 14 to 15 percent range.

when they come due. Periodic payments are made into the sinking fund on a schedule which usually is related to the depreciation of the assets supported by the bonds. A trustee is charged with the responsibility of making sure that the user actually places the right amount of money in the sinking fund each time a payment is due. Periodically, a portion of the bonds outstanding may be retired from monies accumulated in the fund. The trustee will call in selected bonds at par or at par plus a designated call premium.

The majority of corporate bonds issued in recent years have also included *refunding* provisions which allow the issuer to retire bonds in advance of maturity (usually at a premium of 5 to 10 percent over par value) by issuing new securities carrying a lower interest rate. For utility bonds the refundability option generally may be exercised after 5 years, while industrial bonds usually permit refunding after 10 years. Refunding provisions have been one of the most important devices used by U.S. corporations in recent years to shorten the actual maturity of corporate bonds in an era of rapid inflation and high borrowing costs. Just as with call privileges, investors usually demand higher yields on refundable bonds to protect themselves against declining interest rates.

Yields and Costs of Corporate Bonds

Yields on corporate bonds tend to move in line with general business conditions and respond to swings in the credit market between tight and easy money. Yields on the highest-grade corporate issues tend to move closely with yields on U.S. government bonds. In contrast, yields carried by lower-grade corporate bond issues are more closely tied to conditions in the nation's economy and to factors specifically affecting the risk position of each borrowing firm. Bonds issued by the largest U.S. industrial, manufacturing, and utility companies are, with few exceptions, listed and traded on the New York or American Stock Exchange.[3]

As noted in Chapter 7, there are several different ways to measure the rate of return to the investor or the cost to the firm of issuing a bond, note, or other debt security. From the point of view of the issuing company one widely quoted measure of the cost of a bond is its *coupon rate*—the rate of interest the company promises to pay as printed on the face of the bond. However, the coupon rate may understate or overstate the true cost of a bond to the issuing company, depending upon whether the bond was issued at a discount or at a premium from its par value. A better measure of the cost of issuing a bond is to compare the net proceeds available for the borrowing company's use from a bond sale to the present value of the stream of cash payments the firm must make to the bondholders.

For example, suppose a corporation issues $1,000 par bonds, but flotation

---

[3] See Chapter 20 for a description of the workings of these major securities exchanges.

costs reduce the net proceeds to the company from each bond to $950.[4] If the bonds mature in 10 years and carry a 10 percent coupon rate, then the before-tax cost, k, to the issuing company is:

$$\text{Net proceeds per bond} = \frac{\text{Interest cost in year 1}}{(1 + k)} + \frac{\text{Interest cost in year 2}}{(1 + k)^2}$$
$$+ \cdots + \frac{\text{Interest cost in year 10}}{(1 + k)^{10}}$$
$$+ \frac{\text{Principal payment in year 10}}{(1 + k)^{10}}$$

In this example,

$$\$950 = \frac{\$100}{(1 + k)^1} + \frac{\$100}{(1 + k)^2} + \cdots + \frac{\$100}{(1 + k)^{10}} + \frac{\$1,000}{(1 + k)^{10}}$$

A check of the present-value tables in Appendix A indicates that k is 10.85 percent. However, interest charges on debt are tax deductible, making the aftertax cost considerably less than the before-tax cost, especially for the largest and most profitable firms. For corporations which earn over $100,000 per year, the marginal federal income tax rate is 46 percent.[5] Thus, a large company issuing the bond described above would incur an aftertax cost (k′) of

$$k' = k(1 - t)$$

where k is before-tax cost and t is the firm's marginal tax rate. Thus, in this example,

$$k' = 10.85\%(1 - 0.46) = 5.86\%$$

Of course, if the firm were in a lower tax bracket, the aftertax cost of debt would be higher, and in the case of an unprofitable company (whose effective tax rate is zero) would equal its before-tax cost.

---

[4] The major elements of flotation cost for a new bond issue are the underwriting spread of the dealer selling the issue, registration fees, paper and printing charges, and legal fees.

[5] Since passage of the Revenue Act of 1978 U.S. corporations have faced a five-step graduated income tax rate schedule. These five steps are:

If Corporate Taxable Income Is	The Tax Rate Applying to Net Earnings Is
$0–$25,000	17%
$25,001–$50,000	20%
$50,001–$75,000	30%
$75,001–$100,000	40%
Over $100,000	46%

Under the terms of the Economic Recovery Tax Act of 1981 corporate tax brackets below $50,000 are changed to the following marginal rates in the indicated years:

Corporate Taxable Income	1982	1983
$0–$25,000	16%	15%
$25,001–$50,000	19%	18%

The before- and aftertax cost of debt vary not only with each firm's tax rate, but also with conditions in the nation's financial markets. During periods of rapid economic expansion when the supply of credit is scarce relative to the demand for it, the cost of borrowing debt capital will rise. Bonds and notes must be marketed at lower prices and higher yields. Conversely, in periods when the economy contracts and easier credit conditions prevail, the cost of borrowing debt capital tends to decline. The prices of bonds and notes will rise and their yields will fall. It should not be surprising to learn that the volume of long-term corporate borrowings tends to increase markedly during business recessions as companies attempt to lock in the relatively low interest rates available at that time.

Types of Corporate Bonds

Debentures. There are many different types of corporate bonds issued today (see Exhibit 19–1). One of the most popular is the debenture, which is

EXHIBIT 19–1
Principal Types of Corporate Notes and Bonds

Debentures—Long-term debt instruments secured only by the earning power of the issuing corporation and not by any specific property.

Subordinated debentures—Unsecured bonds whose holders receive a claim on the issuing company's assets that ranks behind holders of senior debt securities but ahead of common and preferred stockholders.

Mortgage bonds—Long-term debt secured by a lien on specific assets (normally plant and equipment) held by the issuing corporation.

Equipment trust certificates—A type of lease financing in which the title to certain assets (normally equipment or rolling stock) is held by a trustee and the company issuing the certificates makes lease payments to certificate holders through the trustee.

Collateral trust bonds—Long-term debt representing an interest in a pool of securities held by the issuing corporation.

Industrial development bonds—Debt securities issued by a local government agency to aid a private company in the construction of a plant and/or the purchase of equipment or land.

Convertible bonds—Long-term debt securities which can be exchanged for a specific number of shares of common stock at the option of the bondholder.

Income bonds—Debt instruments used mainly in corporate reorganizations which earn interest for the holder only when the issuing company has sufficient earnings.

Pollution control bonds—Long-term debt securities issued by a local government agency (often on a tax-exempt basis) to assist a private company in purchasing pollution-control equipment or facilities.

not secured by any specific asset or assets owned by the issuing corporation. Instead, the holder of a debenture is a general creditor of the company and looks to the earning power and reputation of the borrower as the main source of the bond's value.

Subordinated Debentures. A related form of bond is the subordinated debenture, frequently called a *junior* security. If a company goes out of business and its assets are liquidated, the holders of subordinated debentures will be paid only after all secured and unsecured senior creditors receive the monies to which they are entitled.

Mortgage Bonds. Debt securities representing a claim against specific assets (normally plant and equipment) owned by a corporation are known as mortgage bonds. These bonds may be either closed end or open end. Closed-end mortgage bonds do not permit the issuance of any additional debt against those assets already pledged under the mortgage. Open-end bonds, on the other hand, do allow additional debt to be issued against pledged assets, and this may dilute the position of the current bondholders. For this reason, open-end mortgage bonds typically carry higher yields than closed-end bonds. Sometimes several different mortgage bonds with varying priorities of claim will be issued against the same assets. For example, the initial issue of bonds against a corporation's fixed assets may be designated *first mortgage bonds,* and later, *second mortgage bonds* may be issued against those same assets. If the company were liquidated and the pledged assets sold, holders of second mortgage bonds would receive only those funds left over after holders of the first mortgage bonds were paid off.

Collateral Trust Bond. A debt instrument secured by stocks, bonds, and notes issued by units of government or by other corporations is called a collateral trust bond. Such a bond is therefore really an interest in a pool of securities held by the bond issuer. The pledged securities are held in trust for the benefit of the bondholders, though the borrowing company usually receives any interest and dividend payments generated by the pledged securities and retains voting rights on any stock that is pledged.

Income Bonds. Bonds often used in corporate reorganizations and in other situations when a company is in financial distress are known as income bonds. Interest on these bonds is paid only when actually earned, making an income bond similar to common stock. However, holders of income bonds do have a prior claim on earnings over stockholders and investors in subordinated debentures. Moreover, some income bonds carry a cumulative feature under which unpaid interest accumulates and must be fully paid before the stockholders receive any dividends.

Equipment Trust Certificates. Resembling a lease in form, equipment trust certificates are used most frequently to acquire industrial equipment or rolling stock (such as trucks, railroad cars, or airplanes). Title to the assets acquired is vested in a trustee (often a bank trust department) who leases these assets to the company issuing the certificates. Periodic lease payments are made to the trustee who passes them along to certificate holders. Title to the assets passes to the borrowing company only after all lease payments are made.

Industrial Development Bonds. In recent years state and local governments have become much more active in aiding private corporations to meet their financial needs. One of the most controversial forms of government-aided, long-term business borrowing is the industrial development bond (IDB), developed originally in the southern states during the Great Depression of the 1930s and used today by local governments scattered throughout the nation. These bonds are issued by a local government borrowing authority in order to provide buildings, land, and/or equipment to a business firm. Because governmental units can borrow more cheaply than most private corporations the lower debt costs may be passed along to the firm as an added inducement to move to a new location, bringing new jobs to the local economy. The business firm normally guarantees bond interest and principal payments by renting the buildings, land, and/or equipment at a rental fee high enough to cover their cost.

Pollution Control Bonds.   Related to industrial development bonds, pollution control bonds are used to aid private companies in financing the purchase of pollution control equipment. In this case local governments frequently will purchase pollution control equipment with the proceeds of a bond issue and lease that equipment to business firms in the area.[6]

INVESTORS IN CORPORATE NOTES AND BONDS

During the 1960s and early 1970s small investors "rediscovered" corporate notes and bonds in their search for higher yields to offset inflation and increased taxes. As the 1970s drew to a close and the 1980s began, however, the interest of small investors in corporate bonds sagged again in the face of soaring inflation and more attractive returns available from money market funds, common stock, real estate, and other assets.

Today, the market for corporate notes and bonds is dominated by insurance companies and pension funds (see Exhibit 19–2). The latter prefer buying corporate bonds in the open market, while insurance companies frequently purchase their corporate securities directly from the issuing company in an "off-the-market" transaction. The stability of cash flows experienced by pension funds and insurance companies permits them to pursue corporate debt obligations with long maturities and lock in their high market yields. Both federal and state laws, however, require these institutions to be "prudent" in their selection of notes and bonds, which generally means buying investment-grade issues in the top four rating categories established by Moody's and Standard & Poor's Corporation.[7]

Commercial banks are not prominent investors in corporate bonds. Gen-

---

[6] Another important type of corporate bond discussed in Chapter 9 is the *convertible bond*. Convertibles may be exchanged for a specific number of shares of common stock at the option of the bondholder. These securities lie midway between stock and corporate debt in their financial characteristics. The value of convertibles to the investor stems as much from the value of the issuing company's stock as it does from the value of the bonds themselves.

[7] As noted in Chapter 8, investment-grade bonds are rated Aaa, Aa, A, and Baa by Moody's. Standard & Poor's assigns ratings of AAA, AA, A, and BBB for these top-quality issues.

EXHIBIT 19–2
Principal Investors in Corporate and Foreign Bonds ($ billions outstanding at year-end)

	1969		1974		1979	
Investor Group	**Amount**	**Percent of Total**	**Amount**	**Percent of Total**	**Amount**	**Percent of Total**
Households	$ 24.8	13.9%	$ 55.2	19.7%	$ 71.6	15.7%
Rest of the world	2.0	1.1	4.0	1.4	10.2	2.2
Commercial banks	1.9	1.1	6.6	2.4	7.7	1.7
Mutual savings banks	6.9	3.9	14.0	5.0	20.8	4.6
Life insurance companies ..	72.7	40.8	96.4	34.4	173.1	38.0
Property-casualty insurance companies	6.3	3.5	10.0	3.6	22.2	4.9
Private pension funds	27.6	15.5	34.0	12.1	55.2	12.1
Government pension funds	30.6	17.2	54.9	19.6	86.2	18.9
Mutual funds	3.6	2.0	3.8	1.4	6.5	1.4
Security brokers and dealers	1.6	0.9	1.8	0.6	2.3	0.5
Totals	$178.0	100.0%	$280.6	100.0%	$455.7	100.0%

SOURCE: Board of Governors of the Federal Reserve System, *Flow of Funds Accounts: Assets and Liabilities Outstanding, 1969–79.*

erally, a banker would prefer to deal personally with his business customer and grant a loan specifically tailored to the borrower's needs rather than enter the highly impersonal bond market. Increasingly in recent years commercial banks have become direct competitors with the corporate note and bond markets through the granting of term loans. A *term loan* is any loan granted by a commercial bank for business purposes which has a maturity of more than one year. Responding to inflation and the soaring cost of business equipment and facilities, bankers have gradually extended the maturity of term loans with many now falling in the 5- to 10-year maturity range. Rates on such loans generally exceed the interest cost on corporate debt sold in the open market, however, especially when banks insist that the borrowing firm keep funds on deposit equal to a specified percentage of the loan.

THE SECONDARY MARKET FOR CORPORATE BONDS

The resale (secondary) market for corporate notes and bonds is relatively limited compared to the market for common stock, municipal bonds, and other long-term securities. Trading volume is thin, even for some bonds issued by the largest and best-known companies. Part of the reason is the small number of individuals active as investors in this market. Individuals generally have limited investment time horizons (holding periods) and tend to turn over their portfolios rapidly when attractive alternative investments appear. In the past secondary market trading in corporate bonds was also held back by the buy and hold strategy of major institutional investors, especially insurance companies and pension funds. Many of these firms purchased corporate bonds exclusively for their interest income and were content to purchase the longest-term issues and simply hold them to maturity. Today, however, under the pressure of volatile interest rates and inflation, many institutions buying bonds have shifted into a new aggressive strategy often labeled "total performance." Institutional portfolio managers are more sensitive today to changes in bond prices and look for near-term opportunities to trade bonds and score capital gains. In fact, a number of insurance companies, pension funds, and mutual bond funds operate their own trading desks and keep a constant tab on developments in the corporate debt markets.

Unlike the stock market, there is no one central exchange for bond trading which dominates the market. While corporate bonds are traded on all major securities' exchanges, including the New York (NYSE) and American (AMEX) exchanges, most secondary market trading in bonds is conducted over the telephone through brokers and dealers. Bond brokers act as middlemen by arranging trades between dealers in return for a small commission. Dealers, on the other hand, commit themselves to take on large blocks of bonds either from other dealers or from pension funds, insurance companies, and other clients. While bond dealers used to carry large inventories of securities in anticipation of customer orders most major dealer houses today have sharply reduced their inventory positions due to rapid and often unpredictable changes in interest rates. Many dealers now try to close out positions taken in individual bond issues in just a few days, frequently act only as middlemen in trades between major institutional investors without commiting their own capital, and often hedge against the risk of large trading losses by using the financial futures markets.

THE MARKETING OF CORPORATE NOTES AND BONDS

New corporate bonds may be offered publicly in the open market to all interested buyers or sold privately to a limited number of investors. The first route, known as a *public sale,* accounts for the largest proportion (about 60 percent) of bond sales each year. Among smaller companies and those firms with unique financing requirements, however, the second route, known as a *private* (or direct) *placement,* has become very popular.

The Public Sale of Bonds

The sale of new corporate bonds and notes in the open market is handled principally by investment bankers. The term *investment banker* is somewhat misleading since these firms have little or nothing to do with banking as we know it. In fact, the Glass-Steagall Act of 1933 prohibits commercial banks from underwriting *any* corporate securities. This law was passed out of fear that commercial bank underwriting of corporate securities would lead either to bank failures or to control of nonfinancial businesses by the banking community.[8]

In contrast to commercial banks which accept deposits from the public, investment bankers underwrite new issues of corporate stocks and bonds and give advice to corporations on their financing requirements. Investment bankers are sometimes called quick intermediaries between the borrower and the ultimate investor in securities. An investment banking firm may singly take on a new issue of corporate securities or band together with other underwriters to form a *syndicate*. Either way, the investment banker's game plan is to acquire new corporate securities at the lowest possible price and sell them to other investors as quickly as possible in order to turn a profit. An investment banker may purchase the securities from the issuing company directly or merely guarantee the issuer a specific price for his securities. With either approach, it is the investment banker who carries the risk of substantial gains or significant losses when the securities are marked for sale in the open market.

The largest issues of corporate bonds and notes sold in the open market are usually bid upon by several syndicates. Competition among syndicates to win a large underwriting contract is usually intense. Investment bankers hope to acquire a new issue at the lowest possible bid price and place the securities with investors at a significantly higher retail price, maximizing the banker's spread. Unfortunately, each new bond issue is always somewhat different from those which have traded before and may involve hundreds of millions of dollars. Moreover, a decision on what price to bid for new securities must be made before the bonds are released for public trading; in the interim, the prices of bonds may change drastically. If the underwriter bids too high a price for the new issue, his firm may not be able to resell the securities at a price high enough to recover its cost and secure an adequate spread. To cite an example, in October 1979 IBM Corporation offered $1 billion in notes and debentures through a collection of Wall Street underwriters. Unfortunately, just as the IBM issue was coming to market, bond prices tumbled and the underwriters lost in excess of $7 million.

Competition in the bidding process tends to narrow the underwriter's spread between bid price and retail (asked) price. If several investment banking houses band together in a syndicate, a *consensus* bid price must be

---

[8] There is currently considerable agitation in the banking community to repeal the Glass-Steagall Act's prohibition against bank underwriting of new corporate securities. The principal reason is that investment banking houses increasingly are competing with commercial banks by offering brokerage accounts, which act as checking and savings deposits and lines of credit. Several investment banking houses, including Merrill Lynch, Bache Halsey, Stuart Shields, and others, have become "symbiotic" financial firms, offering businesses and consumers a wide array of financial services which compete effectively with depository institutions. Many bankers feel this is unfair competition because investment houses face fewer regulations than do commercial banks and other deposit-type financial institutions.

hammered out among the participants. Disagreements frequently arise within a syndicate due to different perceptions on the probable future direction of interest rates and market conditions. Because more than a hundred underwriters may be included in single syndicate, the task of reaching a compromise and placing a unified bid for a new security issue may prove impossible. The old syndicate will break apart with those bidders still interested in the issue hurriedly piecing together a new syndicate and a new bid.

A number of factors are considered in pricing a new corporate bond issue. Certainly the rating assigned by Moody's or Standard & Poor's Corporation is a key item because many investors rely on such agencies for assessing the degree of risk carried by a new security.[9] Another critical factor is the "forward calendar" of security offerings which lists new issues expected to come to market during the next few weeks. Obviously, if a heavy volume of new security offerings is anticipated in the near term, prices will decline unless additional demand appears. Changes in government monetary and fiscal policy also must be anticipated since both can have profound effects on security prices and interest rates. Other factors considered by investment bankers include the overall size of the issue, how aggressive other bidders are likely to be, and the strength of the "book," which consists of indications of advance investor interest in the particular security being offered.

Once the securities are received from the issuing company, the underwriting syndicate will advertise their availability at the price agreed upon by all members of the syndicate. *Delay* in selling new securities is one of the investment banker's worst enemies since he must obtain additional financing to carry his portfolio of unsold securities and there is added risk of price declines. So important to investment bankers are contacts with the retail market for corporate securities that many securities underwriters have merged with retail brokers in recent years in order to maintain close contact with potential customers.

What happens to the market prices of securities being sold by investment banking syndicates is, of course, the key determinant of the success or failure of the underwriting process. If the market price at which a new issue can be sold falls far enough, the syndicate will disband with individual underwriters scrambling to sell their allotments of securities at whatever price the market dictates. The spread between the selling (retail) price of corporate bonds and the proceeds paid to the issuing company (i.e., the flotation cost of a new issue) is usually at or near $7/8$ of a point for top-rated industrial bonds and between $1/2$ and $3/4$ of a point for public utility bonds.[10] Since a spread of $7/8$ of a point is only $8.75 per $1,000 bond, it obviously takes only a small decline in the retail price of a security before the underwriter's profit is eliminated. Moreover, unfavorable price movements can

---

[9] See Chapter 8 and Appendix A for a discussion of security ratings.

[10] See Chapter 7 for a discussion of points in the pricing of bonds.

EXHIBIT 19–3
Type and Industry Source of Bonds and Notes Offered by U.S. Corporations ($ millions)

Type of Issue or Issuer	1977		1978		1979		1980	
	Amount	Percent of Total	Amount	Percent of Total	Amount	Percent of Total	Amount	Percent of Total
Type of offering:								
Public	$24,072	57.39%	$19,815	53.7%	$25,814	64.39%	$41,587	78.2%
Private placements	$17,943	42.7%	$17,057	46.3%	$14,325	35.7%	$11,612	21.8%
Totals	$42,015	100.0%	$36,872	100.0%	$40,139	100.0%	$53,199	100.0%
Industry group:								
Manufacturing	$12,204	29.0%	$ 9,572	26.0%	$ 9,667	24.1%	$15,409	29.0%
Commercial and miscellaneous	6,234	14.8	5,246	14.2	3,941	9.8	6,688	12.6
Transportation	1,996	4.8	2,007	5.4	3,102	7.7	3,329	6.3
Public utilities	8,262	19.7	7,092	19.2	8,118	20.2	9,556	18.0
Communications	3,063	7.3	3,373	9.1	4,219	10.5	6,683	12.6
Real estate and finance	10,258	24.4	9,586	26.0	11,095	27.6	11,534	21.7

Notes: Figures are gross proceeds of issues maturing in more than one year sold for cash in the United States. Offerings of less than $100,000 are excluded as are secondary market sales, intracorporate transactions, open-end investment companies, and employee stock plans.
SOURCES: Securities and Exchange Commission and Board of Governors of the Federal Reserve System.

damage the reputation of the investment banker with both investors and the client companies who issue securities for public sale. The investment banking business is risky, subject to rapid changes with numerous uncertainties, and highly competitive.

Private Placements of Corporate Bonds

In recent years private placements of bonds with one or a limited group of investors have grown rapidly relative to public sales. On average, private placements have amounted to about half of the volume of public offerings of corporate bonds. For example, during the 1977–80 period a total of $61 billion in corporate notes and bonds were privately placed compared to public offering of $111 billion (see Exhibit 19–3). However, the ratio of private to public sales is sensitive to the business cycle and the changing composition of borrowing companies. For example, during periods of rapidly rising interest rates, many public utilities will go into the public market to sell their bonds because utilities usually are able to pass higher borrowing costs along to their customers through rate adjustments. During such periods, sales of corporate bonds in the open market significantly outdistance private placements, as happened in 1979 and 1980. However, periods of falling or relatively stable interest rates often bring out scores of industrial firms seeking borrowed funds, and many of these are smaller companies who cannot go public with their securities. The volume of private sales expands significantly relative to public offerings at these times (as exemplified by the volume of private sales for 1977 and 1978 shown in Exhibit 19–3). For the largest corporations public sales and private placements are substitutes for each other. When interest rates are high or credit is tight in one of these markets, the largest borrowers shift freely and easily to the other market.

Who buys privately placed bonds? Life insurance companies and pension funds are the principal investors in this market. These institutions hope to secure higher yields and protection against call privileges on bonds by engaging in direct negotiation with prospective borrowers. The avoidance of call privileges on corporate securities is of special concern to life insurance companies and pension funds because these institutions often prefer the stable income which comes from purchasing long-term bonds and holding them to maturity. In fact, institutional investors active in the private placement market frequently impose severe penalties in a sales contract for early retirement or refunding of a security by the issuing corporation. Investors other than life insurance companies and pension funds tend to be shut out of the private market due to their lack of financial expertise, small portfolio size, and the absence of a resale market for privately placed securities.[11]

---

[11] Most security offerings in the private placement market are less than $20 million. In contrast, new issues sold in the open market typically range from $20 million on up. Experience has shown that $20 million is just about the minimum amount necessary to develop a good secondary market and give a new security adequate liquidity. At the other extreme, a security

Most private placements are concentrated in the hands of the largest U.S. life insurance companies. Smaller insurance companies, having less technical support, tend to buy most of their securities in the open market or participate with larger companies in private placements. So dominant are life insurance companies in private placements that their financial condition at any particular point in time sets the tone of the whole private market. When these companies are highly liquid and the demand for funds from other sectors of the economy (especially the mortgage market) is weak, life insurers will bid aggressively for new private bonds, and business borrowing costs will drop. During such periods, many large borrowers will switch from public to private sales to take advantage of the ready availability of relatively cheap credit.

The private market is selective by industry type. Corporations active as borrowers in private placements have generally fallen into three groups: (1) public utilities; (2) real estate and financial firms; and (3) industrial companies. Public utilities usually prefer to offer their bonds in the open market. Indeed, restrictions in their charters may require competitive bidding in new public-utility issues. However, when credit conditions tighten, the private placement market is often a more hospitable place to fund the long-term capital needs of utilities. Real estate and financial firms generally have a preference for private placements, over public sales, though they use *both* the public market and the private market extensively. Industrial firms frequently fluctuate between public and private markets in response to interest rates.

There are several *advantages* to the borrower from a private placement. One is the lower cost of distribution since there are no legal registration fees or expenses associated with the issuance of a prospectus as there would be with a public sale. Generally, a more rapid placement of bonds takes place in the private market because only one or a few buyers are involved and the loan is confidential. Special concessions can often be secured by a private sale, such as a commitment for future borrowing. For example, a corporate borrower may negotiate a private sale of $15 million in bonds to an insurance company but also may be granted a line of additional financing in the amount of $2 million a year over the next five years. This kind of future commitment is simply not possible in the impersonal public market where most bonds are highly standardized. Moreover, lenders in the private market usually try to tailor the terms of a loan to match the specific cash-flow and maturity needs of borrowers. This may involve offering a conventional fixed-rate, single-sum credit contract at the prevailing interest rate, a floating-rate loan which can be retired early if cash flows permit, or even a participating loan in which

issue can be too large for public sale with few investment bankers willing to accept the risks involved. For example, during the 1970s several utility bond and stock offerings which exceeded $500 million were positioned through private sale to avoid market risks and large underwriting commissions. While there is much greater variation in security ratings in private as opposed to public sales, most private placements like public sales appear to involve rated securities.

the lender charges a lower interest rate in return for a share of net income from the project financed.[12]

One obvious *disadvantage* is that interest costs are higher in private sales—normally about one percentage point more—than in public sales for bonds of comparable quality and maturity. However, private-sale bonds are less liquid and carry more risk.[13] Still, the larger the size of a corporate issue, the smaller the cost differential between public and private placements.

THE VOLUME OF BORROWING IN THE CORPORATE BOND MARKET

The volume of borrowing through new issues of corporate notes and bonds has grown rapidly in recent years (see Exhibit 19–4). For example,

EXHIBIT 19–4
Growth of Corporate Notes and Bonds in the United States ($ millions)*

Year	New Issues of Corporate Bonds and Notes	Year	New Issues of Corporate Bonds and Notes
1950	$ 4,920	1971	$30,168
1955	7,420	1972	25,774
1960	8,081	1973	20,853
1965	13,719	1974	31,562
1966	15,560	1975	41,664
1967	21,923	1976	41,020
1968	17,384	1977	42,015
1969	18,350	1978	36,872
1970	30,312	1979	40,208
		1980	53,199

* Figures are gross proceeds of issues maturing in more than one year, sold for cash in the United States. Excluded are issues of less than $100,000 and secondary offerings.
SOURCES: U.S. Department of Commerce, *Business Statistics*, 1975 Edition; and Board of Governors of the Federal Reserve System, *Federal Reserve Bulletin*, selected issues.

annual offerings of new corporate debt securities nearly quadrupled between 1960 and 1970, reaching $30 billion in the latter year. Over the next decade, however, the market entered one of the most volatile periods in its history. Faced with record high interest rates and a sluggish recovery from the 1969–70 recession, the volume of new offerings dipped to less than $21 billion in 1973. However, when interest rates declined sharply during the 1975 recession and rose slowly in 1976 and 1977, the volume of long-term corporate borrowings soared. Many companies anticipated significant eco-

---

[12] A participating loan in which the lender shares in a project's net earnings is often called an "equity kicker." Equity kickers are discussed later in this chapter.

[13] Privately placed securities generally carry maturities ranging from 3 years out to 20 years. There is, however, a trend toward shorter maturities, paralleling a similar trend in publicly traded issues.

nomic growth as the 1980s dawned and rushed to borrow in order to expand their facilities. A dip in new borrowings intruded again during 1978 due to a sharp climb in long-term interest rates. During 1980, however, an all-time recorded high in new corporate bond and note offerings was reached—more than $53 billion. This track record reveals quite clearly that the corporate debt market is extremely sensitive to economic conditions (particularly fluctuations in corporate earnings and sales) and to changes in the cost of long-term credit.

Substantial changes have occurred in recent years in the types of firms issuing bonds and notes. The manufacturing and commercial sectors have declined in relative importance as bond issuers with many of these firms turning to commercial banks and the commercial paper market to handle a growing portion of their credit needs. On the other hand, transportation companies and public utilities, confronted with soaring energy and construction costs, have been forced to maintain and even increase their volume of long-term bond offerings. Similarly, the rapid expansion of commercial banks, finance companies, mortgage banking houses, securities dealers, and real estate development corporations has resulted in significantly larger bond issues from these sectors of the economy.

BANK LOANS TO BUSINESS

Commercial banks are direct competitors with the corporate note and bond markets in making both long- and short-term loans to business. At year-end 1980 total commercial and industrial loans extended by banks reached $330 billion, accounting for 35 percent of all loans granted by commercial banks operating in the United States. Business loans are the single largest asset item at most banks, regardless of their size. Moreover, as shown in Exhibit 19–5, commercial banks grant their loans to a wide variety of firms covering all major sectors of the business community.

In recent years the Federal Reserve Board has carried out surveys of business lending practices by banks across the United States. A summary of the findings from a recent business loan survey is shown in Exhibit 19–6. The Federal Reserve survey indicates that bank loans to business firms tend to be short-term or medium-term in maturity. For example, short-term commercial and industrial loans averaged only about two months to maturity, while long-term business loans averaged just under four years. Moreover, the short-term loans—which are used principally to purchase inventories, pay wages and salaries, and meet other current expenses—average considerably larger at most banks than long-term business loans, which are taken out mainly to purchase equipment and expand physical facilities.

The Federal Reserve survey suggests that longer-term business loans tend to carry higher average interest rates than short-term business loans. This is due, in part, to the greater risk associated with long-term credit. Moreover, yield curves have usually sloped upward in recent years, calling for higher

EXHIBIT 19–5
Domestic Commercial and Industrial Loans Granted by Large Weekly Reporting U.S. Banks, June 25, 1980

Industry Group		Volume of Loans Outstanding ($ billions)
Durable goods manufacturing		$ 22.7
Nondurable goods manufacturing		18.3
Food, liquor, tobacco	3.7	
Textiles, apparel, and leather	4.9	
Petroleum refining	2.7	
Chemicals and rubber	3.7	
Other nondurable goods	3.3	
Mining (including crude petroleum and natural gas)		13.8
Trade		24.6
Commodity dealers	1.5	
Other wholesale	11.7	
Retail	11.4	
Transportation, communication, and other public utilities		18.7
Transportation	7.6	
Communication	2.8	
Other public utilities	8.3	
Construction		6.0
Services		20.3
All other business		15.0
Total domestic commercial and industrial loans		$139.4

SOURCE: Board of Governors of the Federal Reserve System, *Federal Reserve Bulletin,* October 1980, Table A22.

average rates on long-term loans.[14] Especially interesting is the high proportion of business loans today which carry *floating* rather than fixed interest rates. The larger and longer-term a business loan is, the more likely its rate will float with market conditions. For example, just 35 percent of the *short-term* business loans included in the August 1980 Federal Reserve Survey of U.S. banks carried floating interest rates, while almost twice as many of the *long-term* business loans—68 percent—had floating rates. Clearly, banks become more determined to protect themselves against unexpected inflation and other adverse developments through floating interest rates as the maturity and average size of a business loan increases.

The Prime or Base Interest Rate

One of the best known and most widely followed interest rates in the financial system is the prime bank interest rate, sometimes called the base

---

[14] See Chapter 8 for a discussion of recent patterns in yield curves and the factors which appear to cause them.

EXHIBIT 19-6
Terms of Lending at U.S. Commercial Banks (Federal Reserve survey of loans made, August 4-9, 1980)

Types of Loans and Terms	Average for Loans of All Sizes ($000)	Loans Arranged by Size ($ thousands)					
		1-24	25-49	50-99	100-499	500-999	1,000 or Over
Short-term commercial and industrial loans:							
Average loan size	$96.7	$ 7.1	$33.3	$63.7	$177.7	$620.9	$4,856.4
Weighted-average maturity in months	2.2	3.0	3.1	3.4	3.5	3.4	1.5
Weighted-average interest rates	11.56%	13.65%	13.53%	13.0%	12.49%	12.01%	10.92%
Percentage carrying floating rate	35.4%	22.1%	30.9%	42.2%	39.2%	68.5%	32.6%
Long-term commercial and industrial loans:							
Average loan size	$75.2		$14.6		$175.6	$649.8	$3,867.6
Weighted-average maturity in months	45.9		33.2		55.1	43.9	47.9
Weighted-average interest rates	12.06%		14.28%		12.57%	12.26%	11.31%
Percentage carrying floating rates	67.8%		20.19%		59.9%	80.9%	81.5%
Construction and land development loans:							
Average loan size	$45.6	$10.5	$37.3	$63.9	$252.9		$1,616.7
Weighted-average maturity in months	8.0	15.2	3.4	4.9	5.2		12.0
Weighted-average interest rates	13.16%	14.87%	13.15%	13.13%	12.74%		12.66%
Percentage carrying floating rate	40.1%	16.8%	14.2%	19.4%	34.2%		87.3%

SOURCE: Board of Governors of the Federal Reserve System, *Federal Reserve Bulletin*, October 1980.

rate.[15] The prime rate is the annual percentage interest rate which banks quote on loans made to their most credit-worthy customers. Most prime loans are unsecured, but the borrower usually is required to keep a deposit at the lending bank equal to a specified percentage of the loan. This so-called compensating balance normally is 15 to 20 percent of the amount loaned. Even for a prime borrower, therefore, the true cost of a bank loan is normally significantly higher than the prime rate itself.[16] Most prime loans are short-term—one year or less—taken out to finance purchases of inventory and meet other working capital needs or to support construction projects. Only a small proportion of U.S. corporations—probably no more than 2,000 of the more than 3 million in existence—have the credit standing needed to qualify as prime-rate customers.

Each bank must set its own prime or base rate, following a vote by its board of directors. Beginning in the 1930s, however, a uniform nationwide prime rate began to appear with differences in rates from bank to bank quickly eliminated by competition. Improvements in communication, the broadening of markets, and the increasing propensity of corporate borrowers to shop around for cheap credit have created a national—even international—market for large corporate loans. Split primes do occur for brief periods, however, due to differences in the formulas used by individual banks to calculate their rates and differences in the availability of bank funds. Thus, a bank strapped for loanable funds may keep its prime temporarily above rates posted by other banks in order to ration the available supply of credit. Similarly, a bank with ample funds to lend may post a prime temporarily below market to encourage its best customers to borrow more frequently and in larger amounts.

Traditionally, the prime rate was set by one or more of the nation's leading banks and other banks played follow the leader in setting their own prime rate. Because changing prime incurs substantial risk for the bank making the

---

[15] *Base rate* is a more general term than prime, referring to that loan interest rate used as the basis for determining the current rate charged a business borrower. Most business loan rates are scaled upward from the base rate. Many commercial loans today, especially those made to the largest corporations, are tied to base rates other than prime. This is frequently the case for large multinational companies that have ready access to the Eurodollar market and other credit markets abroad. For example, the London interbank offering rate (LIBOR) on short-term Eurodollar deposits is often used as a base rate for large corporation loans. In some cases the commercial paper rate or the secondary market rate on bank CDs is also used as a loan base rate.

[16] For example, if a firm borrows $100,000 at a 15 percent prime rate and is required to keep 20 percent (or $20,000) in an interest-free demand deposit, then the effective rate charged by the bank is:

$$\text{Effective loan rate} = \frac{\$15,000}{(\$100,000 - 20,000)} = 18.75\%$$

Thus, the true loan rate in this case is 20 percent higher than the quoted prime rate of 15 percent.

There is a trend away from compensating balances today toward more explicit pricing of bank services. Instead of required deposit balances many banks, at the insistence of their largest corporate customers, are quoting explicit fees for each financial service.

change, shifts in the prime rate prior to the 1970s were infrequent—averaging about once every six months—and usually very gradual (¼ to ½ percentage point) each time a change was made. However, a major innovation in the market for prime-rate loans occurred in October 1971 when First National City Bank of New York (Citibank) announced that it would float its prime. Citibank's basic lending rate was pegged on a weekly basis at ½-percentage point above the yield on 90-day commercial paper. Other major banks soon followed, pegging their prime rates to prevailing yields on U.S. Treasury bills, negotiable CDs, and other money market instruments.

In earlier periods the prime rate was most closely associated with the prevailing yield on high-grade (Aaa) corporate bonds. However, as we observed in Chapter 14, scores of industrial corporations turned to the commercial paper market for funds in the late 1960s and 1970s when banks were unable to meet all their credit needs. Thus, the commercial paper market has provided effective and growing competition for prime-quality bank loans. At the same time, banks have become more heavily dependent on the money market as a source of loanable funds through issuing negotiable CDs and borrowing in the federal funds and Eurodollar markets. For this reason many of the largest banks have found it useful to peg their prime rate to their cost of funds (especially the current yield on negotiable CDs) rather than to rates in the competing commercial paper market. Some banks use both the paper rate and the CD rate in setting prime.

Tying the prime to such active money market rates as those attached to negotiable CDs and commercial paper has resulted in a much more flexible, rapidly changing base lending rate. The prime has come to more accurately reflect the forces of shifting credit demands, fluctuations in government policy, and inflation. For example, as recently as the spring of 1972 the prime rate posted by major U.S. banks dipped to a low of 4.5 percent due to peak loan demand. Spurred on by inflation, sharply higher oil prices, and more rapid economic growth, however, the prime moved up close to 8 percent during 1975, fell back to as low as 6¼ percent in 1977, and then literally soared during the 1978–81 period. For example, in April 1980 the prime reached a record monthly average level of 19.77 percent. It then dropped precipitously during the summer of 1980 to average slightly above 11 percent in August of that year, only to reach for yet another record of 20.35 percent as 1980 drew to a close. These wide swings in prime, while disconcerting to borrowers, have enabled banks to better protect their interest margins—the difference between the return on their loans and the cost of bank funds—and to make credit more readily available to those customers willing to pay the price.

Most business loans today are priced at premiums above prime since only the largest, most financially sound customers qualify for prime itself. Nevertheless, commercial loan rates typically are tied to the base rate through a carefully worked out formula. One popular approach, known as prime-plus, adds on a rate premium for default risk and often an additional premium for longer maturities. Thus, the banker may quote his commercial customer "prime plus 2" with a 1 percent premium above the base rate for default risk and another 1 percent premium for term risk. Other banks use the times-prime method, which multiplies the base rate by a risk factor. For example, the customer may be quoted a loan at 1.5 times prime. If the current prime is 10 percent, this customer will pay 15 percent initially. If the loan carries a floating rate then the interest rate in future periods can always be calculated by multiplying the base rate by 1.5.

Which of the above formulas the banker uses often depends on his forecast of interest rates. In a period of falling rates, interest charges on floating-rate loans figured on a times-prime basis decline faster than those based on prime-plus. And, when interest rates are on the rise, times-prime pricing results in more rapid increases in business loan rates. Therefore, times-prime financing is more sensitive to the changing cost of bank funds over the course of the business cycle.

COMMERCIAL MORTGAGES

The construction of office buildings, shopping centers, and other commercial structures is generally financed with an instrument known as the *commercial mortgage*. Short-term mortgage loans are used to finance the construction of commercial projects, while longer-term mortgages are employed to pay off short-term construction loans, purchase land, and cover property development costs. The majority of long-term commercial mortgage loans are made by life insurance companies, savings and loan associations, and pension funds, while commercial banks are the predominant short-term commercial mortgage lender. Banks support the construction of shopping centers, office buildings, and other commercial projects with loans secured by land and building materials. These short-term mortgage credits usually fall due when construction is completed with permanent mortgage financing of the project then passing to insurance companies, savings and loans, and other long-term lenders.

The growth of commercial mortgages has been quite rapid in recent years, as reflected in Exhibit 19–7. The dollar volume of such loans nearly tripled during the 1970s, rising from about $80 billion to almost $260 billion. However, the market was buffeted by severe problems as the decade of the 80s began. Up to that point, most commercial real estate financing was provided through fixed-rate mortgages. Faced with rapid inflation and soaring interest rates, however, commercial mortgage lenders began searching for new financial instruments to protect their rates of return. Many mortgage lenders today combine both debt and equity financing in the same credit package. The best-known example is the *equity kicker,* where the lending institution grants a fixed-rate mortgage but also receives a share of any net earnings from the project. For example, a life insurance company may agree to provide $10 million to finance the construction of an office building. It agrees to accept a 15-year first mortgage loan bearing a 12 percent annual interest rate

EXHIBIT 19–7
Recent Growth of Commercial Mortgage Loans (end-of-period figures)

Year	Volume of Commercial Mortgages Outstanding ($ billions)
1970	$ 82.3
1971	92.3
1972	112.3
1973	131.3
1974	146.4
1975	158.7
1976	170.8
1977	189.3
1978	212.7
1979	238.4
1980	258.3

SOURCE: Board of Governors of the Federal Reserve System, *Federal Reserve Bulletin,* selected issues.

against the property. However, as a hedge against inflation and higher interest rates, the insurance company may also insist on receiving 10 percent of any net earnings generated from office rentals over the 15-year period.

Another device used recently in commercial mortgage financing is *indexing.* In this case, the annual interest rate on a loan may be tied to the prevailing yields on high-quality U.S. government or public utility bonds of comparable maturity. Lender and borrower may agree to renegotiate the interest rate at certain intervals—every three to five years is common. There is also a trend toward shorter maturity commercial mortgage loans—many as short as five years—with the borrower either paying off the debt or refinancing the unpaid principal with the same or another lending institution.

SUMMARY AND CONCLUSIONS

The majority of funds drawn upon by business firms to meet their working capital and long-term investment needs come not from the financial markets, but from inside the individual firm. In most years well over half of business capital requirements are supplied by net earnings and noncash depreciation expenses—internal cash flow. However, a third to 40 percent of business investment needs in recent years have been met by selling debt and equity securities in the nation's financial markets. The financial system is a backstop for the operations of business firms for those periods when internally generated cash fails to increase fast enough to support the growth of sales and meet customer demands.

The financial markets provide both short-term working capital to purchase inventories and meet current expenses and long-term investment funds to support the purchase of buildings and equipment. The principal external sources of working capital include trade credit (accounts payable), bank loans and acceptances, short-term credits from nonbank financial institutions (such as finance companies and life insurance firms), and sales of commercial paper in the open market. For businesses in need of long-term funding the principal funds sources are the public sale of corporate bonds and notes, the private sale of debt securities to nonbank financial institutions, term loans from banks, and the issuance of common and preferred stock and commercial mortgages.

Corporate bonds have original maturities of more than five years, while notes carry maturities of five years or less. There is a trend today toward shorter maturities of corporate debt securities due to inflation, more rapid changes in technology, and huge federal government deficits which forces corporations into intense competition for funds with the U.S. Treasury. Indexing of corporate bond rates to broader movements in the economy is also becoming more common. A wide variety of different bond and note issues have been developed to provide investors with varying degrees of security and risk protection, including debentures, mortgage bonds, equipment trust certificates, convertible bonds, and government-supported industrial development and pollution control bonds. Each type of bond is accompanied by an indenture spelling out in detail the rights and obligations of borrowers and investors. Corporate notes and bonds are purchased by a wide range of investors today, but the dominant buyers are life insurance companies, public and private pension funds, and households.

New corporate bonds may be offered publicly in the open market where competitive bidding takes place or in a private sale to a limited group of investors. While public sales typically account for the largest portion of annual borrowings, private placements are becoming increasingly popular due to the proliferation of many small firms unable to tap the open market for funds and the unique financing needs of many companies caught in today's turbulent economic and financial environment. Private sales offer the advantages of speed, lower distribution costs, and financing tailor-made to each company's special cash requirements. Public sales offer the advantage of competition as investment bankers, who underwrite new issues of stocks and bonds, bid against each other to win the right to market a new security issue. The process of competitive bidding tends to result in higher security prices and lower interest costs.

The corporate bond market has faced aggressive competition in recent years from commercial banks making long-term business loans. These so-called term loans (about four years in length) are generally used to purchase equipment. Most such loans carry floating, rather than fixed, interest rates tied to the prime lending rate—the interest rate levied on loans made to a bank's most credit-worthy customers. Commercial banks also are the leading financial institution in extending mortgage loans to business. These loans support the construction of office buildings, shopping centers, and other commercial structures. Banks generally specialize in short-term mortgages which finance the construction of commercial facilities, while long-term commercial mortgage financing is provided mainly by insurance companies, savings banks, and pension funds.

Like all long-term debt markets, the trading of commercial mortgages has been profoundly affected by inflation and record-high interest rates in recent years. Traditionally the commercial mortgage, like the corporate bond, has carried a long maturity, a fixed rate of interest, a fixed par principal value, and a fixed maturity. Increasingly, however, institutional lenders are refusing to make long-term commitments of funds on such rigid terms in a volatile economic environment. Participation loans (equity kickers) in which lending institutions receive both interest income and a share of net earnings from business projects are becoming increasingly common. Interest rates on long-term loans frequently are tied to the bank prime rate, yields on high-quality U.S. government or public utility bonds of comparable maturity, or are subject to periodic renegotiation. And, maturities are shortening drastically, placing more and more pressure on business borrowers to refinance their debt and plan more carefully for fluctuating interest rates and credit conditions.

STUDY QUESTIONS

1. Explain what is meant by the phrase, "the financial markets are a supplemental funds source for business." What factors appear to affect the volume of business fund-raising from the money and capital markets?

2. List the principal external sources of business working capital? Of long-term business investment funds? What factors influence which of these various funds sources a business firm will draw upon?

3. Carefully define each of the following terms:
   a. Indenture.
   b. Trustee.
   c. Term bond.
   d. Call privilege.
   e. Sinking fund.
   f. Refunding provision.
   g. Debenture.
   h. Subordinated debenture.
   i. Mortgage bond.
   j. Collateral trust bond.
   k. Income bond.
   l. Equipment trust certificate.
   m. Convertible bond.
   n. Industrial development bond.
   o. Pollution control bond.

4. Explain how the true cost of a corporate bond to the issuing company may be determined.

5. Who are the principal investors in corporate bonds and notes? Why?

6. Describe the role of investment bankers in the corporate bond market. What are the principal risks encountered by these firms? Discuss the factors that must be considered in pricing a new bond issue.

7. What is a private placement? Who buys privately placed bonds and why? What are the principal advantages to the borrower in a private placement of securities?

8. Provide a definition for each of the following terms:
   a. Term loan.
   b. Floating rate.
   c. Prime rate.
   d. Revolving credit.
   e. Stand-by arrangement.
   f. Compensating balance.

9. For what purposes are commercial mortgages issued? What changes have occurred recently in the terms on commercial mortgages. What is an equity kicker?

10. Carefully explain the term *indexing*. Why is this device necessary in today's economy?

SELECTED REFERENCES

1. Block, Ernest. "Pricing a Corporate Bond Issue: A Look Behind the Scenes." *Monthly Review,* Federal Reserve Bank of New York, October 1961.

2. Brimmer, Andrew F. "Credit Conditions and Price Determination in the Corporate Bond Market." *Journal of Finance,* September 1960, pp. 364–70.

3. Budzeika, George "Lending to Business by New York City Banks." *The Bulletin,* New York University, September 1971.

4. Colin, J. W., and Richard S. Bayer. "Calculation of Tax Effective Yields for Discount Instruments." *Journal of Financial and Quantitative Analysis,* June 1970, pp. 365–73.

5. Cook, Timothy Q. "Some Factors Affecting Long-Term Yield Spreads in Recent Years." *Monthly Review,* Federal Reserve Bank of Richmond, September 1973.

6. Crane, Dwight B., and William L. White, "Who Benefits from a Floating Prime Rate?" *Harvard Business Review,* January-February 1972, pp. 121–29.

7. Davidson, Philip H. "Floating the Prime Rate." *Monthly Review,* Federal Reserve Bank of Richmond, August 1972, pp. 10–14.

8. Federal Reserve Bank of Cleveland. "Corporate Bonds, 1960–1968." *Economic Review,* September 1969, pp. 3–16.

9. _____. "Direct Placement of Corporate Debt." *Economic Review,* March 1965, pp. 3–12.

10. Lanza, John W. "Criticism of the Prime Rate." *Journal of Commercial Bank Lending,* February 1973, pp. 48–58.

11. Pye, Gordon. "The Value of Call Deferment on a Bond: Some Empirical Results." *Journal of Finance,* December 1967, pp. 623–36.

12. Ramage, Joseph C. "The Prime Rate." *Monthly Review,* Federal Reserve Bank of Richmond, October 1969, pp. 2–5.

13. Rea, John D. "The Yield Spread Between Newly Issued and Seasoned Corporate Bonds." *Monthly Review,* Federal Reserve Bank of Kansas City, June 1974, pp. 3–9.

14. Wallich, Henry C. "Structural Changes in the Bond Market." Speech before the Second Institutional Investors Bond Conference, New York City, October 8, 1974.

15. White, William H. "The Structure of the Bond Market and the Cyclical Variability of Interest Rates." *International Monetary Fund Staff Papers,* March 1962, pp. 130–37.

16. Wonjnilower, Albert M., and Richard E. Speagle. "The Prime Rate." *Monthly Review,* Federal Reserve Bank of New York, Part I (April 1962), pp. 54–59; Part II (May 1962), pp. 70–73.

20

Corporate Stock

In the preceding chapters we have focused exclusively on debt securities and the extension of credit. In this chapter we examine a unique security which is not debt, but equity. It is a certificate of *ownership* in a corporation, a residual claim against both the assets and earnings of a business firm. Corporate stock grants the investor no promise of return as debt does but only the right to share in the firm's net assets and net earnings, if any.

Corporate stock is unique in one other important respect. All of the securities market we have discussed to this point are intimately bound up with the process of moving funds from ultimate savers to ultimate borrowers in order to support investment and economic growth. In the stock market, however, the bulk of trading activity involves the buying and selling of securities already issued rather than the exchange of financial claims for new capital. Thus, trading in the stock market, for the most part, is *not* closely linked to the saving and investment process in the economy.

Nevertheless, a small portion of trading in corporate shares does involve the sale of new stock to support business investment. Moreover, the stock market has a significant impact on the *expectations* of businessmen when planning future investment, and therefore, stock trading indirectly affects employment, growth, and the general health of the economy.[1] In this chapter

---

[1] One broad index of stock market prices—Standard & Poor's 500 Composite Index—is considered to be a *leading indicator* of subsequent changes in economic conditions, especially of future developments in industrial production, employment, and total spending (GNP). There appear to be several reasons for this. The stock market seems to provide a forecast of business capital spending plans, perhaps reflecting the fact that it captures the expectations of the business community. Stock prices anticipate future changes in corporate profits and, of course,

we take a close look at the basic characteristics of corporate stock and the markets where that stock is traded.

CHARACTERISTICS OF CORPORATE STOCK

All corporate stock represents an ownership interest in a corporation, conferring on the holder a number of important rights and privileges as well as risks. In this section we examine the two types of corporate stock issued today—common and preferred shares.

Common Stock

The most important form of corporate stock is *common stock*. Like all forms of equity, common stock represents a *residual* claim against the assets of the issuing firm, entitling the owner to a share in the net earnings of the firm when it is profitable and to a share in the net market value (after all debts are paid) of the company's assets if it is liquidated. By owning common stock the investor is subject to the full risks of ownership, which means that the business may fail or its earnings may fall to unacceptable levels. However, the risks of equity ownership are limited since the stockholder is liable only for the amount of his or her investment of funds.

If a corporation with outstanding shares of common stock is liquidated, the debts of the firm must be paid first from any assets available. The preferred stockholders then receive their contractual share of any remaining funds. The residual, whatever is left, accrues to common stockholders on a pro rata basis. Unlike many debt securities, common stock is generally a registered instrument with the holder's name recorded on the issuing company's books.

The volume of stock that a corporation may issue is limited by the terms of its charter of incorporation. Additional shares beyond those authorized by the company's charter may be issued only by amending the charter with the approval of the current stockholders. Some companies have issued large numbers of corporate shares, reflecting not only their need for large amounts of equity capital, but also a desire to broaden their ownership base across millions of shareholders. For example, American Telephone and Telegraph (AT&T) has more than 700 million shares of common stock listed on the New York Stock Exchange. International Business Machines (IBM) lists more than 580 million shares.

The *par value* of common stock is an arbitrarily assigned value printed on each stock certificate. Par is usually set low relative to the stock's current

---

these profits are a major source of capital spending which affects the nation's employment and economic growth. In addition, stock prices affect interest rates, which eventually influence business activity. In fact, there is a high *negative* correlation between interest rates (particularly short-term rates) and stock prices. As interest rates on bonds and other fixed-income securities decline, many investors rapidly switch their funds into the stock market.

market value. In fact, today some stock is issued without any par value. Originally, par value was supposed to represent the owners' original investment per share in the firm.[2] The only real significance of par today is that the firm cannot pay any dividends to stockholders which would reduce the company's net worth per share below the par value of its stock. In addition, in the event of liquidation or bankruptcy, the common stockholders may be liable under some circumstances to creditors of the firm for the difference between par value and the subscription price of the stock.[3]

Common stockholders are granted a number of rights when they buy a share of equity in a business corporation. Stock ownership permits them to elect the company's board of directors which, in turn, chooses the firm's officers responsible for day-to-day management of the company. Most companies grant a *preemptive right* when stock is purchased (unless specifically denied by the firm's charter) which gives the individual shareholder the right to purchase any new voting stock, convertible bonds, or preferred stock issued by the firm in order to maintain his pro rata share of ownership. For example, if a stockholder holds 5 percent of all shares outstanding and 500 new shares are issued, this stockholder has the right to subscribe to 25 new shares.[4]

While most common stock grants each shareholder one vote per share, nonvoting common is also issued occasionally. Some companies issue Class A common which has voting rights and Class B common which has a prior

---

[2] The difference between the issue price of stock, which is determined essentially by demand and supply forces in the marketplace, and its par value is known as *capital surplus*. When new common stock is issued, the proceeds of the transaction are recorded in two separate equity accounts—(1) common stock, which shows the par value of each share times the number of shares sold; and (2) additional paid-in capital or capital surplus, which equals the difference between the stock's selling price per share and its par value times the number of shares sold. For example, if a new corporation has just been formed and issues 1 million shares of new common stock at $70 per share, each share having a par value of $20, the equity capital (or net worth) accounts of the corporation would show the following entries:

Equity capital:
Common stock $20,000,000
   (1 million shares at $20 per share)
Additional paid-in capital (or capital surplus)   50,000,000
    Total equity capital $70,000,000

If the issued stock has no par value, the transaction will be entered in the equity accounts at the market value for which the stock was sold.

[3] The critical factor in determining any future liability that might be incurred by current stockholders is the purchase price per share paid by the original investors when the company was formed. If the original investors purchased the company's stock for less than par, subsequent stockholders are liable for the firm's debts in a bankruptcy proceeding up to the amount of the difference between par value and the original purchase price. However, if the original investors purchased the company's shares at par or for more than par, subsequent owners are not liable for the company's debts and can lose no more than the amount they paid for the stock.

[4] Some common stock carries the right of *first refusal,* which means an investor cannot sell his shares to someone other than the current stockholders without offering them the shares first. The right of first refusal is generally used to protect the owners of a small, closely held firm.

claim on earnings but no voting power. The major stock exchanges do not encourage publicly held firms to issue classified common stock, but classified shares are used extensively by privately held firms.

A right granted to all common stockholders is the right of access to the minutes of stockholder meetings and to lists of existing shareholders. This gives the stockholders some power to reorganize the company if existing management or the board of directors is performing poorly. Common stockholders may vote on all matters which affect the firm's property as a whole, such as a merger, liquidation, or the issuance of additional equity shares. This vote may be cast in person or by revocable proxy (which is a temporary assignment of voting power and an instruction on how to vote) granted to a trustee.

Preferred Stock

The other major form of stock issued today is *preferred stock*. Each share of preferred carries a stated annual dividend expressed as a percent of the stock's par value. For example, if preferred shares carry a $100 par value with an 8 percent dividend rate, then each preferred shareholder is entitled to dividends of $8 per year on each share owned, provided the company declares a dividend. Common stockholders would receive whatever dividends remain after the preferred shareholders receive their stated annual dividend.

Preferred stock occupies the middle ground between debt and equity securities, including advantages and disadvantages of both forms of raising long-term funds. Preferred stockholders have a prior claim over the firm's assets and earnings relative to the claims of common stockholders. However, bondholders and other creditors of the firm must be paid before either preferred or common stockholders receive anything. Unlike creditors of the firm, preferred stockholders cannot press for bankruptcy proceedings against a company which fails to pay them dividends. Nevertheless, preferred stock is part of a firm's equity capital and strengthens a firm's net worth account allowing it to issue more debt in the future. It also is a more flexible financing arrangement than debt since dividends may be passed if earnings are inadequate or uncertain and there is no fixed maturity date.

Generally, preferred stockholders have no voice or vote in the selection of management unless the corporation "passes" dividends (i.e., fails to pay dividends at the agreed-upon time). A frequent provision in corporate charters gives preferred stockholders the right to elect some members of the board of directors if dividends are passed for a full year. Dividends on preferred stock, like those paid on common stock, are not a tax-deductible expense. This makes preferred shares nearly twice as expensive to issue as debt for companies in the top-earning bracket. However, IRS regulations specify that 85 percent of the dividends on preferred stock received by a corporate investor are not taxable. This tax-exemption feature makes preferred stock especially attractive to companies seeking to acquire ownership shares in other firms and sometimes allows preferred stock to be issued at a lower net interest cost than debt securities. In fact, corporations themselves are the principal buyers of preferred stock issues.

Most preferred stock is *cumulative,* which means that the passing of dividends results in an arrearage which must be paid in full before the common stockholders receive anything. A few preferred shares are *participating,* allowing the holder to share in the residual earnings normally accruing entirely to the common stockholders. To illustrate how the participating feature might work, assume that an investor holds 8-percent participating preferred stock with a $100 par value. After the issuing company's board of directors votes to pay the preferred shareholders their stated annual dividend of $8 per share, the board also declares a $20-a-share common stock dividend. If the formula for dividend participation calls for common and preferred shareholders to share equally in any net earnings, then each preferred share will earn an additional $12 to bring its total dividend to $20 per share as well. Not all participating formulas are this generous, however, and most preferred issues are nonparticipating since the participation feature is detrimental to the interests of the common stockholders.

Most corporations plan to retire their preferred stock, even though it carries no stated maturity. In fact, the bulk of preferred shares issued today have call provisions. When interest rates decline, the issuing company may exercise the call privilege at the price (which usually includes a premium over par) stated in the formal agreement between the firm and its shareholders. A few preferred issues are *convertible* into shares of common stock at the investor's option.[5] The company retires all converted preferred shares and may force conversion by simply exercising the stock's call privilege. New preferred issues today are often accompanied by a sinking fund provision whereby funds are gradually accumulated and set aside for eventual retirement of preferred shares. A trustee is appointed (usually a bank trust department) who collects sinking fund payments from the company and periodically calls in preferred shares or occasionally purchases them in the open market. While sinking fund provisions allow the issuing firm to sell preferred stock with lower dividend rates, payments into the fund drain earnings and reduce dividend payments flowing to common stockholders.

From the standpoint of the investor, preferred stock represents an intermediate investment between bonds and common stock. Preferred shares often provide more income than bonds but also carry greater risk. Preferred share prices fluctuate more widely than bond prices for the same change in interest rates. Compared to common stock, preferred shares generally provide less total income (considering both capital gains and dividend income) but are, in turn, less risky. They appeal to the investor who is looking for a favorable, but moderate rate of return.

---

[5] See Chapter 9 for a discussion of convertible preferred stock. A convertible preferred issue is usually marked with a "cv" in financial newspapers reporting stock prices. Preferred shares carrying the cumulative feature are often labeled "cum."

Among major corporations preferred stock experienced a resurgence of interest during the 1970s due to high debt financing costs, the greater flexibility of preferred stock financing over bonds, and pressure on many firms (especially public utilities) to rebuild their equity positions. For example, as shown in Exhibit 20–1, the number of issues of preferred stock listed on the

EXHIBIT 20–1
Common and Preferred Stock Listed on the New York Stock Exchange

Year	Common Stock		Preferred Stock	
	Number of Issues Listed at Year-End	Median Dividend Yield*	Number of Issues Listed at Year-End	Median Dividend Yield*
1950	1,039	6.7%	433	4.3%
1955	1,076	4.6	432	4.2
1960	1,126	4.2	402	5.0
1965	1,254	3.2	373	4.7
1970	1,330	3.7	510	6.9
1971	1,399	3.2	528	6.7
1972	1,478	3.0	525	6.7
1973	1,536	5.0	522	8.0
1974	1,534	7.4	537	10.2
1975	1,531	5.0	580	9.3
1976	1,550	4.0	608	8.0
1977	1,549	4.5	628	8.4
1978	1,552	4.8	642	9.4
1979	1,536	5.0	656	10.9

* The dividend yield is calculated by dividing the ratio of cash payments made during the indicated year by the market price at year-end for those equity shares actually paying dividends.
SOURCE: New York Stock Exchange, *Fact Book 1980,* 25th ed., p. 70.

New York Stock Exchange reached a low of 373 in 1965 and then rose to record highs during the 1970s. Many of these new preferred stock issues proved to be extremely popular with investors because of their high dividend yields, which, in several recent periods, have averaged about twice as large as the dividend yields on listed common stock.

STOCK MARKET INVESTORS

Corporate stock is one of the most widely held financial assets in the United States. Only one other financial asset—United States government securities—is held by as large and as diverse a group of individuals and institutions as are common and preferred stock. A shareholder ownership survey conducted by the New York Stock Exchange in 1980 counted 29.8 million stockholders, or about one out of every seven U.S. citizens. While small investors greatly outnumbered institutional holders of stock, financial institutions held about one third of all stock listed on the New York Stock

Exchange in 1980. Institutional investors reporting in the Exchange's ownership survey included life insurance and property-casualty insurance companies, open-end and closed-end mutual funds, private and public pension funds, mutual savings banks, common trust funds, and foreign banks and brokers.[6]

Another important source of information on stockholders in the United States is the Federal Reserve Board's Flow of Funds Accounts.[7] Exhibit 20–2 gives the names of major investor groups and their total holdings of

EXHIBIT 20–2
Principal Investors in U.S. Corporate Stock ($ billions outstanding at year-end)*

	1969		1974		1979	
Investor Group	Amount	Percent of Total	Amount	Percent of Total	Amount	Percent of Total
Households	$746.9	81.7%	$504.8	74.7%	$ 906.9	72.9%
Rest of the world	26.8	2.9	24.2	3.6	49.9	4.0
Commercial banks	0.1	—	0.2	—	0.1	—
Mutual savings banks	2.5	0.3	3.7	0.5	5.5	0.4
Life insurance companies	13.7	1.5	21.9	3.2	40.1	3.2
Property-casualty insurance companies	13.3	1.5	12.8	1.9	25.6	2.1
Private pension funds	61.4	6.7	63.3	9.4	136.4	11.0
Government pension funds	7.3	0.8	16.4	2.4	43.6	3.5
Mutual funds	40.9	4.5	26.3	3.9	33.7	2.7
Security brokers and dealers	1.9	0.2	2.1	0.3	2.7	0.2
Totals	$914.6	100.0%	$675.8	100.0%	$1,244.5	100.0%

* Investor holdings valued at market. Columns may not add to 100 percent due to rounding error.
SOURCE: Board of Governors of the Federal Reserve System, *Flow of Funds Accounts: Assets and Liabilities Outstanding, 1969–1979.*

common and preferred stock at year-end 1969, 1974, and 1979. The exhibit makes clear that households—individuals and families—are the dominant holders of corporate stock in the United States. At year-end 1979, for example, households held about 73 percent of all corporate shares outstanding. Pension funds—both private and government—were a distant second, holding almost 15 percent of available shares. Foreign investors—principally foreign banks, brokers, trusts, and individuals—ranked third with 4 percent of the total. Life insurance companies, mutual funds, and property-casualty insurers each held about 2 to 3 percent of all corporate shares outstanding.

[6] See New York Stock Exchange, *Fact Book 1980,* 25th ed., pp. 49–50.

[7] See Chapter 10 for an explanation of the method of construction and types of information presented in the Flow of Funds Accounts.

The deposit-type financial intermediaries—commercial banks and mutual savings banks—collectively held a meager one half of 1 percent of the total. State laws severely limit savings bank investments in corporate stock, while both state and federal laws prohibit commercial banks from purchasing or underwriting stock. Commercial banks do acquire stock pledged as collateral for loans when the borrower defaults, but such holdings usually must be worked out of the bank's portfolio at the earliest opportunity.

While individuals hold a majority of all equity shares outstanding, their interest in corporate stock has ebbed and flowed with market conditions. For example, as shown in Exhibit 20–3, households were net sellers of equity

EXHIBIT 20–3
Net Purchases of U.S. Corporate Stock by Investor Groups
($ billions at seasonally adjusted rates)

Investor Group	1975	1976	1977	1978	1979	1980*
Households	−$3.5	−$3.2	−$6.1	−$6.2	−$11.9	−$19.1
Rest of the world	4.7	2.8	2.7	2.4	1.6	8.0
Commercial banks	—	—	—	—	—	—
Mutual savings banks	0.2	0.1	0.4	0.1	−0.1	0.8
Life insurance companies	1.9	3.0	1.2	−0.1	—	1.2
Private pension funds	5.8	7.3	4.5	5.3	13.1	15.2
State and local government pension funds	2.4	3.1	3.7	2.7	4.3	7.2
Property-casualty insurance companies	−0.7	0.9	1.2	2.0	2.4	3.8
Mutual funds	−1.1	−2.5	−3.8	−1.6	−2.9	3.7
Security brokers and dealers	1.2	0.4	0.3	−0.9	−1.2	1.1

* Data for first quarter of the year at seasonally adjusted annual rates.
SOURCE: Board of Governors of the Federal Reserve System, *Flow of Funds Accounts,* August 1980.

shares each year of the 1975–80 period. During 1979 individuals and families sold net of any stock purchases almost $12 billion in corporate equities and their net sales of stock accelerated early in 1980. While households were selling large quantities of stock over the 1975–80 period, other investor groups took up the slack with large equity purchases. For example, private pension funds acquired more than $13 billion in corporate shares during 1979, and their purchases accelerated in 1980. State and local government pension funds and property-casualty insurers purchased net almost $7 billion in equity issues during 1979 and stepped up their stock acquisitions as 1980 began.

Fluctuations in the volume of stock purchases have been accompanied by marked changes in the number of shareholders. Periodically, the New York Stock Exchange conducts ownership surveys to determine the number and financial characteristics of stock-market investors. Until recently, the NYSE surveys reported a flight of individuals away from the equity market. For example, the number of individual shareowners declined from 30.8 million in

1970 to 25.3 million in 1975—the first reported decrease in individual stock ownership since the NYSE ownership surveys began in 1952. However, the number of shareholders rose in the late 1970s and early 1980s even as the total dollar volume of household stock investments fell. One reason for the recent increase in the number of equity investors was a rise in first-time stockholders, paralleling the rapid growth of new households in recent years.[8] At the same time, the market posted a strong rally in 1980, though its upward momentum was sharply curtailed by high interest rates in 1981. Other factors arousing recent investor interest in the stock market include a reduction in the federal capital gains tax and a perception on the part of many investors that common stocks are an effective long-run hedge against inflation.

Several financial institutions have increased their participation in the stock market in recent years. As Exhibit 20–2 shows, institutional shareholders held about 23 percent of all equity shares outstanding in 1979 compared to only about 15 percent a decade earlier. Among the various financial institutions, private and public pension funds have expanded their share of the equities market the most with pension-held shares climbing from less than 8 percent of the total outstanding in 1969 to almost 15 percent in 1979. Over the same period, insurance companies increased their holdings from just 3 percent of all equity shares to more than 5 percent. The one financial institution whose share of all equities outstanding fell was mutual funds, traditionally heavy purchasers of common stock. As the stock market behaved erratically during the 1970s, many mutual funds shifted their investment strategy, emphasing bonds and money-market securities instead of equities.[9] By year-end 1979, mutual funds held less than 3 percent of all equity shares available and ranked sixth in total stock holdings behind households, private pension funds, foreign investors, government pension funds, and life insurance companies.

Just as financial institutions as a group have increased their share of total stock ownership, the proportion of daily trading volume in stocks represented by these institutions has also increased. Periodically since 1952, the New York Stock Exchange has conducted a study of the sources of trading volume executed by NYSE member firms in the over-the-counter market and on all U.S. stock exchanges. These periodic studies compare trading activity by dealers and specialists who are members of the NYSE with the volume of trading accounted for by individuals and financial institutions. The latest study conducted in 1976 shows that individuals accounted for 23 percent of the value and 33 percent or the total number of shares traded. Finan-

---

[8] The 1980 New York Stock Exchange ownership survey indicated that the average investor in corporate stock was 45½ years old and held a median stock portfolio of $4,000. A quarter of all shareholders held stock portfolios in excess of $25,000. Forty percent of the stockowners studied in 1980 had acquired their shares through employee stock ownership plans (ESOPs), with the number of such shareholders nearly doubling between 1975 and 1980.

[9] See Chapter 5 for a discussion of the portfolio investment characteristics of mutual funds and other types of investment companies.

cial institutions, on the other hand, represented 55 percent of the value of all stock traded and slightly less than 45 percent of the total number of shares exchanged. On the New York Stock Exchange itself—the core of the public market—individuals represented 30 percent of the dollar volume of daily trades, while financial institutions represented 70 percent of the daily total.[10] The increasing volatility of economic conditions coupled with the stock market's lackluster performance for most of the past decade has given a definite advantage to financial institutions with greater staying power and technical expertise than normally possessed by the small investor.

CHARACTERISTICS OF THE CORPORATE STOCK MARKET

There are two main branches of the market for trading in corporate shares. One is the *organized exchanges* which, in the United States include the New York (NYSE) and American (AMEX) exchanges plus regional exchanges, including the Pacific (PSE), Midwest (MSE), Philadelphia (PHLX), Boston (BSE), and Cincinnati (CSE) exchanges. The regional exchanges historically have served to promote trading mainly in securities of interest to investors in their particular region of the nation. Today, however, the regional exchanges have penetrated the national market and rely to a significant degree upon transactions in securities listed on both AMEX and the NYSE. All the exchanges today use similar procedures for controlling membership, regulating trading, and recording purchases and sales of stock.

Trading on these exchanges is governed by regulations and formal procedures designed to insure both competitive pricing of shares and an active market for the stock of the largest, financially stable companies. In contrast, the second branch of the equities market—the over-the-counter (OTC) market—involves trading of stock through brokers operating off the major exchanges. This "over the telephone" market is much more informal and fluid than exchange trading and includes the stocks and bonds of many small and medium-sized companies and large numbers of banks, mutual funds, and other financial institutions.

The Major Organized Exchanges

Approximately three quarters of all trading in U.S. corporate shares occurs on the organized exchanges. By far the largest and best-known of these is the Big Board—the New York Stock Exchange. In recent years the Big Board has accounted for four fifths or more of both the number of shares and the total market value of all equities traded on U.S. exchanges. The second largest exchange—the American Stock Exchange (ASE or AMEX)—in most years accounts for about one tenth of all shares traded. The NYSE, AMEX, and the regional exchanges overlap each other in trading and function and therefore are competitive markets for the most actively traded U.S.

---

[10] See New York Stock Exchange, *Fact Book 1980*, p. 51.

stocks. For example, more than four fifths of the volume of trading on the regional exchanges is in stocks listed on the New York Stock Exchange. Moreover, in 1978 the Intermarket Trading System (ITS) was set up to electronically link the Big Board with five other exchanges and create additional intermarket competition. Stock brokers and specialists on one exchange now can directly contact traders on the other exchanges in order to find the best prices for their customers.

Each exchange provides a physical location for trading, and trading by member firms must be carried on at that location. On the floor of the NYSE, for example, are 18 counters, each with several windows or *trading posts*. A handful of the more than 1,500 common stock listed and available for trading on the NYSE are traded from each post as prescribed by the Exchange's Board of Governors.[11] The exchanges permit the enforcement of formal trading rules in order to achieve an efficient and speedy allocation of available equity shares.

In order to be eligible for trading on an organized exchange, the stock must be issued by a firm *listed* with the exchange. A substantial number of major U.S. corporations are listed simultaneously on several different exchanges. The listing qualifications demanded by the New York Stock Exchange are the most comprehensive and difficult to fulfill, which serves to limit NYSE trading to stocks issued by the largest and most financially stable companies. The most important listing requirements of the NYSE are summarized in Exhibit 20–4. The basic intent of these rules is to insure that the

EXHIBIT 20–4
Requirements for Listing a Company on the New York Stock Exchange

Minimum Requirements for Initial Listing on the Exchange:

A. Demonstrated earning power, with before-tax earnings of at least $2.5 million in the most recent year and at least $2 million during the previous two years.
B. Adequate size of company operations, with net tangible assets of at least $16 million.
C. Adequate minimum market value of publicly held shares, adjusted for market conditions.
D. A sufficient number (currently 1 million) of common shares held by the public.
E. Shares which are held widely enough to promote an active market—currently at least 2,000 shareholders with 100 or more shares each are required to qualify.

Requirements for Continued Listing

A. Periodic public disclosure of financial condition and earnings.
B. Maintenance of an adequate number of publicly traded shares outstanding. The Exchange would consider suspending or removing a company's security from the trading list if there are fewer than 1,200 round-lot investors, 600,000 or fewer shares in public hands, and the aggregate market value of publicly held shares falls below acceptable limits.

SOURCE: New York Stock Exchange.

---

[11] At year-end 1979 there were 1,536 different issues of common stock listed on the NYSE and a total of 30 billion shares available for trading.

listed company has a sufficient volume of shares available to create an active national market for its stock and discloses sufficient data so that interested investors can make informed decisions. Even if a company meets all of the formal listing requirements shown in Exhibit 20–4, its stock must still be approved for admission to the Exchange by the board of directors, which includes 10 members elected by firms with seats on the exchange.[12] Corporations which are successful in listing their stock must make an annual disclosure of their financial condition, limit trading by insiders, publish quarterly earnings reports, and help maintain an active and deep public market for their shares. If trading interest in a particular firm's stock falls off significantly, the firm may be *delisted* from the Exchange. Under some circumstances a firm may be granted "unlisted trading privileges" if its stock has been previously listed on another exchange.

Member firms of the exchange are the only ones who may trade in listed securities on the exchange floor, either for their own account or for their customers. At year-end 1979 the NYSE had 1,484 members of which 1,366 members actually owned "seats" on the exchange and held claims against the exchange's net assets. The majority of seat owners are directors or partners of brokerage firms, and some of these firms own several seats. Member firms are allowed to sell or lease their seats with the approval of the exchange's governing board. The price of a seat on the NYSE varied between $80,000 to more than $200,000 in 1979.

Member firms fulfill a variety of roles on an exchange. Some act as *floor traders* who buy and sell only for their own account. Floor traders are really speculators whose portfolios turn over rapidly as they drift from post to post on the exchange floor looking for profitable trading opportunities. Other members serve as *commission brokers,* employed by member brokerage firms to represent orders of their customers on the exchange floor, and *floor brokers,* who are usually individual entrepreneurs carrying out buy and sell orders from other brokers not present on the exchange floor.

A few traders holding exchange seats are *specialists* who trade in one or a limited number of stocks. The nearly 100 specialist firms operating on the New York Stock Exchange act as *both* brokers and dealers, buying and selling for other brokers and from their own account when there is an imbalance between the supply and demand for the stocks in which they specialize. Specialists help to create orderly and continuous securities markets and stabilize prices by agreeing to undertake immediate trading to cover unfilled customer orders.[13] However, in return for this service of immediate trading, they profit by purchasing stocks from public sellers at discounts from the market price and by selling stocks at a premium above the market price.

---

[12] Listing of a company which meets all of the NYSE requirements shown in Exhibit 20–4 is not automatic. The NYSE's board of directors also considers the degree of national interest in the company, whether it is in an expanding industry and is likely to at least retain its relative position, and the stability of the industry involved.

[13] The specialist function entails considerable risk of failure in an adverse market. Consequently, most exchanges impose minimum capital requirements on specialist firms.

Finally, a few *odd-lot traders,* typically representing large brokerage firms dealing with the public, also are active on the exchange floor. Odd lots are buy or sell orders involving less than 100 shares, which come primarily from small individual investors. The odd-lot trader typically will purchase 100 or more shares—a *round lot*—and retain any extra shares in his portfolio that are not needed by customers.

Stock exchanges are among the oldest American institutions. The New York Stock Exchange, for example, was set up following an agreement among 24 Wall Street brokers in May 1792, just three years after the U.S. Constitution was adopted. The exchanges provide a continuous market, centered in an established location, for buying and selling equity shares with rigid rules to insure fairness in the trading process. By bringing together buyers and sellers, the exchanges, at one and the same time, make stock a liquid investment, promote efficient pricing of securities, and make possible the placement of huge amounts of financial capital. Without the benefits of exchange trading the volume of investment in the economy undoubtedly would be smaller and the economy's rate of growth much slower.

The Informal Over-the-Counter Market

The large majority of securities bought and sold in the United States, especially debt securities, are traded over-the-counter (OTC) and not on organized exchanges. The customer places a buy or sell order with a bank, broker, or dealer which is then relayed via telephone, by wire, or by computer terminal to the particular dealer or broker with securities to sell or an order to buy. Each broker or dealer seeks the best possible price on behalf of himself or his customer, and the resulting competition to find the "best deal" brings together traders located hundreds or thousands of miles apart. The prices of actively traded securities respond almost instantly to the changing forces of demand and supply so that security prices constantly hover at or near competitive, market-determined levels.

All money market instruments are traded in the over-the-counter markets as are the large majority of government (federal, state, and local) bonds and corporate bonds. While most common stocks are traded on the exchanges, an estimated one quarter to one third of all stocks are traded OTC. The OTC market is generally preferred by financial institutions, especially commercial banks, bank holding companies, mutual funds, and insurance companies, because in many cases their shares are not actively traded and OTC trading and disclosure rules are less restrictive. The presence of financial institutions tends to give the OTC market a more conservative tone than the exchanges.

Many dealers in the OTC market act as *principals* instead of brokers as on the organized exchanges. That is, they take "positions of risk" by buying securities outright for their own portfolios as well as for retail customers.[14]

---

[14] See Chapter 12 for a discussion of the sources and uses of dealer funds and the risks inherent in dealer operations.

Several dealers will handle the same stock so the customer can shop around. All prices are determined by negotiation with dealers acquiring securities at a bid price and selling them at an asked price. The OTC market is regulated by a code of ethics established by the National Association of Security Dealers, a private organization which encourages ethical behavior among its members. Trading firms or their employees who break NASD's regulations may be fined, suspended, or thrown out of the organization.

One of the most important contributions of NASD in recent years has been the development of NASDAQ—the National Association of Security Dealers Automated Quotations System. Launched in 1971, NASDAQ displays bid and asked prices for thousands of OTC-traded securities on video screens connected electronically to a central computer system. All NASD-member firms trading in a particular stock report their bid-ask price quotations immediately to NASDAQ. This nation-wide communications network allows dealers, brokers, and their customers to determine instantly the terms currently offered by major securities dealers.[15]

THE THIRD MARKET: TRADING IN LISTED SECURITIES OFF THE EXCHANGE

The market for securities listed on a stock exchange but traded over the counter is known as the third market. Broker and dealer firms not members of an organized exchange are active in this market, which deals mainly in NYSE-listed stocks. The original purpose of the third market was to supply large blocks of shares to institutional investors, especially mutual funds, bank trust accounts, and pension funds. These investors engage mainly in *block trades,* defined as transactions involving 1,000 shares or more. Presumably, the largest block traders possess the technical know-how to make informed investment decisions and then carry out transactions without assistance from a stock exchange and the high brokerage commissions that may entail. By trading with third-market broker and dealer firms, who, in effect, compete directly with specialists on the exchanges, a large institutional investor frequently can lower transactions costs and trade securities faster. By offering few peripheral services and trading in large volume, the third-market broker or dealer has little overhead and low average costs per transaction.

It has been alleged in the past that the existence of the third market has had a number of undesirable effects. Prices may be more unstable on the organized exchanges due to the presence of third-market activity, creating more risk for the small investor who buys listed stock. The third market, however, provides additional competition for the organized exchanges and

---

[15] NASDAQ is a quotation system designed to report completed transactions rather than a device to carry out actual transactions. To be listed on NASDAQ a minimum number of shares must be publicly held to insure a relatively continuous market, and there must be at least two registered market-makers for the security. In addition, the firm whose securities are included in the NASDAQ system must satisfy NASD's asset-size and equity capital standards.

especially the New York Stock Exchange. Moreover, along with the other over-the-counter markets, the third market has been a catalyst in reducing brokerage fees and promoting trading efficiency. The growth of third market and other OTC trading during the 1970s encouraged the "unbundling" of commissions at many broker and dealer firms to more accurately reflect the true cost of each security trade. Many brokerage firms today, especially those active in odd-lot trading, provide their customers with a wide array of peripheral services—research on market trends, security credit, accounting for purchases and sales, etc.—and often the customer pays for these services whether or not he or she needs them. The largest institutional investors have little need for such services, however, and seek out brokers and dealers offering their services at minimum cost.

The flight of major stock investors into the third market and other OTC markets is gradually bringing about pricing policies in the industry geared more directly to actual services used. However, the third market itself has declined in importance in recent years. While major stockbrokers and dealers used to quote set commissions, the demise of the fixed commission system in May 1975 and the appearance of numerous "discount" brokerage houses during the 1970s[16] have caused many institutional customers to abandon the third market and return to more traditional channels for executing their security orders. Today, about one fourth of all shares traded on the New York Stock Exchange are part of large block transactions.

THE FOURTH MARKET: DIRECT TRADING BETWEEN BUYERS AND SELLERS

Not all the institutions and individuals who buy and sell stock require the services of a broker or dealer. When buyer and seller trade *directly* with each other (usually by telephone or teletype), they become part of the "fourth market" for equity shares. Through a direct exchange of stock, individuals and institutions can escape large brokerage commissions, excess publicity, and security registration requirements. Generally, fourth-market transactions involve large blocks of securities exchanged with the aid of an individual or firm who arranges the terms of trade in return for a small commission or subscription fee. An automated communications system called INSTINET supplies quotations and automatic execution of trades for fourth-market traders. Subscribers to INSTINET can use the automated system to identify likely buyers or sellers of a security and then carry out negotiations over the telephone.

Because the fourth market permits direct negotiation between buyer and

---

[16] Discount brokerage firms offer trading services at commission rates as much as 80 percent less than the rates quoted by so-called full-service brokerage firms. The more than 100 discount houses currently operating cut costs by not giving investment advice or offering personal account management to their customers. One of the most rapidly growing new financial institutions, they represent about 10 percent of all commission business today.

seller, with the potential for substantial cost savings, it offers strong competition to all other segments of the stock market. Many financial analysts believe that the fourth market will capture a larger and larger share of stock market trading in future years due to the expanding role of financial institutions who have little need for specialist firms or brokers.

THE DEVELOPING MARKET FOR STOCK OPTIONS

Paralleling the exchange and over-the-counter markets for common and preferred stock is a growing market for *stock options*. An option is an agreement between two parties granting one party the right (but not the obligation) to purchase an asset from or sell to the other party under specified conditions. In the stock market there are both *call* and *put* options with the call option predominant today.

A *call* option grants the buyer the right to purchase a specified number of shares of a given stock at a specified price up to an expiration date. Call options become attractive when the investor expects the price of a given stock to rise above the price specified in the option contract (known as the "striking price" or "exercise price"). Thus, an option may be available to buy 500 shares of the common stock of Caledonia Manufacturing Company at $6 per share. If the stock rises to a price of $7.50 in the open market, the holder of the option can buy $3,750 worth of stock for only $3,000.

Another potential advantage of options is the amount of financial *leverage* they grant the investor. Less money is required to control a specified number of equity shares than would be necessary if the stock were purchased outright. In addition, even small changes in the price of a stock can lead to magnified changes in the value of an option. It is not uncommon for an option to double or triple in price even though the price of the stock itself may increase by only 15 to 20 percent.

Trading in options gained widespread interest among U.S. investors early in the 1970s, and many corporations today offer stock options to their employees. In 1973, the Chicago Board Options Exchange initiated trading in options for selected stocks listed on the major exchanges. Today, so-called *listed* or exchange-traded options substantially outnumber over-the-counter (OTC) or negotiated options purchased through brokers and dealers. Listed options and their current holders are all recorded on computerized records maintained by the Options Clearing Corporation which also guarantees delivery of the stock in the event the seller defaults. Trading in options is by contract with each agreement covering 100 shares of stock.

Despite their growing popularity, call options are not without some serious disadvantages. One of these is the federal tax treatment of gains from trading in options. If the investor exercises his option, the difference between the option price and the market price of the stock at time of purchase is taxed as ordinary income, not capital gains, up to a maximum of 50 percent. For example, if an investor in the top income bracket uses a call option to purchase 500 shares of Caledonia Manufacturing at $6, currently selling for $7.50 in the market, the $750 total paper gain will be subject to a maximum tax of $375 (i.e., 50 percent of the gain). However, if the stock continues to rise in price after it is purchased, any additional gain will be taxed at the more favorable capital gains rate, provided the stock is held for at least a year. Under IRS rules a call option can be valid for up to 10 years.

The opposite of a call option is known as a *put*. Puts grant the investor the right to *sell* a specified number of equity shares at a set price on or before the expiration date. Unlike a call, the investor in puts hopes the associated stock will drop in price so that he can sell at a price higher than is currently available in the market. In this sense, puts are similar to selling a stock *short* (i.e., the sale of borrowed stock) in the hope that its price will fall. However, puts require less capital and usually result in a lower total brokerage commission than short sales of stock. Also, the investor's potential loss is limited to the price of the put plus brokerage commission regardless of what happens to the price of the underlying stock.

Puts often become quite popular in bear markets when the long-run outlook is for significant declines in stock values. Moreover, as a result of a ruling by the Securities and Exchange Commission in 1980, puts are likely to become even more popular with investors in the future. The SEC granted stock option exchanges permission to increase the number of stocks against which puts could be issued and traded. Prior to that decision put options were available on only 25 stocks. The long-run SEC goal apparently is to permit trading in puts for all those equity shares which have call options. Like calls, puts are traded both over-the-counter and on exchanges.[17]

Traditionally, puts, like call options, have been regarded as a speculative investment since they permit the use of considerable financial leverage. In reality, puts are similar to *insurance* because they enable the investor to place a "floor" under the price of a given stock. Puts may subject the investor to an adverse tax situation in some instances, however, because of their capacity to reduce risk. The IRS may rule in a given situation that the period during which a put was in effect cannot be counted towards establishing long-term capital gains when the associated stock is finally sold.

Some investors will combine put and call options to establish a *straddle* on a given stock. A straddle is simply a combination trade where the investor purchases a put and a call on the same stock, both carrying the same exercise price and maturing on the same date. For example, suppose the stock of Caledonia Manufacturing is selling for $7.50, but the market is so volatile the investor is highly uncertain as to its future direction. To protect against an unexpected move, the investor buys a call option with a strike price of $8 and an $8 put option, each costing $1. Profits will be made if either the call or the

---

[17] Normally the exercise price and number of shares in an option contract are automatically adjusted when stock splits occur or stock dividends are paid on the associated stock. Over-the-counter calls and puts provide extra protection for the investor by reducing the exercise price by the amount of any cash dividends paid on the associated stock.

put increase in value by more than $2. A rise in the market value of Caledonia's stock will cause the call option to rise in value; a fall in the stock's price will cause the put's value to increase. Sometimes, if the market fluctuates violently, *both* the put and call options will turn out to be profitable, though usually one or the other will expire without being used. An option that expires without being exercised is worthless.

THE DEVELOPMENT OF A UNIFIED NATIONAL MARKET FOR STOCK

It is clear from the foregoing discussion that the stock market is fractured into several different parts, each with its own unique collection of brokers and dealers and, in some cases, its own unique collection of customers. However, one of the most significant developments during the 1970s was a movement spurred by government regulation and industry competition to weld all parts of the equities market together into a single national market. In 1975 Congress passed the Securities Acts Amendments, the most sweeping and potentially significant piece of securities legislation since the Great Depression of the 1930s. The amendments instructed the Securities and Exchange Commission to "facilitate the establishment of a national market system for securities" in order to promote the development of nationwide competition. While the new law did not specify what the proposed national market system would look like or what kinds of securities would be involved, the *intent* of Congress was to insure that all investors, regardless of their location, would have ready access to information on security prices and could transact business at the best available price. As the Securities Act Amendments state:

> The linking of all markets for qualified securities through communication and data processing facilities will foster efficiency, enhance competition, increase the information available to brokers, dealers, and investors, facilitate the offsetting of investors' orders, and contribute to the best execution of such orders.[18]

Because the stock market is so popular with both large and small investors and divided into so many fragments, it has become the principal target of reform measures to encourage the development of a true national securities market. Shortly after the Securities Act Amendments became law, the New York Stock Exchange announced that it would begin reporting daily trades of NYSE-listed stocks as they occurred on the principal exchanges. This meant that up-to-the minute information on the latest stock trades would be reported on a *consolidated* or *composite tape,* available through the familiar stock ticker machines, regardless of which of the major American exchanges handled the transaction. The principal equities markets now represented on the consolidated tape include the NYSE, AMEX, Boston, Cincinnati, Midwest, Pacific, and Philadelphia exchanges. More than 12 million separate

---

[18] See Section 11A of the Securities Act Amendments of 1975.

stock transactions, involving 9.3 billion shares, were reported on the consolidated tape in 1979. Data from the consolidated tape is used to compile the composite stock price averages which are reported on radio and television news programs and published in daily newspapers.

While the invention of the consolidated tape was an important step in developing a national market system, it only provided investors with an indication of current trends in the market. No information was provided on the best bid and asked prices available nationwide, even for the most actively traded stocks. The Securities and Exchange Commission responded to this need shortly after the Securities Act Amendments were passed by asking each stock exchange to make their quotations more readily available to brokers and dealers. The first major step in that direction occurred in April 1978 with the development of the Intermarket Trading System (ITS). Through this electronic medium, brokers and specialists can compare bid and ask prices on all the major exchanges for about 700 different stocks through a central computer system which stores and dispenses price information.[19] If the Philadelphia Exchange, for example, is offering a better price for AT&T stock than prevails on the NYSE, a broker or market specialist can immediately place an order through the Philadelphia Exchange without any additional cost. In effect, ITS brings major equities markets into direct price competition with one another for trades in the most popular corporate stocks.

However, there are some problems with the ITS. First, it is separate from the consolidated tape system, and that separation creates time delays. When brokers are pressed by a heavy volume of customer orders, they often simply ignore the Intermarket Trading System. Moreover, ITS does not guarantee that all customer orders will be filled at the best available price. Brokers on the New York Stock Exchange, for example, are not obligated to accept a better deal which might be available on another exchange.

Paralleling the development of ITS, the Cincinnati Stock Exchange has created the National Securities Trading System (NSTS). This system permits automated purchases and sales from the offices of member brokerage firms as well as from the floor of the exchange. Efforts are underway to tie NSTS into ITS and broaden the growing national market. Also aiding the unified market's spread was a recent decision by the Securities and Exchange Commission, issued as Rule 19c-3. This new rule states that any stock not being traded on an organized exchange on or before April 26, 1979 may be traded off the exchange by member firms. Previously, a broker or securities dealer with membership on an exchange could not trade listed stocks anywhere but on the floor of the exchange.[20] Under 19c-3, however,

---

[19] Major exchanges currently participating in the ITS network include the American, Boston, Midwest, New York, Pacific, and Philadelphia Exchanges.

[20] For example, Rule 390 of the New York State Exchange requires NYSE members to execute all dealer orders for NYSE-listed stocks on that particular exchange. NYSE members cannot send their trading orders away from the exchange floor. In July 1980, the SEC, as an

exchange members may trade *newly listed* stocks over the counter or on the exchange itself. This SEC decision brings the exchanges and OTC market into direct competition for the trading of *new* stock.

Among the more recent developments leading to a national market system was a series of decisions by the National Association of Security Dealers (NASD) in 1979 and 1980 to further automate price quotations on over-the-counter stocks. Computer terminals with greatly expanded capacity now include a wide array of information on bid and asked prices offered by traders who may be hundreds or thousands of miles distant. At the same time, NASD and representatives of the ITS have moved to electronically link quotations and trading on the six major exchanges with OTC quotations and trading.

In February 1980, the Securities and Exchange Commission adopted new regulations aimed at improving the flow of stock-price information to both brokers and investors. Previously, the NASDAQ quotation system for securities traded over the counter had carried only "representative" bid and asked prices.[21] Effective July 5, 1980, however, NASDAQ was required to display on its terminals the highest bid prices and the lowest asked prices present in the market. The new rule aids investors in determining what price brokers are actually paying to execute a customer purchase order or what the true sales price is when the customer places his shares on the market. In theory, at least, the rule promotes competition among OTC brokers and makes it easier for customers to negotiate low commission rates.

Another new SEC rule, which took effect in October 1980, requires that the consolidated tape carrying price quotations for stock listed on the major exchanges always includes the best price available on *any* stock, regardless of which exchange is quoting that price. Previously, quotation display screens were linked to a system which made price quotations on the NYSE the easiest to retrieve, granting the Big Board a decided advantage over the regional exchanges. Moreover, under a recent SEC rule, price quotes on the tape or display screens are considered firm and binding commitments to trade.

Despite all of these recent changes, no true national market system for stocks exists at this time. For example, while the consolidated tape reports the best bid and asked prices in the different markets, it does not permit brokers on one market to send orders to other markets. However, it should be obvious from the foregoing discussion that substantial progress has already been made toward a unified market, and a strong commitment on the

experiment, waived Rule 390 for 130 stocks listed on the NYSE. For these particular shares even member brokerage firms can execute their customers' orders without taking them to the exchange floor, and they then merely report any off-floor transactions directly to the consolidated tape. Only time will tell whether this experiment succeeds and whether Rule 390 can be completely waived.

[21] The representative bid price is defined as the median bid of all those made over a certain short period of time. The representative asked price includes the median bid price plus the median trading spread between bid and asked prices.

part of Congress and the regulatory agencies (especially the Securities and Exchange Commission) should insure further progress toward a true national system.[22] Rapid developments in the technology of information transfer are breaking down the barriers to free and open stock trading posed by geography, traditional business practices, and outmoded regulations. The new centralized computer systems, such as ITS, coupled with cheaper electronic methods for information transfer and display permit the United States to preserve and integrate existing markets (including the major exchanges) instead of requiring the creation of an entirely new and untried market system. Thus, the new is gradually merging with the old through the medium of electronics.

RANDOM WALK AND EFFICIENT MARKETS

Stock market behavior has figured prominently in the development of modern theories of what determines the market price or value of securities. One of the most popular of modern theories regarding the valuation of stocks and other securities is the *random-walk hypothesis*.

Random walk is a term used in mathematics and statistics to describe a process in which successive elements in a data series are independent of each other and therefore are essentially random and unpredictable. The theory of random walk applied to the valuation of stocks says that the future path of individual stock prices is no more predictable than is the path of a series of random numbers. Each share of stock is assumed to have an *intrinsic value* based upon investor expectations of the discounted value of future cash flows generated by that stock. The market price per share is an unbiased estimator of a stock's intrinsic value and reflects the latest information available concerning the issuing company's condition and future prospects. Successive changes in the price of a stock are random fluctuations around that stock's intrinsic value, and these changes are independent of the sequence of price changes which occurred in the past. For example, it is impossible to predict this week's stock price from last week's stock price. Knowledge of the sequence of past price changes prior to the current time period is of little or no help in defining the probability distribution of price changes in any current or future period.[23]

The random walk notion is not accepted by all stock-market analysts. Many analysts still subscribe to so-called chartist or *technical analysis* theo-

---

[22] Evidence that a more competitive environment for the pricing of brokerage services has appeared is provided in a recent SEC staff report. The SEC study revealed that between April 1975 and December 1979 brokerage commissions declined by 18 percent for trades involving individual investors and 55 percent for trades involving institutional investors. (See reference 28 at the end of this chapter.) Institutional investors receive lower commission rates due to cost economies on large-scale securities transactions and the superior bargaining power of block traders.

[23] Good explanations of the random-walk hypothesis are provided by Cootner (4) and Fama (9).

ries, which assume that the past behavior of a security's price is rich in information concerning the future behavior of that price. Patterns of past price behavior, technical analysts argue, will tend to reoccur in the future. For this reason, careful analysis of stock price averages and the prices of individual shares will reveal important data concerning future price movements.[24] Unfortunately, existing empirical evidence does not indicate any meaningful degree of dependence of future stock price movements upon those occurring in the past. Important research studies by Fisher and Lorie (12), Mandelbrot (22), Fama (9), Granger and Morgenstern (15), Westerfield (28), and others show that recent changes in stock prices are not significantly related to past price changes.

Another test performed on the technical analysis theory has been to try various mechanical trading or "filter" rules to see if the investor is better off using these rules instead of a simple buy and hold strategy. Filter rules usually require the investor to buy if a security's price goes up at least Y percent and sell when the security's price declines by Y percent or more. Research studies by Alexander (1), Fama and Blume (10), and others have tested values of Y ranging from less than 1 percent to at least 70 percent. The results generally favor the simple buy and hold strategy, especially after brokerage commissions are considered. Average earnings generated by trading rules appear to be no better and often considerably worse than those achieved if the investor randomly selected a group of stocks representative of the market as a whole and held them for his full holding period.[25]

The random walk notion has been supplemented in recent years by a much broader theory of stock price movements known as the *efficient markets hypothesis*. A market is "efficient" if scarce resources are allocated to their most productive uses. In each case those buyers willing and able to pay the highest prices for each resource must receive the resources they require.[26] In a perfectly efficient securities market the prices of securities fluctuate ran-

---

[24] See, for example, Edwards and Magee (6) and Levy (19). Technical analysts focus upon a study of the stock market itself and not upon external factors (such as economic conditions) which influence the market. External factors are presumed to be fully reflected in share prices and the volume of stock exchange trading. Thus, all the relevant information for analyzing and predicting stock price behavior is assumed to be provided by the market itself.

[25] Technical analysts are not the only group which argues that stock price behavior is inherently predictable. Another approach, *fundamental analysis*, attempts to forecast returns from holding certain types of securities or from securities of specific firms or industries. Initially, forecasts are made of general economic conditions and then of supply and demand for the products of certain firms and industries. Complex econometric models may be used which consider such diverse factors as government monetary and fiscal policy, consumer spending and saving, inflation rates, unemployment, etc. The results provided by economic models are usually supplemented by a detailed analysis of individual firm financial statements and a comparison of key financial ratios for the firm with industrywide ratios. This permits the fundamental analyst to estimate future earnings and evaluate the riskiness of investor returns which are assumed to have a direct bearing on stock prices.

[26] It is especially important that security markets be as efficient as possible because, as we have seen in this book, they allocate the scarce resource of investment capital which makes economic growth and a higher standard of living possible.

domly around their intrinsic values and are always in equilibrium. Any temporary deviations from equilibrium prices are quickly (indeed, instantly) corrected. Information relevant to the valuation of securities is simultaneously available to all investors at virtually no cost, and existing security prices reflect fully the latest information available. Moreover, security market prices adjust instantaneously to *new* information, and a new set of intrinsic values results, leading some investors to adjust their portfolios. All of this happens almost instantaneously, however, so that market price always equals intrinsic value in a state of continuous equilibrium.

In recent years the efficient markets hypothesis has been tested on three different levels—each representing a different assumption about how efficient the securities markets really are. In its so-called weak form, the efficient markets hypothesis suggests that successive changes in stock prices are independent of each other. In other words, past stock-price movements are not a reliable guide to future price movements. At a somewhat higher level of abstraction, the semi-strong form of the efficient markets hypothesis declares that all relevant information concerning security prices that is available to the public is fully reflected in the prices actually observed in the marketplace. Thus, security prices hover around their intrinsic equilibrium values which reflect the latest publicly available information. The appearance of new relevant information causes security prices to rapidly adjust to a new set of intrinsic values and a new equilibrium position. Finally, the strong form of the efficient markets theory says that *all* forms of information—that which is publicly available and that which is available to securities analysts through their private inquiries—will be reflected fully in the existing set of security prices. This strong-form hypothesis suggests that such groups as stock specialists, security brokers and dealers, and corporate insiders who often have access to carefully concealed information cannot earn greater profits than those investors who do not have access to such information.

What does the available research evidence have to say about these various levels of market efficiency? How efficient are U.S. securities markets? Research studies generally find that security prices respond promptly to new, publicly available information. Prices do appear to fluctuate around a base (or intrinsic) value in an essentially random and unbiased manner. Moreover, studies of the performance of mutual funds and other professional portfolio management firms indicate that these firms do not consistently outperform randomly selected portfolios of securities bearing comparable risk. In general, the weak and semi-strong forms of the efficient markets hypothesis are validated by recent research findings. However, there is also evidence that traders possessed with inside information (including corporate executives, brokers, and stock specialists) have been able to score impressive gains beyond those available to the average investor. The strong form of the efficient markets hypothesis, therefore, is not consistent with all the facts for all time periods. Nevertheless, the American securities markets must be regarded as highly efficient channels directing the flow of savings into investment. Changes in security prices do appear to conform generally to a random-walk process in which daily price quotations cluster about a security's intrinsic value, reflecting the latest information available.

A buy and hold strategy coupled with a random selection of securities from the entire market's portfolio will, in most cases, yield returns at least as good as those earned by professional traders who rapidly turn over their portfolios. Of course, financial analysts with extraordinary ability to uncover new information and act quickly upon it are likely to achieve above-average rates of return, at least for short periods of time. Moreover, individual investors do differ in their financial goals and circumstances, and professional advice is frequently required to meet these specialized needs. However, those who use technical analysis, looking for patterns and trends in historical security prices, are unlikely to earn above-average rates of return in a random-walk market.

SUMMARY AND CONCLUSIONS

The market for corporate stock is the best known to the general public and the most widely followed of all the securities markets. U.S. corporations have outstanding well over a trillion dollars in equity shares with millions of shares changing hands each day. Prices of the most actively traded stocks are quoted daily in the financial press and watched avidly by millions of investors. Ownership surveys conducted by the New York Stock Exchange indicate there are nearly 30 million stockholders in the United States with the number of first-time equity investors growing rapidly. While the stock market passed through a period of lackluster and often disappointing performance during the 1960s and 70s, there is evidence of a new resurgence of interest by both large and small investors as the decade of the 80s begins. Investors seeking a haven from inflation and high tax rates have found the long-run capital gains potential of stocks an especially attractive use of their funds.

Though one of the oldest of the American securities markets, the market for corporate shares even now is in a period of change and transition. Slowly but surely a unified national market for equity securities is beginning to emerge. Spurred by Congressional legislation and competition within the securities industry, electronic links between the major exchanges and over-the-counter markets are being forged today to insure that all investors, regardless of location, can transact business at the best available prices in the marketplace. Rapid developments in the technology of information transfer are breaking down the barriers to free and open trading posed by geography and outmoded practices and regulations. New centralized computer systems coupled with cheaper electronic methods of data transfer and display have paved the way for integrating existing markets into a new national system, retaining the benefits of experience while allowing ample room for innovation. A true national market for trading in common and preferred stock and stock options does not yet exist, but substantial progress has been made toward that goal. And the benefits of stronger competition and a freer flow of information to all market participants are not likely to be confined to equities alone. Ultimately, all securities markets, all investors, and the financial system as a whole will benefit from the era of change and innovation through which the American stock market is now passing.

STUDY QUESTIONS

1. In what important ways does the stock market differ from the other securities markets we have dealt with up to this point?

2. What are the essential characteristics of *common stock?* What priority do common stockholders have in the event a corporation is liquidated? What limits the amount of shares a company may issue?

3. What are the principal *rights* of common stockholders?

4. Discuss the nature of *preferred stock*. In what ways are preferred shares similar to "debt" and in what ways are they "equity" securities?

5. Explain the meaning of the following terms associated with preferred stock:
   a. Cumulative.
   b. Participating.
   c. Convertible.
   d. Sinking fund.

6. What are the principal differences between trading in stocks OTC and trading on the organized exchanges? How would you rate these two markets in terms of their advantages for the small investor? The large investor?

7. What is the third market? The fourth market? Can you see any significant benefits from the existence of these two market channels?

8. Describe the Dow Jones and Standard & Poor's stock price indexes. What types of securities are included in each series? How have these stock price indexes behaved in recent years? Can you explain why?

9. Explain the possible linkages between economic conditions and the performance of the stock market. Why do stock price movements tend to *lead* changes in general economic conditions?

10. What is the random-walk hypothesis? Does available research evidence tend to support or deny the validity of this hypothesis?

11. Explain the difference between fundamental security analysis and technical analysis. Which approach is likely to yield the best returns to the investor in today's markets, according to recent research findings?

12. What is an efficient market? What are the consequences of market efficiency for the behavior of security prices?

13. Recent research concerning the implications of the *efficient markets hypothesis* focuses on three different theories concerning the degree of market efficiency. These are known as the weak, semi-strong, and strong hypotheses. Explain the basic differences between these three hypotheses. Which of the three is supported by recent research?

SELECTED REFERENCES

1. Alexander, S. "Price Movements in Speculative Markets: Trends or Random Walks." *Industrial Management Review,* May 1961, pp. 7–26.

2. Bear, Robert M., and Anthony J. Curley. "Unseasoned Equity Financing." *Journal of Financial and Quantitative Analysis,* June 1975, pp. 311–26.

3. Berkman, Neil. "Industrial Investors and the Stock Market." *New England Economic Review,* November-December 1977, pp. 60–78.

4. Cootner, Paul H. "Stock Prices: Random versus Systematic Changes." *Industrial Management Review,* Spring 1962, pp. 24–45.

5. Donaldson, Gordon. "In Defense of Preferred Stock." *Harvard Business Review,* July-August 1962, pp. 123–36.

6. Edwards, R. D., and John Magee, Jr. *Technical Analysis of Stock Trends.* 4th ed. Springfield, Mass.: Magee, 1958.

7. Eibott, Peter. "Trends in the Value of Individual Stockholdings." *Journal of Business,* July 1974, pp. 339–48.

8. Elsaid, Hussein H. "The Function of Preferred Stock in the Corporate Financial Plan." *Financial Analysts Journal,* July-August 1969, pp. 112–17.

9. Fama, Eugene F. "The Behavior of Stock Market Prices." *Journal of Business,* January 1965, pp. 34–105.

10. Fama, E. F., and M. E. Blume. "Filter Rules and Stock Market Trading." *Journal of Business,* January 1966, pp. 226–241.

11. Firth, Michael. "The Information Content of Large Investment Holdings." *Journal of Finance,* December 1975, pp. 1265–82.

12. Fisher, L., and J. Lorie. "Rates of Return on Investments in Common Stock: The Year-by-Year Record, 1926–1965." *Journal of Business,* January 1964.

13. Fisher, Donald E., and Glenn A. Wilt, Jr. "Nonconvertible Preferred Stock as a Financing Instrument," *Journal of Finance,* September 1968, pp. 611–24.

14. Friend, Irwin, Marshall Blume, and Jean Crockett. *Mutual Funds and Other Institutional Investors.* New York: McGraw-Hill, 1970.

15. Granger, C. W., and D. Morgenstern. *Predictability of Stock Market Prices.* Lexington, Mass.: Lexington Books, 1970.

16. Guthmann, H. G., and A. J. Bakay. "The Market Impacts of the Sale of Large Blocks of Stock." *Journal of Finance,* December 1965, pp. 617–31.

17. Hayes, Samuel L., III. "Investment Banking: Power Structure in Flux." *Harvard Business Review,* March-April 1971, pp. 136–52.

18. Keane, Simon M. "The Significance of the Issue Price in Rights Issues." *Journal of Business Finance,* 4, no. 3 (1972).

19. Levy, R. A. *The Relative Strength Concept of Common Stock Forecasting.* Larchmant, N.Y.: Investors Intelligence, 1968.

20. Logue, Dennis E. "On the Pricing of Unseasoned Equity Issues: 1965–1969," *Journal of Financial and Quantitative Analysis.* January 1973, pp. 91–104.

21. McDonald, J. G., and A. K. Fisher. "New-Issue Stock Price Behavior." *Journal of Finance,* March 1972, pp. 97–102.

22. Mandelbrot, Benoit, "The Variation of Certain Speculative Prices." *Journal of Business,* October 1963, pp. 394–419.

23. Mulhern, John J. "The National Stock Market: Taking Shape." *Business Review*, Federal Reserve Bank of Philadelphia, September-October 1980, pp. 3–11.

24. New York Stock Exchange, *Fact Book 1980*. New York, 1980.

25. Securities and Exchange Commission. *Report of the Special Study of Securities Markets*. Washington, D.C.: U.S. Government Printing Office, 1963.

26. Securities and Exchange Commission. *Institutional Investor Study Report*. Washington, D.C.: U.S. Government Printing Office, 1971.

27. Stoll, Hans R. "The Pricing of Security Dealer Services: An Empirical Study of NASDAQ Stocks." *Journal of Finance*, September 1978, pp. 1153–72.

28. U.S. Securities and Exchange Commission, Directorate of Economic and Policy Research, *Staff Report on the Securities Industry in 1979*, July 1980.

part seven

Government in the
Financial Markets

21

Central Banking and the
Role of the Federal Reserve

One of the most important financial institutions in any modern economy is the *central bank*. Basically, a central bank is an agency of government which has important public policy functions in monitoring the operation of the nation's financial system and controlling the growth of its money supply. Central banks ordinarily do not deal directly with the public; rather they are "bankers' banks," communicating with commercial banks and securities dealers in carrying out their essential policy-making functions. The central bank of the United States is the Federal Reserve System, a creature of Congress charged with issuing currency, regulating the banking system, and taking measures to protect the value of the dollar and promote full employment. In this and the two succeeding chapters we examine in detail the nature and impact of central bank operations and the major problems of policymaking faced by Federal Reserve money managers today.

THE ROLE OF CENTRAL BANKS IN THE ECONOMY

Control of the Money Supply

Central banks, including the Federal Reserve System, perform several important functions in a modern economy. The first and most important of their functions is *control of the nation's money supply*.

What is money? Money is anything which serves as a medium of exchange in the purchase of goods and services. Money has another important function, however—serving as a store of value, for money is a financial asset that

481

may be used to store purchasing power until it is needed by the owner.[1] If we define money exclusively as a medium of exchange, then the sum of all currency and coin held by the public plus the value of all publicly held checking accounts and other deposits against which drafts may be issued (such as NOW accounts) would constitute the nation's money supply. If we define money as a store of value, on the other hand, then time and savings accounts at commercial banks and other nonbank financial intermediaries, such as credit unions and savings banks, would also be considered important components of the money supply. In Chapter 23 we will note that several different definitions of the money supply may be useful for the purpose of implementing and monitoring central bank policies.

However we define money, the power to regulate its quantity and value was delegated by Congress early in this century to the Federal Reserve System. The Fed has become, not only the principal source of currency and coin (pocket money) used by the public, but also the principal government agency responsible for stabilizing the value of the dollar and protecting its integrity in the international financial markets. Why is control of the nation's money supply so important? One reason is that changes in the money supply are closely linked to changes in economic activity. A number of studies in recent years have found a statistically significant relationship between current and lagged changes in the money supply and movements in the nation's gross national product (GNP).[2] The essential implication of these studies is that, if the central bank carefully controls the rate of growth of money, then it can influence the growth rate of the economy as a whole. We will have more to say on this important issue in Chapter 23.

Another important reason for controlling the money supply is that, in the absence of effective controls, money in the form of paper notes or bank deposits could expand virtually without limit. The marginal cost of creating additional units of money is close to zero. Therefore, the banking system, the government, or both are capable of increasing the money supply well beyond the economy's capacity to produce goods and services. Because this action would bring on severe inflation, disrupt the nation's payments mechanism, and eventually bring business activity to a halt, it is not surprising that modern governments have come to rely so heavily upon central banks as guardians of the quantity and value of their currencies. The Federal Reserve System operates almost daily in the financial markets in an attempt to control domestic price inflation in order to protect the purchasing power of the dollar at home, while occasionally intervening in foreign currency markets to protect the dollar abroad.

---

[1] See Chapter 2 for a discussion of the functions performed by money in the economy.

[2] See, for example, the studies by Burger (2), Carlson (4), Carlson and Hein (5), and Poole and Lieberman (10).

Stabilizing the Money and Capital Markets

A second vital function of central banking is *stabilization of the money and capital markets*. As we have seen, the financial system must transmit savings to those who require funds for investment so that the economy can grow. If the system of money and capital markets is to work efficiently, however, the public must have confidence in financial institutions and be willing to commit its savings to them. If the financial markets are unruly, with extremely volatile fluctuations in interest rates and security prices, or if financial institutions are prone to frequent collapse, the public's confidence in the financial system might well be lost. The flow of capital funds would dry up, resulting in a drastic slowing in the nation's rate of economic growth and a rise in unemployment. All central banks play a vital role in fostering the mature development of financial markets and in ensuring a stable flow of funds through those markets.

Pursuing this objective, the Federal Reserve System will, from time to time, provide funds to major securities dealers when they have difficulty financing their portfolios so that buyers and sellers may easily acquire or sell securities. When interest rates rise or fall more rapidly than seems consistent with the nation's economic goals, the Fed will again intervene in the financial markets. The central bank may change the rates it charges banks on direct loans or engage in securities trading in an attempt to moderate rate movements.

Lender of Last Resort

Another essential function of central banks is to serve as a *lender of last resort*. This means providing liquid funds to those financial institutions in need, especially when alternative sources of funds have dried up. For example, as discussed in Chapter 13, the Federal Reserve through its *discount window* will provide funds to selected deposit-type financial institutions, upon their request, to cover short-term cash deficiencies. As we will soon see, before the Fed was created, one of the weaknesses in the early financial system of the United States was the absence of a lender of last resort to aid financial institutions squeezed by severe liquidity pressures.

Maintaining the Payments Mechanism

Finally, central banks have a role to play in *maintaining and improving a nation's payments mechanism*. This involves the clearing of checks, providing an adequate supply of currency and coin, and preserving confidence in the value of the fundamental monetary unit. A smoothly functioning and efficient payments mechanism is vital for carrying on business and commerce. If checks cannot be cleared in timely fashion or the public cannot get the currency and coin that it needs to carry out transactions, business activity will be severely curtailed. The result might well be large-scale unemployment and a decline in both capital investment and the nation's rate of economic growth.

THE GOALS AND CHANNELS OF CENTRAL BANKING

Central banking is *goal oriented.* Since World War II the United States and several other industrialized nations have accepted the premise that government is responsible to its citizens for maintaining high levels of employment, combating inflation, and supporting sustained economic growth. This is a relatively new idea since, in earlier periods, governments were assigned a much smaller role in the economic system and much less was expected of them by their citizens. It was felt that "automatic" mechanisms operated within the economy to provide stability and high employment in the long run. One of the bitter lessons of the Great Depression of the 1930s was that these mechanisms can break down and that innovative and skillfully managed government policies may be needed to restore the economy's stability and growth.

Central banking in the United States and in most other nations is directed toward four major goals:

1. Full employment of resources.
2. Reasonable stability in the general price level of all goods and services.
3. Sustained economic growth.
4. A stable balance of payments position for the nation vis-à-vis the rest of the world.

Through its influence over interest rates and the growth of the nation's money supply, the central bank is able to influence the economy's progress toward each of these goals. Achievement of all of these goals *simultaneously* has proven to be exceedingly difficult, however, as the recent track record of the economy demonstrates. One reason is that the goals often conflict. Pursuit of price stability and an improved balance of payments position, for example, may require higher interest rates and restricted credit availability—policies which tend to increase unemployment and slow investment spending and growth. Central bank policy making is a matter of accepting *trade-offs* (compromises) among multiple goals. For example, the central bank can pursue policies leading to a lower rate of inflation and a stronger dollar but probably at the price of some additional unemployment and slower economic growth in the short run.

Central banking in most Western nations, including the United States, operates principally through the *marketplace.* Modern central banks operate as a balance wheel in promoting and stabilizing the flow of savings from surplus-spending units to deficit-spending units. They try to assure a smooth and orderly flow of funds through the money and capital markets so that adequate financing is available for worthwhile investment projects. This means, among other things, avoiding panic in the market due to sudden shortages of available credit or sharp declines in security prices. However, most of the actions taken by the central bank to promote a smooth flow of funds are carried out through the marketplace rather than by government order. For example, the central bank may encourage interest rates to rise in order to reduce borrowing and spending and combat inflation, but it does not usually allocate credit to particular borrowers. The private sector, working through demand and supply forces in the marketplace, is left to make its own decisions about how much borrowing and spending will take place at the current level of interest rates and who is to receive credit.

The Channels through Which Central Banks Work

Later on, we will examine in some detail how the Federal Reserve System affects domestic and international economic conditions. It is useful at this point, however, to give a brief overview of the channels through which modern central banks influence conditions in the economy and financial system. Central bank policy affects the economy as a whole by making:

1. Changes in the cost and availability of credit to businesses, consumers, and governments.
2. Changes in the volume and rate of growth of the nation's money supply.
3. Changes in the wealth of investors as reflected in the market value of their security holdings. (See Figure 21–1.)

The central bank has a number of *policy tools* at its command which it can use to influence interest rates, the prices of securities, and the level and growth of reserves in the banking system. In the United States the principal policy tools used by the central bank are open market operations, changes in required reserves held by depository institutions, and changes in the discount rate on central bank loans.[3] In turn, changes in interest rates, security prices, and bank reserves influence the cost and availability of credit. If borrowers find that credit is less available and more expensive to obtain, they are likely to restrain their borrowing and reduce spending for both capital and consumer goods. This results in a slowing in the economy's rate of growth and perhaps a reduction in inflationary pressures. Second, if the central bank can reduce the rate of growth of the nation's money supply, this policy will eventually slow the growth of income and production in the economy due to a reduction in the demand for goods and services. Finally, if the central bank raises interest rates and therefore lowers security prices,

---

[3] Different central banks emphasize different policy tools. For example, the Bank of England relies principally upon changes in its basic lending rate to influence economic and financial conditions, while the Bank of Canada uses changes in reserve requirements as its main policy tool. As we will see in Chapter 22, the Federal Reserve System relies mainly on open-market operations to pursue the goals of U.S. economic policy.

FIGURE 21–1
The Channels of Central Bank Policy

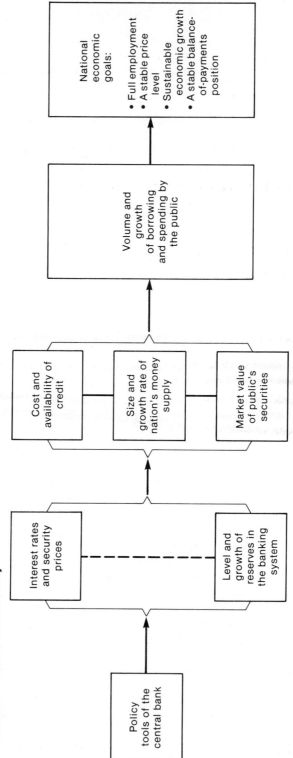

this will tend to reduce the market value of the public's holdings of stocks, bonds, and other securities. The result is a decline in the value of investors' wealth, altering borrowing and spending plans and ultimately influencing employment, prices, and the economy's rate of growth. We will have more to say about these important channels of central bank policy in Chapters 22 and 23.

THE HISTORY OF THE FEDERAL RESERVE SYSTEM

The United States was one of the last major nations in the Western world to charter a central bank. The Bank of England was established in 1694; the Bank of France and the central banks of Switzerland and Italy were founded during the 18th century. Most major industrialized nations early in their history recognized the need for an institution which would provide a measure of stability and control over the growth of money and credit. Public officials in the United States were hesitant to charter a central bank, however, out of fear that it would possess great financial power, would restrict the availability of credit to a growing nation, and might be difficult to control. However, a series of economic and financial crises in the late 19th and early 20th centuries forced Congress to act.

Problems in the Early U.S. Banking System

To fully understand why the Federal Reserve System was created, we must understand the problems that plagued the U.S. financial system throughout much of the nation's early history. Many of these problems were born in the years prior to the Civil War when the states, not the federal government, regulated and controlled the nation's banking system. Unfortunately, with a few notable exceptions, the states did a poor job of regulating the banking industry. Charters for new banks were awarded by state legislatures and were therefore subject to political lobbying and influence peddling. If a new bank's organizers had the right political connections, a charter could be obtained by individuals with little banking experience and with minimal capital invested in the business.

Deposit banking was not as popular then as it is today. Most people preferred hard money (i.e., currency and coin) to deposits. As a result, banks made loans simply by printing and issuing their own paper notes, which circulated as currency. Because few controls existed, there was a tendency to overissue these notes well beyond the financial strength of the bank making the loan. Frequently charters were granted to wildcat banks which would issue a large quantity of notes and then disappear. Some banks, promising to redeem their notes in gold or silver coin, would set up "redemption centers" in locations nearly impossible for the public to reach, such as in the middle of a swamp. Needless to say, there was an extremely high closure rate among these poorly capitalized, ill-managed institutions, resulting in substantial losses to their unlucky depositors.

Responding to these problems and also to the tremendous financial strain imposed by the Civil War, Congress passed the National Banking Act in 1863. This act and its subsequent amendments authorized the open establishment of federally licensed commercial banks, subject to regulations imposed by a newly created office, the Comptroller of the Currency—a part of the United States Treasury Department. Any group of businessmen could organize a so-called *national bank,* provided they could show that the new bank would be profitable within a reasonable period of time (usually within three years), meet the minimum equity capital requirements imposed by the Comptroller's office, and not endanger the viability of banks already operating in the local area. Thus, under the provisions of the National Banking Act, the chartering of commercial banks was, in the main, removed from the political sphere and made subject to carefully spelled-out rules. At the same time, Congress attempted to drive state-chartered banks into the national banking system by imposing a 10 percent tax on state bank notes. It was argued that most bankers would prefer the more-liberal state regulations and avoid seeking national bank charters unless they were forced to do so.

In order to help finance the Civil War, Congress authorized national banks to issue their own notes as circulating currency. However, these notes had to be collateralized by United States government securities. Under the terms of the National Banking Act federally chartered banks could issue notes up to 90 percent of the value of Treasury securities they deposited with the Comptroller of the Currency. The result was to create a money or cash medium under federal control and help pay for the Civil War by creating a demand from banks for U.S. government securities.

Even more important, the National Banking Act created a *dual banking system,* with both federal and state authorities having important regulatory powers over commercial banks. Unfortunately, these authorities were given overlapping powers, and in recent years competition between federal and state bank regulatory agencies has sometimes resulted in actions detrimental to the public interest. Moreover, one of the principal aims of the federal program—to drive out state-chartered banks—was not achieved. The state banks survived only because of the growing popularity of deposit banking which swept the nation in the years following the Civil War. Instead of issuing paper notes, commercial banks increasingly began to make loans by simply creating a deposit on their books in the borrower's name—the practice followed today. The acceptance by the public of deposits instead of notes led to the disappearance of state-bank notes, making the federal government's tax on them ineffective. Although the numbers of state-chartered banks had dwindled to only about 500 out of an estimated bank population of 10,000, the state banks made a dramatic comeback late in the 19th century and soon outnumbered the national banks. As we saw earlier in Chapter 3, there are about twice as many state-chartered banks as national banks today, though the federally chartered institutions average much larger in size and include most of the nation's largest banking institutions.

Problems Leading to Creation of the Federal Reserve System

Several festering problems (including some due to the provisions of the National Banking Act) resulted in the creation of the Federal Reserve System. For one thing, the new national bank notes proved to be unresponsive to the nation's growing need for a money or cash medium. The need for money and credit grew rapidly as the United States became more heavily industrialized and the Midwest and Far West opened up to immigration. Farmers and ranchers in these newly developing areas of the nation demanded an ''elastic'' supply of money and credit—adequate to their needs at relatively low cost. As we will soon see, the new Federal Reserve System would attempt to deal with this problem by issuing a currency of its own and by closer control over the growth of the nation's supply of money and credit.

As deposit banking and the writing of checks became increasingly popular, another serious problem appeared that also limited the nation's growth. The process of clearing and collecting checks was slow and expensive. Then as now, most checks written by the public were *local* in character, moving funds from the account of one local customer to that of another. These checks normally are cleared routinely through the local clearinghouse, which is simply a location where representatives of local banks meet daily to exchange bundles of checks drawn on each other's banks. For checks sent outside the local area, however, the check-collection process is more complicated, with some checks passing through several banks before reaching their final destination.

Before the Federal Reserve System was created, many banks, especially smaller, outlying institutions, charged a fee (exchange charge) for the clearing and redemption of checks. This fee was usually calculated as a percentage of the par (or face) value of each check. Banks levying the fee were called ''no par'' banks because they refused to honor checks at their full face value. To avoid exchange fees, bankers would route nonlocal checks they received only through banks accepting and redeeming them at par. Often this meant routing a check through scores of banks in distant cities until days or weeks had elapsed before the check was finally cleared. Such a delay was not just annoying but served as an impediment to commercial transactions and the speedy allocation of funds within the financial system. Exchange charges resulted in needless inefficiency and increased the true cost of business transactions far above their nominal cost. A new national check-clearing system was needed which honored checks at par and moved them swiftly from payee to payer. As we will soon see, this responsibility was given to the Federal Reserve System.

A third problem with the banking and financial system of that time was recurring liquidity crises. Then as now, money and bank reserves tended to concentrate in the nation's leading financial centers. When the largest banks in the country encountered serious liquidity problems and experienced a drain of reserves, however, there was no way to raise funds except by a massive sell-off of securities, resulting in tremendous losses for investors and a financial panic.

It was in the larger cities, of course, where the greatest need for loanable funds existed and where reserves tended to pile up as smaller banks deposited their reserves with larger banking institutions. However, when the normal pressures for agricultural credit increased in rural areas, many country banks were forced to draw upon their reserves in the cities, and the larger city banks, in turn, had to sell securities and call loans in order to come up with the necessary funds. When the reserve demands of country banks were larger than expected, security prices in major financial centers plummeted due to massive forced selling of bank-held securities. Panic selling by other investors soon followed, leading to chaos in the financial marketplace.

The nation's banking system clearly needed a lender of ready cash to provide liquidity to those banks with heavy cash drains and to protect the stability and smooth functioning of the financial system. A serious financial panic in 1907 finally led to the creation of the Federal Reserve System. In 1908 Congress created a National Monetary Commission to study the financial needs of the nation. The commission's recommendations were forwarded to Congress and ultimately resulted in passage of the Federal Reserve Act, signed into law by President Wilson in December 1913. The Federal Reserve banks opened for business as World War I began in Europe.

The Early Structure of the Federal Reserve System

In the beginning the Federal Reserve System was quite different from the Fed of today. The original Federal Reserve Act reflected a mix of diverse viewpoints—an effort to reconcile competing political and economic interests. There was, on the one hand, great fear that the Fed would have too much control over the nation's financial affairs and operate against the best interests of important segments of American society. For example, small businesses, consumer groups, farmers, and ranchers were concerned that the Fed might pursue restrictive credit policies leading to high interest rates. In addition, it was recognized that the Federal Reserve would become a major financial institution wherever it was located. Any city or state which housed a Federal Reserve bank was likely to become a major financial center.

Responding to these various needs and interest groups, Congress created a truly "decentralized" central bank. Not 1 but 12 Federal Reserve banks were chartered, stretching across the continental United States but located predominantly in the East, where the largest cities and banks were situated. Each Reserve bank was assigned its own district, over which it possessed important regulatory powers. In addition, 24 branch banks were created to better serve local areas and satisfy those not fortunate enough to have a full-fledged Federal Reserve bank in their region. A supervisory board of seven members was set up in Washington, D.C., in an effort to promote a common monetary policy for the nation. In fact, however, the regional Federal Reserve banks possessed the essential monetary tools and made the key policy decisions during the Fed's early history.

Goals and Policy Tools in the Early History of the Federal Reserve System

In order to deal with the economic and financial problems of that day the Federal Reserve Act permitted each regional Reserve bank to open up a discount window where eligible banks could borrow reserves for short periods of time. However, borrowing banks were required to present high-quality, short-term business loans (i.e., commercial paper) to the discount window to secure the loans they needed. The Fed's chief policy tool of the day was the discount rate charged on these loans, with each Reserve bank having the authority to set its own discount rate. By varying this rate, the central banks could encourage or discourage commercial banks' propensity to discount commercial paper and borrow reserves from the Fed. In this way, central bankers could promote easy or tight credit conditions and indirectly influence the overall volume of bank loans.

The Federal Reserve banks were given authority to issue their own paper notes to serve as a circulating currency, but these notes had to be 100 percent backed by Fed holdings of commercial paper plus a 40 percent gold reserve. Almost as an afterthought, Congress authorized the Reserve banks to trade U.S. government securities in the open market, known as open market operations—the Fed's principal policy tool today. Reserve requirements were imposed on deposits held by member banks of the system, but the Fed could not change these requirements. In contrast to the provisions of the earlier National Banking Act, required reserves had to be held on deposit at the Federal Reserve banks instead of in correspondent balances (deposits) with other commercial banks.

Slowly but surely, economic, financial, and political forces combined to amend the original Federal Reserve Act and remake the character and methods of the central bank. The leading causes of change were war, economic recessions, and more recently, persistent inflation. For example, in order to combat economic recessions and fight two world wars, the U.S. government has issued billions of dollars in debt. As we will see in Chapter 24, the total debt of the federal government now approaches $1 trillion. As the debt began to grow, it seemed only "logical" to permit greater use of U.S. government securities in Federal Reserve operations. Banks were quickly authorized to use government securities as backing for loans from the Fed's discount window. The Fed itself was called upon to play a major role in smoothing and stabilizing the market for U.S. government securities so as to ensure that the Treasury would have little difficulty in refinancing its maturing debt. Government securities were made eligible as collateral for the issue of new Federal Reserve bank notes.

More than any other historical event, however, it was the Great Depression of the 1930s that changed the character of the Federal Reserve. Faced with the collapse of the banking system and unprecedented unemployment—some estimates suggest that a quarter of the nation's labor force was thrown out of work during the 1930s—Congress entrusted the Fed with sweeping monetary powers. Significant changes were made in the central bank's operating structure and lines of authority.

The seven-member Board of Governors in Washington, D.C., became the central administrative and policymaking group for the Fed. From 1933 on, any changes in discount rates charged by the Reserve banks have had to be approved in advance by the Board of Governors. The board was granted authority to set minimum reserve requirements on deposits and maximum interest rates which member banks could pay on those deposits. In order to control speculative buying of stocks, the Reserve Board was empowered to set margin requirements specifying what proportion of a security's market value the investor could borrow against to purchase the security. Recognizing that open-market operations in U.S. government securities were rapidly becoming the Fed's main policy tool, a powerful policymaking body—the Federal Open Market Committee—was created to oversee the conduct of open-market operations. And the majority of voting seats on this committee were given to the Federal Reserve Board. In summary, the Great Depression brought about a concentration of power within the Federal Reserve System so that the Fed could pursue a single unified policy and speak with one voice concerning the nation's monetary affairs.

HOW THE FED IS ORGANIZED

The Federal Reserve System today has an organizational structure which resembles a pyramid. As Figure 21–2 shows, the apex of that pyramid is the Board of Governors—the Federal Reserve's chief policymaking and administrative group. At the middle level of the pyramid are the Federal Reserve banks, which carry out system policy and provide essential services to banks and other depository financial institutions in their region, and the Federal Open Market Committee. The bottom of the pyramid contains the member banks of the system, which the Fed supervises and regulates, and the manager of the System Open Market Account, who is responsible for buying and selling securities to achieve the goals of Fed monetary policy.

Board of Governors of the Federal Reserve System

The key administrative body within the Federal Reserve System is the Board of Governors. The board consists of seven persons appointed by the

FIGURE 21–2
How the Federal Reserve System is Organized

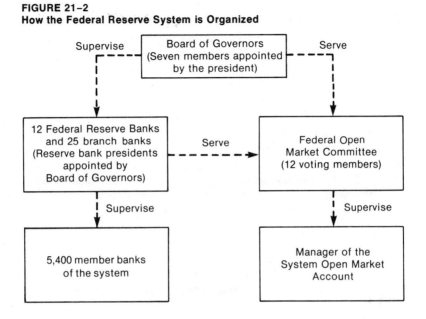

president of the United States and confirmed by the Senate for maximum 14-year terms. Terms of office are staggered, with one board member's appointment ending every two years. When a member of the Federal Reserve Board resigns or dies, the president may appoint a new person to complete the remainder of the unexpired term, and that member may be reappointed to a subsequent full term. However, no member who completes a full term can be reappointed to the Board of Governors. The president designates one member of the board chairman and another, vice chairman, and both serve four-year terms in those appointed offices. In selecting new board members, the president is required to seek a "fair representation of the financial, agricultural, industrial, and commercial interests and geographical divisions of the country" and may not choose more than one member from any one Federal Reserve district.

The powers of the Federal Reserve Board are extensive. The board sets reserve requirements on deposits held by member banks and other depository institutions subject to its rules,[4] reviews and determines the discount rate charged on loans to depository institutions, sets margin requirements on purchases of securities, and provides leadership in the conduct of open-market operations through the Federal Open Market Committee. Besides its monetary policy functions, the board supervises the activities of the 12 Re-

---

[4] As we will note in Chapter 22, any depository institution—commercial bank, savings and loan association, mutual savings bank, or credit union—accepting transactions accounts (such as checking accounts and NOWs) or nonpersonal time deposits must hold legal reserves behind those accounts as specified by the Federal Reserve Board.

serve banks and has supervisory and regulatory control over member banks of the system. It regulates all bank holding companies, foreign banks entering the United States, and the overseas activities of U.S. banks.

In principle, the board is independent of both the Congress and the executive branch of the federal government. This independence is supported by terms of office much longer than the president's term and by the fact that the Fed does not depend upon Congress for operating funds. The Federal Reserve supports itself from revenue generated by selling its services (such as clearing checks and shipping currency and coin), making loans through the discount window, and trading securities in the open market. These monies are not retained by the Fed, since it is operated in the public interest and not for profit. All net income left over after expenses, dividends, and minimal allocations to equity reserves is transferred to the U.S. Treasury.

The Federal Open Market Committee and Manager of the System Open Market Account

Aside from the Federal Reserve Board, the other key policymaking group within the system is the Federal Open Market Committee (FOMC). It has been called the most important committee of individuals in the United States because its decisions concerning the conduct of monetary policy and the cost and availability of credit affect the lives of millions of people. Membership on the FOMC consists of the seven members of the Federal Reserve Board and the presidents of the Reserve banks. Only members of the board and five of the Reserve bank presidents may vote when a final decision is reached on the future conduct of monetary policy, however. The president of the Federal Reserve Bank of New York is a permanent voting member of the FOMC, while the other 11 Reserve bank presidents rotate the four remaining voting seats among themselves. Each Reserve bank president serves a voting term of one year beginning on March 1.

By tradition, the chairman of the Federal Reserve Board and the president of the New York Federal Reserve Bank serve as chairman and vice chairman of the FOMC. The law stipulates that the FOMC will meet in Washington, D.C., at least four times a year. In practice, however, the committee meets at least once every four to six weeks and more frequently if emergencies develop. Between regularly scheduled meetings, telephone conferences may occur, and the members of the FOMC may be asked to cast votes by telephone or telegram. FOMC meetings are not open to the public because confidential financial information frequently is discussed and also because the Fed wants to avoid sending "false signals" to the marketplace. Only Federal Reserve Board members, selected board staff, the Reserve bank presidents and their aides, and the manager and deputy manager of the System Open Market Account are permitted to attend FOMC meetings.

The name *Federal Open Market Committee* implies that this committee's sole concern is with the conduct of Federal Reserve open-market operations in securities, the most important policy tool of the system. In fact, the FOMC reviews current economic and financial conditions and considers *all* aspects and tools of monetary policy at each of its meetings. Once a consensus is reached concerning the appropriate future course for monetary policy, a *policy directive* is given orally and in writing to the manager of the System Open Market Account (SOMA), who is a vice president of the Federal Reserve Bank of New York. The SOMA manager is told in general terms how open-market operations should be conducted in the weeks ahead, and the FOMC's target growth rates for the nation's money supply.[5] Decisions made by the FOMC and actions of the SOMA manager at his securities trading desk in New York are binding on the entire Federal Reserve System.

The Federal Reserve Banks

When the Federal Reserve System was created in 1913, the nation was divided into 12 districts, with one Reserve bank in each district responsible for supervising and providing services to the other member banks there. Reserve banks were established in the cities of Atlanta, Boston, Chicago, Cleveland, Dallas, Kansas City, Minneapolis, New York, Philadelphia, Richmond, San Francisco, and St. Louis. In addition, 24 branches (later expanded to 25) were created to service particular regions within each of the 12 districts. (Figure 21–3 indicates the boundaries of each Federal Reserve District and the locations of the 12 Reserve banks and their branch offices.) The Reserve banks and their branches are an integral part of the Fed's efforts to supervise and regulate the banking system, ensure a smooth flow of payments, and control the growth of money and credit.

Using computers and high-speed sorting machines, the regional Reserve banks route checks and other cash items drawn on financial institutions in one city and deposited in another. While most checks are not cleared through the Fed, it still handles billions of checks and other paper items each year. The Federal Reserve maintains a nationwide electronic network (known as Fed wire) to transfer funds and securities in minutes. Approximately 30 automated clearinghouses (ACHs) are operated by the Reserve banks and their branches to handle the direct deposit of payrolls, mortgage payments, and other funds transfer requests by electronic means instead of through pieces of paper. The Reserve banks ship currency and coin to banks and other depository institutions at those times when the public needs more pocket money and store excess currency and coin in their vaults when less pocket money is needed.

The Reserve banks serve as the federal government's fiscal agent. This involves keeping the operating financial accounts of the U.S. Treasury, delivering and redeeming U.S. government securities, and paying interest on securities issued by the Treasury and various federal agencies. The Reserve

---

[5] See Chapter 22 for an example of a recent FOMC policy directive.

FIGURE 21-3
The Federal Reserve System: Boundaries of Federal Reserve Districts and Their Branch Territories

Boundaries of Federal Reserve Districts	⊙ Federal Reserve Bank cities
Boundaries of Federal Reserve Branch territories	• Federal Reserve Branch cities
⚫ Board of Governors of the Federal Reserve System	· Federal Reserve Bank facility

SOURCE: Board of Governors of the Federal Reserve System, *Federal Reserve Bulletin,* February 1981.

banks also accept deposits of federal income, excise, and unemployment taxes and honor checks drawn against the Treasury. In addition to serving as the federal government's fiscal agent, the Reserve banks closely supervise the activities of member banks within their districts. They conduct field examinations of all state-chartered member banks and supervise bank holding companies headquartered in their region of the nation.

The Reserve banks play a significant role in the conduct of the nation's money and credit policy. Each Reserve bank houses a research division to study regional economic and financial developments and convey this information to the Board of Governors and to the Federal Open Market Committee. While only 5 of the 12 Reserve bank presidents are voting members of the FOMC, all 12 Reserve bank presidents attend FOMC meetings to report on conditions and events in their region and give their views on the appropriate course for monetary policy. The Reserve banks also administer the discount windows where loans are made to financial institutions in their district, and they therefore have a direct impact on the growth of money and credit.

Each Federal Reserve bank is a corporation chartered by Congress. Officially, the Reserve banks are "owned" 100 percent by the member banks of their districts, who select a majority of each bank's board of directors. In fact, the regional Reserve banks are closely controlled by the Federal Reserve Board, which appoints three of their nine directors and approves appointments of all officers. While under the terms of the original Federal Reserve Act, the Reserve banks could set the discount rate on loans to member banks, these rate changes must now be approved by the Board in Washington. The regional banks are required to participate in all open-market transactions on behalf of the system. These purchases and sales are centered in the FOMC, but the Reserve banks must provide the securities needed for open-market sales and also take their pro rata share of any purchases that the system makes.

The Member Banks of the Fed's System

The member banks of the Federal Reserve System consist of national banks, which are required to join the system, and state-chartered banks that agree to conform to the Fed's rules. Today, Federal Reserve member banks constitute a minority of all U.S. banks—about 38 percent of the total. As of year-end 1980 there were 4,425 national banks and 997 state-chartered banks registered as members of the Federal Reserve System compared to approximately 9,000 nonmember banks.

Member banks must subscribe to the stock of the Reserve bank in their district in volume equal to 6 percent of their paid-in capital and surplus accounts. However, only half of this amount must actually be paid, with the rest payable on call to the system. Member banks are bound by Federal Reserve rules regarding their capital structure, deposits, loans, branch operations, formation of holding companies, and policies regarding the conduct of officers and boards of directors. These banks are subject to supervision and examination by the Federal Reserve at any time, though most banks are examined only once a year. Moreover, member banks must hold reserves behind their deposits at levels specified by the Federal Reserve Board.

A number of important *privileges* are granted to member banks. Legally, they are "owners" of the Federal Reserve banks because they hold the stock of these institutions and may elect six of their nine directors. A 6 percent annual dividend is paid to member banks on their holdings of Federal Reserve bank stock. Member banks may borrow reserves through the discount window of the Reserve bank in their district, though the majority of these loans cover only a few days.[6]

---

[6] As a result of the passage of the Monetary Control Act of 1980 any depository institution which holds transactions accounts or nonpersonal time deposits subject to mandatory reserve requirements may borrow from the Fed's discount window on the same terms as member banks.

Member banks may also use the nationwide check-clearing system of the Fed in order to process checks coming from distant cities. However, this is not a particularly distinctive privilege since nonmember financial institutions may also use the Fed's check-clearing facilities, provided they agree to maintain a clearing account with the Reserve bank in the region. An intangible benefit of membership is the *prestige* which comes from belonging to the Federal Reserve System. Many bankers feel that membership in the system attracts large business deposits and correspondent accounts from smaller banks which otherwise might go elsewhere.

MANY ROLES OF THE FEDERAL RESERVE SYSTEM TODAY

In the course of this chapter we have talked about the many roles which the Federal Reserve must play in the financial system of the United States and how those roles have changed over time. In this final section of the chapter we attempt to pull together all of the Fed's responsibilities and roles to give the reader a more complete view of how the central bank interfaces and interacts with the financial markets and the banking system.

The Clearing and Collection of Checks and Other Means of Payment

As we saw earlier in this chapter, one of the earliest tasks of the Federal Reserve System was to establish a nationwide system for clearing and collecting checks. Before the Fed began, all checks were cleared through the correspondent banking system, which was slow, cumbersome, and expensive. When the Fed began its check-clearing operations, it insisted that all checks be honored at full face (par) value. Thus, banks which used the Fed's check-clearing system were not allowed to deduct clearing fees (exchange charges). This regulation rapidly reduced the number of no-par banks and contributed greatly to public acceptance of checks.

When a depository institution receives a check drawn on another institution in a distant city, it can route this check directly through the Federal Reserve banks. The Fed credits an account called Deferred Availability Items on behalf of the institution sending the check and routes that check toward the institution upon which it was drawn for eventual collection. At the end of a specified period (usually two or three days), the depository institution sending in the check will receive credit in its legal reserve account for the amount of that check. Eventually, the check reaches the institution on which it was drawn and is deducted from that institution's reserve account.

Sometimes delays in the clearing system result in the creation of *float*. This occurs when a depository institution receives credit for a check deposited with the Federal Reserve before the institution on which the check was drawn actually loses reserves. When there are strikes or bad weather affecting surface or air transportation, the clearing of checks is delayed, and the volume of float rises. Since float is, in effect, an interest-free loan of reserves that banks can use to create credit, the Fed often has to take action through its open-market operations to offset fluctuations in the volume of float.

Issuing Currency and Coin and Providing Other Services

The Fed helps to promote an efficient payments mechanism, not just through the clearing of checks, but also by issuing its own currency in response to public need. Today nearly all the paper money in circulation consists of Federal Reserve notes, issued by all 12 of the Reserve banks. These notes are liabilities of the Federal Reserve bank issuing them. In fact, Federal Reserve notes are a lien against the assets of the Fed, payable to the holder in the event the Reserve banks are ever liquidated. When the public demands more currency, financial institutions request a shipment of new currency and coin from the Federal Reserve bank in the region, which maintains an ample supply in its vault. Payment for the shipment is made simply by charging the legal reserve account of the institution requesting the shipment. In the opposite situation, when depository institutions receive deposits of currency and coin from the public beyond what they wish to hold in their vaults, the surplus is shipped back to the Reserve banks. Depository institutions receive credit for these return shipments through an increase in their legal reserve accounts.

Prior to 1981, most Federal Reserve services, including the clearing of checks and shipments of currency and coin, were provided free of charge. However, the Monetary Control Act of 1980 required the Fed to publish a set of pricing principles and to assess fees for the following services:

1. Transportation of currency and coin, and coin wrapping.
2. Check clearing and collection.
3. Wire transfer of funds.
4. The use of Federal Reserve automated clearinghouse facilities.
5. Net settlement of debits and credits affecting accounts held by the Federal Reserve.
6. Book entry, safekeeping, and other services connected with the purchase or sale of government securities.
7. Noncash collection (the receipt, collection, and crediting of accounts of depository institutions in connection with municipal and corporate securities).
8. The cost to the Federal Reserve of float (the interest on items—generally, the dollar value of checks—credited by the Federal Reserve to one depository institution before being collected from another).

In December 1980 the Fed began to set fees to users of these services. For example, those desiring to transfer funds over the Fed's electronic wire network were charged fees ranging from $0.80 to $5.30 per use, depending upon whether the user was off-line or on-line and did or did not request additional information. Debits and credits could be settled electronically through the Fed's automated clearinghouses at fees ranging from 0.3 cents to 1.5 cents per item, depending on location.[7] Exhibits 21–1 and 21–2 provide examples of other charges levied by the Fed for keeping records of

EXHIBIT 21–1
Schedule of Fees for Book-Entry Securities Services Provided by the Federal Reserve Banks, Effective October 1, 1981

Security transfers, per transaction:	
Originated on-line	$2.00
Originated off-line	8.50
Received off-line	6.50
Security account maintenance per account per month	6.00

SOURCE: Board of Governors of the Federal Reserve System, *Press Release,* July 20, 1981.

security transfers and security holdings, for the safekeeping of securities, and for the purchase and sale of government securities on behalf of depository financial institutions. Charges for check collection and currency and coin shipments were to be announced during the fall of 1981 or early in 1982.[8]

Why did Congress order the Fed to switch from free services to a fee basis? One reason was the rapid increase in the number of users of Federal Reserve services. The Monetary Control Act of 1980, for the first time in U.S. history, provided for access by *all* nonmember depository institutions to the Fed's facilities and services. With so many new financial institutions eligible to receive Fed services, their cost would soar. Secondly, Congress wanted to encourage as much competition as possible in the provision of these services so that the Fed would not be the only source of supply. Still another motivating factor was a feared loss of revenue to the Treasury. The Monetary Control Act, as we will see in the next chapter, gradually lowers deposit reserve requirements for member banks and requires the Federal Reserve to credit depository institutions with interest on their deposit balances held at the Reserve banks.[9] All of these developments together would have

---

[7] Board of Governors of the Federal Reserve System, *Press Release,* December 31, 1980.

[8] All fees set by the Fed are to be reviewed annually and set at levels which, over the long run, simply recover the total costs of providing each service.

[9] Under a set of procedures announced by the Board of Governors on February 27, 1981, depository institutions will receive "earnings credits" on their Fed balances based on the average federal funds rate each week. However, these credits may only be used to offset charges for Fed services. If the earnings credits exceed a financial institution's bill for Fed services in any given month, it can carry forward the unused credit to cover charges in subsequent months up to one year. All depository institutions must maintain at least a small clearing balance with a Federal Reserve bank in order to obtain these services.

EXHIBIT 21–2
Schedule of Fees for Definitive Securities Safekeeping, Purchase and Sale of Securities, and Noncash Collection Services Provided by the Federal Reserve Banks, Effective October 1, 1981

Federal Reserve District	Definitive Securities Safekeeping				Noncash Collection (Coupon, Bond, or Noncash Item)	
	Deposit Withdrawal or Redemption (per transaction)*	Account Switch (per transaction)	Account Maintenance (per receipt per month)†	Purchase or Sale (per transaction)‡	Per Envelope or Item Processed*	Per $1,000 Coupon Value Shipped
Boston	$12.50	$12.50	$2.65	$12.00	$1.80	$1.00
New York	35.50	13.50	5.35	23.00	1.40	1.00
Philadelphia	15.00	10.00	2.50	17.00	2.90	1.00
Cleveland	11.00	11.00	2.00	27.00	2.85	1.00
Richmond	20.00	12.50	1.50	27.00	2.00	1.00
Atlanta	20.00	10.00	2.50	—	1.40	1.00
Chicago	15.00	10.00	3.20	17.50	2.50	1.30
Detroit	11.00	10.00	1.75	17.50	2.50	1.30
St. Louis	16.00	16.00	1.45	—	2.80	.50
Minneapolis	13.50	11.50	1.70	5.50	2.25	.60
Kansas City	15.00	6.50	1.35	10.50	3.20	1.00
Dallas	12.00	5.00	1.40	26.50	2.25	1.00
San Francisco	—	—	—	22.00	6.85	1.00

* For bonds as well as other noncash items, add shipping expenses, insurance fees, and fees assessed by other Federal Reserve Banks, if any.
† In the New York and Minneapolis districts, the fee shown is *per issue* per month.
‡ Plus brokers' fees, if any.
SOURCE: Board of Governors of the Federal Reserve System, *Press Release*, July 20, 1981.

substantially reduced the Fed's annual net income, most of which flows to the Treasury, if the central bank had not begun charging for its services.

Maintaining a Sound Banking and Financial System

Another important function of the Federal Reserve System today is to maintain a sound banking and financial system. It contributes to this goal by serving as a lender of last resort, providing reserves through the discount window of each Reserve bank. The window represents a source of funds which can be drawn upon without taking reserves away from other banks, and it helps to avoid a liquidity squeeze brought about by sudden changes in economic and financial conditions. The Fed also promotes a sound banking system by regular examinations of member banks, reviewing the quality and quantity of their assets and capital and making sure that federal and state laws are adhered to.

Serving as the Federal Government's Fiscal Agent

The Fed serves as the government's chief *fiscal agent*. In this role, it holds the Treasury's checking account and clears any checks written against that account. The Fed supervises the thousands of Tax and Loan Accounts maintained in banks across the United States which hold the bulk of the Treasury's cash balances.[10] The Federal Reserve banks receive bids when new Treasury securities are offered and provide securities to the purchasers. They redeem maturing U.S. government securities as well. In general, the Fed is responsible for maintaining reasonable stability in the government securities market so that any new Treasury security offerings sell quickly and the government raises the amount of money that it needs.

Carrying Out Monetary Policy

The most critical objective of the Federal Reserve is to carry out monetary policy. Monetary policy may be defined as the use of various tools by the central bank to control the availability of loan funds in an effort to achieve national economic goals, such as full employment and reasonable price stability. The policy tools reserved for the Federal Reserve include *general credit controls* (such as reserve requirements, discount rates, and open market operations) and *selective credit controls* (such as margin requirements on purchases of securities and rate ceilings). General credit controls affect the banking and financial system as a whole and are nondis-

---

[10] See Chapter 24 for a discussion of the nature and purpose of Treasury Tax and Loan Accounts.

criminatory in allocating the available supply of credit. Selective credit controls, on the other hand, are aimed at specific sectors of the economy, influencing their access to credit and their lending and investing policies. We will examine the Fed's credit controls in Chapter 22.

Providing Information to the Public

Another critical function which the Federal Reserve has performed particularly well in recent years is the provision of information to the public. Each Reserve bank has its own research staff, and the Board of Governors maintains a large staff of economists who follow current economic and financial developments and recommend changes in policy. The Fed makes available on a daily, weekly, and monthly basis an impressive volume of statistical releases, special reports, and studies concerning the financial markets, the nation's money supply, long- and short-term interest rates, the volume and composition of borrowing by the public, and national economic developments. In the international sector, the Federal Reserve supplies, on request, information dealing with developments in foreign currency markets, international loans and capital flows, and the U.S. foreign trade and balance-of-payments position. In addition, as we noted in Chapter 10, the Fed prepares the Flow of Funds Accounts each quarter of the year, providing extensive data on borrowing and lending activities among major sectors of the U.S. economy. This information function is often overlooked in discussions of the Federal Reserve's role within the nation's financial system, but it is one of the more important contributions of the central bank.

SUMMARY AND CONCLUSIONS

In this chapter we have examined the important role played by central banks and, in particular, the Federal Reserve System in the financial system and the economy. Central banks must function to control the nation's money supply, maintain stable conditions in the financial markets, serve as a lender of last resort to aid financial institutions in trouble, and maintain and improve the mechanism for making payments for goods and services. In most industrialized countries, including the United States, central banking is goal oriented, aimed principally at the major economic goals of full employment, reasonable price stability, sustainable economic growth, and a strong and stable balance of payments position with the rest of the world. In the Western world, central banks operate mainly through the marketplace, influencing credit conditions but leaving to private borrowers and lenders the basic decisions of whether to create credit, borrow, and spend.

While there is much disagreement today as to how central banks influence the economy through their actions, economists generally argue that these institutions affect the spending, saving, and borrowing decisions of millions of individuals and businesses through at least three interrelated channels. Central bank policies influence the cost and availability of credit, the volume and rate of growth of the money supply, and the market value of securities held by the public. Each of these policy channels ultimately affects the borrowing, consumption, and investment spending decisions of businesses, consumers, and governments.

Central banks around the world use a variety of tools to influence economic and financial decisions. The Bank of Canada, for example, relies heavily upon changes in deposit reserve requirements, while the Bank of England uses its discount rate on loans as a major policy tool. In contrast, the Federal Reserve System depends principally upon open-market operations—the buying and selling of securities—to achieve its policy objectives. As we will see in the next chapter, the Fed's heavy reliance upon open-market operations reflects both the great flexibility of this policy tool and the great breadth and depth of security markets in the United States compared to the limited market systems which exist in the majority of other nations.

Just as the Federal Reserve System's heavy reliance upon open-market operations is distinctive among the world's central banks, its organizational structure is also uniquely American. The main administrative body within the system is the Board of Governors, composed of seven persons appointed by the president of the United States and headquartered in Washington, D.C. The board appoints officers and staff of the system, sets budgets, and controls such important policy tools as deposit reserve requirements, margin requirements on stock, and changes in the discount rate on loans to banks and other deposit-type financial institutions. However, the board's authority over the future course of economic policy and the implementation of that policy is shared with other departments within the Federal Reserve System.

For example, the Federal Open Market Committee, composed of the seven members of the Federal Reserve Board and five presidents of the Federal Reserve banks, discusses all major policy initiatives by the Fed and closely controls the system's major policy tool—open-market operations. The 12 Federal Reserve banks, located in major financial centers across the United States, determine which banks and other depository financial institutions can borrow from the Fed and on what terms. These regional Reserve banks also supervise banks and bank holding company activities within their districts and provide important services, including the clearing and collection of checks, shipment of currency and coin, transfer of funds by wire, and the safekeeping of securities. Moreover, each of the Reserve banks serves as the federal government's fiscal agent, dispensing and collecting government funds, selling and redeeming government securities, and helping to maintain orderly market conditions so that the federal government can borrow new money and refinance its debt as smoothly as possible.

Each part of the Federal Reserve System, therefore, has a key role to play in the operation of the nation's financial system and the functioning of the economy. In the next two chapters we explore more fully what is generally considered the Federal Reserve's most important job, monetary policy—the regulation of money and credit conditions in order to achieve the nation's major economic goals.

STUDY QUESTIONS

1. What functions do central banks perform in a market-oriented economy? Explain why each is important to the efficient functioning of the financial and economic system.
2. What are the principal goals of the Federal Reserve System in its pursuit of monetary policy? To what extent are these goals consistent or inconsistent with each other?
3. What major problems in the late 19th and early 20th century led to the creation of the Federal Reserve System? What problems did the National Banking Act solve, and what problems did it create? How did the creation of the Fed help to solve these problems?
4. In what ways did the early Federal Reserve System differ from the Fed of today? Consider in your answer such factors as the goals pursued, structure, and policy tools used.
5. List the principal functions of the Federal Reserve System today, and explain why each is important.
6. What are the principal responsibilities assigned to:
    a. The Board of Governors of the Federal Reserve System?
    b. The Federal Open Market Committee?
    c. The Federal Reserve Banks?
    d. The manager of the System Open Market Account?

SELECTED REFERENCES

1. Board of Governors of the Federal Reserve System. *The Federal Reserve System—Purposes and Functions.* Washington, D.C., 1974.
2. Burger, Albert E. *The Money Supply Process.* Belmont, Calif.: Wadsworth, 1971, pp. 52–56.
3. Cacy, J. A. "Monetary Policy in 1980 and 1981." *Economic Review,* Federal Reserve Bank of Kansas City, December 1980.
4. Carlson, Keith M. "Money, Inflation, and Economic Growth: Some Updated Reduced-Form Results and Their Implications." *Review,* Federal Reserve Bank of St. Louis, April 1980.
5. Carlson, Keith M., and Scott E. Hein. "Monetary Aggregates as Monetary Indicators." *Review,* Federal Reserve Bank of St. Louis, November 1980.
6. Federal Reserve Bank of Chicago. "The Depository Institutions Deregulation and Monetary Control Act of 1980." *Economic Perspectives,* September-October 1980, pp. 3–23.
7. Lombra, R., and F. Struble. "Monetary Aggregate Targets and the Volatility of Interest Rates: A Taxonomic Discussion." *Journal of Money, Credit, and Banking,* August 1979, pp. 284–300.

8. Luckett, Dudley G. *Money and Banking.* New York: McGraw-Hill, 1976.

9. Pierce, J. L., and T. D. Thompson. "Some Issues in Controlling the Stock of Money." In *Controlling Monetary Aggregates II: The Implementation.* Federal Reserve Bank of Boston, September 1972, pp. 115–37.

10. Poole, William, and Charles Lieberman. "Improving Monetary Control." In *Brookings Papers on Economic Activity,* 1972: 2, edited by Arthur M. Okun and George L. Perry. Washington, D.C.: The Brookings Institution, 1972.

22

The Tools of
Monetary Policy

As we saw in the preceding chapter, the Federal Reserve System has been given the task of regulating the money and credit system in order to achieve the nation's economic goals. Prominent among these goals are the achievement of full employment, a stable price level, sustainable economic growth, and a strong balance of payments position with the rest of the world. As recent experience has demonstrated, these objectives are not easy to achieve and frequently conflict with one another. Still, the central bank has powerful policy tools at its disposal with which to pursue the nation's economic goals. Our purpose in this chapter is to examine the policy tools available to the Federal Reserve in carrying out its task of controlling the nation's supply of money and credit.

RESERVES AND MONEY—TARGETS OF FEDERAL RESERVE POLICY

The principal immediate target of Federal Reserve policy is the *reserves* of the banking system, consisting mainly of deposits held at the Federal Reserve banks plus currency and coin. These reserves are the "raw material" out of which banks and other depository institutions create credit and cause the money supply to grow. And because the growth of the nation's money supply is closely linked to changes in national income, production, prices, and employment, the Fed pays close attention on a daily basis to fluctuations in the quantity of reserves depository institutions have at their disposal. The total supply of reserves can be changed directly by Federal Reserve open-market operations and by making loans to depository institutions through the

Fed's discount window. The Fed can also exert a powerful effect on the growth of money and credit by changing the legal reserve requirements applicable to deposits held by commercial banks and other depository institutions.

While the Fed's primary concern is the volume and rate of growth of reserves held by depository institutions, all of its policy tools have an impact on *interest rates* as well. Whenever the supply of reserves is reduced relative to the demand for reserves, interest rates tend to rise as funds are rationed among competing financial institutions. Conversely, an expansion in the supply of reserves usually leads to lower interest rates because of the increased availability of loanable funds. Why do these changes occur? What are the specific links between bank reserves and the money supply? Between reserves and interest rates?

The Composition of Reserves

To answer these questions, we need to look closely at what makes up the supply of reserves at depository institutions. We recall from Chapter 3 that all depository institutions offering transaction accounts (principally demand deposits and NOWs) or nonpersonal time deposits are required to hold a small percentage of these deposits in an asset account known as *legal reserves*. Legal reserves consist of the amount of deposits each institution keeps with the Federal Reserve bank in its district plus the amount of currency and coin held in its vault.

We noted in Chapter 3 that legal reserves may be divided into two parts— required reserves and excess reserves. In particular,

$$\text{Total legal reserves} = \text{Required reserves} + \text{Excess reserves}$$
$$= \text{Deposits at the Federal Reserve banks}$$
$$+ \text{vault cash} \quad (22-1)$$

Required reserves are those holdings of cash and deposits at the Fed which the depository institution must hold in order to back the public's deposits or face a legal penalty. Excess reserves consist of cash and Fed deposits owned by depository institutions which are not needed to back the public's deposits and may be used to make loans, purchase securities, repay debts, or serve other purposes. Because legal reserve assets earn little or no income, most depository institutions try to keep their excess reserves close to zero. For example, the largest commercial banks today frequently run reserve deficits and must borrow additional legal reserves in the money market to avoid costly penalties.

The Deposit Multiplier

The distinction between excess and required reserves is important because it plays a key role in the growth of money and credit in the economy.

As we observed in Chapter 3, depository institutions offering checkable deposits have the unique ability to create and destroy money at the stroke of a pen. While an individual depository institution cannot create more money than the volume of excess reserves it holds, the banking system as a whole can create a *multiple* amount of money and credit from any given injection of reserves by using excess reserves to make loans and purchase securities.

How much money and credit can the banking system create if it has excess reserves available? The system's money-creating potential can be estimated using a concept known as the *deposit multiplier,* or coefficient of deposit expansion. The deposit multiplier indicates how many dollars of deposits (and loans) will result from any given injection of new excess reserves into the system. If we assume the existence of a very simple financial system in which the public makes all of its payments by check or draft and does not convert any checkbook (demand deposit) money into thrift deposits, and where depository institutions do not wish to hold any excess reserves but loan out immediately all funds received, then:

The transactions deposit multiplier, or coefficient of expansion

$$= \frac{1}{\text{Reserve requirement on transactions deposits}} \quad (22\text{--}2)$$

For example, if the Federal Reserve insists that depository institutions keep $0.12 in required reserves for each new dollar of demand deposits and other transactions deposits they receive, then the deposit multiplier must be 1/0.12, or 8.33.

Then how much money and credit can the banking system create under these circumstances? If all depository institutions continually make loans with any excess reserves they receive, the maximum amount of new deposits and loans that can be created by the entire banking system may be found from the following equation:

Transactions deposit multiplier
$$\times \text{ Excess reserves} = \text{Maximum volume of}$$
$$\text{new deposits and loans.} \quad (22\text{--}3)$$

If banks and other depository institutions receive additional excess reserves in the amount of $1 million and the reserve requirement behind transactions deposits is 12 percent, we have:

$$1/0.12 \times \$1 \text{ million} = 8.33 \times \$1 \text{ million}$$
$$= \$8.33 \text{ million in new deposits and loans}$$

A *withdrawal* of reserves from depository institutions can work in the opposite direction, destroying deposits and loans. For example, a withdrawal of deposits by the public which causes depository institutions to have a $1 million deficiency in their required reserves would eventually lead to a $8.33 million *decline* in deposits, assuming a 12 percent reserve requirement.

Of course, the real world is quite different from the simple deposit expansion model outlined above. Leakages of funds from the banking system greatly reduce the size of the deposit multiplier, so that its actual value is probably somewhat less than two. Among the most important leakages are the public's desire to convert some portion of new checkbook money into pocket money (currency and coin) or into thrift deposits, and the presence of unutilized lending capacity. Banks and other depository institutions may choose to hold substantial excess reserves and not lend out all their excess funds, because they either cannot find enough qualified borrowers or wish to hold a protective "cushion" of reserves.

These various leakages of funds from transactions balances suggest the need for a slightly more-complex model of the deposit and loan expansion process. In this model the deposit multiplier would be represented by the following expression:

Transactions deposit multiplier assuming drains of funds
into cash, time and savings deposits, and excess reserves

$$= \frac{1}{RR_D + CASH + EXR + (RR_T \times TIME)} \quad (22-4)$$

In this instance, RR_D represents the required legal reserve ratio for demand deposits and other transactions accounts, while RR_T is the required legal reserve ratio for time and savings deposits. CASH and TIME represent the amounts of additional currency and coin and time and savings deposits the public wishes to hold for each dollar of new transactions deposits they receive, while EXR stands for the quantity of excess reserves depository institutions desire to hold for precautionary purposes out of each dollar of new transactions deposits. The largest amount of transactions deposits and loans which the banking system can create, assuming all of the above cash drains occur, would be given by this formula:

$$\frac{1}{RR_D + CASH + EXR + (RR_T \times TIME)}$$
$\times$ Volume of new excess reserves = Maximum volume of
new deposits and loans   (22-5)

To illustrate the use of this formula, assume depository institutions have just received an additional $1 million in excess reserves from some source outside the banking system. (One possible source, as we will soon see, is actions by the Federal Reserve lowering legal reserve requirements or buying securities from the public.) We further assume that, for each new dollar of transactions deposits received, the public will convert $0.25 into pocket money (i.e., CASH = 0.25), and $0.60 will be placed in time and savings deposits (i.e., TIME = 0.60). Further, suppose depository institutions elect to hold $0.05 of every new checkable deposit dollar received as excess reserves (i.e., EXR = 0.05) to protect against future contingencies. The reserve requirement on transactions deposits (RR_D) is 12 percent and on time and savings deposits (RR_T), 3 percent. Then the maximum amount of new deposits and loans which depository institutions as a group can create is calculated as follows:

$$\frac{1}{0.12 + 0.25 + 0.05 + (0.03 \times 0.60)}$$
$$\times \$1 \text{ million} = \frac{1}{0.438} \times \$1 \text{ million}$$
$$= 2.28 \times \$1 \text{ million}$$
$$= \$2.28 \text{ million}$$

Clearly, the deposit multiplier is far smaller when we allow for the conversion of checkable deposits into currency, coin, and thrift deposits and when banks and other depository institutions are unwilling to lend all their excess reserves. This would appear to be "good news" for the central bank, charged with controlling the rate of growth of the nation's money supply. A numerically small deposit multiplier implies that the banking system will not be able to significantly increase the size of the nation's money supply unless the supply of excess reserves is also greatly increased. But the central bank has a potent influence on the quantity of excess reserves available to financial institutions.

Unfortunately the existence of cash drains, thrift deposits, and other reserve-absorbing factors, while reducing the size of the deposit multiplier, also makes the forecasting of deposit flows much more difficult. The central bank must be constantly alert to shifts in the public's demand for currency, coin, and savings accounts and also to the demands of depository institutions for excess reserves and other liquid assets. If the central bank cannot accurately forecast changes in the public's money and deposit preferences, control of the nation's money supply will be less precise and subject to erratic fluctuations, so that achievement of the nation's economic goals will be hindered.

The Money Multiplier

While the concept of the deposit multiplier is useful for some purposes, central bankers are more interested in a related concept known as the *money multiplier,* which defines the relationship between the size of the nation's money supply and the size of the total reserve base available to depository institutions. The money multiplier is defined as follows:

$$\text{Money multiplier} = \frac{1 + \text{CASH}}{\text{RR}_D + \text{CASH} + \text{EXR} + (\text{RR}_T \times \text{TIME})} \qquad (22\text{--}6)$$

The terms CASH, EXR, RR_D, RR_T, and TIME are defined as they were in the deposit-multiplier formula.

We note that the money multiplier differs from the deposit multiplier only in the addition of CASH—the proportion of new transactions deposits which the public desires to hold in the form of currency and coin—to the numerator of the multiplier ratio. This change is made because currency and coin held by the public also form an important component of the nation's money supply and must be accounted for in measuring how fast the money supply grows over time. For example, at year-end 1980 the supply of currency and coin held by the public totaled $116.1 billion, which was almost 40 percent of the amount of demand deposits, NOWs and other checkable deposits outstanding. Moreover, with the rapid spread of coin-operated machines, the amount of currency and coin outstanding actually has been growing faster than the volume of checkable deposits. For example, between year-end 1977 and year-end 1980, currency and coin in public hands rose more than 30 percent, while demand deposits and other checkable deposits increased less than 21 percent.

Another important point to note about currency and coin is that fluctuations in the volume held by the public have a direct bearing on the reserves held by depository institutions. For example, when the public wishes to increase its holdings of pocket money—something that routinely occurs around holidays and over weekends—it will write checks against transactions deposits in depository institutions, drawing down both demand accounts and reserves. If the public desires to hold less pocket money, the excess currency and coin typically will be redeposited in transactions accounts, increasing both reserves and demand deposits. Recognizing this important link between currency and bank reserves, economists have developed the concept of the *monetary base,* which is simply the sum of legal reserves plus the amount of currency and coin held by the public.[1] Currency and coin represent almost 70 percent of the monetary base, and legal reserves account for the remaining 30 percent.

Why is the monetary base important? It is one of the principal determinants of the nation's money supply. Specifically,

$$\text{Money multiplier} \times \text{Monetary base} = \text{Money supply} \qquad (22\text{--}7)$$

or,

$$\frac{1 + \text{CASH}}{\text{RR}_D + \text{CASH} + \text{EXR} + (\text{RR}_T \times \text{TIME})}$$
$$\times \text{Monetary base} = \text{Transactions deposits held}$$
$$\text{in depository institutions}$$
$$+ \text{ currency and coin held by the public.}$$

We may use this formula as a device to estimate the size of the money multiplier.[2] For example, in December 1980 the monetary base was $162.5

---

[1] To be more precise, the Federal Reserve defines the monetary base as equal to total reserve balances plus vault cash held by banks plus currency and coin held outside the U.S. Treasury, Federal Reserve banks, and the vaults of commercial banks.

[2] This definition of the money supply is the one labeled M–1A by the Federal Reserve System. Recently, the Fed has developed four other money-supply definitions, which we will examine in Chapter 23. Each money supply concept can be linked directly to the monetary base, provided the components of the money multiplier are altered to reflect the different kinds of deposits or financial assets available to the public under each money-supply definition.

billion, while the sum of checkable deposits and other transactions accounts and currency and coin stood at $422.1 billion. The money multiplier, therefore, was as follows:

$$\text{Money multiplier} = \frac{\$422.1 \text{ billion}}{\$162.5 \text{ billion}} = 2.60$$

On average, each $1 increase in the monetary base resulted in a rise in the nation's money supply of about $2.60. This is one reason the monetary base is frequently referred to as *high-powered money;* a change in the base, working through the money multiplier, produces a magnified change in the nation's money supply.

The monetary base–money multiplier relationship identifies for us the most important factors which explain changes in the nation's money supply, and it also helps us to understand how the Federal Reserve can influence the money supply–creation process. The Fed is one of the principal determinants of the size of the monetary base along with the public and the U.S. Treasury. It can increase or decrease the total supply of reserves to change the size of the base. Alternatively, the Fed may choose merely to offset actions taken by the public or the Treasury in order to keep the size of the monetary base unchanged. Finally, the central bank can change the required reserve ratios behind transactions (RR_D) and time (RR_T) deposits, which will affect the magnitude of the money multiplier. Occasionally, when the central bank wishes to exert a potent impact on economic and financial conditions, it will make changes in *both* the monetary base and the money multiplier. In the next section we take a close look at the tools the Federal Reserve System uses to influence the size of the monetary base, the money multiplier, and ultimately the nation's money supply.

THE POLICY TOOLS OF THE FEDERAL RESERVE SYSTEM

In order to change the volume of reserves available to depository institutions for lending and investing and to influence interest rates in the economy, the Federal Reserve System uses a variety of policy tools. Some of these tools are *general credit controls,* which affect the entire banking and financial system. Included in this list are reserve requirements, the discount rate, and open-market operations. A second set of policy tools may be labeled *selective credit controls* because they affect specific groups or sectors of the financial system. Moral suasion, legal interest-rate ceilings, and margin requirements on the purchase of listed securities are examples of selective credit controls. Of course, *all* the central bank's policy tools have as their ultimate goal the promotion of full employment, sustainable economic growth, price stability, and a stable balance-of-payments position for the United States. Our objective in this section is to look first at the Fed's general credit controls and then at its selective credit controls.

Reserve Requirements

Since the 1930s the Federal Reserve Board has had the power to vary the amount of required legal reserves which member banks must hold behind deposits they receive from the public. With passage of the Monetary Control Act of 1980, nonmember banks and all nonbank depository financial institutions (including credit unions, mutual savings banks, and savings and loan associations) must also conform to the deposit reserve requirements set by the Fed. Early in the Fed's history it was felt that the primary purpose of reserve requirements was to safeguard the public's deposits. More recently, we have come to realize that their principal use is to give the central bank a powerful tool which can be used in emergency situations. Indeed, reserve requirements are probably the most potent policy tool which the Federal Reserve System has at its disposal today. However, changes in reserve requirements are a little-used tool, as we will soon see.

Effects of a Change in Reserve Requirements. A change in deposit reserve requirements has at least three different effects upon the financial system. First of all, it changes the deposit multiplier (or coefficient of expansion) which, as we have seen, affects the amount of deposits and new loans the banking system can create for any given injection of new reserves. A change in reserve requirements also affects the size of the money multiplier, influencing the rate of increase in the nation's money supply. If the Fed increases reserve requirements, the deposit multiplier and the money multiplier are *reduced,* slowing the growth of credit and deposits. On the other hand, a decrease in reserve requirements *increases* the size of both the deposit and the money multiplier. In this instance each dollar of additional reserves available to the banking system will lead to accelerated growth in credit and deposits.

A change in reserve requirements also affects the *mix* between excess reserves and required legal reserves. Suppose all depository institutions are fully loaned up, and excess reserves are zero. If reserve requirements are *reduced,* a portion of what were required reserves now becomes excess reserves. Depository institutions will soon convert all or a portion of these newly created excess reserves into loans and investments, expanding the nation's money supply. Similarly, if all institutions are fully loaned up, with zero excess reserves, an *increase* in reserve requirements will mean that some depository institutions will be short required legal reserves. These institutions will be forced to sell securities, cut back on loans, and borrow reserves from other financial institutions in order to meet their reserve requirements. The money supply will grow more slowly and may even decline.

Interest rates always respond to a change in reserve requirements. A move by the Fed toward higher deposit reserve requirements soon leads to higher interest rates, particularly in the money market, as depository institutions scramble to cover any reserve deficiencies. Credit becomes both less available and more costly. In contrast, a lowering of reserve requirements tends to bring interest rates down as well. Flush with excess reserves, depository institutions are willing to make more loans at lower interest rates, and fewer institutions will have to sell securities or borrow to meet their reserve requirements.

An Illustration.   Exhibit 22–1 illustrates the effects of changes in deposit reserve requirements. Suppose depository institutions are required to keep 12 percent of their deposits in legal reserves. Then, $120 of legal reserves will be needed to support each $1,000 of deposits. If there is sufficient demand for loanable funds, institutions will probably loan or invest the remain-

EXHIBIT 22–1
Changes in Reserve Requirements

Commercial Bank

	Assets		Liabilities	
With a 12% reserve requirement, $120 of reserves are needed to support each $1,000 of deposits.	Loans and investments	$ 880	Deposits	$1,000
	Legal reserves	120		
	Required	120⌉		
	Excess	0⌋		
		$1,000		$1,000

Increase in reserve requirements:

Commercial Bank

	Assets		Liabilities	
If required reserves are increased from 12 to 15 percent, more reserves are needed against the same volume of deposits. Any deficiencies (i.e., negative excess reserves) must be covered by liquidation of loans and investments or by borrowing.	Legal reserves	$ 120	Deposits	$1,000
	Required	150⌉		
	Excess	−30⌋		
	Loans and investments	880		
		$1,000		$1,000

Decrease in reserve requirements:

Commercial Bank

	Assets		Liabilities	
If required reserves are reduced from 12 to 10 percent, excess reserves are created which can be loaned or invested.	Legal reserves	$ 120	Deposits	$1,000
	Required	100⌉		
	Excess	20⌋		
	Loans and investments	880		
		$1,000		$1,000

ing $880. Suppose that the Federal Reserve increases reserve requirements from 12 to 15 percent. As a result, more legal reserves are necessary to support the same volume of deposits, and institutions have a $30 reserve deficit for each $1,000 of deposits. This deficit may be covered by selling loans or investment securities, borrowing funds, or reducing deposits.

On the other hand, suppose required reserves are lowered from 12 to 10 percent. There now are $20 in excess reserves for each $1,000 in deposits, and that excess can be loaned or invested, creating new deposits. We should note that total legal reserves available to the banking system are not affected by changes in reserve requirements. A shift in deposit reserve requirements affects only the *mix* of legal reserves between required and excess, not the total amount.

Current Levels of Reserve Requirements. Today deposit reserve requirements are imposed by the Federal Reserve Board upon all depository institutions that are either federally insured or eligible to apply for federal insurance, including commercial banks, mutual savings banks, savings and loan associations, and credit unions. Under the terms of the Monetary Control Act of 1980 three types of deposits are subject to legal reserve requirements:

1. Transactions accounts, which are those deposits used to make payments and include regular checking accounts, NOW accounts, and any account subject to automatic or telephone transfers of funds.
2. Nonpersonal time deposits, which are interest-bearing thrift deposits held by businesses and governmental units but not individuals.
3. Eurocurrency liabilities, which are borrowings of deposits from banks and branches located outside the United States.

As shown in Exhibit 22–2, the current reserve requirement on transactions accounts of $25 million or less is 3 percent, while the net amount of transactions deposits over $25 million is subject to a 12 percent reserve requirement.[3] Personal time and savings deposits carry no reserve requirement, but nonpersonal time deposits owned by businesses and units of government currently have a 3 percent required reserve. Average reserve requirements are higher on transactions accounts than on time and savings accounts because transactions balances are considered to be less-stable deposits than time and savings deposits.

The largest depository institutions, holding more than $25 million in net transactions balances, carry the heaviest reserve requirements. This is due to the fact that larger financial institutions hold the deposits of thousands of smaller banks and other deposit-type intermediaries. Moreover, the failure

---

[3] The Federal Reserve Board is empowered under the Monetary Control Act to vary reserve requirements on transactions accounts over $25 million between 8 and 14 percent. The $25 million dividing line (known as the "tranche") is indexed and will change each calendar year beginning in 1982 by 80 percent of the percentage change in total transactions accounts of all depository institutions during the previous year ended June 30.

EXHIBIT 22–2
Reserve Requirements of Depository Institutions (percent of deposits)

Type of Deposit and Deposit Interval	Percentage Reserve Requirement	Statutory Range‡
Net transactions accounts:*		
$0–25 million	3%	3%
Over $25 million	12	8 to 14
Nonpersonal time deposits:†		
Original maturity of		
Less than 4 years	3	0 to 9
4 years or more	0	0 to 9
Eurocurrency liabilities		
All types	3	None

* Transactions accounts include all deposits on which the depositor is allowed to make withdrawals by negotiable or transferable instruments, payment orders of withdrawal, telephone and preauthorized transfers (in excess of three per month), for the purpose of making payments to third persons or others.
† Nonpersonal time deposits are interest-bearing thrift deposits, including both time and savings deposits, that are not transactions accounts and in which the beneficial interest is held by a depositor, not a natural person. Also included are certain transferable time deposits held by natural persons and certain obligations issued to depository institutions' offices located outside the United States.
‡ The permissible statutory ranges for reserve requirements were set in the Monetary Control Act of 1980. However, under extraordinary circumstances the board can impose a requirement outside the statutory range on any liability of a depository institution. It can also impose a supplementary reserve requirement of up to 4 percent on transactions accounts and can vary requirements on nonpersonal time deposits by maturity. No reserve requirement ratio or statutory range of permissible ratios was imposed on Eurocurrency liabilities in the Monetary Control Act, leaving the matter to the discretion of the Federal Reserve Board.
SOURCE: Board of Governors of the Federal Reserve System, *Federal Reserve Bulletin*, July 1981, Table 1.15.

of a large bank or other depository institution can send shock waves through the entire financial system and threaten the economic viability of many other institutions and individuals as well.[4]

Proposals to Reform the Reserve Requirement Tool. Over the years there have been a number of proposals to use the reserve requirement tool more aggressively and effectively.[5] It is alleged, for example, that increases in reserve requirements could be an extremely effective tool in putting the brakes on an inflationary expansion of money and credit. One novel proposal which reemerges from time to time calls for the use of reserve requirements to direct credit into areas of the economy where the need appears to be most

---

[4] To make it easier for all depository institutions to adjust to the current reserve requirement schedule, the Monetary Control Act provides for an eight-year, phase-in period. For existing nonmember banks and thrift institutions, the phase-in period for meeting the new reserve requirements ends September 3, 1987. For existing member banks, the phase-in period is approximately three years, depending upon whether their new reserve requirements are greater than or less than the old requirements. All new depository institutions have a two-year phase-in period beginning with the date they open for business.

[5] See, for example, Laurent (9), Poole (11), and Woodworth (14).

critical. The basic idea is to impose reserve requirements on different categories of assets instead of on deposits. If the regulatory authorities decided that an increase in the quantity of mortgage loans is needed, for example, the reserve requirement on mortgage loans might be lowered to stimulate mortgage lending. On the other hand, reserve requirements could be increased on those loans the authorities wished to discourage. This proposal has met with strong opposition in the financial community because it would place the government in the position of determining what types of credit are to be granted by private financial institutions. In the United States, at least, the allocation of credit is generally left to the marketplace, except in times of national emergency.

Uses and Limitations of the Reserve Requirement Tool. At times the Federal Reserve has used the reserve requirement tool aggressively to achieve its goals, especially when severe inflation threatens. Probably the most dramatic example of this occurred on March 14, 1980, when President Jimmy Carter unveiled a new antiinflation package, combining a proposed federal budget surplus with several credit-tightening moves by the Federal Reserve. Acting under the authority of the Credit Control Act of 1969 (which grants the president authority to impose restrictions on the growth of money and credit when needed to fight inflation), the Fed established special deposit reserve requirements for banks, finance companies, oil and gas companies, travel agencies, retail establishments, and other businesses with $2 million or more in consumer loans. These firms were required to set aside cash reserves at the Fed equal to 15 percent of the amount of any new loans made via credit cards, overdraft accounts, or other unsecured credit. Money market mutual funds were required to hold 15 percent of their new assets in reserve. At the same time, the Fed increased to 10 percent from 8 percent the reserve requirement levied in October 1979 on bank-managed liabilities (including large negotiable CDs, RPs, and borrowings of Eurodollars and federal funds). Commercial bankers were asked to voluntarily limit the growth of their loans to no more than 9 percent a year.

These special reserve requirements were reduced to zero in July 1980 when the economy entered a recession. Still, the Carter administration's program illustrates the fact that changes in reserve requirements, combined with other monetary policy measures, can be used to carry out major shifts in government economic policy. The reserve requirement tool is exceedingly powerful, however—even a small change affects hundreds of millions of dollars in legal reserves. Moreover, it is an *inflexible* tool. Required reserve ratios cannot be changed frequently because this would disrupt the nation's banking system. Not surprisingly, changes in reserve requirements do not occur very often, averaging about once every two years since World War II.

Changes in the Federal Reserve's Discount Rate

Any depository institution which accepts transactions accounts or nonpersonal time deposits may borrow reserves from the discount window of the Federal Reserve bank in its region. The Fed's Regulation A states, however, that these loans must be short term (ordinarily no more than 15 days) and serve only as a *temporary* source of funds. In fact, Federal Reserve regulations require depository institutions to alternate their borrowings from the discount window with drawings upon other sources, such as the federal funds market. Frequent borrowing is discouraged and, in the case of the largest borrowers, penalized with a higher interest rate.[6]

The *discount rate* is the interest charge levied against those institutions choosing to borrow from the Fed. The board of directors of each Federal Reserve bank votes to determine what the discount rate should be in its region of the country. However, the Federal Reserve Board in Washington, D.C., must approve the rate charged in each of the 12 Federal Reserve districts. As shown in Exhibit 22–3, the basic rate on short-term loans of

EXHIBIT 22–3
The Discount Rates of the Federal Reserve Banks (percent per annum)

Federal Reserve Bank	Short-term Adjustment Credit*	Extended Credit		Emergency Credit to All Others‡
		Seasonal Credit	Special Circumstances†	
Boston	14%	14%	15%	17%
New York	14	14	15	17
Philadelphia	14	14	15	17
Cleveland	14	14	15	17
Richmond	14	14	15	17
Atlanta	14	14	15	17
Chicago	14	14	15	17
St. Louis	14	14	15	17
Minneapolis	14	14	15	17
Kansas City	14	14	15	17
Dallas	14	14	15	17
San Francisco	14	14	15	17

* Beginning May 5, 1981, a 4 percent surcharge was applied to short-term adjustment loans to institutions with deposits of $500 million or more if borrowing occurred in successive weeks or in more than four weeks in a calendar quarter.
† Credit may be extended for longer periods of time when a particular borrowing institution needs support due to exceptional circumstances or unforeseen problems.
‡ Emergency loans may be provided to individuals, partnerships, and corporations as described in Section 201.3 (c) of Regulation A.
SOURCE: Board of Governors of the Federal Reserve System, *Federal Reserve Bulletin,* July 1981, Table 1.14.

reserves is 14 percent at present. Depository institutions with marked seasonal movements in deposits may apply for extended credit, also at a 14 percent interest rate, while emergency credit may be provided to institutions in trouble but the interest rate is higher. Beginning in May 1981, a 4 percent surcharge was added to the discount rate levied on short-term adjustment

---

[6] For a discussion of the use of the Federal Reserve's discount window as a reserve adjustment device for banks and other depository institutions, see Chapter 13.

loans made to financial institutions with deposits of $500 million or more who borrow in successive weeks or borrow for more than 4 weeks in any calendar quarter.

Borrowing and Repaying Discount Window Loans. The mechanics of borrowing from the Federal Reserve are illustrated in Exhibit 22–4. Depository institutions that borrow regularly at the discount window keep a signed loan-authorization form at the Federal Reserve bank in their district and also keep U.S. government securities or other acceptable collateral on deposit there. Therefore, when a loan is needed, the officer responsible for managing the borrowing institution's legal reserve position will merely contact the district Federal Reserve bank and request that the necessary funds be deposited in that institution's reserve account.

We assume in Exhibit 22–4 that a bank has requested a loan of $1 million and the Fed has agreed to make the loan. The borrowing bank receives an increase in its account "Reserves Held at F. R. Bank" of $1 million. At the same time, the bank's liability account, "Bills Payable," increases by $1 million. On the Federal Reserve bank's balance sheet, the loan shows up as an increase in "Bank Reserves" of $1 million—a liability of the Federal Reserve System—and an increase in a Fed asset account, "Discounts and Advances." When the loan is repaid, the transaction is exactly reversed.

Quite clearly, borrowings from the Fed's discount window increase the total reserves available to the banking system. Repayments of those borrowings cause total reserves to fall.

Effects of a Discount Rate Change. Most observers today feel that at least three effects follow from a change in the Federal Reserve's discount rate. One is the *cost effect.* An increase in the discount rate means that it is more costly to borrow reserves from the Federal Reserve as opposed to using some other source of funds. Other things equal, loans from the discount window and the total volume of borrowed reserves will decline. Conversely, a lower discount rate should result in an acceleration of borrowing from the Federal Reserve and more reserves flowing into the banking system.

Of course, the strength of the cost effect depends upon the *spread* between the discount rate and other money market interest rates. If the Fed's rate remains well below other interest rates even after it is increased, then it would still be cheaper, relatively speaking, to draw upon the Fed for funds. There would be little reduction in loans from the discount window. This has happened frequently in recent years, with the discount rate usually lagging well behind other interest rates in the nation's money market.

A second consequence of changes in the discount rate is called the *substitution effect.* A change in the discount rate usually causes other interest rates to change as well. This is due to the fact that the Federal Reserve is one source of borrowed reserves, but certainly not the only source. An increase in the discount rate, for example, will make borrowing from the Fed less attractive, but borrowing from other sources such as the Federal funds and Eurodollar markets will become relatively more attractive. Banks and other

EXHIBIT 22–4
Borrowing and Repaying Loans from the Fed's Discount Window

Borrowing from a Federal Reserve bank:

Federal Reserve Bank				Commercial Bank		
Assets		Liabilities		Assets		Liabilities
Discounts and advances	$1 million	Bank Reserves	$1 million	Reserves held at Federal Reserve bank	$1 million	Bills payable	$1 million

Repayment of borrowings from the Fed:

Federal Reserve Bank				Commercial Bank		
Assets		Liabilities		Assets		Liabilities
Discounts and advances	−$1 million	Bank Reserves	−$1 million	Reserves held at Federal Reserve bank	−$1 million	Bills payable	−$1 million

borrowers will shift their attention to these other markets, causing interest rates there to rise as well.

A lowering of the discount rate, on the other hand, frequently causes a downward movement in money market rates and, ultimately, capital market rates. This happens because deposit-type financial institutions will begin borrowing more from the Federal Reserve, reducing the demand for credit in other segments of the financial marketplace.

The financial system is really one vast pool of loanable funds. Any disturbance created in one segment of that pool affects other segments. Thus, changes in the Federal Reserve's discount rate soon impact upon virtually all parts of the financial system. Even long-term interest rates in the capital market eventually respond to a change in the discount rate.

The final effect of a discount rate change is called the *announcement effect*. The discount rate has a psychological impact on the financial markets because the Fed's rate is widely regarded as an indicator of monetary policy. If, for example, the Federal Reserve increases the discount rate, many observers regard this as a signal that the Fed is pushing for tighter credit conditions. Market participants may respond by reducing their borrowings and curtailing their spending plans.

Unfortunately, the psychological impact of the discount rate may work against the Fed as well as for it. It is quite likely, for example, that if the Federal Reserve increases the discount rate, borrowers will respond by accelerating their borrowings in an effort to secure the credit they need before interest rates move even higher. Such an action would thwart the Fed's objective of slowing down the growth of borrowing and spending. Because of the possibility of negative psychological effects, the discount rate is changed infrequently and often lags behind rates in the open market. Frequently, the Fed must make a technical adjustment in the rate just to bring it closer into line with other interest rates. Even so, market participants are likely to "read into" discount rate changes either a new policy position or more aggressive pursuit of existing policies by the Fed.

Open-Market Operations

The limitations of the discount-rate and reserve-requirement policy tools have led the Federal Reserve to rely more heavily in recent years upon open-market operations to accomplish its goals. By definition, open-market operations consist of the buying and selling of U.S. government and other securities by the Federal Reserve System to affect the quantity and growth of reserves and, ultimately, general credit conditions. Open-market operations are the most-flexible policy tool available to the Fed and suitable for "fine tuning" of the financial markets when this is necessary.

Effects of Open-Market Operations. The open-market tool has two major effects upon the banking system and credit conditions. First of all, it has an *interest-rate effect* because the Fed usually buys or sells a large quantity (several hundred million dollars worth) of securities in the financial marketplace at any one time. If the Fed is *purchasing* securities, this adds additional demand for these securities in the market, which tends to increase their prices and lower their yields. Conversely, if the Federal Reserve is *selling* securities from its portfolio, this action increases the supply of securities available in the market, tending to depress their prices and raise their yields.

The Fed has claimed for many years, however, that its principal objective is not to influence interest rates, but rather to alter the volume of *reserves* available to the banking system and, through reserves, the availability of credit. Nevertheless, interest-rate effects do follow from open-market operations. Indeed, as we will note in the next chapter, one of the principal indicators of Federal Reserve policy is money market interest rates. Some monetary policy objectives today are still stated in terms of ranges of money market interest rates, especially the daily rate on loans in the federal funds market.

Most authorities agree, however, that the principal day-to-day effect of open-market operations is to change the level and growth of *legal reserves*. Generally, a Federal Reserve *purchase* of securities will increase the reserves of the banking system and expand its ability to make loans and investments. In contrast, a *sale* of securities by the Federal Reserve will decrease the level and growth of reserves and reduce the growth of money and credit. The impact of Federal Reserve open-market operations on the reserve positions of banks and other deposit-type institutions is illustrated in Exhibit 22–5.

Fed Purchases. In the top portion of Exhibit 22–5 we assume that the Fed is making *purchases* of U.S. government securities in the open market from either deposit-type financial institutions, which keep their reserve accounts at the Federal Reserve banks, or from other institutions and individuals.[7] In the case of purchases from deposit-type institutions, the Federal Reserve records the acquisition of securities in the system's asset account—U.S. securities—and pays for the securities by increasing the reserve account of the selling institution. Thus, reserves of depository institutions at the Fed rise, while institutional holdings of securities fall by the same amount. Note that *both* total and excess reserves rise in the wake of a Fed purchase, assuming that depository institutions have no reserves deficiencies to begin with. With these extra reserves, additional loans and investments can be made which will have an expansionary impact on the availability of credit in the economy. Interest rates probably will fall.

An expansionary effect also takes place when the Federal Reserve buys securities from an institution or individual other than a deposit-type financial

---

[7] In reality, all Fed security transactions are conducted with one or more of approximately three dozen primary dealers in U.S. government securities. However, as we will soon see, the effects of each transaction spread rapidly through the money market, affecting the financial position of many individuals and institutions.

EXHIBIT 22–5
Federal Reserve Open-Market Operations

The Fed Buys Securities

Open-market purchase from a bank or other deposit-type financial institution:

Depository Financial Institution		Federal Reserve Bank		Effects
Assets	Liabilities	Assets	Liabilities	
U.S. securities −1,000		U.S. securities +1,000	Reserves +1,000	Total and excess legal reserves increase.
Reserves at Fed +1,000				

Open-market purchase not from a depository financial institution:

Depository Financial Institution		Federal Reserve Bank		Effects
Assets	Liabilities	Assets	Liabilities	
Reserves at Fed +1,000	Deposits +1,000	U.S. securities +1,000	Reserves +1,000	Total and excess legal reserves increase. Deposits increase.

The Fed Sells Securities

Open-market sale to a bank or other deposit-type financial institution:

Depository Financial Institution		Federal Reserve Bank		Effects
Assets	Liabilities	Assets	Liabilities	
U.S. securities +1,000		U.S. securities −1,000	Reserves −1,000	Total and excess legal reserves decrease.
Reserves at Fed −1,000				

Open-market sale not to a depository financial institution:

Depository Financial Institution		Federal Reserve Bank		Effects
Assets	Liabilities	Assets	Liabilities	
Reserves at Fed −1,000	Deposits −1,000	U.S. securities −1,000	Reserves −1,000	Total and excess legal reserves decrease. Deposits decrease.

institution. Legal reserves increase, but total deposits—a component of the nation's money supply—increase as well. Deposits rise because the Fed issues a check to pay for the securities it purchases, and that check will be deposited in some financial institution. Excess reserves rise, making possible an expansion of credit on the part of depository institutions. Note, however, that the rise in excess reserves is *less* in this case than would occur if the Fed bought securities only from institutions which maintain reserve accounts with the Federal Reserve banks. This is due to the fact some of the new legal reserves created by the Fed purchase must be pledged as required reserves behind the newly created deposits. Therefore, Federal Reserve open market purchases of securities have less of an effect on total credit expansion if the Fed's transaction involves only nondeposit financial institutions and individuals.

Fed Sales. Federal Reserve *sales* of securities reduce the growth of reserves and credit. As shown in the bottom half of Exhibit 22–5, when the Fed sells U.S. government securities out of its portfolio to a depository financial institution with a reserve account, that institution adds the securities to its portfolio, and the Fed's security holdings decline. However, the depository institution must pay for these securities by letting the Fed deduct the amount of the purchase from its reserve account. Both total reserves and excess reserves fall. If deposit institutions were fully loaned up with no excess reserves available, the open-market sale would result in a reserve deficiency. Some institutions would be forced to sell loans and securities or borrow funds, reducing deposits and the availability of credit. Interest rates would probably rise.

The Federal Reserve may also sell securities to an individual or a nondeposit institution. As Exhibit 22–5 reveals, in this instance both reserves and deposits fall. Credit becomes less available and usually more expensive.

How Open-Market Operations Are Conducted. All trading in securities by the Federal Reserve is carried out through the system's Trading Desk, located at the Federal Reserve Bank of New York. The Trading Desk is supervised by the manager of the System Open Market Account (SOMA)—a vice president of the New York Fed. The SOMA manager's activities are, in turn, supervised and directed by the Federal Open Market Committee, which meets periodically in Washington, D.C. All Fed security purchases and sales are made through a select list of primary U.S. government securities dealers who agree to buy or sell in amounts called for by the Trading Desk at the time the Fed wishes to trade. About half a dozen of these dealers are commercial banks which have securities departments. The rest—about two dozen—are exclusively dealers in U.S. government and selected private securities.

The Policy Directive. How does the manager of SOMA decide whether or not to buy or sell securities in the open market on a given day? He is guided, first of all, by a policy directive issued to the Federal Reserve Bank of New York following the conclusion of each meeting of the Federal Open Market

Committee (FOMC). The manager of SOMA attends each FOMC meeting and participates in its policy discussion. He listens to the views of each member of the Federal Reserve Board and the Reserve bank presidents, who describe economic conditions in their region of the country. He also receives the benefit of a presentation by staff economists of the Federal Reserve Board which analyzes current economic and financial developments.

An example of a recent Federal Reserve policy directive to the SOMA manager is shown in Exhibit 22–6. This directive summarizes the Federal

EXHIBIT 22–6
Domestic Policy Directive Issued to the Federal Reserve Bank of New York, Federal Open Market Committee Meeting, November 18, 1980

The information reviewed at this meeting suggests that real GNP is recovering further in the fourth quarter from the sharp contraction in the second quarter, while prices on the average continue to rise rapidly. In October industrial production and nonfarm payroll employment expanded substantially for the third consecutive month, and the unemployment rate remained around 7½ percent. The value of retail sales changed little, following four months of recovery. The rise in the index of average hourly earnings over the first ten months of 1980 was somewhat more rapid than in 1979.

The weighted average value of the dollar in exchange markets on balance has risen further over the past month. The U.S. trade deficit was essentially unchanged in September, and the rate in the third quarter was sharply lower than that in the first half.

Growth in M–1A and M–1B moderated further in October but was still relatively rapid; growth in M–2 accelerated slightly, reflecting a pickup in expansion of its nontransactions component. From the fourth quarter of 1979 to October, growth of M–1A was in the upper part of the range set by the Committee for growth over the year ending in the fourth quarter of 1980, while growth of M–1B and M–2 was somewhat above the upper limits of their ranges. Expansion in commercial bank credit was rapid in October, although not so rapid as in August and September. Market interest rates have risen sharply in recent weeks; average rates on new home mortgage commitments have continued upward. On November 14 the Board of Governors announced an increase in Federal Reserve discount rates from 11 to 12 percent and a surcharge of 2 percentage points on frequent borrowing of large member banks from Federal Reserve Banks.

The Federal Open Market Committee seeks to foster monetary and financial conditions that will help to reduce inflation, encourage economic recovery, and contribute to a sustainable pattern of international transactions. At its meeting in July, the Committee agreed that these objectives would be furthered by growth of M–1A, M–1B, M–2, and M–3 from the fourth quarter of 1979 to the fourth quarter of 1980 within ranges of 3½ to 6 percent, 4 to 6½ percent, 6 to 9 percent, and 6½ to 9½ percent respectively. The associated range for bank credit was 6 to 9 percent. For the period from the fourth quarter of 1980 to the fourth quarter of 1981, the Committee looked toward a reduction in the ranges for growth of M–1A, M–1B, and M–2 on the order of ½ percentage point from the ranges adopted for 1980, abstracting from institutional influences affecting the behavior of the aggregates. These ranges will be reconsidered as conditions warrant.

In the short run, the Committee seeks behavior of reserve aggregates consistent with growth of M–1A, M–1B, and M–2 over the period from September to December at annual rates of about 2½ percent, 5 percent, and 7¾ percent respectively, or somewhat less, provided that in the period before the next regular meeting the weekly average federal funds rate remains within a range of 13 to 17 percent.

If it appears during the period before the next meeting that the constraint on the federal funds rate is inconsistent with the objective for the expansion of reserves, the Manager for Domestic Operations is promptly to notify the Chairman, who will then decide whether the situation calls for supplementary instructions from the Committee.

SOURCE: Board of Governors of the Federal Reserve System, *Federal Reserve Bulletin,* January 1981, p. 31.

Reserve's view of current economic developments, particularly those which pertain to the growth of output in the economy and to movements in prices and employment. In line with the Fed's concern over international affairs and especially the value of the dollar in international markets, the directive also contains a synopsis of recent developments in the international money market.

Prominently mentioned in every directive are the *monetary aggregates*—M–1A, M–1B, M–2, and M–3—all measures of the nation's money supply.[8] The FOMC sets target ranges for growth in the nation's money supply and asks the SOMA manager to use the open-market policy tool in an effort to achieve those targeted growth rates. For example, in the directive shown in Exhibit 22–6, the FOMC called for growth in M–1A at approximately a 2½ percent annual rate, in M–1B at 5 percent, and in M–2 at 7¾ percent until the next committee meeting. In addition, a target range for a key money market rate—the average rate on federal funds loans—also is often specified. For example, the directive shown here calls for a weekly average federal funds rate in the 13 to 17 percent range. In the event that rates of growth in the money supply or the federal funds rate drifts outside these ranges, the SOMA manager is to notify the chairman of the Federal Reserve Board for further instructions.

We note that the directive issued to the SOMA manager is extremely *general* in nature, giving specific targets or target ranges but recognizing the need for flexibility as market conditions change. This is a reflection of the crude state of the art in trying to control money market conditions and the nation's money supply. Many factors other than Federal Reserve operations affect both interest rates and the money supply. While the Federal Reserve can have a significant impact on the *direction* of change, it has considerable difficulty in trying to hit specific targets, especially money-supply targets. The Federal Open Market Committee must be flexible and trust the SOMA manager's judgment in responding to daily conditions in the money market, which subsequently may be quite different from those anticipated when the FOMC held its last meeting.

The Conference Call. As an added check on the decisions of the SOMA manager, a conference call between staff economists at the Federal Reserve board, a member of the FOMC, and the SOMA manager is held each day before trading occurs. The SOMA manager will update those sitting in on the conference call concerning current conditions in the money market and then make a recommendation on the type and volume of securities to be bought or

---

[8] These and other money supply measures are discussed in Chapter 23. As noted there, M–1A includes demand deposits held by banks and currency and coin in circulation. M–1B adds to these components NOW accounts and deposits subject to automatic transfer of funds at banks and thrift institutions, credit union share drafts, and demand deposits held by mutual savings banks. M–2 includes all of the foregoing items plus savings and small-denomination time deposits at all depository institutions, overnight RPs at banks, shares in money market mutual funds, and overnight Eurodollar transactions involving U.S. residents. M–3 is defined as M–2 plus large-denomination time deposits at all depository institutions and term RPs at commercial banks and savings and loan associations.

sold that day. At this point the conference call participants may make alternative recommendations for security purchases or sales. Usually, however, the SOMA manager's recommendation is taken, and trading proceeds.

If later in the day the situation changes and it appears that the earlier decision was ill-founded, the trading desk may once again enter the market and carry out purchases or sales of securities to offset its previous action. This great flexibility is what makes the open-market tool the most popular of all the Fed's policy weapons.

Types of Open-Market Operations. There are three basic types of Federal Reserve open-market operations. The so-called *straight* or *outright transaction* refers to the sale or purchase of securities in which outright title passes to the buyer on a permanent basis. In this case, a permanent change occurs in the level of legal reserves, up or down. Thus, when the Federal Reserve wants to bring about a once-and-for-all change in reserves, it will tend to use the straight or outright type of transaction.

In contrast, when the Fed wishes to have a temporary effect on bank reserves it will employ a *repurchase agreement* with a securities dealer. Under a repurchase agreement, or "REPO," the Fed will *buy* securities from dealers but agree to sell them back after a few days.[9] The result is a temporary increase in legal reserves which will be reversed when the Fed sells the securities back to the dealers. Such RPs frequently are used during holiday periods or when other temporary factors are at work which have resulted in a shortfall in reserves.

The Fed can also deal with a temporary excess quantity of reserves by using a matched sale purchase transaction—commonly called a reverse RP or "reverse REPO." In this instance the Fed will agree to *sell* securities to dealers for a brief period and to then buy them back. Frequently, when mail deliveries are slowed by weather or strikes, the result is a sharp increase in the volume of uncollected checks ("float"), giving banks and other depository institutions hundreds of millions of dollars in excess reserves until the checks are cleared. The Fed can absorb these excess reserves using reverse RPs until the situation returns to normal.

The final type of open-market operation is the *run off*. The Federal Reserve may deal directly with the U.S. Treasury in purchasing and redeeming securities. Suppose the Fed has some U.S. Treasury securities which are about to mature. It may redeem these for new securities which are being offered by the Treasury in its latest public auction. The amount of securities which the Fed takes will not then be available to the public, thereby reducing the quantity of securities sold in the marketplace. Other things equal, this would tend to raise security prices and lower interest rates.

On the other hand, the Fed may decide *not* to acquire new securities from the Treasury to replace those which are maturing. This would mean the

---

[9] See Chapter 12 for an explanation of how these repurchase agreements are used as a source of funds for securities dealers.

Treasury would be forced to sell an increased volume of securities in the open market in order to raise cash to pay off the Fed. Other things equal, security prices would fall and interest rates would rise.

The Goals of Open-Market Operations: Defensive and Dynamic. In the use of any of its policy tools, the Federal Reserve always has in mind the basic economic goals of full employment, a stable price level, sustainable economic growth, and a stable international balance of payments position for the United States. However, only a portion of the Federal Reserve's daily open-market activity is directed toward those particular goals. The Fed is also responsible on a day-to-day basis for stabilizing the money and capital markets and avoiding sharp changes in interest rates and credit conditions. A substantial portion (some authorities say most) of its operations are devoted to making fine adjustments in credit conditions and interest rates in order to keep the financial markets functioning smoothly. These technical adjustments in market conditions are often referred to as *defensive* open-market operations. Their basic purpose is to preserve the status quo and to keep the present pattern of interest rates and credit availability about where it is.

In contrast, when the Federal Reserve is more interested in the pursuit of broader economic goals, it will engage in *dynamic* open-market operations. These operations are designed to upset the status quo and to change money and credit conditions to a level the Fed believes is more consistent with the nation's economic goals.

The fact that open-market operations are carried out for a wide variety of purposes makes it difficult to follow the Fed's daily transactions in the marketplace and draw any firm conclusions about the direction of monetary policy. On any given day, the Fed may be buying or selling securities merely to stabilize market conditions without any longer-term objectives in mind. For example, even in periods when the Federal Reserve is pursuing a tight-money policy, it frequently is in the market *buying* securities because (in the Fed's judgment) other factors have been tightening the market too rapidly. The Fed will attempt to slow things down.

The central bank is really a "balance wheel" in the financial system, supplying or subtracting reserves as may be needed on any given day. While experienced Fed watchers find the daily pattern of open-market operations meaningful, many observers argue that, unless the investor possesses inside information on the motivation of Federal Reserve actions, it is exceedingly difficult to "read" daily open-market operations. A longer-run view usually is needed in order to see the direction in which the central bank is trying to move the financial system.

SELECTIVE CREDIT CONTROLS USED BY THE FED

The discount rate, reserve requirements, and open-market operations are often called *general credit controls* because each has an impact on the whole financial system. There is another set of policy tools available to the Federal

Reserve, however, that is more selective in its impact, focusing upon particular sectors of the economy. Nevertheless, use of these selective tools does contribute toward the overall objectives of the Fed to minimize unemployment, stabilize prices, sustain economic growth, and protect the nation's international payments position.

Moral Suasion by Federal Reserve Officials

A selective policy tool which has been used more frequently in recent years than before is moral suasion. This refers to the use of "arm twisting" or "jawboning" by Federal Reserve officials in order to encourage banks and other lending institutions to conform with the spirit of its policies. For example, if the Fed wishes to tighten credit controls and slow the growth of credit, Fed officials will issue letters and public statements urging financial institutions to use more restraint in granting loans. These public statements may be supplemented by personal phone calls from top Federal Reserve officials to individual lending institutions, stressing the need for more-conservative policies. There is evidence that the Federal Reserve has made greater use of moral suasion in recent years, perhaps out of a feeling that its general policy tools have become less effective.[10]

Deposit Interest-Rate Ceilings

Another selective policy tool consists of manipulating legal interest-rate ceilings on deposits. These maximum legal deposit rates are often called "Regulation Q Ceilings," referring to the set of deposit regulations once enforced exclusively by the Board of Governors of the Federal Reserve System.

Since passage of the Banking Act of 1933, interest payments on regular checking accounts have been prohibited by federal law. At the same time, interest rates on time and savings deposits offered by any depository institution could not exceed the maximum (or ceiling) rates set by the regulatory agency responsible for each institution. For example, until 1980, maximum deposit interest rates on time and savings deposits for member banks were set by the Federal Reserve System, while deposit-rate ceilings for non-member insured banks were set by the Federal Deposit Insurance Corporation. Savings and loan associations were required to conform to the legal rate maximums dictated by the Federal Home Loan Bank Board, and credit union deposit interest rates were under the control of the National Credit Union Administration. In most instances these agencies cooperated in setting maximum deposit rates to prevent unfair competition.

On March 31, 1980, the regulation of deposit interest-rate ceilings was turned over to the Depository Institutions Deregulation Committee. Created

---

[10] See especially Kane (7).

by the Depository Institutions Deregulation Act of 1980, this committee includes the chairman of the Federal Reserve Board, the director of the Federal Deposit Insurance Corporation, the chairman of the Federal Home Loan Bank Board, and the chairman of the National Credit Union Administration. The Comptroller of the Currency is a nonvoting member of this committee.

The maximum legal interest rates which commercial banks, savings and loan associations, and mutual savings banks can pay on their time and savings deposits at the present time are shown in Exhibit 22–7. We note that the legal ceilings vary with both the type of deposit and its maturity. Small passbook savings accounts and NOW accounts, against which checks can be written, carry the lowest interest-rate ceilings at 5¼ to 5½ percent. Time accounts, which have fixed maturities ranging from 14 days to eight years or more, carry maximum legal rates of 5¼ to 8 percent. Two deposit plans— six-month money market CDs and 2½-year-or-more small-saver CDs—have ceiling rates which float with the market yields on comparable-maturity U.S. Treasury securities. As we saw in Chapter 13, large ($100,000+) negotiable CDs, purchased primarily by corporations, have no maximum rate ceiling; their yields float with the market.

Why do we have these rate ceilings? The original reason for limiting the interest rates financial institutions could pay on their deposits was to safeguard the public's funds and prevent failures of individual financial institutions. Thousands of banks and savings associations failed during the Great Depression of the 1930s, and many experts felt at the time that excessive competition for deposits had contributed to their collapse. Allegedly, smaller financial institutions, which are more prone to failure even today, are less able to compete for both checking and savings deposits than larger institutions. Thus, the legal rate ceilings are aimed at limiting competition to protect the most vulnerable deposit-type financial intermediaries. Still another purpose is to ensure an adequate flow of funds to the housing industry. As shown in Exhibit 22–7, savings and loan associations and mutual savings banks, which make the bulk of home mortgage loans in the United States, are given an advantage of one fourth of a percentage point over commercial banks for most types of time and savings deposits.

Several times in the past the rate ceilings have been used as a tool of monetary policy. If interest rates on securities sold in the open market are rising rapidly but the ceilings are not adjusted upward, interest-sensitive savers will pull their funds out of savings deposits. Commercial banks, savings and loans, and mutual savings banks may experience a massive loss of funds which cripples their ability to make loans. Therefore, in theory, the ceilings can be used to regulate the flow of credit from depository financial institutions.

Unfortunately, it is not at all certain that the rate ceilings really control the *total* volume of credit available in the economy. To be sure, when market interest rates rise above the legal ceilings, depository institutions are forced

EXHIBIT 22-7
Maximum Interest Rates Payable on Time and Savings Deposits at Federally Insured Institutions (percent per annum)

Type and Maturity of Deposit	Commercial Banks	Savings and Loan Associations and Mutual Savings Banks
Savings	5¼%	5½%
Negotiable order of withdrawal accounts (NOWs)	5¼	5¼
Time accounts:		
14–89 days	5¼	—
90 days to 1 year	5¾	6
1 to 2 years	6	6½
2 to 2½ years	6	6½
2½ to 4 years	6½	6¾
4 to 6 years	7¼	7½
6 to 8 years	7½	7¾
8 years or more	7¾	8
Issued to governmental units (all maturities)	8	8
Individual retirement accounts (IRAs) and Keogh (H.R. 10) plans	8	8
Six-month Money Market CDs 2½-year or more small-saver CDs		[See Notes Below.]

Notes: The maximum rates on time deposits in denominations of $100,000 or more with maturities of 30 to 89 days were suspended in June 1970; such deposits maturing in 90 days or more were suspended in May 1973. Six-month money market CDs must have a maturity of exactly 26 weeks and a minimum denomination of $10,000 and must be nonnegotiable. The interest-rate ceilings on money market CDs are determined by the discount rate (auction average) of most recently issued six-month U.S. Treasury bills with the maximum rate banks can pay one fourth of a percentage point higher than the T-bill rate, and thrift institutions one fourth to half a percentage above the T-bill rate. The ceiling rate on 2½-year CDs is tied to the market yield on 2½-year Treasury securities, generally one fourth of a percentage point below the Treasury yield for banks and up to the Treasury yield for nonbank thrifts.
SOURCE: Board of Governors of the Federal Reserve System, *Federal Reserve Bulletin,* July 1981, Table 1.16.

to reduce their loans to their principal customers—small businesses, household, and state and local governments. However, large corporations, financial institutions, the federal government, and other borrowers who can readily tap the open market have little difficulty in raising funds. Thus, the ceiling rates probably result in credit discrimination rather than credit control.

To many observers legal interest-rate ceilings do far more harm than good. They are inequitable to small savers, who are often forced to place their money in a time or savings deposit because they cannot afford or lack the knowledge to purchase higher-yielding securities in the open market. The ceilings undoubtedly discourage savings when they are not adjusted fast enough to keep pace with market interest rates. They contribute to instability in the home mortgage market. When savers withdraw their funds from lower-yielding time and savings deposits at savings and loan associations and mutual savings banks, mortgage money dries up. Widespread unemployment in the construction industry and high interest rates on home mortgage loans usually follow.

Congress was well aware of these problems when it created the Depository Institutions Deregulation Committee. The opening section of the Depository Institutions Deregulation Act of 1980 states:

> The Congress hereby finds that—(1) limitations on the interest rates which are payable on deposits and accounts discourage persons from saving money, create inequities for depositors, impede the ability of depository institutions to compete for funds, and have not achieved their purpose of providing an even flow of funds for home mortgage lending; and (2) all depositors, and particularly those with modest savings, are entitled to receive a market rate of return on their savings as soon as it is economically feasible for depository institutions to pay such rate.

Accordingly, the Deregulation Committee was instructed to work toward providing a market rate of return on the public's savings, phasing out the legal ceilings over a six-year period. It was required to vote within 18 months after passage of the law on whether to raise the ceilings on passbook savings by at least one fourth of one percentage point. Before the end of the third through the sixth years after enactment, the committee was directed to decide whether to increase the ceilings on all time and savings deposits by at least one half of one percentage point. Therefore, while the deposit-rate ceilings must be phased out gradually in order to protect the safety and soundness of individual financial institutions, it seems clear that their function as a policy tool has ended.

Margin Requirements

A selective credit control still under the exclusive control of the Federal Reserve Board is margin requirements on the purchase of stocks and convertible bonds and on short sales of these securities. Margin requirements were enacted into law with passage of the Securities Exchange Act of 1934. This federal law limited the amount of credit that could be used to purchase and carry certain securities when those same securities were used as collateral for a loan. Regulations G, T, and U of the Federal Reserve Board prescribe a maximum loan value for marginable stocks, convertible bonds, and short sales. That maximum loan value is expressed as a specified percentage of the market value of the securities at the time they are used as loan collateral. The *margin requirement* on a regulated security, then, is simply the difference between its market value (100 percent) and the maximum loan value of that security.

For example, as shown in Exhibit 22–8, the current margin requirement on stock is 50 percent. This means that common and preferred stock can be purchased on credit with the stock itself used as collateral. However, the

EXHIBIT 22–8
Federal Reserve Margin Requirements on Stocks, Convertible Bonds, and Short Sales
(percent of market value and effective date)

Security	3/11/68	6/8/68	5/6/70	12/6/71	11/24/72	1/3/74
Margin stocks	70%	80%	65%	55%	65%	50%
Convertible bonds	50	60	50	50	50	50
Short sales	70	80	65	55	65	50

Note: Regulations G, T, and U published by the Board of Governors of the Federal Reserve System, in accordance with the Securities Exchange Act of 1934, limit the amount of credit to purchase or carry margin stocks when the securities to be purchased are used as collateral. Margin requirements specify the maximum loan value of the securities expressed as a percentage of their market value at the time a loan is made. Margin requirements, therefore, are the difference between the market value of the securities and their maximum loan value.
SOURCE: Board of Governors of the Federal Reserve System, *Federal Reserve Bulletin,* July 1981, Table 1.36.

purchaser can only borrow up to a maximum of 50 percent of the stock's current market value. He or she must put up the remainder of the stock's purchase price in cash money.

As Exhibit 22–8 suggests, margin requirements are not changed very often. The current margin requirements on stocks, convertible bonds, and short sales of these securities have remained unchanged since January 1974. Most observers of the financial markets feel that the imposition of margin requirements was unnecessary. These requirements arose out of the turmoil of the Great Depression of the 30s, when many felt that speculative buying and selling of stocks had contributed to the economy's sudden collapse. While this was probably not the case, margin requirements do ensure that a substantial amount of cash must be contributed by the buyer of securities and that borrowing against these securities is kept within reasonable limits. One serious limitation of this selective tool is that it does not cover purchases of all types of stocks and bonds. For this reason, its future use as a tool of Federal Reserve monetary policy is likely to remain very limited.

SUMMARY AND CONCLUSIONS

The policy tools used by the Federal Reserve affect the quantity and rate of growth of legal reserves in the banking system which, in turn, impact upon the capacity of financial institutions to make loans and investments. Central bank policy also influences the level of and direction of change in interest rates. For example, a policy of tight money and restricted growth in reserves usually results in higher interest rates and a diminished supply of credit available to borrowers. An easy money policy is usually accompanied by lower interest rates and an expanded supply of credit available. Working through both interest rates and reserves, the Federal Reserve has a direct impact upon the size and rate of growth of the nation's money supply.

Because changes in the money supply are highly correlated with changes in economic activity, the Fed ultimately influences *both* the level of economic activity and economic growth.

Over the years the Federal Reserve has developed a number of tools for carrying out the objectives of monetary policy. The Fed's primary policy tool is open-market operations—buying and selling of securities. Open-market operations are used not only to carry out major shifts in policy toward tighter or easier credit conditions (known as dynamic operations), but also to make technical adjustments in market conditions to preserve the status quo (known as defensive operations). Open-market operations are carried out by the Trading Desk of the New York Federal Reserve Bank on behalf of all 12 Federal Reserve banks. Policy guidelines for the conduct of open-market operations are set by the Federal Open Market Committee, which meets every few weeks in Washington, D.C.

When the Federal Reserve wishes to have a quick and powerful impact on the financial system, it may change the amount of legal reserves deposit-type financial institutions must hold behind their deposits. Changes in legal reserve requirements have a direct effect on the volume of funds available to financial institutions for lending and investing and therefore affect both the growth of the money supply and interest rates. However, the impact of reserve requirement changes is so potent that the Fed uses this tool infrequently. A third policy tool—changes in the discount rate charged by the Federal Reserve banks on loans made to depository institutions—is also used infrequently. While this tool affects interest rates in the short run, it has a psychological impact on credit users which often works against the aims of the Fed. Nevertheless, loans to depository institutions provide an important safety valve for the Federal Reserve in the event its policies threaten the safety and soundness of individual financial institutions.

Other, minor tools of monetary policy have been used by the Federal Reserve from time to time to carry out its objectives. Through public speeches and testimony before Congress, private letters, and phone calls, the Fed frequently tries to persuade individuals and groups of the wisdom of its policies. Often called "jawboning" or moral suasion, this policy tool has seen increasing use in recent years to deal with the psychological aspects of the nation's major economic problems, especially inflation. Policy tools which are being phased out include deposit interest-rate ceilings and margin requirements on the purchase of selected stocks and convertible bonds. These infrequently-used tools can affect the flow of credit available from selected financial institutions and discourage speculative borrowing. However, like many regulatory controls, these selective policy tools can lead to distortions in the allocation of scarce resources and discrimination in access to credit, especially for borrowers of limited means.

While it is useful to know what tools the Federal Reserve has at its disposal to deal with the nation's economic problems and what effects these policy tools are likely to have, the student of the financial system needs to know more. When is the Fed likely to use its policy tools? What factors indicate whether a change in monetary policy has occurred or perhaps soon will occur? How successful has the central bank been in helping to achieve the nation's economic goals? We address these critically important questions in the next and final chapter on the Federal Reserve System.

STUDY QUESTIONS

1. What is the principal target of Federal Reserve monetary policy? Why?

2. What are legal reserves? Required reserves? Excess reserves? Explain why these concepts are important.

3. Why are commercial banks and other deposit-type intermediaries able to create money? What factors increase the amount of deposits the banking system can create with any given injection of new reserves? What factors reduce the money-creating capabilities of the banking and financial system?

4. In what ways can the Federal Reserve influence the money-creation process? The public? The U.S. Treasury?

5. How does the reserve requirement tool affect the ability of deposit-type institutions to create money? What are the principal advantages and disadvantages of the reserve-requirement tool?

6. How and why does a depository institution borrow from the Federal Reserve? Explain what happens when the Fed changes the discount rate. What are the principal advantages and disadvantages of the discount mechanism as a policy tool?

7. Why are open-market operations the Fed's most popular and frequently used policy tool? What are the principal effects of open-market operations on the financial system?

8. Describe the relationship between the SOMA manager and the FOMC. What is a policy directive? What types of policy targets does the Fed use?

9. Explain the difference between an RP and a straight (or outright) open-market transaction. Why is each used? What is a "run off"?

10. Explain the difference between defensive and dynamic open-market operations.

11. What is moral suasion? Do you believe this tool can be effective? Explain.

12. What is Regulation Q? How has it been used in recent years as a policy tool? How will the Depository Institutions Deregulation Act affect the future use of deposit interest-rate ceilings as a policy tool? What arguments would you advance in favor of and against interest-rate ceilings?

13. Explain how margin requirements affect the financial system. Why were these requirements instituted by Congress? Could they be effective in promoting the nation's economic goals?

SELECTED REFERENCES

1. Board of Governors of the Federal Reserve System. *The Federal Reserve System—Purposes and Functions*. Washington, D.C.: 1974.

2. _____. *Reappraisal of the Federal Reserve Discount Mechanism.* Washington, D.C.: 1971.

3. Cacy, J. A., Bryon Higgins, and Gordon H. Sellon, Jr. "Should the Discount Rate Be a Penalty Rate?" *Economic Review,* Federal Reserve Bank of Kansas City, January 1981, pp. 3–10.

4. Federal Reserve Bank of Chicago. "The Depository Institutions Deregulation and Monetary Control Act of 1980." *Economic Perspectives,* September-October 1980, pp. 3–23.

5. Gilbert, R. Alton. "Access to the Discount Window for All Commercial Banks: Is It Important for Monetary Policy?" *Review,* Federal Reserve Bank of St. Louis, February 1980.

6. Gilbert, R. Alton. "Lagged Reserve Requirements: Implications for Monetary Control and Bank Reserve Management." *Review,* Federal Reserve Bank of St. Louis, May 1980.

7. Kane, Edward. "The Re-politicization of the Fed." *Journal of Financial and Quantitative Analysis,* Proceedings, November 1974, pp. 743–52.

8. Laufenberg, D. E. "Contemporaneous versus Lagged Reserve Accounting." *Journal of Money, Credit, and Banking,* May 1976, pp. 239–45.

9. Laurent, Robert. "Reserve Requirements: Are They Lagged in the Wrong Direction?" *Journal of Money, Credit, and Banking,* August 1979, pp. 301–10.

10. Lombra, R. E., and R. G. Torto. "Discount Rate Changes and Announcement Effects." *Quarterly Journal of Economics,* February 1977, pp. 171–76.

11. Poole, William. "A Proposal for Reforming Bank Reserve Requirements in the United States." *Journal of Money, Credit, and Banking,* May 1976, pp. 137–47.

12. Poole, William, and Charles Lieberman. "Improving Monetary Control." In *Brookings Papers on Economic Activity,* 1972:2, edited by Arthur M. Okun and George L. Perry, pp. 293–342.

13. Sellon, Gordon H. Jr. "The Role of the Discount Rate in Monetary Policy: A Theoretical Analysis." *Economic Review,* Federal Reserve Bank of Kansas City, June 1980, pp. 3–15.

14. Woodworth, G. Walter. *The Money Market and Monetary Management.* 2d ed. New York: Harper & Row, 1972.

23

Indicators and Goals of Monetary Policy

The Federal Reserve System exerts a powerful impact on the availability and cost of credit in the nation's financial markets. Because the Fed has a great deal to do with the broad changes that occur in interest rates, prices of securities, and the availability of credit, economists and financial analysts spend enormous amounts of time analyzing Federal Reserve actions in an attempt to predict the future course of monetary policy. Indeed, if the experts are able to guess correctly which way the Fed is going, they can make appropriate adjustments in security portfolios and in borrowing and spending plans in order to reduce costs and maximize earnings.

It should be noted, however, that understanding the Federal Reserve's intentions and predicting the direction of monetary policy are not easy tasks. Many factors influence interest rates, security prices, and the flow of loanable funds in the financial markets. For example, if we see interest rates on money market instruments rising, there is often a temptation to assume that this trend reflects government policy and, in particular, the actions of the Federal Reserve. In fact, interest rates are subject to all the forces of demand and supply operating in the financial marketplace. An upward surge in rates may reflect a sharp rise in borrowings by units of government and private investors, the impact of inflation, changes in the public's money-using habits, or a host of other factors. The Federal Reserve System is an extremely important influence on the financial system, to be sure, but only one of many influences.

FACTORS INFLUENCING RESERVES

To fully understand the role of the Federal Reserve in the complex environment of the financial marketplace, we need to focus upon the principal target of Federal Reserve policy—*legal reserves*. We recall from the previous chapter that the reserves of the banking system consist of deposits kept at the Federal Reserve banks plus currency and coin held in the vaults of depository institutions. These reserves are the raw material out of which lenders create credit and cause the money supply to grow. This is why the total supply of reserves is the main target of Federal Reserve monetary policy. However, numerous factors affect the supply of reserves available to banks and other lenders. As shown in Exhibit 23–1, these factors fall into

EXHIBIT 23–1
Factors Affecting the Supply of Legal Reserves in the Banking System

Factors	Effect on Total Reserves
Actions of the public:	
Increase in holdings of currency and coin	−
Decrease in holdings of currency and coin	+
Federal Reserve operations:	
Purchase of securities	+
Sale of securities	−
Loans to depository institutions	+
Repayment of loans to depository institutions	−
Increase in Federal Reserve float	+
Decrease in Federal Reserve float	−
Increase in other assets of the Federal Reserve banks	+
Decrease in other assets	−
Increase in other liabilities	−
Decrease in other liabilities	+
Increase in capital accounts	−
Decrease in capital accounts	+
U.S. Treasury and foreign operations:	
Increase in Treasury deposits at the Federal Reserve banks	−
Decrease in Treasury deposits at the Federal Reserve banks	+
Gold purchases	+
Gold sales	−
Increase in Treasury currency outstanding	+
Decrease in Treasury currency outstanding	−
Increase in Treasury cash holdings	−
Decrease in Treasury cash holdings	+
Increase in foreign and other deposits in Federal Reserve banks	−
Decrease in foreign and other deposits in Federal Reserve banks	+

three groups: (1) actions of the public; (2) operations of the U.S. Treasury Department and foreign investors; and (3) Federal Reserve operations.

Actions of the Public Affecting Reserves

For example, suppose the public desires to increase its holdings of currency and coin (pocket money). It will do so by writing checks or drafts against deposits held in banks and thrift institutions, reducing the legal reserves of these lending institutions. If these institutions were already fully loaned up, with no excess reserves, then the withdrawal of currency would force them to raise additional reserves by selling securities, calling loans, and borrowing. The stock of total reserves and the nation's money supply would begin to contract. On the other hand, if the public wishes to reduce its holdings of currency and coin, pocket money will be redeposited in banks and thrift institutions, increasing the total reserves of these institutions. The volume of lending and investing will rise, resulting in an increase in the nation's money supply, unless, of course, the Federal Reserve uses its policy tools to counteract the inflow of currency and coin.

Operations of the Treasury and Foreign Investors Affecting Reserves

Actions of the U.S. Treasury and foreign investors also affect the level and growth of legal reserves. The Treasury, foreign central banks, and international financial institutions keep large deposits with the Federal Reserve banks. Any *increase* in these deposits generally results in a decline in the reserves of deposit-type financial institutions. This is due to the fact that both the Treasury and foreign institutions frequently receive payments from domestic businesses and households. These payments are nearly always made by check and drain reserves from private banks and thrift institutions as the checks are cleared at the Fed. Federal income tax payments by the public, which periodically flow out of private checkable deposits and into the Treasury's checking accounts at the Fed, are good examples of this process. Similarly, when the Treasury sells securities in the open market, investors write checks against their accounts, which eventually are credited to the Treasury's deposit with the Federal Reserve banks. In both instances, the public's deposits and total reserves of the banking system fall. Conversely, whenever the Treasury or a foreign depositor writes checks against its account, these are normally deposited somewhere in the banking system, causing total reserves to rise.

Occasionally, the Treasury buys and sells gold at the request of foreign governments or to hold in reserve. Payment for Treasury gold purchases is made by checks drawn on the Treasury's accounts at the Fed. Those individuals and institutions selling the gold will deposit the Treasury's checks somewhere in the banking system, leading to an increase in reserves and deposits. Conversely, if the Treasury sells gold, buyers write checks against their deposits, which forces a decline in both reserves and deposits of the banking system when those checks are collected. If the decline in reserves is too great, the Federal Reserve may have to offset the impact of Treasury gold transactions through open-market operations.

The Treasury's minting of new currency and coin also has an impact on reserves and deposits. Newly minted currency and coin are shipped to the vaults of the Federal Reserve banks in return for credit to the Treasury's checking accounts. When the Treasury spends these funds by issuing checks to the public, deposits and reserves in the banking system will rise. Similarly, when there is a decrease in Treasury currency outstanding as currency and coin are retired, total reserves must fall. This happens because the Treasury must pay for redeemed currency and coin by writing checks against its deposits at the Fed. To cover those checks, it must draw down its deposits kept in private banks, which reduces total reserves available to the banking system.[1]

The Treasury does hold small amounts of currency and coin in its own vaults. When these vault deposits rise, the increase in Treasury cash holdings must have come from funds kept somewhere in the private banking system, leading to a decline in total reserves. Similarly, when Treasury cash holdings decline, the released currency and coin flow into the private banking system, and both deposits and total reserves rise.

Federal Reserve Operations Affecting Reserves

The Federal Reserve System can offset *any* of the foregoing actions by the public, foreign institutions, or the U.S. Treasury, keeping total reserves of the banking system at roughly the level it desires. As we observed in the preceding chapter, the Fed can increase total reserves by purchases of securities in the open market, or it can reduce total reserves by sales of securities. Loans made to depository institutions through the discount windows of the Reserve banks will increase reserves, while repayments of those loans will cause reserves to fall.

The Fed often increases reserves unintentionally when the volume of float from uncollected checks rises. Banks and other depository institutions that route their checks through the Federal Reserve banks for collection receive credit in their reserve accounts after a specified period (usually two or three days). However, many of these checks have not been collected at the time the Fed grants credit for them due to delays in processing, transportation, or other problems. Checkbook float is essentially an interest-free loan of reserves from the Fed and has the same effect on the total reserves of the banking system as a loan made through the Fed's discount window.

Finally, when the Federal Reserve banks acquire assets of any kind or issue checks to pay their debts or cover expenses, total reserves of the banking system will rise. In contrast, when the Fed receives payments from banks, securities dealers, and others, total reserves fall as checks written against financial institutions are sent to the Federal Reserve banks. Similarly, when a bank joins the Federal Reserve System, it must contribute up to 6 percent of its capital and paid-in surplus in order to purchase Federal Reserve stock. This action increases the Fed's capital accounts and lowers

---

[1] As we will note in Chapter 24, the Treasury keeps deposits—known as Tax and Loan Accounts—in a majority of the nation's banks. The majority of Treasury receipts flow initially into Tax and Loan Accounts before they are later transferred to the Federal Reserve banks.

the reserves available to private banks. Generally speaking, ~~any Federal Reserve expenditure increases reserves,~~ while any receipt of funds by the Fed reduces the reserves available to the banking system.

The Heart of the Monetary Policy Process—Controlling Reserves

~~The heart of the monetary policy process is to correctly anticipate changes in *all* of the foregoing factors which affect reserves.~~ The Federal Reserve then tries to achieve a level and rate of growth in total reserves which is consistent with the nation's economic goals.

THE FEDERAL RESERVE STATEMENT

One of the most widely followed indicators of what the Federal Reserve System is doing to influence conditions in the financial markets and the economy is known as the Federal Reserve Statement. It is published each week in the financial press and lists the factors which supply reserves to depository institutions and those which absorb reserves. The total amount of reserves held by depository institutions at any time equals the difference between the factors supplying reserves and the factors absorbing reserves. The Federal Reserve Statement shows levels of each reserve-supplying or reserve-absorbing factor for the current and previous month or week and any changes between the two time periods. It is the *changes* in each reserve factor that analysts concentrate upon in attempting to understand what the Federal Reserve is trying to accomplish in the financial marketplace.

Factors Supplying Reserves

A Federal Reserve Statement for the months of December 1980 and January 1981 is shown in Exhibit 23–2. The first item listed on the statement is Reserve Bank Credit, including Federal Reserve purchases of securities, loans from the discount windows of the Reserve banks, float, and other Federal Reserve assets. If each of these items increases, reserves available to depository institutions rise. Other factors held equal, the ability of financial institutions to make loans and investments and expand the nation's money supply also increases. A decrease in any component of Reserve bank credit results in a decline in the reserves of depository institutions.

Looking more closely at the statement, we note that the Federal Reserve held outright $118,795 million in U.S. government securities, $8,734 million in federal agency securities, and a small volume ($68 million) of bankers acceptances in January 1981. In addition, $567 million in U.S. government securities and $73 million in Federal agency securities were held under repurchase agreements with security dealers. The column marked "Changes" tells us that the Fed, on balance, *bought* securities between December 1980 and January 1981. Its total security holdings rose *net* $218 million (i.e., $247 + $41 − $9 − $5 − $56).

EXHIBIT 23–2
Reserves of Depository Institutions ($ millions)

Item	December 1980	January 1981	Change
Factors supplying reserve funds:			
Reserve bank credit:			
U.S. government securities			
Bought outright	$118,548	$118,795	+247
Held under repurchase agreement	526	567	+41
Federal agency securities			
Bought outright	8,752	8,743	−9
Held under repurchase agreement	78	73	−5
Bankers acceptances acquired	124	68	−56
Loans from the discount window	1,617	1,405	−212
Float	5,797	4,161	−1,636
Other federal assets	7,817	9,011	+1,194
Gold stock	11,161	11,160	−1
Special drawing rights (SDRs)	3,313	2,518	−795
Treasury currency outstanding	13,422	13,437	+15
Total—factors supplying reserves ...	$171,146	$169,929	−1,217
Factors absorbing reserve funds:			
Currency in circulation	$135,676	$133,416	−2,260
Treasury cash holdings	446	439	−7
Deposits, other than member bank reserves, with Federal Reserve banks:			
Treasury	2,722	3,172	+450
Foreign	353	380	+27
Other	403	541	+138
Other Federal Reserve liabilities and capital	4,881	4,872	−9
Total—factors absorbing reserves	$144,481	$142,820	−1,661
Reserve balances of all depository institutions	$ 26,664	$ 27,114	+450

Note: Figures in the table may not add exactly to column totals due to rounding error and other factors.
SOURCE: Board of Governors of the Federal Reserve System, *Federal Reserve Bulletin,* February 1981, Table 1.11.

Because Federal Reserve purchases expand the supply of reserves, does this mean the Fed was moving toward an easier, less-restrictive monetary policy as 1981 began? Perhaps, but we also know that much Federal Reserve activity is *defensive* in nature—that is, merely an effort to offset the effects of other factors on reserves and preserve the status quo.[2] Were other factors at work, draining reserves from depository institutions and forcing the Fed to supply more reserves through security purchases just to keep total reserves steady? Exhibit 23–2 suggests the answer is yes. For example, loans of reserves through the discount windows of the Federal Reserve banks

---

[2] See Chapter 22 for a discussion of defensive open-market operations.

dropped $212 million during January, and checkbook float fell more than $1.6 billion. The volume of special drawing rights (SDRs) held by the United States in the International Monetary Fund and used to settle deficits resulting from international trade dropped $795 million.[3] In total, the factors supplying reserves to the banking system fell $1,217 million. The decline in reserve supplies would have been even larger had the Fed not purchased net more than $200 million in securities.

Factors Absorbing Reserves

The second half of the Federal Reserve Statement looks at those factors which absorb reserves, including currency in circulation, Treasury holdings of cash, miscellaneous deposits at the Fed, and the liability and capital accounts of the Federal Reserve banks. If these factors increase, reserve balances held by depository institutions must decline. However, a decrease in reserve-absorbing factors results in an increase in total reserves. Careful inspection of Exhibit 23–2 shows that a massive change occurred in the amount of currency in circulation between December 1980 and January 1981. Following the Christmas–New Year's Day holiday period, the public had less need for pocket money and redeposited (net) in banks and other depository institutions $2,260 million in currency and coin. Without offsetting action by the Fed, a sharp increase in reserves and the nation's money supply would have occurred as depository institutions made loans with these newly acquired reserves. However, on balance, the sum of all factors absorbing bank reserves increased just $1,661 net, as shown on the next-to-last line of Exhibit 23–2.

Interpreting the Federal Reserve Statement

If we compare the sum of changes in factors supplying reserves with changes in factors absorbing reserves, the *net* change is about $450 million (plus or minus a small discrepancy due to rounding error and other influences). Because the factors absorbing reserves declined, on balance, this would have *added* $1,661 million to the reserves of depository institutions. However, reserve-supplying factors also declined, which reduced total reserve balances by $1,217 million. The net difference between these two amounts of approximately $450 million resulted in an *increase* in the total reserves of depository institutions from $26,664 in December 1980 to $27,114 in January 1981, as shown in the last line of Exhibit 23–2.

The Fed can use open-market operations to bring about any change in total reserves that it wishes. Why did it permit the reserves of the banking system to grow by $450 million over the period shown in Exhibit 23–2? A good clue is provided by looking at the state of the economy as 1981 began.

---

[3] See Chapter 26 for a definition and explanation of the role of Special Drawing Rights in international finance.

A recession—one of the deepest since World War II—began in December 1980, with industrial production and auto sales dropping sharply. Unemployment had been at high levels for several months. In fact, by January 1981 the U.S. Department of Labor was estimating that 7.8 million workers were without jobs, representing 7.4 percent of the civilian labor force. Manufacturing plants were operating at less than 80 percent of capacity. Business profits had fallen sharply from the previous year, and demands for credit from all major sectors of the economy had declined significantly. Reflecting weakening credit demands, the nation's money supply was declining, and most interest rates in the money and capital markets were headed downward.

Faced with a deteriorating economic situation, the Fed allowed the reserves of depository institutions to rise in an effort to stimulate the growth of credit and boost spending. The rise in reserves of $450 million was still quite modest—an increase of less than 2 percent. While the economy was weakening, the Fed had to move slowly and carefully because of rapid inflation. Consumer prices had risen at more than a 13 percent annual rate only the month before.

MEASURES OF THE NATION'S MONEY SUPPLY

The Federal Reserve Statement is an important indicator of monetary policy but by no means the only one. Economists, business leaders, and investors look even more closely at weekly, monthly, quarterly, and annual changes in various measures of the nation's money supply. The money supply is the subject of widespread interest and attention for two reasons: (1) changes in money are highly correlated with changes in economic conditions; and (2) the Federal Reserve has a significant impact on money supply growth through its control over the reserves of depository institutions.

Today, economists and other students of the financial system follow, not one definition of the money supply, but several, each reflecting a slightly different view of what money is. The public's money-using habits are changing rapidly, and many new financial instruments have recently appeared, complicating measurement of the nation's money supply. Examples of new money-related financial instruments include automatic transfers of funds from savings to checking accounts (ATS), shares in money market mutual funds, and interest-bearing negotiable-order-of-withdrawal (NOW) accounts. Eurodollar deposits and repurchase agreements, once the exclusive property of the largest banks, securities dealers, and corporations, now are available to individuals and smaller institutions for the rapid investment and transfer of funds. These innovations in money-related assets forced the Federal Reserve Board to announce new definitions of the money supply in February 1980.[4]

---

[4] See "Announcement," Board of Governors of the Federal Reserve System, Washington, D.C., *Press Release*, February 7, 1980.

Money Supply Measures

The narrowest definition of the money supply in use today is known as M–1A—the sum of demand deposits (checking accounts) and currency and coin held by the public. This definition views money exclusively as a *medium of exchange* and includes only non-interest-bearing assets. It excludes demand deposits owned by domestic banks (called "due from" or correspondent deposits), the U.S. government, and foreign banks and official institutions. Similarly, currency and coin held in the vaults of commercial banks, the U.S. Treasury, and the Federal Reserve banks are also excluded from M–1A. As shown in Exhibits 23–3 and 23–4, the narrow M–1A definition of the money supply totaled almost $395 billion at year-end 1980.

EXHIBIT 23–3
Money-Supply Measures

Symbol	Definition	Amount as of December 1980 ($ billions)
M–1A	Demand deposits at commercial banks (except those due other domestic banks, the U.S. government, and foreign banks and official institutions) less cash items in the process of collection and float + currency and coin held by the public.	$ 394.7
M–1B	M–1A + NOW accounts and automatic transfer service accounts at banks and thrift institutions + credit-union share draft accounts + demand deposits at mutual savings banks.	421.8
M–2	M–1B + savings and small-denomination time deposits at all depository institutions + overnight repurchase agreements at commercial banks + overnight Euro-dollars held by U.S. residents other than banks at Caribbean branches of member banks + money market mutual fund shares.	1,675.0
M–3	M–2 + large-denomination time deposits at all depository institutions + term RPs at commercial banks and savings and loan associations.	1,963.0
L	M–3 + Eurodollars held by U.S. residents other than banks + bankers acceptances + commercial paper + U.S. Treasury bills and other liquid Treasury securities + U.S. savings bonds.	2,372.0

Note: In 1982 the Fed dropped M–1A and relabeled M–1B as simply M–1.
SOURCE: Board of Governors of the Federal Reserve System, *Federal Reserve Bulletin,* February 1981, Table 1.21.

While all forms of money serve as a medium of exchange, the newer forms of money today bear interest and therefore serve partly as a *store of value* or temporary repository of savings. Prominent examples include NOW accounts, automatic transfers (ATS), credit-union share drafts, and interest-

EXHIBIT 23–4
Selected Components of Money Supply Measures

Selected Components of the Money-Supply Measures	Amount as of December 1980 ($ billions)
Currency and coin held by the public	$118.5
Demand deposits at commercial banks	276.2
Other checkable deposits (includes ATS and NOW balances, credit union share drafts, and demand deposits at mutual savings banks)	27.1
Overnight RPs and Eurodollars	32.2
Money market mutual funds	75.8
Savings deposits	391.5
Small-denomination time deposits (less than $100,000 apiece)	757.0
Large-denomination time deposits (over $100,000 apiece)	251.4

SOURCE: Board of Governors of the Federal Reserve System, *Federal Reserve Bulletin*, February 1981, Table 1.21.

bearing checking accounts offered by mutual savings banks, which can be as accessible for making payments as conventional non-interest-bearing checking accounts. The version of the money supply known as M–1B adds to M–1A all of the interest-bearing accounts listed above. M–1B, therefore, includes those financial assets held by the public for *both* check-writing and savings purposes. Exhibit 23–3 indicates that the M–1B measure of money amounted to about $420 billion in December 1980.

The focus of M–1A and M–1B is upon those financial assets held *primarily* for making payments for goods and services. Still broader definitions of money in use today include accounts intended primarily as a *reserve of savings*. One example is M–2, which includes all the components of M–1A and M–1B but adds savings deposits and small time deposits (with denominations of less than $100,000) at all depository institutions, overnight RPs issued by commercial banks, overnight Eurodollars owned by U.S. nonbank residents and issued by Carribean branches of member banks, and shares in money market mutual funds. M–2 is notable because it includes the liabilities of so many different financial institutions—commercial banks, credit unions, foreign bank branches and agencies operating in the United States, Edge Act corporations, foreign investment firms, mutual savings banks, and savings and loan associations.

There is considerable debate today as to whether the components of M–2 are transactions accounts or mainly liquid forms of saving.[5] For example, checks may be written against money market mutual funds, though the activity level in these accounts is very low compared to conventional checking accounts because most limit check denominations to a minimum of $500 and some funds impose a penalty for writing more than three or four checks per

_____

[5] See especially Simpson (31), Garcia and Pak (15), and Wenninger and Sivesind (39).

calendar quarter. Similarly, overnight RPs are a device to earn interest on large, surplus checking-account balances by making a short-term loan collateralized by securities. They could be classified as substitutes for demand deposits or as liquid savings.

An even broader measure of money is M–3, which includes all the components of M–2 plus time deposits issued by all depository institutions in denominations of $100,000 or more and term RPs offered by commercial banks and savings and loan associations. Financial institutions, governments, and corporations are the principal holders of large time deposits and term RPs. These two financial assets are regarded as liquid savings. Many of the large time deposits are *negotiable,* with an active resale market.[6] As shown in Exhibit 23–3, the M–3 definition of the money supply totaled $1,963 billion at the end of 1980.

The broadest money supply measure is L, which represents total liquid assets. The critical difference between L and other measures of the money supply is the addition of money market securities—bankers' acceptances, commercial paper, U.S. Treasury bills and other marketable Treasury obligations 18 months or less from maturity, U.S. savings bonds, and Eurodollar deposits other than the overnight Carribean variety included in M–2. L serves as an approximate measure of the nation's total supply of credit resulting from short-term loans and investments made in the money market. As Exhibit 23–3 indicates, the liquid assets measure of money totaled almost $2.4 trillion in December 1980.

Federal Reserve Control of Money-Supply Growth

The Federal Reserve attempts to regulate the growth of these monetary aggregates, particularly M–1B and M–2. As we will soon see, changes in the money supply have been found to be closely correlated with changes in the economy's level of production (GNP) and, through production, both employment and prices. The problem is that the Fed is by no means the only factor determining the size and rate of growth of the nation's money supply. Changes in the public's money-using habits, income levels, and savings patterns and the credit policies of financial institutions also play key roles in monetary growth.

How does the Fed attempt to control growth of the nation's money supply? In October 1979 the central bank adopted new procedures for regulating money which have been called the money supply–reserve aggregates approach.[7] These procedures focus upon the legal reserves of the banking system whose level and rate of growth are regulated through open-market operations. Three steps are involved.

---

[6] See Chapter 13 for a description of the secondary market for large negotiable certificates of deposit.

[7] See especially Cacy (7).

First, the Federal Open Market Committee (FOMC) sets target growth rates for selected money-supply measures (usually M–1A, M–1B, M–2, and M–3) for the coming year and for shorter periods within the year.[8] These targets are stated in the form of annual percentage growth ranges. For example, in 1980, the Fed called for growth in M–1A in the $3\frac{1}{2}$ to 6 percent range, while M–1B was to grow 4 to $6\frac{1}{2}$ percent during the year. As the year progressed and money growth fell above or below the annual target, shorter-run targets were set, covering calendar quarters or periods between FOMC meetings, in an effort to bring money's growth back into line with the annual target.

The second step in money-supply control is to set growth paths for total legal reserves, borrowed reserves, and nonborrowed reserves.[9] We recall from Chapter 22 that total legal reserves of the banking system are linked to the nation's money supply through the *money multiplier*. Thus,

$$\text{Money supply} = \text{Money multiplier} \times \text{Total reserves} \quad (23\text{--}1)$$

where the money multiplier tells us how many dollars of money result from each dollar increase in total reserves. The size of the money multiplier reflects the public's demand for currency and coin, shifts in deposits between transactions accounts and savings accounts, legal reserve requirements, and the credit-granting policies of financial institutions. The money-multiplier relationship suggests that the growth rate of the money supply will be approximately equal to the growth rate of the multiplier plus the rate of growth of total reserves. Therefore, if the Fed is to control the money supply, it must project both the growth of total reserves and expected changes in the money multiplier. The appropriate growth path for total reserves would be as follows:

$$\frac{\text{Growth path}}{\text{for total reserves}} = \frac{\text{Growth path for}}{\text{money supply}} - \frac{\text{Expected change in}}{\text{money multiplier}} \quad (23\text{--}2)$$

The Fed does *not* estimate changes in the money multiplier directly. Instead, it projects a growth path for both total reserves and the money supply. The multiplier may then be estimated from the ratio of the projected money supply growth path to the growth path for total legal reserves.

---

[8] Under the terms of the Full-Employment and Balanced Growth Act of 1978 (known also as the Humphrey-Hawkins Act) the FOMC is required to establish calendar-year growth ranges for money and credit aggregates by February of each year and review these at midyear. These ranges, which must be reported to Congress in February and July, are based upon the period running from the fourth quarter of the previous year to the fourth quarter of the current year. The FOMC is at liberty to change the target growth ranges at any time, however, if it feels that new circumstances warrant a change.

[9] Borrowed reserves are those legal reserves which depository institutions have borrowed from the Fed's discount window. Nonborrowed reserves are the remainder of total legal reserves and their largest component. For example, on December 31, 1980, total legal reserves of all depository institutions held at the Federal Reserve banks were $27.3 billion, of which $1.6 billion were borrowed reserves and $25.7 billion, nonborrowed reserves.

To achieve a target rate of growth for the nation's money supply, therefore, the Fed must set target growth rates for total reserves. How does it do this? A staff paper released by the Board of Governors on January 31, 1980, describes in general terms how the Fed determines its target rates of growth in legal reserves:

> After the objective for money supply growth is set, reserve paths expected to achieve such growth are established for a family of reserve measures. These measures consist of total reserves, the monetary base (essentially total reserves of member banks plus currency in circulation), and nonborrowed reserves. Establishment of the paths involves projecting how much of the targeted money growth is likely to take the form of currency, of deposits at nonmember institutions, and of deposits at member institutions (taking account of differential reserve requirements by size of demand deposits and between the demand and time and savings deposit components of M2). Moreover, estimates are made of reserves likely to be absorbed by expansion in other bank liabilities subject to reserve requirements, such as large CDs, at a pace that appears consistent with money supply objectives and also takes account of tolerable changes in bank credit. . . . Estimates are also made of the amount of excess reserves banks are likely to hold.
>
> The projected mix of currency and demand deposits, given the reserve requirements for deposits and banks' excess reserves, yields an estimate of the increase in total reserves, and the monetary base consistent with FOMC monetary targets.[10]

While the Fed establishes target growth rates for total reserves, it cannot fully control total reserves. This is due to the fact that

Total reserves = Borrowed reserves + Nonborrowed reserves   (23–3)

Borrowed reserves are supplied through the discount window of the Federal Reserve banks and depend upon the demand for loans from depository institutions which hold their reserve accounts with the Fed. The Fed has direct control only over the volume of *nonborrowed reserves,* which are influenced by open-market operations. The central bank must, therefore, make an initial assumption about the behavior of borrowed reserves—known as the *borrowing path.* Then the growth path of nonborrowed reserves needed to achieve the desired growth range for the nation's money supply will be estimated from the following relationship:

$$\text{Growth path for nonborrowed reserves} = \text{Growth path for total reserves} - \text{Assumed growth path for borrowed reserves} \quad (23–4)$$

The third step in the money-supply control process is to undertake daily and weekly open-market operations through the Trading Desk of the Federal Reserve Bank of New York to achieve the desired growth path for nonborrowed reserves. The quantity of nonborrowed reserves is kept as close as

---

[10] See reference 4.

possible to the desired growth path by either buying securities to add more reserves or selling securities through the Trading Desk to reduce reserves.[11] As described in the Fed's staff memorandum quoted above,

> because nonborrowed reserves are more closely under control of the System Account manager for open market operations (though subject to a small range of error because of the behavior of non-controlled factors affecting reserves, such as float), he would initially aim at a nonborrowed reserve target (seasonally unadjusted for operating purposes) established for the operating period between [FOMC] meetings.

If total reserves appear to be growing faster than desired—perhaps because depository institutions have stepped up their borrowings from the discount windows of the Reserve banks—the System Account manager will respond by lowering the nonborrowed reserve growth path. The Federal Reserve banks, with the approval of the Board of Governors, might also decide to increase the discount rate and slow down borrowing. Similarly, if the money multiplier moves away from its expected value, either up or down, the Fed will respond by making corresponding adjustments in nonborrowed reserves through the Trading Desk. The System Account manager will continue to add more nonborrowed reserves or take reserves away until both the money supply and total reserves move back toward their desired growth paths.[12]

Achieving the Fed's Money-Supply Targets

How well has the Fed been doing in achieving its targeted growth rates for money? Overall, the Fed has held quite close to its target ranges on an annual basis. For example, as shown in Exhibit 23–5, the planned growth range for M–1A in 1980 was 3½ to 6 percent, while the actual growth rate was 6¼ percent. M–1B was targeted for a 4 to 6½ percent growth path, and the actual rate turned out to be 6¾ percent. Of course, it should be remembered that the Fed has been in the business of targeting and attempting to closely control money-supply growth a relatively short period of time (since October 1979). More time is needed to gain some perspective and to fairly evaluate the performance of the new money supply reserve targeting approach.

---

[11] The specific procedures used by the Federal Reserve and the System Open Account Manager to control the growth of the money supply are described in more detail by Long (22), Higgins (18), and Sellon (30).

[12] The FOMC and the Trading Desk also pay attention to changes in the size of the *monetary base*. The reader will recall from Chapter 22 that the monetary base is the sum of reserve balances at Federal Reserve banks; vault cash used to satisfy reserve requirements; currency and coin outside the U.S. Treasury, the Federal Reserve banks, and the vaults of depository institutions; and surplus vault cash at depository institutions. The base is sometimes referred to as "high-powered money" because each dollar of base money is translated into multiple dollars available for spending by the public through the act of money creation by the banking system.

EXHIBIT 23–5
Planned and Actual Growth of the M–1 Money-Supply Measures (percent changes, fourth quarter to fourth quarter)

	M–1A	M–1B
Planned for 1980	3½ to 6%	4 to 6½%
Actual for 1980*	6¼	6¾

* The growth rates shown are adjusted for shifts from demand deposits and other assets into new ATS and NOW accounts.
SOURCE: Board of Governors of the Federal Reserve System, *Monetary Policy Objectives for 1981,* p. 5.

The Fed does face a number of serious problems as it attempts to achieve announced money-supply targets, however. Continuing changes in the public's money-using habits, especially shifts from conventional time and savings deposits to NOWs and other interest-bearing payments accounts, distort money-supply measures, particularly M–1A and M–1B. Moreover, judging by the rapid pace of financial innovation over the past decade, many new types of savings and payments instruments will be developed in the years ahead, forcing the Fed to frequently readjust its money-supply definitions, growth targets, and operating procedures.

There is also some evidence that the Fed's greater emphasis today on controlling monetary growth rather than interest rates has resulted in more-volatile interest rates and financial market conditions. In part, this is because monetary growth varies significantly from month to month and quarter to quarter. A good example is provided by the money-supply growth figures shown below for M–1A and M–1B during the four quarters of 1980. Though both money-supply measures averaged 6 to 7 percent growth for the year as a whole, their quarterly growth rates covered a wide range. As we saw earlier, Federal Reserve policy is not the sole determinant of the money supply or of total reserves. Fluctuations in the public's demand for money can lead to enormous changes in the amount of credit creation and interest rates in the financial system. Moreover, many of these changes cannot be anticipated. The Fed frequently is forced to react after the fact, leading to sudden surges or sudden declines in the growth of the nation's money supply.

Money Supply Growth (annualized percentage changes)

	M–1A	M–1B
1980:		
First quarter	4.6%	5.8%
Second quarter	−4.3	−2.4
Third quarter	12.0	15.5
Fourth quarter	8.4	11.3

MONEY MARKET INDICATORS

While control of the money supply and reserves are now the principal focus of central bank policymaking in the United States, the Fed also keeps close watch on conditions in the nation's financial markets, especially the cost and availability of credit in the money market. Indeed, there is evidence that the Federal Open Market Committee also sets target levels or ranges for the interest rate on federal funds loans. One reason is that the Fed is charged with the responsibility for stabilizing conditions in the financial markets to assure a smooth flow of funds from savers to investors. In addition, it must ensure that the government securities market functions smoothly so that adequate supplies of credit are available to dealers and the federal government can market its billions of dollars in debt securities without serious difficulty. This is a burdensome responsibility because the Treasury is in the market every week refunding and offering new bills, and both the Treasury and several federal agencies sell billions of dollars worth of notes and bonds each quarter of the year.

The Federal Funds Rate

We can often gather important clues about the magnitude and direction of Federal Reserve policy by carefully watching changes in the cost of credit in the money market. A key money market indicator for many financial analysts is the daily average rate on federal funds transactions. This interest rate is usually the first to feel the impact of Federal Reserve open-market operations because it reflects the "price" of reserves in the banking system. When the Fed sells securities, the supply of available legal reserves is reduced and, other things equal, the Fed funds rate will tend to rise. On the other hand, a Federal Reserve purchase of securities will increase available reserves, which tends to push the Fed funds rate down. Because the Federal Reserve does not announce its interest-rate targets in advance, however, market watchers try to guess the Fed's target ranges for the federal funds rate by following closely hourly and daily quotations of that rate.

Other Money Market Interest Rates

Other money market rates watched carefully by investors and financial analysts include yields on U.S. Treasury bills, rates charged securities dealers by major New York banks on short-term security loans, and the Federal Reserve's discount rate. When interest rates rise, this is often regarded as an indicator of tightening credit conditions resulting from the Fed's restricting the growth of credit. When rates on T-bills and other money market securities fall, however, this may be regarded as a sign the Fed is easing up, with even lower interest rates soon to follow.

Dealer loan rates and the availability of credit for security dealers are especially sensitive to Federal Reserve policy. As we saw in Chapter 12, dealers in U.S. government securities require millions of dollars in financing each day in order to carry their extensive inventories. These dealers use relatively little of their own (equity) capital to finance their operations, relying heavily upon borrowed funds from major banks and large nonfinancial corporations. Dealer loan rates, like the federal funds rate, are highly sensitive to market conditions and fluctuate daily as credit conditions change.

Fed watchers must take great care in using any interest rate to gauge the direction of Federal Reserve policy, however. A good indicator of monetary policy should meet at least three criteria: (1) the indicator should be controllable (or, at least, heavily influenced) by the Federal Reserve; (2) data on the indicator's movements should be readily available on a timely basis; and (3) the indicator should be linked to factors which influence economic and financial conditions and have a significant impact on the nation's economic goals. While interest-rate data are readily available on a daily basis, and rates profoundly affect economic conditions, all (or even most) interest-rate changes cannot be ascribed to the Federal Reserve. Any interest rate reflects the price of credit and therefore responds to all the forces affecting the demand for and supply of credit.

Nevertheless, the Fed has a powerful influence on interest rates in the economy, especially money market rates. It is safe to say that interest rates are unlikely to move very far up or down unless the Federal Reserve sanctions the move.

Free Reserves

Another popular indicator of money market conditions is the *free reserve* position of the banking system. Free reserves are defined as excess reserve balances of depository institutions held at the Federal Reserve banks minus borrowings from the discount window. (Recall that excess reserves are legal reserve balances kept at the Reserve banks plus vault cash less required reserves.) Both the level and direction of change of free reserves are thought to have meaning.

The dynamic element in free reserves is borrowings by depository institutions from the discount windows of the Federal Reserve banks. When these borrowings increase, depository institutions feel more restricted in their lending and investing until they can repay their debt to the Fed. Credit becomes more difficult to obtain and more expensive. On the other hand, when discount-window borrowings fall relative to excess reserves, depository institutions feel less pressure against their reserves and may become more liberal in extending credit.

Free reserves can be either positive or negative, depending upon whether excess reserves are larger or smaller than borrowings from the Reserve banks. When borrowings exceed excess reserves, a condition of *net borrowed reserves* prevails. On the other hand, if borrowings are less than excess reserves, the banking system has *net free reserves*. Movement from week to week toward deeper net borrowed reserves generally implies that tighter credit conditions are developing. In contrast, a change toward greater net free reserves is usually regarded as an indicator of easier credit conditions.

One problem with the free-reserve indicator is that many forces affect free reserves other than just Federal Reserve policy. For example, individual depository instititutions decide what volume of excess reserves they wish to hold and whether or not to borrow from the Federal Reserve banks. In a period of high interest rates the tendency is for banks and other institutional lenders to hold minimal excess reserves and to borrow heavily from the Fed as one of the cheapest sources of funds available. Conversely, in a period of low interest rates, there is less pressure on lending institutions to reduce their holdings of excess reserves which earn no interest income. Also, in such periods the volume of borrowings from the discount window may decline because lenders find themselves with adequate levels of reserves. This indicator, then, is subject to much the same criticism as the other monetary policy indicators we have discussed—it is influenced by many factors other than just Federal Reserve policy.

Interpreting Money Market Indicators

The use of money market indicators to interpret the current course of monetary policy may be illustrated using the information given in Exhibit 23–6. Movements in the effective Federal funds rate, market yields on U.S.

EXHIBIT 23–6
Money Market Indicators of Federal Reserve Policy

Money Market Indicator	1980			1981 January
	October	November	December	
Effective federal funds rate	12.81%	15.85%	18.90%	19.08%
Interest rate on U.S. Treasury bills, secondary market:				
3-month	11.62	13.73	15.49	15.02
6-month	11.63	13.50	14.64	14.08
1-year	11.30	12.66	13.23	12.62
Federal Reserve Bank of New York discount rate	11.47	12.87	13.00	13.00
Net free (or net borrowed) reserves ($ millions)	(918)	(1,201)	(1,587)	(913)

Notes: Figures for the Federal funds rate are averages of daily effective rates weighted by the volume of transactions at these rates. Treasury bill rates are computed on a bank-discount basis from daily closing bid prices. Discount rates are averages supplied by the Federal Reserve Bank of New York. Free reserves are the difference between excess reserve balances with the Federal Reserve banks less total borrowings from the discount windows of the Reserve banks.
SOURCE: Board of Governors of the Federal Reserve System.

Treasury bills, the Federal Reserve Bank of New York's discount rate, and free reserves between October 1980 and January 1981 are shown in the exhibit. We note that the money market rates rose sharply between October and December, led by a surge of more than six percentage points in the federal funds rate. At the same time, depository institutions keeping their reserve balances at the Federal Reserve banks experienced a deepening net borrowed reserve position, with free reserves dropping from −$918 million to −$1,587 million. This was a signal to many money market analysts that the Federal Reserve was rapidly tightening credit conditions and so credit was becoming less available and more expensive. In part, the Fed appeared to be reacting against an excessively rapid rate of growth in the nation's money supply. (For example, M−1B rose at a 15.5 percent annual rate during the third quarter of 1980 and at an 11.3 percent annual rate during the final quarter of the year.) Moreover, the need for tighter credit conditions was underscored by soaring inflation. The cost-of-living index was increasing at a 13 percent annual rate as 1980 drew to a close.

January 1981 ushered in an entirely different scenario, however. Suddenly the Fed had to reverse itself and pursue easier credit conditions as the economy entered a recession. Predictably, some interest rates began to fall as the new year started. Free reserves became less negative, with the banking system's net borrowed reserve position dropping from −$1,587 to −$913. In just four months, monetary policy had switched from tight credit conditions aimed at slowing the economy down to easier credit conditions designed to stimulate the economy and head off a deep recession.

THE FEDERAL RESERVE AND NATIONAL ECONOMIC GOALS

For many years now, the Federal Reserve System has played an active role in the stabilization of the economy and in the pursuit of the nation's economic goals. These goals include controlling inflation, promoting full employment and sustainable economic growth, and achieving a stable balance of international payments position for the United States. In recent years these goals have proved to be extremely difficult to achieve in practice and in fact have often required conflicting policies. Nevertheless, the Fed remains committed to them and sets its policies accordingly.

The Goal of Controlling Inflation

Inflation—a rise in the general price level for all goods and services produced in the economy—is the number one economic problem in the United States today. Indeed, inflation has become a worldwide problem, with many nations experiencing far higher annual rates of inflation than those currently prevailing in the United States. Moreover, inflation is not new; price levels have been generally rising since the beginning of the Industrial Revolution in Europe nearly 300 years ago. There is also evidence of outbreaks of rampant inflation during the Middle Ages and in ancient times.

What is particularly alarming about inflation is its tendency to *accelerate* in the absence of effective policy controls. For example, between 1960 and 1965 the U.S. consumer price index (CPI) rose an average of only 1.3 percent a year. Then between 1966 and 1973, in the wake of the Vietnam War, large federal budget deficits, and rapid expansion of the nation's money supply, the average annual growth rate of consumer prices more than tripled, to a 4.6 percent annual rate. From 1974 through 1975 the CPI's annual growth rate more than doubled from that base, rising at a 9.4-percent annual rate. In 1980 consumer prices jumped 12.4 percent (see Exhibit 23–7).

EXHIBIT 23–7
Measures of the Rate of Inflation in the U.S. (compound annual rates of change)

Price Level Index	Period			
	1960–65	1966–73	1974–79	1980
Consumer price index (CPI)	1.3%	4.6%	8.0%	12.4%
Producer price index, finished goods	0.4	3.8	7.9	11.7
Implicit price deflator for gross national product	1.6	4.7	7.4	9.6

SOURCES: Federal Reserve Bank of St. Louis, *Annual U.S. Economic Data, Compounded Rates of Change, 1960–79;* U.S. Department of Commerce; and Board of Governors of the Federal Reserve System.

Equally alarming, instead of declining during periods of recession when the economy's growth slowed or turned negative, prices continued to rise. For example, during the 1969–70 recession, consumer prices climbed 5.4 percent; during the 1973–75 recession, consumer prices jumped 11.1 percent. Inflation began from a higher plateau after each major recession in the U.S. economy until the 1980 recession, when the upward surge in consumer prices moderated somewhat. However, the more-moderate growth in prices after 1980 was due, in part, to a sluggish economic recovery and pockets of persistent unemployment, particularly in the auto and housing industries. Indeed, the American economy in recent years has passed through long periods of "stagflation"—i.e., stagnant growth and high unemployment coupled with serious inflation.

What are the causes? During the 1960s and 70s war and government spending were certainly major contributing factors. More recently, soaring energy and food costs, higher home-mortgage rates, and rapid increases in unit labor and medical care costs have played key roles. Another contributing factor until recently was the decline in the value of the U.S. dollar in international markets. The dollar's weakness relative to other major currencies (particularly the German mark and the Swiss franc) raised the price of imports into the United States and lessened the impact of foreign competition on domestic producers.

Still another causal factor is inflationary expectations—the anticipation of continued inflation by businesses and households. Once underway, inflation seems to develop a momentum of its own as consumers spend and borrow more freely to stay ahead of rising prices, sending prices still higher. Businesses and labor unions begin to build inflation into their price and wage decisions, passing higher costs along in the form of higher prices for goods and services. The result is a wage-price spiral where each plateau of increased costs is used as a basis for justifying still further price increases.[13]

Inflation creates distortions in the allocation of the nation's scarce resources and definitely hurts certain groups. For example, it tends to discourage saving and encourages consumption at a faster rate to stay ahead of rising prices. The savings rate in the U.S. economy—the ratio of personal saving to disposable personal income—dropped to about 5 percent in 1978 and remained between 5 and 6 percent as the 1980s began. This was the lowest personal savings rate for U.S. consumers since the Korean War (1950–52), another period of rapid inflation.

Moreover, the decline in the savings rate combined with higher effective tax rates against corporations tended to discourage capital investment. While business spending on plant and equipment in the United States soared during the 1960s, long-term capital spending declined as a percentage of GNP during the 1970s. Businesses found that inflationary cost and tax increases made it cheaper on an aftertax basis to increase their employment and inventory levels rather than purchase new capital equipment. Unfortunately, this meant that the economy's growth in productivity (i.e., output per worker-hour) slowed during the 1970s, and productivity itself actually declined during the 1978–80 period. The fall in productivity meant that the supply of new goods and services could not keep pace with rising demands, putting further upward pressure on prices.

At the same time, workers have sought higher wages to stay ahead of the rising cost of living, leading to a dramatic increase in unit labor costs faced by American business firms. While some workers represented by strong unions or in growth industries have managed to keep pace with inflation, other groups, including many savers, lenders of funds, retired persons, and government employees, whose income is fixed or rises slowly, have experienced a decline in their real standard of living in recent years.

Possible Remedies for Inflation

What are the possible remedies for inflation? How can the Federal Reserve System deal with the inflationary price spiral? There are several differ-

---

[13] One indicator of the strength of inflationary expectations in the U.S. economy is the growth of COLA—cost-of-living-adjustment—clauses built into negotiated agreements between labor unions and employers. The Bureau of Labor Statistics estimates that, in 1979, 9.3 million employees in the United States were subject to major collective bargaining agreements between unions and employers, and 60 percent of these had COLA clauses designed to raise wages automatically with increases in the cost of living. The most common COLA formula called for a wage-rate increase of one cent per hour for each 0.3 point change in the consumer price index.

ent views on what steps must be taken to slow inflation and on what the
Fed's role should be.

The Monetarist View.   An approach to monetary policy growing rapidly
in popularity in recent years is the monetarist school. Among the most important proponents of this particular approach to government policy and
inflation are economists Milton Friedman, Karl Brunner, Alan Meltzer,
David Meiselman, Anna Schwartz, Christopher Sims, and others.[14] These
economists argue that the nation's money supply is a dominant influence on
prices, spending, production, and employment. Friedman and Schwartz, for
example, after analyzing money and business cycles dating back to the Civil
War, concluded that

> Appreciable changes in the rate of growth of the money stock are a necessary
> and sufficient condition for appreciable changes in the rate of growth of money
> income.[15]

Moreover, *changes* in the rate of money-supply growth appear to precede
changes in economic activity and inflation, suggesting that money exerts an
independent causal influence upon economic conditions. They believe that the
economy is inherently stable and tends toward full employment and sustainable growth without inflation if left to its own devices. One of the ways in
which government can aid the economy in achieving noninflationary growth
and full employment is to avoid "fine tuning" the system. Allegedly, attempts at fine tuning do more harm than good, causing instability in the
economy.

According to the monetarist view, monetary policy affects the economy
mainly through changes in the rate of monetary growth. For example, if the
money supply grows too rapidly, exceeding the public's expectations, an
excess stock of money results. Money demand for goods and services will
rise rapidly and put upward pressure on prices.[16] In contrast, when the
money supply grows too slowly relative to the demand for money, the public
attempts to restore its desired money balances by cutting back on spending
and purchases of financial assets. The result is a drop in income and demand
in the economy and a rise in interest rates, so that employment and growth
are slowed. The Federal Reserve can exert its most favorable effect on the
economy simply by allowing the money supply to grow at a relatively *constant rate* (preferably about 4 to 6 percent a year), which approximates the
rate of growth in the economy's capacity to produce goods and services.

---

[14] See especially Friedman and Schwartz (12, 13), Friedman and Meiselman (11), Keran (19),
Anderson and Carlson (1), and Sims (32) in the list of references at the conclusion of this
chapter.

[15] See reference 12, p. 53.

[16] Monetarists base this conclusion on the assumption that each unit (individual or business)
in the economy desires to hold a certain quantity of money. If the money supply grows so large
that it exceeds desired levels, then the cost of holding additional money exceeds its benefits.
Businesses and individuals will attempt to spend away their excess money balances by purchasing goods, services, and other assets. With the economy at or near full employment, prices must
rise due to the added spending.

Fiscal policy—the taxing and spending activities of government—is regarded by monetarists as being much less effective than monetary policy. One reason is that changes in taxes and government spending require legislative approval, which often takes months or years. Moreover, monetarists argue, unless changes in taxes and spending are backed by complementary changes in the money supply, their effects will be nullified. Money taxed away from one group will simply be paid to another, resulting in little net gain to the economy as a whole. Stepped-up government borrowing and spending without an increase in the money supply simply result in higher interest rates, choking off private borrowers. The best remedy for inflation is, according to the monetarists, not higher taxes or reduced government deficits, but slower monetary growth. As we saw earlier, the Federal Reserve has been promoting slower money growth recently, but that growth has not been steady. The money supply often grows modestly in one quarter, only to surge upward the next.

The Credit Availability, or Neo-Keynesian, View. A more traditional approach to fighting inflation is known as the credit-availability, or neo-Keynesian, view.[17] Adherents to this view believe that a wide range of factors—monetary and nonmonetary—influence employment, income, and prices. They argue that the money supply is an important factor in generating business cycles but not necessarily *the* most important factor. Government spending and taxation (i.e., fiscal policy) as well as interest rates also play critical roles in creating or reducing inflation, unemployment, and other problems because of their impact on investment spending.

We recall from Chapter 6 that investment spending includes household expenditures for housing, automobiles, and other durable goods and business expenditures for plant, equipment, and inventories. Investment spending is the most-volatile component of the total demand for goods and services in the economy. When investment falls, a recession usually follows, while rising investment often precipitates an economic boom. Changes in investment expenditures have a multiplier effect on total income in the economy because new investment generates income, which leads to increased consumption and still more income. Thus, even small changes in the volume and mix of investment expenditures can lead to magnified changes in income, spending, employment, and prices.

How can monetary policy affect investment spending and ultimately exert an impact on inflation? According to the neo-Keynesian view, the volume of investment spending is affected directly by the cost and availability of credit,

---

[17] The term *neo-Keynesian* is often used to describe economists who have adopted, amplified, and further refined many of the ideas of British economist John Maynard Keynes. While Keynes wrote several books and many articles covering the period from World War I through World War II, his views on the causes of unemployment, inflation, and other economic problems appear in *The General Theory of Employment, Interest, and Money* (London: Macmillan & Co., 1936). Leading economists who have further refined and developed the original Keynesian theories include Patinkin (23), Tobin (36), Smith (34), and Samuelson (27).

monetary growth, and total wealth. The rate of interest is especially important here because it is a measure of the cost of financing new investment
spending. A rise in interest rates, other things equal, will reduce the demand
for investment funds, slowing not only investment spending but also the
growth of employment, income, and prices. In contrast, lower interest rates
stimulate the demand for investment, which increases income and employment and may cause prices to rise (if the economy is at or near full employment). The Federal Reserve can bring about changes in interest rates, up or
down, by changing the real money supply (i.e., money adjusted for changes
in the price level). For example, rising inflation can be countered by slower
monetary growth. If the money supply grows more slowly than the public's
demand for real money balances, interest rates will rise, leading to a decline
in investment spending. Income and spending in the economy will grow more
slowly, and inflationary pressures will be reduced.

Fiscal policy—government taxing and spending—also has a significant
role to play in cooling inflation, according to the neo-Keynesian view. If total
spending in the private sector of the economy grows too rapidly, generating
inflation, government spending can be reduced, which will soon lead to less
consumption spending and ultimately decrease private investment. In other
words, government spending, like private investment spending, has a multiplier effect, up or down, on employment, income, and prices. Alternatively,
private consumption and investment spending can be choked off by higher
taxes. Through increased tax revenues, federal, state, and local governments
can reduce budget deficits or even run budget surpluses so that the government sector actually withdraws funds from the private spending stream.
Demand for goods and services will fall, leading to reduced inflationary
pressures.

Thus, the neo-Keynesian, or credit availability, view stresses the necessity of using *both* monetary and fiscal policy to achieve the nation's economic
goals. Neo-Keynesians question whether merely maintaining a constant rate
of growth in the money supply will, by itself, solve the problem of inflation.
The appropriate growth rate for money depends upon economic conditions,
the status of government fiscal policy, and especially the public's demand for
money. Under some circumstances (especially if the demand for money were
falling), a 4 percent rate of growth in the nation's money supply could be
highly inflationary. Under other circumstances (such as a rapid rise in money
demand), 4 percent monetary growth could lead to a severe recession. In
either case, suggest the neo-Keynesians, the key factors to watch in gauging
the direction and impact of monetary policy are interest rates and growth of
the real money supply. The way to fight inflation is to reduce the growth rate
of the real money supply and increase interest rates.

Supply-Side Economics. Shortly after President Ronald Reagan took
office in January 1981, the White House announced a new approach to the
problem of inflation. It was labeled *supply-side economics* to differentiate this
strategy from methods employed during most of the postwar period. Both

the monetarist and neo-Keynesian views stress attacking the inflation problem from the *demand* side of the marketplace. That is, inflationary pressures allegedly can be cooled down by choking off excessive demand for goods and services stemming from private investment, consumer spending, and government spending. Higher interest rates, slower money growth, and increased taxes are aimed principally at discouraging demand in the private sector, allowing the aggregate supply of goods and services to catch up with the public's demand for them.

Quite logically, we could also attack inflation from the *supply* side—by increasing the nation's output of goods and services. If the economy produces more, relative to public demand, there is less reason for prices to rise. How can this be done? Basically, by stimulating private investment and saving to finance that investment. As Tatom notes, "supply-side economics is growth- and efficiency-oriented."[18] It argues that economic policy has a direct impact upon the rate of growth in the supply of productive resources and upon technological innovation—factors which determine the economy's capacity to produce. The economy's productive capacity is lowered by government regulations which require the use of inefficient technologies or reduce incentives to save, invest, and use resources. The same is true of an excessive tax burden which transfers resources from the private to the public sector. In an effort to avoid high tax rates, resource owners will divert their resources to lower-taxed but less-efficient uses, such as by substituting labor for capital, retaining rather than replacing old equipment, and spending more on consumption instead of saving. Supply-siders in recent years have recommended (1) a slower rate of monetary expansion; (2) regulatory reform to stimulate competition and technological innovation; (3) reduced tax rates on individual incomes; and (4) accelerated depreciation of business equipment to stimulate both saving and investment.

Following the supply-side approach, the administration of President Ronald Reagan has taken or proposed the following steps to deal with inflation:

1. Lower tax rates on business and personal incomes and on savings,
2. Accelerated depreciation of existing plant and equipment to stimulate the purchase of new investment goods.
3. Cooperation with the Federal Reserve System to promote stable growth in the money supply in order to avoid volatile and unpredictable changes in interest rates.
4. Less government regulation of business to encourage more private initiative and production and reduce the cost burden imposed by rigid, arbitrary rules.
5. A reduction in the size of the government sector relative to the rest of the economy through decreased spending at federal, state, and local levels of government.

---

[18] See Tatom (35), p. 18.

Throughout the postwar period federal government spending has risen faster than the nation's GNP. For example, in 1960 total federal spending of $95 billion represented just slightly less than 19 percent of GNP. By 1970 federal outlays had increased to $204 billion and accounted for 21 percent of GNP, only to soar upward to $600 billion and more than 23 percent of GNP by 1980. The Reagan Administration argues that the inflation problem cannot be solved unless the overall size of government can be reduced, permitting a greater role for the private sector in job hiring and price setting.

Will supply-side economics really work? Can the supply of goods and services increase fast enough, relative to demand, to reduce inflation? No one really knows because it is an experiment that has not been tested in an environment of accelerating inflation. Much depends on the *psychological* impact of the Reagan administration's policies. Will business decision makers be encouraged enough by the prospect of less regulation, reduced taxes, and a generally more "pro-business" environment to step up capital outlays? Certainly if inflationary expectations are dampened, consumers will be less inclined to follow a strategy of buy now and pay later, and perhaps they will save more.

If the personal saving rate does rise, more funds will be available for investment, possibly at lower interest rates. Additional investment spending could halt the recent decline in the nation's industrial productivity. However, lower income tax rates could also fuel more consumption spending as well as lead to larger federal budget deficits. This would force the U.S. Treasury to borrow more heavily, resulting in higher interest rates and possibly more inflation. The essential point is that no one knows for sure whether supply-side effects are really responsive enough or powerful enough to offset soaring inflationary demands. On that point, we must await the verdict of time.

The Goal of Full Employment

The Employment Act of 1946 committed the federal government for the first time to minimizing unemployment as a major national goal. The Federal Reserve, as part of the government structure, is therefore committed to this goal as well. In recent years, the U.S. unemployment rate as determined from monthly surveys conducted by the U.S. Department of Labor has hovered in the 6 to 10 percent range. In terms of numbers of people, between 6 and 11 million workers have been actively seeking jobs but have been unable to find them. The cost of unemployment is high. The nation's output of goods and services and its real standard of living are reduced. Unemployment also breeds social unrest, increased crime, and higher tax burdens on those who are working.

In recent years the U.S. economy has experienced rising plateaus of unemployment. As the 1960s ended, unemployment affected less than 5 percent of the civilian labor force. However, a recession in 1970 led to substantial increases in the number of jobless workers, and there was little improvement until 1973, when the jobless rate returned to the 5 percent range. Following the Arab oil embargo and a deep recession in 1974–75, the nation's unemployment rate rose to a postwar record of almost 9 percent. The recovery of the economy between 1976 and 1979 brought the unemployment rate down to just under 6 percent midway in 1979. However, the recession of 1980 sent it soaring again to a high of 7.8 percent, and the jobless rate remained well above 7 percent as the decade of the 80s began.

Is it possible to have zero unemployment? What is full employment? In a market-oriented economy, where workers are free to change jobs and businessmen are free to hire and fire, some unemployment is inevitable. There is a minimum level of unemployment, known as *frictional unemployment,* which arises from the temporary unemployment of persons who are changing jobs in response to higher wages or better working conditions. *Full employment,* therefore, refers to a situation where the only significant amount of unemployment is frictional in nature. In a fully employed economy, everyone actively seeking work will find it in a relatively short period. During the 1960s the President's Council of Economic Advisers defined full employment as a situation where only 4 percent of the civilian labor force was unemployed, due mainly to frictional factors.

In recent years, however, economists have raised their estimates of the amount of irreducible frictional unemployment. In fact, the Labor Department now considers the economy at full employment if the nation's unemployment rate is 5.1 percent. Why has this significantly higher rate been adopted?

A key factor is the massive shifts which have occurred in the *composition* of the American labor force over the past decade, especially the rapid increase in the number of adult women seeking jobs. Women 20 years of age and older, in fact, have accounted for more than half the net increase in the U.S. labor force since 1977. This upward surge in women's employment may be attributed to a decline in fertility rates, more-varied jobs available to females, and the erosion of family incomes due to inflation. Teenage participation in the labor force also has expanded sharply since the late 1970s under the pressure of inflation, the rising cost of college training, and the spread of vocational schools. Historically, these two groups—women and teenagers—have reported higher average unemployment rates than those of most other workers. Both women and teenagers move in and out of the job market with much greater fluidity than do adult male workers, due to family needs and schooling opportunities.

Other groups also increasing in importance who traditionally report high unemployment rates include nonwhite workers and unskilled labor. One of the most conspicuous failures of U.S. economic policy during the 1970s was its inability to significantly lower the unemployment rate among minority workers and the unskilled. *Structural unemployment*—joblessness due to a lack of necessary skills—has not been reduced to any appreciable extent in the U.S. economy since the mid-1960s.

When unemployment rises above the frictional level, how can monetary policy be used to bring it down? Some economists in the monetarist school would call for a more rapid rate of growth in the nation's money supply.[19] If more money becomes available to the public and exceeds their desired money holdings, the excess money balances will be spent in acquiring goods, services, and securities. This additional spending would tend to increase the demand for labor and reduce the nation's unemployment rate.

The neo-Keynesian, or credit-availability, approach, on the other hand, would call for a combined monetary and fiscal attack on the problem. The growth rate of the real money supply would be increased, leading to lower interest rates. Investment spending would rise in response to the lower cost and greater availability of credit, raising income levels. Out of the higher incomes would come both increased consumption and further investment spending, creating more new jobs. At the same time, tax rates might be reduced to further stimulate consumption and investment. Increased government spending could be used as a supplement to private investment to provide additional employment.

A supply-side approach to the unemployment problem would rely mainly on the private sector, with government reducing taxes, easing burdensome regulations, and cutting back on spending and borrowing in order to make room for more private borrowing and spending. Which of these different methods is used depends, of course, on the severity of the unemployment problem and the preferences of policymakers.

The Goal of Sustainable Economic Growth

The Federal Reserve has declared that one of its most important long-run goals is to keep the economy growing at a relatively steady and stable rate—high enough to absorb increases in the labor force and prevent the nation's unemployment rate from rising, but slow enough to avoid runaway inflation. Most economists believe this implies a rate of growth in the nation's GNP of no less than 4 percent annually on a real (inflation-adjusted) basis. Periodically, however, the economy grows more slowly than this or turns down into a recession, resulting in rising unemployment.

While most U.S. recessions have been relatively brief and mild, they have averaged two each decade, or about one every three or four years. For example, during the 1970s the nation's real output of new goods and services

---

[19] As we noted earlier, however, many monetarists advocate relatively *constant* monetary growth. In theory, this strategy would avoid inflationary pressures during boom periods and prevent a significant rise in unemployment during recessions. For advocates of this approach, a rise in unemployment would be viewed as a temporary phenomenon, and the rate of monetary growth would not be changed unless it dropped below the planned growth path.

EXHIBIT 23–8
Rates of Growth in Real U.S. GNP (compounded annual rates of change)

Period	Annual Rate of Change in GNP (1972 dollars)	Period	Annual Rate of Change in GNP (1972 dollars)
1960–69	3.9%		
1971	3.0	1976	5.9%
1972	5.7	1977	5.3
1973	5.5	1978	4.4
1974	−1.4	1979	2.3
1975	−1.3	1980	−0.3

SOURCE: Federal Reserve Bank of St. Louis, *National Economic Trends*, March 30, 1981.

declined in 1973–75 and again in 1980 (see Exhibit 23–8). The recession of 1973–75 was the longest in postwar history, covering 16 months from peak to trough. In contrast, the 1980 recession was the shortest downturn ever recorded, lasting only six months.

Forecasting the actual starting point of each recession and its duration has proven to be an exceedingly difficult problem for the Federal Reserve. Each downturn in the economy springs from somewhat different causes, though most recessions involve a sharp cutback in investment in inventories as business decision makers come to anticipate lower sales volume. Fears of being caught with a large quantity of unsold goods lead to periodic cutbacks in new orders, throwing people out of work. At the same time, interest rates usually rise to peak levels shortly before a recession begins, gradually choking off private investment. Two recent economic downturns, in 1973–75 and 1980–81, were concentrated in two sectors of the economy—the automobile and housing industries—both dependent on the availability of credit and therefore highly sensitive to movements in interest rates. For example, housing starts declined 34 percent during the 1973–75 recession and 21 percent in 1980. Auto sales plunged 21 percent in 1973–75 and nearly 45 percent during 1980. Unemployment in the construction, auto, and steel industries soared.

Traditional economic theory suggests that a decline in the nation's rate of economic growth should lead to a lower rate of inflation. This follows from the observation that recessions are marked by reduced demand for goods and services and falling incomes. Thus, in theory at least, a recession and slower economic growth are short-run cures for severe inflation, though for those without jobs they are certainly high-cost cures. Interestingly enough, however, recent recessions have not conformed to this pattern. In fact, there is evidence of an increasing rate of inflation during the recessions of the 1960s and 70s. For example, consumer prices rose at a 5.4 percent annual rate during the 1969–70 recession, 11.1 percent during the 1973–75 downturn, and 11.6 percent during the 1980 recession. Many observers believe the bias in the U.S. economy toward inflation even during recessionary periods may be due to the rapid growth of service industries relative to the manufacturing sector, welfare payments (especially unemployment compensation), escalator clauses in many wage contracts, and the expectation that government policy will always respond quickly to protect jobs whenever economic problems appear.

Monetary policy can stimulate the economy to grow faster simply by following a policy of lower interest rates and accelerated growth in the money supply. Larger money holdings will encourage additional consumption spending, while lower interest rates should promote a higher rate of investment spending. Higher levels of spending will, in turn, stimulate still more investment outlays, boosting income and reducing unemployment. If the nation is experiencing a deep recession, fiscal policy measures—lower tax rates and augmented government spending—may also be needed to promote a faster rate of economic growth. Unfortunately, as we have seen, promoting more-rapid growth cannot be the sole concern of policymakers today because those policies favorable to growth also generally increase inflation. Compromises among several worthwhile goals as part of a balanced economic stabilization program must be made if the Fed is to succeed in the long run.

Equilibrium in the U.S. Balance of Payments and Protecting the Dollar

The Federal Reserve must be concerned, not only with domestic economic conditions, but also with developments in the international sector. In this area, the Fed actually pursues two interrelated goals: (1) protecting the value of the dollar in foreign currency markets, and (2) achieving an equilibrium position in the U.S. balance of payments.

When the United States buys more of the goods, services, and securities offered by other nations than those countries spend for what the United States sells, the difference must be made up by giving foreigners claims against U.S. reserves and resources. If the United States persists in purchasing or acquiring more abroad than foreigners purchase or acquire here, a *disequilibrium* position in the nation's balance of payments results. This means that the United States cannot continue to draw down its reserve assets (primarily gold, foreign currencies, and Special Drawing Rights at the International Monetary Fund) indefinitely, nor will it find foreigners willing to accept unlimited amounts of dollars.[20] At some point the federal government and the Federal Reserve must adopt policies which slow down the outflow of U.S. dollars and encourage foreigners to buy more U.S. goods, services, and securities. Failing this, the value of the dollar in international markets begins to weaken.

In recent years the United States has experienced some deep deficits in its international balance-of-payments position. A major cause of these pay-

---

[20] See Chapter 26 for a discussion of reserve assets and disequilibrium problems in the U.S. balance of payments.

ments deficits, as we will see in Chapter 26, has been massive imports of increasingly expensive foreign oil. Petroleum imports now account for nearly a third of total U.S. merchandise imports each year. Other foreign imports into the United States experiencing considerable growth in recent years include European and Japanese autos, steel products, building materials, natural gas, and crude rubber.

How can monetary policy deal with balance-of-payments deficits and threats to the dollar? The traditional remedy is to bring about higher domestic interest rates and slower growth in the nation's money supply. The higher interest rates make U.S. securities more attractive relative to foreign securities, encouraging capital to stay at home and foreigners to invest their funds in the United States. The combination of higher interest rates and slower money-supply growth will also tend to slow down the economy and reduce inflation. The demand for imported goods and services will fall, while U.S. exports will be attractive in overseas markets if inflation can be controlled. Thus, the goal of protecting the dollar is generally consistent with the goal of controlling inflation, but the aggressive pursuit of both these goals may lead to slower economic growth.

THE TRADE-OFFS AMONG NATIONAL ECONOMIC GOALS

The Federal Reserve has not been particularly successful in achieving all of the nation's economic goals, especially in controlling inflation. Lest we reach a hasty conclusion that the central bank has failed in its responsibilities and needs major overhaul, however, it should be kept in mind that the Fed has a difficult, perhaps impossible, task.

For one thing, the goals pursued by the Federal Reserve *conflict* with each other. Controlling inflation and protecting the dollar usually mean slowing down the economy, which frequently leads to a rise in unemployment as well as a slower overall growth rate. A good example of this trade-off problem occurred in July and August 1979, when the Fed raised the discount rate a full percentage point in order to support the dollar in international markets. Domestic interest rates soared to record levels, and a recession began five months later.

Further evidence that the nation's key economic goals frequently conflict with each other, at least in the short run, was provided by British economist A. W. Phillips and American economists Samuelson and Solow more than two decades ago.[21] These researchers found an *inverse* relationship between increases in money wages and prices, on the one hand, and changes in unemployment, on the other. For example, Samuelson and Solow using data from the 1950s, found that stable prices could only be achieved if unemployment remained as high as 5 to 6 percent of the civilian labor force.

---

[21] See, in particular, Phillips (24) and Samuelson and Solow (28).

Unfortunately, these early studies looked only at data on actual price movements and ignored inflationary expectations. However, a more-recent study by Smaistrla and Throop concludes that a significant trade-off still exists between unemployment and inflation when inflationary expectations are considered. These authors found that

> With the inflation rate that prevailed at the beginning of 1977, an unemployment rate of 8 percent would have to be maintained for four years in order to bring the rate of price inflation down to 4 percent and 9½ years to reduce it to 2 percent.[22]

A sustained period of high employment is necessary to eradicate inflation, Smaistrla and Throop conclude, because expectations about future inflation take so long (at least five years) to form and also to eliminate. However, they believe that

> if market participants could be persuaded that the government is going to use monetary and fiscal policies in an effective and consistent manner to reduce inflation, then inflationary psychology could be eliminated mainly by the anti-inflation policies themselves. A longer, drawn-out response to experience, and the associated costs in terms of foregone production and employment, could be avoided. Fashioning a credible policy against inflation, and informing the public of its expected effects, are the great challenges facing government today.[23]

Smaistrla and Throop calculate the frictional or "normal" rate of unemployment to be around 5.6 percent. The rate of inflation, they contend, will accelerate if unemployment falls below that level.

THE LIMITATIONS OF MONETARY POLICY

In addition to conflicts among the nation's economic goals, the Federal Reserve finds that it cannot completely control financial conditions or the money supply. Changes in the economy itself feed back upon the money supply. It becomes exceedingly difficult, especially on a weekly or monthly basis, to sort out the effects of monetary policy from the impact of broad economic forces.

Moreover, until recently the Fed has received little cooperation from Congress in the pursuit of effective taxing and spending programs. Most economists agree that fiscal policy—the taxing and spending activities of the federal government—can have a potent impact upon economic conditions. Unfortunately, changes in tax rates and federal spending programs require the cooperation of both the executive and legislative branches of the government. This kind of cooperation between Congress and the president has only just begun to surface. With the exception of recent tax and spending cuts by the Reagan administration, the Federal Reserve System has been

---

[22] See Smaistria and Throop (33), p. 55.

[23] See Smaistrla and Throop (33), p. 55.

forced to carry the burden of antiinflation policy almost totally alone. Under these circumstances, we should not be too surprised that the Fed's past track record leaves much to be desired.

STUDY QUESTIONS

1. Why are indicators of Federal Reserve policy important to the Fed itself and to managers of financial institutions, corporate treasurers, and the public?

2. What is a money market indicator? Give examples and explain how these indicators reflect changes in credit conditions. What problems can you see in the use of money market indicators to gauge the direction of monetary policy?

3. List and define the various measures of the nation's money supply. Why do we need several different measures of money? Do you really think it matters which form of the money supply the Federal Reserve controls?

4. What are the principal items on the Federal Reserve Statement? Which of these items reflect Federal Reserve activities?

5. Define what is meant by net free reserves and net borrowed reserves. How would you interpret changes in these money market indicators?

6. Explain how the actions of the U.S. Treasury can influence the reserves of depository institutions.

7. What is float? Why is it of concern to Federal Reserve policy makers?

8. List the principal economic goals of Federal Reserve monetary policy and define each. Which of these goals have been reasonably well achieved in recent years, and which have not? Try to explain why.

9. Explain the basic similarities and differences between the monetarist and neo-Keynesian approaches to monetary policy. How would each deal with inflation? With unemployment?

10. What is supply-side economics? Can you foresee any problems in trying to implement the supply-side approach?

11. Outline the steps which the Federal Reserve System goes through in trying to control the growth rate of the money supply and hit its monetary growth targets. What difficulties do you see in the Fed's approach?

12. What trade-offs appear to exist among the nation's key economic goals? Why do you think these trade-offs exist?

SELECTED REFERENCES

1. Anderson, Leonall C., and Keith Carlson. "A Monetarist Model for Economic Stabilization." *Review*, Federal Reserve Bank of St. Louis, April 1970.

2. Berkman, Neil G. "Bank Reserves, Money, and Some Problems for the New Monetary Policy." *New England Economic Review*, Federal Reserve Bank of Boston, July-August 1980, pp. 52–64.

3. Board of Governors of the Federal Reserve System. *The Federal Reserve System—Purposes and Functions*. Washington, D.C., 1974.

4. _____. "The New Federal Reserve Technical Procedures for Controlling Money." Staff Memorandum, January 31, 1980.

5. _____. "Redefining the Monetary Aggregates." *Federal Reserve Bulletin*, January 1979, pp. 13–42.

6. Burger, Albert E. "Alternative Measures of the Monetary Base." *Review*, Federal Reserve Bank of St. Louis, June 1979, pp. 3–8.

7. Cacy, J. A. "Monetary Policy in 1980 and 1981." *Economic Review*, Federal Reserve Bank of Kansas City, December 1980, pp. 18–25.

8. Carlson, Keith M. "Money, Inflation, and Economic Growth: Some Updated Reduced-Form Results and Their Implications." *Review*, Federal Reserve Bank of St. Louis, April 1980.

9. Carlson, Keith M., and Scott E. Hein. "Monetary Aggregates as Monetary Indicators." *Review*, Federal Reserve Bank of St. Louis, November 1980.

10. Friedman, Benjamin M. "Targets, Instruments, and Indicators of Monetary Policy." *Journal of Monetary Economics*, October 1975, pp. 443–73.

11. Friedman, Milton, and David Meiselman. "The Relative Stability of Monetary Velocity and the Investment Multiplier in the United States, 1897–1958." In *Stabilization Policies*, Commission on Money and Credit. Englewood Cliffs, N.J.: Prentice-Hall, 1963.

12. Friedman, Milton, and Anna Jacobson Schwartz, "Money and Business Cycles." *Review of Economics and Statistics*, February 1963.

13. _____. *A Monetary History of the United States, 1867–1960*. Princeton, N.J.: Princeton University Press, 1963.

14. Gambs, Carl M. "Federal Reserve Intermediate Targets: Money or the Monetary Base?" *Economic Review*, Federal Reserve Bank of Kansas City, January 1980, pp. 3–15.

15. Garcia, Gillian, and Dimon Pak. "Some Clues in the Case of the Missing Money." *American Economic Review, Papers and Proceedings*, May 1979, pp. 330–34.

16. Gittings, Thomas A. "The Inflation-Unemployment Tradeoff." *Economic Perspectives*, Federal Reserve Bank of Cleveland, September-October 1979, pp. 3–9.

17. Hafer, R. W. "The New Monetary Aggregates." *Review*, Federal Reserve Bank of St. Louis, February 1980.

18. Higgins, Bryan. "Free Reserves and Monetary Policy." *Economic Review*, Federal Reserve Bank of Kansas City, July-August 1980.

19. Keran, Michael. "Economic Theory and Forecasting." *Review*, Federal Reserve Bank of St. Louis, March 1967.

20. Keynes, John M. *The General Theory of Employment, Interest and Money*. London: Macmillan & Co., 1936.

21. Lombra, R., and F. Struble. "Monetary Aggregate Targets and the Volatility of Interest Rates: A Taxonomic Discussion." *Journal of Money, Credit, and Banking*, August 1979, pp. 284–300.

22. Long, Richard W. "The FOMC in 1979: Introducing Reserve Targeting." *Review*, Federal Reserve Bank of St. Louis, March 1980.

23. Patinkin, Don. *Keynes' Monetary Thought: A Study of Its Development*. Durham, N.C.: Duke University Press, 1976.

24. Phillips, A. W. "The Relation between Unemployment and the Rate of Change of Money Wage Rates in the United Kingdom, 1861–1957." *Economica,* November 1958.

25. Pierce, J. L., and T. D. Thompson. "Some Issues in Controlling the Stock of Money." In *Controlling Monetary Aggregates II: The Implementation.* Federal Reserve Bank of Boston, 1972.

26. Poole, Willliam, and Charles Lieberman, "Improving Monetary Control." In *Brookings Papers on Economic Activity,* 1972: 2, edited by Arthur M. Okun and George L. Perry. Washington, D.C.: The Brookings Institution, 1972.

27. Samuelson, Paul A. *Economics.* 7th ed. New York: McGraw-Hill, 1979.

28. Samuelson, Paul A., and Robert M. Solow. "The Problem of Achieving and Maintaining a Stable Price Level: Analytical Aspects of Anti-Inflation Policy." *American Economic Review,* May 1960.

29. Saving, Thomas R. "Monetary Policy Targets and Indicators." *Journal of Political Economy,* August 1967, pp. 446–56.

30. Sellon, Gordon, Jr. "The Role of the Discount Rate in Monetary Policy: A Theoretical Analysis." *Economic Review,* Federal Reserve Bank of Kansas City, June 1980.

31. Simpson, Thomas D. "The Redefined Monetary Aggregates." *Federal Reserve Bulletin,* February 1980.

32. Sims, Christopher. "Money, Income, and Causality." *American Economic Review,* September 1972, pp. 540–52.

33. Smaistrla, Charles J., and Adrion W. Throop. "A New Inflation in the 1970's?" *Financial Analysts Journal,* March-April 1980, pp. 47–57.

34. Smith, Warren L. "A Neo-Keynesian View of Monetary Policy." In *Controlling Monetary Aggregates.* Federal Reserve Bank of Boston, 1969.

35. Tatom, John A. "We Are All Supply-Siders Now!" *Review,* Federal Reserve Bank of St. Louis, May 1981, pp. 18–30.

36. Tobin, James. "The Monetary Interpretation of History." *American Economic Review,* June 1965.

37. ———. "Money and Income: *Post Hoc Ergo Propter Hoc?*" *Quarterly Journal of Economics,* May 1970.

38. Wachter, Michael L. "The Changing Cyclical Responsiveness of Wage Inflation." *Brookings Papers on Economic Activity,* No. 1, 1976, pp. 115–59.

39. Wenninger, John, and Charles M. Sivesind. "Defining Money for a Changing Financial System." *Quarterly Review,* Federal Reserve Bank of New York, Spring 1979, pp. 1–8.

24

The Treasury in the
Financial Markets

One of the most important financial institutions in any nation's economy is the government treasury. In the United States the Treasury Department exerts a powerful impact on the financial system because of two activities that it pursues on a continuing basis. One of these is *fiscal policy,* which refers to the taxing and spending programs of the federal government designed to promote high employment, reasonable price stability, economic growth, and other worthwhile economic goals. A second area in which the Treasury exerts a potent effect on financial conditions is *debt-management policy,* which involves the refunding or refinancing of the federal government's huge debt. These Treasury policymaking activities influence interest rates, the prices of securities traded in the open market, and the availability of credit to both private and public sectors of the economy. In general, the Treasury pursues policies designed to achieve major economic goals but not to severely disturb the functioning of the nation's financial markets. It must be especially careful not to pursue policies which conflict with the operations of the Federal Reserve System, because both institutions have a profound effect on the cost and availability of loanable funds within the financial system.

THE FISCAL POLICY ACTIVITIES OF THE U.S. TREASURY

Congress dictates the amount of funds which the federal government will spend each year for a variety of federal programs ranging from welfare to national defense, education, the preservation of environmental quality, and the construction of highways, buildings, and other public facilities. Congress also determines the sources of tax revenue and the tax rates which must be paid by individuals, families, and businesses. Frequently, the Congress will vote for a greater amount of spending than is justified by tax revenues and other governmental receipts. Alternatively, due to a slowdown in the economy, tax revenues may fall short of projections and not be sufficient to cover planned government expenditures. Either way, the result is a *budget deficit,* requiring the U.S. Treasury to borrow additional funds in the financial markets. On the other hand, government revenues may exceed expenditures, resulting in a budget surplus, which the Treasury may use to build up its cash balances or to retire debt previously issued.

As shown in Exhibit 24–1, U.S. Treasury budget surpluses have been very rare in recent years. In fact, the federal budget has been in surplus in only three fiscal years since 1931. The last federal budget surplus occurred

EXHIBIT 24–1
Federal Government Revenues, Expenditures, and Net Budget Surplus or Deficit, Fiscal Years 1960–1982 ($ millions)

Year	Total Revenues	Total Expenditures	Net Budget Surplus or Deficit (−)
1960	$ 92,492	$ 92,223	$ 269
1961	94,389	97,795	−3,406
1962	99,676	106,813	−7,137
1963	106,560	111,311	−4,751
1964	112,662	118,584	−5,922
1965	116,833	118,430	−1,596
1966	130,856	134,652	−3,796
1967	149,552	158,254	−8,702
1968	153,671	178,833	−25,161
1969	187,784	184,548	3,236
1970	193,743	196,588	−2,845
1971	188,392	211,425	−23,033
1972	208,649	232,021	−23,373
1973	232,225	247,074	−14,849
1974	264,932	269,620	−4,688
1975	280,997	326,151	−45,154
1976	300,005	366,418	−66,413
1977	357,762	402,710	−44,948
1978	401,997	450,804	−48,807
1979	465,940	493,635	−27,694
1980	520,050	579,613	−59,563
1981e	607,526	662,740	−55,215
1982e	711,780	739,296	−27,516

Notes: Figures based on the unified budget for fiscal years. Prior to 1977 fiscal years ran from July 1 through June 30. Thereafter, the federal budget year runs from October 1 through September 30.
SOURCES: U.S. Department of Commerce; *Business Statistics,* 1977 ed.; *Survey of Current Business,* September 1979; Board of Governors of the Federal Reserve System, *Banking and Monetary Statistics, 1941–1970;* and Council of Economic Advisors, *Economic Report of the President,* January 1981.

during the 1969–70 fiscal year, when revenues exceeded expenditures by about $3 billion. Since that time, the federal budget has been continually in deficit. It seems safe to assume at this point that federal budget deficits will continue to be frequent occurrences in the future, forcing the Treasury to borrow huge amounts of funds annually in the nation's financial markets.

Sources of Federal Government Funds

It is interesting to analyze what sources of revenue the federal government draws upon to fund its activities. Exhibit 24–2 presents information on the principal sources of federal revenue and major spending programs. On the revenue side, the bulk of incoming funds is derived from taxes levied against

EXHIBIT 24–2
Federal Government Revenues, Expenditures, and Net Budget Surplus or Deficit, 1980 (estimate) ($ millions)

Budget Item	Amounts	Percent of Total
Budget revenues by source:		
Individual income taxes	$227,322	45.23%
Corporation income taxes	70,987	14.13
Social insurance taxes and contributions	161,453	32.13
Excise taxes	18,455	3.67
Estate and gift taxes	6,011	1.20
Customs duties	8,447	1.68
Miscellaneous receipts	9,878	1.97
Total budget revenue	$502,553	100.00%
Budget expenditures by function:		
National defense	$125,830	23.67%
International affairs	8,213	1.55
General science, space technology	5,457	1.03
Energy	7,878	1.48
Natural resources and environment	11,456	2.16
Agriculture	4,269	0.80
Commerce and housing credit	3,390	0.64
Transportation	17,609	3.31
Community and regional development	7,281	1.37
Education, training, employment, and social services	30,210	5.68
Health	53,379	10.04
Income security	179,120	33.70
Veterans benefits and services	20,461	3.85
Administration of justice	4,388	0.83
General government	4,412	0.83
General purpose fiscal assistance	8,814	1.66
Interest	57,022	10.73
Allowances	1,398	0.26
Undistributed offsetting receipts	−19,021	−3.58
Total budget expenditures	$531,556	100.00%

SOURCES: Executive Office of the President and Office of Management and the Budget.

individual and family incomes. In 1980, for example, individuals paid $277 billion in income taxes, representing 45 percent of all federal revenues that year. Social security taxes supplied $161 billion—roughly a third of total federal income. Corporate income taxes were a distant third at 14 percent, while other taxes and fees for government services provided less than 10 percent of all federal revenues.

During the 1970s the share of federal revenues produced by corporate and personal income taxes declined. This was due to efforts by the Congress to reduce withholding taxes and increase personal deductions against individual income taxes. For example, the Tax Reduction Act of 1975 increased standard deductions, granted tax credits for low-income families, and provided for direct tax rebates to individuals. At the same time, however, payroll taxes for social insurance rose sharply as Congress attempted to rescue the Social Security system from ever deepening deficits. Responding to this increase in payroll taxes and a desire to stimulate a lagging economy, Congress passed the Tax Reduction Act of 1977, which further reduced personal withholding taxes.

These recent changes in tax rates suggest that the federal government has attempted in recent years to make the federal tax structure somewhat more responsive to the nation's economic problems. When the economy headed down into a recession, or inflation pushed individuals into higher tax brackets, Congress in the 1970s responded quickly with income tax reductions.[1] Unfortunately, scheduled increases in social security taxes and the rapid growth of corporate and individual income taxes associated with inflation outpaced legislated tax reductions. As a result, U.S. citizens were subjected to higher and higher effective tax rates during the 1970s.

The Economic Recovery Tax Act of 1981

In August 1981 Congress and the Reagan administration acted to reverse the trend toward higher tax rates, passing the Economic Recovery Tax Act. This new law brought about the most significant cuts in individual income tax rates in recent U.S. history. In addition, new accelerated depreciation allowances, investment tax credits, and tax incentives for business research and development expenditures were included in the recovery act in an attempt to

---

[1] One of the most serious limitations of fiscal policy in the past has been the long *lag* between the recognition of a need for new fiscal policies and the passage of new legislation. During the 1950s and 60s, for example, it often took several months before tax cuts or budgetary changes were made. By that time, the underlying economic problems might have changed so that the wrong kind of policy was being pursued. For example, a tax cut proposed to stimulate an economy mired in the depths of a recession often was passed several months later when a strong economic recovery was underway, adding fuel to inflation. There is some evidence, however, that fiscal policy lags have shortened drastically in recent years and Congress has become more flexible. For example, the Tax Reduction Act of 1975 was passed during the trough of the 1973–75 recession, only a few weeks after it was proposed. (See especially Board of Governors of the Federal Reserve System [4].)

increase investment spending and create jobs. The new tax law grew out of a comprehensive package of reductions in federal expenditures and tax rates proposed by the Reagan administration to step up production of goods and services as a way of reducing inflation.

While the recovery act is a comprehensive law with numerous sections, some of the more-important provisions may be noted here. The new law reduced individual income tax rates about 23 percent across-the-board over a period of 33 months beginning October 1, 1981. Effective January 1, 1982, the maximum individual income tax rate is reduced from 70 percent to 50 percent.[2] Beginning in January 1985, income tax brackets, standard deductions, and personal exemptions will be adjusted for the effects of inflation as measured by the Consumer Price Index (CPI). This last provision is designed to eliminate "bracket creep"—the tendency for inflation to push individual incomes into higher and higher tax brackets.

The ultimate purpose of the foregoing changes is to stimulate added saving by individuals and families, providing additional funds for business investment. To further encourage household saving, Congress created new tax-exempt savings certificates, which could be offered by depository institutions after September 30, 1981. Up to $1,000 ($2,000 on a joint tax return) in interest from these one-year certificates was exempted from income taxes. Beginning in 1985 individual taxpayers will be allowed to exclude from federal income taxes 15 percent of their net interest income (less interest deductions) up to a maximum of $3,000 (or $6,000 on a joint return). Employees who participate in a qualified retirement plan may deduct from taxable income any contributions to individual retirement accounts (IRAs) or voluntary contributions to their qualified retirement plans up to $2,000 or 100 percent of total compensation, whichever is less. The maximum unified estate and gift tax rate is gradually reduced between 1982 and 1985 from the current 70 percent to 50 percent.

In order to stimulate additional business capital outlays, the Recovery Act instituted an Accelerated Cost Recovery System (ACRS), which permits asset costs to be recovered over a predetermined period less than their estimated useful life. Under the new law most business assets will be depreciated over a 3-, 5-, 10-, or 15-year time period, provided they were acquired after December 31, 1980. Additional research and experimentation outlays made by businesses after June 1981 are eligible for a 25-percent tax credit. Corporations earning less than $50,000 a year will be permitted to retain more funds for investment through lower tax rates. Beginning in 1983, corporate tax rates will be reduced to 15 percent on the first $25,000 of taxable income and 18 percent on taxable income in excess of $25,000 but less than $50,000.

These and other provisions of the Economic Recovery Tax act are de-

---

[2] As noted in Chapter 9, this new top-bracket tax rate reduces the maximum effective tax rate on net long-term capital gains to 20 percent.

signed, not only to lighten current tax burdens carried by businesses and individuals, but also to dampen expectations of continuing inflation and rising taxes in the future. Combined with significant reductions in federal expenditures, also enacted by Congress in 1981, and restrictive monetary policies pursued by the Federal Reserve System, the new tax law represents the first fully coordinated fiscal and monetary attack on the nation's major economic problems in almost two decades.

Federal Government Expenditures

Even with lower tax rates, the federal government still collects an enormous volume of revenue from its citizens. For example, federal revenues exceeded $500 billion in 1980 and are expected to top $700 billion during 1982. Where does the federal government spend this money? What programs account for the bulk of federal expenditures?

Exhibit 24–2 indicates that more than half of all federal spending goes for national defense and income security programs, including social security and unemployment compensation. The latter programs are designed to sustain the spending power and standard of living of individuals retired, disabled, or temporarily unemployed. Income security programs have grown rapidly in recent years in order to provide an expanded menu of services to elderly and disabled Americans. For example, outlays for federal income security programs and federal grants to states and localities arising out of the federal revenue-sharing programs have jumped from about 9 percent of the nation's GNP in 1970 to about 13 percent as the decade of the 1980s began. Federal benefit payments under the social security program more than tripled during the 1970s, while outlays under the federal food stamp program increased almost 10 times over the same period. The growth of federal income security programs and grants has been especially difficult to control because, in many instances, funds can be spent without specific congressional authorization. In contrast, defense spending has fallen in both real terms and relative to total federal outlays, although the Reagan administration in 1981 announced a new program to expand U.S. defense outlays.

Viewing the federal government's budget as a whole, the share of the nation's economic activity accounted for by federal programs has been on a long-term uptrend. Federal expenditures accounted for nearly 22 percent of the nation's GNP in 1980, up from less than 20 percent a decade before. This growth relative to other sectors of the American economy represents both an expansion of existing programs and the recent birth of several new programs designed to deal with pressing social, economic, and environmental needs. Prominent examples include the regulation of energy production and prices administered by the Department of Energy (DOE), the management of natural resources and environmental quality, and the support of housing, community, and regional economic development through the Departments of Commerce and Housing and Urban Development (HUD). Many of these programs are seen as long-term in nature, reflecting the long-term character of the problems they address. It seems likely that balancing the federal budget and avoiding sizable budget deficits will be as difficult a process in the decade ahead as it has been during most of the earlier postwar period.

Effects of Federal Borrowing on the Financial System and the Economy

If the federal government runs a small budget deficit, it is possible for the Treasury to cover the shortfall in revenues by drawing upon its accumulated cash balances held at the Federal Reserve banks or even by issuing new currency. In recent years, however, federal deficits have been so large that substantial amounts of new debt securities have been issued in the money and capital markets. What impact do these Treasury borrowings have upon financial market conditions and the economy? The answer depends upon the *source* of borrowed funds. Exhibit 24–3 summarizes the probable effects of government borrowing designed to cover a budget deficit.

Borrowing from the Nonbank Public. For example, suppose the Treasury needs to borrow $20 billion, which it raises by selling government bonds to the nonbank public. As the public pays for these securities, it writes checks against its deposits held with depository institutions, initially reducing the size of the nation's money supply. As the checks are cleared and deposited in the Treasury's accounts at the Federal Reserve banks, legal reserves held by depository institutions decline by $20 billion.

To gauge the full effects of government borrowing, however, we must consider the fact that the government plans to *spend* its borrowed funds. In our example the Treasury will write checks totaling $20 billion against its Federal Reserve accounts and distribute these checks to the public. Deposits of the public rise by $20 billion, also increasing the legal reserves held by depository institutions.

On balance, after all transactions are completed, there is no change in the nation's money supply or in the total amount of reserves held by the banking system. However, there is likely to be an increase in total spending and income in the economy due to the fact that funds are transferred from those who purchase securities to members of the public receiving government checks. Aggregate consumption spending will probably increase, and, if the economy is at or near full employment, prices may rise. Initially, the increased sale of Treasury securities should put upward pressure on interest rates. Over a longer-run period, however, it is quite possible that interest rates will fall due to the higher levels of income and increased saving out of that income.

Borrowing from Depository Institutions. The effects of government borrowing are somewhat different if the borrowing takes place entirely from depository institutions. If we assume, once again, that the Treasury borrows $20 billion, deposit-type institutions will pay for the securities they purchase by drafts against their legal reserve accounts held at the Federal Reserve

EXHIBIT 24–3
Effects of Government Borrowing on the Financial Markets and the Economy

Borrowing from the Nonbank Public

	Federal Reserve Banks		Depository Financial Institutions	
	Assets	Liabilities	Assets	Liabilities
Sale of securities		Legal reserves of depository institutions −20 Government deposits +20	Legal reserves −20	Deposits of the public −20
Spending of borrowed funds		Government deposits −20 Legal reserves of depository institutions +20	Legal reserves +20	Deposits of the public +20

EFFECTS: No change in the money supply or total reserves; total spending in the economy and interest rates rise.

Borrowing from Depository Institutions

	Federal Reserve Banks		Depository Financial Institutions	
	Assets	Liabilities	Assets	Liabilities
Sale of securities		Legal reserves of depository institutions −20 Government deposits +20	Government securities +20 Legal reserves −20	
Spending of borrowed funds		Legal reserves of depository institutions +20 Government deposits −20	Legal reserves +20	Deposits of the public +20

EFFECTS: The money supply increases; total reserves are unchanged, but excess reserves fall due to increases in deposits; total spending and interest rates rise.

Borrowing from the Federal Reserve Banks

	Federal Reserve Banks		Depository Financial Institutions	
	Assets	Liabilities	Assets	Liabilities
Sale of securities	Government securities +20	Government deposits +20		
Spending of borrowed funds		Government deposits −20 Legal reserves of depository institutions +20	Legal reserves +20	Deposits of the public +20

EFFECTS: The money supply and total reserves increase, while total spending in the economy rises and interest rates tend to fall.

banks. Reserves of depository institutions drop by $20 billion, as shown in Exhibit 24–3, and the Treasury's deposits, of course, rise by a like amount. Once again, however, the Treasury spends these borrowed funds, resulting in an increase in deposits held by the public and in legal reserves. The money supply rises because public deposits increase.

On balance, after all transactions are completed, total legal reserves remain unchanged, but excess reserves fall because of the increase in deposits. There is also likely to be an increase in total spending and income in the economy as the public gains additional funds. Prices may rise if unemployment is low. Interest rates will increase in the short run with the increased quantity of government securities available. However, the gain in total spending should lead eventually to a decline in interest rates.

Borrowing from the Federal Reserve Banks. Still a third route for government borrowing would be to secure credit directly from the central bank. In the United States this could be done by having the Treasury issue securities directly to the Federal Reserve banks. However, borrowing directly from the Federal Reserve is a highly inflationary way for the federal government to raise money. Financially speaking, it is the equivalent of printing money. The Federal Reserve banks acquire securities and increase the Treasury's deposits by the same amount. Initially, there is no withdrawal of reserves from the banking system, nor does the public lose deposits. Instead, both legal reserves and the public's deposits rise by the amount of any borrowed funds actually *spent* by the Treasury.

In the example shown in Exhibit 24–3, the Treasury sells $20 billion in securities to the Federal Reserve banks, and its deposit accounts at the Fed rise by a like amount. As the Treasury spends the $20 billion, public deposits and reserves rise, causing increases in the nation's money supply, total spending, and income. Interest rates tend to fall due to the increase in income, which generates added savings. Because direct Treasury borrowing from the Federal Reserve is potentially inflationary, it is closely monitored by Congress. Only in times of national emergency, such as a major economic recession, would this fund-raising device likely be used on a significant scale.

Effects of the Retirement of Government Debt on the Financial System and the Economy

Occasionally, the federal government collects more in revenue than it spends, running a budget surplus. By definition, a budget surplus implies that the government withdraws a greater amount of funds from the economy in the form of tax collections than it puts back into the economy through spending. The Treasury could save these surplus funds to cover deficits in later years. However, this is usually unpopular from a political standpoint. It is more likely that a budget surplus would be used to retire debt previously issued. But the impact of government debt retirement on the economy and the financial system depends upon who happens to hold the debt securities the government plans to retire.

Retiring Government Debt Held by the Nonbank Public.   Suppose the securities scheduled for retirement are held by individuals and institutions not a part of the banking system. In this case, there will be little or no change in the nation's money supply or in the reserves held by depository institutions.

This is illustrated in Exhibit 24–4, where the act of retiring government debt is separated into two steps. In the first step we assume the U.S. Treasury collects a surplus of $20 billion in tax revenues. This might arise, for example, if the federal government spent $100 billion but collected $120 billion in taxes from the public. Clearly, the public's deposits will drop *net* $20 billion. Moreover, as members of the public write checks against their transactions deposits to pay taxes, legal reserves of depository institutions will also fall a net $20 billion. The Treasury's deposits at the Federal Reserve banks will rise by a like amount.

Assume now that the Treasury uses its surplus funds to retire securities held by the nonbank public. Security holders receive government checks totaling $20 billion, which are deposited in bank and nonbank thrift institutions. Legal reserves of these institutions rise by $20 billion. Of course, the Treasury now loses the same amount of money from its deposits at the Federal Reserve as the government's checks are cleared. The public's deposits and therefore its money supply first decline and then rise by $20 billion, with reserves following the same path. Is there no effect, then, from retiring securities held by the nonbank public? Not likely, because the government has transferred money from the general public (taxpayers), with a high propensity to spend, to security investors who, as a group, tend to be heavy savers. The net effect is probably to *reduce* total spending in the economy. Prices of goods and services may fall and unemployment may rise. It is likely, too, that interest rates will decline because the total supply of securities is being reduced.

Retiring Government Debt Held by Depository Institutions.   What happens if the government uses its budget surplus to retire securities held by banks and other depository institutions? Initially, the effects are much the same. Funds are withdrawn from taxpayer deposit accounts and transferred to the U.S. Treasury's deposits at the Federal Reserve. Legal reserves of depository institutions fall by the amount of the tax surplus (in Exhibit 24–3 by $20 billion). Now, however, the surplus funds are paid to depository institutions, who turn their securities in to the Treasury. Legal reserves rise as the government spends down its $20 billion deposit.

In the short run, the money supply is reduced due to the drain of taxpayer funds. Total legal reserves are unchanged, first falling and then rising. Note, however, that excess reserves must increase because total legal reserves are unchanged when deposits fall. In the long run the nation's money supply will

EXHIBIT 24–4
Effects of Retiring Government Debt on the Financial Markets and the Economy

Retiring Government Securities Held by the Nonbank Public

	Federal Reserve Banks			Depository Financial Institutions			
	Assets	Liabilities		Assets		Liabilities	
Collection of tax surplus		Legal reserves of depository institutions	−20	Legal reserves	−20	Deposits of taxpayers	−20
		Government deposits	+20				
Retiring government securities		Government deposits	−20	Legal reserves	+20	Deposits of security holders	+20
		Legal reserves of depository institutions	+20				

EFFECTS: No change in money supply or in bank reserves; but total spending tends to fall, since funds move from active to passive spenders; interest rates decline.

Retiring Government Securities Held by Depository Institutions

	Federal Reserve Banks			Depository Financial Institutions		
	Assets	Liabilities		Assets	Liabilities	
Collection of tax surplus		Legal reserves of depository institutions	−20	Legal reserves −20	Deposits of taxpayers	−20
		Government deposits	+20			
Retiring government securities		Legal reserves of depository institutions	+20	Government securities −20		
		Government deposits	−20	Legal reserves +20		

EFFECTS: Money supply falls in short run, while total bank reserves are unchanged. Excess reserves increase due to a fall in deposits. Total spending and interest rates decline.

Retiring Government Securities Held by the Federal Reserve Banks

	Federal Reserve Banks			Depository Financial Institutions		
	Assets	Liabilities		Assets	Liabilities	
Collection of tax surplus		Legal reserves of depository institutions	−20	Legal reserves −20	Deposits of taxpayers	−20
		Government deposits	+20			
Retiring government securities	Government securities −20	Government deposits	−20			

EFFECTS: Money supply and total reserves decrease by the amount of the budget surplus; total spending and interest rates decline.

expand due to the gain in excess reserves. With fewer taxpayer funds, however, spending in the economy should decline, which may increase unemployment. Interest rates, too, will probably decline because fewer securities are now available to investors.

It should be clear from the example above that budget surpluses and the retirement of government debt tend to slow down economic activity and therefore could be used as a vehicle to combat inflation. In fact, the announced goal of the Reagan administration is to reduce government expenditures and achieve federal budget surpluses by 1984, "breaking the back" of inflation. If the federal government wanted to have a *maximum* deflationary impact on the economy, whose government securities should it retire? The banking system's? No! The Treasury could have the greatest antiinflationary impact by retiring government securities held by the Federal Reserve banks. This approach would be the equivalent of destroying money.

Retiring Government Debt Held by the Federal Reserve Banks. As the bottom panel of Exhibit 24–3 shows, retiring government securities held by the Federal Reserve drains funds from taxpayers. However, those funds are *not* returned to the private spending stream. Instead, the government uses its increased deposits to pay off the Federal Reserve banks and retrieve securities they hold. Legal reserves of the banking system and the nation's money supply decline by the full amount of the budget surplus. Spending, interest rates, and the prices of goods and services are likely to fall as well.

Treasury Tax and Loan Accounts

In our discussion of the effects of government borrowing and debt retirement, we have omitted a technical detail which does not affect the final outcome of the process but sometimes has interesting effects upon the financial system in the short run. The fact is that monies flowing to the Treasury from the public rarely go directly to the Treasury's checking accounts at the Federal Reserve banks. Instead, federal tax collections and monies from the sale of federal securities are placed temporarily in government-owned accounts kept with commercial banks and other depository institutions. These so-called Tax and Loan Accounts (or T&L Accounts, as they are usually called) reside in approximately 12,000 depository institutions which have qualified to hold Treasury funds. The purpose of the T&L system is to prevent a massive and sudden withdrawal of funds from the banking system each time the Treasury sells securities or collects taxes. In the absence of T&L Accounts, interest rates undoubtedly would soar and credit conditions would suddenly tighten each time the Treasury drew upon the private sector for funds.

MANAGEMENT OF THE FEDERAL DEBT

As we noted at the beginning of this chapter, one of the most important activities of the Treasury today is managing the huge public debt of the

United States. Arising from war and the creation of many new federal spending programs in recent years, the U.S. public debt is the largest single collection of securities available in the financial system today. Securities issued directly by the Treasury, which make up the bulk of the public debt, are regarded by investors as having zero *default risk* because the federal government possesses both taxing power and the power to create money. The government, unless it is overthrown by war or revolution, can always pay its bills.

Government securities do carry *market risk,* however, because their prices fluctuate with changes in demand and supply. In fact, the longer the term to maturity of a government security, the more market risk it possesses. Treasury bills, the shortest-term government IOU, have relatively stable prices compared to long-term government bonds and notes.

The principal role of government securities in the financial system is to provide *liquidity*. Corporations, commercial banks, insurance companies, and other major institutional investors rely heavily on government securities as a readily marketable reserve to be drawn upon when cash is needed quickly. While private debt securities do carry higher explicit yields than government debt of comparable maturity, the greater liquidity and marketability of government securities represents an added return to the investor.

The Size and Growth of the Public Debt

How much money does the federal government owe? As shown in Exhibit 24–5, the gross public debt of the United States totaled more than $930 billion in December 1980. On a per capita basis, the public debt amounts to about $4,000 for every man, woman, and child living in the United States.

EXHIBIT 24–5
The Public Debt of the United States, December 1980 ($ billions)

Types of Securities		Amount
Interest-bearing debt.....................		$928.9
Marketable		$623.2
Bills	216.1	
Notes	321.6	
Bonds	85.4	
Nonmarketable		$305.7
State and local government series	23.8	
Foreign issues	24.0	
Savings bonds and notes	72.5	
Government account series	185.1	
Non-interest-bearing debt		1.3
Total gross public debt............		$930.2

SOURCE: Board of Governors of the Federal Reserve System, *Federal Reserve Bulletin,* various issues.

How did the federal debt become so huge? Wars, recessions, inflation, and the rapid expansion of social programs have been the principal causes. The federal government's debt was insignificant until the Great Depression of the 1930s, when the administration of President Franklin Roosevelt chose to borrow heavily to fund government programs and provide jobs. Even so, the public debt amounted to scarcely more than $50 billion at the beginning of World War II. The public debt multiplied five times over during the war years, however, approaching $260 billion by the end of World War II. Embroiled in the most destructive and costly war in history, the United States government borrowed and taxed away resources from the private sector to build tanks, planes, ships, and other war materials in enormous quantities.

For a brief period following World War II, it appeared that much of the public debt might be repaid. However, the Korean War intervened in the early 1950s, followed by a series of deep recessions when government tax revenues declined. Early in the 1960s the public debt reached $300 billion (see Exhibit 24–6). The advent of the Vietnam War and rapid inflation during the late 1960s and 1970s sent the debt soaring above its earlier levels. During the 70s rising inflation was combined with a sharp expansion in federal programs to provide aid to the elderly, support for research, and funding for social welfare programs. Between 1970 and 1980 the public debt of the United States more than doubled, rising from just under $400 billion to well over $900 billion. As the decade of the 80s began, it seemed certain the public debt would soon climb over $1 trillion.

Is this much debt simply too much? Have we as a society borrowed beyond our means? The answer depends upon the standard (or base) used to gauge the size of the public debt. Measured against the national income (i.e., the earnings of individuals and businesses which can be taxed to repay the debt), the public debt has actually *declined* over the long term. For example, in 1980 the gross public debt amounted to just 44 percent of the U.S. national income, compared to well over 100 percent at the end of World War II. Moreover, other forms of debt in the U.S. economy total as much or more than the public debt. For example, total mortgage debt outstanding in 1980 was $1.45 trillion, while corporate IOUs stood at more than $900 billion. It should be remembered that U.S. government securities are at one and the same time debt obligations and also readily marketable, liquid assets to the millions of investors who hold them.

The Composition of the Public Debt

The public debt consists of a wide variety of government IOUs with differing maturities, interest rates, and other features. A small amount—less than 1 percent—carries no interest rate at all. This *non-interest-bearing public debt* consists of paper currency and coins issued by the U.S. Treasury Department, including silver certificates, greenbacks, and national bank notes,

EXHIBIT 24–6
Public Debt of the United States, 1946–80 ($ billions)

Year	Total Interest-Bearing Debt	Total Non-Interest-Bearing Debt	Total Gross Public Debt	Year	Total Interest-Bearing Debt	Total Non-Interest-Bearing Debt	Total Gross Public Debt
1946	$257.6	$1.5	$259.1	1964	$313.6	$0.7	$314.3
1947	254.2	1.4	255.6	1965	316.5	0.7	317.2
1948	250.6	1.1	251.7	1966	325.0	0.6	325.6
1949	255.0	1.1	256.1	1967	341.2	0.6	341.8
1950	254.3	1.2	255.4	1968	355.2	1.1	356.2
1951	257.1	1.1	258.1	1969	366.2	1.2	367.4
1952	265.3	0.8	266.1	1970	387.3	1.1	388.3
1953	272.9	0.9	273.8	1971	422.4	1.7	424.1
1954	275.7	1.5	277.2	1972	447.3	2.0	449.3
1955	277.8	1.3	279.1	1973	467.8	1.1	469.9
1956	274.2	1.3	275.5	1974	491.6	1.1	492.7
1957	272.9	1.3	274.2	1975	575.7	1.0	576.6
1958	280.8	1.3	282.2	1976	652.5	1.1	653.5
1959	287.7	1.0	288.7	1977	715.2	3.7	718.9
1960	286.8	0.9	287.7	1978	782.4	6.8	789.2
1961	292.7	1.0	293.6	1979	844.0	1.2	845.1
1962	299.2	1.0	300.2	1980	928.9	1.3	930.2
1963	305.2	0.8	306.0				

SOURCES: Board of Governors of the Federal Reserve System, *Banking and Monetary Statistics*, 1941–70; and *Federal Reserve Bulletin*, various monthly issues.

which are gradually being retired as they are turned in by the public. Virtually all paper money in circulation today is Federal Reserve notes, which are not officially a part of the public debt but obligations of the Federal Reserve banks.

More than 99 percent of all federal debt securities are interest bearing and may be divided into two broad groups—marketable securities and nonmarketable securities. By definition, *marketable* securities may be traded any number of times before they reach maturity. In contrast, *nonmarketable* securities must be held by the original purchaser until they mature or are redeemed by the Treasury. It is the marketable debt over which the Treasury exercises the greatest measure of control and which has the greatest impact on the cost and availability of credit in the nation's financial markets.

Marketable Public Debt

The marketable public debt totaled $623 billion at year-end 1980, representing exactly two thirds of all interest-bearing U.S. government obligations. As Exhibit 24–5 reveals, the marketable public debt today is composed of just three types of securities—Treasury bills, notes, and bonds. By law, a U.S. Treasury bill must mature in one year or less. In contrast, U.S. Treasury notes range in original maturity from 1 year to 10 years, while Treasury bonds may carry any maturity, though generally they have a maturity at issue of more than 10 years.[3]

Under federal law, Treasury bonds can carry a maximum interest rate of 4¼ percent, unless special exemption from this legal interest-rate ceiling is granted by Congress. Because only limited exemptions have been granted and interest rates have been far higher than 4¼ percent in recent years, the proportion of long-term bonds making up the Treasury's marketable debt has declined significantly. In contrast, Treasury bills and notes carry no legal interest-rate ceiling. Moreover, with their greater liquidity and marketability, bills and notes have been especially attractive to investors in recent years. As shown in Exhibit 24–7, bills and notes represented about 40 percent of all marketable government obligations in 1960; by 1980, however, these securities accounted for more than 85 percent of the marketable public debt.

---

[3] Both Treasury notes and bonds bear interest at a fixed rate payable semiannually, while bills do not carry a fixed rate. Bonds can carry a call option, allowing the Treasury to redeem them before maturity with four months' notice. Notes and bonds are issued in denominations of $1,000, $5,000, $10,000, $100,000, and $1 million, while bills are available in denominations of $10,000, $15,000, $50,000, $100,000, $500,000, and $1 million. Payment for purchases of Treasury securities generally must be made in cash, immediately available funds, the exchange of eligible securities (accepted at par value), or by check to the Federal Reserve banks or to the Treasury, provided the check is issued early enough to clear by the required payment date.

EXHIBIT 24–7
Volume of Marketable U.S. Government Debt by Type of Security,
Year-End ($ billions)

Year	Total	Bills	Certificates	Notes	Bonds
1960	$189.0	$ 32.4	$18.4	$ 51.3	$ 79.8
1961	196.0	37.4	5.5	71.5	75.5
1962	203.0	45.2	22.7	53.7	78.4
1963	207.6	49.5	10.9	58.7	86.4
1964	212.5	52.5	—	59.0	97.0
1965	214.6	53.7	—	50.2	104.2
1966	218.0	57.4	5.9	48.3	99.2
1967	226.5	61.4	—	61.4	95.2
1968	236.8	66.0	—	76.5	85.3
1969	235.9	71.3	—	85.4	69.9
1970	247.7	80.6	—	101.2	58.6
1971	262.0	97.5	—	114.0	50.6
1972	269.5	103.9	—	121.5	44.1
1973	270.2	107.8	—	124.6	37.8
1974	282.9	119.7	—	129.8	33.4
1975	363.2	157.5	—	167.1	38.6
1976	421.3	164.0	—	216.7	40.6
1977	459.9	161.1	—	251.8	47.0
1978	487.5	161.7	—	265.8	60.0
1979	530.7	172.6	—	283.4	74.7
1980	623.2	216.1	—	321.6	85.4

SOURCE: Board of Governors of the Federal Reserve System, *Banking and Monetary Statistics*, 1941–70; and *Federal Reserve Bulletin*, various issues.

Nonmarketable Public Debt

The nonmarketable public debt consists mainly of Government Account series securities issued by the Treasury to various government agencies and trust funds (see Exhibit 24–5). These agencies and trust funds include the Social Security Administration, the Rural Electrification Administration, the Tennessee Valley Authority, and several smaller government agencies. As these governmental units accumulate funds, they turn them over to the Treasury in exchange for special, nonmarketable IOUs, thus reducing the federal government's activity in the open market.

Another significant component of the nonmarketable debt is United States Savings Bonds and Notes, sold to the general public in small denominations. The volume of Savings Bonds increased during the 60s and 70s, reaching a high of almost $81 billion in 1978. Then, soaring interest rates in the open market encouraged even small savers to invest their funds elsewhere, particularly in money market mutual funds. By year-end 1980 the amount of Savings Bonds outstanding sagged to about $72 billion, or less than 8 percent of the public debt.

As we will discuss later in Chapter 26, holdings of U.S. dollars by foreign governments and investors have expanded enormously in recent years due to oil imports and the flow of American capital to Europe, Asia, the Middle East, and the Far East. Because large foreign holdings of dollars and dollar deposits represent a constant threat to the value of the U.S. dollar in international markets, the Treasury periodically issues nonmarketable dollar-denominated securities to attract these overseas funds. In order to increase U.S. government holdings of foreign currencies which can be used to settle international claims, the Treasury also occasionally issues foreign-currency-denominated securities to investors abroad. These dollar-denominated and foreign-currency-denominated issues totaled $24 billion in 1980, representing about 8 percent of the nonmarketable portion of the public debt.

One of the most rapidly growing segments of the nonmarketable debt consists of special Treasury issues sold exclusively to state and local governments. These securities provide a temporary investment outlet for the funds raised by local governments when they borrow in the open market. Special issues to state and local governments totaled almost $24 billion in 1980, about 8 percent of all Treasury nonmarketable securities.

Investors in U.S. Government Securities

Who holds the public debt of the United States? Each month the Treasury makes estimates of the distribution of its securities among various groups of investors, drawing upon data supplied by the Federal Reserve banks, U.S. government agencies and trust funds, banking associations, trade organizations, and government security dealers. The results from a recent Treasury ownership survey are shown in Exhibit 24–8.

It is evident from the survey that most Treasury debt—about two thirds—is held by private investors. Rather surprising to many observers, however, is the large proportion of the public debt—about one third—held by the federal government itself. For example, in November 1980, U.S. government agencies and trust funds, including the Social Security Trust Fund, Tennessee Valley Authority, and other federal departments, owned almost $190 billion in public debt, or more than one fifth of the total. The Federal Reserve banks held $120 billion in marketable Treasury issues, about 13 percent of all public securities outstanding.

While the ratio of government to private holdings of federal securities has declined over the past decade, the sheer size of the government's holdings of its own debt is viewed with alarm by some analysts. A large volume of government debt out of circulation in federal vaults tends to "thin out" the market for government securities, reducing the volume of trading. Other factors held constant, interest rates and security prices become more volatile and unpredictable, discouraging investment. This can be critical, because the market for United States government securities is the anchor of the whole financial system.

EXHIBIT 24–8
Principal Investors in U.S. Treasury Debt, 1980 ($ billions, end of period)

Investor Group	Amount Held November 1980	Percent of Total Holdings
Federal government:		
U.S. government agencies and trust funds	$189.7	20.8%
Federal Reserve banks........................	120.4	13.2
Private investors:		
Commercial banks	101.8	11.1
Mutual savings banks	5.6	0.6
Insurance companies........................	15.4	1.7
Other companies	24.8	2.7
State and local governments	74.6	8.2
Individuals		
Savings	72.5	7.9
Other securities	52.5	5.7
Total private investors	603.2	66.0
Foreign and international	132.5	14.5
Other investors*	123.4	13.5
Total for all investor groups	$913.3	100.0%

* Includes savings and loan associations, nonprofit institutions, corporate pension trust funds, dealers and brokers, certain government deposit accounts, and government-sponsored agencies.
SOURCE: Board of Governors of the Federal Reserve System, *Federal Reserve Bulletin,* February 1981.

Among private holders of the public debt, commercial banks and individuals are at or near the top of the list. In November 1980 individual investors held $125 billion in public securities, the majority in U.S. Savings Bonds. Commercial banks were close behind with more than $100 billion in government issues. Other financial institutions with significant holdings of U.S. government securities included insurance companies, mutual savings banks, and savings and loan associations. However, these institutions have been reducing their holdings of U.S. government securities relative to other investments in recent years in response to the attractive yields available on private debt securities. Nevertheless, insurance companies, savings banks, pension funds, and other financial institutions still hold substantial dollar amounts of U.S. Treasury securities as a ready reserve of liquid funds. Nonfinancial corporations held almost $25 billion in U.S. Treasury issues on the survey date. As is the case with financial institutions, nonfinancial corporations hold U.S. government securities primarily as a liquidity reserve.

The proportion of the public debt held by foreign and international investors, including foreign central banks, foreign governments, and other international investors, has been rising rapidly in recent years and totaled nearly $133 billion in 1980. The rapid growth of foreign holdings reflects a rise in U.S. imports of goods and services, especially oil imports, which has led foreign investors to build up substantial dollar deposits in banks abroad. These investors have converted many of their dollars into purchases of

Treasury securities in the New York money market and into foreign-currency-denominated securities purchased directly from the U.S. Treasury.

A Trend toward Shorter Maturities

One of the most-serious problems which the Treasury faces today in the debt-management field is a long-term trend toward shorter and shorter maturities. As shown in Exhibit 24–9, the percentage of marketable federal

EXHIBIT 24–9
Distribution of the U.S. Marketable Public Debt by Maturity

	Percent of Total Maturing within:				
Year	1 Year	1–5 Years	5–10 Years	Over 10 Years	Total
1946	31.1%	22.4%	15.5%	31.0%	100%
1950	38.1	21.9	11.4	28.6	100
1955	37.1	23.5	19.2	20.2	100
1960	39.0	38.3	9.9	12.8	100
1965	43.5	28.2	16.3	11.9	100
1970	49.8	32.2	9.1	7.8	100
1975	55.0	30.9	7.3	6.8	100
1980*	47.7	31.7	8.7	12.0	100

* Figures as of November 1980.
SOURCES: U.S. Treasury Department, *Treasury Bulletin;* and Board of Governors of the Federal Reserve System, *Federal Reserve Bulletin*, various issues.

securities over five years to maturity was a full 40 percent in 1950. By 1980, however, this long-term component of the public debt was scarcely more than 20 percent of all marketable issues. The average maturity of the entire marketable public debt in 1980 was about half what it was at the end of World War II. Today, nearly half the debt comes due each year.

This is a potentially serious problem because it requires the Treasury to come to market more frequently to retire or refund debt as securities pile up in shorter maturities. Moreover, in recent years the Federal Reserve has been especially cautious about making significant changes in the posture of monetary policy at a time when the Treasury is actively in the market selling notes and bonds.

If the Treasury must refund and issue debt more frequently, this reduces the period of time over which the Federal Reserve can make significant changes in monetary policy. Suppose, for example, that the Fed wanted to increase interest rates and reduce the availability of credit at precisely the time the Treasury was coming to market with a new issue of bonds. Clearly, the government would have some difficulty in selling its bonds in an environment of rising interest rates and falling bond prices. If maturing securities were coming due and had to be paid off, the Treasury might not be able to raise enough cash to meet its obligations. Conditions in the financial marketplace might border on panic. Therefore, a public debt of short maturity tends to reduce the flexibility of monetary policy. It limits the options open to the Federal Reserve.

Many analysts believe that a substantial buildup of short-term government debt contributes to inflation. Of special concern is the proportion of government securities within one year to final maturity—the so-called floating debt. Treasury obligations coming due within one year totaled $288 billion at the end of 1980, accounting for almost 48 percent of all marketable federal securities. These short-term issues are the most liquid and readily marketable of all securities in the American financial system. Most are held by commercial banks and other lenders of funds, who use them as an extra source of funds when reserves are scarce and credit demand is high. If the Federal Reserve wishes to reduce the growth of money and credit, it must wrestle with the problem that banks and other financial institutions can sell off their floating-debt issues and generate still more credit. Commercial banks alone held nearly $24 billion of such short-term issues in 1980, representing a huge stockpile of ready liquidity. It is perhaps more than just coincidence that both inflation and the short-term federal debt have grown rapidly in recent years.

Methods of Offering Treasury Securities

Management of the public debt is a complicated task. Treasury debt managers are called upon continually to make decisions about raising new money and refunding maturing securities. They must decide what kinds of securities to issue, which maturities would appeal to investors, and the form in which an offering of securities should be made.

Cash Offerings and Exchange Offerings. For example, the Treasury can make a *cash offering,* in which buyers simply pay cash for any securities they receive. On the other hand, if some existing securities must be refunded (rolled over), the Treasury can offer new securities just to holders of the maturing issues. This is called an *exchange offering.* In this type of sale, investors who want to acquire a portion of the new issue must purchase securities from those who hold the maturing issue. The maturing securities are known as "rights" to the new debt being offered.

The choice between a cash offering and an exchange offering can be a difficult one because of changing market conditions. For example, if interest rates rise, holders of maturing securities may not wish to acquire any new Treasury securities offered in exchange; instead, they will seek the higher yields available on other securities sold in the open market. Those investors electing not to exchange with the Treasury will demand cash payment instead. The Treasury may find itself with a substantial amount of unsold securities and in the embarrassing position of not having sufficient cash to pay off holders of maturing issues. A cash offering usually solves this attrition problem. However, cash offerings have a far more powerful impact upon interest rates and security prices than exchange offerings do because they represent a net withdrawal of funds from the financial system. Nevertheless, since 1973 the Treasury has elected to use cash rather than exchange offerings, due primarily to the enormous volume of new securities which it has needed to sell.

Advance Refunding. From time to time the Treasury will conduct *advance refundings,* involving securities which may still be several years from final maturity. For example, during the 1960s the Treasury offered investors holding bonds less than 10 years from maturity the option to exchange these securities for new bonds carrying much longer maturities but also significantly higher yields. While the advance refundings increased the cost of carrying the public debt, they also lengthened its average maturity, reducing the frequency with which the Treasury was forced to borrow. Advance refundings have been discontinued in recent years in favor of cash sales due to the Treasury's heavy borrowing schedule.

The Auction Method. Today the *auction* method is the principal means of selling Treasury notes, bonds, and bills. While there are several different auction methods in use, all such techniques have a number of features in common. Both competitive and noncompetitive tenders are accepted from the public.[4] All noncompetitive bidders receive an allotment of securities from the auction up to a maximum amount determined by the Treasury. As we have seen, federal government agencies and trust funds and the Federal Reserve banks purchase and hold large amounts of Treasury issues. These agencies participate in virtually every auction but pay the price charged noncompetitive bidders. They receive a special allotment of securities in exchange for their maturing issues after the regular auction is conducted.

Types of Treasury Auctions. The Treasury has used three different auction methods in recent years:

1. Price auctions.
2. Dutch auctions.
3. Yield auctions.

The *price auction* is used regularly for sales of Treasury bills and occasionally for note and bond sales. Under this method, the Treasury sets the coupon rate and minimum price it is willing to accept on notes and bonds and

---

[4] Those investors tendering an offer in a Treasury auction must submit a deposit of 5 percent of the amount bid, unless they represent an institution specifically exempt from the required deposit. Institutions that can submit tender offers without deposit include commercial banks, state and local governments, public pension funds, federally insured savings and loan associations, major government securities dealers, Federal Reserve banks, U.S. government agencies and trust funds, foreign central banks and governments, and selected international organizations.

announces the amount of securities available for public sale.[5] Competitive bids are accepted with prices above or below par, accurate to two decimal places (assuming a par value of $100). Securities are allotted first to the highest bidder and then to those investors submitting successively lower bids until the amount available (less any noncompetitive tenders) has been exhausted. Noncompetitive bidders pay the average prices established by the competitive bidder.

On a few occasions, the Treasury has employed the *uniform price,* or *Dutch auction,* method to sell long-term bonds. After the competitive bids are in, the Treasury proceeds to award all available securities (once noncompetitive orders are filled) beginning with the highest bidder on down until all securities are allocated. However, the price actually paid by all bidders is that tendered by the *lowest* accepted competitive bid. Therefore, all investors receiving securities in a Dutch auction pay the same price.

As with the price auction method, however, the Treasury sets the coupon rate on new notes and bonds prior to the date of the auction, and the public must file competitive price bids on the basis of 100. For example, an investor might bid 99.50—which would represent a bid of $9,950 for a $10,000 security. All competitive bids must be accurate to two decimal places and in multiples of 0.05—such as 99.50, 99.55, 99.60, etc. The Treasury always sets a minimum price and will not accept tender offers for less than that price.

The auction method used most often for Treasury notes and bonds is known as a *yield auction.* Neither the price nor the coupon rate on the new securities is set in advance by the Treasury. Instead, it merely announces the amount of securities available and calls for yield bids. Investors submitting competitive bids must express their offers on an annual percentage yield basis accurate to two decimal places. For example, we might place a yield bid of 11.75 percent in the current auction. When the auction closes, noncompetitive bidders will first receive their securities, and next those bidding the lowest annual percentage yield (i.e., the highest price) will be awarded their securities. Awards will continue to be made at successively higher yields (lower prices) until the issue is exhausted. Investors submitting competitive bids pay the price appropriate for the yield they bid, while noncompetitive bidders are assessed the price equivalent to the average yield from all the competitive bids.

Subscription Offerings. Occasionally in the past, when the Treasury has been forced to issue a large volume of notes and bonds, it has employed a *subscription offering.* In this case the Treasury announces in advance the price, interest coupon, required deposits, method of allocating available securities, and amount of the issue. Investors subscribe for the amount of

---

[5] See Chapter 12 for a more-detailed discussion of the weekly price auctions for U.S. Treasury bills. Unlike notes and bonds, the Treasury does *not* set minimum prices in bill auctions, nor do bills carry coupon rates.

securities they wish to acquire based on the announced terms. Frequently such issues are oversubscribed and the Treasury must devise special allotment procedures. Historically, the Treasury has given preference to small investors who, it believes, tend to be *permanent* holders of its securities rather than speculators.

In subscription offerings the Treasury often accepts *preferred tenders,* which are usually limited to a maximum of $500,000. Preferred tenders may be submitted by any investor along with a regular tender offer and have priority in an oversubscribed issue.[6]

Marketing Techniques.   Unlike borrowers in the corporate and municipal bond markets, the Treasury does not use dealers to underwrite its new debt issues. Rather, it places new securities directly with the investing public. New Treasury bills, notes, and bonds can be bought directly from the Treasury Department or from the Treasury's agents—the Federal Reserve banks and their branches. Bids or tender offers are accepted from private and government investors at the Federal Reserve banks until 1:30 P.M., Eastern Standard Time, the day the new securities are sold. Individuals may also file bids for new Treasury securities with the Bureau of the Public Debt in Washington, D.C. Many investors place orders for new Treasury issues through a security broker or dealer, commercial bank, or nonbank financial institution which offers such a service.

Before issuing new notes and bonds, the Treasury will consult with Federal Reserve officials and government securities dealers as to the appropriate terms to be offered. It also frequently is necessary to tailor the terms of a new issue to appeal to investor groups who have the necessary funds to spend.

Book Entry.   More than 80 percent of the marketable public debt is issued today in *book-entry form.* This means that the investor does not receive an engraved certificate representing the Treasury's debt obligation. Instead, the investor's name and amounts of securities held are recorded on the books of a bank or at the Treasury Department. Member banks of the Federal Reserve System are permitted to hold security safekeeping accounts at the Reserve banks where their own security holdings and those of their customers are recorded. As interest is received or securities are sold or purchased, banks will credit or debit their own or their customers' accounts accordingly.

The Treasury also accepts book-entry accounts from the public, subject to a number of restrictions. While there is no charge for the Treasury's bookkeeping services, securities held there cannot be sold until they are transferred to a bank book-entry account held at the Federal Reserve. Moreover,

---

[6] One disadvantage of a preferred tender, however, is that the Treasury's rules require a deposit of 20 percent of the par value of any securities bid for. In contrast, a regular tender carries a deposit requirement of only 5 percent unless the investor is an exempt institution. As we noted earlier, exempt institutions include most federally insured depository institutions; state, local, and foreign governments; pension funds; major securities dealers; the Federal Reserve; and U.S. government accounts.

such transfers are not allowed less than 30 days before a security matures nor sooner than 10 days after issue. When a security matures, the Treasury will mail the investor of record a check in the amount of its par value plus any interest due, unless notified at least 10 days prior to the maturity date that these monies should be reinvested in new securities.

Book entry is the safest form in which to hold any security since this method significantly reduces the risk of theft. Some investors still prefer the much-riskier *bearer* securities, however, in which the engraved certificates are actually kept in the investor's possession. The ownership of such securities is not recorded on the books of a bank or the Treasury Department nor is there any notice to the Treasury of a change of ownership when such securities are traded in the open market.

Bearer notes and bonds with interest coupons attached are known as *coupon securities*. In order for the holder to receive interest, the coupons must be detached and presented to the Treasury Department or to a Federal Reserve bank. Similarly, when bearer securities are redeemed or rolled over at maturity in exchange for new securities, they must be presented to the Treasury or to the Federal Reserve banks for these purposes.

Registered Securities.   A safer way to hold Treasury securities is in *registered* form. A Treasury issue is registered when the securities are engraved with the owner's name, which is also recorded on the Treasury's books. While the owner physically holds registered securities, the Treasury automatically pays (without notice or receipt of coupon) any interest due on these securities to the owner of record.

If Treasury securities held by an investor are lost, stolen, destroyed, or mutilated, the investor *may* be able to recover his or her funds. Each year the Treasury honors a few such claims after careful screening, but usually only after the investor posts an indemnity bond.

Other Services Offered Investors.   In order to encourage greater participation in the government securities market and stimulate demand for new Treasury issues, both the Federal Reserve and the Treasury offer a number of services to investors. Securities held in book-entry accounts at the Federal Reserve banks may be transferred by wire almost anywhere using the Fed's electronic wire transfer network. This device makes it easy to sell Treasury securities before maturity on a same-day basis.

The Goals of Federal Debt Management

Over the years the Treasury has pursued several different goals in the management of the public debt. These goals may be divided into two broad groups: (1) *housekeeping goals,* which pertain to the cost and composition of the public debt; and (2) *stabilization goals,* which have to do with the impact of the debt upon the economy and the financial markets.

Minimize Interest Costs.   The most important housekeeping goal is to keep the interest burden of the public debt as low as possible. The Treasury has not always been successful in the pursuit of this goal, however. Today, the interest burden on the public debt is the third-largest category of federal expenditures, after welfare payments and national defense. As Exhibit 24–2 reveals, interest on the debt reached $57 billion, or more than 10 percent of total federal government spending, in fiscal 1980. This interest burden on the American taxpayer has been rising rapidly in the wake of inflation and record-high interest rates.

Reduce the Frequency of Refundings.   The Treasury also tries to minimize the number of "trips" it must make to the market to refund old securities or issue new ones. As we have seen, this housekeeping goal is particularly important to the Federal Reserve's conduct of monetary policy.

For several decades now the Fed has followed a loosely defined policy known as "even keel" when the Treasury is in the market offering a substantial volume of notes or bonds. Even keel policy calls for the Fed to exert a *steadying* influence on the financial markets, making sure that security trading is orderly and that changes in interest rates are moderate. In principal, "even keel" protects the Treasury's financing operations from catastrophic failure, as might occur if interest rates rose sharply and security prices plunged at the time of a Treasury refunding. Unfortunately, the Fed may be compelled to "even keel" the markets at a time when it should be pursuing a policy of tight money and higher interest rates to fight inflation.

Economic Stabilization.   A much broader goal of debt management is to stabilize the economy—promoting high employment and sustainable growth while avoiding rampant inflation. In strict terms this would involve issuing long-term Treasury securities in a period of economic expansion and issuing short-term securities in a period of recession. The long-term securities would tend to increase long-term interest rates and therefore act as a brake on private investment spending, slowing the economy down. On the other hand, issuing short-term securities during a recession keeps pressure off long-term interest rates and avoids discouraging investment spending which is needed to provide jobs.

Unfortunately, the goal of economic stabilization often conflicts with other debt-management goals, particularly the goal of minimizing the interest burden of the public debt. If the Treasury sells short-term securities in a period of expansion when interest rates are high and then rolls over those short-term securities into long-term bonds during a recession when rates are low, this strategy will tend to minimize the debt's average interest cost. The Treasury will be able to lock in cheap long-term rates.

From a stabilization point of view, however, this is exactly the wrong thing to do. The short-term debt will fuel inflation during an economic expansion, while long-term debt issued during a recession will drive up interest rates and reduce private investment. Like Federal Reserve officials, Treasury debt managers are confronted with tough choices among conflicting goals.

The Impact of Federal Debt Management on the Financial Markets and the Economy

What effect do Treasury debt-management activities have on the financial markets and the economy? This is a subject of heated debate among economists and financial analysts. Most experts agree that in the short run the financial markets become more agitated and interest rates tend to rise when the Treasury is borrowing, especially when new money is involved. A mere exchange of new for old securities usually has minimal effects, however, unless the offering is very large.

The longer-run impact of Treasury debt-management operations is less clear. Certainly the *liquidity* of the public's portfolio of securities changes, though we are uncertain by how much, or what the exact impact might be. For example, suppose $10 billion in Treasury bonds are maturing next month. Treasury debt managers decide to offer investors $10 billion in 10-year notes in exchange for the maturing bonds. The bonds, regardless of what their original maturity might have been, are now short-term securities (with one-month maturities). If investors accept the new 10-year notes in exchange for the one-month bonds, the average maturity of the public's security holdings obviously has lengthened, all else equal. Longer-term securities, as a rule, are less liquid than shorter-term securities.

Will this reduction in public liquidity affect spending habits and interest rates? The research evidence on this question is conflicting, with many studies finding little or no effect from debt-management activities.[7] However, there is some evidence that a lengthening of debt maturities in investor portfolios increases the public's demand for money and raises interest rates. In contrast, if the Treasury offers shorter-term securities, this tends to make the public's portfolio of securities more liquid and may reduce the demand for money. The result would be an increase in total spending for goods and services and, for a time, lower interest rates.

Still another possible debt-management impact is on the *shape of the yield curve*. Lengthening the average maturity of the debt tends to increase long-term interest rates relative to short rates. The yield curve assumes a steeper positive slope, favoring short-term investment over long-term investment. On the other hand, shortening the debt's maturity would tend to reduce longer-term interest rates and raise short-term rates. The yield curve would tend to flatten out, if positively sloped, or even turn down, favoring long-term investment over short-term investment. The net impact on total investment spending would depend upon whether private investment is more responsive to short-term interest rates or long-term interest rates. We believe that long-term rates are more critical than short-term rates for most business investment decisions.

---

[7] See especially the studies by Bowers (5), Lang and Rasche (10), Pierson (16), Roley (18), and Smith (19).

On balance, most authorities are convinced that the debt-management activities of the Treasury do *not* have a major impact upon economic conditions. The effects of debt-management operations appear to be secondary compared to the powerful impact of monetary and fiscal policy on the economy and financial markets. The optimal debt-management policy is probably one which makes Treasury refunding operations as *unobtrusive* as possible, especially where these operations might interfere with the activities of the Federal Reserve System. Nevertheless, debt management represents yet another policy tool that can be used by the federal government in the face of serious economic problems.

SUMMARY AND CONCLUSIONS

In this chapter we have examined the many roles played by the Treasury Department in financing federal expenditures and managing the huge public debt of the United States. We have noted that the federal government affects the nation's financial system through its taxing and spending activities—fiscal policy—and through refunding or refinancing the government's debt—debt management policy. Both tasks involve enormous amounts of money today. The public debt of the United States is rapidly approaching a trillion dollars in total volume, while federal expenditures in 1980 pushed close to $580 billion and are projected to exceed $700 billion in 1982. It should certainly come as no surprise that spending and borrowing of such magnitude can have powerful effects on interest rates, security prices, the availability of credit to all borrowers, and the pursuit of the nation's economic goals.

We have observed in this chapter that government borrowing tends to raise interest rates, increase the money supply, and add to total spending and demand in the economy. In general, the economy will grow faster, with reduced unemployment, when the government borrows and spends additional funds, but often at the price of more-rapid inflation and threats to the dollar abroad. Government budget surpluses, especially where these surpluses are used to retire government debt, often lead to lower interest rates, a decline in the nation's money supply, and reduced spending. A move toward more conservative fiscal policy and toward budget surpluses tends to dampen inflation and strengthen the dollar abroad but increases the risk of high unemployment and slower economic growth.

Management of the public debt can also be used to alter economic conditions, reduce unemployment, and counter inflation. We have noted in this chapter that, if the Treasury refunds maturing short-term securities with longer-term debt, it can reduce the liquidity of the public's security holdings. Interest rates tend to rise, credit becomes more difficult to obtain, and spending and employment tend to fall. Long-term Treasury borrowing, therefore, tends to slow the economy's rate of growth and reduces inflationary pressures. In contrast, a debt-management policy which emphasizes short-term government borrowing often leads to more-rapid economic expansion and reduced unemployment, but these are sometimes purchased at the price of higher inflation.

As we saw in the preceding chapter on the Federal Reserve System, government policymakers face few happy choices. The nation's goals of full employment, reasonable stability in prices, sustainable economic growth, and a stable balance of payments position are elusive targets. Successful fiscal, monetary, and debt-management policies require careful coordination among all branches of government, a farsighted view of national goals, and a firm determination to achieve those goals despite the political pressures of the moment.

STUDY QUESTIONS

1. What exactly is fiscal policy? Debt-management policy?
2. Explain how fiscal policy and debt-management policy might be used to fight inflation. How about unemployment?
3. How frequently have budget surpluses occurred during the past three decades? Can you explain why?
4. List from largest to smallest the principal sources of federal government revenue. What are the principal federal spending programs?
5. Describe the effects of government borrowing on the financial system and the economy. If the federal government wished to increase total spending in the economy the most, from whom should it borrow funds?
6. Describe the effects of retiring government securities on the financial system and the economy. Whose securities should be paid off if the federal government wants to have the maximum contractionary impact on the economy?
7. Explain the function of Treasury Tax and Loan Accounts.
8. What are the principal reasons investors purchase and hold U.S. government securities?
9. Describe the principal types of securities which make up the public debt of the United States. What portions of the debt can the Treasury most closely control?
10. List the principal holders of the public debt. What are the most-important trends in the ownership of federal securities?
11. What is happening to the average maturity of the public debt? Why is this trend important? What measures has the U.S. Treasury employed in the past to deal with the problem?
12. Define the following methods of selling U.S. Treasury securities and explain under what circumstances each might be used:
    a. Advance refunding.
    b. Cash offering.
    c. Exchange offering.
    d. Price auction.
    e. Dutch auction.
    f. Yield auction.
    g. Subscription offering.

13. What factors must Treasury officials consider when coming to market with a new security issue?

14. List the goals of Treasury debt management. What is the essential difference between the so-called housekeeping goals and the stabilization goals? To what extent do these goals conflict?

15. Explain how changes in the maturity structure of the public debt can affect interest rates, the yield curve, and spending for goods and services in the economy.

SELECTED REFERENCES

1. Aaron, Henry J. and A. Joseph Pechman, eds. *How Taxes Affect Economic Behavior*. Washington, D.C.: The Brookings Institution, 1981.

2. Bedford, Margaret E. "Recent Developments in Treasury Financing Techniques." *Monthly Review*, Federal Reserve Bank of Kansas City, July-August 1977, pp. 12–24.

3. Bindes, Alan S., and Robert M. Solow. "Analytical Foundations of Fiscal Policy." In *The Economics of Public Finance*. Washington, D.C.: The Brookings Institution, 1974.

4. Board of Governors of the Federal Reserve System. "The Federal Budget in the 1970's." *Federal Reserve Bulletin*, September 1978, pp. 701–14.

5. Bowers, David A. "The Liquidity Impact of Debt Management." *Southern Economic Journal*, April 1968, pp. 526–37.

6. Cox, William N. "Changes in the Treasury's Cash Management Procedures." *Economic Review*, Federal Reserve Bank of Atlanta, January-February 1978, pp. 14–16.

7. Cullison, William E. "Trends in Federal Taxation since 1950." *Economic Review*, Federal Reserve Bank of Richmond, May-June 1980, pp. 8–18.

8. "Federal Debt Management Policy: A Re-examination of the Issues." *Economic Review*, Federal Reserve Bank of Kansas City, February 1978, pp. 3–13.

9. Gordon, Robert J. "What Can Stabilization Policy Achieve?" *American Economic Review, Papers and Proceedings*, May 1978, pp. 335–41.

10. Lang, Richard W., and Robert H. Rasche. "Debt Management Policy and the Own-Price Elasticity of Demand for U.S. Government Notes and Bonds." *Review*, Federal Reserve Bank of St. Louis, September 1977, pp. 8–22.

11. Meyer, Lawrence H. "Financing Constraints and the Short-Run Response to Fiscal Policy." *Review*, Federal Reserve Bank of St. Louis, June-July 1980.

12. Meyer, Lawrence H., ed. *The Supply-Side Effects of Economic Policy*. Center for the Study of American Business and the Federal Reserve Bank of St. Louis, 1981.

13. Musgrave, Richard A., and Peggy B. Musgrave. *Public Finance in Theory and Practice*. New York: McGraw-Hill, 1973.

14. Ott, David J., and Attiat F. Ott. *Federal Budget Policy*. Washington, D.C.: The Brookings Institution, 1977.

15. Pechman, Joseph A. *Federal Tax Policy*. 3d ed. Washington, D.C.: The Brookings Institution, 1977.

16. Pierson, Gail. "Effect of Economic Policy on the Term Structure of Interest Rates." *Review of Economics and Statistics,* February 1970, pp. 1–11.

17. Pollock, Stephen H. "Off-Budget Federal Outlays." *Economic Review,* Federal Reserve Bank of Kansas City, March 1981, pp. 3–16.

18. Roley, V. Vance. "A Theory of Federal Debt Management." *Research Working Paper,* Federal Reserve Bank of Kansas City, March 1978.

19. Smith, Warren L. "Debt Management in the United States." In *Study of Employment, Growth, and Price Levels,* Joint Economic Committee. Washington, D.C.: U.S. Government Printing Office, 1960.

20. Tatom, John A. "We Are All Supply-Siders Now!" *Review,* Federal Reserve Bank of St. Louis, April 1981, pp. 18–30.

25

State and Local Governments in the Financial Markets

The borrowing and spending activities of state and local governments have been one of the most dynamic, rapidly growing segments of the U.S. financial system in recent years. Pressured by rising population and inflated costs, states, counties, school districts, and other local units of government have been forced to borrow in growing numbers in order to meet increased demands for their services. As we will see later in this chapter, the volume of state and local government borrowing has increased sixfold since 1950, totaling more than $300 billion in 1980.

Despite the rapid growth in borrowing by state and local governments, many investors consider state and local debt obligations a highly desirable investment medium due to their high quality, ready marketability, and tax-exemption feature. As we noted in Chapter 9, the interest income generated by state and local securities is exempt from federal income taxes, and most states exempt their own securities from state income taxes. As a result, these high-quality debt obligations (known as "municipals") appeal to such heavily taxed investors as commercial banks, top-income-bracket individuals, property-casualty insurance companies, and large nonfinancial corporations. In addition, an active secondary market permits the early resale of many state and local government bonds.

GROWTH OF STATE AND LOCAL GOVERNMENT BORROWING

The rapid growth of state and local government borrowing is reflected in Exhibit 25–1, which shows the total volume of municipal securities outstand-

EXHIBIT 25-1
Total Debt Issued by State and Local Governments in the United States, 1940-79 ($ billions)

Year	Debt Outstanding at Year-End	Year	Debt Outstanding at Year-End
1940	$ 20.3	1973	$188.5
1950	24.1	1974	206.6
1960	70.0	1975	219.9
1970	143.6	1976	240.5
1971	158.8	1977	259.7
1972	175.2	1978	282.1
		1979	300.1

SOURCES: U.S. Department of Commerce, Bureau of the Census, *1977 Census of Governments;* and Board of Governors of the Federal Reserve System, *Flow of Funds: Assets and Liabilities Outstanding, 1969-79.*

ing between the years 1940 and 1979. State and local government indebtedness grew slowly until the 1950s, when it nearly tripled. The volume of municipal debt doubled again during the 1960s and during the 1970s as well. In 1980 state and local debt outstanding had climbed above $300 billion, almost a third of the size of the federal government's debt.

What factors account for this strong record of growth in municipal borrowing? Rapid population and income growth are two of the most important causes. The U.S. population, spurred by a postwar baby boom, rose from less than 132 million in 1940 to an estimated 224 million in 1980, a gain of more than 90 million people (i.e., a 70 percent increase) in four decades. Rapid population growth implies that many government services, such as highways, public libraries, and lighting and sewer systems, must also expand rapidly. Tax revenues cannot provide all the monies needed to fund these facilities and services. Borrowings against future state and local government income also must grow commensurately.

Moreover, the nation's population growth has not been evenly spread across the landscape. Beginning in the 1950s a massive shift of the U.S. population began to take place out of the central cities into suburban areas. This demographic change was augmented during the 1970s by a movement of population and industry into small towns and rural areas to escape the social, political, and environmental problems of urban living. Smaller outlying communities were rapidly transformed into moderate-sized cities with a corresponding need for new streets and schools, sewer and lighting facilities, public utilities, expanded police and fire protection, and new airports and freeways to commute back to the central cities for work, recreation, and shopping. The result was an upsurge in borrowing by existing local units of government and the creation of thousands of new borrowing units in the form of sewer and lighting districts, power and water authorities, airport and toll-road boards, and public housing authorities. As shown in Exhibit 25–2, there are nearly 80,000 state, county, municipal, and other units of local government in the United States. And the majority of these governmental units have the authority to issue debt securities.

EXHIBIT 25–2
Number of State and Local Units of Government in the United States, 1977

Governmental Units	Total Number
Municipalities	18,862
Counties	3,042
Townships	16,822
School districts	15,174
Special districts	25,962
States	50
Total governmental units	79,912

SOURCE: U.S. Department of Commerce, Bureau of the Census, *1977 Census of Governments.*

Accompanying the growth and shifting of the U.S. population has come an upgrading of citizens' expectations concerning the quality of government services. We expect much more from government today than even 10 years ago, due in part to higher levels of income and education and greater public concern for the quality as well as the quantity of government services. Particularly noticeable is an increased demand for government services which directly affect the *quality* of life—more modern and better-designed schools, parks, swimming pools, tennis courts, auditoriums, and football stadiums. Instead of gravel roads and narrow highways, local citizens demand paved and guttered streets and all-weather, controlled-access highways. Many municipal governments are active in providing cultural facilities, such as libraries, museums, and convention centers, and are expected to play leading roles in the control of environmental pollution.

All of these public demands have had to be financed in an era of rapid inflation in construction and labor costs, exacerbating the money burdens of local governments. The rapid growth of local government borrowing is expected to continue in future years, with the federal government making smaller contributions to local funding. Adding to local financial needs will be a continuing expansion of suburban and rural communities, especially in the southern and western regions of the United States.

SOURCES OF REVENUE FOR STATE AND LOCAL GOVERNMENTS

Borrowing by state and local governments supplements their tax revenues and income from fees charged users of government services. When tax and fee revenues decline or fail to grow as fast as public demands, municipal borrowings rise. Moreover, when long-term capital projects are undertaken, long-term borrowing rather than taxation is the preferred method of governmental finance.

As we study state and local government borrowing in the financial markets, it is useful to have in mind the principal sources and uses of state and local funds. Where do the majority of state and local government revenues come from? And where does most of the money go? Exhibit 25–3, drawn from a recent census of state and local units of government, provides some answers to these questions.

EXHIBIT 25–3
Sources of Revenue for State and Local Governments, 1976–1977 (percent of total revenues)

Source	State and Local Governments	State Governments	Local Governments
General revenue from own sources	78.1%	71.2%	57.1%
Taxes	61.7	59.8	41.8
Property	21.9	1.3	33.7
Sales and gross receipts	21.3	31.0	4.6
General sales and gross receipts	12.8	18.3	3.1
Selective sales and gross receipts	8.5	12.7	1.6
Motor fuel	3.2	5.4	—
Alcoholic beverages	0.8	1.3	—
Tobacco products	1.3	2.1	—
Public utility	1.5	1.4	1.0
Insurance	0.8	1.4	—
Amusement	—	0.1	—
Parimutuel	0.3	0.4	—
Other	0.7	0.7	0.4
Income	13.5	20.5	2.1
Individual	10.3	15.1	2.1
Corporate	3.2	5.4	—
Motor vehicle license	1.6	2.5	0.2
Death and gift	0.6	1.1	—
Other	2.8	3.4	1.2
Current charges	10.9	7.1	10.7
Miscellaneous general revenue	5.5	4.3	4.6
Intergovernmental revenue	21.9	28.8	42.9
General revenue, total	100.0%	100.0%	100.0%

Note: Blank items are either zero or round to zero.
SOURCE: U.S. Department of Commerce, Bureau of the Census, *1977 Census of Governments.*

As expected, most state and local government revenues are derived from *local* sources of funds—that is, from the citizens these governmental units serve. For example, more than 70 percent of state government revenues and nearly 60 percent of local government revenues were derived from local sources, according to a 1977 Department of Commerce census. However, intergovernmental transfer of funds, including the federal revenue-sharing program and state aid to local schools, also provides a significant share of total revenues. For example, local governments received more than 40 percent of their revenues and state governments almost 30 percent from other governmental units in 1977. Most outside aid for state governments comes from federal sources, while state governments provide the bulk of external assistance for their own local governments, principally school districts.

Not surprisingly, *taxes* are the largest single revenue source for state and local governments. Property taxes are the mainstay of local government support, providing about a third of general revenues. State governments, in contrast, rely principally upon sales and income taxes. During the 1976–77 fiscal year, tax levies against sales and gross business receipts provided nearly a third of state government revenues but only about 5 percent of local government funds. Selective sales taxes on alcoholic beverages, entertainment, gasoline, tobacco, and other specialized products and services are levied almost entirely at the state level and provide about one eighth of state government funds. Income taxes are imposed almost exclusively at the state level and are levied mainly against individuals rather than corporations. Income taxes contributed about 20 percent of state government revenues but only about 2 percent of local government revenues during the 1976–77 fiscal year.

STATE AND LOCAL GOVERNMENT EXPENDITURES

Where do state and local governments spend most of their funds? As Exhibit 25–4 suggests, *education* is the number one item on the budgets of both state and local governmental units. The U.S. Department of Commerce reported that during the 1976–77 fiscal year, nearly 45 percent of local government funds and 40 percent of state revenues flowed into education and library services. Social services, including public welfare and medical care, occupied a distant second place, absorbing nearly a fifth of state revenues and about 7 percent of local outlays. Transportation services, especially highway construction and maintenance, ranked third in the volume of state and local spending.

It is interesting that some of the most-important local government services account for only a minor share of annual public budgets. For example, the cost of insuring public safety—principally police and fire protection—accounted for less than 10 percent of local government expenditures. Sewer services, protection of the environment and natural resources, and housing programs to aid the poor and the disadvantaged represented only about 10 percent of local government costs and less than 5 percent of state government spending. Moreover, despite the tremendous expansion of municipal debt in recent years, interest on that debt represented less than 4 percent of annual state and local government expenditures in the most recent governmental census report.

EXHIBIT 25–4
Annual Expenditures by State and Local Governments, 1976–1977
(percent of total general expenditures)

Function	State Governments	Local Governments
Education and library services	39.1%	44.5%
Social services and income maintenance:		
Public welfare	19.9	7.2
Hospitals	5.3	5.2
Health	2.4	1.7
Social insurance administration	1.0	*
Veterans' service	*	—
Transportation:		
Highway	10.6	5.3
Airport	0.1	0.7
Other	0.2	0.5
Public safety:		
Police protection	1.0	5.1
Other	2.5	3.8
Environment and housing:		
Sewerage	0.4	4.0
Natural resources	2.0	0.6
Housing and urban renewal	0.2	1.9
Other	0.7	3.6
Governmental administration:		
Financial administration	1.4	1.3
General control	1.1	2.6
General public buildings	0.3	1.1
Interest on general debt	3.0	3.6
General government support (all intergovernmental)	3.9	—
Other and combined direct and intergovernmental expenditures	4.7	7.3
General expenditures, total..............	100.0%	100.0%

* Indicates that the percentage figure is less than half the unit of measurement shown.
SOURCE: U.S. Department of Commerce, Bureau of the Census, *1977 Census of Governments.*

State and local government expenditures have grown rapidly in recent years. During 1980, expenditures by state and local units totaled $355 billion, as shown in Exhibit 25–5. This figure was more than 2½ times larger than the level of state and local government spending in 1970.[1] In fact, state and local

_____

[1] It is interesting to compare the size of state and local government expenditures with federal government outlays. Which is larger? Federal expenditures are significantly larger in total. For example, in 1980, federal outlays amounted to nearly $580 billion, while state and local expendi-

EXHIBIT 25–5
State and Local Government Receipts and Expenditures, NIA Accounts ($ billions)

Year	Total Receipts	Total Expenditures	Surplus or Deficit (−)
1946	$ 13.0	$ 11.1	$ 1.9
1950	21.3	22.5	−1.2
1955	31.7	32.9	−1.3
1960	49.9	49.8	0.1
1965	75.1	75.1	−0.0
1970	135.4	133.5	1.9
1975	237.7	232.2	5.5
1980	382.6	355.0	27.6

SOURCE: U.S. Department of Commerce, Bureau of Economic Analysis.

outlays have more than doubled in each decade since World War II. Local tax revenues have simply been inadequate to handle this kind of growth in current and capital expenditures. Borrowing in the money and capital markets against future revenues has become an indispensable supplement to local sources of funds.

MOTIVATIONS FOR STATE AND LOCAL GOVERNMENT BORROWING

There are several reasons why state and local governments borrow money. The first is to satisfy *short-run cash needs*—to meet payrolls, make repairs, purchase supplies and equipment, cover fuel costs, and maintain adequate levels of working capital. Most state and local governments will use tax-anticipation notes and other forms of short-term borrowings from local sources as a supplement to tax revenues to meet these immediate cash needs. Frequently, the construction phase of a building project will be financed out of short-term funds and then permanent financing will be obtained by selling long-term bonds.

The second major reason for state and local government borrowing is to finance *long-term capital investment*—the building of schools, water, gas, and electric systems, highways, public buildings, and similar permanent facilities. Long-term projects of this sort account for the bulk of all municipal securities issued each year. Some governmental units try to anticipate future financial needs, borrowing when interest rates are low even though project

tures totaled $355 billion. In recent years state and local spending has fluctuated between 60 and 70 percent of total federal outlays.

One interesting difference between federal and local government budgets is the frequency of budget deficits. For the most part, state and local governments operate with small budget surpluses each year, while, as we saw in Chapter 24, the federal budget has been in deficit in the majority of recent years. Statistics provided by the U.S. Department of Commerce indicate that during the years 1946–80 the state and local government sector as a whole reported budget surpluses in 22 years and deficits in the remaining 12 years.

construction will not begin for a substantial period of time. Funds raised through anticipatory borrowing will then be "warehoused" in various investments (such as U.S. Treasury bills) until actual construction begins.

Increasingly in recent years local governments have employed *advance refunding* of securities. Advance refundings often occur when a governmental unit has been granted a higher credit rating on its bonds by a rating agency, such as Moody's Investor Service or Standard and Poor's Corporation.[2] Bonds issued previously with lower credit ratings (i.e., higher interest rates) will be called in, and new securities issued at lower cost. Any significant decline in market interest rates usually gives rise to increased advance refunding activity by state and local governments.

USES OF BORROWED FUNDS

Where does the money raised from state and local borrowing go? There have been wide fluctuations in the purposes of municipal borrowing in recent years, but the principal uses of borrowed state and local funds historically have been to provide support for social welfare programs, public utilities, energy conservation, education, and transportation systems (see Exhibit 25–6).

In most recent years, social welfare programs (including public housing) have accounted for 25 to 30 percent of state and local borrowing—the largest single category. Utilities and energy-conservation programs have ranked a close second, accounting for 15 to 20 percent of total tax-exempt borrowings. Public education represents a declining but still important percentage (20 to 25 percent) of state and local borrowing each year. Borrowing for transportation purposes—including airports, bridges, roads, tunnels, and the like—now represents about 10 percent of all state and local borrowing. The remaining proportion of local borrowed funds is distributed among a wide variety of projects, including support for local industry, debt refunding, fire protection, street lighting, and sewer services. There is a trend underway toward increased borrowing for utilities, social welfare programs, and transportation. Rising energy costs have accelerated the need for mass transit systems and for the conversion of electric generating plants from gas and other petroleum-based fuels to coal and lignite.

TYPES OF SECURITIES ISSUED BY STATE AND
LOCAL GOVERNMENTS

There are many different types of securities issued by state and local governments today and, as we will soon see, the variety of municipal securities available to investors is expanding rapidly. One useful distinction is between short-term securities, which are generally issued to provide working

---

[2] See Appendix A for a discussion of municipal and other security ratings.

EXHIBIT 25-6
Uses of Long-Term Borrowings by State and Local Governments, Fiscal 1976-77

Item	Percentage Distribution		
	Total for All State and Local Governments	State Governments	Local Governments
Education:	23.2%	22.2%	23.8%
State institutions of higher education	4.9	13.8	—
Local schools	15.4	4.6	21.2
Other	3.0	3.7	2.5
Highways:	7.8	19.1	1.7
State toll facilities.................	2.5	7.1	—
Other	5.3	12.0	1.7
Housing and urban renewal	6.7	7.9	6.0
Sewerage	3.2	2.0	3.9
Hospitals	2.4	3.7	1.7
Airports	1.4	0.3	1.9
Parks and recreation	1.3	1.6	1.1
Water transport and terminals	0.9	0.6	1.1
Utilities...........................	16.3	3.8	23.1
Electric power	7.3	3.7	9.3
Water supply	6.8	0.2	10.5
Transit system	2.0	—	3.1
Gas supply	0.1	—	0.2
Other and unallocable..............	36.8	38.7	35.8

Notes: Blank items either represent zero or round to zero. Due to rounding error, column entries may not add to totals.
SOURCE: U.S. Department of Commerce, Bureau of the Census, *1977 Census of Governments.*

capital and support construction, and long-term securities, used to fund capital projects.

Short-Term Securities

The two most popular short-term securities issued by state and local governments are tax-anticipation notes and bond-anticipation notes.

Tax-Anticipation Notes. These notes, also called TANs, are used to attract funds in lieu of tax receipts. Governments, like businesses and households, have a daily need for cash to meet payrolls, purchase supplies, make repairs, and so on. However, funds raised through taxes usually flow in only at certain times of the year. In order to satisfy their continuing need for cash between tax dates, state and local governments will issue short-term notes with maturities ranging from a few days to a few months. Most of these short-term issues are acquired by local banks. When tax funds are received, the issuing government simply pays off note holders and retires any outstanding securities.

Bond-Anticipation Notes. These short-term IOUs, also called BANs, are used to provide temporary financing of a long-term project until the time is right to sell long-term bonds. A school district, for example, may need to get construction started on new school facilities due to pressure from rising student enrollments. If interest rates currently are too high to permit the issue of bonds, then construction will be started out of funds raised with bond-anticipation notes. Once the project is under way and interest rates decline to more-modest levels, the school district will then sell its long-term bonds and retire the bond-anticipation notes.

The majority of short-term notes issued by state and local governments are backed by the "full faith and credit" of the issuing governmental unit. They sell at interest rates competitive with current money market yields and reflect the credit rating of the issuer. (As shown in Appendix A, Moody's Investor Service rates investment-grade municipal notes 1, 2, 3, or 4.) Like municipal bonds, interest on short-term local government notes is exempt from federal income taxes. These notes range in original maturity from one month to the more common six-month and one-year maturities.

The volume of municipal notes has been quite large in recent years, reflecting the rising costs of state and local government services. During 1979, for example, nearly $21 billion worth were sold, usually through underwriting syndicates who filed competitive bids for the securities. Short-term tax-exempt notes are issued in marketable bearer form, with denominations ranging typically from $5,000 to $1 million. Both principal and interest are paid at maturity.[3]

Long-Term Securities

The most-common type of municipal borrowing is through long-term bonds. There are two major types of municipal bonds issued today—general obligation and revenue bonds.

General Obligation Bonds. These bonds, known as GOs, are the safest and most secure form of municipal borrowing from the standpoint of the investor because they are backed by the "full faith and credit" of the issuing government and may be paid from any revenue source. State, county, and city governments along with school districts have the power to tax their citizens in order to meet principal and interest payments on any debt issued. GOs are fully backed by this taxing power.[4] The quality or level of risk of GOs depends, therefore, upon the economic base (i.e., income and property values) of local communities and the total amount of debt issued.

---

[3] Tax-exempt notes with maturities longer than a year generally bear coupons. For most tax-exempt notes, interest is computed on the basis of a 30-day month or a 360-day year, like the interest on Treasury bills and bank CDs.

[4] In some cases the issuing government's taxing power is limited by state law to a specified maximum tax rate. In this instance the GOs would be classified as a *limited tax bond*.

Revenue Bonds. In contrast, revenue bonds are payable only from a specified source of revenue, such as a toll road or toll bridge, lighting district, or other revenue-gathering project. These securities are *not* guaranteed or backed by the taxing power of the local unit of government. Instead, revenue bonds depend for their value on the revenue-generating capacity of the particular project they support.[5]

The total amount of general obligation bonds outstanding today exceeds the total supply of revenue bonds. However, as shown in Exhibit 25–7,

EXHIBIT 25–7
New Security Issues of State and Local Governments ($ billions)

	Years		
Type of Issue, Issuer, or Use of Funds	1978	1979	1980
All issues	$48.6	$43.5	$48.5
Type of issue:			
General obligation	17.9	12.1	14.1
Revenue	30.7	31.3	34.3
Housing assistance administration	—	—	—
U.S. government loans	0.1	0.1	0.1
Type of Issuer:			
State	6.6	4.3	5.3
Special district and statutory authority	24.2	23.4	27.0
Municipalities, counties, townships, and			
school districts	17.7	15.6	16.1
Uses of funds raised from issues for new capital:			
Education	5.0	5.1	4.6
Transportation	3.5	2.4	2.6
Utilities and conservation	9.0	8.6	8.1
Social welfare	10.5	16.0	20.0
Industrial aid	3.5	3.8	4.0
Other purposes	6.1	5.5	7.5

Notes: Figures include all state and local government security issues to raise new capital and to refund outstanding debt. Securities are valued at par based on date of sale. Housing Assistance Administration securities are sold according to the terms of the 1949 Housing Act and are secured by contracts requiring that agency to make annual contributions to local housing authorities.
SOURCE: Board of Governors of the Federal Reserve System, *Federal Reserve Bulletin*, July 1981.

[5] Some municipal bonds display characteristics of both GO and revenue securities. For example, a *special tax bond* is payable from the revenues generated by a special tax, such as on gasoline. Many special tax bonds are backed by the full faith, credit, and taxing power of the issuing governmental unit, giving them the character of GOs. *Special assessment bonds* are payable only from assessments against property constructed or purchased from the proceeds of the bond issue and arise from water and sewer projects, street construction, and similar projects. As in the case of special tax bonds, however, special assessment issues may take on the character of GOs when backed by the taxing power of the issuer. *Authority bonds* are issued by special governmental units set up by states, cities, or counties to construct and manage certain facilities, such as airports or water and sewer projects. Sometimes these special governmental units are set up to avoid legal debt limits in state constitutions, and most have taxing power. Authority bonds may be either GOs or revenue issues.

revenue issues have been increasing much faster in recent years. For example, during 1980, $34 billion in revenue bonds reached market, while only $14 billion in GOs were issued. There has been a virtual explosion of different types of revenue bonds within the past decade. Much of the growth in amount and variety of revenue issues is due to welfare programs of the federal government designed to provide housing for low-income groups, improved medical-care facilities, and student loans. In addition, the passage of Proposition 13 in California during the summer of 1978 and the enactment of similar laws by other states has encouraged many local authorities to substitute revenue bonds for GOs. Many of these new revenue bonds are not well known to the majority of investors and may, in some cases, provide a higher rate of return to the well-informed buyer.

Types of Revenue Bonds

One of the most popular new revenue issues is *student-loan bonds* (SLROs) which are issued by state government agencies that lend money to college students. The federal government guarantees 100 percent of the principal and interest of an SLRO, provided the issuing agency's loan-default ratio is less than 5 percent. If a higher percentage of students default on their loans, federal guarantees are limited to only a certain portion (usually 80 to 90 percent) of principal and interest payments on the bonds. SLROs are issued in minimum denominations of $1,000.

In the housing field several new forms of guaranteed and nonguaranteed state and local revenue bonds have appeared in recent years. For example, *life-care bonds,* also known as retirement community bonds, are issued by state and local development agencies to provide housing for the elderly. The housing is not government subsidized but supported by rental fees paid by the tenants. Frequently, nonprofit agencies organized by religious groups administer the property. Investor funds are secured by lease rentals and a mortgage against the property. Life-care bonds are issued in minimum denominations of $5,000.

A related security is the *Section 8 bond* issued under the terms of the Federal Housing Act. These bonds finance low- and middle-income rental housing, usually designed for elderly citizens. Section 8s are not federally guaranteed, but the U.S. Department of Housing and Urban Development (HUD) must accumulate a cash reserve for each project which protects against the failure of project residents to pay their rent. Security for Section 8s is provided by rent subsidies and a mortgage on the housing project. Section 8 bonds carry a minimum denomination of $5,000.

Joint federal and state support for low-income housing is frequently provided through *public housing authority notes* (PHAs). These securities are used to finance the construction of public housing projects for low-income families, many of whom live on welfare. PHAs are attractive to many investors because they are guaranteed by the federal government as well as being tax exempt.

Construction of hospital facilities is frequently supported by *hospital revenue bonds*. These bonds are not guaranteed but are issued by state authorities to build hospitals for lease to public or private operating agencies. Issued in minimum denominations of $1,000, hospital revenue bonds have their principal and interest secured by lease rentals and a mortgage against hospital property. It is likely that the volume of such highly specialized revenue bonds will grow in future years due to the more-conservative attitude of citizens today toward the cost of government.

The late 1970s ushered in widespread use of *mortgage revenue bonds*. Proceeds of these bonds are loaned to low- and moderate-income home buyers who, in turn, eventually pay off the bonds by making monthly mortgage payments. Mortgage revenue bonds typically are issued by cities or counties and carry the tax-exempt privilege, thereby permitting eligible home buyers to borrow at rates below those on conventional residential mortgages. Such issues have aroused a storm of controversy because they represent the use of public funds for private benefit and divert substantial revenues away from the U.S. Treasury. An estimated $12 billion worth of mortgage revenue bonds were sold during 1979.

An unusual type of municipal security which serves both public and private interests is the *industrial development bond* (IDB). These securities are used to finance plant construction and the purchase of land which is then leased to a private company. The purpose is to attract industry into the local area and increase both the number of jobs available and local tax revenues. IDBs were first issued by the state of Mississippi during the Great Depression of the 1930s. Soon the concept of using government credit to promote local industry became common practice across the nation, especially in those areas experiencing declining population or the exodus of large firms. However, the use of public funds raised through the tax-exempt borrowing privilege for private purposes disturbed many members of Congress. Following extensive hearings, Congress in 1968 enacted a new federal law which limits each issue of tax-exempt IDBs to a maximum of $1 million.

Types of Securities Issued by Different Governmental Units

Whether a state or local unit of government issues general obligation or revenue bonds depends upon the type of governmental unit involved. For example, as shown in Exhibit 25–8, school districts issue only general obligation (GO) bonds. In contrast, special districts which provide such services as water, sanitation, bridges and toll roads, street lighting, and electricity tend to use revenue bonds. City and state governments are about evenly split between GO and revenue issues, while counties generally borrow using revenue bonds.

EXHIBIT 25-8
Debt Obligations of State and Local Governments, 1977 ($ billions)

Item	All State and Local Govts.	Governmental Units					
		States	Counties	Municipalities	Townships	School Districts	Special Districts
Total debt outstanding	$259.7	$90.2	$22.7	$71.8	$4.1	$28.4	$42.5
General obligation bonds	136.4	42.9	15.3	39.1	3.2	27.3	8.6
Unguaranteed revenue bonds	110.4	44.3	6.2	28.1	0.2	—	31.6
Total long-term debt	246.8	87.2	21.5	67.2	3.4	27.3	40.2
Short-term debt	12.8	3.0	1.2	4.5	0.7	1.1	2.2
Percentage Distribution							
Total debt outstanding	100.0%	34.7%	8.7%	27.6%	1.6%	10.9%	16.4%
General obligation bonds	100.0	31.5	11.2	28.7	2.3	20.0	6.3
Unguaranteed revenue bonds	100.0	40.1	5.6	25.5	0.2	—	28.7
Total long-term debt	100.0	35.3	8.7	27.2	1.4	11.0	16.3
Short-term debt	100.0	23.5	9.5	35.4	5.6	8.9	17.2

Note: Because of rounding, details may not add to totals.
SOURCE: U.S. Department of Commerce, Bureau of the Census, *1977 Census of Governments.*

KEY FEATURES OF MUNICIPAL DEBT

Tax Exemption

Certainly the outstanding and unique feature of municipal securities is the tax-exemption privilege. The interest income from municipal securities is exempt from federal income taxes under the constitutional doctrine of *reciprocal immunity*. In addition, state law usually exempts municipals from income taxes levied by the state of issuance. Capital gains on municipal securities are *not* tax exempt, however, unless the security is issued at a discount from par. In that special case any increase in price up to par value is considered part of the security's interest return and is tax exempt. However, if the security continues to rise in price, that portion of the gain above par is subject to taxation once the investor realizes the gain.

An Interest Subsidy to High-Income Investors. The tax-exempt feature has been a controversial issue for many years. Clearly, it is a government subsidy to high-tax-bracket investors. This is true because the value of the exemption privilege increases with the investor's marginal income tax rate. Exhibit 25–9 illustrates the impact of the investor's marginal tax rate (or tax bracket) on the relative attractiveness of municipals compared to taxable securities. This exhibit compares the approximate after-tax yield in high-

EXHIBIT 25–9
The Impact of the Tax-Exemption Feature on the After-Tax Yields of Long-Term Corporate and Municipal Bonds (approximate average bond yields reported in January 1981)

Investor Group	Before-Tax Yield on Seasoned Aaa Corporate Bonds	Appropriate Federal Income Tax Bracket for Investor Group	After-Tax Yield on Seasoned Aaa Corporate Bonds	Before-Tax and After-Tax Yield on Aaa Municipal Bonds
Individuals in highest income tax bracket	13%	50%	6.5%	9%
Large corporate investors: Manufacturing and industrial corporations	13	46	7.0	9
Property-casualty insurance companies	13	46	7.0	9
Commercial banks	13	46	7.0	9
Individuals in middle-income tax brackets	13	30–45	9.1–7.2	9
Individuals and institutions in lowest-income tax brackets	13	20–28	10.4–9.4	9
Tax-exempt investors: Governments, pension funds, charities, foundations, and credit unions	13	0	13	9

SOURCE: Yield data obtained from Board of Governors of the Federal Reserve System, *Federal Reserve Bulletin,* March 1981.

grade corporate bonds, which are fully taxable, with the yield on comparable-quality municipal bonds—both for January 1981.

During that month, the before-tax yield of seasoned Aaa corporate bonds averaged about 13 percent, while the before-tax and after-tax yield of Aaa municipals was approximately 9 percent. Because the corporate bond yield is a before-tax rate of return, we must adjust it using the investor's marginal income tax rate to derive the after-tax rate of return. The before-tax corporate yield is multiplied by $(1 - t)$ where t is the investor's applicable federal tax rate.[6] Exhibit 25–9 illustrates the effect of this calculation for investors with marginal tax rates ranging from 0 to 50 percent.[7] For an individual investor in the top, 50 percent, tax bracket, the after-tax return on Aaa corporate bonds was 13 percent $\times$ $(1 - 0.50)$, or 6.5 percent. Clearly, an investor in this high-income group would prefer to purchase municipal bonds yielding 9 percent rather than corporate bonds returning less than 7 percent after taxes, other factors held equal. The same conclusion holds true for large manufacturing and industrial corporations, property-casualty insurance companies, and commercial banks confronted with the top, 46 percent, corporate federal tax rate.

Of course, the foregoing analysis focuses exclusively upon after-tax rates of return, ignoring differences in liquidity and other features of taxable and tax-exempt securities. A corporation which needs to hold securities for liquidity purposes might well hold taxable issues, such as U.S. government securities, which can usually be converted into cash quickly with little risk of loss, even though their after-tax yields may be lower than the yields on municipal bonds.

For income tax brackets below the top rung, corporate bonds and other taxable securities compare more favorably with municipals. For example, life insurance companies, savings banks, and many small private investors whose applicable income tax rate is in the 20 to 30 percent range usually find taxable securities more lucrative and purchase few municipals. In effect, the tax-exempt feature limits the demand for state and local government securities to high-income individuals, commercial banks, property-casualty insurers, and large nonfinancial corporations. This limitation may represent a serious problem in future years when local governments in some areas of the nation must raise an enormous volume of new funds to accommodate rapidly expanding populations.

The tax-exemption feature is an advantage to municipal governments because it keeps their interest costs low relative to interest rates paid by other borrowers. These savings can be passed on to local citizens in the form of lower local tax rates. Of course, the U.S. Treasury is able to collect less revenue from high-tax-bracket investors as a result of the exemption privi-

---

[6] See Chapter 9 for further discussion of the impact of tax exemption on security yields.

[7] The maximum federal income tax rate for individuals was 70 percent until passage of the Economic Recovery Act of 1981, when the maximum rate was reduced to 50 percent. See Chapter 24 for a discussion of recent changes in federal income tax laws.

lege and must tax lower-bracket taxpayers more heavily to make up the difference. Therefore, the total tax bill from all levels of government is probably little affected by the tax-exempt feature of municipals.

Exemption Contributes to Volatility. Because the market for municipal bonds is limited by the tax-exempt privilege to top-tax-bracket investors, prices and interest rates on municipal bonds tend to be highly volatile and unpredictable. Prices of tax-exempt bonds tend to rise during those periods when corporate and individual incomes are rising, because top-bracket investors have a greater need to shelter their earnings from taxation at those times. However, a fall in individual or corporate earnings, especially the earnings of banks and property-casualty insurance companies, often leads to sharp reductions in the demand for municipal bonds. Prices of tax-exempt issues may plummet, and interest costs confronting borrowing governments may rise dramatically during periods when corporate profits are squeezed. This makes financial planning in the state and local government sector an extremely difficult task.

A Market of "Fair Weather" Investors. Another problem which exacerbates the volatility of municipal bond prices is the limited investment horizon of many tax-exempt-bond buyers. For the most part, investors active in the tax-exempt market are "fair weather" friends. Commercial banks, for example, build up their state and local bond holdings when customer loan demand is weak, only to sell off substantial quantities of municipals when loan demand revives. Another major group of tax-exempt investors—high-income individuals—have finite life spans and thus their bonds are often sold after only a short holding period. The net result is to create an active secondary market and relatively high turnover rate for the larger, better-known municipal issues.

Credit Ratings

A feature of municipal securities which makes them especially attractive to investors is their high credit rating. About 10 percent of all municipal securities are AAA-rated by Moody's Investor Service and Standard & Poor's Corporation, while close to 60 percent are AA or A rated. Only about 10 percent of all state and local government securities are rated BA or lower or carry no published rating. This means that the large majority of municipal issues are considered to be of investment quality rather than speculative buys.[8]

Factors behind Setting Credit Ratings. In assigning credit ratings to municipals, Moody's and other investor-rating services consider the past repayment record of the borrowing unit of government, the quality and size of

---

[8] See Chapter 8 and Appendix A for a discussion of published credit ratings for corporate and municipal bonds. Moody's Investor Service rates municipals according to the following scale from high to low quality: Aaa, Aa, A, Baa, Ba, B, and C. Standard & Poor's Corporation uses the following rating symbols: AAA, AA, A, BBB, BB, B, CCC, CC, C, DDD, and D.

its tax base, the volume of debt outstanding, local economic conditions, and future prospects for growth in the local economy. The fact that many municipal issues are backed by taxing authority or may draw upon several different sources of revenue for repayment of principal and interest helps to keep the investment quality of most tax-exempt issues high. This is particularly important for the largest buyer of new municipal bonds and notes—commercial banks. Federal regulations applying to national banks, and most state banking regulations as well, prohibit commercial banks from acquiring debt securities rated below BAA (so-called speculative issues). These restrictive rules encourage state and local governments to keep their credit ratings high in order to encourage active participation by banks in bidding for new municipal bonds.

Recent Credit Quality Problems.   Until recently, state and local governments possessed virtually unblemished credit records. No major defaults on municipal securities had occurred since the Great Depression of the 1930s. However, the turbulent economic and financial environment of the 1970s caused many investors to reassess the credit standing of municipals, especially the bonds and notes issued by some of the largest cities in the nation.

This problem surfaced most dramatically in the financial crisis experienced by New York City in the mid-1970s. Soaring costs for municipal services, excessive reliance on short-term debt, and high unemployment combined to threaten that city with record-high interest costs and financial default. And in the wake of New York City's fiscal crisis, other northeastern cities—Boston, Buffalo, Cleveland, Detroit, Philadelphia, and Newark— also found their credit costs rising to unprecedented levels.

In 1975, at the peak of New York City's financial crisis, the yield spread between the highest-quality (Aaa-rated) and lowest-quality investment-grade (Baa) municipal bonds climbed from about half a percentage point to nearly two full percentage points. Even though there have been few actual defaults on municipal bonds in recent years and the investors involved nearly always have been paid off eventually, risk premiums demanded by investors purchasing lower-grade municipal bonds rose dramatically during the 1970s, significantly exceeding risk premiums on comparable-quality corporate bonds. A massive "flight to quality" rocked the tax-exempt market in a manner not experienced since the Great Depression.

Fortunately, the late 1970s and early 1980s ushered in a more stable economic environment, which aided the finances of many municipal governments. Urban unemployment declined, local tax revenues grew more rapidly, and many cities restructured their debt into longer-term issues, easing a potential liquidity crisis. However, tax-exempt investors have remained more sensitive to the credit-worthiness of borrowing governments than at any time in the past 50 years. This fundamental concern about the investment quality of municipal issues was heightened in December 1978, when Cleveland became the first major U.S. city to default on its debt since the Great Depression. However, Cleveland was able to work out an acceptable agreement with local banks to belatedly pay off approximately $15 million in short-term notes. Nevertheless, investors today remain highly sensitive to the quality of new municipal issues.

Serialization

Most municipal bonds are *serial* securities. Serialization refers to the splitting up of a single bond issue into several different maturities. Thus, an issue of $20 million in bonds to build a municipal auditorium might include the following securities:

Amount	Due in
$1 million	1 year
$1 million	2 years
$1 million	3 years
.	.
.	.
.	.
$1 million	20 years

Splitting a single issue of municipals into multiple maturities contrasts with the practice employed by most corporate borrowers and the federal government. Corporations, for example, generally issue *term bonds* in which all securities in the same issue come due on the same date. In effect, serialization of municipal bonds is a way of amortizing state and local debt.

Why has serialization become so popular in the municipal field? Before serial bonds were widely adopted, state and local bonds were generally term securities. A sinking fund was usually created at the time of issue, and annual contributions were made to the fund until sufficient monies were accumulated to pay off the bond issue at maturity. However, sinking funds proved irresistible to unscrupulous politicians and to governments facing financial emergencies. Accumulated funds often disappeared, leaving virtually nothing to retire municipal debt when it came due. The serial feature seemed to offer an ideal solution to this problem.

Unfortunately, serialization has created as many problems as it has solved. For one thing, splitting an issue into a number of different maturities reduces the liquidity and marketability of municipal securities. The average-sized municipal issue sold publicly contains about $20 to $30 million in securities. Therefore, when such an issue is split into multiple maturities, there is only a small amount outstanding in any one maturity class. The potential volume of trading for particular maturities is therefore extremely limited. Serialization also complicates the offering of new securities because a number of different investor groups must be attracted into the bidding. For example, commercial banks generally prefer the shorter-term (1- to 10-year) securities, while insurance companies, individuals, and other investors often want only the longest-term bonds.

HOW MUNICIPAL BONDS ARE MARKETED

The selling of municipals is usually carried out through a *syndicate* of banks and securities dealers. These institutions underwrite municipals by purchasing them from the issuing unit of government and reselling the securities in the open market, hopefully at a higher price. Prices paid by the underwriting firms may be determined either by competitive bidding among several syndicates or by negotiation with a single securities dealer or syndicate. Competitive bidding normally is employed in the marketing of general obligation (GO) bonds, while revenue bonds more frequently are placed through negotiation.

In competitive bidding, syndicates interested in a particular bond issue will estimate its potential reoffer price in the open market and their desired underwriting commission. Each syndicate wants to bid a price high enough to win the bid, but low enough so that the securities can later be sold in the open market at a price sufficient to protect the group's commission. That is,

Bid price + Underwriting commission = Market reoffer price

The winning bid carries the lowest net interest cost (NIC) to the issuing unit of government. The NIC is simply the sum of all interest payments that will be owed on the new issue divided by its principal amount.

Bidding for new issues of municipal bonds is a treacherous business. Prices, interest rates, and market demand for municipals all change rapidly, often without warning. In fact, the tax-exempt securities market is one of the most volatile of all financial markets. This is due in part to the dominant role of commercial banks, whose demand for municipals fluctuates with their net earnings and loan demand. Legal interest-rate ceilings, which prohibit some local governments from borrowing when market rates climb above those ceilings, also play a significant role in the volatility of municipal trading. These combined factors render the tax-exempt market highly sensitive to the business cycle, monetary policy, inflation, and a host of other economic and financial factors. The spectre of high interest rates often forces the postponement of hundreds of millions of dollars of new issues, while the onset of lower rates may unleash a flood of new security offerings.

There is a trend today away from competitive bidding and toward negotiated sales of new state and local bonds, due partly to the treacherous character of the tax-exempt market. For example, during 1978 an estimated 53 percent of bonds issued in the market for long-term municipals were negotiated, compared with only 15 percent a dozen years before.[9] This trend has aroused some concern among financial analysis because competitive bidding should result in the lowest net interest cost, reducing the burden on local taxpayers. A recent study sponsored by the Municipal Finance Officers Association (MFOA) concluded that taxpayers have borne some added

---

[9] See Byron Klapper, "Negotiated Sales Are on the Increase in Municipal Sector," *The Wall Street Journal,* June 25, 1979.

interest burden as a result of the recent emphasis upon negotiated, rather than competitive, sales.

This problem is especially severe in certain states. For example, the AFOA-sponsored study found that in Pennsylvania, where competitive bidding is not required by law, about 95 percent of all bonds sold by local governments were handled through negotiation with a single underwriter group. It was estimated that Pennsylvania local governments paid approximately $14 million in excess interest costs on bond sales totaling about $360 million. On the other side of the coin, underwriting firms argue that they provide extra services to borrowing governments during the negotiation process—services not generally available through competitive bidding. These include preparing legal offering statements, scheduling the sale of new securities, helping to secure desirable credit ratings, and contacting potential buyers.

PROBLEMS IN THE MUNICIPAL MARKET

Problems and Proposals Regarding Tax Exemption

The municipal market has been plagued by a number of problems over the years, some of these related to its unique tax-exempt character. Many observers question the social benefit of the tax-exemption privilege. As we noted earlier, while state and local governments can borrow more cheaply as a result of tax exemption, the federal government must tax nonexempt groups more heavily to make up the lost revenue. As we have also noted, tax exemption contributes to the cyclical sensitivity of the municipal market, principally because demand for state and local securities comes mainly from commercial banks and individuals, neither of which are permanent investors. Fluctuations in economic conditions frequently lead to large net sales of municipals in the open market and soaring interest rates. Many important investor groups—pension funds, life insurance companies, and mutual funds—display very little interest in municipal bonds because they have little need for this type of tax shelter.

A number of proposals have been advanced over the years for improving the depth and stability of the municipal market and eliminating the tax-exempt feature. One interesting idea calls for reimbursing state and local governments for loss of the tax-exempt privilege through federal interest subsidies. Local governments would be offered the option of selling their debt in either the taxable or tax-exempt security markets. Those choosing taxable securities would be eligible for federal subsidies. This step would open the municipal market to life insurance companies, pension funds, and other active capital market investors. A related idea calls for paying a subsidy directly to investors who choose to buy municipal securities. An *Urbank* has also been proposed which, under federal sponsorship, would issue its own bonds and direct the proceeds of bond sales to municipal governments. One criticism of this approach is the danger of increased federal controls over state and local governments.

California's Proposition 13

The municipal market was rocked to its foundations in 1978 when California voters approved the well-known Proposition 13. This law set maximum real property tax rates in California at 1 percent of the full cash value of taxable property, except for those bonds which had already been approved by the voters. An effective ceiling on tax rates equal to $4 per $100 of assessed value was established—a figure well below the average of $8 to $16 per $100 valuation that prevailed in the state at that time. Proposition 13 also required state officials to roll back their valuation of real property to 1975–76 levels and limited property-value adjustments to only 2 percent a year (except for new construction projects or when property changed hands). The net effect was to reduce funds available to schools and other units of local government by about $7 billion a year.

The state of California was prohibited from enacting a statewide property tax or property transfer tax, and any increase in state taxes required a two-thirds vote of the legislature. In effect, Proposition 13 called for a 60 percent decline in real-property-tax collections without making provision for other sources of funds to take up the slack. Finally, the new law permitted local governments to impose special taxes, provided two thirds of the voters gave their approval. However, *ad valorem* sales and transfer taxes on real property were disallowed.

The success of Proposition 13 in California resulted in the creation of taxpayer lobby groups in many other states (notably Massachusetts, Nevada, Idaho, New Jersey, and South Dakota) intent on enacting similar legislation. Many financial analysts predicted dire consequences for the municipal market stemming from such laws. General obligation bonds were expected to fade away if other states joined California in a move to limit state and local taxing authority. While the new law certainly did not prohibit the issue of municipal bonds, it did prevent increases in taxes to finance many new bond issues. This fact suggested to many observers that revenue bonds rather than GOs would be more heavily used in the future, especially for utilities, lighting districts, and other revenue-generating services.

Laws like Proposition 13 might well encourage the shifting of the local tax base from real property to personal property. Moreover, Proposition 13 appeared to shift a substantial measure of fiscal authority away from state governments toward local governments. Beyond this, there was great concern in California about layoffs of public employees, reduced school hours, and severe limitations on the availability of essential services due to the lack of available funds. One estimate suggested that up to 450,000 people would lose their jobs in California as a result of the passage of Proposition 13. However, few of these "calamities" have materialized as of yet. Indeed, the prospect of lower taxes appears to have stimulated additional private investment, and many new firms have relocated recently in California. The added jobs and tax revenues springing from expanded private investment activity appear to have filled in much of the gap left by Proposition 13's restrictions.[10]

The Growing Burden of Local Taxes and Debt

California's passage of Proposition 13 and strong voter interest in similar laws for other states reflects the tremendous growth in state and local taxes and debt in recent years. The tax burden faced by the average taxpayer today has been worsened by inflation, which pushes individuals into higher and higher tax brackets at both federal and state levels. Moreover, rising property values subject taxpayers to increased tax payments against their homes and other forms of real and personal property. The average family of four in the United States pays more in income, property, and sales taxes today than their total payments for a home, car, and food.

Local property taxes are particularly onerous to the average citizen because they are so visible. Each year, the homeowner is confronted with a large lump-sum property assessment to cover the cost of local schools, street improvements, and other esssential services. The fact is that income and sales taxes have increased more rapidly than property taxes, but they are less visible to the taxpayer and therefore often ignored. An added problem is that many citizens do not see a direct correlation between the size of their tax burdens and the quantity and quality of government services available to them.[11]

The Need for Alternatives to Fixed-Rate Municipal Bonds

The most-serious problem ahead for state and local government securities is the *inflexibility* of the terms on the majority of municipal bonds. Like most corporate bonds, municipals generally carry a fixed interest rate. As bond market yields have soared in recent years, municipal bond prices have

---

[10] There is evidence that California residents were insulated from the budget-cutting effects of Proposition 13 by large budget surpluses due, in part, to the lifting of oil-price controls. Beginning in 1981, however, California faced a serious fiscal crunch as the surpluses melted away. While state employment continues to increase moderately, the number of city government employees in California fell 10 percent between 1978 and 1981, representing a decline of about 20,000 workers. School district budgets were cut by more than $100 million. Perhaps the full, long-run impact of Proposition 13 on the quality and quantity of local government services in California has yet to be felt.

[11] The Reagan administration's cutback of federal aid to cities, counties, and state governments will have a substantial effect on the volume of municipal borrowing in the future. In 1981 the number of civilian government employees at all levels—federal, state, and local—declined for the first time since 1947. In 1980, 18 percent of all civilian jobs were in the government sector, but that figure seems certain to decline. Education, heavily supported by federal grants to the states, will be one of the prime areas affected by recent reductions in federal spending.

plummeted. Except for those investors in the highest tax brackets, many would-be buyers have fled the tax-exempt market in search of more-flexible financial instruments available elsewhere.

There is considerable evidence, however, that many state and local governments are becoming more innovative in their borrowing activities. Several tax-exempt housing-revenue and pollution-control bonds have recently been issued as "floaters." For example, U.S. Steel issued $48 million in government-sponsored pollution-control bonds with a flexible (floating) interest rate to protect investors against future rate changes. Buyers were so attracted by this novel idea that an additional $500 million in floating-rate housing bonds came to market at the end of 1980. These bonds promised a yield tied to changes in the weekly rates on 13-week Treasury bills and 30-year Treasury bonds. Interest is paid semiannually with the investor's yield determined by the average of Treasury bill and bond rates over the preceding six months.

Still another recent innovation is the *option bond*. Option bonds bear a fixed rate of interest but can be sold back to the issuer or his agent at par after a specified period. One example is a $43 million issue of 9 percent, single-family mortgage bonds offered by Denton County, Texas, in December 1980. While these bonds do not come due until the year 2013, a trustee with the backing of First National City Bank of New York has guaranteed to buy back eligible bonds beginning December 1, 1985. More recently, several municipal borrowers have reduced the maturities of their bonds from 30 years into the 10- to 15-year range.

These innovations in state and local government borrowing are not without their risks. Other things equal, they will require more-frequent borrowing by municipal governments and, more than likely, increase the average cost of government funds, further burdening the taxpayer. In effect, floaters, option bonds, and shorter-maturity financial instruments shift risk from investors to borrowers and, ultimately, to the taxpayers. Financial planning becomes more difficult for those local governments electing to use these new financial instruments. Nevertheless, in a rapidly changing economy there is no substitute for financial flexibility. Borrowers who cannot respond to changing investor demands will soon find themselves shut out of the nation's credit markets. This is a bitter lesson which state and local governments have learned all too well in recent years.

STUDY QUESTIONS

1. The market for state and local government bonds has been one of the most rapidly growing financial markets in the United States during the past three decades. Why has this been true? Can you foresee any serious problems on the horizon for the continued growth of the municipal market?

2. What are the principal sources of revenue for state and local governments today? Where do they spend the bulk of their incoming funds?

3. For what reasons do state and local governments borrow short- and long-term funds?

4. Give a concise definition of each of the following state and local government securities, and explain how each is used.
   a. Tax-anticipation notes.
   b. Bond-anticipation notes.
   c. General obligation (GO) bonds.
   d. Revenue bonds.
   e. Special tax bonds.
   f. Special assessment bonds.
   g. Authority bonds.

5. Revenue bonds issued by local governments and public agencies have grown more rapidly than any other type of municipal security in recent years. Moreover, many new kinds of revenue bonds have been developed to deal with specialized public needs. Several different kinds of revenue bonds are listed below. Please explain the principal purpose or function of each of these securities.
   a. SLROs.
   b. Life-care bonds.
   c. Section 8 bonds.
   d. PHAs.
   e. Hospital revenue bonds.
   f. Mortgage revenue bonds.
   g. IDBs.

6. What are the principal features of municipal bonds which have made them attractive to many groups of investors? What factors or features often limit the demand for these bonds?

7. Describe how municipal bonds are marketed. What risks do syndicates face? What advantages do you see for competitive bidding versus negotiated sales?

8. What recommendations would you make to improve the functioning of the municipal bond market? Carefully explain the purpose and probable effects of each of your recommendations.

9. Why do you think Proposition 13 was enacted into law in the state of California? What impact might such laws have on local economies and the municipal market? Would you favor a similar law for your state if it does not already have one? Please explain your answers.

10. In what ways is the municipal bond market dealing with the problem of "inflexibility"? What is a "floater"? An option bond? How might these devices assist the marketability of municipals in future years?

SELECTED REFERENCES

1. Advisory Commission on Intergovernmental Relations. *State and Local Finances in Recession and Inflation: An Economic Analysis.* Washington, D.C.: U.S. Government Printing Office, 1979.

2. Browne, Lynn E., and Richard F. Syron. "Big City Bonds after New York." *New England Economic Review,* Federal Reserve Bank of Boston, July-August 1977.

3. _____. "The Municipal Market since the New York City Crisis." *New England Economic Review*, Federal Reserve Bank of Boston, July-August 1979, pp. 11–26.

4. Federal Reserve Bank of Boston. *Financing State and Local Governments*. Conference Series no. 3, 1970.

5. Fortune, Peter. "Tax-Exemption of State and Local Interest Payments: An Economic Analysis of the Issues and an Alternative." *New England Economic Review*, Federal Reserve Bank of Boston, March-April 1978, pp. 21–31.

6. Humpage, Owen F. "State and Local Budgets during Business Contractions." *Economic Commentary*, Federal Reserve Bank of Cleveland, August 25, 1980.

7. Klapper, Byron. "Negotiated Sales Are on the Increase in Municipal Sector." *The Wall Street Journal*, June 25, 1979.

8. Levin, David J. "State and Local Government Fiscal Position in 1979." *Survey of Current Business*, January 1980.

9. Morris, Frank E. "Restructuring the Municipal Market." *New England Economic Review*, Federal Reserve Bank of Boston, January-February 1971.

10. National Governors' Association. *Understanding the Fiscal Condition of the States*. Washington, D.C., 1978.

11. U.S. House of Representatives. *Tax-Exempt Bonds for Single-Family Housing*, A Study Prepared by the Congressional Budget Office for the Subcommittee on the City of the Committee on Banking, Finance and Urban Affairs, 96th Cong., 1st Sess. Washington, D.C.: U.S. Government Printing Office, 1979.

part eight

The International Financial System

26

The Balance of Payments and International Transactions

In many ways the world we live in is rapidly shrinking in size. Jet planes such as the British Concorde can cross the Atlantic between New York and London in less than four hours, about the same time it takes a Boeing 747 jetliner to travel across the United States. Teletype, telex, and transoceanic cable can move financial information and instructions from one spot on the globe to another in minutes. Orbiting satellites can bring news of major international significance to home television sets the same day an event takes place and make possible video as well as voice communication between those involved in international business transactions.

Accompanying these dramatic improvements in communication and transportation is an enormous growth in world trade and international investment. For example, in 1965 total exports of goods and services worldwide reached $350 billion. Twelve years later, in 1977, the estimated value of world trade had climbed to more than $2 trillion, or roughly equivalent to the United States GNP. In the Eurodollar market, where borrowing and lending of dollar-denominated deposits takes place, total dollar deposits available for trading climbed from $10 billion in 1965 and $110 billion in 1970 to $1,155 billion at year-end 1979.[1] The system of international financial markets which spans the globe has grown enormously just to keep up with burgeoning world trade and investment. Many new financial institutions and financial innovations have appeared in an international environment of dynamic growth and change.

[1] See Morgan Guaranty Trust Company of New York, *World Finance Markets,* selected issues.

Actually, the international financial markets perform the same basic function as do the domestic financial markets. They bring international lenders of funds (savers) into contact with borrowers, thereby permitting an increased flow of scarce funds toward their most productive uses. The volume of capital investment worldwide is made larger because of the workings of the global financial system. And, with increased capital investment, the productivity of individual firms and nations is increased and economic growth in the international sector accelerates. The international financial markets also facilitate the flow of consumer goods and services across national boundaries, making possible an optimal allocation of resources in response to consumer demand on a global scale. With increased efficiency in resource use, the output of consumer goods and services in the international sector is increased and costs of production are minimized.[2]

Just as the domestic financial markets have given rise to a unique collection of financial institutions and methods for transferring funds, so the international financial system has spawned institutions and practices unique to that system. As we will see later in this chapter and in the two chapters to follow, the global financial markets are dominated by huge multinational corporations, central banks, government agencies, the largest commercial banks and financial conglomerates, investment banking houses, security and foreign exchange dealers, and major brokerage houses. Our purpose in this section of the book is to examine the unique roles played by each of these institutions within a rapidly expanding international financial system.

THE BALANCE OF PAYMENTS

One of the most widely used sources of information concerning flows of funds, goods, and services between nations is each country's *balance-of-payments accounts*. This annual statistical report summarizes all the economic and financial transactions between residents of one nation and the rest of the world during a specific period of time. It is a report capturing *flows* (rather than stocks) of payments between nations. Thus, the balance-of-payments accounts reflect *changes* in the assets and liabilities of units— businesses, individuals, and governments—involved in international transactions, rather than the *levels* of their assets and liabilities.[3] The major transac-

---

[2] These benefits from international trade and finance are most likely to occur if each nation involved follows the principle of *comparative advantage*. This principle argues that each country will have a higher real standard of living if it specializes in the production of those goods and services in which it has a comparative advantage in resource costs, while importing those goods and services where it is at a comparative disadvantage. In simplest terms, a country should acquire goods and services from those sources—foreign or domestic—which result in the lowest cost of its own resources. The principle of comparative advantage works best, of course, in an environment of free international trade which permits nations to specialize in their most efficient productive activities.

[3] In this sense the balance-of-payments accounts are analogous to the Flow of Funds Accounts discussed in Chapter 10. The balance-of-payments accounts are really sources and uses of funds statements for a whole nation vis-á-vis the rest of the world.

tions captured in the balance-of-payments accounts include exports and imports of goods and services; tourist expenditures; income from debt and equity investments made abroad; government loans, grants, and military expenditures overseas; and net private capital flows between nations.

In a statistical sense, a nation's balance-of-payments accounts always "balance" because a system of double-entry bookkeeping is used. For example, every payment made for goods and services imported from abroad simultaneously creates a claim on the home country's resources or extinguishes an existing liability. Similarly, every time a domestic business firm receives payment from overseas, either it acquires a claim against resources in a foreign country, or a claim the firm held against a foreign individual or institution is erased. In practice, however, imbalances frequently show up in the balance-of-payments accounts due to unreported transactions or inconsistencies in reporting. These errors and omissions are handled through a Statistical Discrepancy account.

The United States Balance of International Payments

The United States balance of payments accounts are prepared and published quarterly by the Department of Commerce. The quarterly figures usually are annualized to permit comparisons across years. The full set of U.S. international accounts is quite complex because several different groups of international transactions (*balances*) are calculated to meet the varying needs of policymakers and financial analysts. However, the transactions recorded in the U.S. balance of payments (and those for other countries as well) fall into three broad groups:

1. *Transactions on current account,* which include imports and exports of goods and services and unilateral transfers (gifts).
2. *Transactions on capital account,* which include both long-term and short-term investment at home and abroad and usually involve the transfer of financial assets (acceptances, bonds, deposits, stock, etc.).
3. *Official reserve transactions,* which are used by monetary authorities (the Treasury, central bank, exchange stabilization fund, etc.) to settle balance-of-payments deficits, usually through transferring the ownership of official reserve assets (including government foreign currency holdings, gold, special drawing rights at the International Monetary Fund, and government-held securities).

Transactions which bring about an inflow of foreign currency into the home country are recorded as credits ($+$). Transactions resulting in an outflow of foreign currency from the home country are listed as debits ($-$).[4]

---

[4] Therefore, any economic transaction which involves *only* domestic residents and is conducted only in the home currency would not be reflected in the home country's balance-of-payments account.

Thus, credit (+) items in the balance of payments represent *sources of funds*—an increase in a nation's external buying power or ability to command goods and services from abroad or to invest abroad. Debit (−) items represent *uses of funds,* which decrease a nation's buying power abroad. If a country sells goods and services or borrows abroad, these transactions are credit items because they increase a nation's external buying power. On the other hand, a purchase of goods and services abroad or a paydown of a nation's international liabilities is a debit item because that country is surrendering part of its external buying power. A summary of the major credit and debit items making up the balance of payments is shown in Exhibit 26–1.

EXHIBIT 26–1
Principal Credit and Debt Items Recorded in a Nation's Balance of Payments

Credit Entries (inflows of funds, +)	Debit Entries (outflows of funds, −)
Exports of merchandise	Imports of merchandise
Services provided to foreign countries	Services provided to domestic citizens by foreign countries
Interest and dividends due domestic citizens from business firms abroad	Gifts of money sent abroad by domestic citizens
Remittances received from domestic citizens employed in foreign countries	Capital invested abroad by domestic citizens
Foreign purchases of securities issued by domestic firms and units of government	Dividend and interest payments to foreign countries on investments made in the domestic economy
Repayments by foreigners of funds borrowed from domestic lending institutions	

The actual U.S. balance-of-payments accounts for the years 1979 and 1980 as reported by the Department of Commerce are shown in Exhibit 26–2. We have subdivided these international accounts into the three major categories discussed above—the current account, capital account, and official reserve transactions account—to more fully understand how the balance-of-payments bookkeeping system operates.

The Current Account

One of the most highly publicized components of the U.S. balance of payments is the *current account,* which contains three elements:

1. *The merchandise trade balance,* comparing the volume of goods exported to those imported.
2. The *service balance,* comparing exports and imports of services.
3. *Unilateral transfers,* reflecting the amount of gifts made to foreigners by domestic citizens.

The Merchandise Trade Balance. Prior to the 1970s the United States reported a positive merchandise trade balance, with exports exceeding im-

EXHIBIT 26–2
The Balance of Payments of the United States, 1979 and 1980 ($ billions)*

Credit (+) and Debit (−) Items	1979	1980
The current account:†		
Exports of merchandise‡	$182.1	$221.8
Imports of merchandise‡	−211.5	−249.1
Balance on merchandise trade	− 29.4	− 27.4
Exports of services§	104.5	119.1
Imports of services§	− 70.2	− 84.8
Service balance	+ 34.3	+ 34.4
Balance on goods and services	+ 5.0	+ 7.1
Unilateral transfers (excluding military grants), net	− 5.7	− 7.0
Balance on current account	− 0.7	+ 0.1
The capital account:		
Private capital flows:	− 5.0	− 39.8
U.S. bank-reported capital, net (outflow, −).................	6.8	− 35.9
U.S. net purchase (−) of foreign securities	− 4.6	− 3.2
Foreign net purchases (+) of U.S. Treasury securities	4.8	2.7
Foreign net purchases (−) of other U.S. securities	2.9	7.4
U.S. direct investment abroad	− 24.3	− 20.6
Foreign direct investment in the United States	9.7	8.2
Other corporate capital flows, net	− 0.3	NA
Total private capital flows, net	− 5.0	− 39.8
Official reserve transactions:		
Foreign official assets in the United States (increase, +).......	− 14.3	16.2
U.S. government foreign assets, net (increase, −)	− 4.9	− 13.3
Reserve position in IMF	− 0.2	− 1.7
Convertible currencies and other reserve assets.............	− 0.9	− 6.5
U.S. government foreign credits and other claims, net	− 3.8	− 5.1
Allocation of Special Drawing Rights..........................	1.1	1.2
Statistical discrepancy (errors and omissions)	23.8	35.6

* Details may not add to totals due to rounding.
† The current account is seasonally adjusted, but the other accounts are not seasonally adjusted.
‡ These export and import figures exclude military purchases.
§ The service balances include transfers under U.S. military agency sales contracts in the case of exports, and direct defense expenditures in the case of imports.
SOURCES: U.S. Department of Commerce, *Survey of Current Business,* March 1981; and Federal Reserve Board, *Annual Report, 1980,* p. 26.

ports in most years due to substantial demand for American agricultural products, machinery, and equipment overseas. However, uncertainty over the value of the U.S. dollar, rapid inflation, and a dramatic increase in crude oil prices have turned U.S. trade surpluses into substantial deficits in recent years. U.S. sources of external power have generally been less than its uses of external buying power. Moreover, American merchandise trade deficits generally have deepened over time. For example, in 1971 the U.S. merchandise trade balance was −$2.3 billion; in 1976, −$9.3 billion; and in 1979, −$29.4 billion.

There was a slight improvement in the U.S. trade deficit during 1980, as shown in Exhibit 26–2. Merchandise exports totaled $221.8 billion, while imports reached $249.1 billion, resulting in a debit (−) balance in the merchandise account of −$27.4 billion. If oil imports are excluded from U.S. trade figures, a positive merchandise trade balance prevails in most years, suggesting the extremely powerful impact which foreign oil imports have today on the international payments position of the United States.

The Service Balance. Because Americans have purchased more goods from abroad in recent years than they have sold to other countries, how has this deficit (debit balance) in the merchandise trade account been paid for? Funds must be acquired from some source to finance the excess of merchandise imports over exports. Part of the needed funds have come from the service balance, which has been in surplus (credit balance) for many years (see Exhibits 26–2 and 26–3).

EXHIBIT 26–3
U.S. International Service Transactions ($ billions)

Item	1979	1980
Service transactions, net	$ 34.3	$ 34.3
Receipts	104.5	119.1
Payments	−70.1	−84.7
Military transactions, net	−1.3	−3.3
Travel and passenger fares, net	−2.0	−1.4
Other transportation, net	−0.7	−0.1
Investment income, net	32.5	32.5
Direct, net	31.8	28.2
Other, net	0.7	4.3
Fees and royalties, net	5.5	6.2
Other services, net	0.3	0.3

Notes: 1980 figures are preliminary. Net military transactions consist of goods and services transferred under military sales contracts less imports of goods and services by U.S. defense agencies.
SOURCE: U.S. Department of Commerce, Survey of Current Business, March 1981.

Services counted in the balance of payments accounts include insurance policies covering foreign shipments of goods, shipping of ocean freight and other transportation services, hotel accommodations for foreigners visiting the United States, and property management services, entertainment, and medical care for foreign residents. Also included in the service balance are receipts of income from U.S. direct investments abroad (usually in the form of interest and dividends).[5] These income flows are created when U.S. residents purchase foreign securities and acquire equity interests in foreign businesses. When exports of services exceed service imports, the result is a credit (+) balance in the services account. The balance in the service ac-

---

[5] In effect, interest and dividend payments received by domestic residents from international investments reflect services which the nation's capital is providing overseas. The interest and dividend payments increase a country's external buying power.

counts is sometimes called the *balance in invisibles* because services are intangible items. In 1980 the U.S. service balance, or balance in invisibles, was in surplus by $34.4 billion, virtually the same credit (+) balance as the year before.

Balance on Goods and Services. If we combine the merchandise trade balance with the service balance, the resulting figure is labeled the *balance on goods and services*. In 1980 the U.S. reported a merchandise trade deficit of $27.4 billion and a credit balance in services of $34.4 billion, resulting in a credit balance on goods and services of +$7.1 billion.

Unilateral Transfers. The third category of transactions recorded in the current account, labeled unilateral transfers, consists of gifts of goods or money from U.S. residents to foreigners. Gifts of food, clothing, furniture, appliances, money, and other items are referred to as unilateral transfers because they represent a *one-way flow* of resources to the recipient. Nothing is expected in return. Of course, foreigners send gifts to U.S. residents as well as the other way around, but American gift giving abroad far exceeds the return flow. For example, in 1980 gifts to foreigners from Americans (due principally to a sharp rise in transfers to Israel) were $7 billion larger than foreign gifts flowing into the U.S. (see Exhibit 26–2). Each gift sent overseas represents a use of the nation's external buying power and therefore is recorded as a debit (–) item.

The Balance on Current Account. When we put the three components— balance on merchandise trade, balance on services, and net unilateral transfers—together, we derive the *balance on current account*. As Exhibit 26–2 reveals, the U.S. balance on current account in 1980 was a small credit balance of $0.1 billion—the first positive current account balance since 1976. The United States was able to improve its current account position because U.S. exports increased faster than imports and the nation's positive service balance remained strong.

The Capital Account

Flows of funds destined for investment abroad are recorded in the capital account. Investments abroad may be long term, as in the case of an American automobile company building an assembly plant in West Germany, or short term, such as the purchase of six-month British Treasury bills by U.S. citizens. Of course, capital investment flows both ways across national boundaries. For example, in 1980 U.S. citizens and private organizations invested more than $71 billion overseas, but foreign individuals and private institutions, attracted by high interest rates here, invested about $31 billion in U.S. assets. The result was a *net private capital outflow* from the United States of about $40 billion.

Interestingly enough, investments by foreigners in the United States are growing faster today than U.S. investments overseas. The relative prosperity experienced by the American economy over the past decade coupled with political upheavals abroad has brought forth an increasing volume of foreign investment in the continental United States. American banks; hotels; chemical manufacturers; insurance companies; wholesale traders in motor vehicles, metals, and farm products; energy companies; and numerous other businesses have all been acquisition targets for foreign investors. In 1971 direct foreign investment in U.S. assets amounted to just $367 million, but by 1980 foreigners were investing $8.2 billion annually in the U.S. economy. At the same time purchases of U.S. securities—principally blue-chip stocks, U.S. government bonds, and top-rated corporate bonds—expanded from $2.3 billion in 1971 to $10.1 billion in 1980.[6]

Components of the Capital Account. The capital account in the balance of payments includes three different types of international investment: (1) short-term capital flows, (2) direct investment, and (3) portfolio investment. The latter two—direct and portfolio investment—represent a long-term commitment of funds, involving the purchase of stocks, bonds, and other financial assets having a maturity of more than one year. Short-term capital flows, on the other hand, reflect purchases of financial assets with maturities of less than one year. These short-term financial assets are mainly government notes and bills, bank deposits, bills of exchange, and foreign currencies.

What is the essential difference between direct investment and portfolio investment? The key factor is *control*. Portfolio investment merely involves purchasing securities to hold in order to receive interest, dividends, or capital gains. Direct investment, on the other hand, refers to the purchase of land or the acquisition of ownership shares in an attempt to control a foreign business firm.[7]

Claims against Foreigners. In addition to direct investment and purchases of foreign securities, the capital account also records claims against foreigners reported by domestic banks and nonbanking concerns. The bulk of these claims comprises loans extended by domestic banks to firms and governments abroad.

In 1980 U.S. bank claims on foreigners rose a record $46.6 billion. Most of the gain was due to loans made by U.S. banks to their Caribbean branches,

---

[6] The leading foreign nations with ownership interests in U.S.-based firms are the United Kingdom, Canada, the Netherlands, West Germany, and Japan. These five nations accounted for three quarters of the total assets of all U.S. affiliates of foreign firms, according to Department of Commerce estimates. Most of the remaining foreign-controlled U.S. assets were held by Latin American companies.

In general, foreign direct investment in the U.S. is growing significantly faster than U.S. direct investment abroad. For example, during the 1975–79 period, U.S. direct investment overseas increased 55 percent, while foreign direct investment in the United States jumped 97 percent. However, the United States still has a significant edge in direct investment abroad. For example, at year-end 1979, U.S. direct investment in foreign nations totaled nearly $193 billion, while foreign investments in the 50 states were valued at $54 billion.

[7] The U.S. Department of Commerce defines *direct investment* as ownership of 10 percent or more of the voting stock or the exercise of other means of control over a foreign business enterprise by an individual or corporation. Ownership of less than 10 percent of a foreign firm's stock is referred to as *portfolio investment*.

which then turned around and made loans in the global Eurocurrency markets.[8] However, U.S. banks also borrowed heavily abroad to sustain their domestic and international lending operations, giving foreign investors substantial claims against American banks. For example, short-term and long-term liabilities to foreigners reported by U.S. banking and nonbanking concerns totaled $10.7 billion in 1980. If we combine U.S. bank loans abroad of $46.6 billion—a capital outflow or debit (−) item—with U.S. bank borrowings abroad of $10.7 billion—a capital inflow or credit (+) item—the result is a *net* U.S. bank-reported capital outflow of $35.9 billion, the figure shown in Exhibit 26–2.

The Basic Balance

If the current-account balance is added to the long-term investment balance in the nation's international accounts, the net figure is known as the *basic balance*. We can calculate this for the U.S. in 1980:

		$ Billions
U.S. balance on current account		+0.1
Long-term capital flows:		
Net direct investment abroad[9]	−12.4	
Net portfolio investment[9]	+ 6.9	
Net long-term capital outflow		−5.5
Basic balance		−5.4

Therefore, when merchandise trade, services, gifts, and long-term capital flows are taken into account, the U.S. had a $5.4 billion deficit for its basic balance. This deficit has to be covered either by giving up U.S. reserves of gold, foreign currency, and other assets or by giving foreigners larger claims (in the form of securities, bank deposits, etc.) against U.S. resources.

The Cumulative Balance in International Accounts and Short-Term Capital Flows

Actually, the total or cumulative U.S. balance-of-payments deficit may be larger or smaller than the basic balance. The principal reason is that the basic balance fails to consider *short-term capital flows*. Exhibit 26–2 indicates that private investors in the U.S. invested $71.2 billion in assets abroad, while foreign private investors acquired $31.4 billion in U.S. assets—a difference of approximately $40 billion, representing a net outflow from the United

---

[8] See Chapter 15 for a discussion of borrowing and lending activity in the Eurodollar and other Eurocurrency markets.

[9] The net figure is derived by subtracting foreign investments in the U.S. from investments by U.S. residents abroad. The basic balance is designed to capture only basic, long-term trends in a nation's balance of payments. Short-term capital flows, excluded from the basic balance, are assumed to result from temporary factors (such as the financing of current transactions) which will "net out" in the long run.

States of *both* short- and long-term private capital. However, we must also consider the possibility of a *statistical discrepancy* in the reported figures due to thousands of unreported transactions that occur across national borders each day.

As noted earlier, because the balance of payments is based on a double-entry system of bookkeeping, it should always balance out except for errors in recording and reporting transactions and the omission of many unrecorded items. Errors and ommissions are captured in an account called Statistical Discrepancy. Many authorities believe that the Statistical Discrepancy reflects primarily unrecorded short-term capital flows. This account often increases in size when large amounts of short-term capital are known to be in motion from one country to another in response to differences in interest rates or currency values. The 1980 statistical discrepancy was a credit (+) balance of $35.6 billion, suggesting that U.S. security issuers were able to attract large amounts of foreign funds.[10] Particularly notable in 1980 was an upsurge in foreign purchases of U.S. corporate stocks.

After adjusting for foreign capital flowing into the United States, therefore, the *net* amount of short-term and long-term capital which flowed out of the country in 1980 was probably much less than the $39.8 billion private capital outflow (−) shown in Exhibit 26–2. The deficit in the U.S. basic balance of $5.4 billion in 1980 was probably not a true reflection of the cumulative or overall deficit in the American balance of payments.

Official Reserve Transactions

When a nation has a deficit in its international payments accounts, it must settle up by surrendering assets or claims to foreign individuals and institutions. Official reserve transactions, involving transfer of the ownership of gold, convertible foreign currencies, or deposits in the International Monetary Fund (known as special drawing rights or SDRs[11]), are usually the vehicle for settling net differences in international claims between countries.

Official reserve accounts are immediately available assets for making international payments. When these assets increase, this represents a *use* of external buying power by the nation experiencing the increase. On the other hand, a decrease in the official reserve accounts represents a source of exter-

---

[10] The Statistical Discrepancy account has increased dramatically in size in recent years. For example, this catch-all category in the U.S. balance of payments totaled only −$219 million in 1970 and climbed to +$23.8 billion in 1979 before reaching the record level shown for 1980. Several factors have contributed to the account's growth, including political unrest abroad, secret and illegal transactions, errors on the part of clerks filling out or processing government report forms, and concealment by governments of their true international reserve positions. The major problem is probably unreported investment funds flowing in from abroad in search of safety from political upheavals. Many of these funds are secretly invested or are tagged with names not reflecting their true owners. Increased trading in foreign currencies also has been a factor. The floating exchange rates which prevail today have stimulated a huge volume of speculative currency trading, in the range of $40 to $60 trillion a year.

[11] SDRs are discussed later in this chapter.

nal buying power. If a nation has a surplus (credit balance) in its current and capital accounts, the balance in its official reserve accounts generally rises, indicating an excess of sales abroad over foreign purchases. Conversely, a country experiencing a deficit (debit balance) in its current and capital accounts usually will find that the balance in its official reserve accounts is falling.

In 1980 offsetting movements occurred in U.S. and foreign holdings of official reserve assets. Foreign governments and central banks increased their holdings of gold, currencies, and other official assets in the U.S. by $16.2 billion, net, due mostly to increased holdings of dollar assets by OPEC nations. This increase in foreign holdings of American reserve assets was larger than the deficit in the U.S. basic balance. As a result, the U.S. was able to increase its own holdings of official reserve assets. Especially notable was a significant increase in U.S. holdings of convertible currencies. The U.S. government made large purchases of German marks in 1980 to help stabilize the international currency markets.

Disequilibrium in the Balance of Payments

The deficit in the U.S. basic balance account reported in 1980 was not an isolated phenomenon. For several years the United States has displayed a *disequilibrium position* in its balance of international payments. This means that the nation has relied upon foreign credit and its stock of gold, foreign currencies, and other reserve assets to settle continuing balance-of-payments deficits. However, the amount of these financing devices is limited; no nation can go on indefinitely accumulating balance-of-payments deficits, borrowing abroad, and using up its exchange reserves.

To this point foreign central banks and foreign investors have regarded American securities and interest-bearing, dollar-denominated deposits (Eurodollars) as good investments and have been willing to extend an increasing volume of international credits to the United States. At some point, however, when foreign governments, central banks, and private investors are satiated with dollars and dollar claims, the value of the U.S. dollar must begin to decline in the international markets. American purchases of goods and services abroad would also decline because of the dollar's reduced purchasing power. All else equal, the nation's standard of living would begin to fall.

Trends in the U.S. Balance of Payments

Is this long-term disequilibrium position in U.S. international payments likely to continue? What components of the American balance of payments have contributed the most to recent payments deficits?

As Exhibits 26–4 and 26–5 reveal, one of the most-persistent problems has been in the U.S. *merchandise trade account.* Following a series of annual

EXHIBIT 26–4
Annual Series, U.S. International Transactions ($ millions)*

	Trade Flows					Capital Flows†								
Year	Merchandise Exports	Merchandise Imports	Service Exports	Service Imports	Current Account Balance	Direct Investment Abroad	Direct Investment in U.S.	Security Purchases Abroad	Security Purchases in U.S.	Bank Claims on Foreigners	Bank Liabilities to Foreigners	U.S. Government Assets Abroad	Foreign Official Assets in U.S.	Monetary Base Effect
1960	19,650	14,758	9,211	8,971	2,824	2,940	315	663	−82	1,148	678	−1,045	1,473	−2,128
1961	20,108	14,537	9,828	9,054	3,821	2,652	311	762	475	1,261	928	303	765	−1,061
1962	20,781	16,260	11,023	9,518	3,388	2,852	346	969	68	450	336	−450	1,270	−1,012
1963	22,272	17,048	11,942	9,999	4,414	3,483	213	1,105	138	1,556	898	1,284	1,986	−539
1964	25,501	18,700	13,324	10,522	6,822	3,759	322	677	−231	2,505	1,818	1,509	1,660	−114
1965	26,461	21,510	14,625	11,291	5,431	5,010	415	759	−489	−93	503	380	134	−1,378
1966	29,310	25,493	15,250	13,106	3,029	5,416	425	720	550	−233	2,882	973	−672	−879
1967	30,666	26,866	16,649	14,740	2,584	4,806	698	1,308	881	495	1,765	2,370	3,451	1,748
1968	33,626	32,991	18,737	15,809	611	5,295	807	1,569	4,550	−233	3,871	3,144	−774	−1,540
1969	36,414	35,807	21,108	18,322	339	5,690	1,263	1,549	3,062	570	8,886	3,379	−1,301	−72
1970	42,469	39,866	23,204	20,184	2,330	7,589	1,464	1,076	2,270	967	−6,298	−892	6,908	−355
1971	43,319	45,579	25,518	20,090	−1,434	7,617	367	1,113	2,265	2,980	−6,911	−465	26,879	−922
1972	49,381	55,797	28,114	23,638	−5,795	7,747	949	618	4,468	3,506	4,754	1,572	10,475	−39
1973	71,410	70,499	38,831	28,720	7,140	11,353	2,800	671	3,825	5,980	4,702	2,486	6,026	−328
1974	98,306	103,649	48,360	33,708	2,124	9,052	4,760	1,854	1,075	19,516	16,017	1,101	10,546	−34
1975	107,088	98,041	48,641	34,795	18,280	14,244	2,603	6,247	5,093	13,532	628	4,323	7,027	469
1976	114,745	124,051	56,885	38,197	4,384	11,949	4,347	8,885	4,067	21,368	10,990	6,772	17,693	759
1977	120,186	151,689	63,889	42,480	−14,068	12,808	3,728	5,460	3,247	11,427	6,719	4,068	36,575	−414
1978	142,054	175,813	78,982	54,427	−14,259	16,345	7,897	3,450	5,008	33,631	16,259	3,912	33,293	693
1979	182,068	211,454	104,453	70,106	−705	24,319	9,713	4,643	7,772	25,868	32,668	4,916	−14,271	2,039
1980	223,966r	249,308r	120,701r	84,575r	3,723r	18,546r	10,854r	3,310r	8,063r	46,947r	10,743r	13,320r	15,492r	2,947

* See Exhibit 26–5 for explanatory footnotes.
SOURCE: Federal Reserve Bank of St. Louis.

EXHIBIT 26–5
Quarterly Series, U.S. International Transactions, Seasonally Adjusted ($ millions)*

	Trade Flows									Capital Flows†				
Quarters	Merchandise Exports	Merchandise Imports	Service Exports	Service Imports	Current Account Balance	Direct Investment Abroad	Direct Investment in U.S.	Security Purchases Abroad	Security Purchases in U.S.	Bank Claims on Foreigners	Bank Liabilities to Foreigners	U.S. Government Assets Abroad	Foreign Official Assets in U.S.	Monetary Base Effect
1978 II	35,404	43,699	18,752	13,252	-4,102	4,051	2,313	1,106	2,165	-102	1,256	1,009	-5,273	-239
III	36,828	44,336	19,604	14,029	-3,166	3,010	2,620	488	-575	5,179	9,243	1,271	4,777	88
IV	38,900	45,715	22,231	14,923	-820	4,578	1,608	849	2,085	22,284	6,164	809	18,368	503
1979 I	41,806	46,922	23,862	16,016	1,406	5,819	1,120	1,001	3,367	-6,181	7,001	4,687	-8,744	2,310
II	42,816	50,876	24,940	16,988	-1,483	7,214	2,812	513	1,029	7,839	12,082	669	-10,095	888
III	47,207	54,259	27,675	18,009	1,107	7,156	3,217	2,143	2,143	16,997	13,185	-2,013	5,789	-1,281
IV	50,239	59,397	26,063	19,093	-1,735	4,129	2,664	986	1,233	7,213	400	1,574	-1,221	122
1980 I	54,898r	65,024r	30,866r	20,957r	-2,095r	4,863r	2,221r	766r	5,735r	1,203r	6,599r	4,724r	-7,462r	1,165
II	58,667r	62,411r	27,960r	20,419r	-545r	2,710r	3,884r	1,369r	-792r	20,165r	-4,509r	685r	7,557r	-10
III	56,252r	59,164r	30,403r	21,023r	4,975r	3,851r	2,690r	818r	-13r	12,440r	916r	2,536r	7,686r	335
IV	67,149r	62,719r	41,407r	21,183r	1,390r	7,122r	2,060r	356r	3,133r	13,139r	7,737r	5,373r	7,711r	1,457
1981 I	61,117p	65,719p	33,042p	23,841p	3,087p	982p	1,965p	488p	3,854p	11,163p	-3,662p	5,887p	5,384p	2,344

* The signs in this table do *not* indicate whether a particular transaction is an inflow or an outflow. In this table a negative sign indicates a reduction in the stock of a particular class of assets during a particular time period.

† Not seasonally adjusted, quarterly averages of end-of-month data. Beginning first quarter 1979, official U.S. holdings of assets denominated in foreign currencies are revalued monthly at market exchange rates. As of July 1980 the monetary base effect includes the addition of official U.S. holdings of Swiss franc denominated assets. Consequently, this series after July 1980 is not directly comparable to that reported for previous periods.

p—Preliminary   r—Revised

Merchandise Exports and Imports: the current dollar value of physical goods which are exported from and imported into the United States.

Service Exports and Imports: receipts and reinvestment of earnings on foreign investments in the United States (interest, dividends and branch earnings), sales and payments and receipts associated with foreign travel and transportation.

Current Account: the sum of merchandise and service exports less merchandise and service imports and unilateral transfers, which are private transfers representing gifts and similar payments by Americans to foreign residents and government transfers representing payments associated with foreign assistance programs.

Direct Investment: private sector capital transactions which result in the ownership of 10 percent or more of the voting securities or other ownership interests in foreign enterprises by U.S. residents either by themselves or in affiliation with others, including reinvested earnings of incorporated foreign affiliates of U.S. firms; private sector transactions which result in the ownership of 10 percent or more (before 1974, 25 percent or more) of the voting securities or other ownership interests in U.S. enterprises by foreigners, including reinvested earnings of incorporated U.S. affiliates of foreign firms.

Security Purchases: U.S. private sector net purchases of foreign equity and debt securities with no contractual maturity or a maturity of more than one year; foreign private sector and international financial institutions net purchases of U.S. equity and debt securities with no contractual maturities or maturities of more than one year and U.S. Treasury securities.

Bank Claims and Liabilities: changes in claims on private sector foreigners (loans, collections outstanding, acceptances, deposits abroad, claims on affiliated foreign banks, foreign government obligations, and foreign commercial and finance paper) and liabilities to private sector foreigners and international financial institutions (demand, time, and savings deposits, certificates of deposit, liabilities to affiliated foreign banks, and other liabilities) reported by U.S. banks for their own accounts and for the custody accounts of their customers.

U.S. Government Assets Abroad: changes in U.S. official reserve assets (gold, special drawing rights, foreign currency holdings, and reserve position in the International Monetary Fund) and changes in other U.S. government assets abroad.

Foreign Official Assets in U.S.: foreign official agencies' net purchases of U.S. government securities, obligations issued by U.S. government corporations and agencies, securities issued by state and local governments, and changes in liabilities to foreign official agencies reported by U.S. banks.

SOURCE: Federal Reserve Bank of St. Louis.

trade surpluses during the 1960s, the 1970s ushered in a period when merchandise imports substantially exceeded exports. Today, imports account for approximately 12 percent of the U.S. GNP. These U.S. trade deficits have had many causes—sharply higher prices for imported oil, declining industrial productivity, the success of several foreign nations (especially Japan) in marketing their goods in U.S. markets, burgeoning demand for imported automobiles, and the inability of domestic policy makers to solve the problem of inflation. The largest merchandise trade deficit, almost $34 billion, occurred in 1978. Since then, U.S. trade deficits have moderated somewhat due to slower economic growth abroad, the moderating of energy price increases, and evidence as the 1980s began that the U.S. inflation rate had leveled out.

There is some prospect that the U.S. merchandise trade gap will narrow further in the period ahead, though much depends on the success of antiinflation policies and attempts to increase the productivity of American industry. Interestingly enough, however, a new problem appeared as the 1980s began. The value of the dollar in international currency markets rose sharply due to extremely attractive interest rates available in U.S. money and capital markets. The dollar's upward surge in value significantly increased the purchase price of U.S. goods and services abroad. American exports began to grow more slowly, and some sectors of the U.S. economy experienced declining demand for exported goods—notably aircraft, aluminum, coal, office equipment, electric power–generating machinery, machine tools, and wheat grains. At the same time, imports into the United States, particularly from less-developed countries, accelerated as foreign businesses realized that the dollar's rise was making imported goods in the United States relatively cheaper. The prices of a number of key international commodities—copper, gold, lead, silver, and tin—began to decline significantly. The net effect of all these developments, of course, was to create and then deepen a U.S. merchandise trade deficit.

A positive factor in the U.S. international payments position is the long-term surplus in the *service account*. As we noted earlier, exports of services exceeded service imports by nearly $35 billion in 1980. In fact, the U.S. has had a service account surplus each year since 1960, as Exhibit 26–4 reveals, and that surplus has been growing over time. As American shipping lines and airline companies, hotels, travel agencies, insurance companies, and banks continue to expand their service offerings abroad, the U.S. service account should continue to display substantial surplus (credit) balances in the future. A sizable credit balance in the service account coupled with a moderating merchandise trade deficit explains why the U.S. current account balance in 1980 displayed its first surplus (credit) balance since 1976.

A far-more-serious long-term problem for the U.S. balance-of-payments centers on the *capital account*. American investors and lending institutions increasingly are finding foreign markets attractive for both long- and short-term investments, creating each year a massive net outflow of capital funds.

As Exhibit 26–4 indicates, while foreign direct investment in the United States has been growing rapidly in recent years, U.S. direct investment abroad has been far larger in terms of total dollars. Although British, Canadian, Dutch, Japanese, and other investors have begun to invest heavily in American real estate and corporate stock, U.S. direct investments in foreign real estate and businesses are likely to continue at a high level, putting continual pressure on the American balance-of-payments position.[12]

Another problem also likely to persist comprises loans to multinational corporations and foreign governments extended by U.S. banks.[13] When a domestic commercial bank makes a loan overseas, this results in a capital outflow (debit) in the nation's balance of payments. The claims of American banks against foreigners rose almost $47 billion in 1980, a 30 percent increase, after climbing nearly $26 billion the year before. As Exhibits 26–4 and 26–5 show, U.S. bank credit to foreigners has fluctuated widely in recent years due to swings in interest rates, economic conditions, and changes in regulations. An offset to this outflow of capital funds is provided by U.S. bank liabilities to foreigners (mainly in the form of Eurodollar deposits). However, in most years U.S. bank lending abroad (a capital outflow) has far exceeded bank borrowing abroad (a capital inflow), adding to American payments deficits. The future growth of the bank-credit deficit depends critically upon interest rate levels in the United States and abroad, regulations imposed on the foreign activities of American banks, and the strength of the American economy. At present the outlook is for continued rapid expansion of U.S. bank lending in foreign markets as more and more businesses enter the international arena to find new customers and new markets.

---

[12] Capital inflows into the United States have grown faster in recent years than U.S. investments abroad. The most-rapid gains in foreign investment inside the United States have been centered in service-oriented industries—banking and finance, insurance, and trade. However, investments in U.S. trade industries and petroleum affiliates have also continued to grow rapidly. The Netherlands is the leading foreign nation represented in U.S. capital inflows, accounting for about one quarter of the total, followed in relative importance by the United Kingdom, Canada, West Germany, and Japan. Despite much congressional concern, direct investment in the United States by OPEC nations accounts for less than 1 percent of total foreign holdings, and about two thirds of OPEC's holdings are in real estate. A major factor accelerating foreign direct investment is the desire to avoid American import restrictions by developing production facilities inside the United States.

Concern over the speed with which foreign investors are taking over U.S. commercial operations flared into the open in 1975, when President Gerald Ford created the Committee on Foreign Investment, an interagency monitoring group including representatives from the President's Council of Economic Advisers and the Departments of Commerce, Defense, State, and the Treasury. This committee at the present time has confined its monitoring activities to those foreign investments which appear to be politically motivated (i.e., controlled by foreign governments). However, to date it has not blocked any foreign investments in the United States, due largely to a long-standing U.S. policy favoring free international trade and investment. In general, the United States is more receptive to foreign investment than most other nations.

[13] The subject of international banking and international loans is discussed more fully in Chapter 28.

THE PROBLEM OF DIFFERENT MONETARY UNITS

Businesses and individuals trading goods and services in international markets encounter a problem not experienced by those who buy and sell only in domestic markets. This is the problem of different monetary units used as the standard of value from country to country. Americans, of course, use dollars as a medium of exchange and standard of value in domestic markets. British citizens employ pounds sterling for domestic exchange, while the Swiss and the French rely upon the franc as their basic monetary unit. There are more than 100 different monetary units around the world (see Exhibit 26–6). As a result, whenever goods and services are sold or capital flows across national boundaries, it is usually necessary to sell one currency and buy another.

EXHIBIT 26–6
Principal Monetary Units Used in International Trade and Finance

Country	Monetary Unit	Country	Monetary Unit
Australia	Dollar	Japan	Yen
Argentina	Peso	Malaysia	Ringgit
Austria	Schilling	Mexico	Peso
Belgium	Franc	Netherlands	Guilder
Canada	Dollar	New Zealand	Dollar
Denmark	Krone	Norway	Krone
Finland	Markka	Portugal	Escudo
France	Franc	Saudi Arabia	Riyal
Germany	Deutsche mark	South Africa	Rand
Honduras	Lempira	Spain	Peseta
India	Rupee	Sri Lanka	Rupee
Iran	Rial	Sweden	Krona
Ireland	Pound	Switzerland	Franc
Italy	Lira	United Kingdom	Pound sterling
		United States	Dollar

Unfortunately, the act of trading currencies entails substantial risk.[14] Exporters and importers may be forced to purchase a foreign currency when its value is rising while, at the same time, the home country's currency is falling in value. Any profits earned on the sale of goods and services abroad may be outweighed by losses suffered in currency exchange. Moreover, the very existence of different monetary units encourages speculation over future currency values, which in turn increases the instability of exchange rates and adds to the costs of international trade. Differing monetary units also complicate government monetary policy aimed at curbing inflation and ensuring adequate economic growth. Repeatedly during the 1960s and 70s,

---

[14] See Chapter 27 for a discussion of the risks involved in currency trading.

massive flows of funds surged through foreign and domestic markets from speculative buying and selling of dollars, francs, pounds, and other major currencies. These speculative currency flows greatly increased the problems of European economic recovery, the control of inflation, and adjustments to the worldwide shortage of energy.

The Gold Standard

The problem of trading in different monetary units whose prices change frequently is one of the world's oldest financial problems. It has been dealt with in a wide variety of ways over the centuries. One of the most successful solutions prior to the modern era centered upon *gold* as an international standard of value. During the 17th and 18th centuries—a period which gave birth to the Industrial Revolution and the rapid expansion of world trade— major trading nations in Western Europe made their currencies freely convertible into gold. Gold bullion and gold coins could be exported and imported from one country to another without significant restrictions, and each unit of currency was defined in terms of so many grains of fine gold. Nations adopting the gold standard agreed to exchange paper money or gold coins for gold bullion in unlimited amounts at fixed, predetermined prices.

One advantage of the gold standard was that it imposed a common standard of value upon all national currencies. This brought a measure of security to international trade and investment, dampened exchange rate fluctuations, and stimulated the expansion of commerce and long-term investment abroad. A second advantage of the gold standard was economic discipline. Tying national currencies to gold regulated the growth and stability of national economies. A nation experiencing severe inflation or excessively rapid growth in consumption of imported goods and services soon found itself losing gold reserves. Exports declined, unemployment rose, and domestic prices soon began to fall. As a result, the volume of imports was curtailed, and the outflow of gold reduced. Eventually, export industries would recover and the country would begin to rebuild its gold reserves, providing a basis for further expansion of its international trade.[15]

These advantages of security and economic discipline were offset by a number of limitations inherent in the gold standard. For one thing, the gold standard depended crucially upon free trade. Nations desiring to protect their industry and jobs from foreign competition through export or import restrictions could not do so. Moreover, the growth of a nation's money

---

[15] The role of gold in promoting monetary *discipline* may be more important than many financial analysts and policy makers assume. In 1971 the U.S. government severed the link between gold and foreign official holdings of dollars by suspending the convertibility of these holdings into bullion. Following that official break, the volume of Eurodollar deposits in the world monetary system increased by a factor of 10 times during the 1970s, while interest rates and the prices of gold, silver, crude oil, and other commodities soared.

supply was limited by the size of its gold stock. Problems of rising unemployment or lagging economic growth might call for a stimulative monetary policy, leading to lower interest rates and rapid expansion of the domestic money supply. However, such a policy required a suspension of gold convertibility, taking the nation off the gold standard. Thus, the gold standard often conflicted with national economic goals and drastically limited the policy alternatives open to governmental authorities.

The Gold Exchange Standard

While government policy makers were mainly concerned about the effects of the gold standard on domestic economies, investors and commercial traders found that gold bullion was not a particularly convenient medium of exchange. Gold is bulky, expensive to transport, and risky to handle. Moreover, the world's gold supply was limited relative to the rapidly expanding volume of international trade. These problems gave rise in the 19th century to the *gold exchange standard*. Central banks, governments, major commercial banks, and other institutions actively engaged in international commerce began to hold stocks of *convertible currencies*. Each currency was freely convertible into gold at a fixed rate but also was freely convertible into other currencies at relatively stable prices. In practice, virtually all transactions took place in convertible currencies, while gold faded into the background as an international medium of exchange.

Without question, the gold exchange standard provided greater convenience for international traders and investors. However, that monetary standard possessed the same inherent limitations as the original gold standard. National currencies were still tied to gold, and growth in world trade depended crucially upon growth of the international gold stock. The gold exchange standard collapsed during the economic chaos of the Great Depression of the 1930s.

Despite the problems inherent in the gold and gold exchange standards, there is currently a great deal of interest in the United States in returning to some type of gold standard. Congress created a 17-member Gold Commission in 1980 to "study and make recommendations concerning the role of gold in the domestic and international monetary systems." Chaired by the Secretary of the Treasury, the Gold Commission is charged with the responsibility of reviewing systems for linking the dollar's value to gold as a way of controlling monetary growth and stabilizing or eliminating inflation. At least two problems appear to stand in the way of a return to even a modified gold standard. First, while a dollar-gold link may stabilize prices in the long run, a gold standard is likely to produce substantial short-run swings in prices and domestic employment, some of which would be politically dangerous. Second, world production of gold is expected to be essentially flat or possibly even downward over at least the next two decades. The result, in all probability, would be a sharply inflated gold price and significant instability in the international payments system.

The Modified Exchange Standard

Dissatisfaction with international monetary systems tied exclusively to gold resulted in a search for a new payments system following World War II. Major Western countries convened an international monetary conference in Bretton Woods, New Jersey, in 1944 to devise a more stable money and payments system. The conference created a new mechanism for settling international payments, a new system of currency values (known as the Bretton Woods System), and an agency for monitoring the exchange-rate practices of member nations (known as the International Monetary Fund, or IMF).[16]

The centerpiece of the Bretton Woods System was the linking of foreign currency prices to the U.S. dollar and gold. The United States committed itself to buy and sell gold at $35 per ounce upon request from foreign monetary authorities. Other IMF member nations pledged to keep their currency's price within 1 percent of its par value in terms of gold or the dollar. Central banks would use their foreign exchange reserves to buy or sell their own currency in the foreign exchange market. In practice, this usually meant that, if a foreign currency fell in value below par (the lower intervention point), a central bank would sell its holdings of dollars and buy that currency in the market, driving its price up toward par. If the price of a nation's currency rose more than 1 percent above par (the upper intervention point), the central bank involved would sell its own currency and buy dollars, driving the currency's price down toward par. If a currency fell too far in value or rose too high, resulting in market disruption and threatening a massive loss of foreign-exchange reserves, the country involved would simply revalue its currency, establishing a new par value.[17]

Fundamentally, the success of the Bretton Woods System depended upon the ability of the United States to maintain confidence in the dollar and to protect its value. One of the weaknesses of the new system was that the U.S.

---

[16] The IMF establishes rules for settling international accounts between nations and grants short-term loans to member nations who lack sufficient international reserve assets to settle their balance-of-payments deficits. IMF balance-of-payments loans usually are accompanied by strict requirements that the member nation receiving credit must adopt stern economic measures to curtail the growth of its imports and expand sales of goods and services abroad. The IMF's credit guarantee often encourages banks and other nations to grant loans and aid to a member nation in trouble. Most IMF loans are for 4 to 8 years, occasionally stretching out to 10 years, and are designed to give a borrowing country time to restructure its economy to promote greater efficiency and reduced consumption of imports.

A companion organization to the IMF is the World Bank, also created under the Bretton Woods Agreement. The World Bank makes long-term loans to speed the economic development of IMF member nations.

[17] A key advantage of the Bretton Woods System over the gold standard was a severing of the old link between the supply of gold and a nation's money supply. There was no commitment to redeem paper currency with gold in unlimited amounts to anyone filing a claim for gold. Only dollars held by foreign governments could be exchanged for gold (at a fixed price of $35 per ounce). Each nation was expected to create an *exchange stabilization fund*, which held a reserve of gold and currency and stood ready to buy or sell dollars and other currencies to maintain exchange rates within 1 percent of their agreed-upon par values.

dollar was in short supply early in the postwar period, as gold had been in short supply during the 18th and 19th centuries. Initially, there was a substantial excess demand for dollars abroad; however, the system worked well at first because the dollar was by far the most stable money medium around. Moreover, the United States held a strong balance-of-payments position until the late 1950s. Later, however, the United States began to export large amounts of capital to Western Europe and Asia (principally Japan). The result was sizable U.S. trade deficits, which were dealt with by drains on the American gold stock and by a buildup of dollar holdings abroad. In one sense, this was a favorable development because it increased the supply of dollars in foreign hands and alleviated the shortage of dollars needed to finance international trade. In another sense, however, it was an indication of fundamental problems developing in the U.S. economy.

The 1960s and 70s ushered in a massive outflow of U.S. dollars as American investors were attracted by higher interest rates abroad. At the same time the favorable merchandise trade surplus which the U.S. had enjoyed for many years began to erode in the 1960s and turned negative in the 70s, contributing to deepening American balance-of-payments deficits. Presidents Johnson and Kennedy attempted to deal with the problem of capital outflows by creating an Interest Equalization Tax in 1963 and a Voluntary Credit Restraint Program in 1965. Unfortunately, an accelerating rate of inflation in the late 1960s and 70s undermined government efforts to improve the American payments position. Rising prices for domestically produced goods relative to foreign products increased the volume of U.S. imports and restrained the growth of American exports. Inflation appeared to be a permanent feature of the U.S. economic landscape, and foreign observers began to lose confidence in the ability of U.S. policy makers to control it.

Abandonment of the Bretton Woods System

Continuing inflation and other economic weaknesses forced the abandonment of the Bretton Woods System early in the 1970s. The first and most-important step in the dismantling of the old system was taken by the Nixon administration in August 1971, when the dollar was devalued and the convertibility of foreign official holdings of dollars into gold suspended. Gold ceased to be an international monetary medium; it is traded today only as a commodity.

A second step toward a new monetary system was taken in March 1973, when IMF member nations agreed to allow their currencies to float over a wider range, intervening only when currency-exchange rates varied from their par values by more than 2.25 percent. However, volatile economic conditions continued to generate massive speculative flows of capital across national boundaries. Using improved communications and funds-transfer techniques, speculators anticipating changes in official currency exchange rates could now move huge amounts of funds from one nation to another both cheaply and quickly. Central banks, including the Federal Reserve System, soon found themselves compelled to intervene in the currency markets almost daily and to use up huge amounts of foreign exchange reserves.[18] Soon, the largest IMF member countries were allowing their currencies to *float* in value, responding more actively to demand and supply forces in the marketplace.

The Managed Floating Currency Standard

In 1978 a new international payments system—often called a *managed floating currency standard*—was formally adopted by member nations of the IMF. Known as the Second Amendment to the International Monetary Fund's Article of Agreement, the official rules under which today's international money system is supposed to operate allow each nation to choose its own exchange-rate policy, consistent with the structure of its economy and its economic goals. There are, however, three principles which each member country must follow in establishing its exchange-rate policy:

1. When a nation intervenes in the foreign-exchange markets to protect its own currency, it must take into account the interests and welfare of other IMF member countries.
2. Government intervention in the foreign-exchange markets should be carried out to correct disorderly conditions in those markets which are short term in nature.
3. No member nation should intervene in the exchange markets in order to gain an unfair competitive advantage over other IMF members or to prevent effective adjustments in a nation's balance-of-payments position.

DETERMINING CURRENCY VALUES IN THE MODERN WORLD

With nations now free to choose their own exchange-rate policies, many different approaches to establishing the value of national currencies have been adopted around the world (see Exhibit 26–7). Basically, two types of exchange rate policies are followed today—pegging and floating.

Pegging Exchange Rates

Nations which attempt to keep the exchange value of their currencies within a fixed range around the value of some other currency or basket of currencies are known as *peggers*. The majority of pegging nations are developing countries that have strong commercial and financial links with one or

---

[18] See Chapter 27 for a discussion of government intervention in the foreign-exchange markets.

EXHIBIT 26–7
Exchange Rate Policies of Member Countries of the International Monetary Fund

Currencies Pegged to Other Single Currencies				Currencies Pegged to Baskets of Currencies		Floating Currencies and Their Basis		
U.S. Dollar	British Pound	French Franc	Other Currencies	SDRs	Other Basis	Economic Indicators	European Monetary System Management	Other Arrangement
Bahamas, Barbados, Botswana, Burundi, Chile, Costa Rica, Djibouti, Dominica, Dominican Republic, Ecuador, Egypt, El Salvador, Ethiopia, Grenada, Guatemala, Guyana, Haiti, Honduras, Iraq, Jamaica, Korea, Lao People's Dem. Rep., Liberia, Libya, Nepal, Nicaragua, Oman, Pakistan, Panama, Paraguay, Romania, Rwanda, St. Lucia, St. Vincent, Somalia, Sudan, Surinam, Syrian Arab Republic, Trinidad & Tobago, Venezuela, Yemen Arab Republic, Yemen People's Democratic Republic	Gambia	Benin, Cameroon, Central African Republic, Chad, Comoros, Congo, Gabon, Ivory Coast, Madagascar, Mali, Niger, Senegal, Togo, Upper Volta	Equatorial Guinea, Lesotho, Swaziland	Burma, Guinea, Guinea-Bissau, Jordan, Kenya, Malawi, Mauritius, Sao Tome & Principe, Seychelles, Sierra Leone, Uganda, Viet Nam, Zaire, Zambia	Algeria, Austria, Bangladesh, Cape Verde, Cyprus, Fiji, Finland, Kuwait, Malaysia, Malta, Mauritania, Morocco, Norway, Papua New Guinea, Singapore, Soloman Islands, Sweden, Tanzania, Thailand, Tunisia	Brazil, Colombia, Portugal	Belgium, Denmark, West Germany, France, Ireland, Italy, Luxembourg, Netherlands	Afghanistan, Argentina, Australia, Bahrain, Bolivia, Canada, Taiwan, Ghana, Greece, Ireland, India, Indonesia, Iran, Israel, Japan, Lebanon, Maldives, Mexico, New Zealand, Nigeria, Peru, Philippines, Qatar, Saudi Arabia, South Africa, Spain, Sri Lanka, Turkey, United Arab Emirates, United Kingdom, United States, Uruguay, Western Somoa, and Yugoslavia

SOURCE: Exchange rate policies of the 140 member nations of the IMF as reported by the IMF Treasurer's and Exchange and Trade Relations Departments, effective December 31, 1979, and presented in N. Carlozzi, "Pegs and Floats: The Changing Face of the Foreign Exchange Market," *Business Review*, Federal Reserve Bank of Philadelphia, May–June 1980, pp. 22–23.

more industrialized trading partners. Examples include the Bahamas, El Salvador, Panama, and Venezuela, all of which peg the exchange rate on their currency to the U.S. dollar. Madagascar has tied its currency to the French franc, while Gambia's monetary unit is pegged to the value of the British pound sterling.

Frequently, when a small, developing country has strong trade relations with more than one industrialized nation, it will use a *basket* (group) of major currencies to set the value of its own monetary unit in order to "average out" fluctuations in the value of its exports and imports. The currency basket will reflect the current exchange rates for each major trading partner, weighted by the proportion of trade carried on with each partner. A good example is Sweden, which pegs its Krona to a basket of 15 currencies, each representing a trading partner. Other nations relying on baskets of trading-partner currencies to set the value of their own currencies include Austria, Norway, Singapore, and Thailand.

Special Drawing Rights

Several nations peg their currency's exchange rate to a basket of currencies assembled by the International Monetary Fund, known as the special drawing right (SDR). The SDR is an official international monetary reserve unit designed to settle international claims arising from transactions between the IMF, governments of member nations, central banks, and various international agencies. SDRs are really "book entries" on the ledgers of the IMF and are sometimes referred to as "paper gold." Periodically, that organization will issue new SDRs and credit them to the international reserve accounts of member nations. To spend its SDRs, a nation simply requests the IMF to transfer some amount of SDRs from its own reserve account to the reserve account of another nation, usually one whose currency is widely accepted in the international markets. In return, the country asking for the transfer gets deposit balances denominated in the currency of the nation receiving the SDRs. These deposit balances may then be used to make international payments.

The value of SDRs today is based upon a basket of currencies representing the five IMF member nations with the largest volume of exports during the 1975–79 period. These five countries are the United States, the Federal Republic of Germany, France, Japan, and the United Kingdom. In determining the current value of SDRs the currency of each of these five nations is weighted according to the value of their exports and currency holdings. In 1981 the weights applied to these five currencies in the SDR basket were: U.S. dollars, 42 percent; German marks, 19 percent; French francs, 13 percent; Japanese yen, 13 percent; and British pound sterling, 13 percent. Countries that peg their currency's value to the value of the SDR basket include Burma, Guinea, Kenya, Vietnam, Zaire, and Zambia.

Floating Currency Values

Most of the developed nations float, rather than peg, their currencies. This means that the value of any particular currency is determined by demand and supply forces operating in the marketplace. Usually a *managed float* is used, in which governments will intervene on occasion, either buying or selling one or more currencies, to stabilize the value of their home currency. As Carlozzi (5) notes,

> Some nations follow a policy of leaning against the wind—intervening in order to reduce daily fluctuations in their exchange rates without attempting to adhere to any target rate. Others choose target exchange rates and intervene in order to support them. Even nations that do target exchange rates usually do not reveal their targets. Thus, they discourage speculation against these targets and retain greater flexibility to adjust them.

Three nations—Brazil, Colombia, and Portugal—employ economic indicators (such as inflation rates in various countries) to set targets for their exchange rates. Others set currency-value targets based upon the level or growth of their reserve assets or balance-of-payments position. The United States has adopted a managed-float policy but appears now to be moving closer to a "free" floating exchange rate, in which the open market determines the value of the dollar, with U.S. monetary authorities intervening only in emergency situations.[19]

The European Monetary System

A compromise currency-valuation system, including elements of both the peg and the float, has appeared recently among the eight European nations that comprise the European Monetary System (EMS).[20] Known as a "joint float," the EMS arrangement calls for member countries (except Italy) to peg their exchange rates with each other, maintaining EMS currencies within 2¼ percent of their pegged exchange values. However, exchange rates with currencies outside the EMS group are subject to a managed float. EMS member countries intervene in the market as a group to maintain the purchasing power of their group's currencies vis-à-vis those of outside nations. The EMS is viewed as a further step toward economic integration (and, perhaps, eventual political integration) in Western Europe.

Freedom and a Flexible Exchange-Rate System

It should be clear from the foregoing discussion of pegs and floats that wide diversity exists today in the manner in which national monetary units

---

[19] See Chapter 27 for a discussion of recent U.S. policies in the management of the dollar's international value.

[20] The eight countries are Belgium, Denmark, West Germany, France, Ireland, Italy, Luxembourg, and the Netherlands. Great Britain may join the EMS in the near future.

are valued. As Exhibit 26–7 suggests, more than 90 countries currently peg their currency exchange rates (nearly half of these tied to the U.S. dollar), while 45 nations allow their currencies to float (usually with some form of limited government intervention). There is a strong trend today toward greater flexibility and diversity in the management of the international monetary system. And that trend is reinforced by the International Monetary Fund's current rules, which allow each member nation to adjust its exchange policies in line with changing economic and financial conditions.

We must note, however, that in the international field as elsewhere, greater freedom carries greater risk. Trading nations have sought greater freedom in setting their exchange-rate policies in the hope of gaining an increased measure of control over their domestic economies. However, there is now for the first time in history a true international financial system, in which the economic destinies of trading nations are inextricably linked to each other. For the most part capital flows freely across international boundaries today in response to differences in interest rates, currency values, and economic conditions. These unrestricted capital flows have increased the risk that domestic policies designed to fight inflation, counter unemployment, and speed economic growth and development will be thwarted by shifting currents in a largely unregulated international marketplace. Today, successful economic policy at home requires the cooperation and coordinated action of major trading nations.

There are signs that international cooperation on global financial and economic matters is increasing. The emergence of the European Monetary System, the recently negotiated Second Amendment to the IMF's Articles of Agreement, and the coordinated energy policy agreements of the Western oil-importing nations are all indications of a new spirit in international financial affairs. And that spirit will give rise to new institutions designed to deal with conflicts between the desire for national autonomy and independence and the urgent need for international economic and monetary cooperation. The International Monetary Fund—the international agency charged with the responsibility to monitor the international currency and payments policies of member nations—is likely to play an even larger role in the international financial system of the future. SDRs, the reserve asset created by the IMF to settle international claims between nations, will be more widely used to facilitate global payments. Closer government scrutiny and possibly outright regulation of international capital flows, international banking, and the vast Eurocurrency markets will be key issues of global economics and global politics for the 1980s and the decades beyond.

STUDY QUESTIONS

1. What is meant by the term *balance of payments?* Describe the principal components of the balance-of-payments accounts.

2. Please supply a brief definition of each of the following terms associated with the balance of payments:

   a. Current account.

   b. Merchandise trade balance.

   c. Service transactions.

   d. Capital account.

   e. Investment in assets abroad.

   f. Official reserve assets.

   g. Special drawing rights.

   h. Direct investment.

   i. Errors and omissions.

3. Describe and discuss the principal trends which have occurred in the following components of the U.S. balance-of-payments accounts in recent years:

   a. Merchandise trade balance.

   b. Investment in assets abroad by U.S. residents.

   c. Investment in U.S. assets by foreign residents.

4. What is currency risk? Explain how it affects exporters, importers, and securities investors active in the international markets.

5. Why was the gold standard developed? What problems did it solve, and what problems did it create? What is the difference between the gold standard and the gold exchange standard?

6. When and where was the Modified Exchange Standard created? Explain how this system worked to stabilize the value of foreign currencies. Why was the modified exchange standard abandoned in the 1970s?

7. The international monetary system of today has been called a "managed floating currency standard." Briefly and concisely explain what this term means. Why, in your opinion, have we adopted this system today? Can you foresee any problems with this approach?

8. Explain the difference between pegging and floating currency values. What are the advantages of each? What is a basket of currencies?

9. What are SDRs? Describe their function in settling international payments and in determining certain exchange rates.

10. What is a managed float? A joint float? What advantages can you see from each? Any disadvantages?

SELECTED REFERENCES

1. Abrams, Richard K., and Donald V. Kimball. "U.S. Investment in Foreign Equity Markets." *Economic Review,* Federal Reserve Bank of Kansas City, April 1981, pp. 17–31.

2. Anderson, Gerald H. "Turnabout in U.S. Merchandise Trade." *Economic Commentary,* Federal Reserve Bank of Cleveland, June 2, 1980.

3. _____. "U.S. International Economic Performance Measures." *Economic Commentary,* Federal Reserve Bank of Cleveland, September 3, 1979.

4. Barret, Martin. "Eurobonds: An Emerging International Capital Market." *Monthly Review,* Federal Reserve Bank of New York, August 1968, pp. 169–74.

5. Carlozzi, Nicholas. "Pegs and Floats: The Changing Face of the Foreign Exchange Market." *Business Review,* Federal Reserve Bank of Philadelphia, May-June 1980, pp. 13–23.

6. Clarke, Stephen V. O. "Perspective on the United States External Position since World War II." *Quarterly Review,* Federal Reserve Bank of New York, Summer 1980, pp. 21–38.

7. Federal Reserve Bank of Chicago. "Measuring the U.S. Balance of Payments." *Business Conditions,* June 1970, pp. 10–16.

8. Kareken, John, and Neil Wallace. "International Monetary Reform: The Feasible Alternatives." *Quarterly Review,* Federal Reserve Bank of Minneapolis, Summer 1978, pp. 2–7.

9. Kindelberger, Charles P. "Measuring Equilibrium in the Balance of Payments." *Journal of Political Economy,* November-December 1969, pp. 873–91.

10. Kravis, Irving B., and Robert E. Lipsey. "Export Prices and the Transmission of Inflation." *American Economic Review,* February 1977.

11. _____. *Price Competitiveness in World Trade.* New York: National Bureau of Economic Research, 1971.

12. Kuwayama, Patrick H. "Measuring the United States Balance of Payments." *Monthly Review,* Federal Reserve Bank of New York, August 1975, pp. 183–94.

13. Lees, Francis A. *International Banking and Finance.* New York: John Wiley & Sons, 1973.

14. Machlup, Fritz. *International Payments, Debts, and Gold.* New York: Charles Scribner's Sons, 1964.

15. Morgan Guaranty Trust Company of New York. *World Financial Markets,* various issues.

16. Stern, Robert M. *The Balance of Payments.* Chicago: Aldine Publishing, 1973.

17. Williamson, John. *The Failure of World Monetary Reform, 1971–1974.* New York: New York University Press, 1977.

27

The Markets for
Foreign Exchange

As we saw in the preceding chapter, the markets where the world's major currencies, including the U.S. dollar, are traded have changed dramatically in recent years. Major international economic and political developments—inflation, the spiraling price of oil, political revolutions, and a growing spirit of nationalism and independence in the less-developed countries—all have had profound effects on the relative values of the U.S. dollar, the German mark, the British pound, the Japanese yen, and most of the world's other actively traded currencies. So unsettling have been these changes that, during the 1970s, the U.S. government and its major trading partners were no longer able to preserve the official exchange rates among the world's major currencies. Since the early 1970s major international currencies, including the dollar, have floated with relative freedom, their values dependent essentially upon demand and supply forces in the marketplace.

With this newfound freedom for currency prices and the rapid expansion of world commerce, the volume of currency trading and the number of financial institutions actively participating in that trading have virtually exploded. This is especially evident in the New York money market, where brokers have recently opened up their business to bring in currency trading orders from financial institutions all over the globe. U.S. banks today no longer purchase foreign currencies exclusively from domestic sources but deal with foreign exchange brokers in the world's leading financial centers. Trading in foreign currency futures, begun in the United States at the International Money Market in Chicago, now is under development at major commodity exchanges in New York and Toronto.

This phenomenal explosion of activity and interest in foreign-currency trading and prices reflects, in large measure, a desire for self-preservation by businesses, governments, and individuals. As the international financial system has moved toward freely floating exchange rates, currency prices have become significantly more volatile and uncertain. The risks of buying and selling dollars, francs, marks, pounds, and other currencies have increased markedly in recent years. Moreover, fluctuations in the prices of foreign currencies affect domestic economic conditions, international investment, and the success or failure of government economic policies. Governments, businesses, and individuals involved in international affairs find that it is more important today than ever before to understand how foreign currencies are traded and what affects their relative values. A few examples serve to illustrate the importance of the topic.

Consider the problems faced by a corporation headquartered in the United States and selling machinery overseas. This firm frequently negotiates sales contracts with a foreign importer months before the machines are shipped and payment is made. In the meantime, the value of the foreign currency which the U.S. company expects to receive in payment for sales of its product may have declined precipitously, canceling out any expected profits. Similarly, a U.S. importer bringing fine wines, precious gems, petroleum products, or any number of other goods into our domestic markets usually must pay for incoming shipments in the particular currency demanded by a foreign exporter. The American importer's profits could be significantly reduced if the value of the dollar declined relative to the values of foreign currencies used by the importer to pay for goods purchased abroad. Both exporters and importers, then, require practical knowledge of how the foreign-exchange markets operate and how to use those currency markets to their advantage.

The same problem confronts investors in foreign securities who find that attractive interest rates frequently available overseas must be protected from an erosion in currency values by suitable purchases and sales of foreign currencies. Tourists who travel abroad soon find that planning currency purchases and exchanges to match movements in the international markets can spell the difference between an enjoyable visit and extreme financial discomfort. Knowledge of the foreign-exchange markets is the first step toward successful international business, foreign travel, and economic policy. In subsequent sections of this chapter we examine the structure, instruments, and price-determining forces of the world's major currency markets.

THE STRUCTURE OF THE FOREIGN EXCHANGE MARKET[1]

The purpose of the foreign-exchange markets is to bring buyers and sellers of currencies together. It is essentially an over-the-counter market,

---

[1] This section draws heavily upon the booklets *The New York Foreign Exchange Market* by Alan R. Holmes, first published in 1959 and revised in 1965 by Holmes and Francis H. Schott;

with no central trading location and no set hours for trading. Prices and other terms of trade are determined by negotiation over the telephone or via telex. The foreign-exchange market is informal in its operations; there are no special requirements for market participants, and trading conforms to an unwritten code of rules among active traders.

The Role of Banks in the Foreign Exchange Market

The central institution in modern foreign exchange markets is the *commercial bank.* Most transactions in foreign currency of any size represent merely an exchange of the deposits of one bank for the deposits of another bank. That is, if an individual or business firm needs foreign currency, it will contact a bank, which in turn will secure a deposit denominated in foreign money or actually take delivery of foreign currency if the customer requires it. If the bank is a large money-center institution, it may hold inventories of foreign currency just to accommodate its customers. Smaller banks typically do not hold stocks of foreign currency or foreign-currency-denominated deposits. Rather, they will contact larger correspondent banks, who in turn will contact bank and nonbank foreign exchange brokers or dealers.

The largest money-center banks headquartered in New York, London, Zurich, Tokyo, Frankfurt, and other financial capitals of the world not only maintain large inventories of key foreign currencies but trade currencies with each other simply through an *exchange of deposits.* For example, if a major U.S. bank needs to acquire pounds sterling, it can contact its correspondent bank in London and ask that bank to transfer an additional amount of sterling to the U.S. bank's correspondent account. In turn, the U.S. bank will increase the dollar deposit held with it by the London bank. In this way money never really leaves the country of its origin; only its ownership does, as deposits denominated in various currencies are moved from one holder to the next.

The heart of the foreign exchange market in the United States is New York City. Approximately one dozen banks in that city plus a dozen banks headquartered in other U.S. cities keep active positions in 12 to 15 principal currencies, with smaller holdings of less-traded currencies. Most large foreign-exchange transactions take place between the biggest U.S. banks and major banks headquartered abroad. The largest American banks hold dollar and foreign-currency-denominated deposits in banks overseas in order to make foreign-exchange trading possible. At the same time, more than 100 foreign banks maintain offices in the United States to handle the exchange accounts of foreign investors, investors, traders, and government agencies.

Foreign-exchange trading takes place in a *three-tiered market.* Banks trade with their commercial customers who need large amounts of foreign ex-

---

and *Foreign Exchange Markets in the United States,* prepared by Roger M. Kubarych for the Federal Reserve Bank of New York in 1978. See the list of references at the conclusion of this chapter.

change for purchases of imported goods or to convert funds received from abroad into domestic currency. A second tier consists of trading mainly between domestic banks in order to make a market for foreign exchange. This *market tier* includes exchange trading among domestic banks, foreign central banks represented in the United States, and the Federal Reserve System. The market's third tier consists of trading between U.S. banks and foreign banking institutions.

As we noted above, the largest U.S. banks with foreign-exchange departments routinely keep working balances of foreign currencies with major banks abroad. These working balances rise when a bank buys currency for itself or its customers, sells dollars to foreign banks, or purchases financial documents (such as bills of exchange, traveler's checks, bond coupons, etc.) that are denominated in foreign currencies. Transactions affecting a bank's working currency balance are carried out by specialized traders with the aid of telephones, video screens, and teletype equipment to keep them in constant touch with other exchange brokers and dealers. The foreign exchange trader must also keep in close contact with the bank's money desk and senior management because foreign-exchange trading can have a profound effect on the bank's overall financial position.

This last point was brought home dramatically in 1974 when Franklin National Bank of New York, then the nation's 14th-largest commercial bank, was forced into bankruptcy. While numerous factors led to Franklin's demise, massive losses from foreign-exchange trading were one of the primary factors in that bank's ultimate collapse. In an era of freely floating exchange rates, trading in foreign currencies can be exceedingly risky, requiring considerable skill and experience.

Foreign Exchange Brokers

Frequently, currency-trading banks do not deal directly with each other, but rely upon foreign-exchange brokers. Less than a dozen in number, these brokerage firms are in constant communication with the exchange trading rooms of the world's major banks. Their principal function is simply to bring buyers and sellers of foreign exchange together.

For example, a bank wishing to sell foreign currency simply contacts a broker on its active list by telephone, indicating the amount and type of currency for sale. The broker then contacts buyers on his active-customer list, ascertaining the preferred price and quantity of each potential buyer. Once a deal is struck, the selling bank is notified to initiate a transfer of funds, and the broker receives a commission for his efforts. The foreign exchange broker's essential contribution is to reduce the search costs associated with finding buyers of foreign exchange. By providing convenience and an essential flow of trading information, the broker makes the foreign-exchange market more efficient. He ensures that prices for the world's major currencies accurately reflect the forces of supply and demand in the marketplace.

INSTRUMENTS OF THE FOREIGN EXCHANGE MARKET

Cable Transfers

There are several financial instruments which are used to facilitate foreign-exchange trading. One of the most important is the *cable transfer*—an execute order sent by cable to a foreign bank holding a currency seller's account. The seller directs the bank to debit the seller's account and credit the account of a buyer or someone the buyer designates (such as a commercial bank).

For example, suppose a U.S. export firm has just received payment from one of its overseas customers in francs. The U.S. firm is paid in the form of a deposit denominated in francs residing currently in a bank in Paris. The U.S. exporter cables the Paris bank to transfer the francs to the account of a New York bank, receiving a dollar deposit from the New York bank at the current dollar-franc exchange rate. The export firm now has dollars which can be spent in the United States for raw materials, to meet payrolls, pay taxes, etc., while its New York bank now owns a deposit in francs which can be loaned out or used for other purposes.

The essential advantage of the cable transfer is *speed* since the transaction can be carried out the same day or within one or two business days. Business firms selling their goods in international markets can avoid tying up substantial sums of money in foreign exchange by using cable transfers.

Mail Transfers

When speed is not a critical factor, a mail transfer of foreign exchange may be used. Such transfers are simply written orders from a holder of a foreign exchange deposit to a bank to pay a designated individual, firm, or institution upon presentation of a draft. A mail transfer may, of course, require days to execute, depending upon the speed of mail deliveries.

Bills of Exchange

One of the oldest and most important of all international financial instruments is the bill of exchange.[2] Frequently today the word *draft* is used instead of *bill*. Either way, a draft or bill of exchange is a written order requiring a person, business firm, or bank to pay a specified sum of money to the bearer of the bill.

We may distinguish between *sight bills,* which are payable on demand (presentation), or *time bills,* which mature at a future date and are payable only at that time. There are also *documentary bills,* which typically accompany the international shipment of goods. A documentary bill must be ac-

---

[2] A negotiable form of time bill, known as a bankers acceptance, is discussed at length in Chapter 15.

companied by shipping papers (such as bills of lading), allowing importers of goods to pick up their merchandise. In contrast, a *clean bill* has no accompanying documents and is simply an order to a bank to pay a certain sum. The most-common example arises when an importer requests its bank to send a letter of credit to an exporter in another country. The letter authorizes the exporter to draw bills for payment, either against the importer's bank or against one of its correspondent banks. Most bills of exchange drawn in connection with U.S. imports and exports are payable in U.S. dollars.

Foreign Currency and Coin

Foreign currency and coin itself (as opposed to bank deposits) is an important instrument for payment in the foreign exchange markets. This is especially true for tourists who require pocket money to pay for lodging, meals, transportation, etc. Usually this money winds up in the hands of merchants accepting it in payment for purchases and is deposited in domestic banks. For example, many U.S. banks operating along the Canadian and Mexican borders receive a substantial volume of Canadian dollars and Mexican pesos each day. These funds are normally routed through the banking system back to banks in the country of issue, and the U.S. banks receive credit in the form of a deposit denominated in a foreign currency. This deposit may then be loaned to a customer or another bank that needs foreign currency. Some dealers in the New York money market buy and sell foreign bank notes and coins.

Other Foreign Exchange Instruments

There are a wide variety of other financial instruments denominated in various foreign currencies, most of these small in amount. For example, traveler's checks denominated in pounds, francs, dollars, and other convertible currencies may be spent directly or converted into the currency of the country where purchases are being made. International investors frequently receive interest coupons or dividend warrants denominated in various foreign currencies. These documents normally are sold to a domestic bank at the current foreign exchange rate.

FOREIGN EXCHANGE RATES

Exchange Rate Quotations

The prices of foreign currencies expressed in terms of other currencies are called *foreign exchange rates.* There are two markets for foreign exchange: (1) the *spot market,* which deals in currency for immediate delivery; and (2) the *forward market,* which involves the future delivery of foreign currency. Immediate delivery is defined as one or two business days for most transactions. Future delivery typically means one, three, or six months from today.

Exhibit 27–1 cites some recent foreign-exchange rates between the U.S. dollar and world's other major currencies. The exhibit shows, for example, that an American importer or investor could obtain pounds sterling (£) which could be used to buy British goods or British securities at a cost of about $2.3459 per pound (i.e., $2.3459/£) in December 1980. Conversely, a British investor or importer seeking to make purchases in the United States would have to pay 0.42628 pounds (i.e., $1/£2.3459 or £0.4268/$) for each dollar needed. Clearly, the exchange rate between dollars and pounds is the *reciprocal* of the exchange rate between pounds and dollars, which is also true for any other pair of currencies. Exhibit 27–2 illustrates the correct procedures for calculating foreign exchange rates.[3]

Dealers and brokers in foreign exchange actually post not one, but two exchange rates for each pair of currencies. That is, each trader sets a bid (buy) price and an asked (sell) price at which currencies will be exchanged. For example, the dealer department in a large New York bank might be posting a bid price for pounds sterling of £ = $2.3459US (or $2.3459/£) and an asked price of £ = $2.3461US (or $2.3461/£). This means the dealer is willing to buy sterling at $2.3459 per pound and sell it at $2.3461. (These two exchange rates are sometimes referred to as "double-barreled" quotations.) The dealer makes a profit on the *spread* between the bid and asked price, though that spread is normally very small.[4]

Traders in the market continually watch exchange rate quotations in order to take advantage of any *arbitrage* opportunities. Arbitrage refers to the purchase of one currency in a certain market and the sale of that currency in another market in response to differences in price between the two markets. The force of arbitrage generally keeps foreign exchange rates from getting too far out of line in different markets. Thus, if pounds are selling for $2.3461US in New York and $2.3465US in London, professional traders will quickly eliminate this discrepancy by purchasing sterling in the New York market and selling it in London.

Factors Affecting Foreign Exchange Rates

The exchange rate for any foreign currency depends on a multitude of factors reflecting economic and financial conditions in the country issuing the

---

[3] We note that in each quotation of a foreign exchange rate, one currency always serves as a unit of account (i.e., the unit of value) and the other currency functions as the unit for which a price is stated. For example, a quote of $0.40/DM tell us that one deutsche mark costs $0.40. In this instance the dollar serves as the unit of account, and the currency whose price is quoted is the mark. It is customary to place the symbol for the currency serving as the unit of account (in this case, $) before the stated number and the symbol of the currency whose price is being quoted (in this case, DM) following the number.

[4] Dealers will usually quote the bid price first and the asked price second and, as a rule, only the last digits will be quoted to the buyer or seller. Thus, the spot bid and asked rates on pounds might be quoted by a foreign exchange dealer as 59/61. It is assumed the customer is aware of current foreign-exchange rates and knows, therefore, that the bid price being quoted is $2.3459/£ and the asked price is $2.3461/£.

EXHIBIT 27–1
Foreign Exchange Rates (cents per unit of foreign currency)

Country/Currency	1978	1979	1980	1980			1981			
				Oct.	Nov.	Dec.	Jan.	Feb.	Mar.	Apr.
1 Australia/dollar	114.41	111.77	114.00	117.43	116.75	116.86	118.19	116.26	116.29	115.32
2 Austria/schilling	6.8958	7.4799	7.7349	7.6714	7.3433	7.1549	7.0297	6.6033	6.6959	6.5355
3 Belgium/franc	3.1809	3.4098	3.4247	3.3875	3.2457	3.1543	3.0962	2.8972	2.8966	2.8220
4 Canada/dollar	87.729	85.386	85.530	85.538	84.286	83.560	83.974	83.442	83.936	83.966
5 Denmark/krone	18.156	19.010	17.766	17.639	16.962	16.573	16.181	15.152	15.109	14.683
6 Finland/markka	24.337	27.732	26.892	27.122	26.452	25.903	25.752	24.656	24.612	23.059
7 France/franc	22.218	23.504	23.694	23.489	22.515	21.925	21.539	20.142	20.147	19.548
8 Germany/deutsche mark	49.867	54.561	55.089	54.280	52.113	50.769	49.771	46.757	47.498	46.219
9 India/rupee	12.207	12.265	12.686	12.932	12.868	12.608	12.567	12.164	12.131	12.060
10 Ireland/pound	191.84	204.65	205.77	203.88	194.59	189.01	185.54	173.31	173.25	168.46
11 Italy/lira	.11782	.12035	.11694	.11441	.11000	.10704	.10478	.09807	.09699	.09280
12 Japan/yen	.47981	.45834	.44311	.47777	.46928	.47747	.49419	.48615	.47897	.46520
13 Malaysia/ringgit	43.210	45.720	45.967	46.902	46.187	45.406	44.994	44.196	43.830	43.182
14 Mexico/peso	4.3896	4.3826	4.3535	4.3324	4.3166	4.3071	4.2792	4.2544	4.2238	4.1880
15 Netherlands/guilder	46.284	49.843	50.369	50.052	48.102	46.730	45.810	42.870	42.912	41.660
16 New Zealand/dollar	103.64	102.23	97.337	98.069	96.770	95.404	96.137	93.414	91.999	90.273
17 Norway/krone	19.079	19.747	20.261	20.421	19.938	19.370	19.087	18.485	18.540	18.271
18 Portugal/escudo	2.2782	2.0437	1.9980	1.9756	1.9178	1.8773	1.8591	1.7722	1.7621	1.7178
19 South Africa/rand	115.01	118.72	128.54	133.13	133.20	132.83	133.69	129.27	126.50	123.32
20 Spain/peseta	1.3073	1.4896	1.3958	1.3423	1.3085	1.2653	1.2409	1.1686	1.1672	1.1395
21 Sri Lanka/rupee	6.3834	6.4226	6.1947	5.9707	5.8139	5.7379	5.9525	5.5975	5.5527	5.4185
22 Sweden/krona	22.139	23.323	23.647	23.845	23.240	22.722	22.490	21.734	21.704	21.309
23 Switzerland/franc	56.283	60.121	59.697	60.185	57.942	56.022	54.907	51.502	52.043	50.664
24 United Kingdom/pound	191.84	212.24	232.58	241.64	239.41	234.59	240.29	229.41	223.19	217.53
MEMO:										
25 United States/dollar*	92.39	88.09	87.39	86.59	89.31	90.99	91.38	96.02	96.22	98.80

* Index of weighted-average exchange value of U.S. dollar against currencies of other G–10 countries plus Switzerland. March 1973 = 100. Weights are 1972–76 global trade of each of the 10 countries. Series revised as of August 1978. For description and back data, see "Index of the Weighted-Average Exchange Value of the U.S. Dollar: Revision," *Federal Reserve Bulletin*, August 1978, p. 700.
Note: Averages of certified noon buying rates in New York for cable transfers.
SOURCE: Board of Governors of the Federal Reserve System.

EXHIBIT 27–2
Methods for Calculating Foreign Exchange Rates

Exchange Rate Conversion

Suppose the exchange rate between German deutsche marks (DM) and the U.S. dollar ($) is DM/$ = 2.500, or DM 2.50/$.
  What is the $/DM exchange rate?
  Answer: 1 ÷ 2.500 = $0.40/DM.

Exchange Rate Appreciation

Suppose the exchange rate between German marks and the U.S. dollar rises from DM/$ = 2.000, or DM 2.00/$, to DM 2.50/$.
  How much has the dollar appreciated, in percent?
  Answer: 2.500 ÷ 2.000 = 1.25, or 25%.
  Suppose the mark-dollar exchange rate is DM/$ = 2.5000, or DM 2.50/$. If the dollar has appreciated by 3 percent, what is the new mark-dollar exchange rate?
  Answer: 2.500 × 1.03 = 2.5750, or DM 2.575/$.

Exchange Rate Depreciation

Suppose the exchange rate between marks and U.S. dollars rises from DM/$ = 2.000 to DM/$ = 2.5000.
  How much has the mark depreciated, in percent?
  Answer: Note that the $/DM exchange rate has changed from 1 ÷ 2.000 = $0.50/DM to 1 ÷ 2.500 = $0.40/DM. The ratio of these two exchange rates is 0.4000 ÷ 0.5000, or 0.8000. Then, 1 − 0.8000 = 0.2000, or an exchange-rate depreciation of 20%.
  Suppose the mark-dollar exchange rate is DM/$ = 2.50 or DM 2.50/$. If the mark has depreciated 5 percent, what is the new mark-dollar exchange rate?
  Answer: Because 0.4000 × 0.95 = 0.3800, the new exchange rate is 1 ÷ 0.3800 = 2.6316, or DM 2.6316/$.
  Suppose, once again, the mark-dollar exchange rate is DM/$ = 2.5000. If the U.S. dollar has depreciated 5 percent, what is the new mark-dollar exchange rate?
  Answer: 2.5000 × 0.95 = 2.3750, or DM 2.375/$.

Cross Exchange Rates

Suppose the mark-dollar exchange rate is DM/$ = 2.5000, or DM 2.50/$, and the Swiss franc-dollar exchange rate is 2.000, or SF2.00/$. What is the SF/DM exchange rate?
  Answer: 2.000 ÷ 2.500 = 0.8000, or SF 0.80/DM.
  Suppose the mark-dollar exchange rate is DM/$ = 2.500, or DM 2.50/$ and the dollar–Swiss franc exchange rate is $/SF = 0.5000 or 0.50/SF. What, then, is the DM/SF exchange rate?
  Answer: 2.5000 ÷ (1 ÷ 0.5000) = 2.5000 ÷ 2.000 = 1.25, or DM 1.25/SF.

SOURCE: Public Information Center, Federal Reserve Bank of Chicago.

currency. One of the most important factors is the status of a nation's *balance-of-payments position.* When a country experiences a deficit in its balance of payments, it becomes a net demander of foreign currencies and may be forced to sell substantial amounts of its own currency to pay for imports of goods and services. Therefore, balance-of-payments deficits often lead to depreciation of a nation's currency relative to other currencies. During the 1970s, when the United States was experiencing deep balance-of-payments deficits and owed substantial amounts abroad for imported oil, the value of the dollar sagged dramatically. Both the Federal Reserve System and the Treasury were forced to enter the foreign exchange markets with heavy purchases of dollars and offerings of dollar-denominated government securities to create a demand for dollars and prop up the dollar's exchange value.

Speculation. Exchange rates also are profoundly affected by speculation over future currency values. Brokers, dealers, and investors in foreign exchange monitor the currency markets daily, looking for profitable trading opportunities. A currency viewed as temporarily undervalued will quickly bring forth numerous buy orders, driving its price higher vis-à-vis other currencies. A currency considered to be overvalued will soon be greeted by a rash of sell orders, depressing its price. Today the international financial system is so efficient and finely tuned that billions of dollars can flow across national boundaries in a matter of hours in response to speculative fever. As we saw earlier in our review of the Eurodollar market,[5] these massive unregulated flows can wreak havoc with the plans of economic policymakers because currency trading affects interest rates and the money supply.

Domestic Economic and Political Conditions. The market for a national currency is of course influenced by domestic conditions. Wars, revolutions, the death of a major political leader, inflation, recession, and labor strikes have all been observed to have adverse effects on the currency of a nation experiencing these problems. On the other hand, signs of rapid economic growth, industrial development, improving government finances, rising stock and bond prices, and successful economic policies to control inflation and unemployment usually lead to a stronger currency in the exchange markets.

Central Bank Intervention. Overhanging the currency markets today is the ever present possibility that central banks will become active participants. Major central banks around the world, including the Federal Reserve System, the Deutschbank in West Germany, and the Bank of England, may decide on a given day that their national currency is declining too rapidly in value relative to one or more other key currencies. Thus, if the dollar falls precipitously against the mark, support operations by the Federal Reserve in cooperation with the Deutschbank may be employed to stabilize the currency markets. Usually, central bank intervention is temporary, designed to promote a smooth adjustment in currency values toward a new equilibrium level rather than to permanently "prop up" a weak currency. We will have more to say about central bank intervention in the currency markets later in this chapter.

Supply and Demand for Foreign Exchange

The factors influencing a currency's rate of exchange with other currencies may be expressed in terms of the market forces of demand and supply. Figure 27–1, for example, illustrates a demand curve and a supply curve for

---

[5] See Chapter 15 for a discussion of the problems in attempting to regulate the Eurodollar market.

FIGURE 27–1
Demand and Supply of U.S. Dollars in Terms of British Pounds

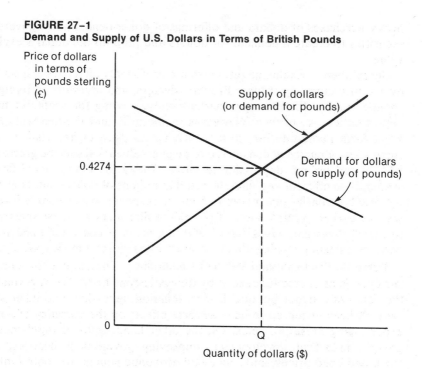

Quantity of dollars ($)

dollars in terms of British pounds (£). Note that the demand curve for dollars is also labeled the supply curve for pounds. This is due to the fact that an individual or institution holding pounds and demanding dollars would be supplying pounds to the foreign-exchange market. Similarly, the supply curve for dollars is identical to the demand curve for pounds. We recall, too, that the price of dollars in terms of pounds is the reciprocal of the price of pounds in terms of dollars.

To illustrate how demand and supply forces operate in the foreign exchange markets, suppose the current exchange rate between dollars and pounds is £ = $2.34. To purchase dollars, we would have to pay 0.4274 pounds per dollar, while to purchase pounds would cost us $2.34 per pound. This exchange rate between dollars and pounds is set in the foreign-exchange markets by the interaction of the supply and demand for each currency. Figure 27–1 indicates that, at an exchange rate of 0.4274 pounds, the quantity of dollars supplied is exactly equal to the quantity of dollars demanded.

If the price of dollars in terms of pounds were to fall temporarily *below* this exchange rate, more dollars would be demanded than supplied. Some buyers needing dollars would bid up the exchange rate toward the point where the demand for and supply of dollars were perfectly in balance. On the other hand, if the price of dollars were temporarily *above* 0.4274 pounds, more dollars would be supplied to the foreign-exchange markets. The price of dollars in terms of pounds would fall as suppliers of dollars willingly accepted a lower exchange rate to dispose of their excess dollar holdings.

Only at that point where the exchange rate stood at 0.4274 pounds per dollar would quantity supplied equal quantity of dollars demanded. Only at that point would there be no reason for future changes in the exchange rate between the dollar and the pound unless and until changes occurred in the demand or supply for either currency.

Effects of Changes in the Relative Supply and Demand for Currencies

As we noted earlier, a number of factors affect the exchange rates between national currencies, including the export and import of goods, services, and capital as reflected in a nation's balance-of-payments position, currency speculation, domestic political and economic developments, and central bank intervention. Each of these factors leads to a *shift* in either the demand for or supply of one currency vis-à-vis another, which brings about a change in their relative rates of exchange.

To illustrate the impact of shifts in currency demand and supply, suppose that consumers in Great Britain increase their demand for U.S. goods and services. As Figure 27–2 indicates, the demand curve for dollars would

FIGURE 27–2
Effects on the Exchange Rate for Dollars of an Increase in Foreign Demand for U.S. Goods and Services

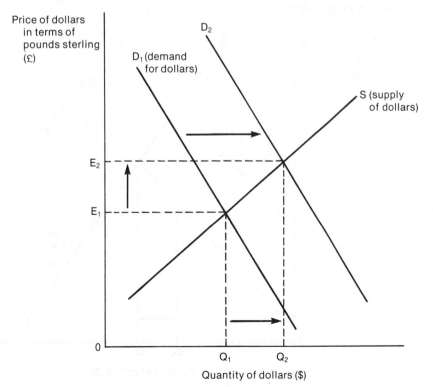

increase from D_1 to D_2. This is equivalent, as noted earlier to an increase in the supply of pounds seeking dollars. The cost of dollars in terms of pounds, therefore, will rise from E_1 to E_2. British importers will be forced to surrender a greater quantity of pounds per dollar in order to satisfy the demands of British consumers for American goods and services. Other things equal, the prices of imported goods from the United States will tend to rise.

The opposite effects would tend to occur if American consumers demanded a larger quantity of British goods and services. In this case the supply-of-dollars (demand-for-pounds) curve slides downward and to the right from S_1 to S_2, as shown in Figure 27–3. Reflecting the increased demand for pounds and associated sales of dollars for pounds by American importers, the dollar's price in pounds sterling falls from E_1 to E_2. At the same time, the market prices of British goods and services imported into the United States will tend to rise.

What happens if a central bank, such as the Bank of England, intervenes to stabilize the dollar-pound exchange rate at some arbitrary level? The answer depends, among other things, on which side of the market the central bank intervenes, which currency is used as the vehicle for central bank intervention, and the particular exchange-rate target chosen.

FIGURE 27–3
Effects on the Exchange Rate for Dollars of an Increase in U.S. Demand for Foreign Goods and Services

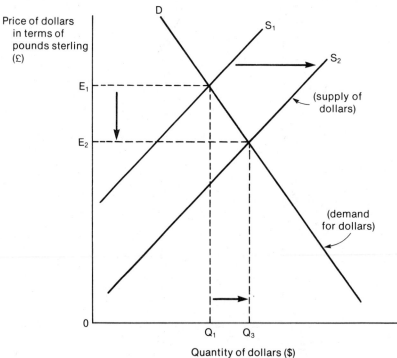

FIGURE 27–4
Effects of Central Bank Intervention to Stabilize the Dollar-Pound Exchange Rate

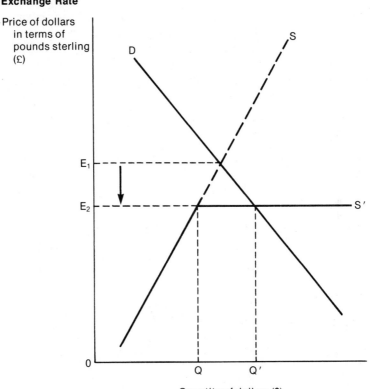

Quantity of dollars ($)

For example, suppose that increased British demand for American goods and services had driven the dollar-pound exchange rate up to E_1, as shown in Figure 27–4. However, this surge in the dollar's value had sharply reduced the purchasing power of the pound for dollar-denominated goods and services and threatened to have damaging effects on British foreign trade and industrial output. Speculators had begun to sell pounds in anticipation of even lower exchange rates. The Bank of England might intervene to force the dollar-pound exchange rate down to E_2 by selling dollars out of its currency reserves and demanding pounds in the foreign-exchange market. In effect, the supply-of-dollars curve would become "kinked" at the stabilization price, E_2. In order to peg the dollar-pound exchange rate at E_2, the central bank would have to spend Q^1-Q of its dollar reserves. Otherwise, the price of dollars would once again rise toward E_1—the level dictated by private demand and supply pressures in the foreign-exchange markets. Conversely, if the dollar were falling to unacceptably low levels against the pound, the Bank of England or the Federal Reserve System might enter on the opposite side of the market, purchasing dollars with pounds and driving the dollar's price higher.

THE FORWARD MARKET FOR CURRENCIES

Knowledge of how the foreign-exchange markets work and the ways in which currency risk can be reduced is indispensable for business managers today. Changes in the relative values of various currencies can wreak havoc with planning by firms engaged in the export or import business. Of course, the problem of fluctuating currency values is not so serious if payment for goods, services, or securities must be made right away. Spot-market prices of foreign currencies normally change very little from day to day. However, if payment must be made weeks or months in the future, there is considerable uncertainty as to what the spot rate will be for any currency on any given future date. When substantial sums of money are involved, the rational investor or commercial trader will try to *guarantee* the future price at which currency can be purchased. This is the function of the forward exchange market—to reduce the risk associated with the future purchase and delivery of foreign currency by agreeing upon a price in advance.

The need for hedging against the risk of fluctuating currency-exchange rates was recognized as early as the 14th century, when forward-market trading first appeared. However, the market developed slowly due to numerous political upheavals, war, and a poorly developed communications network. Following a burst of forward-exchange trading during the 1920s, the forward market almost disappeared during the depression years and World War II. It revived during the 1950s, however, and grew dramatically during the 1970s as currency prices became extremely volatile. Thousands of corporations, foreign governments, and central banks have entered the market during the past decade, responding to problems created by the wide ranges over which national currencies float today.

Spot, Forward, and Option Contracts

Earlier in this chapter we distinguished between the spot market, or market for immediate delivery of a currency, and the forward market, where contracts are made for future currency delivery. Trading in the spot market results in *spot contracts,* which are agreements to deliver a specified amount of foreign currency at an agreed-upon price, usually within one or two business days and sometimes on the same day. In contrast, a *forward contact* is an agreement to deliver a specified amount of foreign currency at a set price on some future date (usually within 30, 90, or 120 days).

In the forward market, therefore, the currency is purchased or sold now at a price agreed upon today, but delivery and payment are made in the future. The actual delivery date is referred to by traders as the *value date.* In the event customers do not know when they will receive or will need foreign currency, then an *option* forward contract frequently is used.[6]

---

[6] Another type of foreign-exchange agreement used frequently is the *swap contract.* Swaps involve the sale (or purchase) of a currency for delivery at a particular date matched by a pur-

Methods of Quoting Forward Exchange Rates

There are several different ways of measuring and quoting forward exchange rates. Suppose the spot rate on German marks today is $0.40US (or $0.40/DM) and that dealers in foreign exchange are selling forward contracts for delivery of marks in six months at $0.3846US. (This means that the spot exchange rate for marks into dollars is DM/$ = 2.500, or $2.50/DM, and the six-month forward rate is DM/$ = 2.600, or $2.60/DM.) We may express the forward exchange rate on marks simply as $0.3846US, or $0.3846/DM,— known as the *outright rate*.

Another popular method is to express the forward rate as a premium or discount from the spot rate, known as the *swap rate*.[7] In this case, marks are selling at a 1.54¢ *discount* in the forward market. Traders in the forward market may be signaling an expectation that the mark will fall in value over the next few weeks.

We may also express forward exchange rates in terms of an annualized percentage rate above or below the current spot price. To use the example above, $/DM spot = 0.4000 and $/DM forward = 0.3846.[8] Then, the discount on forward DM for delivery in six months is:

$$\frac{\text{Forward rate} - \text{Spot rate}}{\text{Spot rate}} \times \frac{12}{\text{Number of months forward}} \times 100$$

$$= \frac{0.3846 - 0.4000}{0.4000} \times \frac{12}{6} \times 100$$

$$= -0.0385 \times 2 \times 100$$

$$= -7.7\%$$

Marks are selling at a 7.7 percent discount from spot in the forward market. Because marks are selling at a discount from their spot price, forward dollars must be selling at a premium over spot.

Suppose we know the current spot-exchange rate between two currencies and the forward premium or discount. We want to know the actual forward exchange rate. What formula should be used? The following will suffice:

Spot rate +

$$\left\{ \frac{\text{Spot rate} \times [\text{Premium } (+) \text{ or discount } (-) \text{ expressed as an annual rate}] \times \text{Number of months forward}}{100 \times \text{Number of months in a year}} \right\}$$

---

chase (sale) of an equivalent amount of the same currency for delivery usually within one week. The majority of foreign-exchange transactions involve spot contracts. For example, a survey by the Federal Reserve Bank of New York of transactions in U.S. foreign exchange markets found that 64 percent were spot contracts, 30 percent were swap contracts, and 6 percent were forward contracts. The German mark was the most actively traded foreign currency in U.S. markets, followed by the British pound, Canadian dollars, Japanese yen, and Swiss franc.

[7] Quite obviously, the current outright rate is the current spot-exchange rate adjusted by the current swap rate.

[8] This example is based upon one developed by the Public Information Center, Federal Reserve Bank of Chicago in their *Exchange Rate Calculation Guide*.

Suppose that $/DM spot $= 0.4000$ and forward marks for delivery in three months are selling at a 4 percent premium over spot. Using the formula above, we have

$$0.4000 + \frac{0.4000 \times 4.0 \times 3}{1,200} = 0.4040 \ \$/DM \ forward.$$

This means DM/$ forward is 2.4752, or DM 2.4752/$.

FUNCTIONS OF THE FORWARD EXCHANGE MARKET

Contracts for the future delivery of currency are employed to cover a number of risks faced by investors and commercial traders. Some analysts group the functions or uses of forward contracts into four categories: (1) commercial covering, (2) hedging an investment position, (3) speculation, and (4) covered interest arbitrage. These four uses of the forward market are discussed below.[9]

Commercial Covering

The export or import of goods and services usually requires someone to deliver payment in a foreign currency or to receive payment in a foreign currency. Either the payor or payee, then, is subject to currency risk, since no one knows for sure what the spot price will be for a currency at the time payment must be made. The forward-exchange market can be used as a buffer against currency risk associated with the export or import of goods and services.

To illustrate, suppose an American importer of cameras has agreed to pay 5,000 marks to a West German manufacturer upon receipt of a new shipment. The cameras are expected to arrive dockside in 30 days. The importer has no idea at this point what 5,000 marks will cost in U.S. dollars 30 days from now. To reduce the risk that the price of marks in terms of dollars may *rise* significantly, the importer negotiates a forward contract with his bank for delivery of 5,000 marks at 0.30/DM in 30 days. When payment is due, the importer simply takes delivery of the marks (usually by acquiring ownership of a deposit denominated in marks) at the agreed-upon price and pays the West German manufacturer. Because the price is fixed in advance, the risk associated with fluctuations in foreign exchange rates has been eliminated. Today, export and import firms routinely cover their large purchases overseas with forward currency contracts.

---

[9] The discussion which follows is indebted to the excellent article by Gerald H. Anderson, "The Nature and Use of Forward Exchange." See reference (1) at the conclusion of this chapter.

Hedging an Investment Position

As we saw in the preceding chapter, thousands of American corporations have invested in long-term capital projects overseas, building manufacturing plants, warehouse and dock facilities, retail stores, shopping centers, and office buildings. In recent years a large return flow of long-term investments by foreign firms in the United States also has occurred. Of course, the market value of these foreign investments may change drastically as the price of a foreign currency changes over time. For example, a drop in the exchange value of the British pound against the dollar may turn an otherwise profitable commercial project launched by a U.S. firm in Britain into a loss, particularly if the firm involved plans to sell the property while currency values are depressed.

To illustrate, suppose an American commercial bank constructed an office building in downtown London. When completed, the office facility had an estimated market value of £2,000,000. The current spot rate on pounds is, let us say, $2.20/£. The bank values the new building on its consolidated financial statement, therefore, at $4.4 million. However, suppose the pound has declined rapidly in value in recent months due to persistent balance-of-payments problems and rapid inflation in the British economy. Some market analysts expect pounds to be selling at $1.98/£ in a few months. In the absence of a hedged position, the bank would take a loss of $440,000 on its building. This is due to the fact that, at an exchange rate of $1.98/£ the office building will have a book value of only $3,960,000.

Can this kind of loss be avoided or at least reduced? Yes, provided the bank can negotiate a sale of pounds forward at a higher price. For example, the bank may be able to arrange with a dealer for the sale of £2 million for future delivery at 210¢US (i.e., $2.10/£). When this forward contract matures, if the spot price has fallen to $1.98/£, the bank can buy pounds at this rate and deliver them to the dealer at 210¢US as agreed. The result is a profit on the foreign-exchange transaction of $240,000, partially offsetting the financial loss on the building due to declining currency values.

Speculation on Future Currency Prices

A third use of the forward-exchange market is speculative investment based on expectations concerning future movements in currency prices. Speculators will *buy* currency for future delivery if they believe the future spot rate will be higher on the delivery date than the current forward rate. They will *sell* currency under a forward contract if the future spot rate appears likely to be below the forward rate on the day of delivery. Such speculative purchases and sales carry the advantage of requiring little or no capital and no borrowing costs in advance of the delivery date. A speculator whose forecast of future spot rates turns out to be correct makes a profit on the spread between the purchase and the sale price.

Covered Interest Arbitrage

One of the most-common transactions in the international financial system arises when an investor discovers a higher interest rate available on foreign securities and invests funds abroad. When the currency risk associated with the purchase of foreign securities is reduced by using a forward contract, this transaction is often referred to as "covered interest arbitrage."

To illustrate the interest arbitrage process, let us suppose that a British auto company is selling high-grade bonds with a promised annual yield of 12 percent. Comparable bonds in the United States offer a 10 percent annual return. While the bonds are of good quality and there is probably little default risk, there is currency risk in this transaction. The U.S. investor must purchase pounds in order to buy the British bonds. When the bonds earn interest or reach maturity, the issuing auto company will pay foreign and domestic investors in pounds sterling. Then the sterling must be converted into dollars to allow the U.S. investor to spend the earnings in the United States. If the spot price of sterling falls, the U.S. investor's net yield from the bonds will be reduced.

Indeed, if the market value of sterling declines far enough, any profit from the bond purchase may be eliminated. Specifically, while the investor expects an interest spread of 2 percent a year over U.S. interest rates by purchasing British bonds, if the spot rate on pounds declines by 2 percent (on an annual basis), the interest gain will be exactly offset by the loss on trading pounds. Clearly, a series of forward contracts is needed to sell pounds at a guaranteed price as the bonds generate a stream of cash payments. In this case the investor will probably purchase sterling spot in order to buy the bonds and sell sterling forward to protect the expected income.

The Principle of Interest-Rate Parity

The foregoing example suggests an important rule regarding international capital flows and foreign-exchange rates: *The rate of return to the investor from any foreign investment is equal to the interest earned plus or minus the premium or discount on the price of the foreign currency involved in the transaction.* The theory of forward exchange states that, under normal conditions, the forward discount or premium on one currency relative to another is directly related to the difference in interest rates between the two countries involved. More specifically, the currency of the nation experiencing higher interest rates normally will sell at a forward *discount* in terms of the currency issued by the nation with lower interest rates. And the currency of the nation with relatively low interest rates normally will sell at a *premium* forward relative to that of the high-rate country. A condition known as *interest-rate parity* exists when the interest-rate differential between two nations is exactly equal to the forward discount or premium on their two currencies.

When parity exists, the currency markets are in equilibrium, and capital funds will *not* flow from one country to another. This is due to the fact that the gain from investing abroad at higher interest rates is fully offset by the cost of covering currency risk in the forward exchange market.

To illustrate the principal of interest-rate parity, suppose interest rates in a foreign country are 3 percent above those in the United States. Then, the currency of that foreign nation will, in equilibrium, sell at a 3 percent discount in the forward exchange market. Similarly, if interest rates are 1 percent lower abroad than in the United States, in equilibrium the foreign currency of the nations involved should sell at a 1 percent premium against the dollar. When such an equilibrium position is reached, movements of funds between nations even with currency risks covered do not generate excess returns relative to domestic investments of comparable risk. Capital funds tend to stay in the domestic market rather than flowing abroad.

It is when interest parity does *not* exist that capital tends to flow across national boundaries in response to differences in domestic and foreign interest rates. For example, suppose interest rates in a foreign nation are 3 percent above U.S. interest rates on securities of comparable quality and the foreign currency involved is selling at a 1 percent discount against the dollar in the forward-exchange market. In this case, investing abroad with exchange risks covered will yield the investor a *net* return of 2 percent per year. Clearly, there is a positive incentive to invest overseas. In the absence of exchange controls, capital will flow abroad.

Is this situation likely to persist for a long period of time? No, because the movement of funds into a country offering higher interest rates tends to increase the forward discount on its currency and lowers the net interest return to the investor. Other factors held constant, the flow of funds abroad eventually will subside, and capital funds will tend to stay at home until further changes in currency prices and interest rates take place.

TRADING CENTERS FOR FORWARD EXCHANGE CONTRACTS

Wherever there are major spot-currency markets operating, forward exchange contracts are usually traded as well. Leading currency markets today are situated in Amsterdam, Brussels, Frankfurt, London, Montreal, New York City, Paris, Toronto, and Zurich. London continues to be the predominant location for spot and forward currency trading, offering forward contracts for Canadian and U.S. dollars, marks, guilders, and both French and Swiss francs. The New York Market specializes in forward trading of Canadian dollars, marks, Swiss francs, and the pound. In 1972 the Chicago Mercantile Exchange inaugurated trading in forward contracts for Canadian dollars, sterling, Swiss francs, marks, yen, lira, and pesos. As in the spot markets, most trading in forward currency contracts occurs between dealer departments of major banks and foreign exchange brokers.

GOVERNMENT INTERVENTION IN THE FOREIGN EXCHANGE MARKETS

The value of a nation's currency in the international markets has long been a source of concern to governments around the world. National pride plays a significant role in this case because a strong currency, avidly sought by traders and investors in the international marketplace, implies the existence of a strong, vigorous, and well-managed economy at home. A strong and stable currency encourages investment in the home country, stimulating its economic growth and development. Moreover, as we observed in Chapter 26, changes in currency values affect a nation's balance-of-payments position. A weak and declining currency makes foreign imports more expensive, lowering the standard of living at home. And a nation whose currency is not well regarded in the international marketplace will have difficulty selling its goods and services abroad, giving rise to unemployment and economic recession at home.

The United States has pursued an active policy of supporting the dollar in international markets for many years. In part, this policy has been motivated by concern over the condition of the U.S. economy, particularly the effects of inflation. Another factor, however, is the key role played by the U.S. dollar in the international financial system. The dollar is a *vehicle currency* which facilitates trade and investment between many nations in addition to the United States. For example, international shipments of crude oil, regardless of their origin or destination, are usually valued in dollars. As noted in Chapter 15, the market for dollar deposits held in banks abroad— Eurodollars—is the world's largest international money market, financing commercial projects and even providing operating funds for many foreign governments around the globe. For all of the foregoing reasons, then, the United States as well as foreign governments and central banks have repeatedly intervened in the foreign-exchange markets to stabilize currency values and insulate domestic economic conditions from adverse financial developments abroad.

As we observed in the preceding chapter, during the years immediately following World War II, the United States agreed to maintain a fixed exchange ratio between the dollar and gold. The Treasury Department stood ready to buy gold from or sell gold to foreign central banks and other monetary authorities at a fixed price of $35 per ounce. The Secretary of the Treasury was also responsible for maintaining the U.S. Exchange Stabilization Fund, to be drawn upon when necessary to intervene in foreign currency markets and protect the dollar. While the United States committed itself to intervene in the currency markets to preserve the desired ratio of dollars to gold, other nations agreed to keep the exchange ratios between their currencies and the dollar centered about a fixed rate. Whenever a currency's exchange rate against the dollar deviated significantly from the agreed-upon rate, central banks and government agencies would intervene (either on the demand side or the supply side of the exchange market) to restore the proper dollar-currency ratio.

U.S. Intervention in the Currency Markets during the 1960s

This relatively passive U.S. foreign-exchange policy, which relied mainly upon other nations to stabilize the international financial system, was modified during the 1960s because of serious economic problems. Massive outflows of capital from the United States into Western Europe, Japan, Latin America, and the Middle East weakened the dollar in foreign markets. High unemployment rates in the United States during the early 60s coupled with significant inflation in later years further eroded the pivotal role of the dollar in the international financial system. Beginning in 1961, the U.S. Treasury, acting in cooperation with the monetary authorities of other Western nations, began to intervene in the currency markets to counter speculative attacks against the dollar.

Later, the Federal Reserve System joined in the cooperative effort to support the dollar and stabilize the currency system. The Fed established a network of *swap agreements* with foreign central banks. These agreements created lines of credit through which a participating central bank could obtain foreign currencies in order to sell them in the exchange markets and protect its home currency. The Federal Reserve pledged to absorb excess dollars that had been accumulated by foreign central banks in their attempts to keep the dollar's value at its officially established level. The Fed would borrow foreign currencies against its swap lines and use these currencies to purchase unwanted dollars held by the Bank of England, the Deutschbank, and other major central banks on a temporary basis. When the exchange markets calmed and the dollar recovered, the Fed would simply repay its swap drawings by purchasing foreign currency from private dealers.

U.S. Foreign Exchange Policy during the 1970s

Federal Reserve swap operations and Treasury intervention in the exchange markets came to an abrupt halt in August 1971, when the Nixon Administration snapped the official link between the dollar and gold. Because the dollar was no longer convertible into gold at a government-guaranteed rate, there seemed little reason to interfere with supply and demand forces in the exchange marketplace. The dollar began to "float." However, concern over the stability of all exchange rates and the possible threats to world trade from unbridled speculation in foreign currencies brought another reversal of U.S. intervention policy in the summer of 1972. The Federal Reserve began actively drawing on its swap lines again to stabilize the currency markets and protect the dollar.

When the Carter administration took office in 1977, it announced a policy of nonintervention, but it abandoned this policy in favor of active intervention only a year later. The Treasury and the Fed jointly announced in January 1978 their renewed intention to "check speculation and reestablish order in the foreign exchange market." The Federal Reserve increased its swap lines with other central banks, while the Treasury drew on the International Monetary Fund for credit, floated foreign-currency-denominated securities to gain additional exchange reserves, and increased its sales of gold. Between January 1978 and January 1979, combined Treasury–Federal Reserve actions to support the dollar totaled $11 billion. Moreover, rising foreign interest rates, higher OPEC oil prices, and rapid inflation at home forced even more strenuous efforts by U.S. monetary authorities to protect the dollar through most of 1979.

The year 1980 brought a complete 180-degree change of direction for U.S. foreign-exchange policies. The dollar began to rise rapidly in value due to record-high interest rates in the United States, which attracted huge amounts of foreign capital. U.S. government securities and American corporate stocks and bonds were among the hottest-selling items in the international financial markets as the 1980s began. U.S. and foreign authorities suddenly had to switch from a time-worn policy of supporting the dollar through heavy dollar purchases in the exchange markets to one of selling dollars and purchasing other beleaguered currencies in order to moderate the greenback's rapidly rising value. As a result, the Federal Reserve and the Treasury began to accumulate large stocks of foreign currencies. For example, between July 1980 and January 1981 the Fed and the Treasury purchased over $12 billion in foreign currencies. The Fed used its share of this vast currency pool to repay past borrowings from the swap network and accumulate funds to redeem foreign-currency-denominated securities issued by the Treasury in earlier years.

A Limited Intervention Policy for the 1980s

The highly favorable market for the dollar in 1980–81 and the inauguration of a new American president in January 1981 ushered in another new foreign exchange policy for the United States. For want of a more convenient label, this latest official foreign-exchange-market approach might be called "Emergency Intervention Only." In May 1981 the Reagan administration announced that U.S. monetary authorities would intervene in the foreign exchange markets only if an emergency developed which threatened to disrupt the smooth functioning of the currency markets. The new policy received its first test almost immediately after its inception when the president was shot in an assassination attempt outside a Washington hotel. The Fed and the Treasury immediately began dollar-support operations to calm the exchange markets amidst worldwide concern over the stability and continuity of U.S. government policies and programs. Other than that limited, short-term operation, however, no additional market intervention was undertaken in 1981. Moreover, the Treasury Department has proposed that foreign currency reserves accumulated in the past for dollar support be gradually disposed of and that Federal Reserve swap lines with foreign central banks be reduced or terminated.

Does this new policy spell the end of active and aggressive U.S. efforts to protect the American dollar in foreign-exchange markets? Perhaps, but many authorities have serious doubts that a policy of nonintervention can last for long in today's markets. Certainly, new and possibly severe tests await the dollar in the future. Another oil embargo comparable to that of 1973–74 would undoubtedly send the dollar, the yen, the mark, and most other Western currencies into a sharp downward spiral, demanding massive central-bank invention, possibly for a considerable period.

Even more ominous for the new "hands off" policy is the current uncertainty over the success or failure of U.S. anti-inflation policies. If the United States cannot bring about a significant reduction in its long-term (base) rate of inflation, that policy failure would almost certainly bring renewed speculative attacks against the dollar. These attacks could disrupt the functioning of the foreign currency markets and create unemployment and slower growth in the domestic economy. Faced with unhappy outcomes of that sort, it seems clear that the U.S. government would not hesitate to intervene as often as necessary to ensure that the foreign-exchange markets functioned smoothly and efficiently.

STUDY QUESTIONS

1. Describe the important role played by commercial banks in the operation of the foreign-exchange market. Why do you think banks are so dominant in this market?

2. The foreign-exchange market consists of three tiers. What are these three divisions of the market?

3. What role do foreign-exchange brokers play in currency trading? Why are broker operations important to the smooth functioning of the foreign-exchange market?

4. Please supply a definition for the following terms:
   a. Cable transfers.
   b. Mail transfers.
   c. Bills of exchange.
   d. Sight bills.
   e. Time bills.
   f. Documentary bills.
   g. Clean bills.

5. What are the principal factors affecting the value of any particular currency in the international exchange markets? What role does a nation's balance of payments position play in affecting the value of its currency?

6. Define "double-barreled" quotations. Arbitrage.

7. Distinguish between the spot and forward markets for foreign exchange. Why is it necessary to have two markets rather than one?

8. How are forward-exchange rates measured? Where is the forward market located?

9. Describe the principal uses of forward-exchange contracts today. Give an example of each use.

10. What is interest-rate parity? How does it influence the flow of capital funds abroad?

11. In recent years central banks (including the Federal Reserve System) have intervened in the foreign-exchange markets from time to time to support one currency or another. Why do you think central bank intervention in the market might be necessary? What impact are central-bank operations likely to have? Would you expect this impact to be temporary or long lasting?

12. What is the latest U.S. government policy regarding intervention in the foreign-exchange markets? Why, in your opinion, was this policy adopted?

SELECTED REFERENCES

1. Anderson, Gerald H. "The Nature and Use of Forward Exchange." *Economic Review*, Federal Reserve Bank of Cleveland, April-May 1972, pp. 7–15.

2. Balback, Anatol B. "The Mechanics of Intervention in Exchange Markets." *Monthly Review*, Federal Reserve Bank of St. Louis, February 1978, pp. 2–7.

3. Batten, Dallas S. "Foreign Exchange Markets: The Dollar in 1980." *Review*, Federal Reserve Bank of St. Louis, April 1981, pp. 22–30.

4. Carlozzi, Nicholas. "Pegs and Floats: The Changing Face of the Foreign Exchange Market." *Business Review*, Federal Reserve Bank of Philadelphia, May-June 1980, pp. 13–23.

5. Chicago Mercantile Exchange. *Understanding Futures in Foreign Exchange*. Chicago, 1977.

6. Einzig, Paul. *A Dynamic Theory of Forward Exchange*. New York: St. Martin's Press, 1967.

7. Gardner, Walter R. "An Exchange Market Analysis of the U.S. Balance of Payments." *IMF Staff Papers* May 1961, pp. 195–211.

8. Grubel, Herbert. *Forward Exchange, Speculation, and the International Flow of Capital*. Stanford, Calif.: Stanford University Press, 1966.

9. Holmes, Alan R., and Francis H. Schott. *The New York Foreign Exchange Market*. New York: Federal Reserve Bank of New York, 1965.

10. Kareken, John, and Neil Wallace. "International Monetary Reform: The Feasible Alternatives." *Quarterly Review*, Federal Reserve Bank of Minneapolis, Summer 1978, pp. 2–7.

11. Kubarych, Roger M. *Foreign Exchange Markets in the United States*. New York: Federal Reserve Bank of New York, 1978.

12. Lary, Hal B. *Problems of the United States as World Banker and Trader*. New York: National Bureau of Economic Research, 1963.

13. Machlup, Fritz. *International Payments, Debts, and Gold*. New York: Charles Scribner's Sons, 1964.

14. Stern, Robert M. *The Balance of Payments*. Chicago: Aldine Publishing, 1973.

15. Westerfield, Janice M. "How U.S. Multinationals Manage Currency Risk." *Business Review,* Federal Reserve Bank of Philadelphia, March-April 1980, pp. 19–27.

16. Weston, J. Fred, and Bart W. Sorge. *International Managerial Finance.* Homewood, Ill.: Richard D. Irwin, 1972.

17. Williamson, John. *The Failure of World Monetary Reform, 1971–1974.* New York: New York University Press, 1977.

28

International Banking

No review of the international financial system would be complete without a discussion of the role of international banking institutions. Along with British and Canadian banks, American commercial banking institutions have led in the development of multinational banking facilities to meet the financial needs of foreign governments, agencies, and multinational corporations. Until recently, the multinational activities of U.S. banks were concentrated principally in foreign offices, due mainly to federal government controls over foreign lending. However, the relaxation of government controls in 1974 and the rapid growth of international trade and commerce have brought a veritable explosion of international banking operations, especially on the part of the largest U.S. banks.

The growth of multinational banking has resulted in several benefits for international trade. One obvious benefit to the public is intense competition in international financial markets, reducing profit margins and prices on loans. The development of multinational banking also has tied together more effectively the various national money markets into a unified international financial system, permitting a more optimal allocation of scarce resources. Funds flow quite freely today across national boundaries in response to differences in relative interest rates and currency values. While these developments undoubtedly have benefited both borrowers and investors, they also have created problems for governments trying to control the volume of credit, interest rates, and inflation.

THE SCOPE OF INTERNATIONAL BANKING ACTIVITIES

Multinational Banking Corporations

The term *multinational corporation* usually is reserved for large nonfinancial corporations with manufacturing or trading operations in several different countries. However, this term is equally applicable to the world's major commercial banks, most of whom have their home offices in Canada, the United States, and Great Britain, but have established offices worldwide. In terms of sheer numbers, however, it is the largest U.S. banks which have accounted for most of the growth in multinational banking during the past 10 years.

Types of Facilities Operated by U.S. Banks Abroad

U.S. banks and other major banks around the world have used several vehicles to expand their international operations. All major banks have international departments, and many operate full-service branches in foreign markets. U.S. banks also operate Edge Act and Agreement Corporations, shell branches, and representative offices in targeted overseas markets. In addition, most multinational banks make direct investments in the stock of foreign companies, either alone or as part of a consortium with other banks.

International Banking Departments. A major bank's international department generally has 20 to 30 officers and staff and maintains close personal contact with customers and correspondent banks overseas. The larger international banking departments buy and sell foreign currencies for immediate or future delivery, issue letters of credit, and engage in acceptance financing.

Shell Branches. Booking offices of major banks, also known as *shell branches,* are located today mainly in the Bahamas and Grand Cayman Islands. These branches have been set up to attract Eurodollars and other Eurocurrency deposits from abroad, making these deposits available to domestic banks.

Representative Offices. These offices attempt to find new loan customers and help meet the financial needs of existing bank customers. However, a representative office cannot accept deposits.

Edge Act and Agreement Corporations. These corporations are special subsidiaries of U.S. banks authorized to offer international banking services.

Which organizational form is adopted by a multinational bank to enter foreign markets depends upon government regulations and the bank's size, goals, and location. Most banks begin with international departments or Edge Acts and then, if business warrants, open shell branches, representative offices, and ultimately full-service branches and subsidiaries. A recent trend toward the liberalization of foreign trade and international lending have stimulated the growth of home-based offices which send officers to call on customers overseas or serve clients by wire. However, many multinational banks today argue that successful international operations require an institution to have a stable presence overseas in the form of branches or representative offices in order to fully meet customer needs.

Growth of U.S. International Banking Activities

U.S. international banking operations really began on a major scale in the early 1960s when the domestic economy was soft and loan demand, relatively weak. Abroad, the demand for credit was strong, particularly from Japanese firms, and rate differentials in the international money market generally favored the United States as a source of loanable funds. By the late 1960s restrictive interest-rate ceilings on domestic deposits encouraged the largest U.S. banks to draw more heavily on the Eurodollar market as a source of reserves. And, when the administration of President Lyndon Johnson imposed restrictions on overseas lending from domestic banking offices through a Voluntary Foreign Credit Restraint Program in 1965, U.S. banks saw the offshore office as a vital link to foreign deposits and loans.

The number of foreign offices operated by American banking organizations rose dramatically. In 1960 only seven U.S. banks operated a total of 132 foreign branches and offices. By 1964 there were 180 foreign branches owned by 11 U.S. banks and by 1974, 125 American banks controlled 732 foreign branch offices. A much-slower growth in the internationalization of U.S. banking then set in as global economic conditions softened in the wake of the energy crisis. By year-end 1979, 130 U.S. banks were represented by close to 800 overseas branch offices. Foreign assets held by U.S. banks had climbed to almost $365 billion as the 1980s began, up from only $9 billion in 1965 and $150 billion in 1974.[1]

As shown in Exhibit 28–1, the majority of assets and deposit liabilities held by U.S. bank branches abroad are concentrated in Western Europe (particularly the United Kingdom), Latin America, and the Caribbean. Assets held by U.S. bank branches in the United Kingdom—most of these headquartered in London, the center of the worldwide Eurodollar market—accounted for about 20 percent of the assets of all U.S. bank branches abroad. Other nations where U.S. bank branches hold substantial assets include Japan, France, Belgium-Luxembourg, West Germany, Brazil, the Bahamas, Mexico, and the Cayman Islands.

In terms of total offices, Latin America leads the list with more than 200 branches and office facilities operated by U.S. banks. Shell branches in the Bahamas and Grand Cayman Islands rank second in total numbers, totaling 153 at year-end 1979. The Far East and continental Europe were not far behind with well over 100 branches, representative offices, and other facilities of American banks in operation there. Significant numbers of U.S.

---

[1] See especially Abrams (1) and Board of Governors of the Federal Reserve System (3).

EXHIBIT 28–1

Geographical Distribution of Assets and Liabilities of Major Foreign Branches of U.S. Banks, Year-End 1980 ($ millions)*

Country of Customer	Assets	Lia-bilities	Country of Customer	Assets	Lia-bilities
Europe:.................	139,631	108,595	Latin America and		
Austria	1,721	1,001	Caribbean—cont'd.		
Belgium-Luxembourg .	12,478	6,713	Venezuela.............	6,647	4,079
Bulgaria	477	20	Others	1,510	1,016
Czechoslovakia	136	61			
Denmark..............	2,125	544	Asia:....................	51,404	52,306
Finland	1,001	211	China (PRC)	79	128
France	12,937	8,726	Hong Kong	7,282	5,678
Germany (East)........	1,032	149	India	156	315
Germany (West)	11,229	4,178	Indonesia	1,635	1,303
Hungary	468	75	Israel	732	890
Ireland...............	1,352	631	Japan	18,031	8,962
Italy	6,614	4,010	Korea (South)	3,065	1,081
Netherlands	4,160	4,993	Malaysia	883	732
Norway	2,432	680	Philippines............	4,263	2,171
Poland	1,189	17	Singapore	5,906	4,215
Portugal	302	153	Taiwan................	2,360	2,727
Romania.............	330	30	Thailand	695	247
Spain	3,184	2,935	Middle East oil-export-		
Sweden...............	2,256	493	ing countries‡	5,837	21,608
Switzerland	3,668	10,260	Others	480	2,249
Turkey	1,405	128			
U.S.S.R.	183	39	Africa:	8,629	5,694
United Kingdom	64,500	57,057	Egypt	699	1,406
Yugoslavia	1,566	123	Liberia	2,654	804
Others†	2,886	5,368	South Africa	837	206
			Morocco..............	465	7
Canada	6,517	5,330	Zaire	82	19
			African oil-exporting		
Latin America and			countries§	2,227	2,687
Caribbean:	72,068	41,378	Others	1,665	565
Argentina	6,153	2,080			
Bahamas	9,519	11,452	Oceania	1,476	340
Bermuda.............	478	2,341	Australia	805	106
Bolivia	336	99	New Zealand	296	8
Brazil	12,087	1,005	Others	375	226
Cayman Islands	9,605	10,660			
Chile	2,489	1,139	Unallocated‖...........	11,705	13,092
Colombia	1,500	403			
Costa Rica	377	118	TOTAL excluding the		
Ecuador	1,279	425	United States, Puerto		
Jamaica	200	35	Rico, and U.S.		
Mexico	11,362	1,945	dependencies	291,430	226,735
Netherlands Antilles ...	1,883	1,200	United States	28,477	91,169
Nicaragua.............	242	64	Puerto Rico and U.S.		
Panama	5,289	2,714	dependencies	4,221	3,559
Peru	1,112	603	Grand Total	324,128	321,463

* Branches submitting the report on which this table is based include all branches in the Bahamas and the Cayman Islands, with total liabilities of $50 million or more and all other branches with total liabilities of $150 million or more. Coverage thus differs from prior to June 1978 data published in the *International Letter* of the Federal Reserve Bank of Chicago. Figures have been adjusted to exclude accounts between branches of the same parent bank.

† Including the Bank for International Settlements.

‡ Bahrain, Iran, Iraq, Kuwait, Oman, Qatar, Saudi Arabia, and the United Arab Emirates.

§ Algeria, Gabon, Libya, and Nigeria.

‖ Including international organizations.

SOURCE: Federal Reserve Bank of Chicago.

banking offices may also be found today in Africa, the Middle East, and U.S. possessions and trust territories.

National laws and regulations play a major role in determining where multinational banking offices are located around the globe. For example, Australia, India, and Saudi Arabia prohibit or severely restrict the operation of branches by foreign banks. In other areas of the world fears of political upheaval or outright expropriation of foreign-owned facilities have severely limited the entry of multinational banks.

For several of the largest U.S. banks, international operations today yield from one third to as much as one half of their income, and a few receive more than half their earnings from international activities. Particularly noteworthy has been U.S.-bank penetration of foreign consumer banking markets, such as the "money shops" operated by New York's Citibank in Great Britain. Much as U.S. banks did in the 19th and early 20th century, many foreign banks today neglect the needs of consumers. American banks entered the consumer lending field in the 1920s, and they have developed considerable expertise in that field. Personal loans and other personal financial services represent extremely attractive opportunities in foreign markets, and U.S. banks have stepped up their efforts to capture a larger share of consumer loan and deposit markets abroad, especially in Great Britain and Western Europe.

SERVICES OFFERED BY INTERNATIONAL BANKS

Multinational banks today offer a wide variety of international financial services to their customers. These services, described briefly below, include issuing letters of credit, buying and selling foreign exchange, issuing bankers' acceptances, accepting Eurocurrency deposits, making Eurocurrency loans, and assisting in the marketing of Eurobonds. Of course, the particular services offered by each bank depend heavily upon its size, location, and the types of facilities—branches, representative offices, etc.—it maintains overseas.

Issuing Letters of Credit (LC)

Most banks enter the international sector to finance trade. A letter of credit is simply an international bank's promise to pay for goods stored overseas or goods shipped between two countries. Such letters may be issued to finance exports and imports or to provide standby credit. Through a letter of credit, the bank merely substitutes its own promise to pay for the promise to pay of one of its customers.[2] However, the bank's promise to pay

---

[2] In return, the customer promises to pay to the bank the amount of funds mentioned in the letter of credit plus credit or commitment fees mutually agreed upon. In a letter-of-credit transaction the individual or business firm applying for the letter (normally an importer of goods) is called the *account party*. The bank issuing the letter is referred to as the *issuing bank*. It

is more readily accepted by a seller of goods than is a buyer's promise of payment. By substituting its promise, the bank acts as a guarantor of payment and thereby reduces the seller's risk, facilitating the flow of goods and services in international markets.

Buying and Selling Foreign Exchange (FOREX)

Major multinational banks, as we saw in the preceding chapter, have dealer departments which specialize in trading foreign currencies. The largest multinationals hold inventories of selected currencies for themselves and for the convenience of their customers. They may also negotiate forward contracts for the future delivery of foreign exchange and speculate on future currency price movements in hopes of turning a profit. Smaller banks usually hold very small currency inventories and concentrate mainly on buying and selling foreign exchange for their customers rather than for speculative purposes. They frequently purchase whatever currency is needed for immediate or future delivery to a customer from larger international banks that maintain active currency positions.

Issuing Bankers' Acceptances

Bankers' acceptances are *time drafts* used mainly to finance the shipment of goods or commodities.[3] Similar to a letter of credit, the acceptance is a bank's promise to pay after a certain number of days, issued on behalf of one of its customers. It substitutes the bank's credit standing in place of the customer's credit standing.

With a banker's acceptance the bank agrees to pay a seller of goods when the time draft expires. For example, an exporter and importer may agree upon "60-day sight" terms on the shipment of certain items. This tells us that the exporter will receive payment from a bank 60 days following the date when the issuing bank affirms that the draft and certain documents associated with the transaction are in good order. Once this is affirmed, the issuing bank will stamp "Accepted" across the face of the draft. The bank's stamp is a guarantee of payment (in our example, in 60 days from date of the draft), and it makes the acceptance a negotiable instrument. The exporter may sell (discount) the acceptance to a bank or other investor and thereby receive payment before the draft's due date.

Acceptances have a number of desirable features for multinational banks and for exporters and importers of goods. They reduce the risk associated

---

promises to pay the sum mentioned in the letter on a specific future date. The individual or firm receiving the letter of credit (normally an exporter of goods) is referred to as the *beneficiary*. The beneficiary will receive payment upon presentation of the letter and other specific documents from the *drawee bank*. The drawee bank is instructed by the issuing bank on how and when to pay the beneficiary, once documents called for in the letter of credit are presented.

[3] See Chapter 15 for a detailed discussion of the creation and uses of bankers' acceptances.

with the shipment of goods by giving exporters a bank's guarantee of payment. That guarantee enables importers to tap numerous sources of supply and find those goods available on the best terms. Acceptances are a high-quality financial instrument used by banks as a reserve of liquidity. As we noted above, they may be discounted in advance of maturity with securities dealers and other commercial banks. Another advantage is that banks selling acceptances do not have to include the contingent liability associated with each acceptance as a deposit for purposes of calculating reserve requirements.

Accepting Eurocurrency Deposits and Making Eurocurrency Loans

As we saw in Chapter 15, international banks accept deposits denominated in currencies other than that of their home country. Thus, London banks will accept deposits denominated in dollars, francs, and other major convertible currencies. Eurocurrency deposits are used to pay for goods shipped between countries, as investment vehicles because they pay a competitive rate of return, and as a source of loanable funds for banks.

Eurocurrency deposits may be loaned in the interbank market, usually on an unsecured basis, to corporations, governments, and other large wholesale borrowers. The majority of Eurocurrency loans carry floating interest rates based, in most cases, on the London Interbank Offer Rate (known in the trade as LIBOR) for three-month and six-month Eurocurrency deposits. The market for Eurocurrency loans is extremely competitive, with the spread over deposit rates averaging no more than one eighth of 1 percent. Eurocurrency credit normally goes to borrowers with impeccable credit ratings. Often, several multinational banks will spread the risk of international lending by forming a syndicate and jointly participating in a single currency loan.

Assisting in the Marketing of Eurocurrency Bonds

In recent years multinational banks have become active as agents, underwriters, and, in some instances, investors in the rapidly growing market for Eurobonds. A *Eurobond* is a debt security denominated in a currency other than those of the countries where most or all of the security is sold. For example, an American automobile company may desire to float an issue of long-term bonds to raise capital for one of its subsidiaries operating in Greece. The company might issue bonds denominated in British pounds (or even dollars) to be sold in several countries in Western Europe through an underwriting syndicate made up of banks, securities dealers, and other firms.

Most Eurobonds are denominated in dollars, though substantial amounts are also denominated today in marks, guilders, pounds, and francs. These bonds generally carry maturities ranging from 11 to 15 years. Eurobonds normally are straight debt offerings, though warrants and conversion features occasionally are attached to improve the marketability of a particular issue. The majority are callable bearer bonds with coupons attached.

Large multinational banks assist the Eurobond market in several ways. Major banks such as Morgan Guaranty Trust Company of New York have established international clearing systems to expedite the delivery of bonds traded in the secondary market. Banks and security brokers are the principal intermediaries through which both old and new Eurobonds find their way to the long-term investor. The borrower—a government or large corporation—usually contacts a major international bank and asks it to organize a syndicate to place a new issue. At this point a consortium will be formed, embracing at least four to five American, British, Belgian, French, or German banks and a bank located in the borrowing country. The consortium typically agrees to subscribe to the Eurobond issue at issue price minus a commission (usually in the 2 to 3 percent range). Institutions in the consortium will then organize a large group of banks and securities dealers as underwriters in several countries. Sometimes more than 100 banks are included in the underwriting syndicate. Once formed, the underwriting group gives the borrower a firm offer for its bonds, and it receives funds immediately. The underwriting institutions will then place the issue with a large, geographically diverse group of investors representing many different countries.

SMALLER BANKS ENTER THE INTERNATIONAL FIELD

One of the unique features of international banking during the past decade is the opening of offshore offices by smaller, essentially regional banks.[4] A recent study by Thompson (14) concludes that more than half the regional banks among the top 300 American commercial banks now operate international departments. Other smaller banks without formal departments still provide such international services as letters of credit and bankers' acceptances. Expansion offshore has granted some of the smaller institutions an opportunity to diversify out of slowly growing domestic markets and to open up entirely new markets. Only the largest regionals actually open foreign branches or set up Edge Act Corporations, and only a handful have purchased majority interests in foreign financial organizations. However, many regional banks have opened shell branches, mainly in the Caribbean area. For example, Abrams (1) found that, as of year-end 1979, 103 U.S. banks, each with assets under $3 billion, were operating shell branches. These shells have provided a convenient source of loanable funds when domestic reserves

---

[4] Regional banks are usually defined as those large banks with a billion or more dollars in assets located in a U.S. city other than New York, Chicago, or San Francisco. Large downtown banks in Atlanta, Boston, Dallas, Houston, Miami, Los Angeles, Seattle, Portland, and New Orleans are examples of regional banks.

are scarce. Moreover, shell operations are low cost compared to most other forms of international banking.

The regional banks have faced some difficult problems in the international field, however. One problem is that some of the smaller banks have rushed into offshore operations without adequate preparation. For example, about 50 U.S. regional banks have entered the London money market since the late 1960s. The foreign affiliates of many of these banks have proven unprofitable because the scale of operations is too small and the range of services offered, too narrow. Moreover, as the number of multinational banks has grown, yield spreads between loans and deposits in the London money market have narrowed. Only in parts of Latin America and the Far East have yield spreads remained high enough and maturity requirements liberal enough to assure profitable lending for the smaller multinational banks. However, experience in lending to underdeveloped countries is extremely limited and, with rising energy costs, the risks are bound to increase.

Another difficulty is the rising cost of operating branches and other overseas facilities. London branches cost at least a million dollars a year to operate, and a representative office in Tokyo may run several hundred thousand dollars a year at minimum. At this rate a London branch must process about $80 to $100 million in loans just to reach the break-even point, while a Tokyo office would need to handle perhaps $15 to $20 million in loans. The rising costs are, in large measure, a function of increased competition for funds prevalent today in the international financial markets. Faced with this competition, many foreign branch operations are, at best, only marginally profitable. In many cases smaller institutions cannot offer a sufficiently broad range of services, generate a large-enough group of loyal customers, or attract the skills necessary to compete successfully with the big multinational banks. Smaller international banks have discovered, much to their surprise, that many of the same corporations which trade with them at home will not trade with them abroad. Instead, multinational corporations generally prefer to deal with the largest international banks, which have established connections and extensive experience in international affairs.

An added problem is that the smaller regional banks have had to rely heavily upon loan participations with better-established multinational lenders. However, participation agreements generally carry a lower rate of return and do not permit the smaller banks to develop the strong customer relationships or specialized knowledge which they need to compete effectively with larger multinationals. In addition, participation loans use up scarce capital and foreclose other, more profitable opportunities that may come along. Some of the smaller banks have become quite successful in international lending by centering their activities on selected industries and developing expertise in only one area or a few areas. Profitable lending opportunities appear to exist today, even for small banks, in ship financing, energy projects, and petroleum exploration. The obvious drawbacks here are the need for experienced personnel and the risks which must be estimated on the basis of limited experience.

FOREIGN BANKS IN THE UNITED STATES[5]

Banks owned by foreign individuals and companies have entered the United States in great numbers in recent years, especially since 1970. The reasons behind the expansion of foreign banking activities in the United States reflect both the growth in international trade and investments and the opportunity for profit in the huge U.S. common market. Originally, foreign-based banks penetrated U.S markets for essentially the same reason U.S. banks established facilities overseas—to follow their customers who had established operations in other countries. Once in the United States, however, foreign banks found the possibility of attracting deposits and loans from major American corporations irresistible. Moreover, the U.S. economy during the postwar period has been more stable and prosperous than many economies abroad.

Recent Growth of Foreign Banks in the United States

The size of foreign bank operations in the United States is impressive. By December 1980, there were 369 foreign banking institutions operating in the United States with assets of $188 billion (see Exhibit 28–2). This asset figure is six times higher than in 1973. During 1980 alone assets of foreign banking institutions in the United States rose 35 percent, while the assets of U.S. domestic banks rose only 14 percent.[6] Such rapid growth has made foreign banks a significant factor in U.S. financial markets, especially in the market for business loans, where their commercial credits now average about 14 percent of the volume of all such loans made by American banks.

Types of Organizations Operated by Foreign Banks in the United States

Foreign banks use a variety of institutional arrangements to establish facilities in the United States. Of course, the particular route used by foreign banks to enter U.S. markets depends upon the financial services they offer, their expected volume of foreign business, and the nature of their domestic operations. British banks generally have set up full-service banking facilities on the American continent by establishing branches and acquiring domestically chartered banks, principally in California and New York.

Canadian banks were the first to enter the United States, establishing agency offices during the last century. The large Canadian-chartered banks

---

[5] This section is based, in part, on an earlier article by the author in *The Canadian Banker and ICB Review*. See reference 12 at the end of this chapter.

[6] See, for example, Board of Governors of the Federal Reserve System (3) and Segala (12).

EXHIBIT 28–2
Assets and Liabilities of U.S. Branches and Agencies of Foreign Banking Institutions,
($ millions)*

	Year-End 1979	Year-End 1980
Assets		
Deposits and cash items:	16,972.8	19,559.3
Deposits and due from unrelated U.S. commercial banks	13,696.5	13,826.6
Deposits and due from unrelated banks in foreign countries	2,778.3	4,758.9
Other cash, CIPC, balances with Federal Reserve	498.0	973.8
Stocks, bonds, and other securities	2,829.7	3,477.1
Loans to unrelated institutions:	70,985.3	91,372.0
Commercial and industrial loans to parties in the U.S.	24,814.7	29,266.2
Commercial and industrial loans to parties in foreign countries	13,776.5	16,535.5
Loans to commercial banks in the United States†	11,178.3	17,015.4
Loans to banks in foreign countries	11,982.7	13,823.4
Loans for purchasing and carrying securities	1,365.4	822.0
Loans to foreign governments and official institutions	5,192.7	8,744.2
All other loans	2,675.0	5,165.3
Loans and due from directly related institutions:	35,167.3	54,770.0
In the U.S.	10,241.6	20,113.8
In foreign countries	24,925.7	34,656.2
Other assets:	13,082.7	18,789.4
Customers' liabilities on acceptances outstanding	4,365.0	7,830.5
Federal funds sold and securities purchased under agreements to resell†	5,746.0	6,678.0
Other assets	2,971.7	4,280.9
Total assets	139,037.8	187,967.8

then and now rely upon the American money market as a source of liquidity. The chartered banks make loans to security brokers and dealers in the market and hold substantial deposits with U.S. money-center banks. Canadian banks in the main have used four devices to carry on their operations in the United States: (1) trust companies in New York to provide for the safekeeping of valuables and the transfer and processing of bank payments; (2) New York and San Francisco agencies; (3) wholesale-retail affiliates, principally in the state of California; and (4) representative offices. Banks in Switzerland and Germany have used branch offices and securities affiliates. Japanese banks have established wholesale banking affiliates in New York, retail banking offices in California, and agency offices in New York which service securities and finance trade.

It is important to maintain some perspective on the relative importance of activities in the United States carried on by foreign banks versus the foreign activities of U.S. banks. U.S. banking activities abroad are enormous in scope—a major factor in foreign credit markets. For example, in the London money market, American banks outnumber British institutions and dominate the market for Eurodollars. It has been estimated that the London branches

EXHIBIT 28–2 (concluded)

	Year-End 1979	Year-End 1980
Liabilities		
Demand deposits or credit balances due to unrelated institutions:	14,116.9	13,964.9
Demand deposits of U.S. individuals, partnerships, and corporations	1,213.4	1,025.0
Demand deposits of foreign individuals, partnerships, and corporations	708.3	759.5
Other demand deposits	506.0	786.8
Due to commercial banks in the United States†	4,679.3	3,798.9
Due to foreign banks	1,339.1	1,204.8
Certified and officers' checks, travelers' checks, etc.	5,670.8	6,389.9
Time and savings deposits due to unrelated institutions:	21,439.7	28,983.1
Time deposits of U.S. individuals, partnerships, and corporations . . .	13,533.5	20,172.3
Foreign time deposits	4,710.5	5,877.8
Savings and other time deposits	3,195.7	2,933.0
Borrowings from unrelated institutions:	29,288.8	43,708.4
From commercial banks in the United States	21,346.7	34,059.0
Other parties in the United States	2,735.4	2,478.3
Parties in foreign countries	5,206.7	7,171.1
Due to directly related institutions:	56.604.1	78,940.7
In the United States	10,863.8	21,059.4
In foreign countries	45,740.3	57,881.3
Other liabilities, reserves, and capital accounts:	17,588.3	22,370.7
Liabilities on acceptances outstanding	4,587.2	8,648.6
Reserves and capital accounts	828.6	n.a.[3]
Federal funds purchased and securities sold under agreements to repurchase†	9,470.9	10,118.9
Other liabilities	2,701.6	3,603.2
Total liabilities, reserves, and capital accounts	139,037.8	187,967.8

* 1980 data are from the quarterly reporting form FFIEC 002, "Report of Assets and Liabilities of U.S. Branches and Agencies of Foreign Banks." This form was first used as of June 30, 1980. From November 1972 through May 1980, U.S. branches and agencies, along with commercial bank subsidiaries, investment companies, and agreement corporations of foreign banks, had filed a monthly FR886a report. 1979 data have been adjusted for general comparability with 1980 data. Some categories, however, may not be strictly comparable due to differences in reporting categories and definitions of balance sheet items.
† Excludes loans to/from U.S. commercial banks maturing in one day and settled in immediately available funds. Such loans are included in the "Federal funds sold/purchased and securities purchased/sold" categories. "Federal funds sold/purchased and securities purchased/sold" categories are not included on the FR886a reporting form, and as a result, 1979 and 1980 data are not strictly comparable.
SOURCE: Federal Reserve Bank of Chicago.

of U.S. banks hold about 10 percent of all bank loans in pounds sterling made to British residents. The foreign branches of American banks hold roughly three times the total assets of all foreign-bank agencies, branches, and affiliates operating in the United States. This figure does not take into account the equity holdings of U.S. banks in various financial institutions abroad—including commercial banks, finance companies, leasing firms, factors, and merchant banks—which are substantial. Clearly, *U.S. commercial banks play a much larger and more significant role in foreign banking markets than do their counterparts that have entered the United States.* In addition, the presence of foreign banks in the United States has strengthened New York City's claim to being the world's major financial center. Moreover, foreign banks bring more capital annually into the United States than they remove. Certainly, the volume of foreign trade financed in the United States is much larger as a result of foreign-bank activity.

Federal Regulation of Foreign Bank Activity

Until recently, there were no federal laws which regulated foreign-bank activity within U.S. borders. However, Congress has been monitoring foreign bank operations since 1966 when IntraBank, a Lebanese institution, collapsed and several U.S. banks suffered severe losses. Passage of the Bank Holding Company Act Amendments of 1970 marked an initial step toward federal regulation of foreign banking. Under the terms of the 1970 amendments, any corporation controlling one or more domestic banks became subject to regulation and supervision by the Federal Reserve Board. An additional step was taken in 1974, when the Federal Reserve began monitoring foreign-bank activities by gathering monthly balance-sheet reports from these banks.[7]

However, with foreign-bank operations within the United States growing more rapidly than domestic banks, the pressure on Congress for regulation of foreign banking institutions intensified. Proponents of restrictive legislation argued that the presence of foreign banks reduced the effectiveness of domestic monetary policy, especially control over the money supply. Moreover, the lack of specific regulations applying to foreign banks seemed unfair to domestic financial institutions, which must conform to an elaborate system of regulations. Allegedly, foreign banks faced significantly lower costs of operation due to less-burdensome regulations and more latitude in investing their funds. (Prior to November 1980, foreign banks were not required to hold reserves behind their deposits or to seek FDIC deposit insurance.) Equally significant, foreign banks could branch across state lines—a privilege denied American banks since passage of the McFadden Act in 1927.

There is also a disparity between foreign and domestic banks in the financial services each group of institutions is permitted to offer. American banks are prohibited from offering services in domestic markets not closely related to traditional banking services—the extension of credit and the taking of deposits. Prior to the 1930s many of the nation's largest banks combined investment banking services with their traditional commercial banking functions. However, congressional passage of the Glass-Steagall Act in 1933 prohibited American banks from investment underwriting of either corporate

---

[7] See Board of Governors of the Federal Reserve System, "Data Series on Foreign-Owned U.S. Banks," (2).

debt or stock issues. Such a prohibition does not apply to foreign-owned financial institutions, and several moved in to take advantage of this loophole. For example, a number of West German and Swiss banks have affiliates engaged in the trading of equity securities in the United States. Securities affiliates of foreign banks are not regulated or prohibited unless the terms of the Bank Holding Company Act apply. (This act does not include investment banking as a permissible nonbank business activity.)

Foreign Banks and the International Banking Act of 1978

Responding to these various arguments, Congress passed the International Banking Act in September 1978 (see Exhibit 28–3). The measure became law with President Carter's signature on September 17, 1978. However, it was not until November 13, 1980, that Federal Reserve regulations governing the interstate operations of U.S. branches, agencies, commercial lending companies, and subsidiaries of foreign banks became effective.

EXHIBIT 28–3
Purposes and Provisions of the International Banking Act of 1978

Purpose:	To promote competitive equality between domestic and foreign banking institutions operating in the United States.
Provisions:	Limited the interstate branching of foreign banks.
	Provided for federal licensing of branches and agencies of foreign banks.
	Authorized the Federal Reserve Board to impose reserve requirements on branches and agencies of foreign banks.
	Provided for foreign-bank access to Federal Reserve services such as the discount window.
	Provided for federal deposit insurance for branches of foreign banks.
	Granted broader powers to Edge Act corporations of U.S. banks so they can compete more effectively with branches and agencies of foreign banks.
	Subjected foreign banks operating branches and agencies to the nonbanking prohibitions of the U.S. Bank Holding Company Act.

SOURCE: Federal Reserve Bank of Chicago, *International Letter*, May 22, 1981.

Under the terms of the International Banking Act, branches and agencies of foreign banks with worldwide consolidated assets of $1 billion or more are subject to reserve requirements and Regulation Q interest-rate ceilings on their deposits. However, the Depository Institutions Deregulation and Monetary Control Act (DIDMCA) of 1980 requires all institutions eligible for deposit insurance to hold legal reserves. Because DIDMCA made all foreign banking institutions active in the U.S. eligible for FDIC deposit insurance, even the smallest foreign branches and agencies are now subject to deposit reserve requirements set by the Federal Reserve Board. And all foreign branches accepting retail deposits from the public must protect those deposits with FDIC insurance. Foreign banks that maintain U.S. offices other than branches or agencies must register with the secretary of the Treasury upon the establishment of such an office. And any foreign bank operating an agency, branch, or commercial lending company in the United States now falls under the provisions of the Bank Holding Company Act and must register with the Federal Reserve Board.

Each foreign bank which has an office accepting deposits from the public must select a "home state." If it does not do so, the Federal Reserve Board designates the home state of the bank. No foreign bank may directly or indirectly establish and operate a federal or state-chartered branch outside its home state. This provision of the law effectively prevents foreign banks from accepting deposits across state lines, especially retail (consumer-type) deposits. A "grandfather" clause exempts those U.S. offices of foreign banks established or applied for before July 28, 1978, however. And agencies that accept credit balances may set up offices outside a foreign bank's home state.

The International Banking Act proved to be a more-lenient piece of legislation than many observers expected. It did not attempt to punish or discriminate against foreign banks relative to their U.S. counterparts. In fact, the act set down in law the principal of *mutual nondiscrimination,* used widely abroad as a regulatory standard. This principal permits foreign-owned banks to operate under the same conditions and to possess the same powers as domestic banks. It is a policy that avoids establishing two sets of banking regulations—one for domestic institutions and the other for foreign-owned banks. Foreign banks can even acquire majority control of U.S. Edge Acts under the terms of the International Banking Act.

REGULATION OF THE INTERNATIONAL BANKING ACTIVITIES OF U.S. BANKS

A far more significant problem than regulating foreign banking activities in the United States is the regulation, supervision, and control of U.S. banks offering their services overseas. As we have seen, U.S. bank involvement abroad is far more extensive than foreign-bank penetration of U.S. domestic markets. What limits should be placed on U.S. banks operating overseas? Who should enforce those limits?

The first of those questions is not yet fully resolved, but the second has a ready answer. The Federal Reserve Board has been designated as the chief regulatory agency for international banking activities, especially where Fed member banks are involved. A member bank choosing to expand its activities abroad through the creation of foreign branches or through investments in foreign firms must secure the approval of the Federal Reserve Board. In contrast, state laws govern the foreign operations of state-chartered banks. However, with the exception of a handful of states (notably

New York), state governments have exerted only nominal control over foreign banking activities.

Of prime concern to the Federal Reserve is the protection of domestic deposits and the stability of the domestic banking system. The Fed has argued that it is difficult, if not impossible, to separate a bank's foreign operations from its domestic activities. If a foreign subsidiary gets into trouble, the danger exists that public confidence in the soundness of the domestic bank will be undermined. For this reason, the Fed, in passing upon applications of American banks to expand abroad, examines closely the condition of their *domestic* offices to determine if their home-based operations are adequately capitalized and if the bank possesses sufficient management skill to support foreign operations.

The regulatory authorities would like to develop ways to "insulate" the foreign activities of U.S. banks from their domestic operations. Such insulation would grant wider latitude to banking activities abroad and, at the same time, shield domestic banks from the hazards associated with foreign operations. As one member of the Federal Reserve Board noted recently, the problem is similar to that of trying to insulate domestic banks from the other business activities of their holding companies. Legally, one subsidiary is not liable for the debts of another. However, in practice, a domestic bank probably would feel compelled (and perhaps required by the authorities) to aid at least its wholly owned affiliates operating in foreign markets. The practical, if not legal, links between foreign and domestic subsidiaries of multinational banks force regulators to keep close tabs on the foreign operations of all commercial banks.

One central problem the Federal Reserve Board faces in regulating multinational banking activities is the wider latitude given most foreign commercial banks by the regulatory authorities of other countries. For example, banks outside the U.S. frequently are permitted to make equity investments in nonfinancial corporations. The Board, therefore, typically allows U.S. banks to offer a greater variety of services in foreign markets than at home. Overseas, American banks have been permitted to offer investment banking services, which, as we have seen, are prohibited in the United States by the Glass-Steagall Act. They also have been allowed to make noncontrolling equity investments in nonfinancial corporations. While American banks do not play an important direct role in our own capital markets, the broader powers available to them for international operations have brought them into the long-term Eurobond market, as we saw earlier in this chapter. The Fed argues that banking regulations in the United States reflect this nation's views on how much competition there should be in the financial system. However, competition in foreign markets depends upon the policies of other nations, and Federal Reserve officials have preferred to leave such questions to the host country. Thus, the Fed tries to balance freedom against risk in deciding upon the proper scope of multinational banking activities.

PROBLEMS AND THE FUTURE OF INTERNATIONAL BANKING

Early in 1974 the administration of President Richard M. Nixon announced the lifting of controls on loans extended by domestic financial institutions for offshore projects. Many experts interpreted the move as encouraging the growth of domestic banks involved in international finance, especially banks headquartered in New York City, which would become even more of a world financial center. In the long run the development of a more efficient, responsive, and viable system of international banking seems likely now that the controls are gone. Since the lifting of controls, however, other developments have raised serious questions about the future stability of multinational banking.

The Risks of International Lending

For one thing, lending funds in the international arena is risky—probably more risky, on average, than domestic lending. Political risk—the risk that government laws and regulations will change to the detriment of business interests—is particularly significant in international operations. Governments are frequently overthrown and confiscation of private property is a common occurrence in many parts of the world. There is also currency risk—the risk associated with changing relative prices of foreign currencies. The value of property pledged behind an international loan will fall if the currency of the home country is devalued, thus eroding the lender's collateral. Geography, too, works against the international lender of funds. The larger distances which frequently separate lender and borrower make it more difficult for the bank loan officer to see that the terms of the loan are being adhered to.

Beginning in the late 70s the Federal Reserve Board, Comptroller of the Currency, and Federal Deposit Insurance Corporation inaugurated semiannual surveys of foreign lending by approximately 140 U.S. banking organizations. The principal concern of these regulatory agencies was that U.S. multinational banks were overly committed to loans in certain countries where political and economic risks were unusually high. If this were the case, it might threaten the confidence of the public in the stability and soundness of this nation's largest banks. By June 1980, the federal banking agencies discovered, nonlocal loan credits extended by the most-active multinational banks totaled $266 billion, while loans to local borrowers in the markets where the banks' foreign offices were located totaled only about $70 billion (see Exhibit 28–4). However, most loans extended by U.S. multinational banks were made to industrially developed nations and to OPEC oil-producing countries. Only $66 billion—about one quarter—of the total of all foreign loans were directed at less-developed, non-oil-producing nations.

Nearly 60 percent of the loans extended by U.S.-based international banks flowed to residents of Switzerland and other developed nations in

EXHIBIT 28–4
Cross-Border and Nonlocal Currency Claims of U.S. International Banks Classified by Residence of Borrower, June 1980 ($ billions)

Residence of Borrower or Borrowing Group	Total Claims	Claims on:			Maturity Distribution of Claims:		
		Banks	Public Borrowers	Other Private Borrowers	One Year and Under	One to Five Years	Over Five Years
Switzerland and other G-10 developed nations	$112.6	$ 79.0	$ 6.3	$27.3	$ 94.0	$13.4	$ 5.2
Non-G-10 developed nations	21.3	7.1	5.6	8.6	11.3	6.8	3.1
Eastern Europe	7.9	4.1	2.9	0.9	3.5	3.5	0.9
Oil-exporting countries	19.9	4.5	7.9	7.5	12.5	6.1	1.2
Non-oil-exporting developing countries in:							
Latin America & the Caribbean	43.0	13.5	13.8	15.7	22.6	15.2	5.2
Asia	19.9	9.1	4.6	6.2	14.2	4.0	1.6
Africa	3.3	0.7	2.1	0.5	2.0	1.2	0.2
Offshore banking centers	38.1	29.3	0.7	8.1	33.2	2.9	2.0
International & regional organizations	0.2	0.0	0.2	0.0	*	*	*
Grand totals	$266.2	$147.4	$44.1	$74.7	$193.4	$53.2	$19.6

* Less than $100 million.

Notes: Cross-border and nonlocal currency claims involve lending from a bank's office in one country to residents of another country and loans in a currency other than that of the borrower. G-10 nations include Belgium-Luxembourg, Canada, France, West Germany, Italy, Japan, Netherlands, Sweden, Switzerland, and the United Kingdom. Non-G-10 developed countries include Australia, Austria, Denmark, Finland, Greece, Iceland, Ireland, New Zealand, Norway, Portugal, South Africa, Spain, and Turkey. Oil-exporting nations include Algeria, Ecuador, Gabon, Indonesia, Iran, Iraq, Kuwait, Libya, Nigeria, Qatar, Saudi Arabia, the United Arab Emirates, and Venezuela. Offshore banking centers include the Bahamas, Bahrain, Bermuda, British West Indies, Hong Kong, Lebanon. Liberia, Macao, the Netherlands Antilles, Panama, and Singapore.

SOURCE: Board of Governors of the Federal Reserve System.

the Group of Ten (G-10)[8] and to offshore banking centers where these large banks regularly conduct their business. In addition, nearly three quarters of the loans to distant nations were short term (maturity of one year or less), with other banks representing the largest borrowing group. It seems clear that, on the whole, multinational banks are relatively conservative lenders, directing their credits mainly to large bank, corporate, and governmental borrowers situated mainly in Europe and among the major oil-producing countries of the Middle East. The combination of regulatory pressure and the inherent risks of international lending have encouraged U.S. multinational bankers to issue mainly short-term loans to established borrowers with strong credit ratings.

Public Confidence and Bank Failures

Another problem in the international banking field is the preservation of public confidence in the banking system. Essentially, this means protecting the major multinationals against ultimate failure. This problem charged into the headlines in 1974 when both Franklin National Bank in New York, then the 20th largest U.S. bank, and the Bankhaus Herstatt of West Germany were forced into bankruptcy. In both instances severe losses in foreign exchange trading and commercial lending precipitated the closings. In the wake of these major bank failures, public confidence in virtually all of the world's multinational banks was shaken. International lending, particularly in the Eurodollar market, was limited to the largest, prime-quality borrowers, and smaller banks were forced to pay substantially higher rates in order to attract funds. Many loan syndicates disbanded, and business investment slowed significantly. All but the largest multinational banking institutions were literally shut out of the Eurocurrency markets for several weeks.

In order to avert future failures among the world's largest banks, regulatory authorities in the United States and elsewhere today look closely at the capital positions of multinational banks. Regulators have urged a slower, more-considered expansion of international loans, avoiding excessive credit exposure in loans to any one country, especially to non-oil-producing nations of the Third World. This is coupled today with an insistence on adequate levels of equity capital, adjusted for differences in loan risk among major banks. Unfortunately, determining what is an adequate capital position to support foreign banking activities is a complicated problem. Fluctuations in foreign-exchange rates, barriers to the flow of information, and foreign political developments add to the risks inherent in international banking. Thus far, there is no evidence that losses on international transactions significantly exceed domestic losses. Then too, a bank diversifying into the international arena may be able to reduce fluctuations in its overall cash flow and there-

---

[8] The Group of Ten countries include Belgium-Luxembourg, Canada, France, West Germany, Italy, Japan, Netherlands, Sweden, Switzerland, and the United Kingdom.

fore may actually need less capital than a bank operating solely in domestic markets. In the aftermath of Franklin and Herstatt, however, the regulatory authorities remain cautious.

The Energy Crisis and Petrodollars

Of all the problems which have confronted the international banking community in recent years, the most widely debated and potentially serious has been the energy crisis. During and immediately following the Oil Embargo of 1973–74, the price of oil sold by member nations of OPEC quadrupled. Between 1974 and 1980, prices per barrel of OPEC oil paid by Western nations rose more than 800 percent. The result in the United States was the severest recession since World War II and a resurgence of inflationary pressures. In Western Europe and Japan, economic growth slowed markedly, unemployment rose, and consumer prices soared.

The sudden surge in oil payments by Western nations was, of course, matched by huge balance-of-payments surpluses for oil-producing countries. During 1974 alone, OPEC countries deposited between $21 and $23 billion in Eurocurrency accounts. The stress associated with these massive flows of "petrodollars" has fallen directly on the international banking system, which has been forced to recycle the receipts of oil-producing nations, mainly back to Western economies, and also draw upon funds—many in short-notice deposits—to make longer-term loans. Without a smoothly functioning international banking system, petrodollars probably would have piled up in the investment accounts of oil-producing nations, resulting in a massive drain of funds from Western economies (including the United States), with disruptive effects on industrial output, employment, and world trade.

Prospects and Issues in the 1980s

Despite the pressures and the problems, the international banking system has recovered rapidly from the disruptive atmosphere of the 1970s. Many multinationals have installed stricter controls over their international operations, especially over foreign-exchange dealings. Others have withdrawn from certain markets or reduced the scale of their operations. The Federal Reserve System seems determined to play a more active role in the problems of individual banks and in monitoring foreign exchange operations. For example, the Federal Reserve Bank of New York, in addition to lending about $1.7 billion to Franklin National Bank when that institution was in trouble, took over Franklin's foreign-exchange operations in order to avoid disruption of international agreements. This move heralds the emergence of a more-conservative supervisory attitude by the Federal Reserve System toward major bank problems.

Another calming factor has been a scaling down of the petrodollar recycling problem. The net oil revenues of OPEC nations have proven to be substantially less than originally anticipated. The cumulative revenue surplus of oil-producing countries through the mid-1980s apparently will be only about a third to a fifth of what had been anticipated originally. In part, this is due to softening petroleum demand, higher energy prices, and effective energy-conservation programs in the industrialized countries.

These recent trends suggest a much-different future for international banking than seemed likely in the 1960s and 70s. Growth—limited by capital and the availability of experienced management—should be considerably more gradual and loan quality more of a factor in future extensions of credit. It is likely, too, that significant expansion of banking facilities—affiliates, branches, representative offices, and subsidiaries—will occur in the OPEC nations. American multinationals, even now, are in the midst of a program to improve their Middle East banking facilities. An unusually rapid expansion of foreign banking activities in the United States also may be anticipated. It is significant, perhaps, that the absorption of New York's Franklin National Bank was carried out by a foreign-owned banking consortium, European-American Bank and Trust Company.

Still, a number of critical issues remain to be resolved in the international sector. These issues cloud the future of international banking and will significantly determine its future development. Among the more important issues are:

1. To what extent can and will the regulatory authorities of different nations cooperate to control foreign banking activities? How can we reconcile different banking rules from one country to the next so as to promote competition and innovation, but also public safety?
2. What is an appropriate capital position for banks engaged in foreign lending, and how does this relate to their domestic capital needs?
3. Where must regulation end and the free play of market forces be allowed to operate in international banking? Should multinational banks be subject to the same rigid controls as domestic banks?
4. What impact are developments in multinational banking, especially in the Eurocurrency market, likely to have on domestic financial markets, and how can domestic monetary policy best deal with that impact?

These are perplexing issues with few clear answers. However, the growing importance of international banking and the increasing penetration of domestic markets all over the globe by foreign banking institutions demand that effective answers be found in the very near future.

STUDY QUESTIONS

1. What are the essential differences between the following types of banking organizations:
   a. International banking departments.
   b. Edge Act corporations.

     c. Agreement corporations.

     d. Shell branches.

     e. Representative offices.

     f. Full-service branches.

     g. Consortiums.

2. In what parts of the world are most U.S. banking offices located? Can you explain why?

3. Explain why many smaller U.S. regional banks have entered the international banking field in recent years. What specific problems is management likely to encounter in trying to establish banking facilities and offer financial services abroad?

4. What are the principal powers and functions of Edge Act Corporations? How did the International Banking Act of 1978 affect Edges?

5. What role have Edge Acts played in the U.S. branch banking controversy? What are LPOs, and why are they important in both domestic and international banking markets?

6. Explain why foreign banks have entered the United States in such large numbers in recent years. What types of organizations do these banks operate in the United States?

7. What federal regulations apply to foreign banks operating in the United States today? What factors motivated Congress to pass the International Banking Act of 1978?

8. What federal agency is the chief regulator of international banking in the United States? What are its principal powers?

9. What is the principal of mutual nondiscrimination? Do you agree with this principal? What problems could it create for regulators?

10. What major problems have been encountered by the international banking community in recent years? How have these problems been dealt with?

SELECTED REFEFENCES

1. Abrams, Richard K. "Regional Banks and International Banking." *Economic Review,* Federal Reserve Bank of Kansas City, November 1980, pp. 3–14.

2. Board of Governors of the Federal Reserve System. "Data Series on Foreign-Owned U.S. Banks." *Federal Reserve Bulletin,* October 1974, pp. 741–42.

3. Board of Governors of the Federal Reserve System. "Implementation of the International Banking Act." *Federal Reserve Bulletin,* October 1979, pp. 785–96.

4. "Edge Act Corporations and International Banking." *Monthly Review,* Federal Reserve Bank of Richmond, June 1967, pp. 2–5.

5. Franklin R. Edwards. *Regulation of Foreign Banking in the United States: International Reciprocity and Federal-State Conflicts.* New York: Columbia University, Graduate School of Business, 1974.

6. Frankel, A. B. "International Banking: Part I." *Business Conditions,* Federal Reserve Bank of Chicago, January 1975, pp. 3–9.

7. Janssen, Richard F. "Crossing the Line—Expanding U.S. Banks Hope Law Allows National Competition." *The Wall Street Journal,* June 21, 1979, pp. 1 and 16.

8. Klopstock, Fred H. "Foreign Banks in the United States: Scope and Growth of Operations." *Monthly Review,* Federal Reserve Bank of New York, June 1973, pp. 140–54.

9. Kvasnicka, Joseph G. "International Banking: Part II." *Business Conditions,* Federal Reserve Bank of Chicago, March 1976, pp. 3–11.

10. Lees, Francis A. *International Banking and Finance.* New York: John Wiley & Sons, 1973.

11. Mitchell, George W. Statement before the Subcommittee on Financial Institutions, Committee on Banking, Housing and Urban Affairs of the U.S. Senate, Federal Reserve Board *Press Release,* January 28, 1976.

12. Rose, Peter S. "Foreign Banking in the United States." *The Canadian Banker and ICB Review,* 1976, pp. 58–61.

13. _____ and Bassoul, Habib G. "Edge Acts: Outside—In." *The Canadian Banker and ICB Review,* 1980, pp. 52–56.

14. Segala, John P. "A Summary of the International Banking Act of 1978." *Economic Review,* Federal Reserve Bank of Richmond, January-February 1979, pp. 16–21.

15. Summers, Bruce J. "Foreign Banking in the United States: Movement toward Federal Regulation." *Economic Review,* Federal Reserve Bank of Richmond, January-February 1976, pp. 3–7.

16. Thompson, I. B. "The International Banking Activities of Regional Banks." *American Banker,* March 23, 1979, pp. 14, 36, and 38.

17. U.S. Congress, *Foreign Bank Act of 1975,* S. 958, 94th Cong., 1st Sess. (1975).

18. U.S. Congress, House Committee on Banking, Currency and Housing. *Financial Institutions and the Nation's Economy (FINE)—Discussion Principles.* 94th Cong., 1st Sess., Title VI (1975).

19. U.S. Congress, Joint Economic Committee. *Foreign Banking in the United States.* Economic Policies and Practices Paper no. 9, Washington, D.C., 1966.

appendix A

Security Credit Ratings

SECURITY CREDIT RATINGS

What Are Credit Ratings?

As discussed in Chapter 8, corporate and municipal debt securities sold in the financial markets today generally must carry a credit rating assigned by one or more rating agencies. The two most widely respected credit-rating agencies in the United States are Moody's Investor Service and Standard and Poor's Corporation, both headquartered in New York City. The ratings assigned by these private companies are generally regarded in the investment community as an objective evaluation of the probability that a borrower will *default* on a given security issue.

Default occurs whenever a security issuer is late in making one or more payments that it is legally obligated to make. In the case of a bond, when any interest or principal payment falls due and is not made on time, the bond is legally in default. While many defaulted bonds ultimately resume the payment of principal and interest, others never do, and the issuing company winds up in bankruptcy proceedings. In most instances, holders of bonds issued by a bankrupt company receive only pennies on each dollar invested, once the company's assets are sold at auction. Thus, the investor who holds title to bankrupt bonds typically loses both principal and interest. It is no wonder, then, that security ratings are so closely followed by investors. In fact, many investors accept the ratings assigned by credit agencies as a substitute for their own investigation of a security's investment quality.

Factors Affecting Assigned Ratings

Each rating assigned to a security issue is a reflection of at least three factors: (1) the character and terms of the particular security being issued; (2) the probability that the issuer will default on the security and the ability and willingness of the issuer to make timely payments as specified in the indenture (contract) accompanying the security; and (3) the degree of protection afforded investors if the security issuer is liquidated, reorganized, and/or declares bankruptcy. As a matter of practice, the investment agencies focus principally upon: (1) the past and probable future cash flows of the security issuer as an indication of the institution's ability to service its debt; (2) the volume and composition of outstanding debt; and (3) the stability of the issuer's cash flows over time. Other factors influencing quality ratings are the value of assets pledged as collateral for a security and the security's priority of claim against the issuing firm's assets. Quality analysts also place heavy emphasis upon interest-coverage ratios and liquidity of the issuing firm.

The rating agencies stress that their evaluations of individual security issues are not recommendations to buy or sell or an indication of the suitability of any particular security for the investor. The agencies do not act as financial advisers to the businesses or units of government whose securities they rate, which helps to promote objectivity in assigning quality ratings.[1] Both domestic and foreign securities are rated using the same criteria.

Standard & Poor's Corporate and Municipal Bond Ratings

The credit ratings assigned to corporate and municipal bonds by Standard & Poor's Corporation are listed below along with the definitions used by S&P for each rating category:[2]

1. AAA—Bonds rated AAA have the highest rating assigned by Standard & Poor's to a debt obligation. Capacity to pay interest and repay principal is extremely strong.
2. AA—Bonds rated AA have a very strong capacity to pay interest and repay principal and differ from the highest-rated issues only in small degree.
3. A—Bonds rated A have a strong capacity to pay interest and repay principal, although they are somewhat more susceptible to the adverse effects of changes in circumstances and economic conditions than bonds in higher-rated categories.
4. BBB—Bonds rated BBB are regarded as having an adequate capacity to pay interest and repay principal. Whereas they normally exhibit ade-

---

[1] Fees are assessed for ratings according to the time and effort expended in gathering sufficient information to determine an appropriate rating. These fees are usually paid either by the security issuer or by the firm or syndicate underwriting the security issue.

[2] See Standard & Poor's Corporation, *Bond Guide*, October 1980, p. 6.

quate protection parameters, adverse economic conditions or changing circumstances are more likely to lead to a weakened capacity to pay interest and repay principal for bonds in this category than for bonds in higher-rated categories.

5. BB, B, CCC, CC—Bonds rated BB, B, CCC, and CC are regarded, on balance, as predominantly speculative with respect to capacity to pay interest and repay principal in accordance with the terms of the obligation. BB indicates the lowest degree of speculation and CC the highest degree of speculation. While such bonds will likely have some quality and protective characteristics, these are outweighed by large uncertainties or major risk exposures to adverse conditions.

6. C—The rating C is reserved for income bonds on which no interest is being paid.

7. D—Bonds rated D are in default, and payment of interest and/or repayment of principal is in arrears.

The ratings from AA to B may be modified by the addition of a plus (+) or minus (−) sign to show relative standing within the major rating categories. A plus (+) sign indicates a bond of better-than-average quality in the particular rating category chosen, while a minus (−) sign denotes a bond that is worse than average in that category. Provisional ratings may also be assigned, as indicated by the letter *P*. According to Standard & Poor's, this may be interpreted as follows:

> A provisional rating assumes the successful completion of the project being financed by the bonds being rated and indicates that payment of debt service requirements is largely or entirely dependent upon the successful and timely completion of the project. This rating, however, while addressing credit quality subsequent to completion of the project, makes no comment on the likelihood of, or the risk of default upon failure of, such completion. The investor should exercise his own judgment with respect to such likelihood and risk.[3] When no rating is requested for a security or the agency feels that insufficient information exists to assign a rating, it will designate the security as NR.

S&P publishes a *Bond Guide* each month which contains data revised through the last business day of the preceding month. The S&P *Bond Guide* gives a brief description of each security issue, including its yield, listing status, eligibility for certain institutional investors, form (coupon or registered), redemption provisions, and earnings coverage.

Moody's Investor Service

Beginning in 1909, John Moody developed and published a simple system of letter grades which indicated the relative investment quality of corporate bonds. Today, Moody's Investor Service rates thousands of issues of corpo-

---

[3] Standard & Poor's Corporation, *Bond Guide,* October 1980, p. 6.

rate and municipal bonds, commercial paper, short-term municipal notes, and preferred stock. These security ratings are reported in *Moody's Bond Record,* which is published monthly. In addition to assigning issue ratings, Moody's also notes for its subscribers the essential terms on each security issue; dates when interest, principal, or dividend payments are due; call provisions (if any); registration status; bid and asked price quotations; yield to maturity; tax status; coverage; and amount of securities outstanding.

Moody's Corporate Bond Ratings

The credit ratings assigned by Moody's to corporate bonds are listed below with the definitions of each rating category:[4]

Aaa

Bonds which are rated Aaa are judged to be of the best quality. They carry the smallest degree of investment risk and are generally referred to as "gilt edge." Interest payments are protected by a large or by an exceptionally stable margin and principal is secure. While the various protective elements are likely to change, such changes as can be visualized are most unlikely to impair the fundamentally strong position of such issues.

Aa

Bonds which are rated Aa are judged to be of high quality by all standards. Together with the Aaa group they comprise what are generally known as high-grade bonds. They are rated lower than the best bonds because margins of protection may not be as large as in Aaa securities or fluctuation of protective elements may be of greater amplitude or there may be other elements present which make the long-term risks appear somewhat larger than in Aaa securities.

A

Bonds which are rated A possess many favorable investment attributes and are to be considered as upper medium-grade obligations. Factors giving security to principal and interest are considered adequate but elements may be present which suggest a susceptibility to impairment sometime in the future.

Baa

Bonds which are rated Baa are considered as medium-grade obligations, i.e., they are neither highly protected nor poorly secured. Interest payments and principal security appear adequate for the present but certain protective elements may be lacking or may be characteristically unreliable over any great length of time. Such bonds lack outstanding investment characteristics and, in fact, have speculative characteristics as well.

Ba

Bonds which are rated Ba are judged to have speculative elements; their future cannot be considered as well assured. Often the protection of interest and principal payments may be very moderate and thereby not well safeguarded during both good and bad times over the future. Uncertainty of position characterizes bonds in this class.

---

[4] See *Moody's Bond Record,* October 1979.

B

Bonds which are rated B generally lack characteristics of a desirable investment. Assurance of interest and principal payments or of maintenance of other terms of the contract over any long period of time may be small.

Caa

Bonds which are rated Caa are of poor standing. Such issues may be in default and there may be present elements of danger with respect to principal or interest.

Ca

Bonds which are rated Ca represent obligations which are speculative in some degree. Such issues are often in default or have other marked shortcomings.

C

Bonds which are rated C are the lowest rated class of bonds and issues so rated are to be regarded as having extremely poor prospects of ever attaining any real investment standing.

Moody's Municipal Bond Ratings

The investment quality of state and local government bonds is rated by Moody's according to the categories shown below:[5]

Aaa

Bonds which are rated Aaa are judged to be of the best quality. They carry the smallest degree of investment risk and are generally referred to as "gilt edge." Interest payments are protected by a large or by an exceptionally stable margin and principal is secure. While the various protective elements are likely to change, such changes as can be visualized are most unlikely to impair the fundamentally strong position of such issues.

Aa

Bonds which are rated Aa are judged to be of high quality by all standards. Together with the Aaa group they comprise what are generally known as high-grade bonds. They are rated lower than the best bonds because margins of protection may be of greater amplitude or there may be other elements present which make the long-term risks appear somewhat larger than in Aaa securities.

Baa

Bonds which are rated Baa are considered as medium-grade obligations; i.e., they are neither highly protected nor poorly secured. Interest payments and principal security appear adequate for the present but certain protective elements may be lacking or may be characteristically unreliable over any great length of time. Such bonds lack outstanding investment characteristics and, in fact, have speculative characteristics as well.

Ba

Bonds which are rated Ba are judged to have speculative elements; their future cannot be considered as well assured. Often the protection of interest

[5] See *Moody's Bond Record*, October 1979.

and principal payments may be very moderate, and thereby not well safeguarded during both good and bad times over the future. Uncertainty of position characterizes bonds in this class.

B

Bonds which are rated B generally lack the characteristics of a desirable investment. Assurance of interest and principal payments or of maintenance of other terms of the contract over any long period of time may be small.

Caa

Bonds which are rated Caa are of poor standing. Such issues may be in default or there may be present elements of danger with respect to principal or interest.

Ca

Bonds which are rated Ca represent obligations which are speculative in a high degree. Such issues are often in default or have other marked shortcomings.

C

Bonds which are rated C are the lowest rated class of bonds, and issues so rated can be regarded as having extremely poor prospects of ever attaining any real investment standing.

Con. (—)

Bonds for which the security depends upon the completion of some act or the fulfillment of some condition are rated conditionally. These are bonds secured by (a) earnings of projects under construction, (b) earnings of projects unseasoned in operation experience, (c) rentals which begin when facilities are completed, or (d) payments to which some other limiting condition attaches. Parenthetical rating denotes probabe credit stature upon completion of construction or elimination of basis of condition.

Like Standard and Poor's Corporation, Moody's Investor Service will sometimes affix an additional symbol to its bond ratings to denote finer gradations of quality. For example, an A-rated municipal bond that appears to be superior to other bonds in this category may be designated as A1. Similarly, a better-than-average Baa municipal obligation may be labeled Baa1.

Moody's Commercial Paper Ratings

Promissory notes sold in the open market by large corporations and having an original maturity of nine months or less are known as commercial paper. Moody's assigns those commercial notes it is willing to rate to one of three quality categories:[6]

Prime-1 (or P-1)—Highest quality
Prime-2 (or P-2)—Higher quality
Prime-3 (or P-3)—High quality

[6] See *Moody's Bond Record,* October 1979.

Moody's Ratings of Short-Term Municipal Notes

Short-term securities issued by states, cities, counties, and other local governments are also rated by Moody's as to their investment quality. For these short-term issues Moody's uses the rating symbol MIG, meaning Moody's Investment Grade. As shown below, only four rating categories are used and speculative issues or those for which adequate information is not available are not rated. The rating categories are as follows:[7]

MIG 1

Loans bearing this designation are of the best quality, enjoying strong protection from established cash flows of funds for their servicing or from established and broad-based access to the market for refinancing, or both.

MIG 2

Loans bearing this designation are of high quality, with margins of protection ample though not so large as in the preceding group.

MIG 3

Loans bearing this designation are of favorable quality, with all security elements accounted for but lacking the undeniable strength of the preceding grades. Market access for refinancing, in particular, is likely to be less well established.

MIG 4

Loans bearing this designation are of adequate quality, carrying specific risk but having protection commonly regarded as required of an investment security and not distinctly or predominantly speculative.

Moody's Preferred Stock Ratings

Beginning in 1973 Moody's extended its rating system to include preferred stock issues. As discussed in Chapter 20, preferred shares occupy middle ground between common stock and corporate bonds in terms of protection afforded the investor. Preferred dividend payments are not required as are interest payments on bonds and, in the event of liquidation, preferred stockholders can recover their funds only after bondholders and other creditors are paid. However, preferred shareholders have priority in claims against both current earnings and assets ahead of common stockholders. Because preferred stock does have a different status than bonds, Moody's stresses that preferred stock ratings should not be compared in absolute terms with bond ratings.

The preferred stock ratings currently assigned by Moody's are as follows:[8]

aaa

An issue which is rated "aaa" is considered to be a top-quality preferred stock. This rating indicates good asset protection and the least risk of dividend impairment within the universe of preferred stocks.

---

[7] See *Moody's Bond Record,* October 1979.

[8] See *Moody's Bond Record,* October 1979.

aa

An issue which is rated "aa" is considered a high-grade preferred stock. This rating indicates that there is reasonable assurance that earnings and asset protection will remain relatively well maintained in the foreseeable future.

a

An issue which is rated "a" is considered to be an upper-medium-grade preferred stock. While risks are judged to be somewhat greater than in the "aaa" and "aa" classifications, earnings and asset protection are, nevertheless, expected to be maintained at adequate levels.

baa

An issue which is rated "baa" is considered to be medium grade, neither highly protected nor poorly secured. Earnings and asset protection appear adequate at present but may be questionable over any great length of time.

ba

An issue which is rated "ba" is considered to have speculative elements and its future cannot be considered well assured. Earnings and asset protection may be very moderate and not well safeguarded during adverse periods. Uncertainty of position characterizes preferred stocks in this class.

b

An issue which is rated "b" generally lacks the characteristics of a desirable investment. Assurance of dividend payments and maintenance of other terms of the issue over any long period of time may be small.

caa

An issue which is rated "caa" is likely to be in arrears on dividend payments. This rating designation does not purport to indicate the future status of payments.

appendix B

Present-Value and Annuity Tables

Present-Value Table
Present Value of $1

Years Hence	1%	2%	4%	6%	8%	10%	12%	14%	15%	16%	18%	20%	22%	24%	25%	26%	28%	30%	35%	40%	45%	50%
1	0.990	0.980	0.962	0.943	0.926	0.909	0.893	0.877	0.870	0.862	0.847	0.833	0.820	0.806	0.800	0.794	0.781	0.769	0.741	0.714	0.690	0.667
2	0.980	0.961	0.925	0.890	0.857	0.826	0.797	0.769	0.756	0.743	0.718	0.694	0.672	0.650	0.640	0.630	0.610	0.592	0.549	0.510	0.476	0.444
3	0.971	0.942	0.889	0.840	0.794	0.751	0.712	0.675	0.658	0.641	0.609	0.579	0.551	0.524	0.512	0.500	0.477	0.455	0.406	0.364	0.328	0.296
4	0.961	0.924	0.855	0.792	0.735	0.683	0.636	0.592	0.572	0.552	0.516	0.482	0.451	0.423	0.410	0.397	0.373	0.350	0.301	0.260	0.226	0.198
5	0.951	0.906	0.822	0.747	0.681	0.621	0.567	0.519	0.497	0.476	0.437	0.402	0.370	0.341	0.328	0.315	0.291	0.269	0.223	0.186	0.156	0.132
6	0.942	0.888	0.790	0.705	0.630	0.564	0.507	0.456	0.432	0.410	0.370	0.335	0.303	0.275	0.262	0.250	0.227	0.207	0.165	0.133	0.108	0.088
7	0.933	0.871	0.760	0.665	0.583	0.513	0.452	0.400	0.376	0.354	0.314	0.279	0.249	0.222	0.210	0.198	0.178	0.159	0.122	0.095	0.074	0.059
8	0.923	0.853	0.731	0.627	0.540	0.467	0.404	0.351	0.327	0.305	0.266	0.233	0.204	0.179	0.168	0.157	0.139	0.123	0.091	0.068	0.051	0.039
9	0.914	0.837	0.703	0.592	0.500	0.424	0.361	0.308	0.284	0.263	0.225	0.194	0.167	0.144	0.134	0.125	0.108	0.094	0.067	0.048	0.035	0.026
10	0.905	0.820	0.676	0.558	0.463	0.386	0.322	0.270	0.247	0.227	0.191	0.162	0.137	0.116	0.107	0.099	0.085	0.073	0.050	0.035	0.024	0.017
11	0.896	0.804	0.650	0.527	0.429	0.350	0.287	0.237	0.215	0.195	0.162	0.135	0.112	0.094	0.086	0.079	0.066	0.056	0.037	0.025	0.017	0.012
12	0.887	0.788	0.625	0.497	0.397	0.319	0.257	0.208	0.187	0.168	0.137	0.112	0.092	0.076	0.069	0.062	0.052	0.043	0.027	0.018	0.012	0.008
13	0.879	0.773	0.601	0.469	0.368	0.290	0.229	0.182	0.163	0.145	0.116	0.093	0.075	0.061	0.055	0.050	0.040	0.033	0.020	0.013	0.008	0.005
14	0.870	0.758	0.577	0.442	0.340	0.263	0.205	0.160	0.141	0.125	0.099	0.078	0.062	0.049	0.044	0.039	0.032	0.025	0.015	0.009	0.006	0.003
15	0.861	0.743	0.555	0.417	0.315	0.239	0.183	0.140	0.123	0.108	0.084	0.065	0.051	0.040	0.035	0.031	0.025	0.020	0.011	0.006	0.004	0.002
16	0.853	0.728	0.534	0.394	0.292	0.218	0.163	0.123	0.107	0.093	0.071	0.054	0.042	0.032	0.028	0.025	0.019	0.015	0.008	0.005	0.003	0.002
17	0.844	0.714	0.513	0.371	0.270	0.198	0.146	0.108	0.093	0.080	0.060	0.045	0.034	0.026	0.023	0.020	0.015	0.012	0.006	0.003	0.002	0.001
18	0.836	0.700	0.494	0.350	0.250	0.180	0.130	0.095	0.081	0.069	0.051	0.038	0.028	0.021	0.018	0.016	0.012	0.009	0.005	0.002	0.001	0.001
19	0.828	0.686	0.475	0.331	0.232	0.164	0.116	0.083	0.070	0.060	0.043	0.031	0.023	0.017	0.014	0.012	0.009	0.007	0.003	0.002	0.001	
20	0.820	0.673	0.456	0.312	0.215	0.149	0.104	0.073	0.061	0.051	0.037	0.026	0.019	0.014	0.012	0.010	0.007	0.005	0.002	0.001	0.001	
21	0.811	0.660	0.439	0.294	0.199	0.135	0.093	0.064	0.053	0.044	0.031	0.022	0.015	0.011	0.009	0.008	0.006	0.004	0.002	0.001		
22	0.803	0.647	0.422	0.278	0.184	0.123	0.083	0.056	0.046	0.038	0.026	0.018	0.013	0.009	0.007	0.006	0.004	0.003	0.001	0.001		
23	0.795	0.634	0.406	0.262	0.170	0.112	0.074	0.049	0.040	0.033	0.022	0.015	0.010	0.007	0.006	0.005	0.003	0.002	0.001			
24	0.788	0.622	0.390	0.247	0.158	0.102	0.066	0.043	0.035	0.028	0.019	0.013	0.008	0.006	0.005	0.004	0.003	0.002	0.001			
25	0.780	0.610	0.375	0.233	0.146	0.092	0.059	0.038	0.030	0.024	0.016	0.010	0.007	0.005	0.004	0.003	0.002	0.001	0.001			
26	0.772	0.598	0.361	0.220	0.135	0.084	0.053	0.033	0.026	0.021	0.014	0.009	0.006	0.004	0.003	0.002	0.002	0.001				
27	0.764	0.586	0.347	0.207	0.125	0.076	0.047	0.029	0.023	0.018	0.011	0.007	0.005	0.003	0.002	0.002	0.001	0.001				
28	0.757	0.574	0.333	0.196	0.116	0.069	0.042	0.026	0.020	0.016	0.010	0.006	0.004	0.002	0.002	0.002	0.001	0.001				
29	0.749	0.563	0.321	0.185	0.107	0.063	0.037	0.022	0.017	0.014	0.008	0.005	0.003	0.002	0.002	0.001	0.001	0.001				
30	0.742	0.552	0.308	0.174	0.099	0.057	0.033	0.020	0.015	0.012	0.007	0.004	0.003	0.002	0.001	0.001	0.001					
40	0.672	0.453	0.208	0.097	0.046	0.022	0.011	0.005	0.004	0.003	0.001	0.001										
50	0.608	0.372	0.141	0.054	0.021	0.009	0.003	0.001	0.001	0.001												

SOURCE: Robert N. Anthony and James S. Reece, *Accounting Principles*, 4th ed. (Homewood, Ill.: Richard D. Irwin, 1979). © 1979 by Richard D. Irwin, Inc.

Annuity Table
Present Value of $1 Received Annually for N Years

Years (N)	1%	2%	4%	6%	8%	10%	12%	14%	15%	16%	18%	20%	22%	24%	25%	26%	28%	30%	35%	40%	45%	50%
1	0.990	0.980	0.962	0.943	0.926	0.909	0.893	0.877	0.870	0.862	0.847	0.833	0.820	0.806	0.800	0.794	0.781	0.769	0.741	0.714	0.690	0.667
2	1.970	1.942	1.886	1.833	1.783	1.736	1.690	1.647	1.626	1.605	1.566	1.528	1.492	1.457	1.440	1.424	1.392	1.361	1.289	1.224	1.165	1.111
3	2.941	2.884	2.775	2.673	2.577	2.487	2.402	2.322	2.283	2.246	2.174	2.106	2.042	1.981	1.952	1.923	1.868	1.816	1.696	1.589	1.493	1.407
4	3.902	3.808	3.630	3.465	3.312	3.170	3.037	2.914	2.855	2.798	2.690	2.589	2.494	2.404	2.362	2.320	2.241	2.166	1.997	1.849	1.720	1.605
5	4.853	4.713	4.452	4.212	3.993	3.791	3.605	3.433	3.352	3.274	3.127	2.991	2.864	2.745	2.689	2.635	2.532	2.436	2.220	2.035	1.876	1.737
6	5.795	5.601	5.242	4.917	4.623	4.355	4.111	3.889	3.784	3.685	3.498	3.326	3.167	3.020	2.951	2.885	2.759	2.643	2.385	2.168	1.983	1.824
7	6.728	6.472	6.002	5.582	5.206	4.868	4.564	4.288	4.160	4.039	3.812	3.605	3.416	3.242	3.161	3.083	2.937	2.802	2.508	2.263	2.057	1.883
8	7.652	7.325	6.733	6.210	5.747	5.335	4.968	4.639	4.487	4.344	4.078	3.837	3.619	3.421	3.329	3.241	3.076	2.925	2.598	2.331	2.108	1.922
9	8.566	8.162	7.435	6.802	6.247	5.759	5.328	4.946	4.772	4.607	4.303	4.031	3.786	3.566	3.463	3.366	3.184	3.019	2.665	2.379	2.144	1.948
10	9.471	8.983	8.111	7.360	6.710	6.145	5.650	5.216	5.019	4.833	4.494	4.192	3.923	3.682	3.571	3.465	3.269	3.092	2.715	2.414	2.168	1.965
11	10.368	9.787	8.760	7.887	7.139	6.495	5.917	5.453	5.234	5.029	4.656	4.327	4.035	3.776	3.656	3.544	3.335	3.147	2.752	2.438	2.185	1.977
12	11.255	10.575	9.385	8.384	7.536	6.814	6.194	5.660	5.421	5.197	4.793	4.439	4.127	3.851	3.725	3.606	3.387	3.190	2.779	2.456	2.196	1.985
13	12.134	11.343	9.986	8.853	7.904	7.103	6.424	5.842	5.583	5.342	4.910	4.533	4.203	3.912	3.780	3.656	3.427	3.223	2.799	2.468	2.204	1.990
14	13.004	12.106	10.563	9.295	8.244	7.367	6.628	6.002	5.724	5.468	5.008	4.611	4.265	3.962	3.824	3.695	3.459	3.249	2.814	2.477	2.210	1.993
15	13.865	12.849	11.118	9.712	8.559	7.606	6.811	6.142	5.847	5.575	5.092	4.675	4.315	4.001	3.859	3.726	3.483	3.268	2.825	2.484	2.214	1.995
16	14.718	13.578	11.652	10.106	8.851	7.824	6.974	6.265	5.954	5.669	5.162	4.730	4.357	4.033	3.887	3.751	3.503	3.283	2.834	2.489	2.216	1.997
17	15.562	14.292	12.166	10.477	9.122	8.022	7.120	6.373	6.047	5.749	5.222	4.775	4.391	4.059	3.910	3.771	3.518	3.295	2.840	2.492	2.218	1.998
18	16.398	14.992	12.659	10.828	9.372	8.201	7.250	6.467	6.128	5.818	5.273	4.812	4.419	4.080	3.928	3.786	3.529	3.304	2.844	2.494	2.219	1.999
19	17.226	15.678	13.134	11.158	9.604	8.365	7.366	6.550	6.198	5.877	5.316	4.844	4.442	4.097	3.942	3.799	3.539	3.311	2.848	2.496	2.220	1.999
20	18.046	16.351	13.590	11.470	9.818	8.514	7.469	6.623	6.259	5.929	5.353	4.870	4.460	4.110	3.954	3.808	3.546	3.316	2.850	2.497	2.221	1.999
21	18.857	17.011	14.029	11.764	10.017	8.649	7.562	6.687	6.312	5.973	5.384	4.891	4.476	4.121	3.963	3.816	3.551	3.320	2.852	2.498	2.221	2.000
22	19.660	17.658	14.451	12.042	10.201	8.772	7.645	6.743	6.359	6.011	5.410	4.909	4.488	4.130	3.970	3.822	3.556	3.323	2.853	2.498	2.222	2.000
23	20.456	18.292	14.857	12.303	10.371	8.883	7.718	6.792	6.399	6.044	5.432	4.925	4.499	4.137	3.976	3.827	3.559	3.325	2.854	2.499	2.222	2.000
24	21.243	18.914	15.247	12.550	10.529	8.985	7.784	6.835	6.434	6.073	5.451	4.937	4.507	4.143	3.981	3.831	3.562	3.327	2.855	2.499	2.222	2.000
25	22.023	19.523	15.622	12.783	10.675	9.077	7.843	6.873	6.464	6.097	5.467	4.948	4.514	4.147	3.985	3.834	3.564	3.329	2.856	2.499	2.222	2.000
26	22.795	20.121	15.983	13.003	10.810	9.161	7.896	6.906	6.491	6.118	5.480	4.956	4.520	4.151	3.988	3.837	3.566	3.330	2.856	2.500	2.222	2.000
27	23.560	20.707	16.330	13.211	10.935	9.237	7.943	6.935	6.514	6.136	5.492	4.964	4.524	4.154	3.990	3.839	3.567	3.331	2.856	2.500	2.222	2.000
28	24.316	21.281	16.663	13.406	11.051	9.307	7.984	6.961	6.534	6.152	5.502	4.970	4.528	4.157	3.992	3.840	3.568	3.331	2.857	2.500	2.222	2.000
29	25.066	21.844	16.984	13.591	11.158	9.370	8.022	6.983	6.551	6.166	5.510	4.975	4.531	4.159	3.994	3.841	3.569	3.332	2.857	2.500	2.222	2.000
30	25.808	22.396	17.292	13.765	11.258	9.427	8.055	7.003	6.566	6.177	5.517	4.979	4.534	4.160	3.995	3.842	3.569	3.332	2.857	2.500	2.222	2.000
40	32.835	27.355	19.793	15.046	11.925	9.779	8.244	7.105	6.642	6.234	5.548	4.997	4.544	4.166	3.999	3.846	3.571	3.333	2.857	2.500	2.222	2.000
50	39.196	31.424	21.482	15.762	12.234	9.915	8.304	7.133	6.661	6.246	5.554	4.999	4.545	4.167	4.000	3.846	3.571	3.333	2.857	2.500	2.222	2.000

SOURCE: Robert N. Anthony and James S. Reece, *Accounting Principles*, 4th ed. (Homewood, Ill.: Richard D. Irwin, 1979). © 1979 by Richard D. Irwin, Inc.

Index

This book has been set VIP in 10 and 9 point Times Roman, leaded 2 points. Part numbers and chapter titles are 18 point Times Roman; part titles are 20 point Times Roman and chapter numbers are 30 point Times Roman. The size of the text area is 28 by 47½ picas.